*Oracle Press*™

# Oracle8*i* Backup & Recovery Handbook

# About the Authors

**Rama Velpuri** is the founder and CEO of ORAMASTERS Inc. Before founding ORAMASTERS, Mr. Velpuri worked with Oracle Corporation for more than 10 years. At Oracle, he was an Executive Director of the Oracle Application Development Center. He has built two offshore development centers for Oracle, one in Bangalore, India (India Product Engineering Center), and the other in Hyderabad, India (Oracle Application Development Center). Before that, he was a Senior Manager of the Mission Critical Support Center. Mr. Velpuri has presented numerous technical papers at various International Oracle Conferences and Oracle user conferences on disaster recovery, and he has trained Oracle support personnel in 22 different countries in problem-solving techniques. You can reach him via email at **rvelpuri@oramasters.com**.

Rama's Oracle Press Books:

- *Oracle8 Backup & Recovery Handbook* (ISBN: 0-07-882389-7; 1998)

- *Oracle8 Troubleshooting* (ISBN: 0-07-882580-6; 1999)

- *Oracle NT Handbook* (ISBN: 0-07-211917-9; 1998)

- *Oracle Troubleshooting* (ISBN: 0-07-882388-9; 1997)

- *Oracle Backup & Recovery Handbook, 7.3 Edition* (ISBN: 0-07-882323-4; 1997)

- *Oracle Backup & Recovery Handbook* (ISBN: 0-07-882106-1; 1995)

**Anand Adkoli** is the cofounder and Chief Technology Officer of Liqwid Krystal Inc. Prior to that, he was a Senior Development Manager in Oracle's Industrial Applications Division. During the course of his long career at Oracle, he as worked for Worldwide Customer Support, the Products Division, and the Worldwide Alliances and Technology Division. Anand has delivered projects for Oracle Corporation in the United States, Australia, and India.

He has published more than 40 technical papers and has made numerous presentations at various international conferences on Performance Tuning and Oracle architecture. He is the coauthor of *Oracle Troubleshooting, Oracle NT Handbook,* and *Oracle8 Backup & Recovery Handbook* from Oracle Press. You can contact him at **anand@liqwidkrystal.com**.

Oracle Press™

# Oracle8*i* Backup & Recovery Handbook

Rama Velpuri and Anand Adkoli

Osborne/**McGraw-Hill**

Berkeley  New York  St. Louis  San Francisco
Auckland  Bogotá  Hamburg  London  Madrid
Mexico City  Milan  Montreal  New Delhi  Panama City
Paris  São Paulo  Singapore  Sydney  Tokyo  Toronto

Osborne/**McGraw-Hill**
2600 Tenth Street
Berkeley, California 94710
U.S.A.

For information on translations or book distributors outside the U.S.A., or to arrange bulk purchase discounts for sales promotions, premiums, or fund-raisers, please contact Osborne/**McGraw-Hill** at the above address.

**Oracle8*i* Backup & Recovery Handbook**

1234567890 CUS CUS 01987654321

ISBN 0-07-212717-1

**Publisher**
   Brandon A. Nordin

**Vice President & Associate Publisher**
   Scott Rogers

**Acquisitions Editor**
   Jeremy Judson

**Project Editor**
   Lisa Theobald

**Acquisitions Coordinator**
   Ross Doll

**Technical Editor**
   Johny Yagappan

**Copy Editor**
   Dennis Weaver

**Proofreaders**
   Tandra McLaughlin
   Paul Medoff

**Indexer**
   Karin Arrigoni

**Computer Designers**
   Jani Beckwith
   Tara Davis

**Illustrators**
   Michael Mueller
   Lyssa Sieben-Wald

**Series Design**
   Jani Beckwith

This book was composed with Corel VENTURA™ Publisher.

# Contents at a Glance

# Contents

# Foreword

The business landscape is dramatically transforming with the explosion of electronic commerce. The Internet has empowered consumers in a way that provides unique challenges for companies, coupled with unparalleled opportunity. Industry experts project that true e-business will emerge, stabilize, and reach the plateau of profits in the next decade. The two most important words for all these businesses are *information* and *availability*.

Information is needed at all levels of the business. The success of a company depends on the availability of its information system, and more often than not, this fact is not realized until it is too late. More and more businesses today are realizing the need for high availability. Minimizing the mean time to recover (MTTR) and maximizing the mean time between failures (MTBF) can be achieved only by continuous improvement.

Despite the level of automation provided by nascent technologies, the need for a good system administrator or database administrator strongly exists. Oracle DBAs who used to manage megabytes of data in the '80s and gigabytes of data in the '90s are now dealing with terabytes and picabytes. With databases increasing in number and size, the demand for good DBAs will continue to increase in the future. As the leader in the database market place, the Oracle RDBMS is robust, scalable, and reliable. Yet, to properly maintain a healthy information system, certain measures must be taken to guard it against physical outages, design outages, environmental outages, and, last but not least, operational outages. These measures include backup planning/testing and proper recovery procedures.

The authors, Rama Velpuri and Anand Adkoli, have worked with mission-critical databases for more than a decade and have amassed a wealth of technical knowledge. In this new edition of the *Backup & Recovery Handbook*, the leading authorities have revealed the power of Oracle8*i* related to backup and recovery. The new chapters added to this book provide a lot of practical information.

This book must be read by every DBA in the world who manages an Oracle database.

Ian Thacker
Executive Vice President
Oracle Support Services
Oracle Corporation

# Acknowledgments

Numerous people have helped us in many ways to make this book a reality. We would like to thank Ian Thacker, Executive Vice President of Oracle Support Services, for encouraging us to write this book and for writing the foreword.

We would like to thank our family and friends—Anuradha, Akhil, Aruna, Raja, Ravi, Subrahmanyam, Smitha, Deepa, and Sudha—for all the support they have given us while we wrote this book. Thanks to our good friend Ramana Gogula for the inspiration he has given us in writing this book. Thanks to Michael Corey for his valuable advice.

Thanks to the crew at Osborne/McGraw-Hill—Lisa Theobald, Project Editor; Jeremy Judson, Lisa McClain, and Ross Doll, the Acquisitions team; Copy Editor Dennis Weaver; the Production team at Osborne; and Proofreaders Tandra McLaughlin and Paul Medoff.

Thanks to Saar Maoz for writing and testing the VMS backup scripts, and to Ravi Krishnamurthy for rewriting and testing the UNIX scripts for Chapter 5.

Thanks to Henry Ong for helping us with the outage analysis survey, done at various Oracle customer sites. And thanks also to Robert Grant, Darryl Presley, Jayashree Rangaswamy, and Anuradha Velpuri for their input. We would like to thank Lawrence To, Brian Quigley, and Basab Maulik for providing valuable information regarding standby databases.

The information in this book was culled from a number of sources. Technical bulletins written by Oracle Support Services' analysts were used. Some of the authors include Moe Fardoost, Ellen Tafeen, Walter Lindsay, Linda Fong, Tuomas Pystynen, Saleem Haque, Harmeet Bharara, Chitra Mitra, Ziad Dahbour, Darryl Presley, Roderick Manalac, Mark Ramacher, Vijay Oddiraju, Ramana Gourinani, and Lawrence To. E-mail messages sent by the staff of Server Technology were also used. Contributors include Jonathan Klein, Terry Hayes, Anurag Gupta, Bill Bridge, Greg Doherty, Greg Pongracz, Gary Hallmark, and Leng Leng Tan. Mary Moran's document on Backup and Recovery has provided the foundation for Chapter 3. We would like to thank Gautam Singhal, Connie Dialeris, Jim Diianni, and Ashok Joshi for providing their input on Oracle8. "An Optimal Flexible Architecture for a growing Oracle database" by Oracle Core Technologies Services was used as a reference. Most of the Oracle8 and Oracle8i Server documentation set was used.

Special thanks to Venkat Mandala for testing the syntax and helping us set up the environment. Last, but not least, thanks to Johny Yagappan for contributing, testing, and reviewing the book so thoroughly. Without him, we couldn't have finished this book.

# Introduction

he heartbeat of any company pulsates through its information system with a vital force that must be maintained for a healthy existence of the company. Much like the human body's health and resiliency to infections depend on the supply of oxygen carried through the blood stream, so does a company's success rely on its information system's ability to supply critical data to all of its organizations for effective response to changing market conditions.

This comparison, though somewhat simplistic, nevertheless seems apt, as a company's success depends on the availability of its information system, and that this fact is often not realized until it is too late and the information systems become unavailable—much like a person may ignore a potential health problem until it becomes a serious problem to be dealt with. With this in mind, proper investment in planning and preparation must be made up front to prepare for the inevitable systems failure whether by hardware, software, natural disaster, or otherwise.

If the information system is the vascular system providing life to a company, the database engine—specifically, the Oracle Relational Database System—is the heart of the system. To properly maintain a healthy information system, certain measures must be taken to guard against systems failures affecting the Oracle RDBMS. These measures include backup planning and proper recovery procedures. The Oracle RDBMS is highly complex and configurable, and to make educated decisions in tailoring the backups to your business environment and information system, it is necessary to understand all the backup options available to you. Such decisions made up front will dictate or limit the options available for recovery if a crash occurs. This book gives details on how to tailor a backup plan and how to deal with systems failures affecting the Oracle RDBMS.

## Audience and Scope

Any Oracle user or any DBA who has installed an Oracle database will find this book useful. The discussions on backup and recovery procedures relate primarily to tools and environments built into Oracle that are available in any operating system. Taking backups in some special environments such as DSS (Decision Support System) and OLTP (OnLine Transaction Processing) is discussed as well. Operating system–specific topics relating to backup and case studies of recovery will also be addressed. Recovery Manager and Logical backups are discussed in detail. In addition to backup and recovery procedures, various diagnostic tools are also available. These tools, which help DBAs debug problems with the RDBMS, are also discussed in this book.

If you are a system administrator, and not an Oracle user or DBA, you can benefit as well from this book by reading the recommendations on how to plan for disaster recovery.

## How to Use This Book

This book focuses on Oracle background and specific operating system information that an Oracle DBA needs to plan a proper backup procedure. It also presents a short introduction to general Oracle concepts, pointing out the mechanisms built into Oracle that will be important for backup planning. General backup principles applicable to all operating systems are provided, with some discussions about the types of backups best suited for VLDB, DSS, OLTP, and OPS environments. Logical backups with the latest features are discussed. You will also find operating system–specific details and issues relating to backups in VMS, MVS, UNIX, NetWare, OS/2, and Windows NT, and recovery principles and hands-on strategies for failure analysis and Oracle recovery. Replication concepts are introduced, and descriptions of available diagnostic facilities are provided. Lastly, you will find a number of case studies based on real-life backup and recovery situations.

The book is divided into 10 chapters and one appendix.

- Chapter 1 gives an overview of Oracle backup and recovery procedures. It should prove to be helpful for any Oracle user or DBA.

- Chapter 2 gives an overview of the Oracle RDBMS from a backup and recovery perspective. The various database files that are installed on your system, database operation, and storage are discussed. In addition, this chapter discusses how to manage control files and online and archived redo log files. Experienced users may be able to skim this chapter or skip it altogether.

■ Chapter 3 is organized into three sections. The first section describes physical backups. The second section presents various backup commands and procedures in different operating systems, including VMS, UNIX, MVS, NetWare, Windows NT, and OS/2. The third section gives some tips on backups while running DSS and OLTP applications.

■ Chapter 4 describes how to use the **export** and **import** utilities. Various modes of export including table mode, user mode, and full database mode are discussed. New features such as transportable tablespaces are also discussed in this chapter.

■ Chapter 5 gives sample scripts to automate backup procedures in the Windows NT, UNIX, and OpenVMS environments. If you use Oracle in one if these environments, you should first go through the scripts to understand the logic, and then tailor them to suit your business needs (be sure to run them on a test machine first). If you use Oracle on an operating system other than Windows NT, UNIX, or OpenVMS, you can still read the scripts to learn the logic and implement a similar scheme on your operating system.

■ Chapter 6 describes the internal concepts and data structures related to recovery and discusses various recovery methods. Some recommendations are also made that will help you plan for disaster recovery. A complete section on Standby Databases are provided. The failure analysis describes different kinds of failures and why systems fail in the real world.

■ Chapter 7 gives details on how to use Recovery Manager and all the features associated with it, such as INCREMENTAL backups. RMAN's backup and recovery procedures and its comprehensive reporting features are described.

■ Chapter 8 discusses replication concepts, configuration requirements, how to configure for basic replication, and database links.

■ Chapter 9 is primarily written to help DBAs understand the various diagnostic tools that Oracle provides. Reading this chapter will prepare you to diagnose all problems related to the RDBMS, such as data corruptions, memory corruptions, and performance issues. New tools in Oracle8*i*, such as LogMiner and the DBMS_REPAIR package, are discussed.

■ In Chapter 10, 22 case studies of backup and recovery are discussed. These case studies are based on different kinds of failures that have occurred in real life at customer sites, and recovery procedures that Oracle Support Services has recommended. This chapter will give you an idea of the various failures that can occur at your site and our perspective on how to resolve such issues.

■ The Appendix describes the new features that are introduced in Oracle8*i*.

# CHAPTER

## 1

## An Overview of Backup and Recovery

I n a last-gasp effort, an Oracle database administrator of a Fortune 500 financial firm escalates a call into Oracle Support Services for a Severity 1 down database issue. The DBA had just spent several hours trying to recover a critical database amidst the turmoil of angry users, nervous managers, and frantic developers. "Help!" cries the DBA, "My database is down and I cannot restart it! People are on my back! Please help me bring the database back up!" The DBA's ability to come out of such systemic apoplexy depends on his or her awareness of disaster recovery procedures.

# Why Plan Backups?

Planning and testing backup procedures for your Oracle database is the only insurance you have against failures of media, operating systems, software, and any other kind of failures that cause a serious crash resulting in loss of vital database files. The better the backup plan, the more choices available during recovery. Furthermore, a solid plan and rigorous testing will give you peace of mind and the tools to handle Oracle database recovery. Much like earthquake and fire drills, a proper backup and recovery procedure will require discipline and practice.

Backup planning is nothing new, but it has grown complicated due to constant adaptation to ever-changing technology. The Internet and network computing are rapidly becoming the computing environment of the 21$^{st}$ century; but, for the information system organization, this change has complicated systems management tasks. Multiple customers call into Oracle Support Services (OSS) every day asking for help in bringing up their down production databases. The DBA's self-confidence in handling down production databases and the time it takes to bring the database back up—even with Oracle Support Services' assistance—will depend on the types of backups that are available.

More often than not, a solid, well-tested backup strategy is *not* practiced at most Oracle sites. In a study conducted by the Core Technology Center within Oracle Support Services, a majority of the Severity 1 recovery-related technical assistance requests result in incomplete recovery (based on the report, "Severity 1/Down System TAR Evaluation," by Core Technology Center, March 1994). Recovering lost database files depends a great deal on the backup strategy employed, and backup strategies vary according to operating systems and application environments.

# What Causes Systems to Fail?

On large systems, managing a multiterabyte database in a complex client/server environment is a daunting task. Software and hardware components must cooperate with precise timing in order to provide information to an end user. Consider, for example, a simple SQL query over SQL*NET. In a split second, the SQL command is parsed in SQL*PLUS, passed from the application to the operating system where it is broken into packets by a network layer, and transmitted over Ethernet to the server. At the server, the packets are recompiled and shipped from the host network layer to the host operating system, finally arriving at the server program. And this is just the transmission process. Once the database server receives the request, there are still many more processes that need to happen before data is finally ready for shipping back to the client machine. Add to that the millions of electronic switches flipping continuously within this split second. What can possibly go wrong?

According to the Institute of Electrical and Electronics Engineers (IEEE), outages are classified into outage types and can be grouped into the following categories:

- Physical
- Design (software bug)
- Operations
- Environment

Physical outages are usually caused by hardware failures, such as media failure or a CPU failure. Design outages are caused by software failures, more commonly known as software bugs. Any software bug, whether in the operating system, database software, or application software, contributes to a design outage. Operational outages, on the other hand, are caused by human intervention. Some examples of operation outages are failures attributed to poor DBA skills, user errors, inappropriate system setup, or inadequate backup procedures. Finally, an environmental outage is an outage due to external environmental concerns, such as earthquakes, power surges, or abnormal temperature conditions.

A DBA can exert the most control over operational outages. While a DBA may not be able to predict physical, design, or environmental problems, he or she must be prepared for outages that they cause. The DBA should plan a solid backup procedure and periodically test the procedure for updating as the database grows. In addition, DBAs can also prepare for outages by practicing recovery methods through simulating outages on test systems.

To err is human, but many of our mistakes can be minimized if we plan for them by preparing appropriately. For example, consider the following operational problems and the steps a DBA can take to minimize outages:

| Problem | Likely Fix |
|---|---|
| Poor DBA skills | Train and certify DBAs, and improve documentation. |
| User errors | Increase database security, bulletproof software. |

| Problem | Likely Fix |
|---|---|
| Inappropriate database setup | Plan upgrades, implement a test system, and control changes. |
| Inadequate backup procedures | Plan and test backup procedures. |
| Inadequate hardware | Plan a prefailure strategy for all hardware involved in the database maintenance. This strategy should include enabling an application that will alert the DBA about possible hardware failures before those may occur. |

# Hardware Protection and Redundancy

Given the growing complexity of today's software—and Oracle is no exception—it is very important to consider protecting hardware and systems by building systems redundancy. Especially with high-availability or mission-critical systems, even a few minutes of downtime can be very costly in terms of business lost. (Consider, for example, the millions of dollars lost when an airline booking system is down during high season.) Many corporations apply various, and sometimes drastic, measures to ensure high availability of systems. Some of these techniques are as follows:

- Uninterrupted power supply (UPS)

- Disk mirroring, or RAID technology

- On-site spare parts

- Redundant switch-over systems or switch-over sites

Obviously, there will be cost and performance factors to consider before implementing one or more of these hardware protection methods. Each site will have to consider this issue and budget accordingly. Some of these techniques are described in Chapter 6.

# ARCHIVELOG Mode vs. NOARCHIVELOG Mode

One of the most important decisions that a DBA has to make is to decide whether to run the database in ARCHIVELOG mode or not. The archive log files contain the changes made to the database. There are advantages and disadvantages to running a database in ARCHIVELOG mode. The advantages are as follows:

- Complete recovery is possible. Since all changes made to the database are stored in the log files, if the database files are lost due to any kind of failure—including media failures—you can use the physical backup (offline or online backup) and the archive log files to completely recover the database without losing any data. All committed transactions can be retrieved. In Oracle version 6, the one way that committed transactions could be lost was by losing the online log files. However, with Oracle7 and above, multiplexing of online redo log files will resolve this problem.

- It is possible to take online (hot) backups. This will allow users to use the database while backup of the database is being performed.

- Tablespaces can be taken offline immediately.

- If all nodes of a distributed database system are running in ARCHIVELOG mode, it's possible to do distributed recovery.

- It gives more recovery options.

- It provides maximum disaster protection by using a standby database.

The disadvantages of running a database in ARCHIVELOG mode are as follows:

- Additional disk space is required to store the archived log files.

- The DBA will have more administrative work to maintain the archive log destination and make sure that the archive log files are copied to tape. If enough disk space is not available in the archive log destination, the database will hang; and unless the online log files are archived, the database will not resume normal operation.

Chapter 2 gives details on managing online redo logs and ARCHIVELOG administration.

The following are the ramifications of running the database in NOARCHIVELOG mode:

- Due to loss of data files, if recovery is required, the DBA can restore only to the last whole offline database backup. Any changes made to the database since then will be lost. Therefore, more frequent offline backups need to be performed.

- The entire database needs to be backed up. You cannot back up only a portion of the database. This will be a big disadvantage if you have a *very large database* (VLDB).

- Since you cannot take online backups, the database is not available during offline backups.

- Tablespaces cannot be taken offline immediately.

- Less administrative work is required for DBAs.

**NOTE**
*The only time you can recover a database while operating in NOARCHIVELOG mode is when you have not already overwritten the online log files that were current at the time of the most recent backup.*

# Diagnostic Facilities and Debugging the RDBMS

The Oracle RDBMS is a complicated piece of software engineering. Its stability depends not only on its internal programming, but also on the environment in which it is running. When error conditions occur while running applications or in the RDBMS, the source of the error may require some investigation to uncover. Error messages printed to the users' terminals often give a good indication of what the problem is, but quite often these messages are cleared from the screen before being recorded by the user.

To allow better problem diagnosing, the Oracle system dumps information to *trace files.* These trace files contain many types of structured information dumps, as well as some standard messages that mark the occurrence of normal events. Errors are internally categorized according to severity. Fatal errors produce stack traces, but some less severe errors might not. While diagnosing such problems, it might be necessary for Oracle Support Services analysts to provide some diagnostic events that will capture diagnostic data during the next failure.

Oracle8*i* provides a wide variety of diagnostic applications such as Trace Manager, diagnostics events, SQL commands, SQL scripts, INIT.ORA parameters, and programs for data capture during failures. The DBA should be familiar with all diagnostic capabilities provided by the Oracle system. Chapter 9 discusses various types of information dumps and messages contained in trace files. Some helpful diagnostic utilities will also be discussed. Familiarity with the basic contents of the trace files and understanding when to use what diagnostic tool/command will allow the DBA to capture and provide complete diagnostic data before calling Oracle Support Services.

# Overview of Backups

Taking backups of an Oracle database is similar to buying insurance on your car—you won't realize the importance of it unless you get into an accident, and the amount of coverage you have depends on the kind of insurance policy you have. Similarly, the type and frequency of your backups determine the speed and success of recovery. Various backup methods exist today; the DBA needs to determine the kind of backup procedures that are required for his or her site. This section gives an overview of various backup types commonly used by Oracle DBAs.

Backups can be broadly categorized into physical backups and logical backups. A physical backup is a backup where the actual physical database files are copied from one location to the other (usually from disk to tape). Operating system backups, backups using Recovery Manager, cold backups, and hot backups are examples of a physical backup. Logical backups are backups that extract the data using SQL from the database and store it in a binary file. This data can be imported back into the same database or a different database at a later time. The **export/import** utility provided by Oracle can be used to take logical backups of a database.

## Backups Using Recovery Manager

Recovery Manager (RMAN) is a command-line interface (CLI) that directs an Oracle server process to back up, restore, or recover the database it is connected to. Throughout this book we will use the terms "Recovery Manager" and "RMAN" interchangeably. The backups taken with the RMAN's **backup** command can be written either to disk or to tape, and must be restored by RMAN, whether on disk or tape. Backups taken with the RMAN's **copy** command are written only to disk, and can be restored using either RMAN or manually as done in Oracle7.

The Recovery Manager program issues commands (like **backup** and **copy** discussed above) to an Oracle server process. The Oracle server process reads the data file, control file, or archived redo logs being backed up, or writes the data file, control file, or archived redo log being restored or recovered.

Recovery Manager gets the required information from either the database's control file or via a central repository of information called a *recovery catalog*, which is maintained by Recovery Manager.

You can perform Recovery Manager backups using Oracle Enterprise Manager. Oracle Enterprise Manager-Backup Management is a GUI interface to Recovery

Manager that enables you to perform backup and recovery via a point-and-click method. Refer to the *Oracle Enterprise Manager Documentation Release 2.0* for details on the Enterprise Manager.

**NOTE**
*All of the Oracle7 backup, restore, and recovery methods are still supported in Oracle8i. For example, Oracle8i still supports Server Manager and its **recover** command to perform recovery.*

Finally, RMAN is very useful if you are backing up files to tape. Backing up files to tape is required in most backup scenarios. This minimizes expensive disk consumption and facilitates sending backups elsewhere for disaster recovery. Recovery Manager supports an application programming interface (API) for data movement between Oracle and other vendors' products. This provides the integration with tape management systems necessary for backup and recovery. In most cases, there is no need to invest in new media management software packages. Oracle8*i*'s backup and recovery facilities interface with most existing media management packages.

## Operating System Backups

This type of backup is the simplest to perform, but is also very time-consuming and requires making the system unavailable. The procedure involves shutting down the database and logging all users off the system. Once all access is removed, the system is brought down and restarted in single-user (maintenance) mode, in which control is only available to the administrator at the system console. This step ensures that no user application software is running, which might modify data on the disks. Since the backup process is the only process reading data from the disk, you are assured that the data on the disk is consistent with the point in time when the system was taken down for backup. If this backup were to be used to restore a system, all changes to system configuration, user data, user files—essentially any modifications made to the disk since the last backup—would be lost.

This backup can be supplemented with other backups to build a more flexible backup strategy. For example, in an environment where the system files remain static and changes are made only to user files, a complete operating system backup can be augmented with more frequent backups of the user files. It is common practice for system managers to do operating system backups, and for DBAs to take backups of the Oracle database files.

A common strategy employs full operating system backups weekly and daily backups of user files. The steps involved in this type of backup procedure are as follows:

 1. Shut down everything.

    ■ Shut down all applications and then the Oracle RDBMS.

- ■ If in a multiuser environment, shut down the system and bring it back up in SINGLE-USER mode.

**2.** Back up all files.

- ■ In SINGLE-USER mode, back up all disks to tape using an OS utility.

**3.** Start up the system.

- ■ Bring the system up in MULTIUSER mode.

- ■ Start up the Oracle database and open it to allow access to user applications.

**NOTE**
*Oracle has a facility that allows you to mark individual tablespaces for hot backups using the* **alter tablespace.. begin backup** *command. You can back up data files belonging to a tablespace using an operating system command or utility. The Recovery Manager also has a feature that allows you to register operating system backups in the recovery catalog. In the above section we are referring to a complete backup of your Oracle and non-Oracle files using the operating system.*

## Cold Database Backups

*Cold* database backups involve shutting down the Oracle database in NORMAL mode and backing up all required Oracle database files. This kind of backup is also known as an *offline* backup. These two terms will be used interchangeably throughout this book. The offline backup procedure is similar to operating system backups, except only a subset of the disk files are backed up to tape—the Oracle-related files. Although users can still access the system at the OS level, access to the Oracle database is not allowed. It is also important to shut down any other in-house or third-party software that may be modifying Oracle files before shutting down the database. Once Oracle is unavailable, back up all Oracle files to tape and start up the Oracle database. In some cases, it might not be possible for DBAs to do a normal shutdown of the database before taking the cold backup. In such cases, the DBAs usually shut down the database using the IMMEDIATE option, then bring the database up in RESTRICTED mode, and finally shut it down gracefully. You can perform offline backups using the Recovery Management utility from Oracle Enterprise Manager V2.0 in Oracle8*i*. However, if the database is running in NOARCHIVELOG mode, first Recovery Manager shuts down the database cleanly, performs whole backup of the database, and then brings back the database online. Backup cannot be performed by RMAN if the database has not been shut down cleanly (i.e., cannot be shut down with the ABORT option). This is because, if the database is not shut down cleanly, the database is considered inconsistent with respect to a point in time and useless to back up.

The steps involved in this type of backup procedure are as follows:

1. Shut down Oracle.

   - Shut down all Oracle-related in-house or third-party software running on top of Oracle.

   - Shut down the Oracle RDBMS with the NORMAL option.

2. Back up required Oracle files.

   - Back up Oracle executables/code, configuration files, and control files.

   - Back up all Oracle data files and online redo log files.

3. Start up Oracle in NORMAL mode.

## Hot Backups

A *hot* backup is one taken while the Oracle database is open and operating in ARCHIVELOG mode. This kind of backup is also known as *online* backup. When using the Recovery Manager to perform online backups, it is called an *open database backup*. Although this allows users to access the database during the backup process, care must be taken to schedule this backup procedure during a time when the load on the Oracle database is low. For example, try not to take a backup of the database when a large update batch job is running, as it would generate more redo compared to the time when the data file is not in HOT BACKUP mode. Another option would be to schedule the batch job, if possible, after the backup procedure is complete.

The hot backup procedure consists of backing up all data files belonging to a particular tablespace or tablespaces, the archived redo logs, and the control file.

The steps involved in this type of backup procedure are as follows:

1. Perform an online backup of the tablespace.

2. Back up the archived redo logs.

3. Back up the control file.

**NOTE**
*The above procedure must be performed for each tablespace in the database, and while the database is up and in ARCHIVELOG mode.*

While using Recovery Manager to perform a backup of the open database, you need not explicitly issue commands such as **alter tablespace.. begin backup**. This will be taken care of by RMAN, which examines blocks before copying them.

# The Logical Backup—Export

The *logical backup,* or export, creates a logical copy of database objects and stores it in a binary file. Unlike physical backups, the **export** utility actually reads the data in the objects using SQL and stores the data in the binary file. The **import** utility uses this file to restore these particular database objects back into the database. So, the **export** utility and the **import** utility together allow DBAs to back up and recover particular database objects within the database and/or move an object from one database into another.

The **export** utility can be used in two modes, CONVENTIONAL PATH and DIRECT PATH. Oracle **export** utility's DIRECT PATH export feature extracts data much faster than a CONVENTIONAL PATH export. DIRECT PATH export achieves this performance gain by reading data directly, bypassing the SQL processing layer. For added performance, the database can be set to DIRECT READ mode, thus eliminating contention with other users for database resources because database blocks are read into the export session's private buffer rather than a public buffer cache. The **export** utility is documented in the *Oracle8i Utilities Guide.*

The export backup mechanism does not provide point-in-time recovery and cannot be used with archived redo log files. There is no notion of importing a table and rolling it forward using redo log files. The archived redo log files are part of the physical online backups that record specific information about changes made to the data blocks on disk. The export file is essentially a file recording the SQL commands that the **import** utility feeds to the Oracle SQL layer for processing. For example, an export of a table would create an export file that contains **create table** and **insert** statements. When the table is recovered using the **import** utility, **import** would use the **create table** command to re-create the table and the **insert** statements to insert the rows back into the table using SQL.

If a particular database block is corrupted on disk for whatever reason, a physical backup would make a copy of the block, and the error would be propagated to the backup copy as well. One of the advantages of using a logical backup is that no such corruption will be propagated to the backup due to the fact that a full table scan is performed while exporting a table. So, in this case, such corruption will be detected while exporting, and the export will fail. At that point, the DBA will need to take corrective action before making a backup again.

The steps involved in this type of backup procedure are as follows:

1.  While the database is running, use the **export** utility to export, for example, a table.

2.  Once an export file is created, copy the export file off to tape.

**NOTE**
*An export of a table will give a read-consistent view of the table at the time the export was initiated. Any changes made to the table during the export will not be incorporated into the export file.*

# Automating Backups

Once backup procedures have been planned and well tested, it may be necessary to automate them—especially for hot backups of a large database. A hot backup of a database with many tablespaces will be tedious and error prone; therefore, automating the process using an OS script will make things more manageable. In Chapter 5, we discuss in detail how to write OS scripts to automate backups, but it is important to note a few rules here.

### Use Recovery Manager

One of the key benefits in Oracle8*i* is that you can automate your backup procedures with RMAN, as they are fully managed by the server. This minimizes the probability of a DBA making an error while backing up or restoring. The RMAN utility manages the process of taking full, partial, or incremental backups of the database and can be automated.

### Flexibility

If you are using OS-specific scripts to automate backups, in order to avoid unnecessary maintenance, do not make the scripts dependent on the object names in the database. To accomplish this, use SQL queries against the database dictionary to dynamically generate backup scripts.

### Logging

It is also very important to tag each backup with a timestamp for proper identification during recovery, and to track the progress through logging. Timestamps for each step in the backup script should be logged into a backup script log file, which can be used by the administrator to verify that a backup procedure ran successfully. All of this is done automatically in Oracle8*i* if you use Recovery Manager.

# What Should You Back Up?

A backup of the database includes the data files, control files, and the archived redo log files. If you are using the Recovery Manager, you can use the **backup** command to create a *backup set*. A backup set contains either archive log files or data files, but not both.

As an alternative to the **backup** command, you can issue a **copy** command in Recovery Manager to create a data file copy on disk. The main difference between a backup set and a data file copy is that data file copies can be used immediately by an Oracle instance—they are already in an instance-usable format. Such copies are also termed *image copies.*

**NOTE**
*Data file copies can only be made to disk.*

You can also direct Recovery Manager to include a control file backup in any data file backup set.

Finally, online redo log files should never be backed up. There is no danger in backing up online log files as long as you don't accidentally apply them during recovery. Our experience tells us that during a media failure, the DBA is under pressure to bring up the database as soon as possible. In such situations, if you restore your entire database from backup, there is a possibility that you could overwrite the existing online log files with the backed-up online log files. This will not allow you to perform complete recovery. So, it is good practice not to back up online log files for any kind of backup.

# Overview of Recovery

Sometimes DBAs might feel that the number of recovery options provided by Oracle is overwhelming. It is true that there are a lot of ways recovery could be performed, even for a particular failure. However, every recovery option provided by Oracle is very important and has its own use, and it is crucial that DBAs understand how each recovery option works. Once the concepts of recovery are understood, then even though a lot of recovery options exist it becomes quite clear to the DBAs what kind of recovery procedure to use during various kinds of failures.

## Types of Errors

A major responsibility of the database administrator is to maintain the uptime of a database, and to prepare for the possibility of hardware, software, network, process, and system failure. In the event of a failure, the DBA should also be prepared to bring the database back to operation as quickly as possible, and with little or no data loss. If properly planned, recovery will be a smooth operation, thereby protecting the users and the database. Recovery processes vary, depending on the type of failure that has occurred, the structures that have been affected, and the type of recovery that is desired.

Some failures might cause the database to go down; some others might be trivial. Similarly, on the recovery side, some recovery procedures require DBA intervention, whereas some of the internal recovery mechanisms are transparent to the DBA. For example, if a process dies abnormally while modifying a block, Oracle will do a block-level recovery, which is automatic and doesn't require human intervention. On the other hand, if a data file has been lost, recovery requires additional steps. Some of the common errors or failures include the following:

- User error
- Statement failure
- Process failure
- Network failure
- Instance failure
- Media failure

### User Error

A user deleting a row or dropping a table is a typical example of user error. There are two issues to be considered here. The users and DBAs should be properly trained on administering the databases and developing applications. Furthermore, the DBAs should have proper backup and recovery procedures for recovering from user errors, which should be tested on test systems at regular intervals. In the above example, recovering a dropped table could be done in several ways; which procedure to choose depends on the amount of data you need to recover. The recovery procedure might be as simple as importing from a logical backup, or might involve a more complicated procedure such as doing point-in-time recovery from a physical backup on a test machine, exporting the table, and, finally, importing it into the production database. If the latter procedure needs to be performed, the DBA should have a physical backup of the database and all the archive log files.

### Statement Failures

A *statement failure* can be defined as the inability by Oracle to execute a SQL statement. While running a user program, a transaction might have multiple statements and one of the statements might fail due to various reasons. Typical examples are selecting from a table that doesn't exist and trying to do an **insert** and having the statement fail due to unavailable space in the table. Such statement failures normally generate error codes by the application software or the operating system. Recovery from such failures is automatic. Upon detection, Oracle usually will roll back the statement, returning control to the user or user program. The user can simply reexecute the statement after correcting the problem conveyed by the error message.

## Process Failures

A *process failure* is an abnormal termination of a process. This could be caused either by Oracle itself or by the user (such as when a user performs a ^C from SQL*PLUS). If the process that is terminated is a user process, a server process, or an application process, the Process Monitor (PMON) performs process recovery. PMON is responsible for cleaning up the cache and freeing resources that the process was using. Some of the work done by PMON includes resetting the status of the transaction table in the rollback segment for that transaction, releasing the locks or latches acquired by the terminated process, and removing the process ID from the list of active processes.

PMON doesn't clean up the processes that have been killed by Oracle. If a background process is terminated abnormally, Oracle must be shut down and restarted. During startup, crash recovery is automatically performed to do the roll forward, and transaction recovery will roll back any uncommitted transactions.

## Network Failures

*Network failures* can occur while using a client/server configuration or a distributed database system where multiple database servers are connected by communication networks. Network failures such as communications software failures or aborted asynchronous (phone) connections will interrupt the normal operation of the database system. Sometimes, network failures will in turn cause process failures. In such cases, PMON will roll back the uncommitted work of the process. If a distributed transaction were involved in a network failure, this would create an in-doubt transaction on one or more nodes. (A distributed transaction includes one or more statements that updates data on two or more distinct nodes of a distributed database.) Once the connection is reestablished, the RECO background process resolves such conflicts automatically.

## Instance Failures

An *instance failure* can be caused by a physical (hardware) or a design (software) problem—for example, when one of the database background processes (DBWR) detects that there is a problem on the disk and can't write to it. In situations like this, an error message is written to a log file (and might also create a trace file, depending on the severity of the problem) and the background process terminates. In this case, you need to shut down the instance and restart it. Crash recovery or instance recovery is automatic.

Depending on the amount of work that is being done at the time of the failure, database instance failures might take a long time to recover. For example, suppose a transaction has updated a huge table and decided to roll back, but before the transaction finished rolling back, the instance fails. Crash recovery has to do roll forward and then transaction recovery has to roll the transaction back, which might take a long period of time.

### Media Failures

*Media failures* are the most dangerous failures. Not only is there potential to lose data if proper backup procedures are not followed, but it usually takes more time to recover than with other kinds of failures. In addition, the DBA's experience is a very important factor in determining the kind of media recovery procedure to use to bring the database up quickly with little or no data loss. A typical example of a media failure is a disk controller failure or a disk head crash, which causes all Oracle database files residing on that disk (or disks) to be lost. Every DBA needs to plan appropriate backup procedures to protect against media failures. This is probably the most important responsibility of a DBA.

A lot of factors determine recovery time, such as how fast data can be transferred from tape to disk, how often backups are taken, the size of the database, the kind of failure that occurred, and what kind of media recovery needs to be applied.

A detailed look at outage classes, and specifically backup and recovery-related errors, will be discussed in the "Failure Analysis" section of Chapter 6.

# Types of Recovery

There are three types of recovery mechanisms that Oracle uses: block-level recovery, thread recovery, and media recovery.

*Block-level recovery* is the simplest type of recovery, and is automatically done by Oracle. It is done when a process dies just as it is changing a buffer. The online redo logs for the current thread are used to reconstruct the buffer and write it to disk.

*Thread recovery* is done automatically by Oracle when it discovers that an instance died leaving a thread open. Thread recovery is performed as part of either crash recovery or instance recovery. If the database has a single instance, then crash recovery is performed. This requires the DBA simply to start up the database, and crash recovery is automatically performed by Oracle. If multiple instances are accessing the database and if one of the instances crashes, the second instance automatically performs instance recovery to recover the first thread. Either way, the goal of thread recovery is to restore the data block changes that were in the cache of the instance that died, and to close the thread that was left open. Thread recovery always uses the online redo log files of the thread it is recovering.

The third type of recovery is *media recovery*. It is only done in response to a recovery command. It is used to make backup data files become current, or to restore changes that were lost when a data file went offline without a checkpoint. During media recovery, archived logs—as well as online log files—can be applied.

Though all media recovery procedures use the same algorithm, choosing the right kind of recovery procedure can reduce the mean time to recover. Chapter 6 discusses in detail the fundamental concepts of recovery and describes various recovery strategies. In addition, Chapter 10 gives some real-life examples.

## Recovery with Physical Backups

If the database is operating in NOARCHIVELOG mode, recovery with physical backups involves restoring from recent whole offline backup and starting up the database. There is no roll forward involved. If the database is operating in ARCHIVELOG mode, recovery involves multiple steps. First, the lost data files need to be restored from tape to disk (or disk to disk). The next step is to apply the changes from redo log files to the data files. You can do this in one of three ways: *database recovery, tablespace recovery,* or *data file recovery.* There are special SQL commands for each of the above methods.

Which recovery method to use primarily depends on which files are lost as part of the media failure. For example, if you lose your online or archived log files, and you don't have a mirror copy, then you must do *incomplete recovery,* which means that some of the data will be lost. Incomplete recovery can be done only at a database level in Oracle7, but incomplete recovery is possible while recovering tablespaces in Oracle8 and above. There are some restrictions in using each of the above methods. For example, if you decide to perform database recovery, the database needs to be mounted but not open. However, if you decide to do data file recovery, you can take the data file in question offline, start up the database, and recover the data file. The advantage in doing this is that users can use a portion of the database while you perform recovery on a specific data file.

To summarize, two factors that influence the DBA in choosing one recovery method over the others are as follows:

- Can I do complete recovery, or do I have to do incomplete recovery?

- Do I want part of the database open while doing recovery or not?

All recovery options provided in Oracle8*i* are identical to Oracle7 and Oracle8 with lot of enhancements and new features. Tablespace Point-In-Time Recovery (TSPITR) enables recovery of one or more non-SYSTEM tablespaces to a point in time that is different than that of the rest of the database. Chapter 6 gives a detailed discussion of the various recovery methods and how to decide which method to choose.

**NOTE**
*Oracle has a table-partitioning feature that allows
you to partition tables. Partitions allow tables to
span tablespaces. This was not possible in releases
prior to Oracle8. In Oracle8i, it is therefore possible
to have a situation where one or more partitions of a
table are unavailable while the remaining partitions
are available for use. More information on partitions
is available in Chapter 2.*

## Recovery with Logical Backups

The **export/import** utility is very easy to use, and a lot of DBAs use this utility to
back up and recover their databases. Some DBAs do weekly exports in addition
to the physical backups that they normally perform. For customers with large
databases or high availability requirements, the **export/import** utility for backup
and recovery purposes might not be feasible due to performance reasons. One
should note that the CONVENTIONAL PATH **export** and **import** (unlike the fast
loader) use the SQL layer for data transfer. Chapter 4 discusses the feasibility of
using logical backups.

## Replication—A Backup Option

Apart from having various backup options, it is worth considering Oracle replication
as one more backup facility that keeps mission-critical applications running round
the clock. The replication feature in Oracle8*i* provides users with fast, local access
to shared data, and protects availability of applications in a distributed environment,
because alternate data access options exist in replication setup. Even if one site
becomes unavailable in the event of failure, users can still continue to query or
update the databases that are on different locations. This feature is more appropriate
where information distribution is crucial across the network. Different types of
replication options can be chosen, depending on the business needs. Oracle
supports two types of replication environments:

- Basic replication
- Advanced replication

The basic replication can be employed where information distribution and
availability are considered to be crucial for decision support applications. This type
of replication provides read-only access (at local site) to data that originates from a

master site. This setup reduces the network traffic and increases the availability of data even if the primary site goes down.

Advanced replication environment provides update access in addition to read-only access from anywhere in the distributed setup. This type of replication is appropriate for businesses that involve disconnected business execution and maintaining mission critical databases as well. We will be discussing more about replication in Chapter 8.

# CHAPTER
## 2

The Oracle
Architecture and
Configuration

efore we discuss backup and recovery strategies, it is important to understand some basic concepts of Oracle and the Oracle system's architecture. This information is detailed in the *Oracle8i Concepts*, but will be briefly presented here with a perspective on backup and recovery.

# Oracle Files on Your System

An understanding of the various Oracle files and their locations on the disk is necessary for backup planning. Oracle supports Optimal Flexible Architecture (OFA). It is a set of file naming and placement guidelines for Oracle software and databases. The OFA-compliant databases have the following advantages over non-OFA-compliant databases:

- It simplifies database administration and management by categorizing various Oracle files, executables, database files, network files, etc., and placing them into well-defined directory structures.

- It ensures protection against disk failures by allowing Oracle files to span across more than one hard disk.

- It reduces performance bottlenecks as compared to a non-OFA complaint database.

- It supports concurrent execution of application software by enabling the DBA to install different versions of Oracle in a home with certain restrictions, without affecting one another. For more details, refer to the Oracle documentation, *Oracle8i Server, Release 8.1.5*.

- It helps maintain better, simple, and yet distinctive naming conventions for better maintenance.

During Oracle installation, the Oracle Universal Installer creates all the Oracle-related subdirectories and files under one main directory called **ORACLE_BASE**. This base directory holds all Oracle products except the products that are not associated with an Oracle home such as Microsoft Management Console. Host programs that enable administrators to manage their database, network, etc. such as Oracle Administration Assistant for Windows NT (known as Oracle snap-ins), Oracle Universal Installer, Java Runtime Environment, and Remote Configuration Assistant are installed into an Oracle home under program files in Windows NT. This home should not be confused with that of the Oracle home under the **ORACLE_BASE** directory. This home is entirely different from that of the Oracle executables and data files. A sample OFA-compliant database structure is shown in Figure 2-1 for Windows NT. You, the DBA, should take time to locate and note where these files reside. The most important files to note are the control files, data files, online redo log files, archive redo log files, the initialization parameter file (INIT.ORA), and the Oracle code. A full operating system backup will include all of these files; however, for partial backups, subsets of these files will be backed up in varying frequencies.

Let's take a closer look at how each of these types of files fits into the big picture.

## The Oracle Code

When the Oracle software is installed on your system, Oracle Universal Installer creates various subdirectories and files in the **ORACLE_BASE** directory. In addition, one subdirectory is created in the **ORACLE_BASE** directory for each Oracle product installed in your system. For example, a directory called **ora_oem** is created for the Oracle Enterprise Manager. Installation procedures are operating system dependent. For example, on the UNIX operating system and on Windows NT, the installer creates many subdirectories in the home, which include **dbs**, **bin**, **rdbms**, **network**, and so on. These subdirectories include files such as the Oracle executables and various SQL scripts, which are crucial for database operation and administration and are generally referred to as the *Oracle code*. The Oracle executables are the set of program files that make up the database engine and the various tools that work with the engine to provide a data access channel to the data in the database. These are the files that start up the Oracle processes and run applications such as Oracle Server Manager (SVRMGR), SQL*PLUS, and numerous other tools that are included in the installation package. Since these files do not change, a one-time backup of these files should be adequate. Every time the software version of Oracle is upgraded, or a patch is applied, these executables are replaced by new ones. An initial full operating system backup or partial backup of just the executables taken after an install would be advisable. The backup strategy should also include backing up these files after every Oracle version upgrade.

## The Data Files

The *data files* make up the physical repository for all the data in the database. Oracle divides the data files into numerous logical entities, with the smallest unit being an Oracle block. As part of the database creation, Oracle creates the SYSTEM tablespace and associated data files, which contain system tables known as the *data dictionary*. As the database grows and more space is needed, the DBA needs to create and add more data files to the database. These files are a major concern for backup and space management (space management and data files are discussed later in this chapter). In addition to the SYSTEM tablespace (**system01.dbf**), Oracle also creates a USER tablespace (**users01.dbf**) to store user data, an INDEX

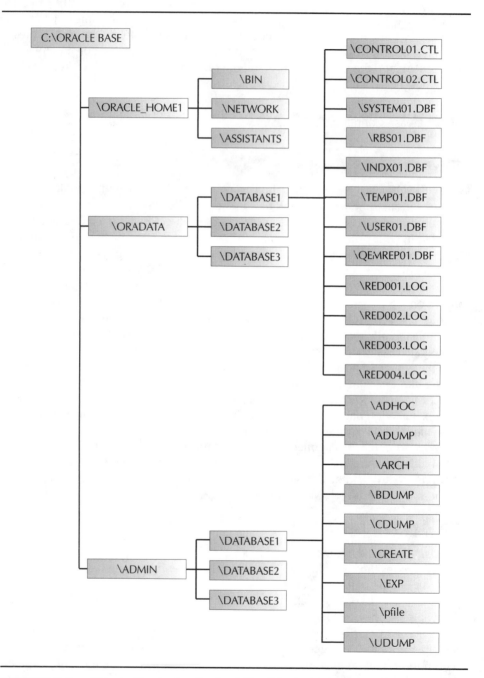

**FIGURE 2-1.** *Oracle files in the Optimal Flexible Architecture*

tablespace (**indx01.dbf**) to store index data, a ROLLBACK_SEGMENT tablespace (**rbs01.dbf**) to store rollback segments, and, finally, a TEMPORARY tablespace (**temp01.dbf**) that can be used for sort operations. On your operating system, all these tablespaces are created by default if you choose to create the database using the Database Configuration Assistant. You can also modify the names and locations of the data files that belong to the respective tablespaces using the custom option in the Database Configuration Assistant.

## The Redo Log Files

The *redo log files* are used by Oracle to record changes made to the database during normal operation. Since these files are open, or *online,* during normal operation of the database, they are commonly referred to as the *online redo log files.* These files are used by Oracle during recovery to reapply the changes made to the database in the event such changes were not permanently written to the data files on disk at the time of the failure. Oracle provides the facility of multiplexing online redo log files. This is very similar to the concept of mirroring provided by some operating systems. Oracle allows you to create redo log groups, each consisting of at least one redo log member. The members in a redo log group are exact images of each other. It is essential that redo log members in each group are spread across disks, preferably mounted under different disk controllers. This avoids loss of data if one of the disks containing the online redo log groups fails or a controller crashes.

Oracle DBAs also have a choice to run the database in the ARCHIVELOG mode or in NOARCHIVELOG mode. If the former is chosen, contents of the online redo log files are copied to an archive area by an Oracle background *processes Archiver (ARCn).* These archive files are known as the *archived redo log files, archived redo logs,* or simply *archived redo.* These files are sometimes referred to as the *offline redo log files* since they are not open during normal operation of the database and are required only during media recovery. The redo log files (online and archived) are essential for database recovery since they contain information on all changes made to the database. If the database is chosen to operate in NOARCHIVELOG mode, *online backups* and database media recovery will not be possible. The backup strategy you design should include copying archived redo log files to tape periodically.

## The Control File

The control file is a very important piece of the database. This file contains the schema of the database. The names, locations, status, and states of all the data files and online redo log files are recorded in the control file. Similar to the data files and online log files, the control file is essential for normal operation of the database. As part of the database startup procedure, Oracle reads the control file to locate the data files and online log files. If the control file is lost due to a media failure, a new control file can be created. This is discussed in detail in Chapter 6. This would cause some downtime of the database, so you should maintain at least three copies of the control file, each on a separate disk drive mounted under different controllers. Oracle allows multiplexing of control files. Mirror images of the control files as defined by the CONTROL_FILES parameter in the INIT.ORA are maintained automatically. The control file should be backed up along with the data and log files. A special SQL command is available to back up the control file while taking online backups.

## The INIT.ORA File

As part of the software distribution, Oracle provides an initialization parameter file called INIT.ORA. In all OFA-compliant databases, the name of this parameter file is INIT.ORA, which you can locate in the directory **ORACLE_BASE\ admin\ databasename\pfile,** where *databasename* is the name of the database. For example, on Windows NT, the default database name will be **ora8i** and its initialization parameter file INIT.ORA will be copied to the **c:\ORACLE_BASE\ admin\ora8i\pfile** directory. We will refer to the initialization parameter file as INIT.ORA throughout this book. This file contains the Oracle system parameters and should be used by the DBA to customize the RDBMS configuration at a specific site. Oracle reads this file during database startup to determine the size of the system global area (SGA, discussed later in this chapter) and to locate the control files, among other things. Since the control and INIT.ORA files are crucial for database startup, they should be backed up frequently. Since the size of these files is negligible, you should keep online copies of these files. For a complete listing of the INIT.ORA parameters, refer to the *Oracle8i Reference Release 8.1.5* manual. Among other things, the INIT.ORA parameters are used to do the following:

- Tune the memory

- Set diagnostic events to obtain trace files

- Trace the SQL statements

- Indicate the location of the control files and the trace files

- Distribute the PCM locks if using the PARALLEL SERVER option

- Configure Multi Threaded Server (MTS)

- Configure Parallel Query Servers

- Set database wide Audit

- Enable or disable archiving

To view the INIT.ORA file, you can issue the command **show parameters** from an SQL*PLUS session. A partial listing is shown here:

```
SQL> show parameters;
NAME                                TYPE    VALUE
----------------------------------- ------- --------------------
O7_DICTIONARY_ACCESSIBILITY         boolean TRUE
always_anti_join                    string  NESTED_LOOPS
always_semi_join                    string  standard
aq_tm_processes                     integer 0
audit_trail                         string  NONE
background_dump_dest                string  C:\Oracle\admin\ora8
backup_tape_io_slaves               boolean FALSE
bitmap_merge_area_size              integer 1048576
blank_trimming                      boolean FALSE
buffer_pool_keep                    string
buffer_pool_recycle                 string
commit_point_strength               integer 1
compatible                          string  8.1.0
control_file_record_keep_time       integer 7
control_files                       string  C:\Oracle\oradata\or
cpu_count                           integer 1
create_bitmap_area_size             integer 8388608
cursor_space_for_time               boolean FALSE
db_block_buffers                    integer 8192
db_block_checking                   boolean FALSE
db_block_checksum                   boolean FALSE
```

If you are using the Oracle Enterprise Manager GUI, you can enable the Instance Manager and view the INIT.ORA parameters as shown in Figure 2-2. You can view the *basic tuning, instance specific, advanced tuning,* and *derived* parameters in separate windows.

# The Oracle Trace Files

For purposes of problem diagnosis and application tuning, Oracle creates text files called *trace files*. Each Oracle background process can write to an associated trace file when appropriate. These files are commonly known as *background trace files*. The user processes can create trace files as well, and these files are called the *user trace files*. The location where the background and user trace files are created can be controlled by setting the appropriate INIT.ORA parameters. All the background trace files are created in a directory specified by the BACKGROUND_DUMP_DEST parameter. Similarly, the USER_DUMP_DEST parameter determines where the user trace files are created. Oracle automatically creates trace files when internal

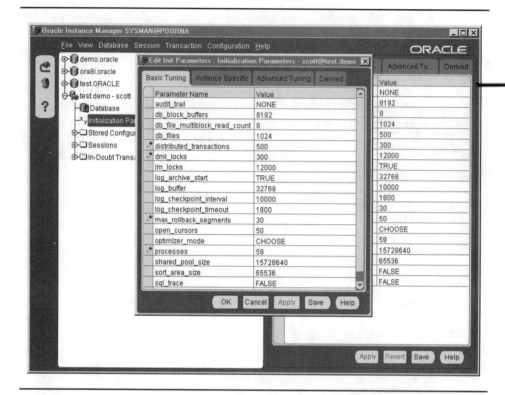

**FIGURE 2-2.** *Viewing INIT.ORA parameters*

Oracle errors occur. In addition, a DBA can force Oracle to create trace files by setting various *diagnostic events* in the INIT.ORA file or by issuing the **alter session** statement while connected to the database, from SQLPLUS or SQL*PLUS Worksheet. Note that if the INIT.ORA file is used to create trace files, tracing will be turned on at a database-wide level, whereas the **alter session** command will turn on tracing only at a session level. Chapter 9 deals with setting diagnostic events and various other diagnostic tools that are available to the DBA for debugging the RDBMS.

One of the common INIT.ORA parameters used by application developers is SQL_TRACE. When this parameter is set to TRUE, every SQL statement that is executed in the database will be traced and the information written to a trace file. Alternatively, SQL tracing can be turned on at a session level by typing the following command:

```
SQL> ALTER SESSION SET SQL_TRACE = TRUE;
```

The trace directory needs to be regularly examined every day to see if Oracle has created any important trace files. DBAs should delete the unwanted trace files and save the ones that are important. It is a good practice to archive the trace files to tape on a regular basis. Some DBAs automate these procedures.

Oracle Corporation also provides a utility called **tkprof** (the executable is called **tkprof73.exe** on Oracle version 7.3, **tkprof80.exe** on Oracle8, and **tkprof.exe** on Oracle8*i* for Windows NT) that can be used to obtain formatted reports from Oracle trace files. For example, a trace file called **ora00483.trc** was generated from a simple SQL statement **select * from emp.** (The name of the trace file is determined by the process ID, 483 in this example.) You can generate a formatted report by using **tkprof.exe**:

```
D:\oracle\admin\ora8i\udump> TKPROF ORA00483.TRC test.txt
```

A portion of the resulting formatted report in **test.txt** is shown below:

```
TKPROF: Release 8.1.5.0.0 - Production on Tue Apr 17 07:13:42 2000
(c) Copyright 1999 Oracle Corporation.  All rights reserved.
Trace file: ora00289.trc
Sort options: default
********************************************************************************
count    = number of times OCI procedure was executed
cpu      = cpu time in seconds executing
elapsed  = elapsed time in seconds executing
disk     = number of physical reads of buffers from disk
query    = number of buffers gotten for consistent read
current  = number of buffers gotten in current mode (usually for update)
rows     = number of rows processed by the fetch or execute call
********************************************************************************
ALTER SESSION SET SQL_TRACE = TRUE
call     count       cpu    elapsed       disk      query    current       rows
-------  ------  --------  ---------- ----------  ---------- ----------  ----------
Parse        0      0.00       0.00          0          0          0          0
Execute      1      0.00       0.00          0          0          0          0
Fetch        0      0.00       0.00          0          0          0          0
-------  ------  --------  ---------- ----------  ---------- ----------  ----------
total        1      0.00       0.00          0          0          0          0
Misses in library cache during parse: 0
Misses in library cache during execute: 1
Optimizer goal: CHOOSE
Parsing user id: SYS
********************************************************************************
select obj#,type#,ctime,mtime,stime,status,dataobj#,flags,oid$
from obj$ where owner#=:1 and name=:2 and namespace=:3 and(remoteowner=:4 or
remoteowner is null and :4 is null)and(linkname=:5 or linkname is null and :5 is
null)and(subname=:6 or subname is null and :6 is null)

call     count       cpu    elapsed       disk      query    current       rows
-------  ------  --------  ---------- ----------  ---------- ----------  ----------
Parse        1      0.00       0.00          0          0          0          0
Execute      1      0.00       0.00          0          0          0          0
Fetch        1      0.00       0.00          0          4          0          1
-------  ------  --------  ---------- ----------  ---------- ----------  ----------
total        3      0.00       0.00          0          4          0          1
```

```
Misses in library cache during parse: 1
Misses in library cache during execute: 1
Optimizer goal: CHOOSE
Parsing user id: SYS    (recursive depth: 1)
```

```
******************************************************************************
```

For other important configuration files specific to your environment, refer to the *Oracle8i Enterprise Edition Installation Release 8.1.5* manual for your operating system.

# Database Operation

It is important that you understand the functions of the various Oracle processes and the different players involved during database operation. These processes, files, and shared memory areas make up the Oracle database server, and a basic understanding of the roles of each player will be vital in problem diagnostics during database recovery.

## The System Global Area

The *system global area* (or SGA) is a piece of memory allocated by Oracle. All the memory structures that reside in the system global area are shared by concurrent users connected to the instance. This is why the system global area is commonly referred to as the *shared global area*. When the database is started, information regarding the SGA is displayed by Oracle. The following example shows the output when the Oracle database is started:

```
C:\>sqlplus connect internal/oracle
SQL*Plus: Release 8.1.5.0.0 - Production on Wed Apr 19 07:20:01 2000
(c) Copyright 1999 Oracle Corporation.  All rights reserved.
Connected to:
Oracle8i Enterprise Edition Release 8.1.5.0.0 - Production
With the Partitioning and Java options
PL/SQL Release 8.1.5.0.0 - Production
SQL> startup
ORACLE instance started.
Total System Global Area    36437964 bytes
Fixed Size                     65484 bytes
Variable Size               19521536 bytes
Database Buffers            16777216 bytes
Redo Buffers                   73728 bytes
Database mounted.
Database opened.
```

**NOTE**
*Though Oracle8i supports Server Manager Line Mode (SVRMGRL), it is recommended that you move from Server Manager to Oracle Enterprise Manager or SQL\*PLUS, as the SVRMGRL is provided for backward compatibility only. Versions of SQL\*Plus before SQL\*Plus release 8.1 will not support Server Manager Line Mode commands. SQL\*PLUS supports all SVRMGRL commands. If you want SQL\*PLUS to behave in the same way as Server Manager, use the NOLOG option when you start SQL\*PLUS by entering the* **SQLPLUS /NOLOG** *command at the command prompt.*

While the database is open, the DBA can issue a **show sga** command from SQL\*PLUS to examine the SGA size. For example:

```
SQL> show sga
Total System Global Area      38322124 bytes
Fixed Size                       65484 bytes
Variable Size                 21405696 bytes
Database Buffers              16777216 bytes
Redo Buffers                     73728 bytes
SQL>
```

Alternatively, if you are using the Instance Manager GUI, you can select the database and click on the "information" folder to view archive information and the SGA size, as shown in Figure 2-3.

The INIT.ORA file is read during database startup. The size of the SGA is also determined at this time. The SGA contains a *fixed-size* portion and a *variable-size* portion. The fixed-size portion of the SGA contains the database- and instance-specific information that is needed by the background processes. This portion of the SGA is not tunable. The size of the fixed portion of the SGA might change between different versions of the database. This size could also vary between different UNIX platforms due to different *alignment procedures.* The variable-size portion of the SGA consists

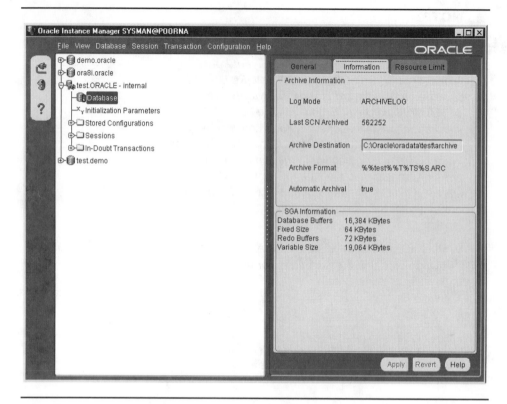

**FIGURE 2-3.** *Viewing SGA size from Instance Manager*

of data structures that are allocated based upon some INIT.ORA parameters. This variable size of the SGA is tunable using the INIT.ORA parameters. The INIT.ORA parameters that most affect the SGA size are the following:

- DB_BLOCK_SIZE
- DB_BLOCK_BUFFERS
- LOG_BUFFERS
- SHARED_POOL_SIZE

The DB_BLOCK_SIZE is specified in bytes and represents the size of an Oracle block. DB_BLOCK_BUFFERS is the total number of buffers in the SGA, each with a size of DB_BLOCK_SIZE, so DB_BLOCK_SIZE * DB_BLOCK_BUFFERS gives the total amount of space allocated in the SGA to cache data blocks. Since this portion of the SGA caches the database information, this area is also known as the *buffer* *cache.* Data blocks are usually read into the buffer cache for two reasons: either to read the buffer, or to modify the buffer. The modified buffers in the SGA are commonly referred to as the *dirty buffers.* There are various lists that Oracle maintains for the buffers in the buffer cache. The *dirty list* contains the list of all the dirty buffers that haven't yet been written back to the disk. All the dirty buffers will be flushed back to the disk at a later time, and this event is called a *checkpoint.* There are various ways in which a checkpoint can be triggered. We will discuss this concept in greater detail in Chapter 6.

LOG_BUFFERS is specified in bytes and represents the amount of space allocated for the redo log buffer. This is the area where any changes made to the data blocks are recorded before they are flushed to the redo log file on disk. The SHARED_POOL_SIZE is specified in bytes as well, and this is the amount of space in the SGA allocated to shared SQL and PL/SQL statements.

The following INIT.ORA parameters minimally impact the size of the SGA. For a complete listing and explanation of the INIT.ORA parameters, refer to the *Oracle8i Reference Release 8.1.5* manual.

- DB_FILES
- DB_FILE_MULTIBLOCK_READ_COUNTS
- DML_LOCKS
- ENQUEUE_RESOURCES
- PROCESSES
- SEQUENCE_CACHE_ENTRIES
- SEQUENCE_CACHE_HASH_BUCKETS
- SESSIONS
- TRANSACTIONS
- TRANSACTIONS_PER_ROLLBACK_SEGMENT

## Oracle Processes

A *process* of an operating system is a thread of control that executes a piece of code. Every process has a private memory area in which it runs. Some operating systems support running multiple processes concurrently, and some don't. In a single-process Oracle instance, the Oracle code is executed by a single process. This means only one user can access the database at any given point in time—multiple users cannot access the database concurrently. MS-Windows 3.1 is an example.

On the other hand, in a multiprocess Oracle instance, several processes execute different parts of the Oracle code concurrently, and each process has a specific job to do. In this environment, the processes can be categorized into two groups: *user processes* and *Oracle processes*. A process that is created to run a user application or an Oracle tool is called a user process. Oracle processes can be further subdivided into two types: *Oracle server processes* and *Oracle background processes*. In some operating systems such as VMS (single-task environment), the user process and the server process are combined into a single process. On operating systems such as UNIX (two-task environment), for every user process, a server process exists (Oracle also provides for an MTS configuration that allows user processes to share server processes). The Oracle background processes, along with the SGA, are generally called the *Oracle instance*. Let's take a closer look at the various tasks handled by the Oracle processes.

The server process (in a two-task environment) or user process (in a single-task environment) is responsible for parsing and executing the SQL statements issued by the application. Also, when the user issues a **select** statement and the blocks to be read are not in the SGA, the server/user process is responsible for reading those blocks from disk into the SGA. Once a SQL statement is parsed and executed, data is fetched from the block. The server/user process is responsible for returning this data back to the application.

In a multiprocess Oracle instance (with the two-task environment), the DBA can configure the database to operate with a *dedicated server* or a *Multi Threaded Server (MTS)*. In the former, every user process will have a dedicated server process to execute the Oracle code on its behalf. The dedicated server serves only one user process. In the latter, multiple user processes are serviced by a few *shared server processes*. All the user processes are connected to a special process known as the *dispatcher process*. The dispatcher process routes user process requests to the next available shared server process. The advantage of using MTS is to reduce the overhead of running too many processes on the system. For example, if 50 user processes are running applications in a dedicated server configuration, 50 server processes need to be established to serve the user processes, taking the total number of processes running on the system to 100. If the database is configured to operate as a multithreaded server with 10 shared servers, then the total number of processes running on the system will be 61 (50 user processes + 10 shared processes +1 dispatcher). We have assumed in this example that the user processes are running on the same machine as the server processes. Various INIT.ORA parameters are available to configure MTS. For a complete listing of the INIT.ORA parameters, refer to the *Oracle8i Reference Release 8.1.5* manual.

The Oracle background processes have different tasks and interact with different parts of the database. Note that all the Oracle background processes are not present in all environments. The number of Oracle background processes running on a server depends on the type of database configuration chosen by the DBA. The following is a complete list of all the Oracle background processes, followed by a brief description of each process:

- Database writer (DBWR)

- Log writer (LGWR)

- Checkpoint (CKPT)

- System monitor (SMON)

- Process monitor (PMON)

- Archiver (ARCH)

- Recoverer (RECO)

- Dispatcher (Dnnn)

- Server (Snnn)

- Lock (LCKn)

The *database writer process* (DBWR) is responsible for writing data blocks from the database buffer cache to the data files on disk using an LRU (least recently used) algorithm. Committed transactions do not force DBWR to write blocks to disk; however, DBWR is optimized to minimize disk I/O by only writing to disk when needed due to demand on SGA memory by other transactions. While using the PARALLEL SERVER option (the PARALLEL SERVER option is discussed at the end of this chapter), it might be necessary for one instance's DBWR process to write a dirty buffer to disk because a user needs to modify the same buffer from another instance. This operation is known as *pinging*. Pinging is a major concern in designing applications on a database running with the Parallel Server option because pinging will keep the DBWR process very busy, thus degrading database performance. The DBWR process is essential for normal operation of the database and is automatically started when the instance is started.

The *log writer process* (LGWR) is responsible for writing redo log entries from the redo log buffer to the redo log files on disk. LGWR also updates the headers of control files and data files to reflect the latest *checkpoint* when the checkpoint process is not present. The LGWR process is required for normal operation of the database and is automatically started when the instance is started.

The *checkpoint process* (CKPT) sends a signal to the DBWR at the checkpoint and updates the headers of control files and data files. In Oracle8*i*, the CKPT process is automatically started and is one of the background processes.

The *System Monitor* process (SMON) of an instance performs recovery when another instance belonging to this database (Parallel Server) has crashed or has terminated abnormally. The SMON process also cleans up *temporary segments* not in use, and recovers dead transactions skipped during crash/instance recovery. The concept of temporary segments is discussed later in this chapter, and Chapter 6 discusses in detail the concepts of crash and instance recovery. The SMON process is started automatically by Oracle and is required for normal operation of the database.

The *process monitor* (PMON) performs process recovery on failed user processes and frees up any resources the failed process was using. The PMON process also checks the *dispatcher* and *server* processes to restart them if necessary. The PMON process is essential for normal operation of the database and is automatically started when an instance is started.

The *archiver process* (ARCH) is present if the database is operating with *automatic archiving* enabled. Automatic archiving can be enabled by using the INIT.ORA parameter LOG_ARCHIVE_START or issuing the SQL*PLUS command **archive log start**. Note that the database needs to be in ARCHIVELOG mode to take advantage of the ARCH process (you can start the ARCH process even when the database is in NOARCHIVELOG mode, but this doesn't achieve anything). The ARCH process is responsible for copying the redo entries from the online redo log files to the archive area. If automatic archiving is not enabled, then the DBA needs to manually archive the redo log files when they become full. The INIT.ORA parameter LOG_ARCHIVE_START can be used to enable the ARCH process on database startup.

The *recoverer process* (RECO) is responsible for resolving failures involved in distributed transactions. In a distributed environment, Oracle may have multiple databases on multiple machines connected by a network. When a network or a node fails, some transactions will be put in an *in-doubt* state, depending on when the failure occurred. The RECO process attempts to establish communication with remote servers. When a connection between the database servers is reestablished, the RECO process automatically resolves all the in-doubt transactions. If an instance is not permitted to do distributed transactions, this process doesn't need to be enabled. The INIT.ORA parameter DISTRIBUTED_TRANSACTIONS is used to enable the RECO process.

As discussed earlier, the *dispatcher processes* (Dnnn) are present only if you are operating the database with a multithreaded server configuration. The dispatcher processes manage requests to/from user processes and shared server processes. Multiple dispatcher processes can be started by the DBA. At least one dispatcher process is required for each network protocol being used by users to communicate with Oracle. The parameters MTS_DISPATCHERS and MTS_MAX_DISPATCHERS in the INIT.ORA pertain to dispatcher configuration.

The *server processes* are responsible for communicating with user processes and interacting with Oracle to carry out tasks on behalf of the associated user processes. If you are operating the database with a multithreaded server configuration, each server process will service multiple user processes, thereby minimizing system resources. If you are operating the database with a dedicated server configuration, every user process will have a dedicated server process. The INIT.ORA parameters MTS_SERVERS MTS_MAX_SERVERS, MTS_DISPATCHERS, and MTS_MAX_DISPATCHERS can be used to configure server processes in an MTS configuration.

The *lock processes* (LCKn) are used for interinstance locking in an Oracle Parallel Server environment. The Parallel Server option is described at the end of this chapter. For more details on this background process, refer to the *Oracle8i Parallel Server Setup and Configuration Guide Release 8.1.5.*

Parallel Query Servers are processes that are used in parallel queries. These processes are defined by the parameters PARALLEL_MIN_SERVERS, PARALLEL_MAX_SERVERS, and PARALLEL_SERVER_IDLE_TIME in the INIT.ORA file. Oracle8 provides full support for all parallel DML (PDML) operations. The number of query server processes associated with an operation is known as the *degree of parallelism.* This can be specified as a hint in the SQL statement or defined in the table definition itself.

## Database Startup and Shutdown

During the Oracle database startup and shutdown, a number of events occur that take the Oracle database through various stages. The *Oracle8i SQL Reference Release 8.1.5* manual gives the complete syntax to start up and shut down the Oracle database. To access the Oracle database, the DBA needs to open the database. If you have configured Oracle Enterprise Manager and registered your database with OEM, you can control the startup and shutdown activities of the database using Oracle Instance Manager. The following example shows how to open an Oracle database:

```
C:\>sqlplus connect internal/oracle
SQL*Plus: Release 8.1.5.0.0 - Production on Tue Apr 18 14:01:02 2000
(c) Copyright 1999 Oracle Corporation.  All rights reserved.
Connected to an idle instance.
SQL> startup open
ORACLE instance started.
Total System Global Area    36437964 bytes
Fixed Size                     65484 bytes
Variable Size               19521536 bytes
Database Buffers            16777216 bytes
Redo Buffers                   73728 bytes
Database mounted.
Database opened.
SQL>
```

Figure 2-4 shows the status of a shutdown database in the Oracle Instance Manager GUI. You can start the instance and open the database by selecting the radio button as shown in Figure 2-4. Figure 2-5 shows the completion of opening a database in Oracle Instance Manager.

When the **startup open** command is issued, the database passes through three stages—**nomount**, **mount**, and **open**—before becoming available. The DBA can also manually start up the database to a particular stage using the SQL*PLUS **startup**

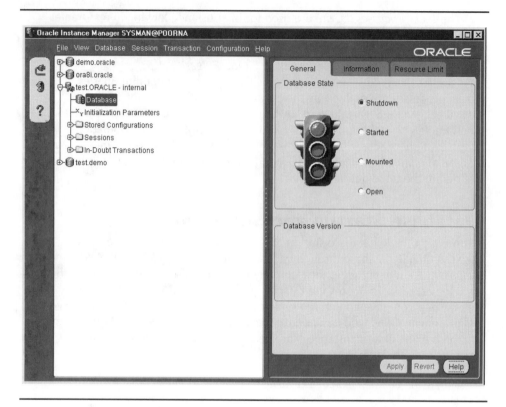

**FIGURE 2-4.**   *Viewing a shutdown database from Instance Manager*

command or Oracle Instance Manager. Oracle8*i* SQL*PLUS supports all Server
Manager commands. This is necessary during particular operations. For example, if
database recovery needs to be performed, the database has to be mounted and the
**recover database** command issued. The following example shows how to set the
database to **nomount** and **mount** stages, respectively:

```
SQL> startup nomount
ORACLE instance started.
Total System Global Area                           36437964 bytes
Fixed Size                                             65484 bytes
Variable Size                                       19521536 bytes
Database Buffers                                    16777216 bytes
Redo Buffers                                           73728 bytes
SQL> SQL> startup mount
ORACLE instance started.
Total System Global Area                           36437964 bytes
Fixed Size                                             65484 bytes
```

```
Variable Size                                        19521536 bytes
Database Buffers                                      16777216 bytes
Redo Buffers                                            73728 bytes
Database mounted.
SQL>
```

During the **nomount** stage, Oracle reads the INIT.ORA file, locates the control files, creates and initializes the SGA, and, finally, starts all Oracle background processes. As mentioned earlier, the combination of the Oracle background processes and the SGA is referred to as an Oracle instance. As shown in the above example, when the database is at the **nomount** stage, Oracle displays a message saying that the instance has started. You need to set the database to the **nomount** stage while creating the database for the first time or while re-creating a control file after losing the current control file. During the **mount** stage, Oracle opens the control files to identify the location of the data files and the online redo logs. However, no verification checks are performed on the data files and log files at this time. The instance mounts the

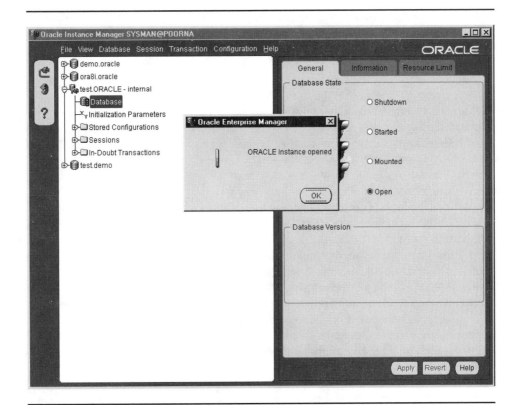

**FIGURE 2-5.**   *Viewing an open database from Instance Manager*

database and gets an instance lock, and it verifies that no other instance has mounted this database. After this is done, Oracle displays a message to the user screen saying that the database is mounted. There are a number of reasons why you might want to set the database to a mounted state. In general, any SQL command that starts with the keywords **alter database** can be executed while the database is mounted (note that some of these commands can be executed while the database is open as well). Some of the database operations that can be performed while the database is mounted are as follows:

- Performing media recovery
- Taking a data file offline or online
- Relocating data files and redo log files
- Creating a new redo log group (or member) or deleting an existing redo log group (or member)

During the **open** stage, the instance opens the database, gets a lock on the data files, and opens all the online redo log files. (If it is the first instance to open the database, it gets a *startup* lock as well.) If the instance is opening the database after an abnormal termination or after a database crash, crash recovery will be performed automatically by Oracle using the online redo log files. After the database is opened, Oracle displays a message to the user screen saying that the database is open. Figure 2-6 gives a schematic diagram of the various stages that the Oracle database goes through during startup.

Three options are available to DBAs while shutting down the database: NORMAL, IMMEDIATE, and ABORT. The NORMAL shutdown process stops all user access to the database, waits until all users complete their requests and disconnect from the server, purges data buffer and redo log caches and updates data files and online redo logs, drops file locks, completes ongoing transactions, updates file headers, closes thread, drops the database instance lock, and synchronizes control files and data files. In short, the shutdown NORMAL option closes the database, dismounts the database, and shuts down the instance gracefully. The NORMAL shutdown should be done before a cold database backup—it ensures complete consistency of the database and will not require crash recovery during the next startup. The NORMAL option is always recommended while shutting down the database.

In certain situations, it might be necessary for you to choose the IMMEDIATE option while shutting down the database. For example, the DBA might decide to increase the PROCESSES parameter in the INIT.ORA file. If this needs to be done immediately, the DBA should use the IMMEDIATE option. If this option is used to shut down the database, the current SQL statements that are being processed by Oracle are terminated immediately, any uncommitted transactions are rolled back, and the database is shut down. The only disadvantage of using this option is that

Oracle doesn't wait for the current users to disconnect. However, the database will be consistent and no recovery is required during the next startup.

Likewise, in emergency situations and when all else fails, a shutdown with the ABORT option can be used. An example would be when one of the background processes dies and you cannot shut down the database using the NORMAL or IMMEDIATE option. When the ABORT option is used, current SQL statements are immediately terminated and the uncommitted transactions are not rolled back.

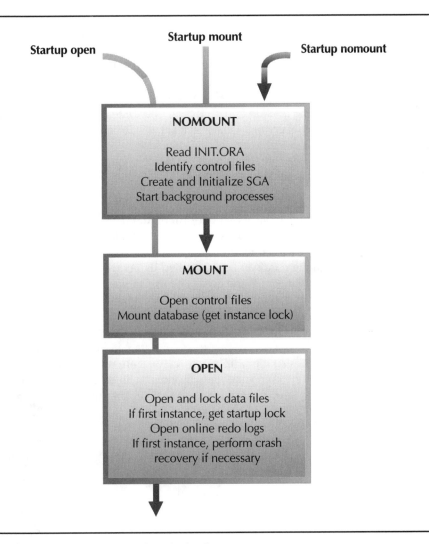

**FIGURE 2-6.**   *Three stages during database startup*

Shutdown with the ABORT option will require *crash recovery* on the next startup of the database, and this option should be used only when it is absolutely necessary. The stages of the shutdown and paths taken for NORMAL, IMMEDIATE, and ABORT are shown in Figure 2-7.

# Data Storage

The database's data is collectively stored in the tablespaces. A *tablespace* is a logical entity that corresponds to one or more physical data files on disk or disks. The database is divided into one or more tablespaces. Each tablespace can have one or more physical data files. Figure 2-8 depicts a typical database storage structure. The primary reason for this logical grouping of data is to increase the flexibility in performing database operations. In this section, we look at some of the database administrative operations corresponding to tablespaces and data files that are necessary while doing backup and recovery. The *Oracle8i Concepts Release 8.1.5 and Oracle8i Administrator's Guide Release 8.1.5* manual gives a complete description of managing the tablespaces and data files.

## Tablespaces and Data Files

A tablespace is used by DBAs to perform space management tasks, control the availability of data in the database, and perform partial backup and recovery of the database. The space management tasks include, among other things, controlling disk allocation and usage by users.

The availablility of the data can be controlled by taking a specific tablespace offline so that users cannot access the data. The first tablespace in the database is always the SYSTEM tablespace. This tablespace has to be available *all* the time for normal operation of the database because it contains the data dictionary information of the database. After initial creation of the database, it is recommended that additional tablespaces be created so that the user data can be separated from the data dictionary data. Also if multiple applications are running on the database, you might want to keep the data separately. Following is an example showing how you can use Oracle Storage Manager and SQL*PLUS utility to create a new tablespace called NEW_USERS that is 20MB in size.

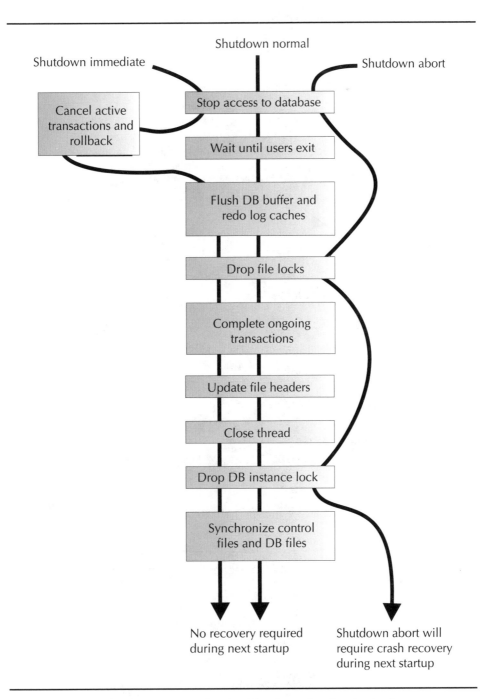

**FIGURE 2-7.** *The three options for shutting down the Oracle database*

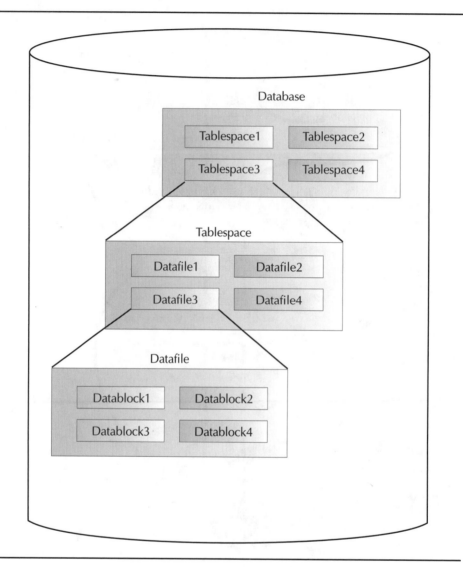

**FIGURE 2-8.** *Database storage structure*

**1.** Select Object │ Create from the Oracle Storage Manager main menu. You will see a pop-up menu. Select the Tablespace option and click the Create button.

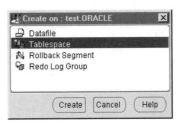

**2.** In the Create Tablespace window's General tab, type the name of the tablespace you want to create; then click the Create botton.

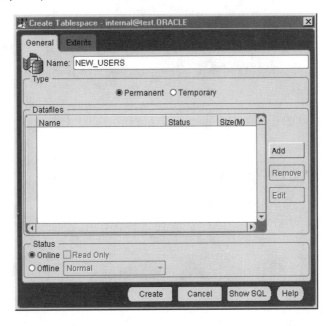

**3.** In the Create Datafile Window, type the datafile name and the size of the file in MB or KB. The illustration shows that the filename is USR_DATA and the file size is 20MB. Click OK.

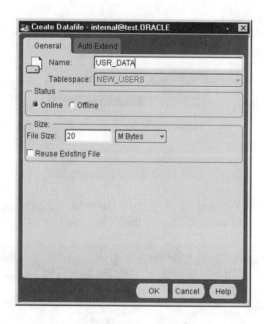

4. You will again see the Create Tablespace window, with the data filename, size, and status that you have selected shown in the Datafile Name area. Click the Create button.

**5.** Oracle will display a dialog box that indicates the operation was successful.

The **create tablespace** command should be used for creating a tablespace if using SQL*PLUS. For example,

```
SQL> CREATE TABLESPACE tablespace_name DATAFILE 'datafile_name' SIZE 50M ONLINE;
```

The above command will create a tablespace with one data file with a size of 50MB. The *tablespace_name* and *datafile_name* parameters represent the tablespace name and the full path name of the data file, respectively. When creating a tablespace, you have to specify what type of space management you want to set for the tablespace. Oracle gives you two options: dictionary managed and locally managed tablespaces.

## Dictionary Managed Tablespaces

When you choose this method, Oracle uses the data dictionary to manage the tablespaces' extents. Whenever a change is made to the tablespace, Oracle updates the appropriate tables in the data dictionary. You should be aware that this method involves recursive space management operations, thereby resulting in resource contention in accessing the data dictionary. If you don't specify a type while creating a tablespace, this method will be the default.

## Locally Managed Tablespaces

In this method, a tablespace manages its own extents by maintaining a bitmap in each data file to keep track of the free or used status of blocks in that data file. Oracle changes the bitmap values to show the new status of the blocks whenever space allocation and deallocation happens on the tablespace. Choosing this method has the following advantages:

- Avoids recursive space management operations in the data dictionary

- Reduces user dependence on the data dictionary

- Eliminates the need to coalesce free extents in the tablespace

- Supports temporary tablespace management in standby databases

Once you assign a space management method while creating a tablespace, it cannot be changed to other space management methods later on.

The new feature in Oracle8*i*, *transportable tablespaces,* enables you to move a subset of an Oracle database from one Oracle database to another by copying the physical data files and changing the meta-data in the data dictionary of the target database. Transporting tablespaces has the following advantages:

■  Transporting data from OLTP systems to data warehouse staging systems

■  Loading data marts from central data warehouses

■  Archiving OLTP and data warehouse systems efficiently

■  Data publishing to internal and external customers

Each tablespace has a default *storage* parameter that determines how much space should be allocated for each object created in that tablespace. Note that at least one physical data file should be created with each tablespace. If more space needs to be allocated to the tablespace after creation, the tablespace can be altered to add one or more physical data files to it. The **alter tablespace** command should be used for this purpose. For example, the command

```
SQL> ALTER TABLESPACE tablespace_name
ADD DATAFILE 'datafile_name' SIZE 20M;
```

adds a data file with a size of 20MB to an existing tablespace. If the data files of a tablespace need to be relocated, this can be done either with the **alter tablespace** command or the **alter database** command. If **alter tablespace** is used, the tablespace should be taken offline first. If **alter database** is used, the database needs to be in a mounted state, but not open. Before issuing either of the above commands, the data files need to be copied to the destination. While relocating the data files that belong to the SYSTEM tablespace, **alter database** is the only way since the SYSTEM tablespace can never be taken offline. Consider the following examples:

```
SQL> ALTER TABLESPACE tablespace_name
RENAME DATAFILE 'old_filename' TO 'new_filename';

SQL> ALTER DATABASE RENAME FILE 'old_filename' TO 'new_filename';
```

**NOTE**
*It is always a good practice to take a complete backup of the data files, log files, and control files before and after any schema changes to the database.*

## Taking Tablespaces Offline

Taking a tablespace *offline* means making the data in the tablespace unavailable to
users. When a tablespace is taken offline, Oracle will take all the associated data files
offline as well. The SYSTEM tablespace can never be taken offline. Figure 2-9 shows all
tablespaces available in a database and their status, size, and space usage. Sometimes,
it is necessary to take a non-SYSTEM tablespace offline because Oracle signaled a
*write error* on one of the data files of the tablespace. In other cases, the DBA might
have to take the tablespace offline for regular maintenance. For example, if the DBA
needs to relocate a data file that belongs to a tablespace called USERS, then the USERS
tablespace needs to be taken offline. After the appropriate work is done, the DBA
needs to make the tablespace available to the users again. This is known as bringing
the tablespace *online*. While running a production database, you need to be very
careful when taking tablespaces offline as it might impede the database users'
work. Such operations should normally be done during scheduled database
maintenance time.

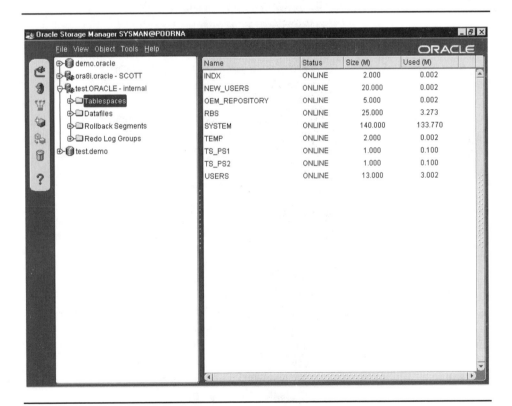

**FIGURE 2-9.** *A typical database storage structure from Storage Manager*

There are four *modes* in which a tablespace can be taken offline: NORMAL, TEMPORARY, IMMEDIATE, and FOR RECOVERY. If no error conditions occur on any of the data files, it is always recommended to take a tablespace offline in the NORMAL mode. In this mode, Oracle would do a checkpoint for the tablespace before taking it offline gracefully.

If a tablespace is taken offline with the TEMPORARY option, Oracle checkpoints all the data files that are available and then takes the tablespace offline. If one of the files has a corruption and you can't write to it, then the NORMAL option will fail and the TEMPORARY option needs to be used. You should use the TEMPORARY option only when one of the data files has a write error and you can't write to it. For example, let's assume that tablespace T1 contains two data files, D1 and D2, and that file D1 was taken offline by Oracle due to a write error. If the TEMPORARY option is used to take tablespace T1 offline, then Oracle checkpoints data file D2 before taking T1 offline. After the problem is fixed, while bringing the tablespace online, Oracle will do recovery for data file D1.

The IMMEDIATE option can be used only if the database is operating in ARCHIVELOG mode. If the tablespace is taken offline with this option, no checkpointing is done before taking the tablespace offline, and Oracle requests *media recovery* for this tablespace when it is brought online. You should use this option only when all the data files of a tablespace have a write error and you can't write to them. Chapter 6 gives details on media recovery. The FOR RECOVERY option is used for taking the production tablespaces in the recovery set offline for performing a tablespace point-in-time recovery operation. This can be used when one or more data files of a tablespace are unavailable. This option will be applicable only when you run your database in ARCHIVELOG mode. In the following example, tablespace USERS is taken offline with the NORMAL option:

```
SQL> ALTER TABLESPACE users OFFLINE NORMAL;
```

## Taking Data Files Offline

It is not normal to take data files offline and online. If a specific data file is damaged, you need to take it offline, get it repaired, and bring it online again. If the file is lost and a backup file is restored, recovery needs to be done on the data file before bringing it online again. The following example will illustrate why it might be necessary to take a non-SYSTEM data file offline.

Let's assume that a tablespace called USER_DATA contains two data files: **c:\oracle\database\usr1.ora** and **d:\oracle\database\usr2.ora**. Let's further assume that **usr1.ora** contains user tables and **usr2.ora** contains the indexes for tables that are in **usr1.ora**. Let's say that drive D crashed, making **usr2.ora** unavailable. At this time, using the **alter database** command, **usr2.ora** can be taken offline. The advantage of this is that the users can still access the tables in **usr1.ora** but cannot use the indexes that reside in **usr2.ora**. Once disk D is restored and **usr2.ora** is recovered, the data file can be brought online again. If an older

copy of **usr2.ora** is restored, you need to apply recovery to **usr2.ora** by using the
**recover datafile** command before bringing the file online. The **recover datafile**
command is described in Chapter 6. In this example, we have assumed that the
objects are not spanning data files, but in a relational model it is possible for objects
to span data files within a tablespace. The following syntax takes data files offline.

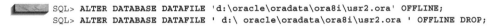
```
SQL> ALTER DATABASE DATAFILE 'd:\oracle\oradata\ora8i\usr2.ora' OFFLINE;
SQL> ALTER DATABASE DATAFILE ' d:\ oracle\oradata\ora8i\usr2.ora ' OFFLINE DROP;
```

The first command should be used only if you are operating the database in
ARCHIVELOG mode. If operating in NOARCHIVELOG mode, you should use the
second command. If you want to know if a specific data file is online or offline,
select the STATUS column from the V$DATAFILE view.

The Oracle Storage Manager that is included with the Oracle Enterprise Manager
provides an easy-to-use GUI that allows you to manage tablespaces and data files.
Figure 2-10 shows how Storage Manager can be used to modify a tablespace so that it

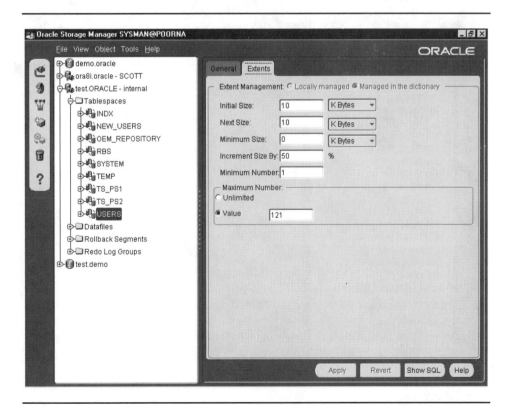

**FIGURE 2-10.**   *Modifying tablespace characteristics with Oracle Storage Manager*

has *unlimited extents* (equivalent to the AUTOEXTEND option in the **alter tablespace** command) and Figure 2-11 shows how Storage Manager can be used to take a data file offline.

## Partitions

When it comes to managing very large tables, a DBA is concerned about issues such as data access, storage, performance, file contention, etc. In order to address these problems, Oracle offers a mechanism called *partitioning* that allows DBAs to split large tables into smaller pieces called *partitions* in order to achieve high performance. Oracle offers two basic partitioning schemes: *range partitioning* and *hash partitioning*. The range partitioning allows users to select the data ranges that Oracle will use to create the partitions. The hash partitioning uses a hash function on the partitioning columns to stripe data into small partitions as per function definition.

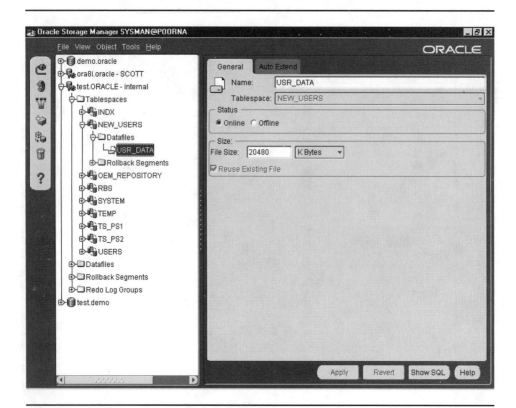

**FIGURE 2-11.** *Taking a data file offline with Oracle Storage Manager*

Hash partitioning allows data that does not lend itself to range partitioning to be easily partitioned for performance reasons when parallel DML, partition pruning, and partition-wise joins are performed on the partition tables. Oracle also offers one more partition method, namely *composite partitioning*, which is a combination of both range and hash methods. The composite partitioning method partitions the data by range and further subdivides the data into subpartitions using a hash function. Furthermore, Oracle allows a table or index segment to span tablespaces. This is made possible by the fact that partitions belonging to a table or an index can be placed in separate tablespaces. This eases maintenance operations and improves performance, as well as providing for partial failures. Partitioning only applies to nonclustered tables and indexes. All partitions of a table or index share the same column, index, and constraint definitions while the physical storage attributes such as PCTFREE, PCTUSED, INITRANS, and MAXTRANS can vary for each partition. Users can decide if they want to partition the index belonging to the table or not. Users can also choose if they want a matching index partition for each table partition (termed *equipartitioning*).

Partition maintenance operations are much faster than similar operations for the entire table. For example, you can rebuild indexes for a partition using the **create index** statement. This is much faster than rebuilding the index for the entire table.

Performance is improved, as partitioning allows partitions belonging to a table to span tablespaces. Disk striping allows for better performance. The new extended ROWID format in Oracle includes the OBJECT_ID, which allows faster access to data as partitions have their own unique OBJECT_ID.

Since partitions can span tablespaces, Oracle provides for partition independence. Tablespaces that hold partitions can be placed on separate disks to allow for partial availability. You can take a tablespace offline for maintenance even as the remaining partitions in the table are available for use.

We will highlight some of the advantages of partitioning with the following sample script. The script creates a test table ABC with two partitions P1 and P2 in tablespaces USER_DATA and TEMPORARY_DATA, respectively. In the second half of the script, we will take the TEMPORARY_DATA tablespace offline and verify that partition P1 is still available. This demonstrates the concept of partial failure by use of partitions.

```
PROMPT General Setup
set echo on
drop table abc;
set echo off
set feedback on
set lines 80
set pause off
col partition_name format a10
col index_name format a12
col tablespace_name format a16
```

```
col table_name format a10
col high_value format a10
set echo off
PAUSE Create a partition table with partitions p1 in the
PAUSE user's default tablespace and partition p2 in the temporary
PAUSE tablespace
set echo on
create table abc(a number, b varchar2(10))
partition by range(a)
(partition p1 values less than(10) tablespace user_data,
 partition p2 values less than(20) tablespace temporary_data);
set echo off
PAUSE Verify through the Data Dictionary
set echo on
select table_name, partition_name, high_value, tablespace_name
from user_tab_partitions where table_name ='ABC';
set echo off
PAUSE Insert rows using the partition-extended name
set echo on
insert into abc partition (p1) values (1,'Rama');
insert into abc partition (p2) values (11,'Double A');
commit;
set echo off
PAUSE Now take the temporary tablespace offline
set echo on
connect system/aa
alter tablespace temporary_data offline;
set echo off
PAUSE Verify that partial data in partition p1 is still available
set echo on
connect scott/tiger
select * from abc partition (p1);
set echo off
PAUSE You cannot do a full table scan
set echo on
select * from abc;
```

The output of the above script is shown here:

```
SQL> @d:\aa\b2\working\partition
SQL> PROMPT General Setup
General Setup
SQL> set echo on
SQL> drop table abc;
Table dropped.
SQL> set echo off
Create a partition table with partitions p1 in the
user's default tablespace and partition p2 in the temporary
tablespace
```

```
SQL> create table abc(a number, b varchar2(10))
  2  partition by range(a)
  3  (partition p1 values less than(10) tablespace user_data,
  4   partition p2 values less than(20) tablespace temporary_data);
Table created.
SQL>
SQL> set echo off
Verify through the Data Dictionary

SQL> select table_name, partition_name, high_value, tablespace_name
  2  from user_tab_partitions where table_name ='ABC';
TABLE_NAME PARTITION_ HIGH_VALUE TABLESPACE_NAME
---------- ---------- ---------- ----------------

ABC        P2         20         TEMPORARY_DATA
ABC        P1         10         USER_DATA
2 rows selected.
SQL>
SQL> set echo off
Insert rows using the partition-extended name
SQL> insert into abc partition (p1) values (1,'Rama');
1 row created.
SQL> insert into abc partition (p2) values (11,'Double A');
1 row created.
SQL> commit;
Commit complete.
SQL> set echo off
Now take the temporary tablespace offline
SQL> connect system/aa
Connected.
SQL> alter tablespace temporary_data offline;
Tablespace altered.
SQL> set echo off
Verify that partial data in partition p1 is still available
SQL> connect scott/tiger
Connected.
SQL> select * from abc partition (p1);
        A B
--------- ----------
        1 Rama
1 row selected.
SQL> set echo off
You cannot do a full table scan
SQL> select * from abc;
ERROR:
ORA-00376: file 4 cannot be read at this time
ORA-01110: data file 4: 'D:\ORANT\DATABASE\TMP1ORCL.ORA'
```

You can refer to the *Oracle8i Administrator's Guide Release 8.1.5* manual for more details on partitioning.

## Segments, Extents, and Blocks

The data in the database is stored in *Oracle blocks.* An Oracle block is the smallest unit of physical space and is a multiple of operating system blocks. The Oracle block size is usually 2,048 bytes, but can be set as high as 8KB. The DB_BLOCK_SIZE parameter in the INIT.ORA file determines the size of the Oracle block. Keeping the Oracle block size high could result in a better buffer cache hit ratio because an individual physical read gets more data, which increases the likelihood that the next read will find what it needs without going to disk, especially in online transaction processing (OLTP) environments. Some DBAs find general read throughput improvements by migrating from a 2KB database block size to a 4KB database block size. However, with a bigger Oracle block size, it takes more space in the SGA to have the same DB_BLOCK_BUFFERS. If memory is constrained, it is recommended that you have more Oracle blocks of a smaller size than fewer Oracle blocks of a larger size. Refer to Figure 2-8, which depicts the building blocks of a typical Oracle database. It also shows the relationship between tablespaces, data files, and data blocks in a database.

A contiguous collection of Oracle blocks is called an *extent.* This is a logical unit of space. A collection of extents is called a *segment,* which is the next level of logical storage unit. There are different kinds of segments in the database. Figure 2-12 shows how segments, extents, and data blocks make up a tablespace. For example, the data of a table is stored in a *data segment.* Similarly, an *index segment* contains the data of an index. Other segments in the database are *temporary segments, rollback segments,* and *bootstrap segments.* When an object (such as a table, index, or rollback segment) is created, an extent is allocated to the object's segment. As the object grows, more space is required and extra extents are allocated to the segment. The first Oracle block of the first extent contains the *segment header.* For example, when table EMP is created, the first Oracle block of the first extent of the EMP table contains the data segment header. If you choose to partition a table, then each new partition allocates an initial extent that contains a header. Among other things, the segment header contains information about freelists and also the *extent map.* The extent map contains information about the number of extents allocated to the segment and each extent's size. Note that while using the PARALLEL SERVER option, if the FREELIST GROUPS is set to a number greater than 1 while creating a table, the segment header doesn't contain the freelist information, but another Oracle block is allocated to maintain the freelist information. We will discuss the PARALLEL SERVER option at the end of this chapter.

While designing a database, careful consideration should be given to sizing the database and anticipating the growth of tables and data. Sizing is essential for

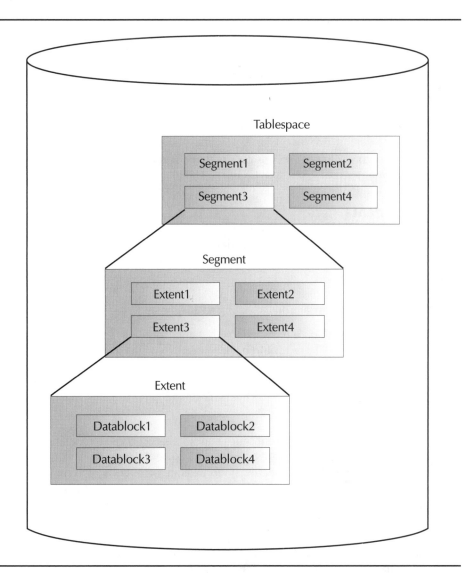

**FIGURE 2-12.**   *Relationship among segments, extents, and data blocks*

implementing a production (or test/development) database that will be around for a long time. The space requirements for database objects should be carefully calculated and accounted for before the database goes into production.

Accurate sizing of the data dictionary, user tables, user indexes, rollback segments, and redo logs depends on accurate estimates of the following:

- The number and size of rows stored (or to be stored) in user tables

- The transaction mix

- The sizes and performance characteristics of database objects

The next section gives some tips on space management issues for different database segments.

## Data Segments

Consideration should be made for the larger tables that will reside in the database, as well as for tables that will grow considerably over time. To size the transactions, you will need to ascertain the nature of your transactions. These can fall into three basic categories:

- Short update transactions affecting relatively small amounts of data

- Long-running update transactions that alter significant amounts of data before committing or rolling back

- Long-running read-only transactions that only query data but require that read-consistent snapshots of tables remain available until the last fetch of the query is completed

The transaction mix for different times should also be considered, since it may vary throughout the day. For example, during the daytime work hours users might perform short update transactions, whereas in the evening you may execute longer-running batch jobs doing updates or queries. Both cases should be investigated and planned for in the production system. This transaction mix may also change over time as the number of users increases or decreases and the amount of data to be processed changes. Once the row and transaction information is gathered from an analysis of the application, object sizes for the database can be estimated.

**Data Dictionary/System Tablespace**　　The data dictionary space should remain relatively constant, growing only as the database objects increase. Whenever the database is in operation, the Oracle RDBMS updates the data dictionary in response to every DDL statement, reflecting changes in database structures, auditing, grants, and data. The data dictionary generally requires only a small percentage of space when compared with application requirements. It is critical to allow enough room for the data dictionary to grow and for other objects such as *deferred rollback segments* to exist in the SYSTEM tablespace.

To ensure that space remains available for the data dictionary and other objects that must reside in the SYSTEM tablespace, place all other user tables, indexes, temporary segments, and rollback segments in other tablespaces. In addition, make the SYSTEM tablespace large enough so that it has at least 50 to 75 percent free space. Finally, ensure that your users do not have privileges on the SYSTEM tablespace for creating objects or temporary segments.

**Tables**     In Oracle8*i*, the space required for tables will vary considerably depending on the partitioning scheme adopted and the degree of parallelism used in Parallel DML (PDML) operations. For partitioned tables, the space requirements will be proportional to the number of partitions created since each partition allocated initial extents and next extents. Statements such as parallel appends multiply the space requirements for data segments as each parallel server allocates extents separately.

Table size increases proportionally with the number of rows in the table, assuming the average row length remains constant. It is very important to know the types of transactions that will affect the data in the tables. This will help you size the storage clause parameters PCTFREE and PCTUSED accordingly when the table is initially created. A detailed description of the storage clause is given in the *Oracle8i SQL Reference Release 8.1.5* manual. For example, as the rows lengthen in a block, *row chaining* may result if PCTFREE is not set sufficiently high. (Row chaining is when pieces of a single row reside in multiple Oracle blocks.)

Oracle8*i* has new data types for *large objects* (LOBS) like BLOB, CLOB, and NCLOB. LOB data can be stored inline or out of line. Users can choose the tablespace that is used for out-of-line storage. This allows users to choose appropriate storage parameters for the tablespace that holds LOB data.

### Index Segments

Indexes are objects that are associated with tables and clusters, and are used to speed up the execution of a SQL statement. Dropping or creating indexes doesn't affect the associated tables. Indexes increase in size slightly faster than the corresponding table if the data in the table is modified frequently, so you should estimate the size of the index carefully.

Space management is more efficient if you maintain indexes for large tables in separate tablespaces—it decreases fragmentation and also makes managing the index growth easier if re-creating the index is necessary.

Oracle also supports partitioning on index segments. Users can decide if they want to create an index partition for each table partition (termed *equipartitioning*) or create their own combination of index partitions.

## Rollback Segments

A rollback segment is a segment in the database that stores the before image information of data when a transaction modifies a block. The information in the rollback segment is used for read consistency, transaction rollback, and during transaction recovery. For example, if a transaction modifies a block by changing the key value of a column from 10 to 20, then the old value of 10 needs to be stored in the rollback segment and the data block will have a new value of 20. If the transaction is rolled back, then the value 10 is copied from the rollback segment back to the data block.

**Contents of Rollback Segments**     It's important to understand what is stored in the rollback segment when a transaction modifies a block. The rollback segment does not store the whole data block—only the before image of the row or rows that were modified. Information in the rollback segment consists of several rollback entries called *undo*. For example, if a row is inserted into a table, the undo created by that transaction would include the ROWID of that row, among other information. This is because the undo operation of an **insert** is a **delete**, and all you need to delete a row is the ROWID. If a **delete** operation is performed on a table, the complete row will be part of the undo. For update transactions, we store the old value of the updated columns. If the transaction modifies an index as well, then the old index keys will also be stored as part of the undo. Rollback segments guarantee that the undo information is kept for the life of a transaction.

Every rollback segment has a *transaction table*. When a transaction modifies a data block, it updates the data block header, which points to the rollback segment that has the undo information for that transaction. The transaction also inserts an entry into the transaction table of the rollback segment. Among other information, the transaction table entry gives the address of the data block that was modified, status of the transaction (commit or active), and the location within the rollback segment where the undo for that transaction is stored.

**Operation of Rollback Segments**     A rollback segment, like any other segment, consists of multiple extents. However, the main difference between a data segment and a rollback segment is that the rollback segment uses its extents in an ordered, circular fashion, moving from one extent to the next after the current extent is full. A transaction writes a record to the current location in the rollback segment and advances the current pointer by the size of the record. The current writing location of the undo is called the *head* of the rollback segment. The location of the oldest active undo record is called the *tail* of the rollback segment. The undo generated by a transaction is guaranteed to remain in the rollback segment until the transaction commits or rolls back.

Some important rules in allocating space for rollback segments are as follows:

■ A transaction can only use one rollback segment to store all of its undo records. In other words, a transaction cannot span rollback segments.

■ Multiple transactions can write to the same extent of a rollback segment.

■ Only one active transaction can be in a rollback segment block. This reduces contention on the rollback segment block.

■ The head of the rollback segment never wraps into an extent currently occupied by the tail.

■ Extents in the ring are never skipped over and used out of order as the head tries to advance.

■ If the head cannot wrap into the next extent, it allocates a new extent and inserts it into the ring between the two original extents.

The following example illustrates the space allocation in rollback segments.

A transaction has started and is updating blocks in a table. The undo generated by the transaction is being written to the rollback segment. Let's assume the current head of the undo is in block 5 of extent 1 (which is the current extent) and needs to generate more undo records. If extent 1 has no more blocks, it will look at the next extent (either extent 2 or 0), say extent 2. If all the undo records in extent 2 belong to transactions that are already committed, then the transaction can use the first block of extent 2. A new transaction or continuing transaction that needs more space can then use the next available block in extent 2 without doing the same checks, because *extent 2* is now the head.

Now let's discuss the algorithm used in selecting a rollback segment. The following steps will make this algorithm clear:

**1.** If forced to use SYSTEM (for a certain operation), go to step 6.

**2.** If using the **set transaction use rollback segment** command, go to step 7.

**3.** Skip rollback segment SYSTEM to consider other rollback segments if present; otherwise, go to step 6.

**4.** Skip a rollback segment if marked OFFLINE, NEEDS RECOVERY, or PENDING OFFLINE.

**5.** Find and select the rollback segment with the least number of active transactions. In case of a tie between multiple rollback segments, select the rollback segment after the one last used (round-robin) and go to step 7.

6. Select SYSTEM rollback segment.

7. Use the selected rollback segment if possible. If the rollback segment already has the maximum number of active transactions, then wait and loop back to step 2.

Note that the PCTINCREASE parameter of the storage clause cannot be used with the **create rollback segment** statement. This has been replaced by a parameter called OPTIMAL. This specifies the optimal size of a rollback segment in bytes. It can also be specified in kilobytes or megabytes. The RDBMS tries to keep the segment at its specified optimal size. The size is rounded up to the extent boundary, which means that the RDBMS tries to have the fewest number of extents such that the total size is greater than or equal to the size specified as OPTIMAL. If additional space is needed beyond the optimal size, it will eventually deallocate extents to shrink back to this size. The process of deallocating extents is performed when the head moves from one extent *(n)* to the next *(n + 1)*. At the time, the segment size is checked and the RDBMS checks if the *n + 2* extent can be deallocated. The extent can only be deallocated if there are no active transactions in it. If necessary, the RDBMS will deallocate several extents at a time until the segment has shrunk back to its optimal size. The RDBMS always deallocates the oldest inactive extents, as they are the least likely to be used for read consistency.

The optimal size can be set on the SYSTEM rollback segment as well. This is important because the SYSTEM rollback segment can grow like any other rollback segment, but can never be dropped by the DBA since it belongs to the user SYS. There are two main reasons why SYSTEM rollback segments can grow: either there are no non-SYSTEM rollback segments created by the DBA, or the user has specifically requested Oracle to use the SYSTEM rollback segment by issuing the following command before executing the transaction:

```
SQL> set transaction use rollback segment SYSTEM;
```

In either case, the SYSTEM rollback segment will grow, and the only way to shrink it is to use the OPTIMAL parameter. However, it's very important to note that the OPTIMAL parameter should not be set too small for the SYSTEM rollback segment. The initial size of the SYSTEM rollback segment is 100K, and the OPTIMAL for it should not be smaller than that. If the OPTIMAL value is set less than the MINEXTENTS size, you will get an error. Setting the OPTIMAL parameter too small for the SYSTEM rollback segment (or any rollback segment) may degrade the system's performance because the rollback segment keeps shrinking too often, which is an expensive operation.

Oracle allows *dynamic onlining* and *offlining* of rollback segments. What this means is that the database doesn't need to be shut down and started up to change the status of a rollback segment. By default, whenever a rollback segment is created it is offline and must be acquired by the instance or brought online. If a rollback segment has to be brought online, the SQL command **alter rollback segment** with the ONLINE option can be used. To take a rollback segment offline, you can use the OFFLINE option. If a rollback segment is taken offline and the specified rollback segment does not have any active transactions, it is immediately taken offline. But if the specified rollback segment contains rollback data (undo) for active transactions, it is taken offline once all the active transactions are either committed or rolled back. No new transactions are written to a rollback segment that is either marked offline or is waiting for other transactions to complete so that it can be brought offline. To become available again, a rollback segment that is taken offline has to be explicitly brought back online or it has to be specified in the INIT.ORA file when the instance is started. This means that when a public rollback segment is taken offline it remains offline, even if the database is shut down and restarted.

**Configuration of Rollback Segments**    What should the size of a rollback segment be? How many rollback segments should I have? These are two questions commonly asked by DBAs.

There are two issues that need to be considered when deciding the size of the rollback segment. First, you need to make sure that transactions will not cause the head to wrap around too fast and catch the tail. This causes the segment to extend in size. Second, if you have long-running queries that access frequently changing data, you want to make sure that the rollback segment doesn't wrap around and prevent the construction of a read-consistent view. In this case, the ORA-01555-*Snapshot Too Old* error occurs.

The size needed for a rollback segment depends directly on the transaction activity in a database. DBAs should be concerned about the activity during normal processing of the database, not with rare or infrequent large transactions. These special cases will be discussed later in this section.

The number of rollback segments needed to prevent contention between processes can be determined by monitoring the rollback segments through the SQL*PLUS *monitor* screen and with the use of the V$WAITSTAT view. The rollback monitor column HEADER WAITS/SEC gives an indication of the current transaction table contention. Waits are a definite indication of contention. The following V$WAITSTAT query will display the number of waits since instance startup:

```
SQL> SELECT CLASS, COUNT FROM V$WAITSTAT WHERE UPPER(CLASS)
IN ('SYSTEM UNDO HEADER', 'SYSTEM UNDO BLOCK', 'UNDO HEADER',
'UNDO BLOCK');
```

The query above gives an indication of the number of times that a session had to wait to acquire a system or user-defined rollback segment.

To find out the size and number of rollback segments needed to handle normal processing on the database, DBAs need to do some testing. A good test is to start with small rollback segments and allow your application to force them to extend. Here are the steps to run such a test:

1. Create a rollback segment tablespace.

2. Select a number of rollback segments to test and create them in the tablespace.

3. Create the rollback segments so that all extents are of the same size. Choose an extent size that you suspect will need between 10 to 30 extents when the segments grow to full size.

4. Each rollback segment should start with two extents before the test is run. This is the minimum number of extents any rollback segment can have.

5. Activate only the rollback segments that you are testing by making the status ONLINE. The only other segment that should be ONLINE is the SYSTEM rollback segment.

6. Run transactions to simulate a typical load of the application.

7. Watch for rollback segment contention.

8. Watch for the maximum size a rollback segment extends to.

The maximum size any one of the rollback segments reaches during the test is the size you should use when configuring. We will call this size the *minimum coverage size*. If you see contention, adjust the number of segments and rerun the test. Also, if the largest size requires fewer than 10 extents or more than 30, it is a good idea to lower or raise the extent size, respectively, and rerun the test. Otherwise, you may be wasting space.

For sizing rollback segment extents, Oracle strongly recommends that each extent be of the same size. In fact, for all strategies listed below, we assume that all rollback segments have extents of the same size and that the size of the rollback tablespace is some multiple of the common extent size. The number of extents for an individual segment should be between 10 and 30.

You now have some good base estimates for the size and number of rollback segments needed for normal data processing. After calculating the size and the number of rollback segments required, it is time to plan for the configuration of the rollback segment tablespace. To do this, you first need to understand the amount of undo that is being generated and the transaction pattern that is being executed.

You can estimate the amount of undo generated by a transaction with the help of the following script, **undo.sql**. Note that this script should be run from SQL*PLUS only.

```
REM: UNDO.SQL
set  feedback off
set termout  off
column name format A40
define undo_overhead = 54
DROP TABLE undo$begin;
DROP TABLE undo$end;
CREATE TABLE undo$begin ( writes number );
CREATE TABLE undo$end ( writes number );
INSERT INTO undo$begin
SELECT sum(writes) FROM v$rollstat;
set termout on
set feedback on
REM: The following statement runs a script called TEST.SQL, which
REM: contains the test transactions
@TEST.SQL
set termout off
set feedback off
INSERT INTO undo$end
SELECT sum(writes) FROM v$rollstat;
set termout on
set feedback on
SELECT  ( ( e.writes - b.writes) - &undo_overhead) "number of bytes generated"
FROM undo$begin b, undo$end e;
set termout off
set feedback off
DROP TABLE undo$begin;
DROP TABLE undo$end;
```

The value reported by this script is the undo generated during the transaction. You need to make sure that this is the only running transaction in the database. The UNDO_OVERHEAD defined in the script is a constant that compensates for the unavoidable overhead of the **insert into undo$begin...** statement.

Now you need to examine the *transaction pattern* that you run on your database. There are primarily three different transaction patterns:

■ A steady average transaction rate

■ Frequent large transactions

■ Infrequent large transactions

For databases with a *steady average transaction rate* (i.e., there are no abnormally large transactions), create a tablespace that will fit your calculated number of rollback segments with the minimum coverage size you have determined. Make all extents the same size. As a safety net, allocate some additional space in the tablespace to allow segments to grow if they need to. If you elect to do this, use the OPTIMAL feature to force all rollback segments to free up any additional space they allocate beyond their determined size requirement. You do not want to make OPTIMAL smaller than the minimum coverage size; otherwise, performance will suffer due to excessive segment resizing.

Databases with *frequent large transactions* are the hardest cases to deal with. By *frequent,* we mean that the time between large transactions is less than the time needed to allow all rollback segments to shrink back to optimal size. A large transaction is one in which we don't have enough space to create all rollback segments of the size necessary to handle its rollback information. Since we can't depend on the segment shrinking in time to allow repeated large transactions, OPTIMAL is not really an option for this environment.

There are basically two options that you can choose from for your rollback segment tablespace. One is to reduce the number of segments so that all are large enough to hold the largest transactions. This option will introduce contention and will cause some degradation in performance. It is a reasonable choice if performance is not extremely critical. The second option is to build one or more large rollback segments and make sure that large transactions use these segments. The **set transaction use rollback segment** command is necessary to control the placement of these large transactions. This option is difficult to implement if large transactions are being run with ad hoc queries and there is no systematic control of large transactions. This option is recommended in an environment where the large transactions are issued from a controlled environment (i.e., an application that will set the transaction to the appropriate rollback segment).

For databases with *infrequent large transactions,* you can use the OPTIMAL feature to set up a flexible rollback segment scheme, one in which you are not concerned about which rollback segment the large transaction falls upon. The key is to leave enough free space in the rollback segment tablespace that the largest transaction's rollback information can fit entirely into it. To do this, create the rollback segment tablespace with the space needed for your calculated number of segments and the minimum coverage size plus this additional space. Then set the OPTIMAL for each segment equal to the minimum coverage size. What you will see is that the large transactions will randomly make one of the segments grow and eat up the free space, but the segment will release the space before the next large transaction comes along. Note that you are sacrificing some performance for this flexibility.

Finally, you need to remember two points from this discussion. First, though the use of the OPTIMAL clause is a very handy tool, beware that the extent allocation and deallocation are expensive operations with regard to performance. This means that an OPTIMAL setting may decrease performance if it is too low. The second point is that there is no guarantee when a rollback segment will shrink down to its optimal size, because a rollback segment only shrinks when a transaction attempts to move into another extent and sees that the extent meets the requirements for deallocation.

**Maintenance of Rollback Segments**    As a DBA, you need to monitor the rollback segment activity from time to time in the database. This is necessary to maintain the correct number of rollback segments and the correct OPTIMAL size for each rollback segment. Monitoring also helps you identify the long-running transactions and the users running these transactions. For example, the following SQL script identifies all users with active transactions and the rollback segment each transaction is using:

```
SELECT  r.name "ROLLBACK SEGMENT NAME",
l.sid "ORACLE PID",
p.spid "SYSTEM PID",
NVL ( p.username , 'NO TRANSACTION'),
p.terminal
FROM v$lock l, v$process p, v$rollname r
WHERE  l.sid = p.pid(+)
AND TRUNC (l.id1(+)/65536) = r.usn
AND l.type(+) = 'TX'
AND l.lmode(+) = 6
ORDER BY r.name
```

The following gives you the output of the above script:

```
SQL> set transaction use rollback segment rb5;
Statement processed.
SQL> insert into x values (90);
1 row processed.
SQL> @d:\rvelpuri\rb
SQL> SELECT r.name "ROLLBACK SEGMENT NAME",
     2> l.sid "ORACLE PID",
     3> p.spid "SYSTEM PID",
     4> NVL ( p.username , 'NO TRANSACTION'),
     5> p.terminal
     6> FROM v$lock l, v$process p, v$rollname r
     7> WHERE  l.sid = p.pid(+)
     8> AND TRUNC (l.id1(+)/65536) = r.usn
     9> AND l.type(+) = 'TX'
    10> AND l.lmode(+) = 6
    11> ORDER BY r.name
    12> ;

ROLLBACK SEGMENT NAME            ORACLE PID SYSTEM PI NVL(P.USERNAME, TERMINAL
-------------------------------- ---------- --------- --------------- -----------
RB1                                                   NO TRANSACTION
RB3                                                   NO TRANSACTION
RB4                                                   NO TRANSACTION
RB5                                        16 0012D   rvelpuri        RAMA
RB6                                                   NO TRANSACTION
RB7                                                   NO TRANSACTION
RB_TEMP                                               NO TRANSACTION
SYSTEM                                                NO TRANSACTION
8 rows selected.
```

Also, note that V$ROLLSTAT gives some valuable information regarding the rollback segments and amount of redo being generated.

The rollback segment monitor screen has been enhanced to help you determine how successfully you have chosen your OPTIMAL size. Some of the statistics give you information such as the highest number of extents that were allocated to the rollback segment, the OPTIMAL size, and the number of shrinks performed. Based on these statistics, you can analyze the OPTIMAL setting for a rollback segment. If the cumulative number of shrinks is low and the average size of shrinks is high, that's an indication that the OPTIMAL value is set appropriately. If the cumulative number of shrinks is high and the average size of shrinks is low, the OPTIMAL size needs to be increased. If the number of shrinks is very low, then you should decrease the OPTIMAL value.

If you are using Oracle Storage Manager (GUI), you can view the list of rollback segments, their status, and other information by clicking on the Rollback Segments button. Figure 2-13 gives the output.

## Temporary Segments

Oracle often requires temporary workspace for intermediate stages of data processing. These areas are referred to as *temporary segments* and are allocated as needed during a user operation. A DBA may occasionally need to find additional database space on disk for temporary segments that are larger than normally anticipated. This section describes a procedure in which disk space currently allocated to the database can be managed or even *borrowed* to accommodate the creation of large temporary segments. Let's first examine when and how temporary segments are created.

The following SQL operations may require the use of a temporary segment:

- **create index**

- **select** with DISTINCT, ORDER BY, GROUP BY, UNION, INTERSECT, and MINUS clauses

- Nonindexed JOINs

- Certain correlated subqueries

If the table/index can be sorted in memory, then the sorting method is called *internal*. If the table is very large, the sorting process is *external* to main memory and requires disk storage. The INIT.ORA parameter SORT_AREA_SIZE influences whether the sort is performed in memory or on disk. If the amount of data to be sorted is greater than the allocated sort area, the data is divided into smaller pieces. Each sort piece is then sorted individually and stored on disk in the form of a

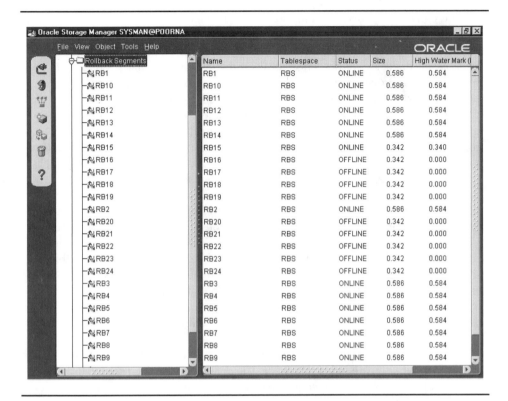

**FIGURE 2-13.** *List of rollback segments from Oracle Storage Manager*

temporary segment. These temporary segments are merged among numerous sort passes called *runs* and eventually merged into a final sorted result.

Increasing SORT_AREA_SIZE will reduce the creation of temporary segments on disk and therefore the amount of disk storage space needed. Some operating systems impose limits on the allocation of main memory. In these situations, the creation of large temporary segments on disk is inevitable. For example, creating a large index requires temporary segments. To satisfy the **create index** SQL statement, the RDBMS performs a sort operation to populate the index in the desired order. If resource constraints on main memory exist, the sort operation will result in the creation of one or more temporary segments on disk.

Temporary segments, like any other segments, can consist of multiple extents. If the sort requirements are great, temporary segments will grow by allocating additional extents. If there's insufficient contiguous space on the database to allocate the next extent, the following error will occur:

```
01652, 00000, "unable to extend temp segment by %s in tablespace %s"
```

You can provide adequate temporary storage in a number of ways. One approach is to allocate another data file to the tablespace, thereby increasing the amount of contiguous free space in the tablespace. This space is now permanently allocated to the tablespace whether or not the space is normally needed. Another option is to use the **alter user** command to point the given user's temporary segments to another tablespace that contains more contiguous free space. However, space may not be adequate in the other tablespaces. Perhaps disk space outside the database can be temporarily borrowed by creating a new tablespace, altering the user's definition to point to this tablespace for the creation of temporary segments, and then subsequently dropping the tablespace after the operation completes. If the additional disk space is not available, a more complex form of the tablespace shuffle is required.

The *tablespace shuffle* is useful for creating indexes on large tables, especially in database environments that haven't been sized for exceptionally large temporary segments. First, identify a user tablespace that doesn't contain database objects relevant to the creation of a specific index. Specifically, the tablespace should not be SYSTEM, contain the target table, or contain any rollback segments that are IN USE. In addition, the DBA should approximate whether the elimination of this tablespace will free up enough storage. The tablespace is then taken offline. After the tablespace is taken offline, an operating system backup is performed on all associated data files. After verification, delete those data files at the operating system level.

Next, create a new tablespace that will be used exclusively to build temporary segments for your **create index** statement. The data file(s) specified should point to the same disk that contained the recently deleted data file(s). You may also want to access space from additional disks. Once the tablespace is created, alter the user's definition to point to this tablespace for the default creation of his or her temporary segments. During index creation, monitor temporary segment space requirements by issuing the following statement:

```
SQL> SELECT SEGMENT_NAME, BYTES, EXTENTS FROM SYS.DBA_SEGMENTS
WHERE SEGMENT_TYPE='TEMPORARY';
```

Determine how much free space remains in the tablespace by issuing the following command:

```
SQL> SELECT MAX(BYTES) FROM SYS.DBA_FREE_SPACE
WHERE TABLESPACE_NAME= tablespace_name;
```

After the index is successfully created, modify the user definition to point back to that user's original temporary tablespace default and drop the recently created tablespace. Delete these data files and restore the above backups. Bring the offline tablespace online and, if necessary, perform media recovery.

We recommend that you create a separate tablespace with type TEMPORARY and designate this as the temporary tablespace for users. Temporary tablespaces are able to deallocate extents that are not being used very efficiently.

```
SQL> CREATE TABLESPACE temp_data DATAFILE '/oracle/temp.ora' SIZE 10M TEMPORARY
```

# Database Configuration

When configuring the database, three major areas of concern are control files, online redo log files, and archived redo log files. While designing the database layout, the DBA also needs to consider *disaster recovery* and the *performance* of the database. For example, placing all the data files that contain indexes on one disk might be a good thing to do from a recovery point of view. If the disk crashes and you lose all the index data files, online recovery can be performed on the index tablespace, thereby minimizing the downtime of the database. But from a performance point of view, this might not be pragmatic if all the applications heavily read and write to the index data files. This might create an I/O bottleneck since all data files reside on the same disk drive. So, the database design and configuration primarily depends on the business requirements and resources available. Once the business requirements are known, the database needs to be designed correctly, and proper operational procedures should be put in place to meet the business needs.

## Managing Control Files

The control file contains the schema of the database. This is one of the most important and essential files for normal operation of the database. In this section, we will look at some of the guidelines for managing control files. Control file administration is probably the easiest, and takes very little time. However, if the DBA doesn't do the initial setup correctly, losing the control file may cause a significant amount of database downtime. This is a concern for customers running mission-critical applications with high availability requirements. This section discusses some of the basic operations, such as adding, renaming, relocating, and dropping control files.

The INIT.ORA parameter CONTROL_FILES lists the names of all the control files that are being used by the database. As mentioned earlier, when the database is started up, during instance startup, Oracle reads the INIT.ORA file to find out how many control files are being used with the database and where their locations are. During the mount stage, the control file is opened to read the schema of the database, so it's necessary for the DBA to include all the names of the control files in the CONTROL_FILES parameter, separated by commas. Oracle will write to all the control files during normal operation of the database. However, only the first control file listed in INIT.ORA is read by Oracle.

To protect against media failures, it is suggested that at least two control files be maintained; it is a good practice to maintain three or four copies of the control file on different disks. Keeping multiple copies of the control file on the same disk drive defeats the purpose of mirroring control files. The idea of mirroring is to plan for media failures. If a disk crashes, you may lose all files on that disk. For this reason, maintaining copies of the control file on different disks is essential. Also, if multiple disk controllers are being used, it is a good idea to keep control files on different disks that are mounted under different disk controllers. This will protect control files against disk controller failures as well.

Oracle strongly recommends mirroring of control files. There is only a slight overhead in maintaining multiple copies of the control files. Every time the database checkpoints or the schema of the database changes, all the control files are updated. This will take a little longer if more copies of the control file are maintained. Also, additional disk space is required if control files are mirrored (the size of the control file is determined by the parameters MAXDATAFILES, MAXLOGFILES, MAXLOGMEMBERS, MAXLOGHISTORY, and MAXINSTANCES, which are specified during the creation of the database). However, the performance overhead is really insignificant and the size of the control file is negligible compared to the total database size.

At the current time, even if the control file is mirrored, if one of the control files becomes unavailable because of a disk failure, you need to shut the database down with the ABORT option. Once the database is shut down, the INIT.ORA file needs to be edited such that the unavailable control file is not specified in the CONTROL_FILES parameter. Then, the database can be started up. Once the disk drive is repaired, shut down the database one more time, copy the current control file to the new disk, edit the INIT.ORA file to reflect this change, and, finally, start up. This is not very practical, yet it is necessary for shops running with high availability requirements. This is probably one of the areas where Oracle should consider changing the functionality in the future releases. If a control file were to become unavailable, it would be nice if Oracle notified the DBA that a specific control file is not available and continued to function normally, ignoring the bad control file.

## Creating, Adding, and Renaming Control Files

When a database is created, the initial control file is created as part of the database. Before creating the database, the INIT.ORA file can be edited to specify the names of the control files to be created. The file specification is operating system dependent. This would create all the requested control files as part of the database creation. For a given database, if you want to add a new control file, or change the name or location of an existing control file, execute the following steps:

1. Using SQL*PLUS, shut down the database using the NORMAL option. If the database had to be shut down with the IMMEDIATE or ABORT option,

restart the database in RESTRICT mode and shut it down cleanly using the NORMAL option.

**2.** Exit SQL*PLUS.

**3.** Using the appropriate operating system command, copy an existing control file to a different location. If the existing control file's name needs to be changed, rename the control file.

**4.** Edit the CONTROL_FILES parameter in the INIT.ORA file and add the new control file's name. Rename the existing control file, if necessary.

**5.** Log on to a SQL session.

**6.** Restart the database.

If all control files of the database are permanently damaged and no backups of the control file exist, then the **create controlfile** command can be used to create a new control file. Alternatively, if one of the database settings needs to be modified, this can be achieved by creating a new control file as well. The parameters, MAXLOGFILES, MAXLOGMEMBERS, MAXLOGHISTORY, MAXDATAFILES, and MAXINSTANCES are specified when the database is originally created. To modify any of these values, you might assume that the database needs to be rebuilt. However, using the **create controlfile** command, the values of these parameters can be changed without rebuilding the database.

For example, let's assume that you have created the database with MAXDATAFILES =20. This means that you cannot have more than 20 data files in the database. At a later time, if you realize that this value is set too low, you might want to change this by setting a new value for this parameter while re-creating the control file using the **create controlfile** command (the **create controlfile** command is described in detail in Chapter 6).

## Dropping Control Files

A DBA might decide to drop a particular control file for a number of reasons. For example, there may be too many control files, or multiple control files may exist on the same disk drive. Or, due to a system reconfiguration, a particular disk drive may no longer be available. In such cases, the DBA can drop the control file, but note that there should always be a minimum of two control files. The following example gives you the steps involved in dropping a control file from the database:

**1.** Using SQL*PLUS utility, shut down the database gracefully, using the NORMAL option.

**2.** Exit SQL*PLUS utility.

3. Edit the CONTROL_FILES parameter in the INIT.ORA file to delete the old control file's name.

4. Restart SQL*PLUS.

5. Restart the database.

6. Delete the control file at the operating system level by using the appropriate OS command.

# Managing Online Redo Log Groups

A single point of failure in version 6 of Oracle was to lose the online log file. Oracle7 and Oracle8 provide a *mirroring* mechanism that allows you to create redo log *groups*. Each group contains redo log *members*, which are identical to each other (multiplexed). This is very similar to having multiple copies of your control file—the main difference is that the database will not become inoperable when one of the online log file members is damaged or inaccessible. Oracle very strongly suggests multiplexing the online redo log files. By multiplexing the redo log files, you will eliminate the chance of a single point of online redo log failure.

## Normal Operation

Oracle needs a minimum of two log file *groups* for normal operation of the database. Each log file group needs a minimum of one log file *member*, and can contain multiple log file members. Every member within a log file group is identical and contains exactly the same information. When mirrored, since the LGWR process needs to write to multiple members of a log group, performance will be affected. However, this can be mitigated or almost eliminated by setting up the mirrors across disk controllers. The LGWR process does parallel writes to members of a log group. If members are on the same device, the writes would actually be serial. The LGWR process waits until the write completes—log blocks are always synchronously written. If the *parallel write* call returns an error, LGWR checks the status of each open log member to see which file gave the error. Also, the LGWR process keeps a counter of errors on each log file member. When an error occurs, it marks the log member as STALE in the control file and you should see the ORA-00346 error in the LGWR trace file. The STALE status indicates that the contents of the file are incomplete. If the LGWR process encounters more than four errors on a file, it simply closes the file and does not write to it anymore. A message is written in the trace file with the ORA-00345 error. It is possible to write to a STALE file until the error count hits four. If the LGWR process can't write to any one of the members, then it kills itself with the ORA-00340 error. After this error is encountered, you need to shut the database down with the ABORT option.

After the cause for write errors is investigated and the problem rectified, the database needs to be started up again.

## Configuring the Online Redo Log Files

It is important to choose the right size for an online log file. If the proper log file size is not chosen, then the LGWR process has to switch log files too often, which will affect the performance. On the other hand, if the log file size is too big, then during recovery Oracle needs to recover a lot of transactions and recovery will take a longer time. Though Oracle allows the DBA to maintain different file sizes for different groups, there is no advantage in doing so. For most Oracle shops, the default log file size is sufficient; the default size is operating system dependent. Even if the wrong file size is chosen for an online log file, it can be dropped and re-created at a later time. When you drop log files, Oracle will make sure that you have a minimum of two groups at any given time.

Choosing the number of online log groups is also very important. Having too few log groups could become a serious problem while using the database in ARCHIVELOG mode in some shops with a high transaction rate. Consider the case where there are two log groups. When the LGWR process fills up the log file in group 1 (say logA ), it switches to the log file in group 2 (say logB). At this time, the ARCH process starts copying the redo from logA to an archived log file. If the LGWR process finishes filling up logB, it cannot switch to logA until the ARCH process finishes archiving logA. In the meantime, the database will hang because logA cannot be written to until it is archived. In this case, adding additional groups would help. For most shops, keeping the number of online log files between 2 and 10 is sufficient. The total number of log groups cannot exceed MAXLOGFILES. Similarly, the total number of members per group cannot exceed MAXLOGMEMBERS. These parameters are specified in the **create database** command and can be changed later by either rebuilding the database or re-creating the control file.

## Creating and Relocating Online Redo Log Files

The **alter database** command can be used to add log groups or add a member to an existing group. Consider the following example:

```
SQL> ALTER DATABASE ADD LOGFILE GROUP 3
('c:\oracle\oradata\ora8i\newlog1.ora',
'd:\oracle\database\newlog2.ora') SIZE 500K;
SQL> ALTER DATABASE ADD LOGFILE MEMBER
'e:\oracle\database\newlog3.ora' TO GROUP 3;
```

In this example, the first statement would create a group with two online log file members, one on each disk. The second statement would add a third member to that group on another disk.

Similar to the control files, the online log files need to be relocated for various reasons. Files need to be relocated for load balancing or due to removal of existing disk drives. To relocate the online log files, the following steps need to be taken:

1. Shut down the database gracefully, using the NORMAL option.

2. Take a complete backup of the database, including the log files, data files, and control files.

3. Copy the online log files to the new location using the appropriate OS command.

4. Start up SQL*PLUS and mount the database.

5. Rename the online redo log members.

6. Open the database for normal operation using the **alter database** command.

7. Back up the control file since the schema of the database has changed now.

## Dropping Online Redo Log Groups and Members

You might want to drop a redo log group for various reasons. For example, the application's transaction rate might change, thereby generating less redo. This is a dangerous operation and should be executed cautiously. If the online redo log group is the *active* log group (which means the LGWR process is currently writing to this group), it cannot be dropped. Also, as mentioned earlier, there has to be a minimum of two redo log groups at any given time for database operation. The above restrictions apply while dropping a member of a redo log group as well. In addition, note that there has to be at least one member for each group available to the database. Consider the following example:

```
SQL> ALTER DATABASE DROP LOGFILE MEMBER 'e:\oracle\database\newlog3.ora';
SQL> ALTER DATABASE DROP LOGFILE GROUP 3;
```

Here, the first statement drops a log file member from the log file group. The second statement drops the entire redo log group 3.

Three views help the DBA administer the online log files: V$LOG, V$LOGFILE, and V$THREAD. The STATUS column in the V$LOGFILE view gives the status of the log file member. As discussed earlier, a status of STALE shows that the log member is not complete. A status of INCOMPLETE indicates that the file is not accessible by Oracle. If there is no status for the online log file, or the status is CURRENT, this indicates that the file is in use.

# Managing Archive Redo Log Files

*Archiving* is the process of copying a filled online redo log file to a different disk drive or a tape drive by the ARCH process. As discussed earlier, the DBA can configure the database to operate in ARCHIVELOG mode or NOARCHIVELOG mode. Oracle writes to the online redo log files regardless of the mode the database is operating in. If the database is configured to run in ARCHIVELOG mode, the online redo log files are saved (archived) before being overwritten by the LGWR process. In NOARCHIVELOG mode, the redo log files are overwritten each time a redo log file is filled and a log switch occurs. In other words, the past changes made to the database are not available in the log files.

This section discusses some of the advantages of running the database in ARCHIVELOG mode, as well as the costs involved. A procedure to turn on *manual archiving* and *automatic archiving* is also described.

## Normal Operation

The ARCH process has been made robust in Oracle8 and 8*i*. In Oracle7, every block of the online log file is verified before copying. This ensures that if a block is bad in the online redo log file, the ARCH process signals an error *before* copying, and the DBA would know of it immediately instead of realizing it during recovery. Oracle doesn't check the contents of the online redo log data blocks. The algorithm for archiving begins by attempting to open all log members. If none can be opened, an error is signaled. Otherwise, Oracle opens as many members of the log group as possible. Next, the headers of the log file members are read and validated. Oracle keeps switching between members, reading a range of blocks from each member at a time. If the read is successful, Oracle remembers that log as an anchor point so that if a read fails on a range of blocks later for some other member, it can switch to any good member. This round-robin reading procedure helps to distribute the disk I/O.

## Archive Destination

In Oracle8*i*, the INIT.ORA parameter LOG_ARCHIVE_DEST can be set to point to the primary destination where the archive log files need to be created. Oracle allows you to duplicate the archive logs automatically to a second destination. The INIT.ORA parameter LOG_ARCHIVE_DUPLEX_DEST can be used to define the second archive destination. In addition, the INIT.ORA parameter LOG_ARCHIVE_MIN_SUCCEED_DEST can be used to ensure the success of archiving to the primary destination specified by LOG_ARCHIVE_DEST and the secondary destination specified by LOG_ARCHIVE_DUPLEX_DEST. In Oracle8*i* Enterprise Edition, the INIT.ORA parameter LOG_ARCHIVE_DEST has been replaced with LOG_ARCHIVE_DEST_n parameter that allows the background archive process (ARCH) to archive online redo log files up to five different destinations. The destinations can be either local or remote directories. Access to remote destination is done via Oracle net8 SERVICE_NAME. Before specifying the remote destination, you should ensure that Oracle could establish a net8 session to the remote destination using the net8 SERVICE_NAME.

**NOTE**
*Oracle8i Edition is different from Oracle Enterprise Edition, which has many additional features as mentioned above.*

Archiving to disk and tape is supported on some operating systems (e.g., UNIX). Archiving to tape is not supported on all operating systems, but it was the only way supported on IBM VM until Oracle7 release 7.1. Operating systems such as VMS, Macintosh, Novell NetWare, OS/2, Windows, and DOS do not support archiving to tape directly unless it looks like a normal volume (i.e., you can do a directory listing command on the tape drive). Oracle supports only local tape archiving on some operating systems such as UNIX System V, and on others (UNIX BSD, for example), remote archiving to tape is supported. Table 2-1 gives a listing of some of the major operating systems and their supported archive destinations.

| Operating System | Archiving to Disk | Archiving to Tape |
|---|---|---|
| UNIX | Yes | Yes |
| VMS | Yes | No |
| Windows NT | Yes | Not normally |
| Windows 3.1 | Yes | Not normally |
| MAC | Yes | No |
| OS/2 | Yes | Not normally |
| Novell NetWare | Yes | Not normally |
| VM | Not until 7.1 | Yes |
| MVS | Yes | Yes |

**TABLE 2-1.** *Major Operating Systems and Their Supported Archive Destinations*

**Archiving To Disk**     If you are archiving the redo log files to disk, here are some recommendations:

- Archive the redo logs to a dedicated disk with sufficient disk space.

- Copy the archived redo log files to tape at least once per day.

- Once on tape, archived redo log files may be removed from disk.

**Archiving To Tape**     Backing up large databases to disk can be prohibitively expensive. The Recovery Manager on Oracle8 has a facility to back up files to tape directly. This minimizes the disk consumption considerably. You can also protect yourself from natural disasters like earthquakes by sending copies of the tapes elsewhere. Recovery Manager supports the API that allows it to integrate with tape management systems provided by third-party vendors. Third-party vendors provide a media manager that can be linked in with Oracle. Details can be found in the platform-specific Oracle documentation.

### Enabling Manual Archiving

The ARCHIVELOG mode can be set up on database creation or by using the **alter database archivelog** command. To issue this command, the database needs to be mounted but not open. Once ARCHIVELOG mode is set, it remains in effect until you explicitly set the database to run in NOARCHIVELOG mode. Redo log files will be archived, by default, to the destination specified by the INIT.ORA parameter LOG_ARCHIVE_DEST_1. Once the database is operating in the ARCHIVELOG mode, there are two ways in which online redo log files can be archived: *manual* and *automatic*. Manual archiving allows you to choose and control at what time archiving is done. You must issue a SQL*PLUS command each time you want to archive a redo log file. All or specific redo log files can be archived manually with the **archive** command. The **archive log all** command archives all the online redo log files that haven't been archived yet.

   Assuming that the database is running in NOARCHIVELOG mode, executing the following series of commands in the specified order will put the database in ARCHIVELOG mode with the *manual archiving* option:

```
SQL> shutdown
SQL> startup mount [dbname]
SQL> alter database [dbname] archivelog;
SQL> alter database [dbname] open;
SQL> archive log all
```

When the database is operating in the ARCHIVELOG mode with the manual archiving option, the SQL*PLUS command **archive log list** should show the database log mode as ARCHIVELOG and automatic archival as DISABLED. For example,

```
SQL> archive log list;
Database log mode              Archive Mode
Automatic archival             Disabled
Archive destination            C:\Oracle\Oradata\ora8i\archive
Oldest online log sequence     578
Next log sequence to archive   578
Current log sequence           581
SQL>
```

## Enabling Automatic Archiving

Alternatively to the manual archiving option, you can choose to run with the automatic archiving option. Enabling automatic archiving starts the ARCH process. The ARCH process archives the online log files automatically every time the LGWR process switches log files. Automatic archiving can be enabled in either of two ways: by using the INIT.ORA parameter LOG_ARCHIVE_START (it should be set to TRUE) or by using the SQL*PLUS command **log archive start**. If the database is operational with manual archiving, and if you decide to enable automatic archiving using the INIT.ORA parameter, note that the database has to be shut down and restarted again. While running the database with automatic archiving enabled, the SQL*PLUS command **archive log list** should show automatic archival as ENABLED, as shown here:

```
SQL> archive log list;
Database log mode              Archive Mode
Automatic archival             Enabled
Archive destination            C:\Oracle\Oradata\ora8i\archive
Oldest online log sequence     578
Next log sequence to archive   581
Current log sequence           581
SQL>
```

## Advantages and Costs of Archiving

Configuring the database to operate in ARCHIVELOG mode allows you to do complete and point-in-time recovery from media failures using offline or online backups. For customers running mission-critical applications where loss of data is not acceptable, this is the mode of operation recommended by Oracle. Shops that don't configure their database to run in ARCHIVELOG mode can restore the database from a backup in case of failure, but cannot roll forward from that point.

For example, let's assume that you take a cold backup of the database every Sunday night and run the database in NOARCHIVELOG mode. Let's further assume that a media failure occurred on Friday and all the database files were lost. The only option you have is to restore the database from Sunday night's backup and restart the database. All the data entered or transactions done between Sunday and Friday are lost. Had you operated the database in ARCHIVELOG mode, you could have restored the database and then applied all the changes made to the database, thus not losing any data. In summary, operating the database in ARCHIVELOG mode allows you to recover the database completely.

Operating the database in ARCHIVELOG mode requires extra disk space (if archiving to disk) and adequate tape facilities. The DBA will have additional administrative work to do, such as space management and log file tracking.

# Configuring the Oracle PARALLEL SERVER Option

The majority of Oracle installations today are single-instance configurations; that is, one instance on one system provides access to one Oracle database for all users of that database. The PARALLEL SERVER option, using shared disk access and a lock manager, allows two or more Oracle instances running on independent systems to share coordinated access to one shared database, thus allowing users connected to different systems to submit transactions that will be executed by the system to which the user is connected against the shared database. The shared disk access is a capability provided by some platform vendors to allow multiple systems to share concurrent physical access to the same set of disk drives. A lock manager is a component, also provided by platform vendors, that is used by the PARALLEL SERVER option to coordinate Oracle activities globally across multiple systems.

The implications of such a capability are that more computing resources (the aggregate CPU and memory structures of all systems sharing the database) can be provided to access the same physical database, enabling increased capacity, increased performance, more users supported, and more available database service since the failure of one system affects other systems only for a brief period without interrupting user transactions on surviving systems. The PARALLEL SERVER option is available on platforms that provide both shared disk access and a lock manager. Some of the platforms that currently support the PARALLEL SERVER option are DEC Open VMS, Sequent, Pyramid, NCR, nCUBE, Parsys, Meiko, KSR, Encore, and IBM, and Windows NT Support is expected to be forthcoming from other vendors as well.

To realize the benefits of using the PARALLEL SERVER option, database and application designers and DBAs need to take into account various attributes of the PARALLEL SERVER option. These include deciding which applications are appropriate for the PARALLEL SERVER option (and which are not), partitioning of data access, space management, understanding and managing global locks used by the PARALLEL SERVER option, measuring and alleviating contention, and configuring a Parallel Server for high availability. *TheOracle8i Parallel Server Setup and Configuration Guide Release 8.1.5* manual gives details on all of these issues.

Each instance in a Parallel Server has its own *thread* of redo log files. Each thread will have a minimum of two log groups. Some concepts—such as *thread switching* and *instance recovery*—are unique to databases operating with the PARALLEL SERVER option and are discussed in detail in Chapter 6.

# Architecture of Oracle Enterprise Manager—An overview

In the world of Internet computing, managing huge databases spread across the globe needs special kinds of tools. Oracle addresses this ever-growing issue by introducing the powerful tool called Oracle Enterprise Manager (OEM), an easy to use user-friendly tool that makes database administrators' tasks easier. OEM provides an integrated, comprehensive systems management platform for managing Oracle products. OEM's architecture has extended to allow system management through a Web browser, allowing system and database administrators greater access and control of their database environments.

This functionality is made possible by a three-tier architecture. The three-tier architecture brings all functions related to Oracle database management under three well-defined structures called tiers. This architecture enables administrators to globally manage complex, interconnected databases and services from an industry-standard Web browser from most machines anywhere in the world. Figure 2-14 shows the simple Enterprise Manager architecture.

The three tiers of Oracle Enterprise Manager are as follows:

- The first tier of OEM is the Java-based console and management applications (clients).

- The second tier is the Oracle Management Server(s).

- The third tier consists of managed nodes containing databases and other related services.

## Clients

The client part of the OEM consists of Java console and management applications that communicate with one or more Oracle Management Servers (second tier) via standard Common Object Request Broker Access (CORBA) interfaces and Internet Inter-Orb Protocol (IIOP) protocol. The sole function of the first tier is to act as an

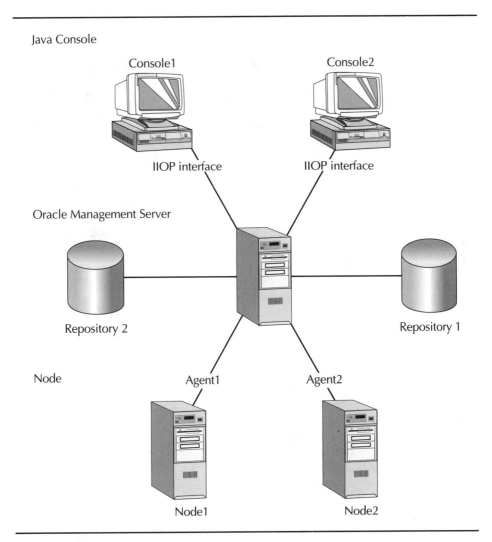

Java Console

Oracle Management Server

Node

**FIGURE 2-14.**    *Enterprise Manager architecture*

interface between the database administrator and the Oracle Management Servers. To run the Java console from a thin client (standard Web browsers), you have to have Oracle Enterprise Manager Web site installed on your Web server and your Web browser must also be configured by installing the required Java plug-ins (Jinit11781.exe for windows 95/98/NT). If you don't install the plug-ins, the error "Cannot load class sun/plugin/JavaRunTime; the bridge was never installed and The CLASSPATH does not include the bridge directory" will occur. Figure 2-15 shows OEM running from a Web browser.

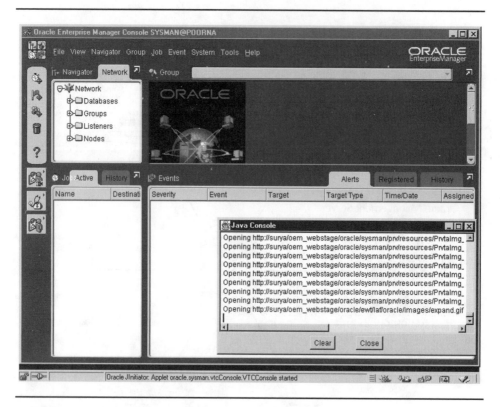

**FIGURE 2-15.** *Running OEM from a Web browser*

## Oracle Management Server

The Oracle Management Server is the second tier, which has the application logic and distributed control between the console (first tier) and the managed nodes (third tier), and processes system management tasks sent by the console. The Oracle Management Server stores all system data, application data, and information about the state of managed nodes in a repository, which is a set of database tables that can be stored in any Oracle database connected to the Oracle Management Server. Though the repository can reside on the production database, it is recommended to keep it on a separate server. One of the most important responsibilities of the Oracle Management Server is distributing tasks to the Oracle Intelligent Agents, which run on managed nodes in the third tier. Intelligent Agent is a function that works independently of the database or services they serve, as well as being independent of the Management Server and Console clients. The Intelligent Agents are responsible for the execution of tasks and the ongoing monitoring of networked systems.

## Managed Nodes

The third tier of Oracle Enterprise Manager is comprised of managed nodes, which contain databases and other managed services. Residing on each node is an Oracle Enterprise Manager Intelligent Agent, which gathers data and communicates with the Oracle Management Server(s) and performs tasks sent by consoles and client applications. Figure 2-16 shows all the nodes managed by a Management Server. For more information, refer to the *Oracle Enterprise Manager Concepts Guide Release 2.0*, *Oracle Enterprise Manager Configuration Guide Release 2.0*, and *Oracle Enterprise Manager Administrator's Guide Release 2.0*.

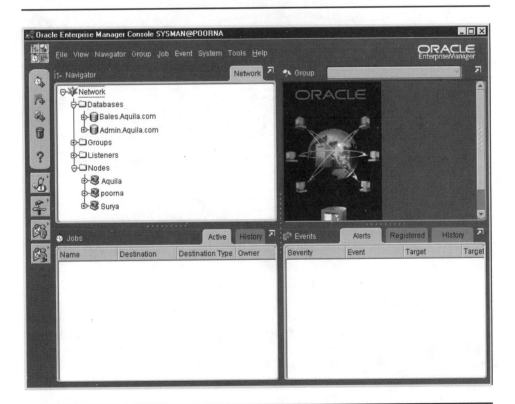

**FIGURE 2-16.** *Nodes managed by the OEM Management Server*

# CHAPTER
## 3

## Physical Backups

valid backup is, quite simply and generally, a copy of the necessary information in a database that can be used to rebuild the database should the database reach an unusable state. The loss of a disk device and the accidental removal of a database file or table are two examples of how a database could be brought to an unusable state. Naturally, if the backup scheme relies upon image backups of the database and archiving of the log files, copies must be maintained of the data files, control files, online redo log files, and archived redo log files. If you lose one of the archived redo log files, you can say that there is a *hole* in the sequence of files. A hole in the archived log files invalidates a backup but does allow the database to be rolled forward up to the beginning of the hole. For example, if you have 25 archived redo log files to roll forward and archived redo log file 15 is missing, then you can roll forward only until log 14.

A robust backup scheme is the method used to ensure that valid backups occur. Fundamental to a robust backup scheme is an understanding of the physical location of database files, the order of events during the backup process, and the handling of certain errors that occur during backups. A robust backup scheme is one that is resilient in the face of media, programmatic, and operator failures.

*Physical* and *logical* backups are generally the two types of backups that are used by DBAs. A physical backup involves copying the physical database files to a backup destination, whereas a logical backup uses an Oracle utility (**export**) to read the data in the database using SQL and stores the data and definitions in a binary file at the OS level. The Oracle database and the operating system where Oracle runs together offer a rich set of features that allow a wide range of robust backup schemes. This chapter gives an overview of the physical backup procedures that Oracle provides and the backup commands that you can use with various operating systems. In addition, some of the design considerations while planning physical backup procedures are discussed for decision support systems (DSS) and online transaction processing (OLTP) shops using very large databases (VLDB). The next chapter deals with logical backups of Oracle databases.

# Database Design and Basic Backup Rules

Before we can discuss online and offline backup procedures, it is very important to understand certain rules about placing the database files and other design considerations, which greatly affect the backup scheme. Following are some simple rules that will make a backup scheme robust in case of a disk or tape drive failure and will decrease the length of time needed for recovery:

1. It's recommended that you archive the log files to disk (i.e., set the archive destination such that the archived redo log files are created on disk) and later copy them to tape. However, the archived log destination should not reside on the same physical disk device as any database file or online redo log file. If a database file or the currently active redo log file is lost, the archived log files will be needed for recovery. If the archived redo log file or an online redo log file that is not currently active is lost, the current database should be backed up using an online or offline backup procedure that copies the database files to a backup device (disk or tape). Operations can then safely continue. When creating the database using the **create database** command, setting the MAXLOGFILES parameter to a value greater than 2 will simplify recovery from the loss of an inactive but online redo log file. We will discuss the recovery procedures in greater detail in Chapter 6.

2. If database files are being backed up to disk, a database file residing on the same physical device as its backup copy is not adequately backed up. You should have a separate disk or disks to maintain the backup copy of the database files. Backing up database files to disk can speed recovery, since the file need not be restored from tape. Also, backing up to disk often allows recovery to run in a shorter amount of time.

3. You should multiplex the control file; a copy of the control file should be placed on several different disk devices mounted under different disk controllers. A control file can be added to the database by shutting down the database, copying the control file, altering the INIT.ORA parameter CONTROL_FILES, and restarting the database. For details, refer to Chapter 2.

4. Online log files should be multiplexed, and a minimum of two members for each group should be maintained. Two members of a log group should not reside on the same physical device, as it defeats the purpose of multiplexing log files.

5. Many systems may benefit from keeping a *hot spare* disk. A hot spare is an unused empty disk sitting in the disk cabinet that can be brought online should any other disk fail.

6. Multiplexing archived redo log files will, in many cases, allow recovery from multiple media failures. For example, if the log files are archived to disk,

periodically copied to tape, and then removed from disk, data loss could result if the tape and a database file are both lost. It is recommended to maintain a backup copy on disk as well as on tape. Oracle8*i* allows you to multiplex archived log files automatically using the LOG_ARCHIVE_DEST_*n* INIT.ORA parameter, where *n* is an integer from 1 to 5. We recommend that you archive it to at least two destinations.

7. The procedure of rolling forward a database or database file from a backup can, in many cases, be simplified and made faster by keeping on disk all archived redo log files needed to roll forward the least recently backed up database file of a database. For many systems, much of the time necessary for recovery is spent restoring archived redo log files from tape.

8. Whenever the database structure is changed by adding, renaming, or dropping a log file or a data file (you can drop a data file only by dropping the tablespace that the data file belongs to), the control file should be backed up since the control file stores the schema of the database. In addition, any data file that is added should be backed up as well. The control file can be backed up while the database is open using the following command:

```
SQL> alter database backup controlfile to 'filespec';
```

9. If you have multiple Oracle databases in your enterprise, you should use the Oracle Recovery Manager with a recovery catalog. This will help you minimize risks due to user errors in the backup and recovery procedures. Chapter 7 details the features of Oracle Recovery Manager.

10. Last, but not least, identification of tapes that have been backed up (that are kept in a cabinet or shelf) is very important. Choosing the right naming convention and labeling the tapes is extremely important as it could decrease the mean time to recover (MTTR). We give details on labeling later in this chapter.

Keeping the above rules in mind, the following is an example of a typical backup strategy:

1. Operate the database in ARCHIVELOG mode.

2. Perform offline backups at least once a week if you don't need to operate your database 24 hours a day, 7 days a week (24x7). However, if your shop is operational 24x7, take daily online backups.

3. Back up all archived redo log files at least once every four hours. The number of archived log files to back up depends on the log file size and the amount of redo generated. The amount of redo generated is dependent on the transaction rate.

4. Perform a weekly full database export (or incremental, cumulative, or table-level export for large databases) in RESTRICT mode. For shops with 24x7 requirements, perform full exports when no database access or reduced database access is expected.

# Physical Backups

A *physical backup* is a backup in which the actual physical blocks of the database files are copied from one location to the other. You can copy the database files from disk to tape or from disk to disk, depending on the type of backup procedure you use. Oracle gives you two options while using physical backups to back up your database.

The first option is to back up the database files after the database is shut down clean with the **shutdown normal** command. This is known as an *offline*, or *cold*, backup since the database is offline (shut down) while the backup is being performed. Some DBAs perform an offline backup of the Oracle database as part of the operating system backup. This means that when the system administrator takes a backup of the entire system, the Oracle files get backed up as part of it. The DBA just needs to make sure that the database is shut down before the system manager takes the OS backup.

The second option is to take a physical backup of your database while the database is open and operational. This is the preferred backup procedure if, due to high availability requirements, you can't shut the database down. This kind of physical backup is called an *online*, or *hot*, backup due to the fact that the database is online while the backup is being performed. There are some special steps that you need to take while performing online backups.

## Offline (Cold) Backups

The first step in taking an offline backup is to shut down the database with the NORMAL option. If you shut the database down with the ABORT or IMMEDIATE option, you should restart the database in RESTRICT mode and shut it down again with the NORMAL option before copying the database files. Then, use an OS backup utility to copy all the database files and control files. Any archived log files that haven't yet been backed up must be copied as well. Oracle strongly recommends that you do not back up the online log files because you really don't need the online log files to recover your database.

In general, it is recommended that you take an offline backup of your database at least once a week. However, the frequency of your backups should really be determined from your business needs.

Some DBAs tend to take backups manually instead of automating the backup procedures. However, there are some problems with this approach. First, after shutting down the database, you may not remember how many files exist in this database or where they are located. Next, if you have added a new data file recently, you might not remember to take a backup of that file. In situations like this, some DBAs dump the control file to obtain the information of the data files and the log files (i.e., $ strings *controlfile* for UNIX; $dump *controlfile* for VMS). Instead, in such cases, the best thing to do is to open the database and get the information you need. The data dictionary views, DBA_DATA_FILES or V$DATAFILE, V$LOGFILE, and V$CONTROLFILE will list, respectively, all the data files, redo log files, and control files associated with the database. (You don't need to open the database to select from these V$ views; you can mount the database and select the information.) Automating the backup procedures alleviates the administrative work for you and minimizes human errors. Note that automating the backup procedures requires writing backup scripts. Some example scripts are given in Chapter 5.

While taking offline backups (or online backups), since blocks are physically copied from the source to the destination, some data block corruptions might go undetected while copying the data files. In other words, the corruptions will be propagated to the backup copy of the data file. The only time you will realize this is when you restore the data files and try to recover the database. For this reason, testing your database backups is very important—the procedure to do so includes restoring the database files from a backup and rolling forward. You can also simulate a failure before doing recovery. Chapter 10 gives you several examples on how to perform such tests. It is recommended that you test your backups at least once every three months, or as frequently as your business allows you to.

### Offline Backup Procedure
The following steps are required to take an offline backup of the database:

1. Prepare for the backup.

   A. Create a text file at the OS level that marks the start of the backup.

   B. Disable logon to the application.

   C. Provide warning messages that the database will be unavailable.

   D. Shut down the database with the **shutdown normal** or **shutdown immediate** command.

**2.** Perform the backup.

    **A.** Remove the day-old archived redo logs from the day-old disk area. (The term "day-old" presumes you are doing daily backups.)

    **B.** Move the current day's archived logs to the day-old area.

    **C.** Perform the image copy of the data files, control files, and online log files to their backup disk locations.

**3.** Finish the procedure.

    **A.** Start the database.

    **B.** Enable login to the applications.

    **C.** Copy the database image (data, control, online log, and archived log files) to tape.

    **D.** Finish the backup by removing the file that indicated the backup was started.

Step 1A can be used to ensure that the backup procedure is not inadvertently run twice at the same time for a database. Steps 2A and 2B keep the archived redo log files on disk until they are no longer needed for online recovery, but do not provide for keeping multiple copies on disk. Multiple copies could be kept on disk by copying the "day-old" logs to a "two-day-old" disk area, and copying the "two-day-old" disk area to tape during step 3C.

In an Optimal Flexible Architecture (OFA)–compliant database, all database files can be manipulated with a single command. The operating system backup procedures and the commands used to back up the operating system files are given in Table 3-1. Some of these commands will be discussed later in this chapter.

# Online (Hot) Backups

If your business requires you to operate the database 24 hours a day, 7 days a week, you should take online, or hot, backups. To use online backups, you should operate the database in ARCHIVELOG mode. Otherwise, Oracle will give you an error and will not allow you to use the online backup procedure. The online backup procedure is very similar to taking offline backups, but there are two additional steps involved. You should issue a **begin backup** command before you start the backup and an **end backup** command after the backup is completed. However, the **begin backup** and **end backup** commands are not necessary if you are using Recovery Manager. For example,

```
SQL> alter tablespace users begin backup;
SQL> alter tablespace users end backup;
```

| Operating System | OS Procedure | Commands |
|---|---|---|
| UNIX | Cron job | obackup, cpio, tar, dd, fbackup, ... |
| VMS | Batch job | backup |
| Windows NT | Interactive | Backup Manager (in Oracle8 and lower versions only)or OCOPY utility |
| MAC | Interactive | GUI Finder to copy to disk, third-party software |
| OS/2 | Interactive | Standard DOS/OS2 copy commands |
| Novell NetWare | Interactive | NBACKUP utility, third-party software |
| MVS | JCL submit | DFDSS or IDCAMS using e EXPORT (not REPRO) |

**TABLE 3-1.**   *Backup Procedures and Commands in Various Operating Systems*

These commands are issued, respectively, before and after the hot backup of the USERS tablespace is taken.

Unlike offline backups, which back up the entire database, the unit of an online backup is a tablespace, and any or all tablespaces can be backed up as needed. The online backup includes a backup of the data files (for one or more tablespaces), the current control file, and all archived redo log files created during the period of the backup. All archived redo log files generated after the online backup are also required for complete recovery. Though the unit of backup for online backups is a tablespace, all tablespaces need to be backed up eventually, and this is very important. The following example should make this point clear.

Let's assume that you have three tablespaces—T1, T2, and T3—in your database, and you take partial online backups of your database every night. That means you take an online backup of T1 on Monday, T2 on Tuesday, and T3 on Wednesday. You repeat this procedure by taking an online backup of T1 again on Thursday, T2 on Friday, and so on. That means that at the end of every three days (on Wednesday and Saturday, in this example), you will have a complete backup of the database, though not all tablespaces are backed up at the same point in time, as in the case of offline backups. In this example, if you have a media failure on Friday after the online backups are done and lose all your database files, you need to restore your entire database from backups. Since you have only two tablespaces (T1 and T2 from Thursday and Friday, respectively), and T3 has not been backed up yet, you need to restore T3 from the Wednesday night's backup. That means you also need to restore all the archived redo log files starting from Wednesday night's backup.

From the above example, you can see that recovery using partial backups (data files backed up at different times) begins with the oldest database file being restored. Therefore, you must preserve archived redo log files dating back to the time of the least recently backed up database file. Also, you need to make sure that full database backups are periodically performed to ensure that a backup of all the database files is available.

The advantages of using online backups compared to offline backups are as follows:

■   The database is completely accessible to users while backups are being made, including access to tablespaces that are being backed up.

■   All data files do not have to be backed up at the same time—partial backups can be obtained. Redo logs can be applied to partially backed up tablespaces to perform full database recovery.

### Sample Online Backup Procedure
The following are the steps involved in taking an online backup:

1. The database should be in ARCHIVELOG mode. If not, mount the database and issue the following commands:

```
SQL> alter database archivelog;
   SQL> archive log start
   SQL> alter database open;
```

The first command sets the database to ARCHIVELOG mode. The second command enables automatic archiving (creates ARCH process), and the third command opens the database.

2. The next step is to obtain the oldest online log sequence number by issuing the following command:

```
SQL> archive log list
    Database log mode              ARCHIVELOG
    Automatic archival             ENABLED
    Archive destination            /oracle/oradata/test/archive
    Oldest online log sequence     59
    Next log sequence to archive   61
    Current log sequence           61
```

You need to keep all the archived log files starting from sequence number 59 as part of the online backup. Though recovery will start from the SCN (system change number) where backup has started (which will be in log sequence number 61), as a precautionary measure you should keep all the archived log files starting from the *oldest online log sequence* number. (SCN is discussed in Chapter 6.)

**3.** Set the tablespace you want to back up to HOT BACKUP mode as follows:

```
SQL> ALTER TABLESPACE tablespace_name BEGIN BACKUP;
```

**4.** Back up all database files associated with the tablespace using an operating system command.

**5.** Set the tablespace back to NO HOT BACKUP mode by using the following command:

```
SQL> ALTER TABLESPACE tablespace_name END BACKUP;
```

Repeat steps 3–5 for each tablespace that you want to back up.

**6.** Execute the **archive log list** command again to obtain the *current* log sequence number. This is the last redo log file you must keep as part of the online backup. Force a log switch so that Oracle will create an archived log file, using the **alter system** command as follows:

```
SQL> ALTER SYSTEM SWITCH LOGFILE;
```

**NOTE**
*While recovering a database using online backups, you need to apply a minimum of all the archived log files that were created between the **begin backup** command and the **end backup** command, so it's very important to back up all the archived log files. If complete recovery is required, all archived redo log files are required.*

**7.** Back up all the archived log files (determined from steps 2 and 6) using an OS command. You should never take a backup of the online redo log files, as the online log file has the *end of backup* marker and would cause corruptions if used during recovery.

**8.** Back up the control file using the following command:

```
SQL> ALTER DATABASE BACKUP CONTROLFILE TO 'filespec';
```

If you are backing up the control file to disk, make sure you copy the backup control file to tape as well.

**NOTE**
*Control files should be backed up after a database schema change such as when a log file or data file is added, removed, or renamed in the database. New database files (if added to the database) should be backed up immediately after they are added.*

## Internal Operation of Hot Backups

It is important to understand some of the internal mechanisms of hot backups. When an **alter tablespace begin backup** command is issued, the data files that belong to the tablespace get flagged as *hot-backup-in-progress*. Taking the backup before issuing the **alter tablespace begin backup** command would make the backup data files useless. This command would checkpoint all the data files that are in HOT BACKUP mode. This means that any dirty buffers that belong to the data files in HOT BACKUP mode are flushed to disk. The file header's *checkpoint SCN* (checkpoint SCN is discussed in Chapter 6) is advanced to the SCN captured when the **begin backup** command is issued. This is important because the checkpoint SCN in the backup files must be the same as when the backup started, and Oracle cannot guarantee that the file header is the first block that the OS backup utility would copy. Now, after the initial checkpoint, succeeding checkpoints will cease to update the file headers when in HOT BACKUP mode.

The **alter tablespace begin backup** command will begin logging entire block images on the first change to the block if the INIT.ORA parameter _LOG_BLOCKS_DURING_BACKUP is set to TRUE (which is the default value). Why? Because it might be necessary to have a copy of the whole block while applying recovery. To explain this, you need to understand a phenomenon called *split blocks*. If the Oracle block size is a multiple of OS blocks, then, depending on how the OS copies blocks, it is possible for a hot backup to contain an inconsistent version of a given data block. For example, if a block is updated on disk between the reads, the copy in the backup file could be useless since the front and back halves of a block may be written at different times. By logging the before image of a data block to the redo log file before the first change, it can be used later to reconstruct a fractured block during recovery.

The checkpoint done during the execution of the **alter tablespace begin backup** command ensures that only blocks that are changed during the hot backups are written to the redo log file. This explains why excessive redo would be generated for data files in HOT BACKUP mode. Note that if a block remains in cache for a long period of time, it will be logged only once; but if it is flushed to disk and read into cache again while still in HOT BACKUP mode, the before image of the block is logged again.

To verify the consistency of the block before recovery, the version number at the beginning of the block is compared to the version number at the end of the block to determine whether the block has been split during a hot backup. If the version of the block at the beginning and end are the same, then the block is consistent. If not, a consistent version of the block is required and the before image of the block in the redo is copied to disk before applying redo changes.

What this means is that if more DML (i.e., **insert**, **update**, or **delete** operations) is performed on the data files during hot backup, more redo will be generated during this period. This is why Oracle Support Services recommends that you take hot backups when there is less DML activity in the database. This also suggests that you should end the hot backup of a tablespace by issuing the **alter tablespace end backup** command before you take a hot backup of the next tablespace. For example, if two tablespaces need to be backed up, it is recommended that you issue a **begin backup** command for the first tablespace, take the backup at the operating system level, then issue the **end backup** command before taking the backup of the second tablespace—rather than issuing a batch of **begin backup** commands, followed by a batch of backups, and finishing with a batch of **end backup** commands. In summary, you should keep the tablespaces open in HOT BACKUP mode for as little time as possible under the lightest usage conditions.

The file copy during hot backups is done by utilities that are not part of Oracle. The presumption is that the manufacturer of the hardware will have backup facilities that are superior to any portable facility that Oracle would develop. It is the responsibility of the DBA to ensure that copies are only taken between the **begin backup** and **end backup** commands.

The **alter tablespace end backup** command creates a redo record containing the begin backup checkpoint SCN. The SCN is also in the header of the hot backup data files. This is how Oracle knows when all the redo generated during the backup has been applied to the data files. In other words, while using hot backups, during recovery, the DBA needs to apply *at least* the redo generated between the **begin backup** and **end backup** commands to make the backup data files consistent. If you stop the recovery before applying the redo and try to open the database, an error will be signaled. Also, when the **end backup** command is issued, logging of block images is stopped and the data file checkpoints are advanced to the database checkpoint. Chapter 6 discusses checkpoints in detail.

While taking a hot backup, Oracle will not allow you to shut the database down using the NORMAL or IMMEDIATE option. Also, you cannot take a tablespace that is in HOT BACKUP mode offline with the NORMAL or TEMPORARY option. A message is displayed to the DBA indicating that the files are in HOT BACKUP mode and thus the DBA cannot shut the database down or take the tablespace offline. This is to ensure that an *end backup* marker is generated and to remind the DBAs to issue the **end backup** command. Chapter 10 describes a case study on how to deal with situations when the database crashes while you are taking a hot backup of the database.

## Labeling and Naming Conventions

Though the Oracle Recovery Manager can identify and maintain the backup set information in its metadata, it is not sufficient to support a DBA while doing disaster recovery. You have to follow certain well-defined and yet suitable identification methods and naming conventions.

The backup tape cartridges should be labeled in a consistent way so that if they are needed to restore from the backup, the point of recoverability is clearly identified. You should mark the backup tapes with certain well-defined coloring and naming conventions for easier identification for managing the backup sets. For example, the starting letters of the name should be *M* or *W* or *D* indicating monthly, weekly or daily backups respectively. The second letter should indicate the type of backup whether it is full (F), or cumulative, (C) or incremental (I) and so on. The next four letters should indicate the name of the database. The next six digits should indicate the date in *dd/mm/yy* format. The last three letters should indicate the initials of the person taking the backup. For example if DBA "Johnny" has taken a complete backup of the database **SALES.AQUILA** on the 5th of July, 2000, the label should clearly say in bold letters DF-SAAQ-050700-JOH.

When it comes to marking the tapes with color codes, you should maintain the defined color codes for daily, weekly, and monthly backup sets and different types of backups like full, incremental, etc. with different color codes. This kind of practice will definitely relieve you from confusion that can arise during recovery time and guide you in avoiding user errors and improving your recovery time.

# Backup Commands in Various Operating Systems

This section focuses on various operating-system-specific commands that are used to back up and restore the database files during an offline or online backup. In some operating systems, such as IBM MVS, some of the basic concepts (such as archiving redo log files) are different compared to other operating systems. Such mechanisms are described in this section.

## Backup/Restore in VMS Environment

The data files in the VMS environment have a **dbs** extension. The control files have a **con** extension, and the archived and online redo logs have an **rdo** extension. **backup** and **copy** are the two commands used in VMS to back up and restore database files. Wildcards can be used while backing up with the **backup** and **copy** commands. If the database layout is OFA compliant, all the data files can be backed up with one command using wildcards (i.e., wildcards can be used for the disk, part of the file path, and for the filename without the extension). Refer to Chapter 2 for an OFA-compliant database layout.

**NOTE**

*The **backup** command does some file verification, whereas, the **copy** command does not.*

The following examples show how to back up the data files, log files, and control files, respectively, from disk to disk:

```
$ backup/log/ignore=(interlock, nobackup) -
DiskA:[dir_path]*.dbs DiskB:[backup_dir_path]*.dbs

$ backup/log/ignore=interlock DiskA:[dir_path]*.rdo -
DiskB:[backup_dir_path]*.rdo

$ backup/log/ignore=interlock DiskA:[dir_path]*.con -
DiskB:[backup_dir_path]*.con
```

The following commands should be used if backing up from disk to tape:

```
$ mount/foreign tape_device:
$ backup/log/ignore=interlock DiskA:[dir-path]*.dbs -
tape_device:db_test.bck/sav
```

The **copy** command does not do any verification or ignore lock contentions to access files-11 copy to tape. The **copy** command is given below to copy to tape:

```
$ mount/over=id tape_device:
$ copy  DiskA:[backup_dir_path]*.dbs  tape_device:
```

The **backup** or the **copy** command can be used to restore the database files from tape to disk as well. Again, wildcards can be used. The **backup** command must be used if the tape is mounted with the FOREIGN option. The **copy** command is used if the tape is mounted files-11. The following example shows how to use the **backup** command to restore files from tape to disk:

```
$ mount/foreign tape_device:
$ backup/rewind/list tape_device:*/sav
```

To retrieve a file from tape, the following command should be issued:

```
$ backup/rewind tape_device:db_test.bck/sav/select=(test.dbs,..) -
disk:[dir_path]file/new_version/owner=parent/log
```

The following command shows how to use the **copy** command to restore files from tape to disk:

```
$ mount   tape_device:   volume_label      !OR you can use the following command:
$ mount/over=id tape_device:
$ dir tape_device:                          ! To list all the files on tape
$ copy tape_device:file   disk:[dir_path]file  ! To retrieve a file from tape
```

## Backup/Restore in UNIX Environment

In this section, we will describe some of the commands that are used in UNIX to take physical backups of the database files.

### cpio

The **cpio** is a standard utility on UNIX System V platforms. It's a nonstandard utility on UNIX BSD platforms, but many BSD vendors include it. This command is used to copy files and directory structures in and out of archive files and to copy directory structures from one location to another. To generate a required single-column list of path names, use the **cat**, **ls**, or **find** command. The **cpio** command can back up files describing devices (special files), as well as data files.

There are three **cpio** modes:

1. Copy out mode, which creates an archive file, as in:

   **cpio -o** [aABcLvV ] [ -C size ] [ -H hdr ] [ -O file ] [-M msg ]

2. Copy in mode, which allows you to retrieve a previously archived file, as in:

   **cpio -i** [ 6bBcdfkmrsStuvV ] [ -C size] [ -E file ] [ -H hdr ] [ -O file ]
   [ -I file ] [ -M msg ] [ -R ID ] [ patterns ]

3. Pass mode, which passes a copy of a directory structure from the source to a new destination. It works like copy out, except the files are copied to a new *directory tree.* For example,

   **cpio -p** [adlmruvV ] [ -R ID] *directory*

Please refer to the **man** pages in UNIX for an explanation of the various options used with **cpio**.

The following three examples show how to copy a directory tree from the source location to a new directory location on disk. The first command is used to back up all files in the same directory path, the second example is used to back up all data files and control files, and the last example is used to back up the redo log files.

```
$ ls /dsk*/ORACLE/prod/*.*   |   cpio -pdk new-dir

$ ls /dsk*/ORACLE/prod/*.dbf  |   cpio -pdk new-dir

$ ls /dsk*/ORACLE/prod/*.rdo  |   cpio -pdk new-dir
```

To restore files from an archive file (**arch010194**) on disk, use the following command:

```
$ cpio -ic < /bck/arch010194
```

or

```
$ cat /bck/arch010194 | cpio -ic
```

On *some* platforms, the -r option (not used with -p) can be used to interactively rename files. To restore and rename files from an archive file (**arch010194** ) on disk, use the following command:

```
$ cpio -icr < /bck/arch010194
```

While copying from disk to tape, if **cpio** reaches the end of the tape it will prompt you for the device name, allowing you to insert a new tape to continue or press ENTER to exit. To copy files in the directories to tape, use the following command:

```
$ ls /dsk*/ORACLE/*.*  | cpio -ocBv  >  tape_device
```

To copy the current directory and all subdirectories (directory trees) to tape, use the following command:

```
$ find . -depth -print | cpio -ocBv  >  tape_device
```

While restoring from tape, first identify the tape that contains the files needed by issuing the following command:

```
$ cpio itBv < tape_device
```

Then copy the file or directory tree of files from tape to disk using the following command:

```
$ cpio -icBv file  < tape_device
$ cpio -icdBv file < tape_device
```

## tar

The **tar** command is a standard utility on System V and BSD UNIX. This command is used to archive files from disk to tape or used to retrieve archived files from tape. It can also be used to copy directory structures from one directory to a new directory. Some BSD systems do not support a hyphen preceding the options to the **tar** command. If the device is a hyphen (-), **tar** writes to the standard output or reads from the standard input. For a detailed description of the options for the **tar** command, refer to the **man** pages in UNIX.

The following is an example of using the **tar** command to back up one directory structure to a new directory location on disk:

```
$ tar cf - . | ( cd to_dir; tar xf - )
```

In the above example, the **tar** command is used to create a tar file to the standard output (the device argument is a hyphen). The output is piped to a subshell that changes directories (**cd**) to the directory you want to copy the files to. The second **tar** command extracts the files back out into a hierarchical structure.

The following example shows how to back up files from one directory to tape:

```
$ tar -cvf  /dev/rmt0h  /dsk*/ORACLE/*.*
```

where **rmt0h** is the tape device.

Similarly, to list the contents of an archive tape and restore files from the tape device, use the following commands, respectively:

```
$ tar -tvf tape_device
```

```
$ tar -xvf tape_device
```

### tar versus cpio

The advantages of using the **tar** command are as follows:

- It has relatively simple syntax.

- It allows you to replace archived files with different versions and append new files to the end of an archive without having to rewrite the file from the beginning.

The advantages of using the **cpio** command are as follows:

- It can back up files describing devices (special files), as well as data files.

- It writes data in a stream format, saving space and time when creating a tape backup; **cpio** tends to be faster than **tar** and stores data more efficiently than **tar**.

- **cpio**, unlike **tar**, will attempt to read a tape several times if it encounters problems.

- **cpio** will skip a bad area on tape.

### cp

**cp** is a System V and BSD UNIX command to copy files or directory structures from one location on disk to another. The syntax is

**cp** [-ip] *source_file destination_file*
**cp** [-ipr] *source_file_list destination_directory*
**cp** -r [-ip] *source_directory destination_directory*

where option -i is used if interactive confirmation is required. You are prompted if the copy will overwrite an existing file. If you answer *yes* to the prompt, the copy is done. Option -p is used to preserve the characteristics of the source file. The contents, modification times, and permission modes of the source file are copied to the destination file. Option -r recursively copies any source directories. If a directory is given as the source file, then all of its files and subdirectories are copied. The destination must be a directory.

The following examples show how to back up a file and a directory structure to another location on disk, respectively:

```
$ cp datafile   /bck/datafile

$ cp -r data_file_dir    bck_dir
```

### volcopy

This is a System V command that makes a literal copy of the file system using block size matched to the device. The syntax is

$ **volcopy** *[option] fsname srcdevice volname1 destdevice volname2* where *option* can be -a or -s. If you use the option -a, it invokes a verification sequence requiring a positive operator response instead of the standard 10-second delay before the copy is made. The -s is the default option that aborts the operation if a wrong verification sequence occurs. The program requests length and density information if not given on the command line or not recorded on an input tape label. **fsname** represents the mounted name (i.e., root) of the file system being copied. **srcdevice** and **volname1** represent the device and physical volume name from which the file system copy is extracted. **destdevice** and **volname2** represent the target device and volume.

### dump and restor

**dump** and **restor** are standard BSD UNIX commands. The **dump** command copies all files changed after a certain date from a specified file system to a file, a pipe, magnetic tape, or disks. This utility supports EOF handling, which allows the use of multiple media. The utility prompts for the next volume when the current one is filled. The syntax is

$ **/etc/dump** [*key* [*argument* ...] *file_system* ]

where the *key* specifies the date and other options about the dump; some keys require an *argument*. The various options for the *key* are

[0123456789aBdFfnsSuWw]

where 0 through 9 is the dump level. Level 0 means dump the entire system. Level 1 dumps only those files modified since the last level 0 dump. Level 2 dumps only those files modified since the last level 0 or 1 dump, and so on. Refer to the **man** pages in UNIX for detailed descriptions of all the options (i.e., **man** dump).

The following example dumps the entire file system (**/bck/db_files**) to the device (**/dev/rra2a**) with a size of 400 blocks and each block of 1,024 bytes:

```
$ dump 0Bf 400 /dev/rra2a  /bck/db_files
```

The following example dumps the entire file system (**/bck/db_files**) to a 6,250-bpi tape on a TU78 tape drive:

```
$ dump 0undf /dev/rmt0h /bck/db_files
```

The **restor** command performs an incremental file system restore for BSD UNIX. The **restor** command obtains files from a file, magnetic tape, or disk that was saved by a *previous* dump. You can restore all or part of a corrupted file system, or retrieve individual files overwritten by users. Only a *superuser* may restore a file system containing special files. You must be in stand-alone mode to restore the root file system, and the **restor** command does not accept any arguments; the -r argument is implicit. The syntax is as follows:

   $ **restor** *key [ argument ] [ file-system ]*

The following command creates an empty file system on the disk device, destroying the existing file system, and then restores a complete dump to the same device. The device cannot contain the root device, since after the **mkfs** command the root file system wouldn't exist.

```
$ restor r device          (This assumes the default device)
$ restor r /dev/da0        (The file system is restored on disk, da0)
```

To restore a file from the previous dump, use the command

```
$ restor x file
```

where *file* is the inode number of the file extracted from the dump.

### backup and restore
**backup** and **restore** are standard System V UNIX commands. The **backup** utility is a front end for **cpio**. You should use the **restore** command to restore backups made with this utility. The syntax is

   $ **backup**  [-t]  [-p|-c|-f *files* |-u "*user1* [*user2*]" ]  -d *device*
   $ **backup** -h

where -h produces a backup history, informing the user when the last complete and incremental/partial backups were done. The option -c generates a complete backup—all files changed since system installation. The -p option does an incremental/partial backup—only files modified since the last backup. The -f files backs up specified files. Filenames may contain characters to be expanded—i.e., asterisk (*) and period (.). Note that the argument must be in quotes. The -u option backs up all files in the user's home directory. At least one user must be specified. If more than one user is specified, the argument must be in quotes. The argument *all* backs up all users' home directories. Option -d specifies the backup device.

Option -t indicates that the backup device is a tape. The -t option must be used with the -d option when a tape device is specified.

The **restore** command performs an incremental file system restore of a previous backup made with the System V **backup** utility. This utility acts as a front end to **cpio**. The syntax is

$ **restore** [-c] [-i]  [-o] [-t] [-d *device*] [*pattern* [*pattern*] ...]

where the -c option does a complete restore. All files on the tape are restored. The -i option gets the index file off of the medium. The -o option overwrites existing files. If the file to be restored already exists, it will not be restored unless this option is specified. The -t option indicates that the tape device is to be used. The option must be used with the -d option when restoring from tape. The **-d** device option indicates the device to be used.

### fbackup and frestore
The **fbackup** and **frestore** commands are used on HP-UX System V. The **fbackup** command is used to selectively transfer files to an output device. **fbackup** combines the features of **dump** and **ftio** to provide a high-speed, flexible file system backup mechanism. The syntax is as follows:

$ **/etc/fbackup** -f *device* [-f *device..*] [-0-9] [-uvyAH] [ -i *path*]
[-e *path*] [-g *graph_file*] [-l *path*] [-V *path*] [-c *config*]
$ **/etc/fbackup** -f *device* [-f *device..*] [-R *restart_file*] [-uvyAH] [-l *path*] [-V *path*]
[-c *config*]

The Return Value is 0 upon normal completion, 1 if it is interrupted but allowed to save its state for possible restart, and 2 if error conditions prevent the session from completing. The output device can be a file, standard output, a raw magnetic tape drive, a DDS-format tape, or a rewritable magneto-optical disk.

The selection of files to back up is done by explicitly specifying trees of files to be included or excluded from a **fbackup** session. The user can construct an arbitrary graph of files by using the -i (include) or -e (exclude) option on the command line, or by using the -g option with a graph file or multiple graph files. For backups being done on a regular basis, the -g option provides an easier interface for controlling the backup graph. **fbackup** selects files in this graph and attempts to transfer them to the output device. The selectivity depends on the mode in which **fbackup** is being used (i.e., full or incremental backups).

When doing full backups, all files in the graph are selected. When doing incremental backups, only files in the graph that have been modified since a previous backup of that graph are selected. If **fbackup** is used for incremental backups, a database of past backups must be kept. By default, **fbackup** maintains the data in the text file **/usr/adm/fbackupfiles/dates**. The directory **/usr/adm/fbackupfiles** must be created prior to the first incremental backup. The -d option can be used to specify another database file. Entries for each session are recorded on separate pairs of lines. The first line of each pair contains the graph filename, backup level, starting time, and ending time. The second line of each pair contains the same information, but in strftime (3C) format, **fbackup** does not use this line and it is included for readability. Graph filenames are compared character by character upon checking the previous backup database file to determine when a previous session was run for that graph.

The following example shows how to back up to tape a file that contains directories of files. Following that, we list the files that should be included in or excluded from the backup.

```
$ /etc/fbackup -f tape_device - g graph_file -u -0
$ /etc/fbackup -0I /usr -e /usr/lib -f /dev/rmt0h
$ cd /usr/adm/fbackupfiles
$ /etc/fbackup -0uc config -g graphs -I indices -f /dev/rmt0h
# graphs file
i        /dsk1
i        /dsk2
i        /dsk3/oracle
i        /dsk4/usr
e        /dsk1/usr/class
e        /dsk2/usr/test
```

The **frestore** command reads media written by the **fbackup** command. The syntax is as follows:

$ **/etc/frecover** -r [-hmosvyAFNOX] [-c *config*] [-f *device*] [-S skip]
$ **/etc/frecover** -R *path* [-f *device*]
$ **/etc/frecover** -x [-hmosvyAFNOX] [-c *config*] [-e *path*] [-f *device*]
[-g *graph*] [-i *path*] [-S skip]

Refer to the **man** pages in UNIX for descriptions of the various options.

## dd

This command copies the specified input file to the specified output file with possible conversions. It can read input from a file or from standard input. It writes to a file or to standard output. The **dd** command is very useful because it allows raw device backups that cannot be done with the **tar** and **cpio** commands. With the **dd** command, you can specify the input and output block size to perform raw physical I/O.

The **dd** command lets you copy data from one device to another that does not have the same block size, where **cpio** and **tar** might fail; you could use the **dd** command as a front-end command that would extract the data from tape and convert it to a block size **cpio** and **tar** can utilize. The syntax is as follows:

$ **dd** [*option = value ...* ]

Some of the important options are described below:

- bs=*n*   Sets the input and output block size to *n* bytes.

- count=*n*   Allows only *n* blocks of input to be copied.

- ibs=*n*   The input block size is set to *n* bytes. If the ibs option is not specified, a 512-byte block is used. Data corruption can occur on some systems if the ibs exceeds 1,024 when copying data from tape to disk. As a workaround, use the bs option.

- if=*file*   Specifies the input file, *file*. If the if option is not used, standard input is used.

- obs=*n*   The output block size is set to *n* bytes. If the obs option is not used, a 512-byte block is used.

- of=*file*   Specifies the output file, *file*. If the of option is not used, standard output is used.

- seek=*n*   Skips over the first *n* blocks of the output file before it starts to write the data.

- skip=*n*   Skips forward the first *n* blocks of the input file before copying.

To back up from a raw device to a raw tape device, you have two options:

1. You can copy the raw device data to a regular UNIX file using the **dd** command and then use the normal UNIX backup commands such as **cpio** and **tar**.

2. Copy the raw device data directly to a raw tape device. The **dd** command does not handle multiple drives, so if the partition exceeds one tape,

multiple commands will need to be used. Check to see if **dd** requires special block size values to be used. The following steps will make the procedure clear:

■  Mount the first tape and back up the raw device to tape using the command

```
# dd if=raw_device of=tape_device bs=block_size
count=number
```

■  If additional tapes are needed, enter the following when prompted. *skip* is incremented by the *count* value for each successive tape.

```
# dd if=raw_device of=tape_device skip=number bs=
block_size count=number
```

To restore data from a raw tape device onto a raw partition, use the following steps:

1.  Mount the tape and then enter the following:

```
# dd if=tape_device of=filename bs=block_size count=number
```

2.  Mount subsequent tapes if needed, incrementing **seek** or **oseek** by **count**:

```
# dd if=tape_device of=raw_device [seek|oseek]=number bs=block_size
count=number
```

## crontab—UNIX Automated Scheduler Command

You can schedule physical backups or exports using **crontab**, an automated scheduler command. Chapter 5 gives an example of a UNIX script to do cold and hot backups. The script is scheduled to run using **crontab**. In this section, we describe how this scheduler works.

The **crontab** command is used to designate a file whose lines schedule commands to be executed at regular intervals. The cron program reads, interprets, and executes the crontab file. The commands are usually executed by the Bourne shell (sh). The following is the syntax:

> # **crontab** [ *file* ]
> # **crontab** -e [ *username* ]
> # **crontab** -l [ *username* ]
> # **crontab** -r [ *username* ]

where *file* is the crontab file. Option -e lets you edit your **crontab** file using the editor defined by the EDITOR variable. The -r option removes your current **crontab** file. If username is specified, it removes that user's **crontab** file. Only the *superuser* can remove other users' **crontab** files. The -l option lists the contents of your current

**crontab** file. The argument *file* is the name of the file you want to use as your **crontab** file. The file is copied to a file named *username* in the system crontab directory. If you do not specify a filename for **crontab** to read as input, **crontab** reads the standard input until you press CTRL-D.

The **crontab** command reads a file or the standard input to a directory that contains all users' crontab files: **/usr/spool/cron/crontabs/username**. You can use **crontab** to remove your **crontab** file or display it. You cannot access other users' **crontab** files in the **crontab** directory. If you do not redirect the standard output and standard error of a command executed from your **crontab** file, the output is mailed to you. The **crontab** file contains lines that consist of six fields separated by blanks (tabs or spaces). The first five fields are integers that specify the time the command is scheduled. The sixth field contains the command that is executed by **cron**. Table 3-2 shows the first five fields of a line in the **crontab** file.

Each field can contain the following:

- An integer

- A range

- A list (of integers or ranges)

- An asterisk (*) (indicates all legal values, i.e., all legal times)

The days of the week and the day of the month fields are interpreted separately if both are defined. To specify days to run by only one field, the other field must be set to an asterisk (*). Table 3-3 provides some examples.

The sixth field contains the command that is executed by **cron** at the specified times. The command string is terminated by a newline or a percent sign (%). Any text following the percent sign is sent to the command as standard input. The

| Field | Range | Meaning |
|-------|-------|---------|
| 1 | 0 to 59 | Minutes |
| 2 | 0 to 23 | Hours (midnight is 0; 10 P.M. is 22) |
| 3 | 1 to 31 | Day of the month |
| 4 | 1 to 12 | Month of the year |
| 5 | 0 to 6 | Day of the Week (Sunday is 0; Saturday is 6) |

**TABLE 3-2.**    *Description of the First Five Fields of a Line in the crontab File*

| | |
|---|---|
| 10 0 * * 3 | Run the command only on Wednesday at 12:10 A.M. |
| 0 6 1,9 * 1 | Run the command at 6 A.M. on the first and ninth of each month and every Monday. |
| 0,30 7-20 * * * | Run the command every 30 minutes from 7 A.M. to 8 P.M. every day. |

**TABLE 3-3.** *Examples of crontab Entries*

percent sign can be escaped by preceding it with a backslash (\%). Lines beginning with a # sign are comment lines. To use the **crontab** command, you must have access permission. The system administrator can make the **crontab** command available to all users, specific users, or no users. Two files that are used to control access are **/usr/sbin/cron.d/cron.allow** and **/usr/sbin/cron.d/cron.deny**. If the **cron.allow** file exists but is empty, then all users can use the **crontab** command. If neither file exists, then no users other than the *superuser* can use **crontab**.

Other related files are given here:

| | |
|---|---|
| **/usr/sbin/cron.d** | The main directory for the cron process |
| **/usr/sbin/cron.d/log** | Accounting information for cron processing |
| **/usr/sbin/cron.d/crontab.allow** | A file containing a list of users allowed to use crontab |
| **/usr/sbin/cron.d/crontab.deny** | A file containing a list of users not allowed to use crontab |
| **/usr/spool/cron/crontabs** | The location of crontab text to be executed |

# Backup/Restore in IBM MVS Environment

Backup and recovery procedures for Oracle on MVS are exactly the same as any other operating system. Externally, however, there are some differences because there are differences between MVS and other operating systems. In essence, Oracle for MVS files are VSAM files, and the ARCH process submits a batch job to archive online redo log files.

## Backing Up Data Files

Oracle files are backed up using *physical image* type backup utilities like IBM's DF/DSS or FDR. You can back up the database files using IDCAMS EXPORT with the CIMODE parameter. IDCAMS REPRO will not work because Oracle works on the CI level and does not use VSAM records. Files belonging to a tablespace should be backed up as a unit by submitting a batch job. The following is an example of a *physical image* type backup:

```
//BACKUP    JOB (0000,O7),'ORACLE IMAGE COPY',CLASS=A
//STEP1     EXEC PGM=ADRDSSU
//SYSPRINT DD  SYSOUT=*
//DUMPOUT   DD  DSN=ORACLE.ORA1V.IMAGE.COPY,DISP=(NEW,CATLG,DELETE),
//              UNIT=TAPE,VOL=(,99,SER=(BKUP01,BKUP02,BKUP03,BKUP04)),
//              LABEL=(1,SL,EXPDT=98000)
//SYSIN     DD  *
  DUMP DATASET(INCLUDE(ORACLE.ORA1V.**))
       OUTDD(DUMPOUT)
/*
//
```

## Archiving Redo Log Files

Archiving redo log files is done differently on MVS compared to UNIX or other operating systems. If you are operating in the ARCHIVELOG mode, Oracle for MVS sets a timer of MAXWAIT duration and submits a batch job to archive the filled online log file. If the archive job hasn't completed by the time the MAXWAIT timer expires, Oracle submits another batch job to archive the same log. Occasionally your robotic (or other) tape mount request may get delayed and a second job submitted before the tape gets mounted. The second job will recognize that the redo log it has been asked to archive has already been processed and will terminate. Oracle for MVS uses the INIT.ORA parameter ACS (Archive Control String) to control archiving. The following is an example of an ACS parameter:

```
ACS="TYPE=SUBMIT,INCJCL=/DD/ARCH,ODSN1=/DD/O1,ODSN2=/DD/O2,MAXWAIT=30"
```

This instructs the archiver to do the following:

1. Set a timer for 30 minutes.

2. Read the skeleton JCL from the ARCH DD statement.

3. Replace the substitute keywords with the appropriate values.

4. Submit a batch job to archive the recently filled online redo log file to the O1 DD statement and to the O2 DD statement. (Yes, Oracle for MVS has had dual archiving for years!)

5. When the timer expires, Oracle checks to see whether the online redo log was archived. If not, the process is repeated until it is archived.

The following is an archive JCL example:

```
//ARCHIVE   JOB (0000,O7),'ORACLE ARCHIVE',CLASS=A
//STEP1     EXEC PGM=ARCHIVE,PARM='++/DD/SYSPARM'
//STEPLIB   DD  DISP=SHR,DSN=ORACLE.ORA1.AUTHLOAD
//SYSERR    DD  SYSOUT=*
//SYSOUT    DD  SYSOUT=*
//SYSIN     DD  DUMMY
//O1        DD  DISP=(NEW,CATLG,DELETE),
//              DSN=ORACLE.AL%LOGSEQ%.LOG,
//              UNIT=SYSDA,DCB=(RECFM=FB,LRECL=4096,BLKSIZE=24576),
//              SPACE=(4096,(200,350),RLSE),VOL=SER=ORA001
//ORA$MMIO DD  DUMMY
//SYSPARM  DD  *
%LOGSEQ%
%LOGNAME%
%ODSN1%
%ODSN2%
/*
//
```

In the above JCL,

■   %LOGNAME% is the online redo log to be archived.

■   %LOGSEQ% is the redo log sequence number.

■   %ODSN1% is the ODSN1 string from the ACS parameter.

■   %ODSN2% is the ODSN2 string from the ACS parameter.

## Backing Up Control Files

Control files should be backed up as part of the normal cold backup process in exactly the same way as the rest of the database and online redo log files. You can also do backups of the control file using the **alter database backup controlfile to 'file'** command. If you decide to back up the control file using this command, the file that will hold the backup control file is a VSAM file that has to be precreated using the IDCAMS utility before the **alter database** command can be issued. If you want to submit a batch job to create the VSAM file, it is a good idea to do the backup of the control file as a second step in the same batch job. The following JCL example creates a VSAM file to hold a control file and then issues the **alter database** command to take a control file backup:

```
//ORACLE1  JOB (0000,ORA),'ORACLE',CLASS=A,
//          MSGCLASS=X,PRTY=15,MSGLEVEL=(1,1),
//          REGION=4096K
//*-----------------------------------------------------------*
//*        CREATE A VSAM FILE                                  *
//*        TO HOLD A CONTROL FILE BACK                         *
//*-----------------------------------------------------------*
//STEP1    EXEC PGM=IDCAMS
//SYSPRINT DD SYSOUT=*
//SYSIN    DD *
   DELETE (ORACLE.ORA1V.C020295)                    -
          CLUSTER PURGE
   DEFINE CLUSTER                                    -
      (                                              -
      NAME(ORACLE.ORA1V.C020295)                     -
          VOLUMES(ORA001)                            -
          CONTROLINTERVALSIZE(4096)                  -
          RECORDS(400)                               -
          RECORDSIZE(4089 4089)                      -
          NONSPANNED                                 -
          UNIQUE                                     -
          NONINDEXED                                 -
          SPEED                                      -
          SHR(3 3)                                   -
      )                                              -
      DATA                                           -
      (                                              -
      NAME(ORACLE.ORA1V.C020295.DATA)                -
      )
//*-----------------------------------------------------------*
//*        RUN SVRMGR TO BACKUP THE CONTROL FILE              *

//*        TO A VSAM FILE AND TO TRACE                        *
//*-----------------------------------------------------------*
//STEP2    EXEC PGM=SVRMGR
//STEPLIB  DD DSN=ORACLE.ORA1.CMDLOAD,DISP=SHR
//SYSMDUMP DD SYSOUT=*
//SYSOUT   DD SYSOUT=*,DCB=(LRECL=132,BLKSIZE=1320,RECFM=VB)
//SYSERR   DD SYSOUT=*,DCB=(LRECL=132,BLKSIZE=1320,RECFM=VB)
//ORAPRINT DD SYSOUT=*
//DBAINIT  DD DUMMY
//ORA@ORA1 DD DUMMY
//SYSIN    DD *
CONNECT SYSTEM/MANAGER
ALTER DATABASE BACKUP CONTROLFILE TO '/DSN/ORACLE.ORA1V.C020295';
ALTER DATABASE BACKUP CONTROLFILE TO TRACE;
/*
//
```

Note that the last **alter database** command creates a trace file with the SQL script to create a new control file. On MVS, the trace files are created using the MPM TRACEDS parameter as a model. The INIT.ORA parameters USER_DUMP_DEST and BACKGROUND_DUMP_DEST are not used. The following is an example of the TRACEDS parameter:

```
TRACEDS="ORA1.PROD1.TRACE** UNIT=SYSDA"
```

## Backup/Restore in Windows NT

Windows NT 4.x provides a utility called **backup** that allows users to back up files on hard disk to either floppies or tapes. The **backup** command is available on the command line and with a GUI. To use the GUI, choose Start | Programs | Administrative Tools | Backup. To use the command-line interface, type **backup** at the command line. You must ensure that the database is shut down normally for a cold backup, or ensure that the tablespace is offline for a hot backup, before copying the files using the Windows NT Backup utility.

Windows NT allows you to schedule tasks using the **at** command. You can create a batch file that contains all the commands required for a backup and schedule the execution of this batch file using the **at** command. To schedule the execution of a batch file named **orabak.bat** at 2:00 A.M., use

**C:> at 02:00 c:\oracle\orabak.bat**

One of the Windows NT database-management tools you can use with Oracle7 release 7.1 up to Oracle8 (NOT available in Oracle8*i* for NT), is the Oracle for Windows NT Backup Manager. Click on Start | Programs | Oracle for Windows NT to see this program. The password for the user *internal* is required to use this utility (the default password is *oracle*). The Backup Manager runs in two modes, depending on whether you are operating the database in ARCHIVELOG mode or NOARCHIVELOG mode. Figure 3-1 and Table 3-4 provide details on the Backup Manager if the database is running in ARCHIVELOG mode.

If the database is operating in NOARCHIVELOG mode, or the database is shut down, a different Backup Manager dialog appears, as described in Table 3-5. Figure 3-2 shows the dialog box in this case.

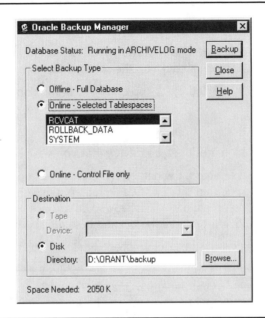

**FIGURE 3-1.** *Backup Manager dialog box for ARCHIVELOG mode*

| Dialog Element | Explanation |
|---|---|
| Database Status | Indicates the status of the database. |
| Offline - Full Database | If selected, this option does an offline backup for you. If the database is not open, it just takes a backup of the data files, log files, and control files. If the database is open, it shuts down the database, performs backup, and restarts database. |

**TABLE 3-4.** *Elements of the Backup Manager Dialog Box when Operating in ARCHIVELOG Mode*

| Dialog Element | Explanation |
|---|---|
| Online - Selected Tablespace | If selected, this allows you to do an online, partial database backup. It backs up the selected tablespaces for you. |
| Online - Control File only | If selected, backs up one copy of the control file. |
| Tape | If selected, backs up to tape. |
| Device | Indicates the tape device that stores the backup database files. |
| Disk, Directory and Browse | If selected, the database file is backed up to the directory specified on disk. Oracle recommends that you specify the complete path. The Browse button can be used to select the location where the backup data file should be stored. |
| Backup | Initiates the backup procedure. |

**TABLE 3-4.**    *Elements of the Backup Manager Dialog Box when Operating in ARCHIVELOG Mode* (continued)

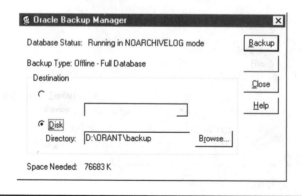

**FIGURE 3-2.**    *Backup Manager dialog box for NOARCHIVELOG mode*

| Dialog Element | Explanation |
|---|---|
| Database Status | Indicates the status of the database: NOARCHIVELOG mode or not running. |
| Backup Type | Indicates that only offline backup is possible in this mode. |
| Tape | If selected, backs up to tape. |
| Device | Indicates the tape device that stores the backup database files. |
| Disk, Directory and Browse | If selected, the database file is backed up to the directory specified on disk. Oracle recommends that you specify the complete path. The Browse button can be used to select the location where the backup data file should be stored. |
| Backup | Initiates the backup procedure. |
| Files | This button is enabled only when the database is not operating. You can use this button to review and change the list of database files before performing a backup. |

**TABLE 3-5.**   *Elements of the Backup Manager Dialog Box when Operating in NOARCHIVELOG Mode*

If you choose the Files button to review or modify the database files, another dialog box appears. Using this dialog box, you can list all the database files and validate the file list by adding and/or deleting filenames.

The following backup procedure shows how to use the Backup Manager:

1. Open the Backup Manager. The Backup Manager dialog box appears.

2. When prompted, enter the password for the user *internal* and choose OK. The default password is *oracle.*

3. If operating with NOARCHIVELOG mode or the database is not operating, skip this step. Otherwise, select either Offline Full Database, Online

Selected Tablespace, or Online Control File Only, depending on what you want to back up.

4. Select either Tape or Disk as the destination for the backup database files.

5. If you selected Disk in the previous step, specify a full path name in the Directory field or by using the Browse button.

6. If the database is open, skip this step. Otherwise, choose the Files button to verify that you are backing up the right data files, log files, and the control files.

7. Choose Backup to begin the backup procedure. Note that if the database is open and an offline backup is requested, then the database is automatically shut down before the backup and restarted after the backup.

If you want to manually copy the data files during hot backups, you can use the **OCOPYnn** command (where **nn** is the version of **OCOPY**) to back up to disk or to a diskette.

**NOTE**
*OCOPYnn is used in Oracle8 and lower versions only. This is called the **OCOPY** command in Oracle8i.*

If copying to multiple diskettes, you can use the /B option to split large files. While restoring from multiple diskettes, you should use the /R option. The following examples show you how to back up to disk, back up to multiple diskettes, and how to restore from multiple diskettes to disk on Oracle8i, respectively.

```
C:\> OCOPY current_file backup_file
C:\> OCOPY /B current_file a:
C:\> OCOPY /R a: restore_dir
```

# Backups in Special Environments

Before designing the appropriate backup procedure for your site, it is important that you understand the applications that are run at your site. First, determine if your applications are online transaction processing/query processing (OLTP/OLQP) or DSS-type applications. It is not wise to mix the two types of applications if you can help it. For OLTP/OLQP, there will be some sustained transactions per second (TPS) rate and, as the DBA, you must know where those changes (which tablespaces/data files) propagate to. Let's look into the various backup strategies for databases running these kinds of applications.

# Backup Considerations in an OLTP Environment

In an OLTP environment, there are several options that one can choose for backup strategy. Irrespective of the application type, if the databases are small (less than 5 gigabytes), and high availability is not a requirement (for example, you don't need to have the database available 24 hours a day, 7 days a week), then cold backups can be considered. However, if you operate your database 24 hours a day, 7 days a week, cold backups may not be feasible since the time to perform backups is longer than the window of time for maintenance. In such cases, the majority of the sites prefer using hot backups. Many sites elect to back up some tablespaces on one particular day and the others on another day. This is cycled until all tablespaces have been backed up. While designing such a backup strategy, careful thought must be given to mean time to recover (MTTR), because the determining factor for the time to recover is the recovery of the oldest data file with the most changes. For this reason, if the online backups are chosen, ensure that the rollback segment tablespace(s) and all other tablespaces that undergo heavy changes are backed up frequently. The key issue with most of these sites is high availability. Let's look at some of the approaches that are used to maintain high availability and redundancy from a backup and recovery perspective.

One approach for ensuring availability of large OLTP systems is the deployment of RAID 1 or *mirroring* architecture, which provides fault tolerance. With disk mirroring, two drives store identical information so that one is a mirror of the other. Thus, for every disk **write** operation, the OS must write to both the disks. Mirroring of data files is not an Oracle feature, but should be achieved at the OS or hardware level, depending upon the platform. Redo log files, control files, and all data files are mirrored. This is an expensive approach, as the number of disks is doubled.

The second approach is to take advantage of the *read-only* tablespaces, available in Oracle 7.1 and later. Make the tablespaces read-only for tablespaces that contain data that does not undergo changes, such as lookup tables and monthly rollup data. Refer to Appendix A for details on read-only tablespaces. This means that the application must split up the data into appropriate tablespaces. However, you would still need to mirror redo log files, rollback segments, SYSTEM tablespaces, and tablespaces that undergo changes. If you have a lot of read-only tablespaces, backup and restore time is significantly reduced since you don't have to take backups of the read-only tablespaces. It also reduces the number of disks because only the read-write tablespaces have to be mirrored.

The third approach to minimize database downtime and increase fault tolerance is by using triple mirrors. Basically, the idea is to have a three-way mirror of a tablespace, and when you want to take a hot backup, simply issue the **alter tablespace begin backup** command and then break the mirror. You now have an on-disk hot backup while a two-way mirror is still in place. The broken mirror can be copied off to tape. This approach, though expensive, adds the benefit of having an on-disk hot backup of tablespaces, which drastically reduces MTTR because you don't need to restore data files from tape.

The last approach to minimize database downtime and maximize availability is to use a *hot standby database*. This is feature is available from Oracle7 release 7.3 and higher. The concept of standby databases is given in the last section of this chapter. Oracle8*i* has some good enhancements with hot standby databases. For complete details on planning and maintenance of standby databases, refer to the "Disaster Recovery" section in Chapter 6.

## Backup Considerations in a DSS Environment

Typically, in DSS-class databases, such as data warehouses, many of the tablespaces will not undergo change, and thus can be made read-only. This means that backups need to be done only once for these tablespaces. This reduces the need to implement RAID unless availability is a factor. For DSS applications, backups will depend upon how often batch loads are completed. With some architectural improvements in Oracle7 release 7.2 and later, it is possible to add data through a parallel direct path loader and rebuild the indexes with the PARALLEL CREATE INDEX option.

In a DSS environment, the backup and recovery strategy *must* dictate the overall operations of the system. For example, don't build a table with large amounts of data; instead, partition it into several smaller and more manageable pieces (for example, a few gigabytes), so that you have the ability to back up and restore the individual pieces in a reasonable amount of time.

Before you design a backup procedure for a very large database (VLDB), you should come up with a test model for predicting the length of time it takes to recover the database or portion of the database, given some failure scenario. The intent of such a model is to derive a set of best-practice activities that can help you reduce MTTR and increase mean time between failures (MTBF).

## Hot Standby Database

The growing need for high-availability systems and the enormous expense resulting from downtime of database systems have given rise to many different approaches that are focused towards maximizing uptime. Oracle Corporation recognizes the importance of high availability and reporting and has come up with the standby database. While this concept is introduced in Oracle7 release 7.3, Oracle8*i* provides some new features such as being able to read the data in the standby database in a READ-ONLY mode. The objective of the standby database is to support the capability of maintaining a duplicate, or "standby," database of a "primary" or online production database for recovering from disasters at the production site. The goal is to be able to switch over from the primary database to the standby database in the case of a disaster in the least amount of time with as little recovery to perform as possible. The standby database can be maintained in a STANDBY mode or a READ-ONLY mode. You can switch between these two modes at any time. For example, to start a standby database in READ-ONLY mode, you do the following. First you start the database with the nomount option.

```
SQL> STARTUP NOMOUNT pfile=initSTANDBY.ora
```

Next you mount the standby database with the following command:

```
SQL> ALTER DATABASE MOUNT STANDBY DATABASE;
```

Finally, you can open the database in READ-ONLY mode:

```
SQL> ALTER DATABASE OPEN READ ONLY;
```

A brief description of standby databases follows. For a complete description on how to plan for disaster recovery and maintain standby databases, please refer to the "Disaster Recovery" section in Chapter 6.

A hot standby database is a backup copy of the production database that is maintained on an identical but different machine. Let's call the production database you use the *primary* database and the hot standby database the *standby* or *backup* database. Typically, an offline or online backup of the primary database is made and copied to the secondary machine (standby). The secondary machine has a similar configuration as the primary (names of disk drives, directory paths, etc.) and the standby database is mounted but not opened. If keeping the same directory path is not feasible, Oracle provides DB_FILE_NAME_CONVERT and LOG_FILE_NAME_CONVERT parameters that you can use for filename conversion at the secondary machine, so that renaming the files is not necessary. The archive log files are copied to the secondary machine and applied to the standby database at regular intervals. This means that the standby database is always synchronized with the primary database and is always in *mounted* but not *open* stage.

You can make use of the Multiple Remote Archive Destinations feature of Oracle8*i* to duplicate the archived redo log files from primary to secondary. This feature provides an INIT.ORA parameter called LOG_ARCHIVE_DEST_N. You can use this parameter to define the destination and attributes for the archive redo. For example,

```
LOG_ARCHIVE_DEST_1='SERVICE=standby1 OPTIONAL REOPEN=300'
```

where the attribute SERVICE specifies a standby destination. In this example, it is defined as standby1, which corresponds to an appropriate service name in the **TNSNAMES.ORA** file. Net8 will be used to transmit the archivelog files. You should ensure that the Net8 service name is working properly before you define this service. See the *Oracle8i Reference Manual* for details on using LOG_ARCHIVE_DEST_N.

**NOTE**
*LOG_ARCHIVE_DEST_N parameter is valid only if you have installed the Oracle Enterprise Edition.*

Using this feature, a standby database can be automated for automatic archival. This allows the standby database to remain synchronized with the production database, without the intervention of a DBA for transporting the archived redo log files from the primary database to the standby database and applying manually. When you keep a standby database in READ-ONLY mode, you should remember that you can query the database but it's unavailable for managed recovery and will be out of sync with the primary database. This will limit the standby's role as a disaster recovery database. One option is to consider two standby databases. This may not be an option if you are using a VLDB.

When the primary database fails (for example, due to a media failure), the secondary database can be opened or *activated* and all users can now be switched to the second machine and can continue to do work while the primary database is being recovered. After such a switch, the standby database becomes the primary database. Then, you will need another standby site. The mechanisms you use to deploy and maintain a standby database must be flexible. You should use environmental variables (in UNIX, for example) to identify the primary and standby sites. This way, you will not need to modify the scripts. Thus, after activation, you can create a new standby database simply by changing the variables to point to the new site names and running the scripts. This is particularly useful if you want to use the original site as the standby. Furthermore, you will need to make the original site the standby site if you wish that original site to once again house the production database.

A lot of things can go wrong with this administration-intensive procedure if it is not implemented correctly. For example, if the primary database renames a data file, what are the ramifications of this on the standby database? A detailed description of design considerations, planning, and maintenance of standby databases is given in Chapter 6.

# CHAPTER

## 4

## Logical Backups

*logical backup* is defined as a backup that copies the data in the database and does not record the physical location of the data. The **export** utility offered by Oracle can be used to take logical backups of the database. The **export** utility copies the data and database *definitions* and saves them in a binary operating system file in Oracle internal format. It is complemented by the **import** utility that can be used to put data from the binary file back into an Oracle database. To use the **export** or the **import** utility, the database must be open. Since a snapshot of the table is taken before exporting, read consistency for individual tables is guaranteed, but intertable consistency is not. So, if you want a snapshot of all the tables in the entire database, then no changes should be made to the database while taking an export of the database. This can be achieved if you open the database in RESTRICT mode (so users cannot access the data) and export the database. You can also specify the parameter CONSISTENT=Y before exporting a table, when you anticipate that other applications will be updating the data in the table after your export starts. Please refer to the *Oracle8i Utilities* document to see all the parameters of the **export** utility.

Export backup usually takes more time than a physical backup. If you are exporting to disk, or if you have multiple tape drives and are exporting to tape, you can run parallel export sessions to decrease the time to obtain a full export. When there is not enough local disk space, you can export to tape or copy multiple export files across the network.

# Advantages of Logical Backups

The following are some of the advantages of taking an export backup.

- One of the biggest advantages of using a logical backup is that data block corruptions can be detected while exporting and the export procedure will fail. Then, you need to fix the corruption in the table before you can attempt to take a logical backup again.

- Export provides an extra level of protection from user errors or structural failures. For example, if a user accidentally drops a table, it is very easy to use the **import** utility to restore the table compared to doing incomplete recovery with physical backups.

- Export offers a great deal of flexibility in choosing what data and definitions you want to export.

- You can take COMPLETE, INCREMENTAL, or CUMULATIVE exports.

- Export backups are portable and can be imported into any database on the current machine. The export file can also be transferred through the network (i.e., using **ftp**) to another machine, and data can be imported into another database on the remote machine.

■ You can reduce fragmentation by doing an export and import of a database.

■ In Oracle8*i*, you can change the partitioning scheme using the **export** and **import** utilities.

■ You can upgrade to newer versions of Oracle.

One of the disadvantages of using an export to take logical backups is that it could be very slow if exporting large amounts of data. It is recommended that you take a full database export (in addition to your physical backups) at least once a month, if possible. This will help you maintain high database availability if object-level recovery is required. Depending on the kind of transaction rate and pattern, you can take INCREMENTAL, CUMULATIVE, or COMPLETE **export** backups. We will discuss some of the **export** parameters and **export** modes in the next two sections. For complete details, refer to the *Oracle8i Server Utilities User's Guide* or *Oracle8i Server Utilities* manual.

To summarize, logical backups should be taken *in addition* to the physical backups that you take. Depending on the failure, sometimes it is quicker to use the physical backups to recover the database—for example, a data file loss. In other cases, you can recover more quickly using an **export** backup. An example is when a user accidentally drops a table and point-in-time recovery needs to be performed on the database to recover the table.

# Before Using Export Utility

You need to perform the following steps before you start using the **export** utility.

1. When you create a database, you should run the **catexp.sql** script. If you have created a database using SQL scripts, you should ensure that you run the SQL script **catexp.sql**. It creates the necessary internal views for the **export/import** utility and assigns all necessary privileges—such as **select any table, backup any table, execute any procedure, execute any type**— to the EXP_FULL_DATABASE role. This role will then be assigned to the DBA role for proper execution of export on the database. You can verify the creation of the role EXP_FULL_DATABASE and privileges assigned to it using Oracle Security Manager. If you have run the script **catalog.sql** while creating your database, you need not run the script **catexp.sql**, because **catalog.sql** automatically runs **catexp.sql**.

**NOTE**
*The actual names of the script files may vary on your operating system. The script file names and the method for running them are described in your Oracle operating-system-specific documentation.*

2. As a DBA, when you want to assign a user to perform entire database exports and imports, he or she has to be granted the EXP_FULL_DATABASE and IMP_FULL_DATABASE roles. By default both these roles are assigned to the DBA role.

3. If you plan to use the Oracle Enterprise Manager V2.0 GUI for automating and scheduling exports on a database, you need to ensure that Oracle Intelligent Agent is running on that database and is registered with the Management Server for the **export** utility to work.

4. Disk space or tape storage should also be checked for sufficient space before you invoke **export**. The export would fail if sufficient space is not available for export file(s).

5. To use the **export** utility, you must have the CREATE SESSION privilege on the Oracle database.

## Export Methods

The **export** utility provides two methods to export table data. The CONVENTIONAL PATH **export** uses the SQL layer to create the export file. The data is read into the database buffers and first stored in an evaluation buffer. An export client then writes the data to a file after expression evaluation of the SQL statements. The DIRECT PATH **export** skips the SQL layer entirely and is much faster. Data is written from the database buffers directly to file using the export client. You can specify a DIRECT PATH **export** by using the command-line option *DIRECT=YES*. Details on the export methods are available in the *Oracle8i Utilities* manual.

## Export Parameters

Table 4-1 gives a list of parameters you can use to control an export plus a brief description of each parameter. For more information, refer to the *Oracle8i Utilities Release 8.1.5* manual.

| Parameter | Default Value | Description |
|---|---|---|
| USERID | None | The username/password of the user performing the export. Optionally, you can specify the @connect_string clause for Net8 to perform export on a remote database. |
| BUFFER | OS dependent | The size in bytes of the buffer used to fetch data rows. If zero is specified, or if the table contains LONG data, only one row at a time is fetched. Tables with LONG, LOB, BFILE, REF, ROWID, LOGICAL ROWID, DATE, or type columns are fetched one row at a time. **Note:** The BUFFER parameter applies only to CONVENTIONAL PATH **export**. It has no effect on a DIRECT PATH **export**. |
| FILE | expdat.dmp | The name of the binary output file created by export at the OS level. Oracle8*i* **export** supports multiple export files and **import** can read from multiple export files. The value of FILESIZE is operating system specific. |
| GRANTS | Yes | A flag to indicate whether to export grants. |
| INDEXES | Yes | A flag to indicate whether to export indexes. |
| ROWS | Yes | A flag to indicate whether to export rows in the tables. If set to NO, only table definitions are exported without data. |
| CONSTRAINTS | Yes | A flag to indicate whether to export constraints. |
| COMPRESS | Yes | A flag to indicate whether to compress table data into one extent upon import. If you specify COMPRESS=N, the export uses the current storage parameters specified in the **create table** or **alter table** statements, including the values of initial extent size and next extent size. In case of LOB data, compression will not take place. |

**TABLE 4-1.** *Description of Export Parameters*

| Parameter | Default Value | Description |
|---|---|---|
| FULL | No | A flag to indicate whether to export data in the entire database. |
| OWNER | Undefined | A list of usernames whose objects are exported. Specify OWNER=(*userlist*) to export in USER mode. |
| TABLES | None | A list of table names and partition and subpartition names to export. Specify TABLES=(*tablelist*) to export in TABLE mode. |
| RECORDLENGTH | OS dependent | The length in bytes of the file record. You can use this parameter to specify the size of the export I/O buffer. |
| INCTYPE | None | The type of INCREMENTAL export. Valid values are COMPLETE, CUMULATIVE, and INCREMENTAL. |
| RECORD | Yes | A flag to indicate whether to record an INCREMENTAL export in database tables, SYS.INCVID, and SYS.INCEXP. |
| PARFILE | Undefined | The name of a parameter file that contains one or more export parameters. |
| CONSISTENT | No | Specifies whether or not the export uses the SET TRANSACTION READ ONLY statement to ensure that the data is consistent to a single point in time and does not change during the execution of the **export** command. |
| DIRECT | No | Specifies whether you use DIRECT PATH or CONVENTIONAL PATH **export**. |
| FEEDBACK | 0 | Specifies that the export should display a progress meter in the form of a dot for *n* number of rows exported. |
| HELP | No | Displays a help message with descriptions of the export parameters. |

**TABLE 4-1.** *Description of Export Parameters* (continued)

| Parameter | Default Value | Description |
|---|---|---|
| LOG | None | Specifies a file name to receive informational and error messages. |
| QUERY | None | This parameter allows you to select a subset of rows from a set of tables when doing a TABLE mode export. The value of the query parameter is a string that contains a WHERE clause for a SQL **SELECT** statement that will be applied to all tables (or table partitions) listed in the TABLE parameter. |
| STATISTICS | ESTIMATE | Specifies the type of database optimizer statistics to generate when the exported data is imported. |
| TABLESPACES | None | This parameter allows you to export a list of the tablespaces from a database into the export file. |
| TRANSPORT_ TABLESPACE | No | When this parameter is set to Yes, it enables the export of transportable tablespace metadata. |
| VOLSIZE | | Specifies the maximum number of bytes in an export file on each volume of tape. The VOLSIZE value is operating system dependent. |

**TABLE 4-1.** *Description of Export Parameters* (continued)

**NOTE**
*Tablespace point-in-time recovery is available only in Oracle8 and higher. DIRECT PATH **export** is available in Oracle Version 7.3 and higher.*

# Export Modes

There are four modes in which you can export the data. The FULL **export** mode is the first one; it can be enabled by using the FULL=YES option in the **export** command. The second mode is the USER **export** mode. Using the OWNER parameter, you can export tables owned by certain users in the database. The third mode is the TABLE mode, where you can use the TABLES parameter to export selected tables in the database. The fourth mode is TABLESPACE mode that allows you to move a set of tablespaces from one Oracle database to another with certain restrictions that will be discussed later in this chapter. Table 4-2 shows the objects exported for the four export modes. These exports can be run in parallel to speed up the process of obtaining an export of the entire database or when there is not enough time to obtain a FULL **export**.

| TABLE Mode | USER Mode | FULL Database Mode | TABLESPACE Mode |
|---|---|---|---|
| Table definitions | TABLE mode + | USER mode + | Cluster definitions |
| Table data | Clusters | Roles | Pretable procedural actions |
| Owner's grants | Database links | All synonyms | Object type definitions used by the table |
| Owner's indexes | Views | System privileges | Table definition (table rows are not included) |
| Table constraints | Private synonyms | Tablespace definitions | Table grants |
| Table triggers | Sequences | Tablespace quotas | Table indexes |
| | Snapshots | Rollback segment definitions | Referential integrity constraints |
| | Snapshot logs | System audit options | Column and table comments |
| | Stored procedures | All triggers | Triggers |
| | | Profiles | Post-table actions |
| | | | Post-table procedural actions and objects |

**TABLE 4-2.**   *Modes of Export*

# FULL Database Export

The FULL database **export** mode can be further divided into *COMPLETE,* *CUMULATIVE,* and *INCREMENTAL* exports. CUMULATIVE and INCREMENTAL exports take less time than COMPLETE exports and allow you to get an export of just the changed data and definitions. Which type of export to use depends on how the data is modified in your tables. For example, if your applications modify only one table or a small set of tables, you can back up only those tables using the INCREMENTAL **export**. All three modes should be used in a robust backup scheme. Table 4-3 provides a closer look at these different export options.

## COMPLETE

A COMPLETE export should be done as part of an INCREMENTAL database **export** backup scheme. In a typical incremental backup scheme, instead of taking a FULL database **export** every day, you will start with a COMPLETE backup on day one (say, Sunday), and take INCREMENTAL exports for the rest of the week. This way, only the tables in the database that are modified are exported from Monday through Saturday, thereby saving export time. A COMPLETE **export** performs an export of all

| Option | Value | Function |
|---|---|---|
| DIRECT | No | A value of Yes will specify DIRECT PATH **export**. |
| LOG | None | Name of a log file that will record the errors from the export. |
| FEEDBACK | 0 | Specifies that a progress meter be displayed. A dot is displayed for every *n* rows exported. For example, FEEDBACK=10 will display a dot for every 10 rows exported successfully. |
| POINT_IN_ TIME_RECOVER | N | Specify Y to export tablespaces. You can recover these tablespaces to a point in time using the **import** utility. |
| RECOVERY_ TABLESPACES | Undefined | A list of tablespaces that will be used for point-in-time recovery. |

**TABLE 4-3.** *Export Options*

the tables in the database and resets the INCREMENTAL **export** information for each table. In other words, this type of export is the same as a FULL database **export**, but it also updates some bookkeeping information regarding exports. To perform this kind of export, you should set the parameter INCTYPE=COMPLETE in the **exp** command. If the INCTYPE parameter is specified, information is written to tables SYS.INCVID (reset to 1 if INCTYPE=COMPLETE), SYS.INCFIL, and SYS.INCEXP. After each COMPLETE **export**, both the preceding CUMULATIVE and INCREMENTAL export files are no longer required. For example:

```
C:\exp userid=system/manager full=Y inctype=complete constraints=Y
file=full_export_filename
```

You can also use a parameter file that allows you to specify export parameters in a text file, which can easily be modified or reused. You need not type all the parameters at the command prompt every time you want to invoke **export** with different parameter settings. For example the above command-line parameter can be specified in a parameter file (**db_export.txt**). The contents of the **db_export.txt** files will look as below:

```
Full=y
Inctype=complete
Constraints=y
File=c:\export\db_exp.dmp
```

The parameters specified in the parameter file can be passed on to the **export** utility by using the command-line option PARFILE=filename. Assume that the parameter file is placed in **c:\utility** directory. Look at the following command:

```
C:\exp system/manager parfile=c:\utility\fullexp.txt
```

In this example, the **export** utility uses the login credential of system to perform a database-wide FULL INCREMENTAL **export**. Before performing the actual export of the schema objects, it looks for the parameter file **fullexp.txt** in the directory **c:\utility** as specified in the command line. Once it finds the parameter file, it reads the parameter values for the export and performs the export as per the value supplied in the file.

Oracle also allows you to perform exports and imports on a remote database using the Net8 service name. In the above example, the **export** operation is performed on the database residing on the local machine. You can modify the same command to perform an export on a remote database by supplying the Net8 service name in the **export** command syntax as follows:

```
C:\exp system/manager@prod.aquila.com parfile=c:\utility\fullexp.txt
```

In this case, Oracle uses the Net8 service name "prod.aquila.com" to log on to the remote database as SYSTEM and performs an export on the remote database. You should note that the export file and log files would be generated in the local machine from where you are issuing the **export** command. Similarly, you can also perform the **import** operation on the remote machine using the service name. If the service name is not configured for the remote database, you will get following error message:

```
"EXP-00056: ORACLE error 12560 encountered
ORA-12560: TNS:protocol adapter error
EXP-00222:
System error message 2
 System error message: No such file or directory
EXP-00000: Export terminated unsuccessfully"
```

When you specify the location of file parameter in the **export** command, you should not leave any blank space in the file path string, as the **export** utility considers file names and directory names to be invalid if a blank space is present. In some operating systems, your directory name contains spaces. For example, in Windows NT, the export file may be placed in **c:\program files\users data\expfile**. In this case, you have to enclose the full path in the FILE= parameter in triple quotes. For example:

```
c:\exp userid=system/manager full=Y inctype=complete constraints=Y
file="""c:\program files\export file1.dmp"""
```

# CUMULATIVE

The CUMULATIVE database **export** exports only tables that have been modified or created since the most recent CUMULATIVE or COMPLETE **export**, and records the export details for each table exported. To perform this kind of export, you should set the parameter INCTYPE=CUMULATIVE in the **export** command. After each CUMULATIVE export, any preceding INCREMENTAL export files are no longer required and may be archived/deleted. For example:

```
C:\exp userid=system/manager full=Y inctype=cumulative constraints=Y
file=cumulative_export_filename
```

# INCREMENTAL

The INCREMENTAL database **export** exports all tables modified or created since the most recent INCREMENTAL, CUMULATIVE, or COMPLETE **export**, and records the export details for each table exported. To perform this kind of export, you should set the parameter INCTYPE=INCREMENTAL in the **export** command. INCREMENTAL exports are beneficial in environments where users are able to create their own tables.

In this case, many tables will remain static for periods of time, while others will be updated and need to be backed up. Also, INCREMENTAL exports allow a table that has been accidentally dropped or modified to be quickly restored. For example:

```
C:\exp userid=system/manager full=Y inctype=incremental constraints=Y
file=incremental_export_filename
```

You may use any of the following export combinations:

COMPLETE alone
COMPLETE with CUMULATIVE
COMPLETE with INCREMENTAL
COMPLETE with CUMULATIVE and INCREMENTAL

**NOTE**
*A COMPLETE* **export** *is needed in order to do INCREMENTAL or CUMULATIVE exports. The FULL=Y export parameter, in addition to the INCTYPE parameter, should be specified when performing COMPLETE, CUMULATIVE, or INCREMENTAL exports.*

## Restrictions

■ INCREMENTAL, CUMULATIVE, and COMPLETE exports can be performed only in FULL database mode (FULL=Y).

■ Only users who have the role EXP_FULL_DATABASE can run INCREMENTAL, CUMULATIVE, and COMPLETE exports.

■ You cannot specify INCREMENTAL exports as read-consistent.

## Invoking Export as SYSDBA

Invoking **export** as SYSDBA is not advisable as it has database-wide implications. During normal operation, you need not invoke an export through SYSDBA. However, you should do this at the request of Oracle Services only as you may have to do so under specific circumstances. When you want to invoke an export as SYSDBA, you have to mention the string "AS SYSDBA" with a username in the **export** command-line syntax. For example:

```
C:\ exp 'sys/oracle as sysdba'

Export: Release 8.1.5.0.0 - Production on Fri May 12 14:42:41 2000

(c) Copyright 1999 Oracle Corporation.  All rights reserved.


Connected to: Oracle8i Enterprise Edition Release 8.1.5.0.0 - Production
With the Partitioning and Java options
PL/SQL Release 8.1.5.0.0 - Production
Enter array fetch buffer size: 4096 >

Export file: EXPDAT.DMP > dba.dmp

(1)E(ntire database), (2)U(sers), or (3)T(ables): (2)U > 1

Export grants (yes/no): yes >

Export table data (yes/no): yes >

Compress extents (yes/no): yes >

Export done in WE8ISO8859P1 character set and WE8ISO8859P1 NCHAR character set

About to export the entire database ...
. exporting tablespace definitions
. exporting profiles
. exporting user definitions
. exporting roles
. exporting resource costs
. exporting rollback segment definitions
. exporting database links
. exporting sequence numbers
. exporting sequence numbers
. exporting directory aliases
. exporting context namespaces
. exporting foreign function library names
. exporting object type definitions
. exporting system procedural objects and actions
. exporting pre-schema procedural objects and actions
. exporting cluster definitions
. about to export SYSTEM's tables via Conventional Path ...
. . exporting table                    DEF$_AQCALL             0 rows exported
. . exporting table                    DEF$_AQERROR            0 rows exported
. . exporting table                    DEF$_CALLDEST           0 rows exported
. . exporting table                    DEF$_DEFAULTDEST        0 rows exported
```

**NOTE**
*Since the string "AS SYSDBA" contains a blank, most operating systems require that entire string 'username/password AS SYSDBA' be placed in quotes or marked as a literal by some method: otherwise, the export will fail. Please see your operating-system-specific documentation for information about special and reserved characters on your system.*

## Sample Export Procedure for FULL Database Export

The following export procedure assumes that you don't want any changes made to the database while taking a FULL database **export**, so the database will be shut down and started in RESTRICT mode before taking the FULL database **export**. The steps are as follows:

1. Shut down any applications or third-party tools running on top of Oracle, and then shut down the database using the following command:

   ```
   SQL> shutdown immediate
   ```

2. So that users can't access the data, start up the database with the RESTRICT option by using the following command:

   ```
   SQL> startup restrict open
   ```

3. Obtain the export with the following **export** command:

   ```
   C:\exp username/password full=y file=full_exp.dat constraints=Y
   ```

4. Use the following command to give the users access to the database again:

   ```
   SQL> alter system disable restricted session;
   ```

Oracle Corporation also provides a GUI tool called Data Management along with Oracle Enterprise Manager. This allows users to use **export** (also **import** and SQL*Loader) with a graphical wizard interface.

**NOTE**
*INCREMENTAL, CUMULATIVE, and COMPLETE exports are obsolete features that will be phased out in subsequent releases. You should begin now to migrate to Oracle's Backup and Recovery Manager (**rman**) for database backups.*

# USER Mode Export

This mode of **export** utility can be used to export one or more database user's schema. It allows the user who invokes the **export** utility to back up his or her own schema objects. If you have been assigned the EXP_FULL_DATABASE role, then, apart from exporting tables in your own schema, you can also export tables from another user's schemas as well. USER mode is also appropriate for users who want to move objects from one owner to another.

For example, let's assume that you have been assigned the EXP_FULL_DATABASE role for taking a backup of the objects from your schema as well as that of other users. The following steps illustrate how you should perform the export operation using the Data Management GUI utility from Oracle Enterprise ManagerV2.

1. Start Oracle Schema manager from the Tools | Database Applications menu of the Oracle Enterprise Manager.

2. Start the Export Wizard GUI from Tools | Data Management menu of the Oracle Schema Manager, and click the Next button on the introduction page of the Export Wizard.

3. In the Export File screen, specify export parameters, such as the name of the export file(s) and their location. Oracle8*i* allows you to place the export file into four different locations. If you need to control the export file size, you can do so by entering a desired file size in the Maximum File Size field in this screen. Oracle defaults to 2GB for each export file. See Figure 4-1 for a sample output. Once you are finished with this screen, click on the Next button.

4. In the Export Type screen, tell Oracle what type of export you want to do. Select the desired type of export mode to be performed. For our example, select User Mode Export. Figure 4-2 shows a sample output. Now click the Next button to go to the next screen.

5. In the User Selection screen, specify which users' schemas you want to export. Select the user schemas from the available users list as shown in Figure 4-3.

6. If you want to specify what type of objects should be exported, click the Next button. However, if you want to export everything for the given schemas, click the Finish button.

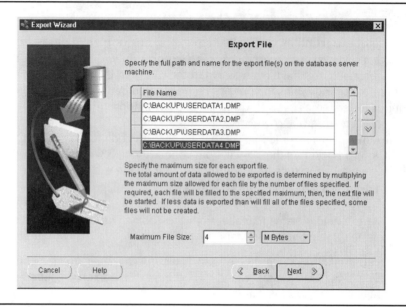

**FIGURE 4-1.** *Specifying the export file names and size*

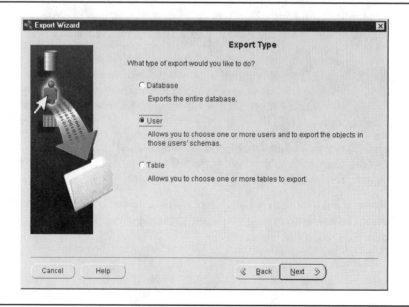

**FIGURE 4-2.** *Selecting the export mode*

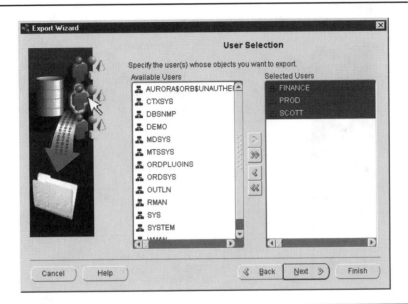

**FIGURE 4-3.** *Selecting database users*

If you click the Next button, you will see the Associated Objects screen. In this screen, the Export Wizard gives you the options to export schema associations such as Table Index, Grants associated with the schema, table Constraints, and so on, as shown in Figure 4-4. You can then click the Advanced button or the Finish button.

7. In the Advanced Options screen, you can override the default buffer size, record length, and choose the type of database optimizer statistics you want. You can also choose to do Direct path export. Figure 4-5 shows the Advanced Options screen in the Export Wizard.

8. When you are finished with the Advanced Option screen, click OK. In the Schedule screen, you can run the export job immediately, as shown in Figure 4-6, or you can schedule it to run at a later time. Click Next to schedule it later, or click Finish to submit the job immediately.

9. After you click Finish, the Job Information screen appears. You should specify a relevant name and description for the export job and when to submit the job to the Oracle Enterprise Manager, as shown in Figure 4-7. Click Finish to complete the export job specifications.

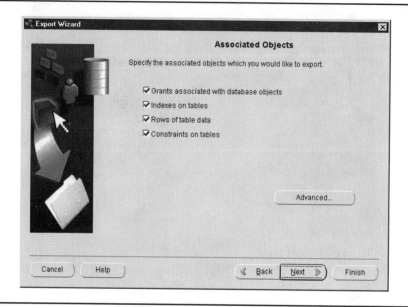

**FIGURE 4-4.** *Specifying the associated objects to export*

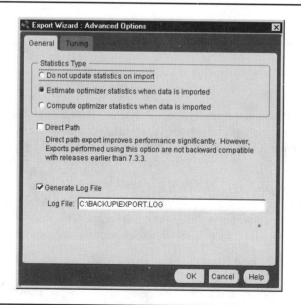

**FIGURE 4-5.** *Selecting advanced options*

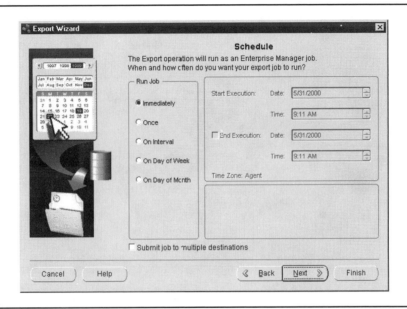

**FIGURE 4-6.** *Scheduling the Oracle Enterprise Manager job*

**10.** In the Summary screen, verify that all the export parameters you specified are correct. Click Cancel if you want to go back and change something. Otherwise, click OK to complete the operation. Figure 4-8 shows the output of the Summary screen.

**11.** Click on the job that you have submitted to the OEM to view its execution details, as shown in the Figure 4-9.

You can make use of the new feature of Oracle8*i* for the **export** utility by writing to multiple dump files at different locations. If you specify a value for the FILESIZE parameter, the export will write only the number of bytes you specify to each dump file. The Oracle8*i* **export** utility can write to as many as four dump files on different disks with equal sizes. The Oracle8*i* **export/import** utility has the ability to export and import precalculated optimizer statistics instead of recomputing the statistics at import time. This ability to export precalculated optimizer statistics during export helps the **import** operation to be much faster, as the import doesn't need to estimate statistics at the time of import. The **import** utility can use the table statistics available in the export file at the time of import.

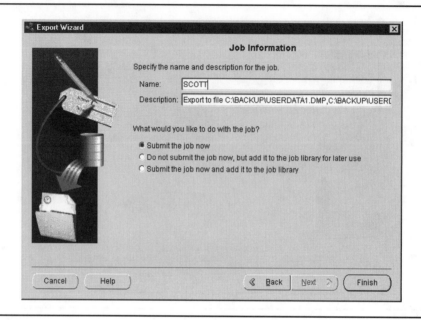

**FIGURE 4-7.** *Specifying the job name*

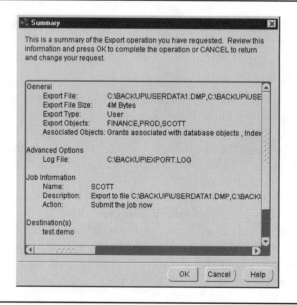

**FIGURE 4-8.** *Viewing the summary of an export job*

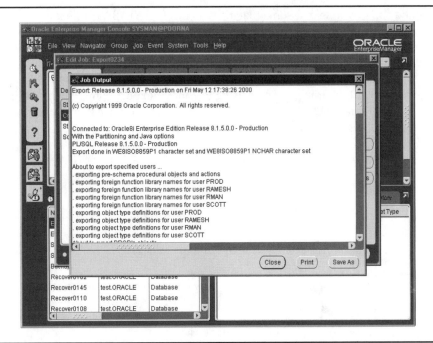

**FIGURE 4-9.** *Export job completion view from OEM*

# TABLE Mode Export

TABLE mode **export** allows you to back up table data and/or its definitions. This mode of export is appropriate when you want to take only a backup of tables from one's user schema. In this mode, users can export tables owned by them. By default, when you invoke the **export** utility, you can export your tables but you can't export table definitions that are referenced to other objects on which you do not have any privileges. If the EXP_FULL_DATABASE role is assigned to you, then you can export tables from any user's schema in the database by specifying TABLES=schema.tablename. If schema is not specified, the export defaults to the previous schema from which an object was exported. If there is not a previous object, the export defaults to the exporter's schema. For example, a TABLE mode **export** can be invoked as follows:

```
C:\exp prod/password tables=(Emp_Details, John.Fin_Rcp, Jack.Material_Desp,
Jack.Goods_Rcp) rows=Y log=prodexp.log
```

In the above example, assume that the EXP_FULL_DATABASE role is assigned to the user. User PROD is exporting a table (EMP_DETAILS) owned by him, a table (FIN_RCP) from JOHN's schema and two more tables (MATERIAL_DESP and GOODS_RCP) from JACK's schema. You need not mention your own schema name.

Assume that the user PROD doesn't have the EXP_FULL_DATABASE role assigned to him. If he tries to export using the above **export** command, the utility only exports the table EMP_DETAILS that belongs to his own schema and gives an error for the other objects. Following is an example:

```
C:\exp scott/tiger@ora8i.oracle tables=(DEMO.employee, SYS.WWW, emp) log=prodexp.log


Export: Release 8.1.5.0.0 - Production on Sat May 13 16:13:03 2000

(c) Copyright 1999 Oracle Corporation.  All rights reserved.


Connected to: Oracle8i Enterprise Edition Release 8.1.5.0.0 - Production
With the Partitioning and Java options
PL/SQL Release 8.1.5.0.0 - Production
Export done in WE8ISO8859P1 character set and WE8ISO8859P1 NCHAR character set

About to export specified tables via Conventional Path ...
EXP-00009: no privilege to export DEMO's table EMPLOYEE
EXP-00009: no privilege to export SYS's table WWW
. . exporting table                       EMP        14 rows exported
Export terminated successfully with warnings.
```

The **export** utility in Oracle8*i* supports the QUERY parameter to select a set of rows from tables to export. When you want export only a set of selected rows—for example, to export data based on a region—you can do so by specifying the WHERE clause for a SQL **select** statement that selects the rows of our interest. The QUERY is applied to all tables (or table partitions) listed in the TABLE parameter. So, for example:

```
exp prod/password tables=emp_cat,division query="""where job='SUPPORT ENG' and sal<55000"""
```

In this example, the QUERY option enables the **export** utility to export rows in both EMP_CAT and DIVISION that match the query.

**NOTE**
*Since the value of the QUERY parameter contains blanks, most operating systems require that the entire string of the QUERY be marked as a literal by some method. In Windows NT, the QUERY can be placed in triple quotes as shown in the above example. On UNIX systems, a backslash (\) will be used to separate the special characters such as single quote (') and double quotes (").*

For more information on special and reserved characters, refer to your operating-system-specific documentation.

## Restrictions

While the QUERY parameter is extremely useful (this enhancement was requested by the Oracle user community from Oracle V5 days), there are some restrictions in using it:

- The QUERY parameter cannot be specified for FULL, USER, or transportable TABLESPACE mode exports.

- This parameter must be applicable to all specified tables.

- It cannot be specified in a DIRECT PATH **export** (DIRECT=Y).

- It cannot be specified for tables with inner nested tables.

# TABLESPACE Mode Export

A TABLESPACE mode export allows you to move a subset of an Oracle database and "plug" it in to another Oracle database. Moving data via transportable tablespaces can be much faster than performing either an import/export of the same data, because transporting a tablespace requires copying of data files and integrating the database schema information into the data dictionary. You can also use transportable tablespaces to move index data, thereby avoiding the index rebuilds. Before transporting tablespaces between databases, you should make the set of tablespaces read-only. This is because no transaction should alter the data that's in the tablespace. If the tablespace is not set to READ-ONLY mode, and if you try to export the tablespace to another database, you will get the following error:

```
EXP-00008: ORACLE error 29335 encountered
ORA-29335: tablespace 'DATA_TS' is not read only
ORA-06512: at "SYS.DBMS_PLUGTS", line 411
ORA-06512: at line 1
EXP-00000: Export terminated unsuccessfully
```

The following example shows how to transport a tablespace from one database to another database using TABLESPACE **export**:

```
C:\EXP TRANSPORT_TABLESPACE=Y TABLESPACES=DATA_TS  FILE=DATATS.DMP  LOG=DATATS.LOG

Export: Release 8.1.5.0.0 - Production on Sun May 14 10:50:46 2000
(c) Copyright 1999 Oracle Corporation.  All rights reserved.
Username: SYS AS SYSDBA
```

```
Password:
Connected to: Oracle8i Enterprise Edition Release 8.1.5.0.0 - Production
With the Partitioning and Java options
PL/SQL Release 8.1.5.0.0 - Production
Export done in WE8ISO8859P1 character set and WE8ISO8859P1 NCHAR character set
Note: table data (rows) will not be exported
About to export transportable tablespace metadata...
For tablespace DATA_TS ...
. exporting cluster definitions
. exporting table definitions
. . exporting table                     USER_TATA
. exporting referential integrity constraints
. exporting triggers
. end transportable tablespace metadata export
Export terminated successfully without warnings.
```

Note above that Oracle asks you username and password before performing export. You have to connect as "SYS AS SYSDBA". If you are not connected as SYS AS SYSDBA, you can still export the tablespace if you have been assigned the EXP_FULL_DATABASE role. However, in this case, the **export** utility will work, but at the time of import the **import** utility will give an error and you can't import the tablespaces. So, you must connect as SYS AS SYSDBA only. During TABLESPACE **export**, the **export** utility records the database schema changes from the data dictionary regarding the tablespace. It will not export any rows from the tablespace. Once the export is over, you should copy the data files that belong to the tablespace(s) and the export dump file to the destination database and "plug in" using the **import** utility as shown here:

```
C:\IMP TRANSPORT_TABLESPACE=Y DATAFILES='C:\LOB\DATA1'
TABLESPACES=DATA_TS TTS_OWNERS=PROD FROM USER=PROD TOUSER=SCOTT
FILE=C:\LOB\PROD.DMP LOG=DATATS.LOG

Import: Release 8.1.5.0.0 - Production on Sun May 14 12:13:05 2000
(c) Copyright 1999 Oracle Corporation.  All rights reserved.
Username: SYS AS SYSDBA
Password:
Connected to: Oracle8i Enterprise Edition Release 8.1.5.0.0 - Production
With the Partitioning and Java options
PL/SQL Release 8.1.5.0.0 - Production
Export file created by EXPORT:V08.01.05 via conventional path
About to import transportable tablespace(s) metadata...
import done in WE8ISO8859P1 character set and WE8ISO8859P1 NCHAR character set
Import terminated successfully without warnings.
```

In the above **import** command, TABLESPACES, TTS_OWNERS, FROMUSER, and TOUSER are optional parameters. If you do not specify FROMUSER and TOUSER, all database objects will be created under the same user as in the source database. When you don't specify the FROM USER and TO USER parameters, you must ensure that the username exists in the destination database. If not, the import will return an error.

## Restrictions

TABLESPACE mode export is an excellent way to move large amounts of data very fast between databases. Please note that this mode of export is not normally used for logical backup purposes. The following restrictions apply when you use TABLESPACE mode export:

■ You can only transport a set of tablespaces that are *self-contained*. In this context, self-contained means that there are no references from inside the set of tablespaces pointing outside of the tablespaces.

■ The source and target databases must be in a homogenous environment. For example, you cannot transport a tablespace from an HP-UX Oracle database to an NT Oracle database. You can transport tablespaces between two HP-UX Oracle databases, or between two NT Oracle databases. However, the source and target databases *must* have the same database block size.

■ The source and target databases must use the same character set.

■ You cannot transport a tablespace to a target database in which a tablespace with the same name already exists.

■ Currently, transportable tablespaces do not support the following:

■ Snapshot/replication

■ Function-based indexes

■ Scoped REFs

■ Domain indexes (a new type of index provided by extensible indexing)

■ 8.0-compatible advanced queues with multiple recipients

## Advantages

TABLESPACE mode **export** helps you in the following situations:

■ Feeding data from OLTP systems to data warehouse staging systems

■ Updating data warehouses and data marts from staging systems

■ Loading data marts from central data warehouses

- Archiving OLTP and data warehouse systems efficiently
- Data publishing to internal and external customers

# Exporting Special Objects and Considerations

This section gives you tips when you export particular database objects. For example, special care should be taken while you're exporting LONG or LOB datatypes due to memory restrictions. Similarly, if you have multiple Oracle databases installed at your side (created with different versions of Oracle), you need to know the ramifications of using multiple **export** utilities and their compatibilities.

## Partition-Level Export

A partition-level export lets users export one or more specified partitions or subpartitions within a table. FULL database, USER, and transportable TABLESPACE mode exports do not support partition-level export; only a TABLE mode **export** does. For example:

```
C:\exp prod/password tables=(inventory:p1, dispatch:sp2) rows=Y
```

In this example, all rows in the partition (p1) of the table inventory and subpartition (sp2) of the table dispatch will be exported. Partition-level export helps you maintain very large tables with ease.

## Exporting LONG and LOB Datatypes

While exporting tables that contains LONG and LOB datatypes, the **export** utility fetches those datatypes in pieces. However, enough memory must be available to hold all of the contents of each row, including the LONG data.

**NOTE**
*All data in a LOB column does not need to be held in memory at the same time. LOB data is loaded and unloaded in pieces.*

## Exporting Offline Bitmapped Tablespaces

If the data you are exporting contains offline bitmapped tablespace(s), the export will not be able to export the complete tablespace definition and will display an error message. You can still import the data; however, you must precreate the offline bitmapped tablespace(s) before importing to prevent DDL commands (that may reference the missing tablespaces) from failing.

## Exporting BFILE

When you use **export** utility to back up BFILE columns, the export will only record the names and directory aliases referenced by the BFILE columns. BFILE contents will not be recorded in the export file. If you move the database to a location where the old directories cannot be used to access the included files, you must create the directories at O/S level and copy the BFILE files to the new location.

## Compatibility Between Different Versions of Export

When you want to move database objects between different versions of Oracle databases, such as between Oracle7.3, and 8*i*, you should consider the ramifications. A lower version of the **import** utility cannot import from an export file that was created using a higher version of the **export** utility. In order to move tables and database objects, you should use lower versions of export/import that will be compatible with your destination database. For example, if you want to move objects from Oracle8*i* databases to an Oracle8 database, you should use the Oracle8 **export/import** utility on Oracle8*i* Server to create export files so that the **import** utility in Oracle8 can read the file.

**NOTE**
*Whenever a lower-version **export** utility runs with a higher version of the Oracle Server, categories of database objects that did not exist in the lower version are excluded from export.*

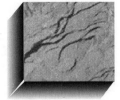

# CHAPTER
## 5

Backup Scripts in
Windows NT, UNIX,
and OpenVMS
Environments

his chapter presents sample scripts that you can use to automate your backup procedures in the OpenVMS, UNIX, and Windows NT environments. First, in the OpenVMS environment, a generic backup script is presented. Due to the flexible design, this script should work at most shops without customizing it. For example, most of the variables—such as the data files that need to be backed up—are generated dynamically from the database. Hence, after adding a new file, you don't need to modify your backup scripts to include the new data file. However, you should customize the scripts and test them thoroughly before using them to back up your production database. For this purpose, every script contains a *USER_PARAMETERS* section, where you can modify certain parameters to customize the scripts. We have added a section on Windows NT in this edition. Simple scripts and batch files that will allow for automation of backups are presented for Windows NT. In the UNIX environment, we have automated scripts as well. However, we suggest you customize the scripts according to your environment. All the assumptions made are clearly documented in the scripts and should be changed to fit your needs.

**NOTE**
*The OpenVMS scripts should work on any Oracle7 version running on OpenVMS. Note that Oracle8 doesn't exist in OpenVMS. The UNIX and Windows NT scripts should run for all versions of Oracle7, Oracle8, and Oracle8i.*

# Backup Scripts in the OpenVMS Environment

This script assumes that you are running a single-instance configuration. If you are running with the PARALLEL SERVER option, you should modify the script. The detailed operation of each script is documented in the script header. We assume that all the script files are located in a directory called ORACLE_UTILS, and we further assume that you are familiar with the OpenVMS-specific directories.

The main command procedure that you should run is called BACKUP_MAIN.COM. Depending on the day of the week, this procedure calls other procedures to take either a cold backup, a hot backup, or a full database export. Note that this procedure doesn't copy from disk to tape, so you should run additional scripts to do this. The following tree of execution shows how the scripts are related. These command procedures can be executed separately as well.

BACKUP_MAIN.COM
    oracle_utils:env_symbols_sample.com
    oracle_utils:export_database.com
    oracle_utils:hot_backup.com
    oracle_utils:cold_backup.com
EXPORT_DATABASE.COM
    oracle_utils:env_symbols_sample.com
    oracle_utils:*db_name*_devices_sample.com
    oracle_utils:instance_up.com
    oracle_utils:startup_dbamode.com
    ora_db:shutdown_*db_name*.com
HOT_BACKUP.COM
    oracle_utils:env_symbols_sample.com
    oracle_utils:*db_name*_devices_sample.com
    oracle_utils:instance_up.com
    oracle_utils:tbs_hotbackup.sql
    oracle_utils:tablespace_state.sql
    oracle_utils:hot_backup_cmd_*db_name*.com
        oracle_utils:env_symbols_sample.com
        oracle_utils:backup_tablespace.com
        oracle_utils:instance_up.com
        ora_db:ora_db_*db_name*.com
COLD_BACKUP.COM
    oracle_utils:env_symbols_sample.com
    oracle_utils:*db_name*_devices_sample.com
    oracle_utils:instance_up.com
    oracle_utils:shutdown_immediate.com
    oracle_utils:startup_dbamode.com
    oracle_utils:tbs_coldbackup.sql
    oracle_utils:backup_tablespace.com
    ora_db:ora_db_*db_name*.com
    ora_db:shutdown_*db_name*.com
    ora_db:startup_exclusive_*db_name*.com
SHUTDOWN_IMMEDIATE.COM
    ora_db:ora_db_*db_name*.com
    oracle_utils:shutdown_immediate_*db_name*.com
        oracle_utils:shutdown_immediate_*db_name*.sql
STARTUP_DBAMODE.COM
    ora_db:ora_db_*db_name*.com
    oracle_utils:startup_dbamode_*db_name*.com
        oracle_utils:startup_dbamode_*db_name*.sql

# BACKUP_MAIN.COM

This script performs cold and hot backups and an export of an Oracle database. We will get the current day of the week and perform the correct operation(s) on that day determined by the user-configurable symbols (export_days, hot_backup_days, cold_backup_days). Look in the "USER_PARAMETERS" section of this script for details on these symbols. After the operation is complete we will check and, if necessary, resubmit this script for the following day at the same time. For more details, refer to the other DCL command procedures that this script is using.

```
$!
$!
$!
$ vvv = 'f$verify(0)'  ! set noverify and remember what it was before
$! FILE:     ORACLE_UTILS:BACKUP_MAIN.COM
$!
$!           by: Saar Maoz, Oracle Worldwide Support
$!
$! PURPOSE: Perform a cold/hot backup and export of an Oracle database.
$!
$! USAGE:     submit backup_main.com -
$!              /parameters=("<dbname>","<export mode>","<resubmit flag>")
$!           OR
$!             @oracle_utils:backup_main <dbname> [<export mode>] -
$!                                               [<resubmit flag>]
$!
$!           Example:  @backup_main TESTDB COMPLETE YES
$!
$! PARAMETERS:
$!           P1 The database name to perform operation on.
$!
$!           P2 Type of export to do: "INCREMENTAL", "CUMULATIVE" or "COMPLETE".
$!
$!           P3 Resubmit flag, optional: "YES","NO"  default=YES
$!              If set to NO, job will not resubmit itself for the next day.
$!
$! CALLS:    oracle_utils:env_symbols_sample.com     ! Set up symbols to point to DB
$!           oracle_utils:export_database.com ! Export the database
$!           oracle_utils:hot_backup.com    ! Perform hot backup on the DB
$!           oracle_utils:cold_backup.com     ! Perform cold backup on the DB
$!
$! CALLED BY: Possibly called by submit_backup_<dbname>.com
$!            There is a sample file (submit_backup_TESTDB_sample.com) for
users
$!             to modify.
$!
$! INPUT:    Symbols: Check the "USER_PARAMETERS" section of this script for
$!                    a list of symbols that you can change to control the
$!                    operation.
$!
$!           Logical Names: ORACLE_UTILS must point to a directory with all
$!                          the backup scripts.
$!
$!           Files: None.
```

```
$!
$! OUTPUT:    Symbols: None.
$!           Logical Names: None.
$!           Files: None directly, but may include all or part of files created
$!                  by the calls that it makes to export_database.com,
$!                  hot_backup.com and oracle_utils:cold_backup.com.
$!
$!
$! KNOWN LIMITATIONS:
$!
$! PRIVILEGES: There were no privileges checks done for assuming this script
$!             is run from the Oracle account.
$!
$!
$! HISTORY:
$!   Date         Name          Comments
$!   20-MAR-1995  Saar Maoz     Created
$!
$!
$!
$!!!!!!!!  This section could be changed by user to configure backup procedure
$ USER_PARAMETERS:
$!
$! These are the recommended values for the *_days symbols
$!
$  export_days := "/Sunday/"
$  hot_backup_days := "/Monday/Tuesday/Wednesday/Thursday/Friday/"
$  cold_backup_days := "/Saturday/"
$  userpasswd :== system/manager
$  logfile :== sys$scratch:save_database
$  mailuser == "SMAOZ"          ! set to "" if not interested in mail messages
$!
$! define oracle_utils <location of all backup scripts>
$!!!!!!!!!!
$!
$ set noon
$!
$! Save time that we begun running, so we can resubmit at same time tomorrow.
$!
$ begin_time = f$time()
$!
$! Local symbols to this script
$!
$ say := write sys$output
$ wo := write outfile
$ delfile := delete/noconfirm/log
$ sendmail :== mail nl: 'mailuser' /subject=
$ something_done =0
$!
$! Check for correct usage
$!
$ if p1 .eqs. "" then goto HELP
$ db_name = f$edit(p1,"UPCASE")
$ export_mode = f$edit(p2, "UPCASE")
$ submit_flag =  f$edit(p3, "UPCASE")
$ if submit_flag .eqs. "" then submit_flag := YES ! default value to submit
flag
$!
```

```
$! Setup environment
$!
$ if f$trnlnm("oracle_utils") .eqs. "" then goto NO_LOGICAL
$ @oracle_utils:env_symbols_sample.com
$!
$! The following command will point us to the right database, note that there
$! must be a symbol as the database name defined in
$! ORACLE_UTILS:ENV_SYMBOLS_SAMPLE.COM which will run the correct
$! ORA_DB:ORAUSER_<DBNAME>.COM which will point us to the right database.
$!
$ 'db_name'
$ if .not. $status then goto NO_SYMBOL
$ show logical ora_sid
$!
$ today = f$cvtime("TODAY","WEEKDAY")    ! get day of week.
$!
$! According to day of week, and the user defined days branch to the right
place
$! Note that it is possible to perform more than one task per day.
$!
$ if f$locate("/''today'/",export_days) .ne. -
    f$length(export_days) then            call DO_EXPORT
$!
$ if f$locate("/''today'/",hot_backup_days) .ne. -
    f$length(hot_backup_days) then        call DO_HOT_BACKUP
$!
$ if f$locate("/''today'/",cold_backup_days) .ne. -
    f$length(cold_backup_days) then       call DO_COLD_BACKUP
$!
$! Go to resubmit this script for tomorrow if needed
$!
$ goto RESUBMIT
$!
$! If nothing done give an informational message
$!
$ if something_done then goto FINISH
$ say " "
$ say "INFORMATION ** ORACLE_UTILS:BACKUP_MAIN.COM **"
$ say " There was no backup/export defined to be done today, if this is a"
$ say " mistake check the USER_PARAMETERS section in"+-
    " ORACLE_UTILS:BACKUP_MAIN.COM"
$ goto FINISH
$!
$ DO_EXPORT: SUBROUTINE
$!
$! Call the export routine
$!
$ something_done =1
$ @oracle_utils:export_database 'db_name' 'export_mode'
$ EXIT
$ ENDSUBROUTINE
$!
$ DO_HOT_BACKUP: SUBROUTINE
$!
$! Call the hot backup routine
$!
$ something_done =1
$ @oracle_utils:hot_backup 'db_name'
```

```
$ EXIT
$ ENDSUBROUTINE
$!
$ DO_COLD_BACKUP: SUBROUTINE
$!
$! Call the cold backup routine
$!
$ something_done =1
$ @oracle_utils:cold_backup 'db_name'
$ EXIT
$ ENDSUBROUTINE
$!
$ RESUBMIT:
$!
$! Submit this script for tomorrow if needed
$!
$ if .not. submit_flag  then goto FINISH
$ submit oracle_utils:backup_main.com -
      /parameters=("'''db_name'","'''export_mode'","'''submit_flag'") -
      /after="''begin_time'+23:59:59" -
      /log='logfile'_'db_name'.log -
      /queue=sys$batch -
      /retain=error -
      /noprint
$ if f$search("'''logfile'") .nes. "" then purge/nolog/keep=8 'logfile'
$!
$ goto FINISH
$!
$! ERROR HANDLING SECTION
$!  Note: The rest of this script is an error handling routine.  After each
$!  error message we branch to MAIL_FINISH (will send an email) or to FINISH
$!  (will NOT send an email).  Feel free to change the labels in case you
$!  are not interested in a mail message in that case, or vice versa.
$!
$ NO_SYMBOL:
$  say " "
$  say "ERROR ** ORACLE_UTILS:BACKUP_MAIN.COM **"
$  say " a. No symbol found with the database name that runs the"
$  say "    ORAUSER_<dbname>.COM which will point us to the right database,"
$  say "     add it to ORACLE_UTILS:ENV_SYMBOLS_SAMPLE.COM"
$  say " b. Some other error has occurred while attempting to run the"
$  say "    ORAUSER_<dbname>.COM file, check the preceding OpenVMS error message"
$  goto MAIL_FINISH
$!
$ NO_LOGICAL:
$  say " "
$  say "ERROR ** ORACLE_UTILS:BACKUP_MAIN.COM **"
$  say " The logical name ORACLE_UTILS is not defined please define it to point"
$  say " to the directory where all the backup scripts reside."
$  goto MAIL_FINISH
$!
$ HELP:
$  say " "
$  say "Usage of ORACLE_UTILS:BACKUP_MAIN.COM is:"
$  say " @ORACLE_UTILS:BACKUP_MAIN <db_name> [<export mode>] [<submit>]"
$  say " <db_name> : Database name"
$  say " <inc type> : INCREMENTAL, CUMULATIVE or COMPLETE"
$  say " <submit> : YES | NO (default=YES)"
```

```
$  goto FINISH
$!
$ MAIL_FINISH:
$  if mailuser .eqs. "" then goto FINISH
$!
$! Send correct mail whether run in interactive or batch mode
$!
$  msg = "Backup procedure run in interactive mode failed"
$  if f$mode() .eqs. "BATCH" then msg = "Backup procedure terminated"+-
        " with errors check ''logfile'_''db_name'.log for details"
$  sendmail "'''msg'"
$  goto FINISH
$!
$ FINISH:
$  vvv='f$verify(vvv)'
$  Exit
```

# EXPORT_DATABASE.COM

Given a database name and export incremental type (either INCREMENTAL,
CUMULATIVE, or COMPLETE) as parameters, this script performs a full export of
that database. This is a logical backup of the database that can only be used in
conjunction with **import**. The algorithm works as follows:

1. Make sure there is a device to export to.

2. Check whether database is up. If YES, go to step 4.

3. Bring database up in restricted mode to export it.

4. Delete the previous export files from the export device.

5. Perform the actual export.

6. If database was down when export started (step 2), bring it back down.

7. Done.

```
$!
$!
$!
$ vvv = 'f$verify(0)'  ! set noverify and remember what it was before
$! FILE:    ORACLE_UTILS:EXPORT_DATABASE.COM
$!
$!          by: Saar Maoz, Oracle Worldwide Support
$!
$!
$! USAGE:    Usually called by oracle_utils:backup_main
$!
$!          OR (if you want to use it separately)
$!
$!            @oracle_utils:export_database <dbname> <inc type>
$!
```

```
$!           Example:  @export_database TESTDB COMPLETE
$!
$! PARAMETERS:
$!           P1 The database name to perform export on.
$!           P2 Incremental type can be: INCREMENTAL, CUMULATIVE or COMPLETE
$!              if not specified, defaults to COMPLETE
$!
$! CALLS:   oracle_utils:env_symbols_sample.com        ! Set up symbols to
point to DB
$!           oracle_utils:<db_name>_devices_sample.com ! Get backup devices
names
$!           oracle_utils:instance_up              ! Check if instance is up/down
$!           oracle_utils:startup_dbamode          ! Startup in restricted mode
$!           ora_db:shutdown_'db_name'             ! Shutdown normal


$!
$! CALLED BY:
$!           Usually this script will be called by BACKUP_MAIN.COM however it
$!           could be called independently.
$!
$! INPUT:    Symbols: Check the "USER_PARAMETERS" section of this script for
$!                    a list of symbols that you can change to control the
$!                    operation of this script
$!
$!           Logical Names: ORACLE_UTILS must point to a directory with all
$!                          the backup scripts.
$!
$!           Files: None.
$!
$! OUTPUT:   Symbols: None.
$!           Logical Names: None.
$!           Files:
$!                export_location:export_<inc_type>_<db_name>.dmp
$!                  The export file of the specified incremental level.
$!
$!
$! PRIVILEGES: There were no privileges checks done for assuming this script
$!             is run from the Oracle account.
$!
$!
$! HISTORY:
$!   Date        Name         Comments
$!   24-JAN-1997 DJ Cover     Added "GOTO" to export mode test
$!   20-MAR-1995 Saar Maoz    Created
$!
$!
$!!!!!!!!  This section could be changed by user to configure export
procedure
$ USER_PARAMETERS:
$  export_buffer = 524288      ! make sure you have enough BYTLM for this
user
$! userpasswd := system/manager
$! mailuser == "SMAOZ"        ! set to "" if not interested in mail messages
```

```
$!!!!!!!!!!
$!
$ set noon
$!
$! Local symbols to this script
$!
$ say := write sys$output
$ wo := write outfile
$ delfile := delete/noconfirm/log

$ sendmail :== mail nl: 'mailuser' /subject=
$!
$! Check for correct usage
$!
$ if p1 .eqs. "" then goto HELP
$ db_name = f$edit(p1,"UPCASE")
$ export_mode = f$edit(p2,"UPCASE")
$ if export_mode  .eqs. "" then export_mode := COMPLETE  !default value
$!
$ if export_mode .nes. "INCREMENTAL" .and. export_mode .nes. -
     "CUMULATIVE" .and. export_mode .nes.  "COMPLETE" then goto HELP
$!970124 "CUMULATIVE" .and. export_mode .nes.  "COMPLETE" then HELP
$!
$ if f$type(userpasswd) .eqs. "" .or. f$type(mailuser) .eqs. "" -
     then goto NO_SYMS
$!
$ say " "
$ say "ORACLE_UTILS:EXPORT_DATABASE.COM begins a ''export_mode' export on"
$ say " ''db_name' database at: "+f$time()
$ say " "
$!
$! Setup environment
$!
$ if f$trnlnm("oracle_utils") .eqs. "" then goto NO_LOGICAL
$ @oracle_utils:env_symbols !just to make sure
$!
$! The following command will point us to the right database, note that there
$! must be a symbol as the database name defined in
$! ORACLE_UTILS:ENV_SYMBOLS_SAMPLE.COM which will run the correct
$! ORA_DB:ORAUSER_<DBNAME>.COM which will point us to the right database.
$!
$ 'db_name'
$ if .not. $status then goto NO_SYMBOL
$ show logical ora_sid
$ @oracle_utils:'db_name'_devices_sample.com    ! Define export location
$!
$! Check if export location exists and is a disk
$!
$ show logical export_location
$ if .not. f$getdvi("export_location","EXISTS") then goto NO_EXPORT_LOCATION
$ if f$getdvi("export_location","DEVCLASS") .ne. 1 then goto NOT_A_DISK
$ show device export_location
$!
$! Check whether instance is up
$!
```

```
$ @oracle_utils:instance_up 'f$trnlnm("ora_sid")'
$!
$ if instance_up then goto EXPORT
$!
$ say " "
$ say "ORACLE_UTILS:EXPORT_DATABASE.COM"
$ say " Instance was shutdown and an export is due so starting database
up..."
$ say " "
$ @oracle_utils:startup_dbamode 'db_name'
$!
$ EXPORT:
$ say " "
$ say "ORACLE_UTILS:EXPORT_DATABASE.COM is now deleting last week's export"
$ say " "
$ if f$search("export_location:export_''db_name'_''export_mode'.dmp") .nes.
""
$ then
$    directory/date=(created,backup)/size=all -
        export_location:export_'db_name'_'export_mode'.dmp
$    delfile export_location:export_'db_name'_'export_mode'.dmp;*
$ endif
$!
$! Performing the actual export
$!
$ on error then goto EXPORT_ERROR
$ exp userid='userpasswd' -
      buffer='export_buffer' -
      file=export_location:export_'db_name'_'export_mode'.dmp -
      inctype='export_mode' -
      full=y -
      grants=y -
      indexes=y -
      rows=y -
      constraints=y -
      compress=n -
      statistics=none
$!
$ say " "
$ say "ORACLE_UTILS:EXPORT_DATABASE.COM finished a ''export_mode' export on"
$ say " ''db_name' database at: "+f$time()
$ say " "
$ if mailuser .nes. "" then  sendmail -
      "''export_mode' export finished successfully at ''f$time()'"
$!
$ if .not. instance_up
$ then

$    say " "
$    say "ORACLE_UTILS:EXPORT_DATABASE.COM"
$    say " The database was shutdown when export begun, so bringing it back
down"
$    say " "
$    @ora_db:shutdown_'db_name'
```

```
$ endif
$ goto FINISH
$!
$! ERROR HANDELING SECTION
$!  Note: The rest of this script is an error handling routine.  After each
$!  error message we branch to MAIL_FINISH (will send an email) or to FINISH
$!  (will NOT send an email).  Feel free to change the labels in case you
$!  are not interested in a mail message in that case, or vice versa.
$!
$ NO_SYMS:
$   say " "
$   say "ERROR ** ORACLE_UTILS:EXPORT_DATABASE.COM **"
$   say " The local symbols userpasswd or mailuser are not defined"
$   say " This usually means that this script was called independently and the"
$   say " USER_PARAMETERS section of this script was not updated"
$   say " "
$   goto FINISH
$!
$ NO_LOGICAL:
$   say " "
$   say "ERROR ** ORACLE_UTILS:EXPORT_DATABASE.COM **"
$   say " The logical name ORACLE_UTILS is not defined please define it to point"
$   say " to the directory where all the backup scripts reside."
$   goto MAIL_FINISH
$!
$ NO_SYMBOL:
$   say " "
$   say "ERROR ** ORACLE_UTILS:EXPORT_DATABASE.COM **"
$   say " a. No symbol found with the database name that runs the"
$   say "    ORAUSER_<dbname>.COM which will point us to the right database,"
$   say "    add it to ORACLE_UTILS:ENV_SYMBOLS_SAMPLE.COM"
$   say " b. Some other error has occurred while attempting to run the"
$   say "    ORAUSER_<dbname>.COM file, check the preceding OpenVMS error message"
$   goto MAIL_FINISH
$!
$ NO_EXPORT_LOCATION:

$   say " "
$   say "ERROR ** ORACLE_UTILS:EXPORT_DATABASE.COM **"
$   say " The logical name EXPORT_LOCATION which controls where the export file"
$   say " will be created is not defined."
$   goto MAIL_FINISH
$!
$ NOT_A_DISK:
$   say " "
$   say "ERROR ** ORACLE_UTILS:EXPORT_DATABASE.COM **"
$   say " The export location pointed to by EXPORT_LOCATION logical name is not"
$   say " a disk.  Sorry, we currently didn't implement exporting to tape in"
$   say " this script."
$   goto MAIL_FINISH


$!
$ EXPORT_ERROR:
$   st=$status
$   say " "
```

```
$  say "ERROR ** ORACLE_UTILS:EXPORT_DATABASE.COM **"
$  say " An error has occurred during the export, final OpenVMS error code: ''st'"
$  say " Text: "+f$message(st)
$  goto MAIL_FINISH
$!
$ HELP:
$  say " "
$  say "Usage of ORACLE_UTILS:EXPORT_DATABASE.COM is:"
$  say " @ORACLE_UTILS:EXPORT_DATABASE <db_name> <inc type>"
$  say " <db_name> : Database name to export"
$  say " <inc type> : INCREMENTAL, CUMULATIVE or COMPLETE"
$  goto FINISH
$!
$ MAIL_FINISH:
$  if mailuser .eqs. "" then goto FINISH
$!
$! Send correct mail whether run in interactive or batch mode
$!
$  msg = "''export_mode' export run in interactive mode failed"
$  if f$mode() .eqs. "BATCH" then msg = "''export_mode' export terminated"+-
        " with errors check ''logfile'_''db_name'.log for details"
$  sendmail "''msg'"
$  goto FINISH
$!
$ FINISH:
$ vvv= 'f$verify(vvv)'
$  Exit
```

# HOT_BACKUP.COM

Given a database name as a parameter, this script performs a hot backup of that
database. It copies all data files and one control file to backup devices designated
for that purpose, and creates a DCL script that restores the files from the backup to
their original locations. The algorithm works as follows:

1. Make sure there is at least one backup device.

2. Make sure the database is up; otherwise, stop.

3. Call **oracle_utils:tbs_hotbackup.sql** to generate a list of all data files and
   their sizes ordered by tablespace name.

4. Read this file and create a DCL script that will go into SVRMGRL and
   perform an **alter tablespace begin backup**, followed by a host command
   that will invoke **backup_tablespace.com** (with the tablespace as parameter)
   and then an **alter tablespace end backup** for each tablespace in the
   database to be backed up.

5. Delete the previous backup files from the backup devices.

6. Start creating the **restore_database.com** file needed to recover from this backup.

7. Call **oracle_utils:tablespace_state.sql** to show the status of all data files (any that have ACTIVE status are in backup mode; they should all have NOT ACTIVE status).

8. Invoke **oracle_utils:hot_backup_cmd_*db_name*.com**, which in turn issues the **alter tablespace** command and calls **backup_tablespace.com** for each tablespace.

9. Again call **oracle_utils:tablespace_state.sql** to show the status of all data files (any that have ACTIVE status are in backup mode; they should all have NOT ACTIVE status).

10. Search all the logs generated from the **alter tablespace** command and issue an error if the string "ORA-" is found.

11. Add final helpful notes to the **restore_database.com** file.

12. Done.

```
$!
$!
$!
$ vvv = 'f$verify(0)'  ! set noverify and remember what it was before
$! FILE:     ORACLE_UTILS:HOT_BACKUP.COM
$!
$!           by: Saar Maoz, Oracle Worldwide Support
$!
$!
$! USAGE:    Usually called by oracle_utils:backup_main
$!
$!           OR (if you want to use it separately)
$!
$!             @oracle_utils:hot_backup <dbname>
$!
$!           Example:  @hot_backup TESTDB
$!
$! PARAMETERS:
$!           P1 The database name to perform hot backup on.
$!
$! CALLS:   oracle_utils:env_symbols.com       ! Set up symbols to point to DB
$!          oracle_utils:<db_name>_devices.com ! Get backup devices names
$!          oracle_utils:instance_up           ! Check if instance is up/down
$!          oracle_utils:tbs_hotbackup.sql  ! Generate tbs/datafiles list
$!          oracle_utils:tablespace_state.sql  ! view tablespace states
$!          oracle_utils:hot_backup_cmd_'db_name'.com ! Perform the hot backup
$!             |-> oracle_utils:env_symbols.com
$!             |-> oracle_utils:backup_tablespace ! Backup one tablespace
```

```
$!              |-> oracle_utils:instance_up.com
$!              |-> ora_db:ora_db_<db_name>.com   ! Get the ora_control* logicals
$!
$! CALLED BY:
$!              Usually this script will be called by BACKUP_MAIN.COM however it
$!              could be called independently.
$!
$! INPUT:     Symbols: Check the "USER_PARAMETERS" section of this script for
$!                     a list of symbols that you can change to control the
$!                     operation of this script
$!
$!            Logical Names: ORACLE_UTILS must point to a directory with all
$!                     the backup scripts.
$!                     ORA_CONTROL* The logical names of the control files
$!                     defined by ora_db:ora_db_<db_name>.com


$!            Files:
$!               backup_location_1:tbs_to_datafiles.lis  !
Tablespaces/datafiles
$!                                                        ! to backup.
$!
$! OUTPUT:    Symbols: None.
$!            Logical Names: None.
$!            Files:
$!              * oracle_utils:hot_backup_cmd_'db_name'.com
$!                    This is a dynamically created DCL script that goes into
$!                    SVRMGRL, alters the tablespaces to begin/end backup and
$!                    hosts out to backup that tablespace by calling
$!                    oracle_utils:backup_tablespace.  It does this for all
$!                    tablespaces, after finishing, it saves a copy of the
$!                    control file.
$!
$!              * backup_location_1:restore_database.com
$!                    This is a dynamically created DCL script that will perform
$!                    the restore operation of this hot backup.  If you plan
$!                    to use this file please remember that you will need to
$!                    perform the actual database recovery after this script
$!                    restores the copy of this database.
$!                    Keep this file because here it remembers to which backup
$!                    device it copied each file of the database during backup.
$!                    Look in this file for more details.
$!
$!              * backup_location_1:tbs_to_datafiles.lis
$!                    This is an output of a SELECT statement for the purpose
$!                    of identifying the tablespaces, the datafiles, and their
$!                    sizes in OpenVMS blocks. Sample record of this file:
$!         "SYSTEM|DISK$AXPOpenVMSSYS:[ORACLE7.ROOT71.DB_TESTDB]ORA_SYSTEM.DBS|12288"
$!                    This file is created by oracle_utils:tbs_hotbackup.sql
$!
$!              * One control file of this database will be backed up to
$!                the first backup device.
$!
$!
$! PRIVILEGES: There were no privileges checks done for assuming this script
```

```
$!              is run from the Oracle account.
$!
$!
$! HISTORY:
$!   Date        Name         Comments
$!   24-JAN-1997 DJ Cover     Replaced all refs to SQLDBA with SVRMGRL

$!                            Bug fix to backup location device count test
$!   20-MAR-1995 Saar Maoz    Created
$!
$!
$!
$!!!!!!!! This section could be changed by user to configure backup procedure
$ USER_PARAMETERS:
$!
$! uncomment the following 2 lines, if you plan to use this script by itself
$! userpasswd := system/manager
$! mailuser = "SMAOZ"              ! set to "" if not interested in mail messages
$!!!!!!!!!
$!
$ set noon
$!
$! Local symbols to this script
$!
$ say := write sys$output
$ wo := write outfile
$ wo2 := write outfile2
$ delfile := delete/noconfirm/log
$ backupfile := backup/log/ignore=(interlock,nobackup)/new
$ sendmail :== mail nl: 'mailuser' /subject=
$!
$! Check for correct usage
$!
$ if p1 .eqs. "" then goto HELP
$ db_name = f$edit(p1,"UPCASE")
$!
$ if f$type(userpasswd) .eqs. "" .or. f$type(mailuser) .eqs. "" -
    then goto NO_SYMS
$!
$ say " "
$ say "ORACLE_UTILS:HOT_BACKUP.COM begins a hot backup on"+-
    " ''db_name' database at: "+f$time()
$ say " "
$!
$! Setup environment
$!
$ if f$trnlnm("oracle_utils") .eqs. "" then goto NO_LOGICAL
$ @oracle_utils:env_symbols  !just to make sure
$!
$! The following command will point us to the right database, note that there
$! must be a symbol as the database name defined in
$! ORACLE_UTILS:ENV_SYMBOLS.COM which will run the correct

$! ORA_DB:ORAUSER_<DBNAME>.COM which will point us to the right database.
$!
```

```
$ 'db_name'
$ if .not. $status then goto NO_SYMBOL
$ show logical ora_sid
$ @oracle_utils:'db_name'_devices.com     ! Define available backup locations
$!
$! Count the available devices (disks only)
$!
$ show log backup_location_*
$ device_cnt=1
$ DEV_LOOP:
$   if .not. f$getdvi("backup_location_''device_cnt'","EXISTS") -
      then goto DEV_VER  ! Make sure the device exists
$   if f$getdvi("backup_location_''device_cnt'","DEVCLASS") .ne. 1 -
      then goto DEV_VER  ! Make sure it's a disk
$   show device backup_location_'device_cnt'
$   device_cnt= device_cnt+1
$ goto DEV_LOOP
$!
$ DEV_VER:
$   device_cnt= device_cnt-1
$   if device_cnt .eq. 0 then goto NO_BACKUP_DEVICES ! if we have no devices
$!
$   say " "
$   say "ORACLE_UTILS:HOT_BACKUP.COM has recognized ''device_cnt' devices to"+-
      " use for backup."
$   say " "
$!
$! Check whether instance is up
$!
$ @oracle_utils:instance_up 'f$trnlnm("ora_sid")'
$ if .not. instance_up then goto UP_FOR_HOT     ! DB must be up for hot backup
$!
$! Generate the tablespace/datafiles listing file & delete old ones
$!
$ if f$search("backup_location_1:tbs_to_datafiles.lis") .nes. "" -
    then delfile/nolog backup_location_1:tbs_to_datafiles.lis;*
$ if f$search("oracle_utils:hot_backup_cmd_''db_name'.com") .nes. "" -
    then purge/nolog/keep=2 oracle_utils:hot_backup_cmd_'db_name'.com
$!
$ sqlplus -s 'userpasswd'  @oracle_utils:tbs_hotbackup.sql
$!
$! Open tablespace/datafiles listing file.  If it doesn't exist then something
$! went wrong.

$!
$ close/nolog infile
$ open/read/error=OPEN_TBS_ERROR infile backup_location_1:tbs_to_datafiles.lis
$ read/end=EMPTY_TBS_LIST infile rec  ! Skip first line in file it's a comment
$!
$! Start writing the script that will go into SVRMGRL and perform the actual
$! ALTER TABLESPACE BEGIN BACKUP; followed by the OpenVMS backup; followed by an
$! ALTER TABLESPACE END BACKUP
$!
$ close/nolog outfile
$ open/write outfile oracle_utils:hot_backup_cmd_'db_name'.com
$!
```

```
$ wo "$! FILE:  oracle_utils:hot_backup_cmd_''db_name'.com"
$ wo "$! Dynamically created by ORACLE_UTILS:HOT_BACKUP.COM at: ''f$time()'"
$ wo "$! to perform hot backup of ''db_name' database"
$ wo "$ set noon"
$ wo "$ if f$search(""backup_location_1:alter_tbs_begin_end.log"") -"
$ wo " .nes. """" then delfile/nolog backup_location_1:tbs_tbs_begin_end.log;*"
$ wo "$ vvv = 'f$verify(1)' ! Turn verify on so we can see commands in SVRMGRL"
$ wo "$ SVRMGRL"
$ wo "connect internal"
$ wo "alter system archive log current;"  ! To switch from and archive the
$!                                         ! current redolog
$ wo "  REM It is normal to get warning messages from backup in the form of"
$ wo "  REM %BACKUP-W-ACCONFLICT, <file name> is open for write by another
user"
$!
$! Process each tablespace at a time
$!
$ prv_tbs = ""
$LOOP:
$ read/end=END_INFILE infile rec
$ tbs = f$element(0,"|",rec)                 ! extract tablespace name
$ file = f$element(1,"|",rec)                ! extract the file specification
$ size = f$element(2,"|",rec)                ! extract the size of this file
$!
$ if tbs .eqs. prv_tbs then goto LOOP     ! skip it if we already did it
$!
$ if prv_tbs .eqs. ""
$ then
$   wo "spool backup_location_1:alter_tbs_begin_end.log"
$   wo "alter tablespace ''tbs' begin backup;"
$   wo "spool off"
$ else
$   wo "spool backup_location_1:alter_tbs_begin_end.log"

$   wo "alter tablespace ''prv_tbs' end backup;"
$   wo "spool off"
$   wo "spool backup_location_1:alter_tbs_begin_end.log"
$   wo "alter tablespace ''tbs' begin backup;"
$   wo "spool off"
$ endif
$!
$ wo "host @oracle_utils:backup_tablespace ''tbs' ''db_name' ''device_cnt'"
$ prv_tbs = tbs
$!
$ goto LOOP
$END_INFILE:
$!
$! Add end backup command to last tablespace and save a copy of the controlfile
$!
$ wo "spool backup_location_1:alter_tbs_begin_end.log"
$ wo "alter tablespace ''tbs' end backup;"
$ wo "spool off"
$ wo "alter database backup controlfile to "+-
  "''''backup_location_1:ora_control_''db_name'.con'''';"
```

```
$ wo "exit"
$ wo "$ vvv = 'f$verify(vvv)'"
$ wo "$ exit"
$ close/nolog outfile
$ close/nolog infile
$!
$ say "ORACLE_UTILS:HOT_BACKUP.COM is now deleting previous backup files"
$ say " on all devices with the name BACKUP_LOCATION_*"
$ say " "
$ dev_cnt=1
$ DELETE_YESTERDAYS_BCK:
$!
$ delfile backup_location_'dev_cnt':*.*.* - ! dont delete the tbs/datafile
          /exclude=(*.lis.*,*.dmp.*)         ! listing file we just created
$!                                           ! and the export file
$ dev_cnt=dev_cnt+1
$ if dev_cnt .LE. device_cnt then goto  DELETE_YESTERDAYS_BCK
$!
$! Start writing the RESTORE_DATABASE.COM which will be used to restore from
$! this backup.
$!
$ close/nolog outfile2
$ open/write outfile2 backup_location_1:restore_database.com
$ wo2 "$!FILE: backup_location_1:restore_database.com"

$ wo2 "$!Dynamically created by ORACLE_UTILS:HOT_BACKUP.COM at: "+-
       f$time()
$ wo2 "$!"
$ wo2 "$ type sys$input"
$ wo2 " This script will restore all database files from their backup
location"
$ wo2 " to their location on production environment. It will first delete the"
$ wo2 " database file if it exists in the production environment and then
will"
$ wo2 " copy a backup of that file to that location."
$ wo2 " After that it will copy all the controlfiles to their location in"
$ wo2 " the same fashion (deleting the production ones first)."
$ wo2 " "
$ wo2 " This script should be run only if you plan to perform a database"
$ wo2 " recovery from a HOT backup."
$ wo2 " To invoke this script edit it and remove the EXIT statement following"
$ wo2 " this notice"
$ wo2 "$!"
$ wo2 "$ EXIT"
$ wo2 "$!"
$ wo2 "$ db_name := ''db_name'"
$ wo2 "$ if f$trnlnm(""oracle_utils"") .eqs. """" then goto NO_LOGICAL"
$ wo2 "$ @oracle_utils:env_symbols"
$ wo2 "$ ''''db_name''''"
$ wo2 "$ @ora_db:ora_db_''''db_name''''" ! to get ora_control* logicals
$ wo2 "$ if f$trnlnm(""ora_control1"") .eqs. """" then goto NO_CTL_LOGICALS"
$ wo2 "$!"
$ wo2 "$ @oracle_utils:instance_up ''''f$trnlnm(""ora_sid"")'''"
$ wo2 "$ if instance_up then goto INSTANCE_UP"
```

```
$ wo2 "$!"
$ wo2 "$ @oracle_utils:''db_name'_devices"
$ wo2 "$!"
$ wo2 "$ set noon"
$ wo2 "$!"
$ wo2 "$ delfile := ''delfile'"
$ wo2 "$ backupfile := ''backupfile'"
$ wo2 "$!"
$ close/nolog outfile2
$!
$! Call the script we just created which will backup all tablespace
$! one at a time
$!
$ sqlplus -s 'userpasswd'  @oracle_utils:tablespace_state.sql  ! state before
$ @oracle_utils:hot_backup_cmd_'db_name'.com

$ sqlplus -s 'userpasswd'  @oracle_utils:tablespace_state.sql  ! state after
$!
$! Search all the begin/end backup logs for any errors, if yes then report them
$!
$ search backup_location_1:alter_tbs_begin_end.log;* "ORA-"/exact/win=1
$ if $status .ne. %X08D78053 then goto HOT_BACKUP_PROBLEM
$!
$! Write final helpful notes to restore_database file.
$!
$ close/nolog outfile2
$ open/append outfile2 backup_location_1:restore_database.com
$ wo2 "$!"
$ wo2 "$ type sys$input"
$ wo2 "  Restoring of all datafiles files of database ''db_name' has"
$ wo2 "  been completed, please review the logfile or screen for any errors."
$ wo2 "  Since this restore was from a HOT backup, you will need to recover"
$ wo2 "  the database before you will be able to use it.  Go into SVRMGRL"
$ wo2 "  and issue:"
$ wo2 "  1. connect internal"
$ wo2 "  2. startup MOUNT ''db_name';"
$ wo2 "  3. set autorecovery ON;"
$ wo2 "  4. recover database; (or add the until clause)"
$ wo2 "  5. Then ALTER DATABASE OPEN; (use RESETLOGS in case of an"+-
     " incomplete recovery)"
$ wo2 " "
$ wo2 " Note: The controlfiles were not restored, if you need to use them"
$ wo2 "         please do so manually."
$ wo2 " "
$ wo2 "  Good Luck!"
$ wo2 "$ goto FINISH"
$ wo2 "$!"
$ wo2 "$ INSTANCE_UP:"
$ wo2 "$ type sys$input"
$ wo2 "ERROR ** BACKUP_LOCATION_1:RESTORE_DATABASE.COM **"
$ wo2 "  The database is UP.  One or more processes belonging to this database"
$ wo2 "  is still running.  This script should be run when the database is"
$ wo2 "  DOWN.  Make sure the database is down, if necessary, issue a SHUTDOWN"
$ wo2 "  ABORT then rerun this script to restore a backup of this database."
```

```
$ wo2 "$ goto FINISH"
$ wo2 "$!"
$ wo2 "$ NO_LOGICAL:"
$ wo2 "$ type sys$input"
$ wo2 "ERROR ** BACKUP_LOCATION_1:RESTORE_DATABASE.COM **"
$ wo2 " The logical name ORACLE_UTILS is not defined please define it to point"
$ wo2 " to the directory where all the backup scripts reside."

$ wo2 "$ goto FINISH"
$ wo2 "$!"
$ wo2 "$ NO_CTL_LOGICALS:"
$ wo2 "$ type sys$input"
$ wo2 "ERROR ** BACKUP_LOCATION_1:RESTORE_DATABASE.COM **"
$ wo2 "  Can't find the controlfiles logicals (ORA_CONTROL*)"
$ wo2 "  They are usually defined in ORA_DB:ORA_DB_''db_name'.COM as opposed"
$ wo2 "  of hardcoding controlfilenames in the init.ora file"
$ wo2 "$ goto FINISH"
$ wo2 "$!"
$ wo2 "$ FINISH:"
$ wo2 "$ Exit"
$ close/nolog outfile2
$!
$ say " "
$ say "ORACLE_UTILS:HOT_BACKUP.COM finished a hot backup on"+-
      " ''db_name' database at: "+f$time()
$ say " "
$ if mailuser .nes. "" then sendmail -
  "HOT backup operation for ''db_name' database completed at: ''f$time()'"
$!
$ goto FINISH
$!
$! ERROR HANDLING SECTION
$!  Note: The rest of this script is an error handling routine.  After each
$!  error message we branch to MAIL_FINISH (will send an email) or to FINISH
$!  (will NOT send an email).  Feel free to change the labels in case you
$!  are not interested in a mail message in that case, or vice versa.
$!
$ NO_SYMS:
$  say " "
$  say "ERROR ** ORACLE_UTILS:HOT_BACKUP.COM **"
$  say " The local symbols userpasswd or mailuser are not defined"
$  say " This usually means that this script was called independently and the"
$  say " USER_PARAMETERS section of this script was not updated"
$  say " "
$  goto FINISH
$!
$ NO_LOGICAL:
$  say " "
$  say "ERROR ** ORACLE_UTILS:HOT_BACKUP.COM **"
$  say " The logical name ORACLE_UTILS is not defined please define it to
point"
$  say " to the directory where all the backup scripts reside."
$  goto MAIL_FINISH
```

```
$ !
$ NO_SYMBOL:
$   say " "
$   say "ERROR ** ORACLE_UTILS:HOT_BACKUP.COM **"
$   say " a. No symbol found with the database name that runs the"
$   say "    ORAUSER_<dbname>.COM which will point us to the right database,"
$   say "     add it to ORACLE_UTILS:ENV_SYMBOLS.COM"
$   say " b. Some other error has occurred while attempting to run the"
$   say "    ORAUSER_<dbname>.COM file, check the preceding OpenVMS error message"
$   goto MAIL_FINISH
$ !
$ NO_BACKUP_DEVICES:
$   say " "
$   say "ERROR ** ORACLE_UTILS:HOT_BACKUP.COM **"
$   say " No backup locations with the name BACKUP_LOCATION_* found."
$   say " Please define some backup locations in ''db_name'_DEVICES.COM"
$   say " and verify that the devices exist."
$   goto MAIL_FINISH
$ !
$ UP_FOR_HOT:
$   say " "
$   say "ERROR ** ORACLE_UTILS:HOT_BACKUP.COM **"
$   say " The database ''db_name' is down, and a hot backup was attempted"
$   goto MAIL_FINISH
$ !
$ OPEN_TBS_ERROR:
$   say " "
$   say "ERROR ** ORACLE_UTILS:HOT_BACKUP.COM **"
$   say " An error has occurred opening the tablespace datafiles mapping file."
$   say " It's located in BACKUP_LOCATION_1:TBS_TO_DATAFILES.LIS"
$   say " Please verify that the location is a valid directory owned by Oracle"
$   say " or the person running this script.  Also make sure that the Oracle"
$   say " shareable images are installed using ORA_RDBMS:INSORACLE.COM which"
$   say " is required to run sqlplus"
$   goto MAIL_FINISH
$ !
$ EMPTY_TBS_LIST:
$   say " "
$   say "ERROR ** ORACLE_UTILS:HOT_BACKUP.COM **"
$   say " Found tablespace listings file empty"+-
$        " (BACKUP_LOCATION_1:TBS_TO_DATAFILES.LIS)"
$   goto MAIL_FINISH
$ !
$ HOT_BACKUP_PROBLEM:
$   say " "

$   say "ERROR ** ORACLE_UTILS:HOT_BACKUP.COM **"
$   say " ALTER TABLESPACE BEGIN or END BACKUP command was issued."
$   say " Please check logfile or backup_location_1:alter_tbs_begin_end.log;*"
$   say " for more details."
$   goto MAIL_FINISH
$ !
$ HELP:
$   say " "
```

```
$  say "Usage of ORACLE_UTILS:HOT_BACKUP.COM is:"
$  say " @ORACLE_UTILS:HOT_BACKUP <db_name>"
$  goto FINISH
$!
$ MAIL_FINISH:
$  if mailuser .eqs. "" then goto FINISH
$!
$! Send correct mail whether run in interactive or batch mode
$!
$  msg = "HOT backup procedure run in interactive mode failed"
$  if f$mode() .eqs. "BATCH" then msg = "HOT backup procedure terminated"+-
        " with errors check ''logfile'_''db_name'.log for details"
$  sendmail "'''msg'"
$  goto FINISH
$!
$ FINISH:
$  close/nolog infile
$  close/nolog outfile
$  close/nolog outfile2
$  vvv= 'f$verify(vvv)'
$  exit
```

# COLD_BACKUP.COM

Given a database name as a parameter, this script performs a cold backup of that database. This means that the database must be shut down for the duration of the backup. This script will copy all data files and redo logs, one control file, and the parameter files (**INIT.ORA** and ***nodename_SID*_INIT.ORA**) to backup devices designated for this purpose. It will also create a DCL script that will restore the files from this backup to their original locations. The algorithm works as follows:

1. Make sure there is at least one backup device.

2. Check if database is up; if NO, go to step 7.

3. Notify users that database is going down in 10 minutes.

4. Shut down the database with the IMMEDIATE to force a database shutdown.

5. Wait for PMON to clean up.

6. If waited more than user-defined wait period, stop; something is wrong.

7. Bring database up in restricted mode to SELECT the data file and redo log filenames to back up and shut the database down clean.

8. Generate a list of all datafiles and redo logs and their sizes by calling **oracle_utils:tbs_coldbackup.sql**.

9. Shut down the database with the NORMAL option.

10. Delete the previous backup files from the backup devices.

11. Start creating the **restore_database.com** file needed to recover from this backup.

12. Read the file created in step 8 and for each new tablespace call **backup_tablespace.com**, which will back up all files associated with that tablespace.

13. When getting a null for tablespace name, it will recognize that it is a redo log file and back it up while adding records to the **restore_database.com**.

14. After finishing all the redo logs, it will back up the control file indicated by ORA_CONTROL1.

15. Back up the **INIT.ORA** and *nodename_SID_***INIT.ORA** files to the first backup device.

16. Add final records to the **restore_database.com** file.

17. If the database was up when the backup was started (step 2), bring it back up.

18. Done.

```
$!
$!
$!
$ vvv = 'f$verify(0)'  ! set noverify and remember what it was before
$! FILE:     ORACLE_UTILS:COLD_BACKUP.COM

$!
$!            by: Saar Maoz, Oracle Worldwide Support
$!
$!
$! USAGE:     Usually called by oracle_utils:backup_main
$!
$!            OR (if you want to use it separately)
$!
$!               @oracle_utils:cold_backup <dbname>
$!
$!            Example:  @cold_backup TESTDB
$!
$! PARAMETERS:
$!            P1 The database name to perform cold backup on.
$!
$! CALLS:     oracle_utils:env_symbols.com         ! Set up symbols to point to DB
$!            oracle_utils:<db_name>_devices.com ! Get backup devices names
$!            oracle_utils:instance_up.com         ! Check if instance is up/down
$!            oracle_utils:shutdown_immediate.com! Shutdown immediate
$!            oracle_utils:startup_dbamode.com     ! Startup in restricted mode
$!            oracle_utils:tbs_coldbackup.sql       ! tbs/datafile/redo logs list
$!            oracle_utils:backup_tablespace.com ! Backup one tablespace
```

```
$!           ora_db:ora_db_<db_name>.com        ! Get the ora_control* logicals
$!           ora_db:shutdown_'db_name'.com      ! Shutdown normal
$!           ora_db:startup_exclusive_'db_name' ! Startup database
$!
$! CALLED BY:
$!           Usually this script will be called by BACKUP_MAIN.COM however it
$!           could be called independently.
$!
$! INPUT:    Symbols: Check the "USER_PARAMETERS" section of this script for
$!                    a list of symbols that you can change to control the
$!                    operation of this script
$!
$!           Logical Names: ORACLE_UTILS must point to a directory with all
$!                          the backup scripts.
$!                          ORA_CONTROL* The logical names of the control files
$!                          ORA_PARAMS points to the <node>_<SID>_INIT.ORA file
$!                           both defined by ora_db:ora_db_<db_name>.com
$!           Files:
$!               backup_location_1:tbs_to_datafiles.lis  !
Tablespaces/datafiles
$!                                              ! to backup.
$!
$! OUTPUT:   Symbols: None.

$!           Logical Names: None.
$!           Files:
$!           * backup_location_1:restore_database.com
$!               This is a dynamically created DCL script that will perform
$!               the restore operation of this cold backup.  After using
$!               this file to restore from the cold backup, the database
$!               could be opened with no recovery needed.
$!               Keep this file because here it remembers to which backup
$!               device it copied each file of the database during backup.
$!               Look in this file for more details.
$!
$!           * backup_location_1:tbs_to_datafiles.lis
$!               This is an output of a SELECT statement for the purpose
$!               of identifying the tablespaces, the datafiles, and their
$!               sizes in OpenVMS blocks.  In cold backup mode this file also
$!               contains the redo logs names and sizes.
$!               Sample records of this file are:
$!     "SYSTEM|DISK$AXPOpenVMSSYS:[ORACLE7.ROOT71.DB_TESTDB]ORA_SYSTEM.DBS|12288"
$!     "       |DISK$AXPOpenVMSSYS:[ORACLE7.ROOT71.DB_TESTDB]ORA_LOG1.RDO|1000"
$!               This file is created by oracle_utils:tbs_coldbackup.sql
$!
$!           * The redo logs of this database will be backed up on to
$!             one of the available backup devices.
$!
$!           * One control file of this database will be backed up to
$!             the first backup device.
$!
$!           * The parameter files INIT.ORA and <nodename>_<SID>_INIT.ORA
$!             will be backed up to the first backup device.
$!

$!
$! PRIVILEGES: There were no privileges checks done for assuming this script
$!             is run from the Oracle account.
```

```
$!
$!
$! HISTORY:
$!    Date         Name         Comments
$!    24-JAN-1997  DJ Cover     Bug fix to backup location device count test
$!    20-MAR-1995  Saar Maoz    Created
$!
$!
$!!!!!!!!! This section could be changed by user to configure backup procedure
$ USER_PARAMETERS:
$   shutdown_immediate_wait = 20 ! wait for shutdown immediate to complete
$!

$! uncomment the following 2 lines, if you plan to use this script by itself
$! userpasswd := system/manager
$! mailuser = "SMAOZ"            ! set to "" if not interested in mail messages
$!!!!!!!!!!
$!
$ set noon
$!
$! Local symbols to this script
$!
$ say := write sys$output
$ wo := write outfile
$ delfile := delete/noconfirm/log
$ backupfile := backup/log/ignore=(interlock,nobackup)/new
$ sendmail :== mail nl: 'mailuser' /subject=
$!
$! Check for correct usage
$!
$ if p1 .eqs. "" then goto HELP
$ db_name = f$edit(p1,"UPCASE")
$!
$ if f$type(userpasswd) .eqs. "" .or. f$type(mailuser) .eqs. "" -
     then goto NO_SYMS
$!
$ say " "
$ say "ORACLE_UTILS:COLD_BACKUP.COM begins a cold backup on"+-
     " ''db_name' database at: "+f$time()
$ say " "
$!
$! Setup environment
$!
$ if f$trnlnm("oracle_utils") .eqs. "" then goto NO_LOGICAL
$ @oracle_utils:env_symbols  !just to make sure
$!
$! The following command will point us to the right database, note that there
$! must be a symbol as the database name defined in
$! ORACLE_UTILS:ENV_SYMBOLS.COM which will run the correct
$! ORA_DB:ORAUSER_<DBNAME>.COM which will point us to the right database.
$!

        $ 'db_name'
        $ if .not. $status then goto NO_SYMBOL
```

```
$ show logical ora_sid
$ @oracle_utils:'db_name'_devices.com      ! Define available backup locations
$!
$! Get the logical names of the control files so we can back them up later.
$!

$ @ora_db:ora_db_'db_name'
$ if f$trnlnm("ora_control1") .eqs. "" then goto NO_CTL_LOGICALS
$!
$! Count the available valid devices (disks only)
$!
$ show log backup_location_*
$ device_cnt=1
$ DEV_LOOP:
$  if .not. f$getdvi("backup_location_''device_cnt'","EXISTS") -
     then goto DEV_VER  ! Make sure the device exists
$  if f$getdvi("backup_location_''device_cnt'","DEVCLASS") .ne. 1 -
     then goto DEV_VER  ! Make sure it's a disk
$  show device backup_location_'device_cnt'
$  device_cnt= device_cnt+1
$ goto DEV_LOOP
$!
$ DEV_VER:
$  device_cnt= device_cnt-1
$  if device_cnt .eq. 0 then goto NO_BACKUP_DEVICES  ! if we have no devices
$!
$  say " "
$  say "ORACLE_UTILS:COLD_BACKUP.COM has recognized ''device_cnt' devices to"+-
     " use for backup."
$  say " "
$!
$! Check whether instance is up, and remember that for later
$!
$ @oracle_utils:instance_up 'f$trnlnm("ora_sid")'
$ instance_was_up = instance_up
$ if instance_up
$ then
$! If instance UP we need to shut it down to perform COLD backup
$  say " "
$  say "ORACLE_UTILS:COLD_BACKUP.COM"
$  say " The ''db_name' database is UP and we need to perform a COLD backup,"
$  say " therefore we must shut it down first."
$  say " "
$!
$! Notify all users and shutdown immediate after 10 minutes.
$!
$   reply/node/all/urgent/bell -
    "Database ''db_name' shutting down in 10 minutes for backup, please logout!"
$   say " "
$   say "ORACLE_UTILS:COLD_BACKUP.COM"
$   say "Now waiting 10 minutes before shutting down immediate"

$   say " "
$   wait 0:10:0.0
$   @oracle_utils:shutdown_immediate 'db_name'
```

```
$   wait 0:02:0.0
$   min = 2
$!
$! Wait for instance shutdown immediate to complete
$!
$   SHUTDOWN_WAIT:
$     @oracle_utils:instance_up 'f$trnlnm("ora_sid")'   ! Check if it's up?
$     if .not. instance_up then goto BRING_DB_UP
$     wait 0:05:0.0
$     min = min + 5
$     if min .ge. shutdown_immediate_wait then -
          goto SHUT_IMMED_TIMEOUT   ! Waited too long, something is wrong
$     goto SHUTDOWN_WAIT
$ endif
$!
$ BRING_DB_UP:
$!
$! Now bring db up in dba mode for two reasons:
$! 1. To get the datafiles redo logs listing file
$! 2. To later shut it down normal to get a clean COLD backup
$! Note that this will guarantee a backup of a normal shutdown database
$!
$ say " "
$ say "ORACLE_UTILS:COLD_BACKUP.COM"
$ say " Bringing ''db_name' database up to get the list of datafiles/redo logs"
$ say " and also to make sure it is shut down normal before this backup"
$ say " "
$ @oracle_utils:startup_dbamode 'db_name'
$!
$! Generate the tablespace/datafiles listing file & delete old ones
$!
$ if f$search("backup_location_1:tbs_to_datafiles.lis") .nes. "" -
    then delfile/nolog backup_location_1:tbs_to_datafiles.lis;*
$ sqlplus -s 'userpasswd'  @oracle_utils:tbs_coldbackup.sql
$!
$ say " "
$ say "ORACLE_UTILS:COLD_BACKUP.COM"
$ say " Finally shutting down ''db_name' database for the cold backup"
$ say " which is coming next"
$ say " "
$ @ora_db:shutdown_'db_name'   ! Shutdown normal for a clean cold backup.

$!
$! Open tablespace/datafiles listing file.  If it doesn't exist then something
$! went wrong.
$!
$ close/nolog infile
$ open/read/error=OPEN_TBS_ERROR infile backup_location_1:tbs_to_datafiles.lis
$ read/end=EMPTY_TBS_LIST infile rec  ! Skip first line in file it's a comment
$!
$ say "ORACLE_UTILS:COLD_BACKUP.COM is now deleting previous backup files"

$ say "  on all devices with the name BACKUP_LOCATION_*"
$ say " "
$ dev_cnt=1
```

```
$ DELETE_YESTERDAYS_BCK:
$!
$ delfile backup_location_'dev_cnt':*.*.* - ! dont delete the tbs/datafile
        /exclude=(*.lis.*,*.dmp.*)          ! listing file we just created
$!                                          ! and the export file
$ dev_cnt=dev_cnt+1
$!970124 if dev_cnt .lt. device_cnt then goto  DELETE_YESTERDAYS_BCK
$ if dev_cnt .LE. device_cnt then goto  DELETE_YESTERDAYS_BCK
$!
$! Start writing the RESTORE_DATABASE.COM which will be used to restore from
$! this backup
$!
$ close/nolog outfile
$ open/write outfile backup_location_1:restore_database.com
$ wo "$!FILE: backup_location_1:restore_database.com"
$ wo "$!Dynamically created by ORACLE_UTILS:COLD_BACKUP.COM at: "+-
      f$time()
$ wo "$!"
$ wo "$ type sys$input"
$ wo "  This script will restore all database files from their backup location"
$ wo "  to their location on production environment. It will first delete the"
$ wo "  database file if it exists in the production environment and then will"
$ wo "  copy a backup of that file to that location. The same will be done to"
$ wo "  restore all the logfiles."
$ wo "  After that it will copy all the controlfiles to their location in"
$ wo "  the same fashion (deleting the production ones first)."
$ wo "  "
$ wo "  This script should be run only if you plan to restore a database"
$ wo "  from a COLD backup."
$ wo "  To invoke this script edit it and remove the EXIT statement following"
$ wo "  this notice"
$ wo "$!"
$ wo "$ EXIT"
$ wo "$!"
$ wo "$ db_name := ''db_name'"
$ wo "$ if f$trnlnm(""oracle_utils"") .eqs. """" then goto NO_LOGICAL"
$ wo "$ @oracle_utils:env_symbols"
$ wo "$ ''''db_name''''"
$ wo "$ @ora_db:ora_db_''''db_name'''' ! to get ora_control* logicals"
$ wo "$ if f$trnlnm(""ora_control1"") .eqs. """" then goto NO_CTL_LOGICALS"
$ wo "$!"
$ wo "$ @oracle_utils:instance_up ''''f$trnlnm(""ora_sid"")'''' ! is db up?"
$ wo "$ if instance_up then goto INSTANCE_UP"
$ wo "$!"
$ wo "$ @oracle_utils:''db_name'_devices  ! define available backup devices"
$ wo "$!"
$ wo "$ set noon"
$ wo "$!"
$ wo "$ delfile := ''delfile'"
$ wo "$ backupfile := ''backupfile'"
$ wo "$!"

$ close/nolog outfile
$!
$! Process the datafiles listing file and backup all tablespaces
```

```
$!
$ prv_tbs = ""
$LOOP:
$ read/end=END_INFILE_ERROR infile rec
$ tbs = f$element(0,"|",rec)              ! extract tablespace name
$!
$! If tablespace name is blank that's a logfile, go there.
$!
$ if f$edit(tbs,"compress") .eqs. " " then goto BACKUP_LOGFILES
$!
$! If it's a "new" tablespace then call the script that saves it
$!
$ if tbs .nes. prv_tbs then -
   @oracle_utils:backup_tablespace 'tbs' 'db_name' 'device_cnt'
$ prv_tbs = tbs
$ goto LOOP
$!
$ BACKUP_LOGFILES:
$  open/append outfile backup_location_1:restore_database.com
$  wo "$! Restore all logfiles, by first deleting originals and then"
$  wo "$! copying the saved files onto the production environment."
$  wo "$!"
$!
$ LOG_LOOP:

$  file = f$element(1,"|",rec)            ! extract the file specification
$  size = f$element(2,"|",rec)            ! extract the size of this file
$!
$! Announce file to be backed up.
$!
$  say " "
$  say "Attempting to backup ''file'"
$  dev_cnt = 1
$  FIND_DEVICE_LOOP:
$!
$!   Is there enough space on this disk?  Always leaving ~2000 free blocks
$!   just in case (important not to fill location_1 completely)
$!
$    if f$getdvi("backup_location_''dev_cnt'","FREEBLOCKS") - 2000 .gt. size
$    then
$      say "                    to "+f$trnlnm("backup_location_''dev_cnt'")
$      say " "
$      backupfile 'file'; backup_location_'dev_cnt':/by=original
$      st = $status
$      if st .eq. %X10A38410 then goto BACKUP_OK  ! open for write by someone
$      if .not st then goto BACKUP_ERROR          ! some other backup error
$!
$      BACKUP_OK:
$!
$!      Get full filename that we wrote, this is to make sure we get the
$!      version number of the file we just copied, in case there are files
$!      with the same name.
$!
$      fname=f$parse(file,,"NAME")+f$parse(file,,"TYPE")
```

```
$       full_name=f$search("backup_location_''dev_cnt':''fname'")
$!
$!      Write the commands to restore this redolog
$!
$       wo "$ if f$search(""''file'"") -"
$       wo " .nes. """" then -"
$       wo "       delfile ''file';"
$       wo "$ backupfile    ''full_name' -"
$       wo "                ''file'/by=original"
$       wo "$!"
$    else
$      dev_cnt = dev_cnt + 1                         ! skip to the next device
$      if dev_cnt .gt. device_cnt then goto NO_SPACE ! no space on any device
$      goto FIND_DEVICE_LOOP
$    endif
$  read/end=COPY_CONTROLFILES infile rec   ! Finished copying redo logs

$  goto LOG_LOOP
$!
$ COPY_CONTROLFILES:
$!
$ close/nolog infile    ! We don't need this file anymore
$!
$! All we need is one controlfile
$!
$ backupfile ora_control1 -
            backup_location_1:ora_control_'db_name'.con/by=original
$ st = $status
$ if st .eq. %X10A38410 then goto COPY_PARAMS   ! open for write by someone
$ if .not. st then goto BACKUP_ERROR            ! some other backup error
$!
$ COPY_PARAMS:
$!
$! Find and backup INIT.ORA and <nodename>_<SID>_INIT.ORA
$!
$ initora=f$parse("ora_params",,"device")+-     ! Get init.ora location in
         f$parse("ora_params",,"directory")     ! case it's not in ora_db:
$ initora=f$search(initora+"init.ora")
$ backupfile ora_params:;,'initora'-
            backup_location_1:/by=original
$ st = $status
$ if .not. st then goto BACKUP_ERROR             ! some backup error
$!
$! Write the commands to restore all controlfiles and write final notes to
$! the restore file
$!
$ wo "$!"
$ wo "$! Now restore all control files"
$ wo "$!"
$ wo "$ cnt=1"
$ wo "$ REPLACE_CTL:"
$ wo "$ backupfile backup_location_1:ora_control_''''db_name''''.con; -"
$ wo "                ora_control''''cnt''''/by=original"
$ wo "$ cnt=cnt+1"
```

```
$ wo "$!"
$ wo "$ if f$trnlnm(""ora_control""+f$string(cnt)) .nes. """" then "+-
     "goto REPLACE_CTL"
$ wo "$!"
$ wo "$ type sys$input"
$ wo " Restoring of datafiles, logfiles and control files of database"+-
     " ''db_name'"
$ wo " has been completed, please review the logfile or screen for any errors."

$ wo " Since this restore was from a COLD backup, you can proceed to startup"
$ wo " the database."
$ wo " Please note that the parameter files INIT.ORA and <node>_<SID>_INIT.ORA"
$ wo " were not restored, although they have been originally backed up."
$ wo " If you wish to restore them, please do so manually."
$ wo " "
$ wo "  Good Luck!"
$ wo "$ goto FINISH"
$ wo "$!"
$ wo "$ INSTANCE_UP:"
$ wo "$ type sys$input"
$ wo "ERROR ** BACKUP_LOCATION_1:RESTORE_DATABASE.COM **"
$ wo "  The database is UP.  One or more processes belonging to this database"
$ wo "  is still running.  This script should be run when the database is"
$ wo "  DOWN.  Make sure the database is down, if necessary, issue a SHUTDOWN"
$ wo "  ABORT then rerun this script to restore a backup of this database."
$ wo "$ goto FINISH"
$ wo "$!"
$ wo "$ NO_LOGICAL:"
$ wo "$ type sys$input"
$ wo "ERROR ** BACKUP_LOCATION_1:RESTORE_DATABASE.COM **"
$ wo " The logical name ORACLE_UTILS is not defined please define it to point"
$ wo " to the directory where all the backup scripts reside."
$ wo "$ goto FINISH"
$ wo "$!"
$ wo "$ NO_CTL_LOGICALS:"
$ wo "$ type sys$input"
$ wo "ERROR ** BACKUP_LOCATION_1:RESTORE_DATABASE.COM **"
$ wo "  Can't find the controlfiles logicals (ORA_CONTROL*)"
$ wo "  They are usually defined in ORA_DB:ORA_DB_''db_name'.COM as opposed"
$ wo "  of hardcoding controlfilenames in the init.ora file"
$ wo "$ goto FINISH"
$ wo "$!"
$ wo "$ FINISH:"
$ wo "$ Exit"
$ close/nolog outfile
$!
$ say " "
$ say "ORACLE_UTILS:COLD_BACKUP.COM finished a cold backup on"+-
     " ''db_name' database at: "+f$time()
$ say " "
$ if mailuser .nes. "" then sendmail -

   "COLD backup operation for ''db_name' database completed at: ''f$time()'"
$!
$! If db was up, then bring it back up and we are done!
```

```
$!
$ if instance_was_up
$ then
$   say " "
$   say "ORACLE_UTILS:COLD_BACKUP.COM"
$   say " The database was up when COLD backup started, so bringing it back up"
$   say " "
$   @ora_db:startup_exclusive_'db_name'
$ endif
$ goto FINISH
$!
$! ERROR HANDLING SECTION
$!  Note: The rest of this script is an error handling routine.  After each
$!  error message we branch to MAIL_FINISH (will send an email) or to FINISH
$!  (will NOT send an email).  Feel free to change the labels in case you
$!  are not interested in a mail message in that case, or vice versa.
$!
$ NO_SYMS:
$   say " "
$   say "ERROR ** ORACLE_UTILS:COLD_BACKUP.COM **"
$   say " The local symbols userpasswd or mailuser are not defined"
$   say " This usually means that this script was called independently and the"
$   say " USER_PARAMETERS section of this script was not updated"
$   say " "
$   goto FINISH
$!
$ NO_LOGICAL:
$   say " "
$   say "ERROR ** ORACLE_UTILS:COLD_BACKUP.COM **"
$   say " The logical name ORACLE_UTILS is not defined please define it to
point"
$   say " to the directory where all the backup scripts reside."
$   goto MAIL_FINISH
$!
$ NO_SYMBOL:
$   say " "
$   say "ERROR ** ORACLE_UTILS:COLD_BACKUP.COM **"
$   say " a. No symbol found with the database name that runs the"
$   say "    ORAUSER_<dbname>.COM which will point us to the right database,"
$   say "     add it to ORACLE_UTILS:ENV_SYMBOLS.COM"
$   say " b. Some other error has occurred while attempting to run the"
$   say "    ORAUSER_<dbname>.COM file, check the preceding OpenVMS error message"
$   goto MAIL_FINISH
$!
$ NO_CTL_LOGICALS:
$   say " "
$   say "ERROR ** ORACLE_UTILS:COLD_BACKUP.COM **"
$   say " Can't find the controlfiles logicals (ORA_CONTROL*)"
$   say " They are usually defined in ORA_DB:ORA_DB_''db_name'.COM as opposed"
$   say " of hardcoding controlfilenames in the init.ora file"

$   goto MAIL_FINISH
$!
```

```
$ NO_BACKUP_DEVICES:
$   say " "
$   say "ERROR ** ORACLE_UTILS:COLD_BACKUP.COM **"
$   say " No backup locations with the name BACKUP_LOCATION_* found."
$   say " Please define some backup locations in ''db_name'_DEVICES.COM"
$   say " and verify that the devices exist."
$   goto MAIL_FINISH
$!
$ SHUT_IMMED_TIMEOUT:
$   say " "
$   say "ERROR ** ORACLE_UTILS:COLD_BACKUP.COM **"
$   say " Waited for instance "+f$trnlnm("ora_sid")+" to shutdown immediate for"
$   say " ''min' minutes, but instance has not shutdown yet."
$   goto MAIL_FINISH
$!
$ BACKUP_ERROR:
$   say " "
$   say "ERROR ** ORACLE_UTILS:COLD_BACKUP.COM **"
$   say " Received an OpenVMS backup error final error code: ''st'"
$   say " Text: "+f$message(st)
$   goto MAIL_FINISH
$!
$ NO_SPACE:
$   say " "
$   say "ERROR ** ORACLE_UTILS:COLD_BACKUP.COM **"
$   say " Not enough space for ''file'"
$   say " on any backup device. please assign more backup devices or clear some"
$   say " space on existing ones"
$   goto MAIL_FINISH
$!
$ OPEN_TBS_ERROR:
$   say " "
$   say "ERROR ** ORACLE_UTILS:COLD_BACKUP.COM **"
$   say " An error has occurred opening the tablespace datafiles mapping file."
$   say " It's located in BACKUP_LOCATION_1:TBS_TO_DATAFILES.LIS"
$   say " Please verify that the location is a valid directory owned by Oracle"
$   say " or the person running this script.  Also make sure that the Oracle"
$   say " shareable images are installed using ORA_RDBMS:INSORACLE.COM which"
$   say " is required to run sqlplus"
$   goto MAIL_FINISH
$!
$ EMPTY_TBS_LIST:
$   say " "
$   say "ERROR ** ORACLE_UTILS:COLD_BACKUP.COM **"
$   say " Found tablespace listings file empty"+-
$       " (BACKUP_LOCATION_1:TBS_TO_DATAFILES.LIS)"
$   goto MAIL_FINISH
$!
$ END_INFILE_ERROR:
$   say " "
$   say "ERROR ** ORACLE_UTILS:COLD_BACKUP.COM **"
$   say " Unexpected end of file BACKUP_LOCATION_1:TBS_TO_DATAFILES.LIS"

$   say " The file is created by this script, and contains all the tablespaces"
$   say " names and their associated files, followed by the logfiles names."
```

```
$   say " The first argument of a logfile record should be blank"
$   goto MAIL_FINISH
$!
$ HELP:
$   say " "
$   say "Usage of ORACLE_UTILS:COLD_BACKUP.COM is:"
$   say " @ORACLE_UTILS:COLD_BACKUP <db_name>"
$   goto FINISH
$!
$ MAIL_FINISH:
$   if mailuser .eqs. "" then goto FINISH
$!
$! Send correct mail whether run in interactive or batch mode
$!
$   msg = "COLD backup procedure run in interactive mode failed"
$   if f$mode() .eqs. "BATCH" then msg = "COLD backup procedure terminated"+-
            " with errors check ''logfile'_''db_name'.log for details"
$   sendmail "''msg'"
$   goto FINISH
$!
$ FINISH:
$   close/nolog infile
$   close/nolog outfile
$   vvv = 'f$verify(vvv)'
$   exit
```

# BACKUP_TABLESPACE.COM

Given the parameters *tablespace name*, *database name*, and *the number of backup devices available*, this routine will find all the data files associated with this tablespace and back them up. It will also add records to the **restore_database.com** file to restore the files being backed up. This uses the following algorithm:

1. Open **backup_location_1:tbs_to_datafiles.lis** in READ mode.

2. Read one record from the file in step 1 and check to see if the tablespace name matches the one that was passed as a parameter.

3. Find out if the first device has enough space to hold the file to be backed up; if YES, go to step 6.

4. Advance to the next device and check to see if there is enough space for this data file; if YES, go to step 6.

5. Repeat step 4 until you find a device with space; otherwise, generate an error stating that there is not enough space on any of the backup devices.

6. Back up the file to the chosen backup device number denoted by **backup_location_X**, where *X* is the number of that device.

**7.** Append records to the **restore_database.com** file, which will delete the old copy of the file and restore the backup version of it.

**8.** If there are more records in the file from step 1, go to step 2; otherwise, go to step 9.

**9.** Done.

```
$!
$!
$!
$ vvv = 'f$verify(0)'  ! set noverify and remember what it was before
$! FILE:     ORACLE_UTILS:BACKUP_TABLESPACE.COM
$!
$!          by: Saar Maoz, Oracle Worldwide Support
$!
$!
$! USAGE:    @oracle_utils:backup_tablespace <tbs> <db_name> <num of devs>
$!


$!          Example: @oracle_utils:backup_tablespace SYSTEM TESTDB 6
$!
$! PARAMETERS:
$!          P1 The tablespace to backup
$!          P2 The database name that tablespace belongs to
$!          P3 The number of backup devices available
$!
$! CALLS:   None.
$!
$! CALLED BY: oracle_utils:cold_backup
$!             oracle_utils:hot_backup
$!
$! INPUT:    Symbols: None.
$!          Logical Names: ORACLE_UTILS must point to a directory with all
$!                         the backup scripts.
$!          Files:
$!              backup_location_1:tbs_to_datafiles.lis  !
Tablespaces/datafiles
$!                                                      ! to backup.
$!
$! OUTPUT:   Symbols: None.
$!          Logical Names: None.
$!          Files:
$!           * backup_location_1:restore_database.com
$!                This is a dynamically created DCL script that will perform
$!                the restore operation of this backup.  This script will
$!                append to this file whether it be cold/hot backup which
$!                created it.
$!
$!           * The datafiles, of a specific tablespace will be backed up
$!                on to one of the backup devices.
$!
$!
$!
```

```
$! HISTORY:
$!   Date          Name          Comments
$!   20-MAR-1995  Saar Maoz      Created
$!
$!
$ set noon
$!
$! Local symbols to this script
$!
$ say := write sys$output
$ wo := write outfile

$ delfile := delete/noconfirm/log
$ backupfile := backup/log/ignore=(interlock,nobackup)/new
$!
$! Check for correct usage
$!
$ if p1 .eqs. "" then goto HELP
$!
$ tbs_to_copy = p1
$ db_name = p2
$ device_cnt = p3
$!
$! Open tablespace/datafiles listing file.  If it doesn't exist then something
$! went wrong.
$!
$ close/nolog infile2
$ open/read/error=OPEN_TBS_ERROR infile2 backup_location_1:tbs_to_datafiles.lis
$ read/end=EMPTY_FILE infile2 rec  ! Skip first record in file which is a
comment
$!
$! Append commands to the RESTORE_DATABASE.COM which will be used to restore
$! from this backup
$!
$ close/nolog outfile
$ open/append outfile backup_location_1:restore_database.com
$!
$ wo "$! Restore all files of tablespace ''tbs_to_copy' by first deleting"
$ wo "$! originals and then copying the saved files to the production"
$ wo "$! environment."
$ wo "$!"
$!
$! Identify the files for this tablespace
$!
$ MAIN_LOOP:
$    read/end=CLOSE_FILES infile2 rec
$    tbs = f$element(0,"|",rec)            ! extract tablespace name
$    if tbs .nes. tbs_to_copy then goto MAIN_LOOP
$!
$!   found file to copy now find a disk for it.
$!
$    file = f$element(1,"|",rec)           ! extract the file specification
$    size = f$element(2,"|",rec)           ! extract the size of this file
$!
```

```
$! Announce file to be backed up.
$!
$   say " "
$   say "Attempting to backup ''file'"
$   dev_cnt = 1
$   FIND_DEVICE_LOOP:
$!
$!    Is there enough space on this disk?  Always leaving ~2000 free blocks
$!    just in case (important not to fill location_1 completely)
$!
$    if f$getdvi("backup_location_''dev_cnt'","FREEBLOCKS") - 2000 .gt. size
$    then
$      say "                     to "+f$trnlnm("backup_location_''dev_cnt'")
$      say " "
$      backupfile 'file'; backup_location_'dev_cnt':/by=original
$      st = $status
$      if st .eq. %X10A38410 then goto BACKUP_OK  ! open for write by someone
$      if .not st then goto BACKUP_ERROR
$!
$      BACKUP_OK:
$!
$!      Get full filename that we wrote, this is to make sure we get the
version
$!      number of the file we just copied, in case there are files with the
$!      same name.
$!
$      fname=f$parse(file,,"NAME")+f$parse(file,,"TYPE")
$      full_name=f$search("backup_location_''dev_cnt':''fname'")
$!
$!      Write the commands to restore this datafile
$!
$      wo "$ if f$search("""''file'""") -"
$      wo "   .nes. """" then -"
$      wo "       delfile ''file';"
$      wo "$ backupfile   ''full_name' -"
$      wo "              ''file'/by=original"
$      wo "$!"
$      goto MAIN_LOOP
$    endif
$    dev_cnt = dev_cnt + 1                           ! skip to the next device
$    if dev_cnt .gt. device_cnt then goto NO_SPACE ! no space on any device
$    goto FIND_DEVICE_LOOP
$!
$ CLOSE_FILES:
$ close/nolog infile2
$ close/nolog outfile
$!
$ goto FINISH    !Done


$!
$! ERROR HANDLING SECTION
$! Note: The rest of this script is an error handling routine.  After each
$! error message we branch to MAIL_STOP (will stop execution send an email)
$! It's important to stop, because other scripts are relying on this script
```

```
$!  to complete successfully.
$!
$ OPEN_TBS_ERROR:
$  say " "
$  say "ERROR ** ORACLE_UTILS:BACKUP_TABLESPACE.COM **"
$  say " An error has occurred opening the tablespace datafiles mapping file."
$  say " It's located in BACKUP_LOCATION_1:TBS_TO_DATAFILES.LIS"
$  say " Please verify that the location is a valid directory owned by Oracle"
$  say " or the person running this script.  Also make sure that the Oracle"
$  say " shareable images are installed using ORA_RDBMS:INSORACLE.COM which"
$  say " is required to run sqlplus"
$  goto MAIL_STOP
$!
$ EMPTY_FILE:
$  say " "
$  say "ERROR ** ORACLE_UTILS:BACKUP_TABLESPACE.COM **"
$  say " Tablespace datafiles mapping file is empty.  The file is created by"
$  say " ORACLE_UTILS:HOT/COLD_BACKUP.COM which calls"
$  say " ORACLE_UTILS:TBS_HOTBACKUP.SQL or ORACLE_UTILS:TBS_COLDBACKUP.SQL"
$  say " respectively."
$  goto MAIL_STOP
$!
$ BACKUP_ERROR:
$  say " "
$  say "ERROR ** ORACLE_UTILS:BACKUP_TABLESPACE.COM **"
$  say " Received an OpenVMS backup error final error code: ''st'"
$  say " Text: "+f$message(st)
$  goto MAIL_STOP
$!
$ NO_SPACE:
$  say " "
$  say "ERROR ** ORACLE_UTILS:BACKUP_TABLESPACE.COM **"
$  say " Not enough space for ''file'"
$  say " on any backup device. please assign more backup devices or clear some"
$  say " space on existing ones"
$  goto MAIL_STOP
$!
$ HELP:
$  say " "
$  say "Usage of ORACLE_UTILS:BACKUP_TABLESPACE.COM is:"
$  say " @ORACLE_UTILS:BACKUP_TABLESPACE.COM <tbsname> <db_name> <num_devs>"
$  say " look in ORACLE_UTILS:HOT/COLD_BACKUP for correct usage"
$  goto FINISH
$!
$ MAIL_STOP:
$  if mailuser .nes. "" then  sendmail -
     "Backup procedure terminated with error check logfile for details"
$!
$  STOP ! Exit this script and all calling scripts because of serious error
$!
$ FINISH:
$  vvv = 'f$verify(vvv)'
```

# INSTANCE_UP.COM

Given the SID (system identifier) name of an instance, this script sees if any of the
background processes of that instance are up. The algorithm is as follows:

**1.** Set the global symbol instance_up to 1, assuming it is up.

**2.** Scan all processes on this node (requires WORLD privilege) for any
processes with the name of ORA_*sid*_*

**3.** If no processes are found in step 2, set instance_up to 0 to signal that the
instance is down.

```
$!
$!
$!
$! FILE:      ORACLE_UTILS:INSTANCE_UP.COM
$!
$!            by: Saar Maoz, Oracle Worldwide Support
$!
$!
$! USAGE:     @oracle_utils:instance_up <SID>
$!
$!            Example: @oracle_utils:instance_up TEST
$!
$! PARAMETERS:
$!            P1 The System Identifier (SID) of the instance
$!
$! CALLS:   None.
$!
$! CALLED BY: oracle_utils:cold_backup
$!            oracle_utils:hot_backup
$!            oracle_utils:export_database
$!
$! INPUT:   Symbols: None.
$!          Logical Names: None.
$!          Files: None.
$!
$! OUTPUT:  Symbols: instance_up    1 for up, 0 for down.
$!          Logical Names: None.
$!          Files: None.
$!
$!
$! HISTORY:
$!   Date         Name          Comments
$!   20-MAR-1995  Saar Maoz     Created
$!
$!
$ set noon
$!
$! Check for correct usage
$!
```

```
$ if p1 .eqs. "" then goto HELP
$ sid = p1
$!
$ instance_up == 1
$ ctx = ""
$!
$! Look for any process with a name ORA_<sid>_* on this node, this would mean
$! that this is one of the background processes belonging to this instance
$!
$ tmp = f$context("PROCESS",ctx,"NODENAME","'''f$getsyi("nodename")'","EQL")
$ tmp = f$context("PROCESS",ctx,"PRCNAM","ORA_''sid'_*","EQL")
$ pid = f$pid(ctx)
$ if pid .eqs. "" then instance_up == 0
$ goto FINISH
$!
$ HELP:
$  say " "
$  say "Usage of ORACLE_UTILS:INSTANCE_UP.COM is:"
$  say " @ORACLE_UTILS:INSTANCE_UP <SID>"
$  goto FINISH
$!
$ FINISH:
$  exit
```

# ENV_SYMBOLS_SAMPLE.COM

This script defines the symbols that will point to the right **orauser_*dbname*.com** file.
The symbol should be the database name and should point to the **orauser_*dbname*.com**
located in the **ora_db** directory.

```
$!
$!
$!
$! FILE:     ORACLE_UTILS:ENV_SYMBOLS_SAMPLE.COM
$!
$!           by: Saar Maoz, Oracle Worldwide Support
$!
$! PURPOSE: Setup a symbol for each database.
$!
$!
$! USAGE:    @oracle_utils:env_symbols
$!
$! PARAMETERS:  None.
$!
$! CALLS:   None.
$!
$! CALLED BY: Preferably by login.com or sylogin.com
$!
$! INPUT:    Symbols: None.
$!           Logical Names: None.
$!           Files: None.
```

```
$!
$! OUTPUT:    Symbols: <db_name>
$!            Logical Names: None.
$!            Files: None.
$!
$!
$! HISTORY:
$!   Date          Name           Comments
$!   20-MAR-1995   Saar Maoz      Created
$!
$ set noon
$!
$! Setup a symbol for each database on this node as follows:
$!
$! dbname :== @<location of orauser file>.com
$!
$! Example:
$!
$! testdb :== @sys$sysdevice:[oracle7.root71.db_testdb]orauser_testdb
$!
$ Exit
```

# SHUTDOWN_IMMEDIATE.COM

Given a database name, this script generates the DCL and SVRMGRL scripts
necessary to shut down the database with the IMMEDIATE option. It does so in the
following way:

1. Create **oracle_utils:shutdown_immediate_*db_name*.com** with the DCL
   commands to go into SVRMGRL, and call
   **oracle_utils:shutdown_immediate_*db_name*.sql**.

2. Create the SVRMGRL command file that will connect as the user
   INTERNAL, and then issue a shutdown with the IMMEDIATE option.

3. Invoke the DCL file created in step 1.

4. Done.

```
$!
$!
$!
$! FILE:      ORACLE_UTILS:SHUTDOWN_IMMEDIATE.COM
$!
$!            by: Saar Maoz, Oracle Worldwide Support
$!
$!
$! USAGE:     @oracle_utils:shutdown_immediate <db_name>
$!
$!            Example: @oracle_utils:shutdown_immediate TESTDB
```

```
$!
$! PARAMETERS:
$!          P1 The database name to shutdown immediate
$!
$! CALLS:    ora_db:ora_db_'db_name'.com
$!           oracle_utils:shutdown_immediate_'db_name'.com
$!           |->oracle_utils:shutdown_immediate_'db_name'.sql
$!
$! CALLED BY: oracle_utils:cold_backup
$!
$! INPUT:    Symbols: None.
$!           Logical Names: ORACLE_UTILS must point to a directory with all
$!                          the backup scripts.
$!                          ORA_PARAMS points to the <node>_<SID>_INIT.ORA file
$!                          defined by ora_db:ora_db_<db_name>.com
$!           Files: None.
$!
$! OUTPUT:   Symbols: None.
$!           Logical Names: None.
$!           Files:
$!             * oracle_utils:shutdown_immediate_'db_name'.sql
$!                   This is a dynamically created script that contains the
$!                   SVRMGRL commands necessary to shutdown immediate that
$!                   database.
$!             * oracle_utils:shutdown_immediate_'db_name'.com
$!                   This is a dynamically created DCL script that goes into
$!                   SVRMGRL, and calls the above mentioned file to shutdown
$!                   the database.
$!
$!
$! HISTORY:
$!   Date        Name          Comments
$!   24-JAN-1997 DJ Cover      Replaced all refs to SQLDBA with SVRMGRL
$!   20-MAR-1995 Saar Maoz     Created
$!
$ set noon
$!
$! Local symbols to this script
$!
$ say := write sys$output
$ wo := write outfile
$ wo2 := write outfile2
$!
$! Check for correct usage
$!
$ if p1 .eqs. "" then goto HELP
$ db_name = p1
$ @ora_db:ora_db_'db_name'                   ! to get ora_params logical
$ if f$trnlnm("ora_params") .eqs. "" then goto NO_PARAM_FILE
$!
$! Purge old logs
$!
$ if f$search("oracle_utils:shutdown_immediate_''db_name'.*") .nes. "" then -
```

```
      purge/nolog/keep=3 oracle_utils:shutdown_immediate_'db_name'.*
$!
$! Create the DCL script and SQL script which will actually do the shutdown

$!
$ close/nolog outfile
$ close/nolog outfile2
$ open/write outfile oracle_utils:shutdown_immediate_'db_name'.com
$ open/write outfile2 oracle_utils:shutdown_immediate_'db_name'.sql
$!
$ wo "$!Dynamically created by ORACLE_UTILS:SHUTDOWN_IMMEDIATE.COM at: "+-
      f$time()
$ wo "$!This script will go into SVRMGRL and call a SQL script that will
shutdown"
$ wo "$!the ''db_name' database with the immediate option"
$ wo "$!"
$ wo "$ SVRMGRL"
$ wo "@oracle_utils:shutdown_immediate_''db_name'"
$ wo "exit"
$ wo "$exit"
$ close/nolog outfile
$!
$ wo2 "rem Dynamically created by ORACLE_UTILS:SHUTDOWN_IMMEDIATE.COM at: "+-
      f$time()
$ wo2 "rem This script issues the SQL statements to shutdown the ''db_name'"
$ wo2 "rem database with the immediate option"
$ wo2 "set echo on"
$ wo2 "connect internal"
$ wo2 "shutdown immediate"
$ close/nolog outfile2
$!
$! Execute the created script - to shutdown immediate the database
$!
$ @oracle_utils:shutdown_immediate_'db_name'.com
$ goto FINISH
$!
$ NO_PARAM_FILE:
$  say " "
$  say "ERROR ** ORACLE_UTILS:SHUTDOWN_IMMEDIATE.COM **"
$  say " The logical name ORA_PARAMS which points to the init.ora file of"
$  say " this ("+f$trnlnm(""ora_sid"")+") instance is not defined. The usual"
$  say " place where this logical is defined is ora_db:ora_db_''db_name'.com"
$  say " Please check why this logical was not defined and rerun this script."
$  goto FINISH
$!
$ HELP:
$  say " "
$  say "Usage of ORACLE_UTILS:SHUTDOWN_IMMEDIATE.COM is:"
$  say " @ORACLE_UTILS:SHUTDOWN_IMMEDIATE <db_name>"

$  goto FINISH
$!
$ FINISH:
$  Exit
```

# STARTUP_DBAMODE.COM

Given a database name, this script generates the DCL and SVRMGRL scripts necessary to bring the database up in restricted mode. It does so in the following way:

1. Create **oracle_utils:startup_dbamode_*db_name*.com** with the DCL commands to go into SVRMGRL, and call **oracle_utils:startup_dbamode_*db_name*.sql**.

2. Create the SVRMGRL command file, which will connect as the user *internal* and issue the **startup restrict** command.

3. Invoke the DCL file created in step 1.

4. Done.

```
$!
$!
$! FILE:      ORACLE_UTILS:STARTUP_DBAMODE.COM
$!
$!            by: Saar Maoz, Oracle Worldwide Support
$!
$!
$! USAGE:     @oracle_utils:startup_dbamode <db_name>
$!
$!            Example: @oracle_utils:startup_dbamode TESTDB
$!
$! PARAMETERS:
$!            P1 The database name to bring up in dba mode
$!
$! CALLS:     ora_db:ora_db_'db_name'.com
$!            oracle_utils:startup_dbamode_'db_name'.com
$!            |->oracle_utils:startup_dbamode_'db_name'.sql
$!
$!
$! CALLED BY: oracle_utils:cold_backup
$!             oracle_utils:export_database
$!
$! INPUT:    Symbols: None.

$!           Logical Names: ORACLE_UTILS must point to a directory with all
$!                          the backup scripts.
$!                          ORA_PARAMS points to the <node>_<SID>_INIT.ORA file
$!                          defined by ora_db:ora_db_<db_name>.com
$!           Files: None.
$!
$! OUTPUT:   Symbols: None.
$!           Logical Names: None.
$!           Files:
```

```
$!              * oracle_utils:startup_dbamode_'db_name'.sql
$!                   This is a dynamically created script that contains the
$!                   SVRMGRL commands necessary to start that database
$!                   up in restricted mode.
$!              * oracle_utils:startup_dbamode_'db_name'.com
$!                   This is a dynamically created DCL script that goes into
$!                   SVRMGRL, and calls the above mentioned file to bring
$!                   the database up in restricted mode.
$!
$!
$! HISTORY:
$!   Date        Name          Comments
$!   24-JAN-1997 DJ Cover      Replaced all refs to SQLDBA with SVRMGRL
$!   20-MAR-1995 Saar Maoz     Created
$!
$ set noon
$!
$! Local symbols to this script
$!
$ say := write sys$output
$ wo := write outfile
$ wo2 := write outfile2
$!
$! Check for correct usage
$!
$ if p1 .eqs. "" then goto HELP
$ db_name = p1
$ @ora_db:ora_db_'db_name'                ! to get ora_params logical
$ if f$trnlnm("ora_params") .eqs. "" then goto NO_PARAM_FILE
$!
$! Purge old logs
$!
$ if f$search("oracle_utils:startup_dbamode_''db_name'.*") .nes. "" then -
   purge/nolog/keep=3 oracle_utils:startup_dbamode_'db_name'.*
$!
$! Create the DCL script and SQL script which will actually do the startup
$!

$ close/nolog outfile
$ close/nolog outfile2
$ open/write outfile oracle_utils:startup_dbamode_'db_name'.com
$ open/write outfile2 oracle_utils:startup_dbamode_'db_name'.sql
$!
$ wo "$!Dynamically created by ORACLE_UTILS:STARTUP_DBAMODE.COM at:
''f$time()'"
$ wo "$!This script will go into SVRMGRL and call a SQL script that will start"
$ wo "$!the ''db_name' database in restricted mode"
$ wo "$!"
$ wo "$ SVRMGRL"
$ wo "@oracle_utils:startup_dbamode_''db_name'"
$ wo "exit"
$ wo "$exit"
$ close/nolog outfile
$!
$ wo2 "rem Dynamically created by ORACLE_UTILS:STARTUP_DBAMODE.COM at: "+-
```

```
        f$time()
$ wo2 "rem This script issues the SQL statements to startup the ''db_name'"
$ wo2 "rem database in restricted mode."
$ wo2 "set echo on"
$ wo2 "connect internal"
$ wo2 "startup restrict open """'db_name'"""
$ close/nolog outfile2
$!
$! Execute the created script - to startup the database in restricted mode
$!
$ @oracle_utils:startup_dbamode_'db_name'.com
$ goto FINISH
$!
$ NO_PARAM_FILE:
$  say " "
$  say "ERROR ** ORACLE_UTILS:STARTUP_DBAMODE.COM **"
$  say " The logical name ORA_PARAMS which points to the init.ora file of"
$  say " this ("+f$trnlnm(""ora_sid"")+") instance is not defined. The usual"
$  say " place where this logical is defined is ora_db:ora_db_''db_name'.com"
$  say " Please check why this logical was not defined and rerun this script."
$  goto FINISH
$!
$ HELP:
$  say " "
$  say "Usage of ORACLE_UTILS:STARTUP_DBAMODE.COM is:"
$  say " @ORACLE_UTILS:STARTUP_DBAMODE <db_name>"
$  goto FINISH
$!
$ FINISH:
$ Exit
```

# SUBMIT_sample.COM

This is a sample file that shows how to submit **oracle_utils:backup_main.com** to run
as a batch job. Copy this script and modify all that is in uppercase to match your
environment and needs. If you specify the resubmit flag (third parameter) as YES,
you will need to run this script only once. After that, the backup script will run a
similar command to resubmit itself every day at the same time.

```
$ submit oracle_utils:backup_main.com -
    /parameters=("TESTDB","COMPLETE","YES") -
    /after="23:00" -
    /log=sys$scratch:save_database_TESTDB.log -
    /queue=sys$batch -
    /retain=error -
    /noprint
```

# db_name_DEVICES_SAMPLE.COM

This is a sample file that defines the backup and export devices for a database.
This file should be copied from this sample form and named **oracle_utils:db_
name_devices_sample.com**. Currently only disks are supported as backup and
export devices.

```
$! HISTORY:
$!   Date         Name            Comments
$!   24-JAN-1997  DJ Cover        Added "/JOB" to backup location logical defs
$!   20-MAR-1995  Saar Maoz       Created
$!
$! Define only one export location which is a valid directory on a disk
$!
$ define/nolog export_location userdisk1:[export_testdb]
$!
$! Define as many backup directories as you wish
$!
$ define/nolog/job  backup_location_1  sys$sysdevice:[hot_backup_testdb]
$ define/nolog/job  backup_location_2  userdisk21:[hot_backup_testdb]
$ define/nolog/job  backup_location_3  userdisk33:[hot_backup_testdb]
$ define/nolog/job  backup_location_4  userdisk14:[hot_backup_testdb]
$ define/nolog/job  backup_location_5  userdisk5:[hot_backup_testdb]
$ define/nolog/job  backup_location_6  userdisk4:[hot_backup_testdb]
$!
$!
```

# Tbs_hotbackup.sql

The following SQL script is used by the hot backup script to create a list of the
tablespace and data filenames. The output contains a list of all data files that are
part of the database.

```
REM  DJ Cover/Saar Moaz    970124    added "set timing off"
set feedback off
set pagesize 0
set heading off
set echo off
set termout off
set timing off
spool backup_location_1:tbs_to_datafiles

SELECT '! Dynamically created by ORACLE_UTILS:HOT_BACKUP.COM at: '||
       to_char(sysdate,'dd-mon-yyyy hh:mi:ss')
FROM dual;

rem Get all the datafiles for this database

SELECT tablespace_name||'|'||file_name||'|'||ceil(bytes/512)
FROM   sys.dba_data_files
ORDER BY tablespace_name,bytes desc;

spool off;

EXIT
```

# Tbs_coldbackup.sql

The following SQL script is run by the cold backup script. The output file lists all the
data files as well as the online log filenames.

```
REM  DJ Cover/Saar Moaz    970124     added "set timing off"
set feedback off
set pagesize 0
set heading off
set echo off
set termout off
set timing off
spool backup_location_1:tbs_to_datafiles

SELECT '! Dynamically created by ORACLE_UTILS:COLD_BACKUP.COM at: '||
       to_char(sysdate,'dd-mon-yyyy hh:mi:ss')
FROM dual;


rem Get all the datafiles for this database

SELECT tablespace_name||'|'||file_name||'|'||ceil(bytes/512)
FROM   sys.dba_data_files
ORDER BY tablespace_name,bytes desc;

rem Get all the redo logs for this database

SELECT ' '||'|'||member||'|'||ceil(bytes/512)
FROM   v$log,v$logfile
WHERE  v$log.group# = v$logfile.group#;
spool off;

EXIT
```

## Tablespace_State.sql

```
rem This will show if the tablespaces are in backup mode, done before and
rem after a hot backup.  All rows should show as NOT ACTIVE
select * from v$backup;
exit;
```

## Hot_Backup_Sample_Run.log

This is a sample run of a *hot* backup. The reason why we are recognizing only one backup device is because the rest of the logicals 2 through 6 are of devices that do not exist. Also note that the "no strings matched" message at the end is normal—it means that the logs have been searched for errors and none were found.

```
ORACLE_UTILS:HOT_BACKUP.COM begins a hot backup on TESTDB database
                      at: 24-MAR-1995 23:00:32.29

%DCL-I-SUPERSEDE, previous value of ORA_SID has been superseded
   "ORA_SID" = "TEST" (LNM$PROCESS_TABLE)
```

```
(LNM$PROCESS_TABLE)

    "BACKUP_LOCATION_1" = "SYS$SYSDEVICE:[HOT_BACKUP_TESTDB]"
    "BACKUP_LOCATION_2" = "USERDISK21:[HOT_BACKUP_TESTDB]"
    "BACKUP_LOCATION_3" = "USERDISK33:[HOT_BACKUP_TESTDB]"
    "BACKUP_LOCATION_4" = "USERDISK14:[HOT_BACKUP_TESTDB]"
    "BACKUP_LOCATION_5" = "USERDISK5:[HOT_BACKUP_TESTDB]"
    "BACKUP_LOCATION_6" = "USERDISK4:[HOT_BACKUP_TESTDB]"
```

| Device | Device | Error | Volume | Free | Trans | Mnt |
|---|---|---|---|---|---|---|
| Name | Status | Count | Label | Blocks | Count | Cnt |
| MCAOpenVMS$DKA0: | Mounted | 0 | AXPOpenVMSSYS | 90408 | 422 | 1 |

```
ORACLE_UTILS:HOT_BACKUP.COM has recognized 1 devices to use for backup.

ORACLE_UTILS:HOT_BACKUP.COM is now deleting previous backup files
 on all devices with the name BACKUP_LOCATION_*

%DELETE-I-FILDEL, SYS$SYSDEVICE:[HOT_BACKUP_TESTDB]ORA_CONTROL_TESTDB.CON;1 deleted (312 blocks)
%DELETE-I-FILDEL, SYS$SYSDEVICE:[HOT_BACKUP_TESTDB]ORA_DATA_1.DBS;4 deleted (2048 blocks)
%DELETE-I-FILDEL, SYS$SYSDEVICE:[HOT_BACKUP_TESTDB]ORA_DATA_2.DBS;4 deleted (2048 blocks)
%DELETE-I-FILDEL, SYS$SYSDEVICE:[HOT_BACKUP_TESTDB]ORA_SYSTEM.DBS;3 deleted (12288 blocks)
%DELETE-I-FILDEL, SYS$SYSDEVICE:[HOT_BACKUP_TESTDB]ORA_SYSTEM1.DBS;2 deleted (8192 blocks)
%DELETE-I-FILDEL, SYS$SYSDEVICE:[HOT_BACKUP_TESTDB]RESTORE_DATABASE.COM;2 deleted (12 blocks)
%DELETE-I-FILDEL, SYS$SYSDEVICE:[HOT_BACKUP_TESTDB]RESTORE_DATABASE.COM;1 deleted (12 blocks)
%DELETE-I-TOTAL, 7 files deleted (24912 blocks)
```

| FILE# | STATUS | CHANGE# | TIME |
|---|---|---|---|
| 1 | NOT ACTIVE | 7151 | 03/24/94 12:31:30 |
| 2 | NOT ACTIVE | 7151 | 03/24/94 12:31:30 |
| 3 | NOT ACTIVE | 7150 | 03/24/94 12:31:26 |
| 4 | NOT ACTIVE | 7150 | 03/24/94 12:31:26 |

```
$ vvv = 0 ! Turn verify on so we can see commands in SVRMGRL
$ SVRMGRL

SVRMGRL: Release 7.1.3.2.0 - Production on Fri Mar 24 23:00:40 1995

Copyright (c) Oracle Corporation 1979, 1995.  All rights reserved.

Oracle7 Server Release 7.1.3.2.0 - Production Release
With the distributed, parallel query and Parallel Server options
PL/SQL Release 2.1.3.2.0 - Production

SVRMGRL>
connect internal
Connected.
SVRMGRL>
alter system archive log current;
Statement processed.
SVRMGRL>
  REM It is normal to get warning messages from backup in the form of
SVRMGRL>
  REM %BACKUP-W-ACCONFLICT, <file name> is open for write by another user
SVRMGRL>
spool backup_location_1:alter_tbs_begin_end.log
```

```
File SYS$SYSDEVICE:[HOT_BACKUP_TESTDB]ALTER_TBS_BEGIN_END.LOG opened
SVRMGRL>
alter tablespace SAAR begin backup;
Statement processed.
SVRMGRL>
spool off
File SYS$SYSDEVICE:[HOT_BACKUP_TESTDB]ALTER_TBS_BEGIN_END.LOG closed
SVRMGRL>
host @oracle_utils:backup_tablespace SAAR TESTDB 1

Attempting to backup DISK$AXPOpenVMSSYS:[ORACLE7.ROOT71.DB_TESTDB]ORA_DATA_1.DBS
               to SYS$SYSDEVICE:[HOT_BACKUP_TESTDB]

%BACKUP-W-ACCONFLICT, DISK$AXPOpenVMSSYS:[ORACLE7.ROOT71.DB_TESTDB]ORA_DATA_1.DBS;4
 is open for write by another user
%BACKUP-S-CREATED, created SYS$SYSDEVICE:[HOT_BACKUP_TESTDB]ORA_DATA_1.DBS;4

Attempting to backup DISK$AXPOpenVMSSYS:[ORACLE7.ROOT71.DB_TESTDB]ORA_DATA_2.DBS
               to SYS$SYSDEVICE:[HOT_BACKUP_TESTDB]

%BACKUP-W-ACCONFLICT, DISK$AXPOpenVMSSYS:[ORACLE7.ROOT71.DB_TESTDB]ORA_DATA_2.DBS;4
 is open for write by another user
%BACKUP-S-CREATED, created SYS$SYSDEVICE:[HOT_BACKUP_TESTDB]ORA_DATA_2.DBS;4

$  vvv = 0

SVRMGRL>
spool backup_location_1:alter_tbs_begin_end.log
File SYS$SYSDEVICE:[HOT_BACKUP_TESTDB]ALTER_TBS_BEGIN_END.LOG opened
SVRMGRL>
alter tablespace SAAR end backup;
Statement processed.
SVRMGRL>
spool off
File SYS$SYSDEVICE:[HOT_BACKUP_TESTDB]ALTER_TBS_BEGIN_END.LOG closed
SVRMGRL>
spool backup_location_1:alter_tbs_begin_end.log
File SYS$SYSDEVICE:[HOT_BACKUP_TESTDB]ALTER_TBS_BEGIN_END.LOG opened
SVRMGRL>
alter tablespace SYSTEM begin backup;
Statement processed.
SVRMGRL>
spool off
File SYS$SYSDEVICE:[HOT_BACKUP_TESTDB]ALTER_TBS_BEGIN_END.LOG closed
SVRMGRL>
host @oracle_utils:backup_tablespace SYSTEM TESTDB 1

Attempting to backup DISK$AXPOpenVMSSYS:[ORACLE7.ROOT71.DB_TESTDB]ORA_SYSTEM.DBS
               to SYS$SYSDEVICE:[HOT_BACKUP_TESTDB]

%BACKUP-W-ACCONFLICT, DISK$AXPOpenVMSSYS:[ORACLE7.ROOT71.DB_TESTDB]ORA_SYSTEM.DBS;3
 is open for write by another user
%BACKUP-S-CREATED, created SYS$SYSDEVICE:[HOT_BACKUP_TESTDB]ORA_SYSTEM.DBS;3

Attempting to backup DISK$AXPOpenVMSSYS:[ORACLE7.ROOT71.DB_TESTDB]ORA_SYSTEM1.DBS
               to SYS$SYSDEVICE:[HOT_BACKUP_TESTDB]

%BACKUP-W-ACCONFLICT,
```

```
DISK$AXPOpenVMSSYS:[ORACLE7.ROOT71.DB_TESTDB]ORA_SYSTEM1.DBS;2
 is open for write by another user
%BACKUP-S-CREATED, created SYS$SYSDEVICE:[HOT_BACKUP_TESTDB]ORA_SYSTEM1.DBS;2

SVRMGRL>
spool backup_location_1:alter_tbs_begin_end.log
File SYS$SYSDEVICE:[HOT_BACKUP_TESTDB]ALTER_TBS_BEGIN_END.LOG opened

SVRMGRL>
alter tablespace SYSTEM end backup;
Statement processed.
SVRMGRL>
spool off
File SYS$SYSDEVICE:[HOT_BACKUP_TESTDB]ALTER_TBS_BEGIN_END.LOG closed
SVRMGRL>
alter database backup controlfile to
'backup_location_1:ora_control_TESTDB.con';
Statement processed.
SVRMGRL>
exit


        FILE# STATUS              CHANGE#    TIME
        ---------- ------------------- ---------- --------------------
            1 NOT ACTIVE          7163       03/24/94 23:00:45
            2 NOT ACTIVE          7163       03/24/94 23:00:45
            3 NOT ACTIVE          7162       03/24/94 23:00:41
            4 NOT ACTIVE          7162       03/24/94 23:00:41

%SEARCH-I-NOMATCHES, no strings matched

ORACLE_UTILS:HOT_BACKUP.COM finished a hot backup on TESTDB database
                    at: 24-MAR-1995 23:01:03.15

Job BACKUP_MAIN (queue SYS$BATCH, entry 43) holding until 25-MAR-1995 23:01
    SMAOZ         job terminated at 24-MAR-1995 23:01:03.89

    Accounting information:
    Buffered I/O count:          1843      Peak working set size:  18096
    Direct I/O count:             643      Peak page file size:    73344
    Page faults:                 3442      Mounted volumes:            0
    Charged CPU time:      0 00:00:04.43   Elapsed time:      0 00:00:33.19
```

# Backup Scripts in a Windows NT Environment

In this section we will provide examples that will demonstrate a partial and a full backup. You can use the Backup utility on Windows NT to back up files to secondary and tertiary storage. You must ensure that the database is shut down normally for a cold backup, or ensure that the tablespace is offline for a hot backup, before copying the files using the Windows NT Backup utility. Be sure to back up all the database files, log files, and control files for a cold backup and all the data files belonging to the tablespace that is offline for a hot backup. We will illustrate a hot backup of the tablespace USER_DATA in the following example:

```
REM First get a listing of all datafiles belonging to the tablespace user_data
REM Connect to Oracle using SQL*Plus with a DBA Account
SQL> select file_id, tablespace_name, status, file_name from dba_data_files
2  where tablespace_name='USER_DATA';
FILE_ID    TABLESPACE_NAME    STATUS        FILE_NAME
---------  -----------------  ---------     ---------
2 USER_DATA                   AVAILABLE     C:\ORANT\DATABASE\
                                            USR1ORCL.ORA
3 USER_DATA                   AVAILABLE     C:\ORANT\DATABASE\
                                            USR2ORCL.ORA
```

We have determined that the files **c:\orant\database\usr1orcl.ora** and **c:\orant\database\usr2orcl.ora** are the only data files belonging to this tablespace.

```
REM Now take the tablespace USER_DATA offline
SQL> alter tablespace user_data offline;
Tablespace altered.
```

From the Windows NT command line, you can use the **backup** command to take a backup of the files **usr1orcl.ora** and **usr2orcl.ora.** Finally, you can bring the tablespace online again.

```
C:\ORANT\DATABASE > backup usr1orcl.ora a:
C:\ORANT\DATABASE > backup usr2orcl.ora a:
SQL> alter tablespace user_data online;
Tablespace altered.
```

We will now present a step-by-step approach for a cold backup using the **at** command. The **at** command can be used to schedule tasks in Windows NT.

**I.** Create a file called **shutdown.sql** that contains the following:

```
connect internal/<password>
shutdown immediate
startup restrict
shutdown normal
exit
```

**2.** Create a file called **startup.sql** that contains the following:

```
connect internal/<password>
startup
exit
```

**3.** Create a batch file called **orabak.bat** that contains the following:

```
c:\orant\bin\svrmgr30.exe @shutdown.sql
backup c:\orant\database\*.* <tape or floppy device>
c:\orant\bin\svrmgr30.exe @startup.sql
```

Be sure to add all the database files, log files, and control files to the **backup** command, using multiple statements if necessary. Finally, you can schedule your backup job in Windows NT. To schedule the execution of the batch file **orabak.bat** at 2:00 A.M., use the following:

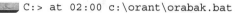

```
C:> at 02:00 c:\orant\orabak.bat
```

# Backup Scripts in a UNIX Environment

In this section we give a very similar script to the OpenVMS section. The main backup script reads the schedule to determine the kind of backup to be taken. Then it calls other procedures to actually take a cold backup, a hot backup, or an export of the database. The scripts should give you an idea on the kind of logic to use while automating backup procedures. We have tried not to hardcode any values in the scripts. Some commands like **awk** that are used in these examples may not be available on your UNIX implementation. Instead, we have obtained the information from the database whenever possible, or used environment variables that can be set to suit your needs. However, you should customize the scripts for your business needs and test them before using them in a production environment.

The main procedure is called **dbbackup**. This procedure always does the following:

- Sets up the environment variables specific to the database by running the shell script **$TOOLS/db_admin/common/crontab.env**

- Reads the backup schedule from **$TOOLS/db_admin/common/ dbbackup_sched.dat** file to determine whether to take a hot backup, a cold backup, or an export of the database

- Calls the procedure **dbbackup_begin** to do a hot or cold backup

- Calls the procedure **dbexport_begin** to do a full database export

The procedure **dbbackup_begin** does the following:

- Builds a dynamic listing of database files, control files, and location of archive log files for use by hot and cold backups

- Performs hot backups by executing the following steps:

    **1.** Each tablespace is put into hot backup mode.

    **2.** Data files are copied.

**3.** Ends hot backup mode for the tablespace being backed up.

**4.** A log switch is forced before the archive logs are copied.

**5.** Only a single control file backup is made.

■ Performs cold backups by executing the following steps:

**I.** Sends warning messages to users notifying them of the impending database shutdown.

**2.** The database is shut down.

**3.** Copies all database files, control files, and archive logs.

**4.** Optionally, starts the database in RESTRICTED mode and performs DBA tasks, and shuts down again.

**5.** Restarts the database, and sends message to users.

The procedure **dbexport_begin** does the following:

■ Takes a backup of the previous export file by copying it from the current location to a backup location

■ Deletes the export file in the current location

■ Performs the export using the parameter file **$TOOLS/db_admin/db_*dbname*/export.par**

| Directory, Routine, or File Name | Description |
| --- | --- |
| $TOOLS/backup/dbbackup | Main routine |
| $TOOLS/backup/dbbackup_begin | Called by dbbackup |
| $TOOLS/ /backup/dbexport_begin | Called by dbbackup |
| $TOOLS/db_admin/common/dbbackup_sched.dat | Backup schedule file |
| $TOOLS/db_admin/common/crontab.env | Sets environment variables |
| $TOOLS/db_admin/db_dbname/log | Directory containing logs written by the backup and export scripts |
| $TOOLS/db_admin/db_dbname/export.par | Export parameter file |

The directory structure that is required by these scripts is shown here:

| Directory Name | Description |
| --- | --- |
| $TOOLS | Top-level directory, needs to be set in the environment before the scripts are executed |
| $TOOLS/backup | Location of backup scripts |
| $TOOLS/db_admin/common | Administrative files common to all databases |
| $TOOLS/db_admin/db_dbname | Administrative files specific to each database |
| $TOOLS/db_admin/db_dbname/log | Log files |

While creating scripts in UNIX, always remember the following general rules:

- Never use **cd** in a script; always use absolute paths of files.
- Use wildcards in files with caution.
- Always verify file copies using the **cksum** command.
- Always check the return status of shell commands to verify their success or failure.
- Always check whether a file or directory exists with the **-f** option.

**NOTE**
*This assumes that all the backup files are kept in the same directory. You may want to modify this such that the directory structure of the original database files is maintained. You also need to determine whether you want to copy all data files to one disk, to more than one disk, or to tape, and customize the scripts accordingly.*

The scripts **dbbackup**, **dbbackup_begin**, and **dbexport_begin** are described below.

# dbbackup

Following is the main backup script. It reads the backup schedule and calls scripts to take hot and cold backups and exports.

```
#! /bin/sh
#
# name          $TOOLS/backup/dbbackup
# modified      11/4/97 Ravi Krishnamurthy
# Note: $TOOLS variable is set to the directory where all system
# administration scripts are present.
#
# purpose    Perform a backup of a database.
#
# usage         $TOOLS/backup/dbbackup <dbname>
# parameters    $1=dbname
#
#               Calls $TOOLS/db_admin/backup/common/crontab.env
#                     to set required environment variables
#         Calls $TOOLS/backup/dbbackup_begin or

#                     $TOOLS/backup/dbexport_begin
#                     depending on the schedule
#
# .........................................................
# set local variables: Files to log messages, errors, etc.
# .........................................................
BEGIN_JOB="`date`"
ERRMSG="Usage: `basename $0` <dbname>"

if [ "$1" ]
then DBNAME=$1
else echo $ERRMSG
     exit
fi

LOGDIR="$TOOLS/db_admin/db_${DBNAME}/log"

LOGFILE="${LOGDIR}/backup_`date '+%y%m%d'`.log"
ERRFILE="${LOGDIR}/backup_`date '+%y%m%d'`.err"
ERRFILE2="${LOGDIR}/backup_`date '+%y%m%d'`_old.err"
MSGFILE="${LOGDIR}/backup_`date '+%y%m%d'`.msg"

#
# .........................................................
# set environment
# .........................................................

# This should define ORACLE_HOME, ORACLE_SID, PATH, BACKUPDIR
# BACKUPDIROLD, EXPORTDIR, EXPORTDIROLD, ARCOLD
#
. $TOOLS/db_admin/common/crontab.env $DBNAME


# ADMIN_FILE is a file that can be used to run some administrative commands
# on a given database. One such task could be changing a parameter in
# init<sid>.ora. Uncomment the line if required.
#
# ADMIN_FILE="$TOOLS/db_admin/db_$DBNAME/tools/${DBNAME}_backup_admin.sh"

#
# SCHED_FILE is the file containing backup schedule.  A typical line in
# this file is:
```

```
#
# V8iPROD Sun hot export /V8iPROD/db_management/restrict1.sh
#

# where V8iPROD is name of the database, Sun is for Sunday, hot is the
# backup type, and export is the additional backup procedure.  The last
# column is a special task you want to perform, for example cleanup
# of some files etc.
#
# JOBNAME is the current script.
# DBBACKUP_BEGIN is the backup script that performs hot or cold backup
# based on the schedule of the day.
# DBEXPORT_BEGIN is the script for exporting the database.
# dbbackup_begin and dbexport_begin are shown in this section.
#


SCHED_FILE="$TOOLS/db_admin/common/dbbackup_sched.dat"
JOBNAME="$TOOLS/backup/dbbackup"
DBBACKUP_BEGIN="$TOOLS/backup/dbbackup_begin"
DBEXPORT_BEGIN="$TOOLS/backup/dbexport_begin"
TODAY="`date`"
THIS_DAY="`date '+%a'`"
MSG="$DBNAME Backup succeeded at `date`"

# This has to be nawk for most platforms, except HP-UX
AWK=/usr/bin/nawk
# bdf works on HP-UX, df -k on Solaris 2.x, df on SunOS 4.x
# You might also want to add other options, like 'df -kF ufs' for Solaris.
DF="/usr/bin/df -k"

# ........................................................
# begin
# ........................................................
if [ -f "$ERRFILE" ]; then
  #
  # Save old log file
  #
  cat $ERRFILE >> $ERRFILE2
fi
#
# Read backup schedule
#
$AWK -v dbname=$DBNAME -v this_day=$THIS_DAY '{
    #
    # get a record
    #
    cmd=$0

    sizeofarray=split(cmd,rec," ")
    dbname2=rec[1]
    day_of_week=rec[2]
    backup=rec[3]
    export=rec[4]
    special_task=rec[5]

    if (( dbname2 == dbname ) && ( this_day == day_of_week ))
    print " " backup " " export " " special_task
```

```
}' $SCHED_FILE | while read BACKUP EXPORT SPECIAL_TASK
do

  #
  # Print all parameters before beginning backup.
  #
  PARAMETER_MSG="
\n..............................................................
\nBackup Job Parameters:
\n
\nDatabase Name = $DBNAME
\nBackup Type   = $BACKUP
\nExport Type   = $EXPORT
\nSpecial Task  = $SPECIAL_TASK
\n
\nEnvironment Variables:
\nORACLE_HOME   = $ORACLE_HOME
\nORACLE_SID    = $ORACLE_SID
\nPATH          = $PATH
\n..............................................................
\n
"
  echo $PARAMETER_MSG >> $LOGFILE 2> $ERRFILE
  echo $PARAMETER_MSG >> $MSGFILE
  $DF >> $LOGFILE 2> $ERRFILE
  echo " " >> $LOGFILE 2> $ERRFILE

  #
  # Backup
  #
  if [ "$BACKUP" != "nobackup" ]; then
    echo "................................." >> $LOGFILE 2>> $ERRFILE
    echo "Begin backup at `date`" >> $LOGFILE 2>> $ERRFILE
    echo "................................." >> $LOGFILE 2>> $ERRFILE
    $DBBACKUP_BEGIN $DBNAME $BACKUP $SPECIAL_TASK >> $LOGFILE 2>> $ERRFILE
    echo "$DBBACKUP_BEGIN $DBNAME $BACKUP $SPECIAL_TASK >> $LOGFILE 2>> $ERRFILE"

    echo
    echo
    echo "................................." >> $LOGFILE 2>> $ERRFILE
    echo "End backup at `date`" >> $LOGFILE 2>> $ERRFILE
    echo "................................." >> $LOGFILE 2>> $ERRFILE
  fi

  #
  # Export
  #
  if [ "$EXPORT" != "noexport" ]; then
    echo "................................." >> $LOGFILE 2>> $ERRFILE
    echo "Begin export at `date`" >> $LOGFILE 2>> $ERRFILE
    echo "................................." >> $LOGFILE 2>> $ERRFILE
    $DBEXPORT_BEGIN $DBNAME $EXPORT $SPECIAL_TASK >> $LOGFILE 2>> $ERRFILE
    echo "$DBEXPORT_BEGIN $DBNAME $EXPORT $SPECIAL_TASK >> $LOGFILE 2>> $ERRFILE"
    echo
    echo
    echo "................................." >> $LOGFILE 2>> $ERRFILE
    echo "End export at `date`" >> $LOGFILE 2>> $ERRFILE
    echo "................................." >> $LOGFILE 2>> $ERRFILE
  fi
```

```
echo " " >> $MSGFILE
echo "Backup log file errors and warnings:" >> $MSGFILE

echo " " >> $LOGFILE 2>> $ERRFILE
$DF >> $LOGFILE 2>> $ERRFILE
echo " " >> $LOGFILE 2>> $ERRFILE

#
# Errors
#
egrep -e error -e warning -e ORA- -e EXP- -e fatal $LOGFILE | grep -v "No errors."
>> $MSGFILE
ERRCNT=`egrep -e error -e ORA- -e EXP- -e fatal $LOGFILE | grep -c -v "No errors."`
egrep -e error -e warning -e ORA- -e EXP- -e fatal $ERRFILE | grep -v "Export
terminated successfully" >> $MSGFILE
ERRCNT2=`egrep -e error -e ORA- -e EXP- -e fatal $ERRFILE | grep -c -v "Export
terminated successfully"`
END_JOB="`date`"
if [ "$ERRCNT" -gt 0 -o "$ERRCNT2" -gt 0 ]
then MSG="$DBNAME backup failed at ${END_JOB}"

else MSG="$DBNAME backup succeeded at ${END_JOB}"
fi

echo " " >> $MSGFILE
echo "Log files: " >> $MSGFILE
echo "Log file=$LOGFILE" >> $MSGFILE
echo "Error file=$ERRFILE" >> $MSGFILE
echo "Message file=$MSGFILE" >> $MSGFILE

# Create database Space Report
# The space_report script should contain SQL statements needed to get
# information about the available space in the database. One example:
#
#    svrmgrl <<EOF
#    connect internal
#    spool <file_name>
#    select tablespace_name, sum(bytes) from dba_free_space
#     group by tablespace_name;
#    exit
# EOF
#
# Uncomment the next line if you have set up the script.

# $TOOLS/sql/space_report $DBNAME

#
# Send mail to all DBAs
# Uncomment the next line if you want a mail to be sent to all DBA's
# at the end of a backup job. We assume that a mailing list or alias
# "${DBNAME}_dbas" exists in your system. If not, modify the sender name
# appropriately. The mail command also may have to be changed depending
# on the platform.
#    /usr/bin/mailx -s "$MSG" ${DBNAME}_dbas < $MSGFILE

#
# Uncomment the next line if you have set the ADMIN_FILE variable.
#  . $ADMIN_FILE
done
```

# dbbackup_begin

```
#! /bin/sh
# name          $TOOLS/backup/dbbackup_begin
#
# purpose     Perform a backup of a database.
#
# usage         $TOOLS/backup/dbbackup_begin <dbname> <backup>
#               <special task>
#
# parameters    $1=dbname
#        $2=backup type
#        $3=special task
#
#
# ...........................................................
# set local variables
# ...........................................................
ERRMSG="
`basename $0`: syntax error:
    dbbackup_begin <dbname> <hot|cold|nobackup> <special task>.
"
#
# parameters
#
if [ "$1" ]
then DBNAME=$1
else echo $ERRMSG   >&2
     exit 1
fi
if [ "$2" ]
then BACKUP=$2
else echo $ERRMSG   >&2
     exit 1
fi
if [ "$3" ]
then SPECIAL_TASK=$3
else SPECIAL_TASK=" "
fi

#
# booleans
#
TRUE=0
FALSE=1
SHUTDOWN_FAILED_B=1
RESTART_FAILED_B=1

#
# local variables
#

JOBNAME="$TOOLS/backup/dbbackup_begin"
JOBNAME_SHORT="dbbackup_begin"
LOGDIR="$TOOLS/db_admin/db_$DBNAME/log/"
DBBACKUP="$LOGDIR/datafile_`date '+%y%m%d'`.log"
```

```
CTLFILES="$LOGDIR/control_`date '+%y%m%d'`.log"
ARCHLOGS="$LOGDIR/archlog_`date '+%y%m%d'`.log"
ALERTLOG="$LOGDIR/alertlog_`date '+%y%m%d'`.log"
SPECIALOG="$LOGDIR/special_`date '+%y%m%d'`.log"

# Location of these commands is system dependent
WALL="/usr/sbin/wall"
CKSUM="/bin/cksum"
CMP="/bin/cmp"

BANNER="$TOOLS/db_admin/db_${DBNAME}/banner/status"
CKSUM_SIZE_ERR="${JOBNAME_SHORT}: fatal error in cksum size comparison."
CKSUM_VALUE_ERR="${JOBNAME_SHORT}: fatal error in cksum value comparison."
CKSUM_VALUE_WAR="${JOBNAME_SHORT}: warning in cksum value comparison."
CMP_ERR="${JOBNAME_SHORT}: fatal error in cmp."
ARCERR="${JOBNAME_SHORT}: fatal error in archive log copy."
THISNODE=`uname -n`


# ........................................................
# begin
# ........................................................


#
# check for database online
# Using 'grep -w' so that database name is exactly matched
# *** grep in HP-UX 9.x doesn't have the '-w' switch ***
# You may have to change this as 'grep "ora_[a-z]*_${DBNAME}\$"'
#
STATUS=`ps -fu oracle | grep -w "ora_[a-z]*_${DBNAME}" `
if [ $? != 0 ]; then
   # There are no background processes running, or database is down
   if [ "$BACKUP" = "hot" ]; then
     # hot backup does not make sense.
     echo "${JOBNAME_SHORT}: Database is not online. Switching to cold backup"
     echo "${JOBNAME_SHORT}: Database is not online. Switching to cold backup">&2
     BACKUP="cold"
   else
     # for cold backup this is fine
     echo "${JOBNAME_SHORT}: Database is already down.  Continuing."
   fi
else
   # since database is already up
   if [ "$BACKUP" = "cold" ]; then

     #
     # broadcast shutdowns, write your own banners
     #
     # $WALL $TOOLS/db_admin/db_${DBNAME}/banner/shutdown_15min.banner
     # sleep 300
     # $WALL $TOOLS/db_admin/db_${DBNAME}/banner/shutdown_5min.banner
     # sleep 240
     # $WALL $TOOLS/db_admin/db_${DBNAME}/banner/shutdown_1min.banner
     # sleep 60
     #
     # shutdown using appropriate shutdown scripts
     # Before the shutdown ensure that the logfile being used is archived
     #
     echo "${JOBNAME_SHORT}: Shutting down immediate."
```

```
    svrmgrl >/dev/null <<EOF
    connect internal
    alter system switch logfile;
    shutdown immediate;
    exit
EOF
    # Using 'grep -w' so that database name is exactly matched
    # *** grep in HP-UX 9.x doesn't have the '-w' switch ***
    # You may have to change this as 'grep "ora_[a-z]*_${DBNAME}\$"'
    #
    STATUS=`ps -fu oracle | grep -w "ora_[a-z]*_${DBNAME}" `
    if [ $? = 0 ]; then
    echo "${JOBNAME_SHORT}: Error in database shutdown. Exiting."
    exit
    fi
    #
    # kill sqlnet processes
    #
    echo "${JOBNAME_SHORT}: killing sqlnet v2 processes."
    #
    # Using 'grep -w' so that database name is exactly matched
    # *** grep in HP-UX 9.x doesn't have the '-w' switch ***
    # You may have to change this as 'grep "oracle${DBNAME} ("'
    #
    PROCS=`ps -ef |grep -w oracle${DBNAME} |grep -v grep |awk '{print $2}'`
    if [ x$PROCS = x ]; then
    echo "${JOBNAME_SHORT}: no processes to kill"
    else
    echo "${JOBNAME_SHORT}: killing processes $PROCS"
    kill $PROCS
    fi
    echo " "
  fi
fi

if [ "$BACKUP" = "cold" ]; then
    echo "${JOBNAME_SHORT}: Starting up restrict."
    svrmgrl >/dev/null <<EOF
    connect internal
    startup mount restrict
    exit
EOF
    # Using 'grep -w' so that database name is exactly matched
    # *** grep in HP-UX 9.x doesn't have the '-w' switch ***
    # You may have to change this as 'grep "ora_[a-z]*_${DBNAME}\$"'
    #
    STATUS=`ps -fu oracle | grep -w "ora_[a-z]*_${DBNAME}" `
    if [ $? != 0 ]; then
    echo "${JOBNAME_SHORT}: Error in database startup. Exiting."
    exit
    fi

fi

# ..................................................................
# begin backup
# ..................................................................
#
# build database file list
```

```
#

echo "${JOBNAME_SHORT}: building dynamic parameter file."

if [ $BACKUP = "hot" ]; then
  svrmgrl >/dev/null <<EOF
  connect internal
  set termout off
  spool $DBBACKUP;
  select file_name,tablespace_name from sys.dba_data_files
  order by tablespace_name,file_name;

  spool off;
  exit;
EOF

else
  svrmgrl >/dev/null <<EOF
  connect internal
  set termout off
  spool $DBBACKUP;
  select name from v\$datafile;
  spool off;
  exit;
EOF

fi

svrmgrl >/dev/null <<EOF
connect internal
set termout off
spool $CTLFILES;
select name from v\$controlfile;
spool off;
spool $ARCHLOGS;
select value from v\$parameter where name='log_archive_dest';
spool off;
spool $ALERTLOG;
select value from v\$parameter where name='background_dump_dest';
spool off;
exit
EOF

# Check the dynamic parameter file size
if [ -z $DBBACKUP ]; then
   echo "${JOBNAME_SHORT}: fatal error during backup file creation.  Backup aborting."
   return
fi

#
# shutdown
#
if [ $BACKUP = "cold" ]; then
  echo "${JOBNAME_SHORT}: Shutting down immediate."
svrmgrl >/dev/null <<EOF
connect internal
```

```
shutdown immediate
exit
EOF

# Using 'grep -w' so that database name is exactly matched
# *** grep in HP-UX 9.x doesn't have the '-w' switch ***
# You may have to change this as 'grep "ora_[a-z]*_${DBNAME}\$"'
#
  STATUS=`ps -fu oracle | grep -w "ora_[a-z]*_${DBNAME}" `
  if [ $? = 0 ]; then
    echo "${JOBNAME_SHORT}: error in shutdown. Cold backup aborting."
    SHUTDOWN_FAILED_B="$TRUE"
  else
    echo "${JOBNAME_SHORT}: Database is shutdown."
    echo "${JOBNAME_SHORT}: move alert log."
    ALERT=`sed -e 's/[    ]*$//' -e '/selected\.$/d' \
     -e '/^---.*—$/d'  -e '/^VALUE/d' $ALERTLOG`
    mv ${ALERT}/alert_${DBNAME}.log \
    ${ALERT}/alert_${DBNAME}.log_`date '+%y%m%d'`
  fi

fi


#
# Begin backup
#
if [ $SHUTDOWN_FAILED_B = $FALSE ]; then
  echo " "
  echo "${JOBNAME_SHORT}:  Starting $BACKUP backup using $DBBACKUP..."
  #
  # Move BACKUPDIR to BACKUPDIROLD
    # Files from the old backup are moved to a different location
    # before starting another backup job.
    # If you have backed up these files to tape (recommended), you
    # might want to remove these files instead of moving.
  #
  if [ `ls ${BACKUPDIR} | wc -l` != 0 ]; then
    for FILE in ${BACKUPDIR}/*
    do
    mv $FILE $BACKUPDIROLD
    done
  fi
  #
  # Make a backup copy of alert log
  #

  if [ $BACKUP = "cold" ]; then
   cp ${ALERT}/alert_${DBNAME}.log_`date '+%y%m%d'` \
   ${BACKUPDIR}
  fi
  #
  # check hot backup status
  #
  if  [ $BACKUP = "hot" ]; then
    svrmgrl <<EOF
    connect internal
    select * from v\$backup;
    exit
```

```
EOF
  fi
 #
 # begin reading dynamic parameter file
 #
 if [ $BACKUP = "hot" ]; then
   SED="sed -e '/selected\.$/d' -e '/^---.*-$/d'  -e '/^FILE_NAME/d' \
   $DBBACKUP"
 else
   SED="sed -e '/selected\.$/d' -e '/^---.*-$/d'  -e '/^NAME/d' $DBBACKUP"
 fi

 eval $SED | while read FILE TABLESPACE
 do
   if [ $BACKUP = "hot" ]; then
     svrmgrl <<EOF
     connect internal
     alter tablespace $TABLESPACE begin backup;
     exit
EOF
   fi
   #
   # copy a database file
   #

   echo "${JOBNAME_SHORT}: cp $FILE $BACKUPDIR"
   DATAFILE=`basename $FILE`

   # It is possible that database files under different directories have the
   # same name. We have to take care that we don't accidentally overwrite
   # a file because of this. One possible way to do this is:
   #    if [ -f ${BACKUPDIR}/${DATAFILE} ]; then
   #        NEWNAME=`dirname $FILE | tr / _`

   #        cp $FILE ${BACKUPDIR}/${DATAFILE}${NEWNAME}
   #    fi

   cp $FILE $BACKUPDIR
   STATUS=$?
   if [ "$STATUS" != 0 ]; then
     echo  "${JOBNAME_SHORT}: error during file copy $FILE."
   fi
   if [ $BACKUP = "hot" ]; then
     echo "${JOBNAME_SHORT}: $CKSUM $FILE $BACKUPDIR/$DATAFILE"
     $CKSUM $FILE $BACKUPDIR/$DATAFILE
     CKSUM_OUT=`$CKSUM $FILE $BACKUPDIR/$DATAFILE`
     echo $CKSUM_OUT | read VALUE1 SIZE1 NAME1 VALUE2 SIZE2 NAME2
     if [ "$VALUE1" != "$VALUE2" ]; then
       echo "$CKSUM_VALUE_WAR"
     fi
     if [ "$SIZE1" != "$SIZE2" ]; then
       echo "$CKSUM_SIZE_ERR"
     fi
   else
     echo "${JOBNAME_SHORT}: $CMP $FILE $BACKUPDIR/$DATAFILE"
     $CMP $FILE $BACKUPDIR/$DATAFILE
     STATUS="$?"
     if [ "$STATUS" != 0 ]; then
```

```
        echo "$CMP_ERR"
      fi
    fi
    if [ $BACKUP = "hot" ]; then
      svrmgrl <<EOF
      connect internal
      alter tablespace $TABLESPACE end backup;
      exit
EOF
    fi
  done
  #
  # check hot backup status
  #
  if  [ $BACKUP = "hot" ]; then
    svrmgrl <<EOF
    connect internal
    select * from v\$backup;
    exit
EOF
  fi


  #
  # Backup control files
  #
    #
    # control files
    #
 if [ $BACKUP = "hot" ]; then
    echo "${JOBNAME_SHORT}: backing up controlfile to \
        ${BACKUPDIR}/${DBNAME}_control01.ctl"
    svrmgrl <<EOF
    connect internal
    alter database backup controlfile to '${BACKUPDIR}/control01.ctl';
    exit
EOF
    #
  else
    sed -e '/rows selected\.$/d' -e '/^---.*-$/d'  -e '/^NAME/d' $CTLFILES \
    | while read FILE
    do
      #
      # copy a control file
      #
      echo "${JOBNAME_SHORT}: cp $FILE $BACKUPDIR"
      DATAFILE=`basename $FILE`

      # It is possible that control files under different directories have the
      # same name. We have to take care that we don't accidentally overwrite
      # a file because of this. One possible way to do this is:
      #   if [ -f ${BACKUPDIR}/${DATAFILE} ]; then
      #     NEWNAME=`dirname $FILE | tr / _`
      #     cp $FILE ${BACKUPDIR}/${DATAFILE}${NEWNAME}
      #   fi

      cp $FILE $BACKUPDIR
      STATUS=$?
      if [ "$STATUS" != 0 ]; then
```

```
        echo  "${JOBNAME_SHORT}: error during file copy $FILE."
      fi
      echo "${JOBNAME_SHORT}: $CMP $FILE $BACKUPDIR/$DATAFILE"
      $CMP $FILE $BACKUPDIR/$DATAFILE
      STATUS="$?"
      if [ "$STATUS" != 0 ]; then
         echo "$CMP_ERR"
      fi
    done

  fi

  #
  # archive logs
  #
  # Make sure that you backup archive logs only and not the online
  # redo logs.
  #
  # force a log switch
  #
  if [ $BACKUP = "hot" ]; then
    svrmgrl <<EOF
    connect internal
    alter system switch logfile;
    exit
EOF
  # Sleep for sometime, till the log file is copied.
  sleep 120
  fi
  # copy archive logs
  #
  ARC=`sed -e 's/[    ]*$//' -e '/selected\.$/d' \
    -e '/^---.*-$/d'  -e '/^VALUE/d' $ARCHLOGS`
  if [ -f $ARCOLD/* ]; then
   echo " "
   echo "${JOBNAME_SHORT}: Delete previous backup archive logs..."
   for I in $ARCOLD/*
     do
      ls -l $I
       ARCNAME=`basename $I`
       rm $ARCOLD/$ARCNAME
       STATUS="$?"
       if [ "$STATUS" != 0 ]; then
        echo "${JOBNAME_SHORT}: error deleting old archive log: $ARCOLD/$ARCNAME"
       fi
    done
  else    echo " "
          echo "${JOBNAME_SHORT}: No old archive logs to delete."
  fi

  if [ -f $ARC/* ]; then
    echo " "
    echo "${JOBNAME_SHORT}: Copying archive logs..."
    for I in $ARC/*
      do

        ls -l $I
          ARCNAME=`basename $I`
```

```
         echo "${JOBNAME_SHORT}: cp $ARC/$ARCNAME $ARCOLD"
              cp $ARC/$ARCNAME $ARCOLD
       STATUS="$?"
              if [ "$STATUS" != 0 ]; then
                  echo "$ARCERR"
       fi
       echo "${JOBNAME_SHORT}: $CMP $ARC/$ARCNAME $ARCOLD/$ARCNAME"
       $CMP $ARC/$ARCNAME $ARCOLD/$ARCNAME
            STATUS="$?"
            if [ "$STATUS" != 0 ]; then
                echo "$CMP_ERR"
                echo "${JOBNAME_SHORT}: Archive log deletion skipped."
              else echo "${JOBNAME_SHORT}: $CKSUM $ARC/$ARCNAME $ARCOLD/$ARCNAME"
            $CKSUM $ARC/$ARCNAME $ARCOLD/$ARCNAME
              CKSUM_OUT=`$CKSUM $ARC/$ARCNAME $ARCOLD/$ARCNAME`
              echo $CKSUM_OUT | read VALUE1 SIZE1 NAME1 VALUE2 SIZE2 NAME2
              if [ "$VALUE1" != "$VALUE2" -o "$SIZE1" != "$SIZE2" ]; then
                  echo "$DIFFERR"
                  echo "${JOBNAME_SHORT}: Archive log deletion skipped."
                else rm $ARC/$ARCNAME
                  if [ $? != 0 ]; then
                      echo "${JOBNAME_SHORT}: Archive deletion failed."
                  fi
                fi
            fi
        done
   else echo "${JOBNAME_SHORT}: Found no archives to copy."
   fi


if [ $BACKUP = "cold" ]; then
  # startup
  #
    #
    # dba mode tasks
    #
    if [ "$SPECIAL_TASK" != " " ]; then
        echo "${JOBNAME_SHORT}: Running DBA mode task..."

      svrmgrl >/dev/null <<EOF
      connect internal
      startup restrict
      exit

EOF
      STATUS=`ps -fu oracle | grep -w "ora_[a-z]*_${DBNAME}"`
      if [ $? != 0 ]; then
        echo "${JOBNAME_SHORT}: error in database startup."  >&2
        echo "Skipping ${SPECIAL_TASK}."  >&2
      else
          . ${SPECIAL_TASK} > $SPECIALOG 2>&1

      svrmgrl >/dev/null <<EOF
      connect internal
      shutdown
      exit
EOF
      fi
```

```
    fi
     #
     # startup
     #
    svrmgrl >/dev/null <<EOF
    connect internal
    startup mount;
    alter database archivelog;
    alter database open;
    exit
EOF
    STATUS=`ps -fu oracle | grep -w "ora_[a-z]*_${DBNAME}" `
    if [ $? != 0 ]; then
      echo "${JOBNAME_SHORT}: error in database startup."
      echo "${JOBNAME_SHORT}: error in database startup."  >&2
      RESTART_FAILED_B=0
    else
      echo "${JOBNAME_SHORT}: Database restarted."
      # $WALL $TOOLS/db_admin/db_${DBNAME}/banner/db_online.banner
    fi
  fi

fi
```

# dbexport_begin

```
#! /bin/sh
# name          $TOOLS/backup/dbexport_begin
#
# purpose       Perform a backup of a database.
#
# usage         $TOOLS/backup/dbexport_begin <dbname>
#               <export> <special task>
#
# parameters    $1=dbname
#         $2=export
#         $3=special task
#
#
# ..............................................................
# local variables
# ..............................................................
ERRMSG='
$0: syntax error:
    dbexport_begin <dbname> <export|noexport> <special task>.
'
#
# parameters
#
if [ "$1" ]
then DBNAME=$1
export DBNAME
else echo $ERRMSG  >&2
     exit 1
fi
if [ "$2" ]
```

```
then EXPORT=$2
else echo $ERRMSG  >&2
     exit 1
fi
if [ "$3" ]
then SPECIAL_TASK=$3
else SPECIAL_TASK=" "
fi


#
# booleans
#
TRUE=0
FALSE=1
SHUTDOWN_FAILED_B=1
RESTART_FAILED_B=1


#
# local variables
#

JOBNAME="$TOOLS/backup/dbexport_begin"
JOBNAME_SHORT="dbexport_begin"


CMP="/bin/cmp"
PARFILE="$TOOLS/db_admin/db_$DBNAME/export.par"
CMP_ERR="${JOBNAME_SHORT}: fatal error in cmp."
EXPERR="${JOBNAME_SHORT}: fatal error in export file copy."


# ..........................................................
# begin
# ..........................................................


#
# check for database online
# Using 'grep -w' so that database name is exactly matched
# *** grep in HP-UX 9.x doesn't have the '-w' switch ***
# You may have to change this as 'grep "ora_[a-z]*_${DBNAME}\$"'
#
STATUS=`ps -fu oracle | grep -w "ora_[a-z]*_${DBNAME}" `
if [ $? != 0 ]; then
  echo "${JOBNAME_SHORT}: error - database not online."
  echo "${JOBNAME_SHORT}: error - database not online."  >&2
  echo "${JOBNAME_SHORT}: process listing is to follow..."  >&2
  echo "${JOBNAME_SHORT}: ps -fu oracle | grep -w \"ora_[a-z]*_$DBNAME\""  >&2
  ps -fu oracle | grep -w "ora_[a-z]*_${DBNAME}"  >&2
  echo "${JOBNAME_SHORT}: exiting."  >&2
  exit 1
fi


# ..........................................................
# Export
# ..........................................................
echo " "
echo "${JOBNAME_SHORT}: List previous export files..."
```

```
ls -l $EXPORTDIR/${DBNAME}.exp*
ls -l $EXPORTDIROLD/${DBNAME}.exp*

#
# delete old export
#
if [ -f $EXPORTDIROLD/${DBNAME}.exp_old ]; then
  rm $EXPORTDIROLD/${DBNAME}.exp_old
  if [ $? != 0 ]; then
    echo "${JOBNAME_SHORT}: error deleting previous export."
  else
    echo "${JOBNAME_SHORT}: Deleted previous export file."
  fi
else echo "${JOBNAME_SHORT}: Found no previous export file."
fi
#
# copy current export to old
#
if [ -f $EXPORTDIR/${DBNAME}.exp ]; then
  chmod 644 $EXPORTDIR/${DBNAME}.exp
  echo "${JOBNAME_SHORT}: cp $EXPORTDIR/${DBNAME}.exp $EXPORTDIROLD"
  cp $EXPORTDIR/${DBNAME}.exp $EXPORTDIROLD
  if [ $? != 0 ]; then
    echo "$EXPERR"
  else echo "${JOBNAME_SHORT}: $CMP $EXPORTDIR/${DBNAME}.exp
$EXPORTDIROLD/${DBNAME}.exp"
    $CMP $EXPORTDIR/${DBNAME}.exp $EXPORTDIROLD/${DBNAME}.exp
    STATUS="$?"
    if [ "$STATUS" != 0 ]; then
      echo "$CMP_ERR"
    fi
    echo "${JOBNAME_SHORT}: mv ${EXPORTDIROLD}/${DBNAME}.exp
${EXPORTDIROLD}/${DBNAME}.exp_old"
    mv ${EXPORTDIROLD}/${DBNAME}.exp ${EXPORTDIROLD}/${DBNAME}.exp_old
    if [ $? != 0 ]; then
      echo "$EXPERR"
    fi
    rm $EXPORTDIR/${DBNAME}.exp
    if [ $? != 0 ]; then
      echo "${JOBNAME_SHORT}: error deleting export file."
      exit
    fi
  fi
else echo "${JOBNAME_SHORT}: Found no current export file to copy."
fi

#
# Begin export
#
exp parfile=$PARFILE
echo " "
echo "${JOBNAME_SHORT}: Export complete.  "
ls -l $EXPORTDIR/${DBNAME}.exp*
ls -l $EXPORTDIROLD/${DBNAME}.exp*
```

## dbbackup_sched.dat

This section presents a sample schedule file that describes the schedule for taking physical and logical backups. A typical line in this file has the following format:

```
V8iPROD    Sat    cold    export    /bugdev/db_management/bug_restrict1.sh
```

where *V8iPROD* is the name of the database, *Sat* is the day of the week, *cold* is the physical backup type (hot or cold), and *export* is the logical backup procedure. You can specify a shell script in the last column to perform additional administrative tasks, such as deleting certain files.

```
bkup_tst Sun hot export
bkup_tst Mon hot export
bkup_tst Tue hot export
bkup_tst Wed hot export
bkup_tst Thu hot export
bkup_tst Fri cold export
bkup_tst Sat nobackup export
V8iPROD Sun hot noexport
V8iPROD Mon hot noexport
V8iPROD Tue hot noexport
V8iPROD Wed hot noexport
V8iPROD Thu hot noexport
V8iPROD Fri cold export /bugdev/db_management/bug_restrict1.sh
V8iPROD Sat cold export /bugdev/db_management/bug_restrict1.sh
```

You should modify this schedule and the backup procedures to fit your business needs. For example, in addition to the full export backup, you might want to take a USER or TABLE mode export as well. Or you might want to take a COMPLETE export once a week and an INCREMENTAL export every night.

## crontab.env

```
#!/bin/sh
#
# This is a sample file only. Please customize this file
#
# Name:              crontab.env
#
# purpose          Sets environment variables for a given database
#                  that needs to be backed up or exported. This file
#                  also supplies directory information

if [ $# -lt 1 ]
then
```

```
echo "Database name required"
exit 1
fi

# Variables to be set for each database.
# ORACLE_HOME, ORACLE_SID, PATH
# EXPORTDIROLD (Directory to move old export files)
# EXPORTDIR (Directory for keeping exporting files)
# BACKUPDIR (Directory for keeping backup files)
# BACKUPDIROLD (Directory for moving old backup files - may not be required
#            if you have moved old backups to tapes)
# ARCOLD (Directory for keeping archive log files)

case $1 in
    bkup_tst) ORACLE_HOME=/home3/oradata/app/oracle/product/7.3.2;
         ORACLE_SID=bkup_tst;
         PATH=/usr/bin:/usr/sbin:$ORACLE_HOME/bin ;
         EXPORTDIROLD=/home3/oracle/bkup/db_${1}/old_export.dir;
         EXPORTDIR=/home3/oracle/bkup/db_${1}/export.dir;
         BACKUPDIR=/home3/oracle/bkup/db_${1}/backup.dir;
         BACKUPDIROLD=/home3/oracle/bkup/db_${1}/old_backup.dir;
         ARCOLD=/home3/oracle/bkup/db_${1}/archive.dir;
            ;;

    *)      echo "No such database";
         exit 1 ;;
esac

export ORACLE_HOME ORACLE_SID PATH EXPORTDIR EXPORTDIROLD
export BACKUPDIR BACKUPDIROLD ARCOLD
```

# sample_run.log

```
File name: sample_run.log
Description: A log file generated during a sample run of the scripts.

.................................................................
Backup Job Parameters:

Database Name = bkup_tst
Backup Type = cold
Export Type = noexport
Special Task =

Environment Variables:
ORACLE_HOME = /home3/oradata/app/oracle/product/7.3.2
ORACLE_SID = bkup_tst
PATH = /usr/bin:/usr/sbin:/home3/oradata/app/oracle/product/7.3.2/bin
```

```
. . . . . . . . . . . . . . . . . . . . . . . . . . . . . . . . . . . . . . . . . . . . . . . . . . . . . . . . . . .
Filesystem                kbytes      used    avail capacity  Mounted on
/dev/dsk/c0t0d0s0          67815     41908    19127     69%   /
/dev/dsk/c0t0d0s6         336863    202467   100716     67%   /usr
/proc                         0         0        0      0%    /proc
fd                            0         0        0      0%    /dev/fd
/dev/dsk/c0t0d0s5         28959      9343    16726     36%    /var
/dev/dsk/c0t0d0s7       1389366    367679   882757     30%    /home1
swap                     170976       656   170320      1%    /tmp
/dev/md/dsk/d0          3895250    458964  3046766     14%    /home2
/dev/md/dsk/d1          1947253   1335645   416888     77%    /home3
/dev/dsk/c1t11d0s6      1952573   1100733   656590     63%    /home4


. . . . . . . . . . . . . . . . . . . . . . . . . . . . . . . . . . .
Begin backup at Sat May 17 14:22:17 IST 1997
. . . . . . . . . . . . . . . . . . . . . . . . . . . . . . . . . . .
dbbackup_begin: Database is already down.  Continuing.
dbbackup_begin: Starting up restrict.
dbbackup_begin: building dynamic parameter file.
dbbackup_begin: Shutting down immediate.
dbbackup_begin: Database is shutdown.
dbbackup_begin: move alert log.

dbbackup_begin:  Starting cold backup using
/home3/oracle/bkup/db_admin/db_bkup_tst/log//datafile_970517.log...
dbbackup_begin: cp /home3/oradata/bkup_tst/system01.dbf
/home3/oracle/bkup/db_bkup_tst/backup.dir
dbbackup_begin: /bin/cmp /home3/oradata/bkup_tst/system01.dbf
/home3/oracle/bkup/db_bkup_tst/backup.dir/system01.dbf
dbbackup_begin: cp /home3/oradata/bkup_tst/rbs01.dbf
/home3/oracle/bkup/db_bkup_tst/backup.dir
dbbackup_begin: /bin/cmp /home3/oradata/bkup_tst/rbs01.dbf
/home3/oracle/bkup/db_bkup_tst/backup.dir/rbs01.dbf
dbbackup_begin: cp /home3/oradata/bkup_tst/temp01.dbf
/home3/oracle/bkup/db_bkup_tst/backup.dir

dbbackup_begin: /bin/cmp /home3/oradata/bkup_tst/temp01.dbf
/home3/oracle/bkup/db_bkup_tst/backup.dir/temp01.dbf
dbbackup_begin: cp /home3/oradata/bkup_tst/tools01.dbf
/home3/oracle/bkup/db_bkup_tst/backup.dir
dbbackup_begin: /bin/cmp /home3/oradata/bkup_tst/tools01.dbf
/home3/oracle/bkup/db_bkup_tst/backup.dir/tools01.dbf
dbbackup_begin: cp /home3/oradata/bkup_tst/users01.dbf
/home3/oracle/bkup/db_bkup_tst/backup.dir
dbbackup_begin: /bin/cmp /home3/oradata/bkup_tst/users01.dbf
/home3/oracle/bkup/db_bkup_tst/backup.dir/users01.dbf
dbbackup_begin: cp /home3/oradata/bkup_tst/tools02.dbf
/home3/oracle/bkup/db_bkup_tst/backup.dir
dbbackup_begin: /bin/cmp /home3/oradata/bkup_tst/tools02.dbf
/home3/oracle/bkup/db_bkup_tst/backup.dir/tools02.dbf
```

```
dbbackup_begin: cp /home3/oradata/bkup_tst/control01.ctl
/home3/oracle/bkup/db_bkup_tst/backup.dir
dbbackup_begin: /bin/cmp /home3/oradata/bkup_tst/control01.ctl
/home3/oracle/bkup/db_bkup_tst/backup.dir/control01.ctl
dbbackup_begin: cp /home3/oradata/bkup_tst/control02.ctl
/home3/oracle/bkup/db_bkup_tst/backup.dir
dbbackup_begin: /bin/cmp /home3/oradata/bkup_tst/control02.ctl
/home3/oracle/bkup/db_bkup_tst/backup.dir/control02.ctl
dbbackup_begin: cp /home3/oradata/bkup_tst/control03.ctl
/home3/oracle/bkup/db_bkup_tst/backup.dir
dbbackup_begin: /bin/cmp /home3/oradata/bkup_tst/control03.ctl
/home3/oracle/bkup/db_bkup_tst/backup.dir/control03.ctl

dbbackup_begin: Delete previous backup archive logs...
-rw-r-----   1 oracle   dba          50688 May 17 14:07
/home3/oracle/bkup/db_bkup_tst/archive.dir/1_88.dbf

dbbackup_begin: Copying archive logs...
-rw-r-----   1 oracle   dba           5120 May 17 14:12
/home3/oradata/bkup_tst/archlog/1_89.dbf
dbbackup_begin: cp /home3/oradata/bkup_tst/archlog/1_89.dbf
/home3/oracle/bkup/db_bkup_tst/archive.dir
dbbackup_begin: /bin/cmp /home3/oradata/bkup_tst/archlog/1_89.dbf
/home3/oracle/bkup/db_bkup_tst/archive.dir/1_89.dbf
dbbackup_begin: /bin/cksum /home3/oradata/bkup_tst/archlog/1_89.dbf
/home3/oracle/bkup/db_bkup_tst/archive.dir/1_89.dbf
3991599986    5120    /home3/oradata/bkup_tst/archlog/1_89.dbf
3991599986    5120    /home3/oracle/bkup/db_bkup_tst/archive.dir/1_89.dbf
dbbackup_begin: Database restarted.

`  ...................................
End backup at Sat May 17 14:22:49 IST 1997
...................................
```

| Filesystem | kbytes | used | avail | capacity | Mounted on |
|---|---|---|---|---|---|
| /dev/dsk/c0t0d0s0 | 67815 | 41908 | 19127 | 69% | / |
| /dev/dsk/c0t0d0s6 | 336863 | 202467 | 100716 | 67% | /usr |
| /proc | 0 | 0 | 0 | 0% | /proc |
| fd | 0 | 0 | 0 | 0% | /dev/fd |
| /dev/dsk/c0t0d0s5 | 28959 | 9343 | 16726 | 36% | /var |
| /dev/dsk/c0t0d0s7 | 1389366 | 367679 | 882757 | 30% | /home1 |
| swap | 163064 | 664 | 162400 | 1% | /tmp |
| /dev/md/dsk/d0 | 3895250 | 458964 | 3046766 | 14% | /home2 |
| /dev/md/dsk/d1 | 1947253 | 1337664 | 414869 | 77% | /home3 |
| /dev/dsk/c1t11d0s6 | 1952573 | 1100733 | 656590 | 63% | /home4 |

Remember, building a robust backup procedure will help you reduce the mean time to recover (MTTR) during a failure.

# CHAPTER

## 6

## Recovery Principles

o understand recovery principles and strategies, you need to understand the underlying data structures used in recovery. This chapter is divided into three sections. First, we define the fundamental data structures of the Oracle RDBMS, followed by a detailed discussion of some of the basic concepts that relate to recovery. An overview of the contents of the control file, log files, and data files is given. Later, we shift our focus to the various recovery options provided by Oracle. We discuss the three main options of recovery—database, tablespace, and data file recovery. In addition to learning the syntax, you will also learn when and how to apply different recovery procedures, depending on the kind of failure. Chapter 7 talks about the Recovery Manager utility and various backup and recovery options it provides.

The final section is on *failure analysis*. In this section, we first discuss a survey that was done with several Oracle customers regarding system outages. The results show the mean time between failures (MTBF) of various systems and the mean time to recover (MTTR) when a failure occurs. When a production or a development database goes down, Oracle customers usually call Oracle Support Services and open a priority 1 Technical Assistance Request (TAR). An analysis was done on a sample of priority 1 TARs that shows how the databases are recovered (i.e., what kind of recovery method was chosen). The results of this analysis are given in detail. Based on this information and the real-life experience that we have gained while dealing with mission-critical applications, some recommendations are made on how to plan for a disaster recovery site.

# Definitions and Internal Recovery Concepts

The following definitions introduce some fundamental data structures that are used in recovery. Each definition is followed by a discussion or an example to make the concepts clear.

## Redo Generation and Estimation

As mentioned in Chapter 2, the redo log files contain changes made to the database. In this section, we will discuss some of the basic concepts, such as change vectors and redo records, that relate to redo. Some SQL scripts are also provided that help you estimate the amount of redo generated at your site. This is very important, because when you design a backup procedure to back up the archived redo log files, the frequency of this backup depends on it.

## Change Vector

A *change vector* describes a single change made to any single block in the database. Among other information, the change vector contains a *version number*, the operation code of the transaction, and the address of the data block that this change belongs to. The version number is copied from the data block when the change vector is constructed. During recovery, Oracle reads the change vector and applies the change to the appropriate data block. When a change vector is applied to the data block, the data block's version number is incremented by 1.

**NOTE**
*A data block can belong to a data segment, an index segment, or a rollback segment in the database. Redo is not generated for temporary segments.*

## Redo Record and Its Contents

A *redo record* is a group of change vectors describing a single atomic change to the database. Some transactions may generate multiple redo records, and each redo record can have a collection of change vectors. Recovery guarantees that all or none of the change vectors of a redo record are applied, no matter what type of system failure occurs. In other words, a *transaction* is the unit of recovery, so, as a unit, all changes are either applied or not applied.

To illustrate the creation of change vectors and redo records, consider the following example transaction, which updates one record in the EMP table:

```
SQL> update emp set empno=1234 where empno = 9999;
```

When this **update** statement is executed, the sequence of operations is as follows:

1. Change vectors of the redo record are generated.

2. The redo record is saved in a redo log buffer (which eventually gets flushed to the redo log file on disk).

3. The change vectors are applied to the data blocks.

In the example we are using here, the redo record generated in step 1 contains three change vectors:

1. The transaction has to write an undo entry to the transaction table of the rollback segment (refer to Chapter 2 for the contents of a rollback segment). Since the transaction table is also another block in the database, entering an undo entry would modify this block and thus generate redo. So, the first change vector of the redo record contains the change for the transaction table.

**2.** Next, the old value of EMPNO (which is 9999) has to be stored in a block within the rollback segment. This is another modification to a block within the database and therefore generates redo. So, the second change vector contains redo for the undo block.

**3.** The last and most obvious change is the change to the data block where the EMPNO value is changed to 1234. So, the third change vector is the redo for the data block.

To summarize, the redo record for this transaction contains three change vectors:

■ Change to the transaction table of the rollback segment

■ Change to the rollback segment data block

■ Change to the data segment block belonging to the EMP table

Of course, this may not be the only redo record generated. If, for example, the EMP table has an index on the EMPNO column, then the index key needs to be modified as well and will generate a second redo record (also containing multiple change vectors). Similarly, if a **commit** statement is issued after this transaction, a third redo record will be created. So, if you lose the data files and have to restore a backup and roll forward, since the unit of recovery is a transaction, *all* three of these redo records will be applied to keep the database consistent, or none will be applied at all.

Starting with Oracle7, some optimization has been done to generate less redo. If more space is available in the rollback segment block, the transaction uses it without modifying the transaction table again. This way, fewer change vectors are created.

## Estimating the Amount of Redo

To estimate how much redo is generated at your site, use the following two procedures. The first procedure estimates the amount of redo generated in one day; the second procedure gives you the amount of redo generated for a specific transaction. Knowing this information and the transaction rate, you can calculate the amount of redo generated at your site.

**Amount of Redo per Day**    The **archive log list** command gives information regarding the online log sequence number. For example,

```
SQL> archive log list
Database log mode               ARCHIVELOG
Automatic archival              ENABLED
Archive destination             D:\ORACLE\ORADATA\TEST\ARCHIVE
Oldest online log sequence      1742
Next log sequence to archive    1744
Current log sequence            1744
```

Issuing this command on two consecutive days at the same time each day and taking the difference between the *current log sequence* numbers will give a general idea of how many redo log files are created in 24 hours. Multiply that number by the redo log file size to estimate the amount of redo generated at your site (in bytes).

**Amount of Redo per Transaction**    This procedure calculates the amount of redo generated for a particular transaction. You can then multiply this value by the transaction rate (the number of transactions that are run on the database in 24 hours) to estimate the amount of redo generated at your site, in bytes. Use the following steps to estimate the amount of redo generated by a specific transaction.

1. Run the following script before executing your transaction. This will mark the redo's "begin value" (taken from the V$SYSSTAT view) before you run the transaction in step 2.

```
SQL> column name format a40
   SQL> column redo_i new_value redo
   SQL> set termout off
   SQL> select value redo_i from v$sysstat where statistic#=71;
      REDO_I
   ---------
       3460
```

2. Execute your transaction. At this time, we assume that this is the only transaction that is running in your database.

3. Run the following script, which gives the difference between the "end value" of the redo and the "begin value" taken from step 1. This number gives you the amount of redo generated (in bytes) by running the transaction in step 2.

```
SQL> select (value - &redo) redo from v$sysstat where statistic#=71;
   old   1: select (value - &redo) redo from v$sysstat where statistic#=71
   new   1: select (value -    3460) redo from v$sysstat where statistic#=71
       REDO
   ---------
        719
```

Note that the *statistic#* in step 3 can change in future releases of Oracle.

# System Change Number (SCN)

The *System Change Number* (or simply the *SCN*) is a crucial data structure that defines a committed version of the database at a precise moment in time. When a transaction commits, it is assigned an SCN that uniquely identifies the transaction. SCNs provide Oracle's internal clock mechanism and can be viewed as logical clocks, but must not be confused with the system clock—think of SCNs as a way to provide read-consistent *snapshots* of the database that are crucial for recovery operations (Oracle performs recovery based on SCNs only). For example, if transaction 1 does an UPDATE and commits, it will be assigned an SCN value of, say, 20. The next transaction that commits five minutes later will receive an SCN value of 21 or greater. If the second transaction receives a higher value than 21—say, 25—that means between the two transactions, Oracle has done some work internally (for example, block cleanout) that has used SCNs 21 through 24. So, SCNs are guaranteed to be unique to a database and increase with time, but may not be sequential. SCN values never get reset to zero unless the database is re-created. You don't need to worry about running out of SCNs—even if you were to commit 16,000 transactions per second, it would take more than 500 years to run out of SCN numbers.

SCNs play a very important role in distributed transactions. When a distributed transaction is committed, the highest SCN of all the database instances involved is given to the distributed transaction. Thus, there will never be a problem with read consistency. For example, if database 1 has an SCN value of 200 (i.e., the next transaction that commits in this database gets an SCN value of 200), and database 2 has an SCN value of 20,000, and if you do a distributed transaction from database 1 and commit, this transaction will be given an SCN value of 20,000 instead of 200. This means that for some databases (involved in distributed transactions), the SCN value can jump from one value to another, much higher value.

In times of high activity, multiple transactions may commit simultaneously. Then, the LGWR process may write multiple commit records to the online redo log file for each write I/O. These are known as *group commits*. (Using group commits has some effects on time-based recovery and will be discussed in Chapter 10.)

While using the PARALLEL SERVER option, since there are multiple instances accessing the same database, Oracle maintains some information in the SGA of each instance for controlling the allocation of redo and SCNs. Each instance stores a *local SCN* value, and there is one *global SCN* value for all the instances. This global SCN is protected by a global lock. Every time a transaction does a commit on any instance, it updates the global SCN and copies the global SCN value to the local SCN. This way, the SCN value is still unique to the database, and two transactions running on two different instances will never get the same SCN value.

SCNs are used in transaction tables, block headers, control files, data file headers, and redo records. Let's now look at some of the important data structures that store SCNs in the redo log files (low and high SCNs), data files (offline normal SCNs and checkpoint SCNs), and the control file (stop SCNs).

## Low and High SCN

Every redo log file has a *log sequence number* to identify that file uniquely. When a redo log file gets filled with redo records, it gets closed and a new redo log file is opened. The redo log file is marked with a *low SCN*, which is one greater than the *high SCN* of the previous log file, and the high SCN value of the current log is set to infinity, since Oracle doesn't know how many SCNs will be recorded in the current log file. The low SCN represents the lowest value of the change number that is stored in that log file. Similarly, when the log file gets closed, the high SCN marker is set to the highest SCN recorded in the log file. This information can be obtained by selecting from the V$LOG_HISTORY view:

```
SQL> select * from v$log_history where rownum < 3;
    RECID      STAMP    THREAD# SEQUENCE# FIRST_CHANGE# FIRST_TIM NEXT_CHANGE#
--------- ---------- --------- --------- ------------- --------- ------------
        1 316115149         1         1             1 01-NOV-97          108
        2 316115154         1         2           108 01-NOV-97          130
```

In this example, where we have used a newly created database, log sequence number 1 belongs to thread number 1 (its name and time that the log file was created are also given). The lowest SCN recorded in this log file is 1 and the highest SCN is 108. Note that since the log files are used in a cyclic order, the high SCN of log sequence 1 is equal to the low SCN of log sequence 2. If any one of these changes is required in the future to do recovery, Oracle will request that this log file be applied to roll forward the backup of the database.

### Offline Normal SCN

An *offline normal SCN* is an SCN that is kept in the data dictionary table **ts$** for each tablespace that is taken offline with the NORMAL option. When a tablespace is taken offline with the NORMAL option, a checkpoint is performed on all the data files that belong to the tablespace; at this point the offline normal SCN is assigned. The offline normal SCN is used by Oracle while bringing a tablespace online. This is especially useful while bringing a tablespace online after the database is opened with the RESETLOGS option (we will discuss the RESETLOGS option in greater detail later in this chapter).

The offline normal SCN will be zero if the tablespace is taken offline with the IMMEDIATE or TEMPORARY option. This way, you cannot bring the tablespace online after the database is opened with the RESETLOGS option.

There is an SCN value stored in every data file header, called the *checkpoint SCN*, which gets updated when a checkpoint is done on a data file. We will discuss this data structure in detail later in this chapter when we discuss checkpoint structures.

### Stop SCN

In the control file, corresponding to every data file, there is a *stop SCN* that is recorded. When a data file is online and any instance has the database open, the stop SCN for that corresponding data file will be set to infinity. When you take a tablespace offline, the stop SCN is recorded in the control file for each data file that belongs to the tablespace. This means that no redo will be generated for the data file after the stop SCN is allocated.

The stop SCN is used while doing media recovery to ensure that media recovery will end when recovery reaches an SCN value equal to the stop SCN of the data file when recovering an offline data file.

# Redo Threads

An online redo log file contains the changes made to the database. The redo records that are created by modifying data are stored in these online log files. Online log files are essential for normal operation of the database. As discussed in Chapter 2, each instance of an Oracle database has at least two online redo log groups; a *redo log group* contains one or more online log files (known as members) that are identical and reside on different disk drives. Oracle recommends maintaining at least two members for each group to protect against online redo log file failures.

A collection of online redo log files is referred to as a *thread of redo log files.* Each instance records changes in its own set of online log files or its own thread of redo. If you have a single-instance database, Oracle creates the first thread of redo log files when you create the database. If you are using the PARALLEL SERVER option, you have to create a thread of redo log files for each instance (except for the first one). Each thread is uniquely identified by a thread number. After creating a thread of redo log files, you have to enable the thread using the PUBLIC or PRIVATE option. The PUBLIC option indicates that the redo thread may be used by any instance. If the keyword PUBLIC is omitted, the thread is enabled PRIVATE. This means that you have to specifically include the **init.ora** parameter THREAD = *n,* where *n* is the thread number, to use the thread. Every instance that opens a database needs a thread of redo log files. The following example illustrates how to create a thread of redo log files.

Let's assume that instance A has opened the database and uses thread 1. Thread 1 has three log groups with one member each. From instance A, we issue the following commands in SQL to create a second thread:

```
SQL> alter database add logfile thread 2 group 3 c:\oracle\oradata\test\log3.ora' size 200k;
Database altered.
SQL> alter database add logfile thread 2 group 4 'c:\ oracle\oradata\test\log4.ora' size 200k;
Database altered.
SQL> alter database enable public thread 2;
Database altered.
SQL> alter database disable thread 2;
Database altered.
```

The first two commands create a new thread (thread number 2) with two redo log groups. Each log group has one member. By default, the new thread is disabled after creation. The thread then needs to be enabled before it can be opened by an instance. The last two commands in the above example show how to enable and disable a thread, respectively. Note that the thread is publicly enabled. When an instance opens the database, it needs to open a thread of redo log files to store the changes made to the database by that instance.

If multiple threads are available to the database, one of the threads is chosen at mount time. The **init.ora** parameter THREAD can be specified if you want the instance to open a specific thread number. Otherwise, any publicly enabled thread can be used if it is available. A *thread mount lock* is used to prevent two instances from mounting the same thread at the same time. When a thread is opened, a new checkpoint is done and used as the *thread checkpoint*. If this is the first instance to open the database, this becomes the new *database checkpoint*, and Oracle ensures that all the online data files have the same checkpoint SCN in their headers. We will discuss *thread checkpoints* and *database checkpoints* in detail later in this section.

A thread must have at least two online redo log files (groups) while it is enabled. An enabled thread always has one online log file as its current log file. The *high SCN* value of the current log file is set to infinity so that any new SCN allocated will be recorded within the current log file. A special redo record is written when a thread is enabled. This record is used by media recovery to start applying redo from the new thread. For example, given two threads of a database, if you want to enable thread 2, you have to enable it by issuing the command from thread 1, which implies that it takes an open thread to enable another thread.

This chicken-and-egg problem is resolved by having the first thread automatically enabled publicly at database creation time. Only if you are running the database with the PARALLEL SERVER option will you need to create/enable a second thread. If you are running a single-instance database, you don't need a second thread.

When an instance closes the database or when a thread is recovered by instance/crash recovery (discussed later in this chapter), the thread is closed. The first step in closing a thread is to ensure that no more redo is generated in it. Next, all the changes to the online files must be in the data files. For a normal database close, Oracle accomplishes this by doing a checkpoint. Thread recovery does this by applying the redo since the previous thread checkpoint. Once all the changes are in the data files, the thread's checkpoint is advanced to the end of the thread. This may advance the database checkpoint just like a normal thread checkpoint. If this is the last thread to close, the database checkpoint will be left pointing at this thread even after it is closed.

If a thread is not going to be used for a long time, it is best to disable it. A thread must be closed first before it can be disabled. This ensures that all the changes have been written to the data files. Then, as part of the disable process, a new SCN is allocated as the *next SCN* for the current log file. The log header is marked with this SCN and flags saying that it is the end of a disabled thread. Similar to enabling a thread, when you disable a thread, you need to issue the **disable thread** command from SQL*PLUS. This means that a thread must be open in order to disable another thread. Thus, it is not possible to disable all the threads of a database. Once you have disabled a thread, it means that crash recovery will not expect any redo to be found in the thread. However, you need to be very careful in discarding redo log files of a disabled thread, as the log files might be required if media recovery is done later. The following example should make this concept clear.

Consider that a new thread—say, thread 2—is created with two log files, log4.ora and log5.ora, and by default the thread is disabled. Then we perform the following two commands in the order given:

```
SQL> alter database enable thread 2;
Statement processed.
SQL> alter database disable thread 2;
Statement processed.
```

The first command above enables the thread. In other words, in the control file, the *low SCN* value is set for log4.ora, and the log is marked *current*. Let's assume that the low SCN value is 200. The second command disables the thread. This sets the *high SCN* value in the control file for log4.ora to, say, 201. Note that thread 2 is never opened by any instance, so no redo is recorded in log file log4.ora. However, if you ever do media recovery starting at an SCN that is less than 200, log4.ora is required as part of the recovery.

The above example shows that you need to be careful in discarding the redo files once a thread is disabled because redo from a thread that was once enabled but is currently disabled is required for media recovery, but not required for crash recovery.

## Redo Log Switching

*Log switching* is the process whereby the LGWR process stops writing to the current log file and switches to the next available online log file. When Oracle creates redo, it uses the redo log buffer in memory and the redo log files on disk. The redo log buffer is flushed to disk to the redo log files, and the redo log buffer is reused to store further redo. The same is true for the redo log files on disk. As the log file on disk fills up, Oracle switches to the next available log file while the ARCH process archives the filled log file. Each log has a sequence number to identify it. As mentioned earlier, Oracle needs a minimum of two log files on disk, and a redo buffer in memory. The LGWR process writes to only one log file on disk at a time, but the redo buffer can be written to by several processes concurrently.

A log switch is triggered on one of the following two conditions:

■ Foregrounds are no longer able to allocate space in the redo log buffer.

■ The **alter system switch logfile** command is issued by the DBA.

The processing of the log switch, no matter which event triggers it, causes redo generation to resume in the next allocated log file. The steps are summarized here:

1.  *Select a log file to switch into.* Oracle gets the thread information from the control file and scans the log files. Using criteria including the checkpoint information, the archiving status, and the availability, Oracle selects a log file to switch into. If several log files are good candidates for switching into, Oracle chooses the one with the lowest log sequence number. Once a log file is chosen, Oracle sets various status flags to make it the next log file. These changes are made in a manner such that if the process doing the changes dies, crash recovery will recognize that the switch was not complete.

2.  *Flush the current log and disable redo generation.* Oracle maintains information in the SGA regarding several structures, including information to indicate whether redo can be generated or disabled. During a log switch, redo generation is disabled. Once this information is written in the SGA, redo generation by foregrounds is stopped. The buffers filled so far are then written out to disk. While the LGWR process is taking care of the log switch, processes that are allocated redo space in the redo log buffer continue to generate redo. Once Oracle flushes the last buffer, it closes the log.

3.  *Perform the switch in the control file/data file headers and close the log.* The information in the thread record and also for the log file entries is updated. This is written out to disk so that it is visible to other threads. A new SCN is allocated and used during the operation. The log file is now closed.

4.  *Open the new log file.* This opens the new log group for access as the current log. All the members are attempted, including members previously marked as STALE (members that could not be written to). If there is a write error with a specific log file member, LGWR doesn't write to it and updates the status of the member accordingly. For the members that it can write to, the log header status is set to OPEN, indicating that the log switch is complete.

## Archiving Log Switches

Each thread switches log files independently. Thus, when running the PARALLEL SERVER option, the SCN ranges in the current log can vary. However, it is desirable to have roughly the same range of SCNs in the archived log files of all enabled threads. This ensures that the last log archived in each thread is reasonably current. For example, we don't want a situation in which instance A has a low SCN value of 200 in its current online log file and instance B has a low SCN value of 2,000,000. In this situation, if the current online log file of instance A is lost due to a media failure, you can apply media recovery to a backup of the database, but you can only roll forward up to an SCN value of 200. This means that all changes made to the database from SCN = 201 to SCN = 2,000,000 are lost.

This problem is solved by forcing log switches in other threads when their current SCNs are significantly behind the log just archived. For example, if instance A has two log files and instance B has five, and if instance B is a very active instance, then for every five log switches at instance B, instance A will be forced to switch once. This way, instance A will keep up with the SCN range and you will not lose a significant amount of data should you lose an online log file of an inactive or less active instance.

**NOTE**
*Multiplexing online log files is very strongly recommended, as it addresses the single point of failure caused by losing the online log files.*

What happens if there is a thread that is closed but enabled? For open threads, a lock is used to trigger the other inactive instances, which then will do a log switch and archive as soon as they can. For a closed thread, the ARCH process of the active thread (instance B in the above example) will do a log switch of the closed thread. It will then archive the log files for the closed threads. You don't need to worry about wasting disk space because all the archived redo log files that are created by the closed threads will have only a file header, since no redo is generated in those threads. So the archive log files are very small and don't take up much disk space.

To implement the above feature of archiving redo log files from disabled threads, Oracle maintains a *force SCN* in the control file. Oracle will archive any log file that contains an SCN that is less than the *force SCN*. In general, the log file with the lowest SCN is archived first.

Note that you can manually archive the current log files of all enabled threads by using the **archive log next** command from SQL*PLUS. This command forces all threads (open and closed) to switch to a new log file. All necessary log files of all threads are archived. This command doesn't return to the prompt until all redo generated before the command was entered is archived. This is useful for ensuring that all redo log files necessary for the recovery of a hot backup are archived.

## Checkpoints

A *checkpoint* is a database event that flushes the modified data from cache to disk and updates the control file and data files. After a checkpoint, the redo in the redo log files is no longer useful for crash/instance recovery. If the redo log file size on disk were unlimited and crash recovery time were not a consideration, perhaps checkpoints wouldn't be needed; all we would do is apply the changes to the backup database using all the archive log files generated. But given the circular nature of the redo log file, there is a need to guarantee that before we allocate space in the redo log file and overwrite redo, the redo is copied to an archived log file.

In the recovery scheme, Oracle makes sure that before a change to the data block is made, the redo for the change has made its way into the redo log buffer;

and before the data block is flushed to the data file on disk, its redo is flushed to the redo log file. So to determine that a particular piece of redo is no longer useful for crash/instance recovery, Oracle makes sure that all the blocks changed up to the cutoff point in the log file do actually make it to the disk and into the database files. This is sufficient to guarantee that the redo is no longer of use and the redo log files can be allocated for reuse.

## Events Triggering Checkpoints

Checkpoints are triggered automatically when an event occurs during the normal operation of the database, but can be triggered manually by issuing a SQL*PLUS command. For example, the command

```
SQL> alter system checkpoint local;
Statement processed.
```

will explicitly trigger a checkpoint from the instance that is executed from. When a log file gets full and the log is switched, this operation implicitly triggers a checkpoint. *The Oracle8i Concepts Release 8.1.5* manual gives a good explanation of checkpoints and the events that trigger them. There are three types of checkpoints:

- **Local (thread) checkpoint**   A particular instance performs a checkpoint on all the data files of the database. In other words, all the dirty buffers from a specific instance are written to all the data files of the database. For example, the **alter system checkpoint local** command will perform a local checkpoint.

- **Global (database) checkpoint**   All the instances perform a checkpoint on all the data files of the database. For example, the **alter system checkpoint global** command performs a global checkpoint.

- **File checkpoint**   All the instances perform a checkpoint on a subset of the data files. For example, the command **alter tablespace SYSTEM begin backup** performs a global checkpoint on all the data files that belong to the SYSTEM tablespace.

Global checkpoints are specific to Parallel Server configuration (multiple threads). Local checkpoints are instance specific and restricted to the local thread. A global checkpoint may be done in response to a SQL command or when a database-wide checkpoint is done. Local checkpoints may be started due to a log file switch, execution of a SQL command, or on reaching the checkpoint interval specified by the **init.ora** parameter LOG_CHECKPOINT_INTERVAL. Global and local checkpoints are always done on all data files of the database. On successful completion, the redo prior to the checkpoint is no longer useful, except during media recovery. A file checkpoint is always done in response to a SQL command. For example, database operations such as hot backups or taking a tablespace offline require the RDBMS to do a checkpoint from all the instances, but only on a specific tablespace. The command **alter tablespace *tablespace_name* offline** requires that all the dirty buffers in cache (of all instances) that belong to the tablespace be written to the disk. Similarly, when you issue an **alter tablespace begin backup** command, all the dirty buffers from all instances that belong to this tablespace are flushed.

Checkpoints can be triggered with *fast* or *slow* priority and are discussed in detail later in this section. There are certain occasions when completion of a checkpoint becomes critical. A good example is when a log switch occurs and the LGWR process has to wait because the log file it has to write to is still involved in the checkpoint process.

Checkpoints are an integral part of the normal functioning of the database. You can control the frequency of checkpoints, but be aware that performing a checkpoint can be an I/O- and CPU-intensive operation, and should be tuned carefully.

Since checkpoints can be triggered by users or by database events, and checkpoint processing is done concurrently with normal activity in the database, there can be multiple checkpoints triggered in an overlapped fashion. To avoid this, each type of checkpoint event carries with it a privilege to *override* or be *ignored* when it is activated. When a checkpoint with override is triggered, the earlier checkpoint is replaced by the current checkpoint. This means that no matter where you are in processing the earlier checkpoint, Oracle will start another one as if the previous one did not exist. Overriding of checkpoints can be done for local or global checkpoints only.

Table 6-1 gives all the SQL commands, database events, and **init.ora** parameters that trigger checkpoints. The global, local, and file checkpoints are denoted by G, L, and F, respectively (N/A in the table means "not applicable"). The table also gives the priority of the checkpoints (fast or slow) and if they have override privilege.

In Table 6-1, the operation *log file switch stuck* means that a log file switch may be unsuccessful if a checkpoint has started and not yet finished. A typical case is when you have two log files, the second log file is completely filled, and the instance needs to switch to log 1. If log 1 is still involved in a previous checkpoint, then it needs to be sped up. To do this, another checkpoint is not started—starting another checkpoint would only delay things. Instead, the process requests that Oracle speed up the checkpoint process.

For single-process databases, all the work is done by the same process; messaging is done away with. Blocks are written out immediately upon being found to be checkpoint-marked.

| Checkpoints Triggered by Foreground and Background Processes | Fast/Slow | Override | G/L/F |
|---|---|---|---|
| alter system switch logfile | Slow | Yes | L |
| alter system checkpoint (local or global) | Fast | Yes | G/L |
| alter tablespace begin backup | Fast | N/A | F |
| alter tablespace offline (*normal, temporary*) | Fast | N/A | F |
| instance shutdown (*normal, immediate*) | Fast | Yes | L |
| log file switch *normal* | Slow | Yes | L |
| log file switch *stuck* | Fast | N/A | L |
| INIT.ORA parameter: LOG_CHECKPOINT_TIMEOUT | Slow | No | L |
| INIT.ORA parameter: LOG_CHECKPOINT_INTERVAL | Slow | No | L |

**TABLE 6-1.** *Checkpoints and Their Attributes*

## Checkpoint Processing

The work done in processing a checkpoint is more or less the same in any case; which process doing the work depends on the event triggering the checkpoint. If a checkpoint is initiated by a user command such as **alter system checkpoint local**, then a checkpoint is performed by the foreground process. In all other cases, the checkpoint processing is done either by the CKPT process or by the LGWR process. In Oracle7, the CKPT process is enabled by using the CHECKPOINT_PROCESS parameter in the **init.ora**. In Oracle8*i*, the CKPT process is started automatically.

For a global checkpoint, the work done to process the checkpoint involves the following steps:

1. **Getting/holding the instance state enqueue** The instance state enqueue is acquired during instance state transitions. Oracle acquires this enqueue to ensure that the database is kept open over the duration of the checkpoint processing.

2. **Capturing the current checkpoint information** This step involves setting up a structure to record information, including the current checkpoint time, the active threads at this time, the current thread doing the checkpoint, and

(most importantly) the address in the redo log file that will be the cutoff point for recovery.

3. **Identifying the dirty buffers**   The next step is to identify all the dirty buffers. This is done by scanning each buffer in cache and looping through until all dirty buffers are found. If Oracle finds a dirty buffer within the range of files that are being checkpointed, the buffer header is marked as *to be flushed.* Oracle skips temporary segment buffers and unmodified (read-only) buffers, since no redo is generated for them. Once the dirty buffers are identified, the DBWR process is posted to do the writes.

4. **Flushing the dirty buffers**   This step involves flushing all the dirty buffers to disk using the DBWR process. (How this works is explained in the section on fast/slow checkpoints, which will be discussed presently.) Once the DBWR flushes all the buffers, it sets a flag to indicate that it has finished flushing the buffers to disk. The LGWR (or CKPT) process continuously keeps checking until it recognizes that the DBWR process is done.

5. **Updating the data files and control files**   The last step is to update the data file headers and the control file with the information captured in step 2. The control file contains a checkpoint structure for each enabled thread. Each data file header contains a checkpoint structure as well. The information in these structures is updated as part of this step. Later in this chapter, we will discuss the checkpoint structure in greater detail.

In two cases, the checkpoint information (captured from step 2 above) is not updated in the file header. The first case is when the data file is in HOT BACKUP mode. In this case, Oracle doesn't know when the OS backup will read the file header, and the backup copy must have the checkpoint SCN when the copy started. The second case is if the checkpoint SCN is less than what is in the file header. This means that the changes made by the checkpoint are already on the disk. This can happen if a hot backup fast checkpoint updates the file header when a global checkpoint is in progress. Remember that Oracle captures the checkpoint SCN before it really gets into doing the hard work of processing the checkpoint, and it's quite possible that a command like **begin backup**, which does a fast tablespace checkpoint, might beat it.

Oracle verifies the data file headers for consistency before updating them. Once verified, the data file headers are updated to reflect the current checkpoint. Unverified files, and files that error out while doing the update write, are ignored. A file would need media recovery if the log files get overwritten, and in this case, the DBWR process takes the data file offline.

Taking a data file offline is always performed by the DBWR process. A data file cannot be taken offline if you are operating the database in NOARCHIVELOG mode or if the data file belongs to the SYSTEM tablespace. If Oracle can write all dirty blocks (in step 4 above) or if nothing needs to be written (because the data blocks are in the future of the redo, hence all changes already exist in the data file on disk), then no damage has been done.

Oracle keeps a counter of checkpoints in the data file headers. This is used to verify that you are using the current version of the data file during normal operation and to prevent you from restoring the wrong version of a data file during recovery. This counter is incremented even if the data files are in HOT BACKUP mode. The checkpoint counter for each data file is also kept in the control file for the corresponding data file entry.

### Checkpoint Processing in Oracle8*i*

A brief description is given here.

The dirty buffers in the cache are linked on a new queue called the checkpoint queue. Every change to the buffer has a redo value associated with it. The checkpoint queue contains dirty, logged buffers ordered according to the position in the log file; that is, the buffers in the checkpoint queue are ordered according to their low redo value. Note that since the buffer is linked into the queue in the order it is first dirtied, it does not move if additional changes are made to the buffer before it is written out. In other words, once a buffer is linked into the checkpoint queue, it stays in the same place until it is written out.

In response to a checkpoint request, DBWR writes out the buffers on this queue in ascending low redo order. Every checkpoint request specifies a redo value. Once DBWR writes out buffers whose redo values are equal to or greater than the checkpoint's redo value, the checkpoint is declared complete and recorded in the control file and file headers.

Since buffers on the checkpoint queue are ordered by low redo value and DBWR writes out checkpoint buffers in low redo order, it is possible to have multiple checkpoint requests active; as DBWR writes out the buffers, it checks the redo value of the buffer at the head of the queue with the checkpoint redo value. All checkpoint requests whose redo value is less than the low redo value of the buffer at the head of the checkpoint queue can be declared completed. DBWR continues to write out batches of checkpoint buffers while there are outstanding active checkpoint requests.

The new algorithm is an improvement over the old algorithm in several respects:

- DBWR always knows exactly which buffers need to be written in order to satisfy a checkpoint request.

- Every checkpoint write ensures that it makes progress towards completing the earliest checkpoint (the one with the lowest redo value).

- It is possible to distinguish between multiple checkpoint requests based on their checkpoint redo values and to complete them in that order.

## Fast and Slow Checkpoints

The speed of performing a checkpoint is really determined by the DBWR process and not by the LGWR or CKPT process, as it may seem. The LGWR (or CKPT) process merely conveys to the DBWR process how it needs to handle the writes for the buffers marked for checkpoint write. Once the DBWR process is posted, it starts scanning all buffer headers looking for dirty buffers that need to be flushed to disk. In doing the scan, all the buffers that are read in CONSISTENT READ mode (i.e., blocks that are read into memory with the **select** statement) and temporary segment buffers are ignored, as no redo is generated for them. All other buffers are scanned, and if a buffer is found dirty, it is saved for write. If Oracle is doing a *slow* checkpoint, the DBWR process stops to process the checkpoint if one of the two following conditions occurs:

- If the threshold size of the **db_checkpoint_write_batch** (number of buffers) is reached

- When over 1,000 buffers are scanned and a dirty buffer can't be found to write to disk

The idea is to give up the CPU, which would otherwise get wasted, affecting the foreground response. Also, if large values are set for **db_checkpoint_write_batch**, I/O will clobber the foregrounds. If, however, Oracle is doing a *fast checkpoint,* the DBWR simply continues scanning all the buffers in cache. In this case, such things as the overhead of message handling and passing and possible context switching, are avoided. Once started, the DBWR process will not do anything else until all the dirty buffers are written to disk as part of the fast checkpoint process.

## Fast-Start Checkpoint

The Fast-Start Checkpointing feature of Oracle8*i* limits the number of dirty buffers in the cache that need to be applied for the instance to recover from instance failures and thereby limits the amount of time required for instance recovery. Fast-Start Checkpointing records the position in the redo log from which crash or instance recovery would need to begin. The oldest dirty buffer in the buffer cache determines this position. During roll forward operation, Oracle does I/Os (defined by the FAST_START_IO_TARGET parameter value) to hard disk in order to read that many number of data blocks for applying the changes to the database. If Oracle must process an excessive number of I/O operations to perform instance recovery, performance can be adversely affected.

## Thread Checkpoint

When an instance checkpoints, it's called a *thread checkpoint*. Every thread will perform checkpoints independent of other threads; and every time a thread checkpoints, it updates the checkpoint information in the control file.

There is a *checkpoint structure* that is maintained in the control file for each thread. This means only dirty buffers from the instance that is performing the checkpoint are guaranteed to be written to disk. Oracle guarantees that all the redo generated in this thread before the checkpoint SCN has been applied to the online data files, and the blocks are written to the data files on disk. Among other things, the checkpoint structure contains the following information:

- The *current SCN* at which the checkpoint occurred

- The thread that did the checkpoint

- All threads that are enabled at the time

- The timestamp at which the current SCN is recorded

- Other information regarding redo

When a checkpoint occurs, Oracle records the SCN value and timestamp as of that point in the control file. Oracle guarantees that all changes made to the database before this checkpoint SCN are on disk. This means that in the event of a database crash, crash recovery will apply changes only from that SCN value.

## Database Checkpoint

When a database has multiple threads, there is one checkpoint structure for each thread in the control file. One of these checkpoint structures is also written to the data file headers and is referred to as the *database checkpoint structure, database checkpoint information,* or simply the *database checkpoint.* The thread checkpoint structure that is chosen to be the database checkpoint structure is the one with the lowest checkpoint SCN. For example, if there are three open threads with thread checkpoint SCN values of 300, 350, and 400, the database checkpoint SCN will be equal to 300 since that's the lowest value of all the thread checkpoint SCNs.

Oracle guarantees that all the changes that have an SCN value lower than the database checkpoint SCN have been written to the database files on disk. In the case of a single-instance database, the thread checkpoint in the control file is the same as the database checkpoint in the data files. If there are no open threads, the database checkpoint is the highest thread checkpoint of all the enabled threads, because all changes before the database checkpoint are written to the online data files. The database checkpoint is used to update the file headers when an instance checkpoints its thread.

### Data File Checkpoint

Every data file header contains the checkpoint information (checkpoint structure). The SCN corresponding to the checkpoint guarantees that all changes previous to this SCN are on disk. The checkpoint information in all the online data files gets updated when a *file checkpoint* or a *global checkpoint* is performed. The only exception is when a hot backup is in progress. For example, if the checkpoint SCN of a data file is 500, then when the data file is put in HOT BACKUP mode, this value doesn't change until the **end hot backup** command is issued. Since this SCN value is not updated, the backup data file is guaranteed to have the same checkpoint SCN value of 500. So, if we ever restore this data file to do media recovery, recovery starts from SCN 500 for this file. As discussed earlier, the checkpoint SCN value is stored in the control file for every data file as well.

## Log History

The control file can be configured to contain the history records for every redo log file that is used by the database. Each record in this table gives information about one redo log file. Each history record, among other things, contains the thread number, log sequence number, low SCN, and high SCN. This information can be obtained by selecting from the V$LOG_HISTORY view. The parameter MAXLOGHISTORY can be used while creating a database to specify how much history you want to store in the control file.

The purpose of maintaining this information is to reconstruct archived log file names from the SCN and thread number. Since the log sequence number is part of the checkpoint information, databases opened with single instances don't need this log history table to reconstruct the log file names during recovery.

With the PARALLEL SERVER option, when media recovery processes a data file, it reads the thread number from the checkpoint information recorded in the data file header and starts recovery with that thread. However, when Oracle switches threads (the concept of *thread switching* is discussed later in this chapter in the section "Thread Recovery"), it needs the names of the log files for the other threads. The log history table is used for this purpose. The log history table is a circular table, which means that the records are overwritten in a fashion such that the oldest information is lost first.

# Structures of Control Files, Data Files, and Log Files

The *control file* describes the schema of the database. It holds state information about the other database files. Several types of records are stored in the control file. Control file transactions allow updates to the control file to be committed atomically. It is recommended that you maintain redundant copies of the control file.

The *data files* contain the data blocks that hold the users' data. Each tablespace contains one or more data files. The first block of the data file is the file header and is not used for user data. This block stores structures to keep track of the state of the data file. The rest of the file is a collection of blocks that can be accessed through the buffer cache.

Log files contain redo that is generated in the process of modifying the data blocks. A log file is divided into blocks that must be the same size as the operating system block size. The first block of the redo log file is the header and doesn't contain redo.

For a detailed description of the contents of a control file, log file, and data file header in Oracle8i, see the "Debugging the RDBMS" section in Chapter 9. An overview is given next.

## Contents of a Control File in Oracle7

The information in the control file is divided into five parts. The first part contains information about the database. It has information about the total number of data files, log files, and threads that are enabled and open. If you are not using the PARALLEL SERVER option, you will have only one thread.

The second part of the control file gives information about the redo threads. Among other things, it contains information such as whether it is privately or publicly enabled. Information about each log group and the current log group that the LGWR is writing to is also recorded.

The third part of the control file contains information about each log member of each log group. The size of each log file, its full path name, the log sequence number, the low and high SCN values, and the thread to which each log file belongs are some of the important data structures.

The fourth part contains the data file information. A text string giving the fully expanded file name is recorded, along with its size in Oracle blocks and the Oracle block size in bytes. In addition, each data file has a status indicating whether the file is readable, writable, online or offline, whether media recovery is required, and so on. The stop SCN for each data file is also recorded.

The last part of the control file contains the log history information (discussed earlier in this chapter).

## Contents of a Control File in Oracle8*i*

In Oracle8*i*, the control file contains 17 parts. In addition to the five parts discussed above for Oracle7, the control file contains the following information:

- *Checkpoint progress information*, which gives information about the current SCN that hasn't checkpointed since the last checkpoint for each thread. This information is used during thread recovery.

- *Tablespace records*, which contain the tablespace name and information regarding tablespace point-in-time recovery. If you have done TSPITR on a particular tablespace, the SCNs at the beginning and end of TSPITR of this tablespace are recorded.

- *Offline range records* are created when a tablespace is taken *offline normal* or is made *read-only* and brought back *online* or made *read-write*.

- *Archived log records* contain archived logs that were successfully archived. They are also created when an archive log is restored from a backup set or a copy.

- *Backup set records, backup piece records, backup data file records,* and *data file copy records* have information pertaining to Recovery Manager. For example, *backup set records* contain one record for each backup set. Each record contains information about the backup set key, the contents of the backup set, whether it's part of the incremental backup, and the number of pieces in the backup set.

- *Backup data file corruption records* and *data file copy corruption records* contain information regarding corrupted blocks that RMAN has found while taking a backup set or data file copy, respectively. This information can be queried by the views V$BACKUP_CORRUPTION and V$COPY_CORRUPTION, respectively.

- *Deletion records* contain information on deletions made on a backup set. This information is used by RMAN to speed up the catalog *resync* operation.

- *Proxy copy records* contain details of each proxy-copied file in the control file. RMAN uses this information to resynchronize the recovery catalog.

Chapter 9 contains more detailed information on Oracle8*i* control file dumps.

## Contents of a Data File

As discussed earlier, the first block of the data file contains the file header information. Almost all of the information that is stored in the data file header is also stored in the control file for each data file. This includes, among other things, the file size, checkpoint information, block size, and creation timestamp. In addition, there is some information stored in the file header to indicate whether the data file is in HOT BACKUP mode or not.

Every data block contains header information such as the data block address, the block type (whether it's a data segment block, index segment block, and so on), and the version of the data block. The version of the block always increases by 1 when the block is read into cache for modification. This is crucial during recovery because the redo needs to be applied to a block with a specific version. It also contains information regarding the tablespace that the file belongs to and hot backup information.

If the **init.ora** parameter **_db_block_compute_checksum** is set to TRUE, the block header will also contain some checksum information. This is used for special debugging purposes and is discussed in Chapter 9. Finally, at the end of the Oracle block, the version number is recorded. This is used to determine if the front and back halves of a block match. This is especially useful while recovering from hot backups, because there is a possibility of a block split (as discussed in Chapter 3).

In Oracle8*i*, some portions of the data files that are allocated to locally managed tablespaces are set aside for bitmaps to manage the space availability. Space availability information is stored in segment headers and bitmap blocks for each locally managed tablespace. Each bit (0 and 1) in the bitmap represents a block of 64KB. Oracle does the space management by changing the bit value from either 0 to 1 or 1 to 0. Zero represents space allocation of 64KB and 1 represents deallocation of 64KB. This tablespace management feature has the following advantages over dictionary-managed tablespaces:

- Reduces user reliance on the data dictionary for tablespace space management

- Eliminates recursive space allocation and deallocation, which needs rollback segments and data dictionary tables during space management operations

- Improves concurrence of space operations

- Eliminates the need to coalesce free extents

## Contents of a Log File

The contents of an online redo log file and an archive log file are identical. (Note that each log file only holds redo for one thread.) The first block of the log file is the log file header. It contains the log sequence number, the thread number it belongs to, the low SCN, the high SCN, and some other flags to indicate the thread status.

One of the interesting data structures is the *resetlogs counter*. This is the same value from the database portion stored in the control file. It is used to prevent applying log files that were generated before the *resetlogs SCN*. Opening the database with the RESETLOGS option is discussed later in this chapter and in Case 11 of Chapter 10.

# Recovery Methods

This section focuses on the recovery methods using physical backups used by Oracle and various options available to the DBA. There are three basic types of recovery— *online block recovery, thread recovery,* and *media recovery.* In all three cases, the algorithm that applies the redo records against an individual block is the same. But first, you need to understand the concepts of *redo application, roll forward,* and *rollback* mechanisms and how Oracle determines that recovery is required for a data file(s). The next section discusses how to do logical recovery using the **import** utility.

## Redo Application

When a database is started with the **startup** command from SQLPLUS, there are various stages that the database goes through. The database first goes into the *nomount* state. In this state, Oracle reads the **init.ora** file to determine the size of the SGA, creates the SGA, and starts the background processes. The DBA sees a message on the terminal at this time that says "instance started."

Next, the instance *mounts* the database. In this state, the control file is opened and the "database mounted" message is displayed. In the mounted state, commands such as **recover database** or any **alter database** command can be issued. The **alter session** command can be used to dump trace information from the control file, redo log file headers, data file headers, and data blocks to trace files.

In the third and final stage, the instance *opens* the database displaying the "database opened" message to the user screen. In this stage, it is verified that all the data and log files can be opened. If the instance is opening the database for the first time after a database crash, crash recovery needs to be performed. There are two steps to crash recovery. The first is to roll forward the database, where all the redo stored in the redo log files will be applied to the database files and a new thread will be opened. As part of the second step (known as *transaction recovery*), all uncommitted transactions are rolled back.

A common question asked is "How does Oracle know when to apply recovery to a particular data file or data files?" We have learned that each data file, in its header, has a checkpoint counter that gets incremented every time Oracle performs a checkpoint on the data file. The control file keeps a checkpoint counter for every data file as well. We have also learned that every data file header contains an SCN as part of its checkpoint structure. This is called the *start SCN*. Corresponding to every data file, the control file has a *stop SCN*. During normal operation of the database, the stop SCN in the control file is set to infinity. The start SCN in the data file is incremented every time a checkpoint is done.

When the database is shut down with the NORMAL or IMMEDIATE option, the checkpoint that is issued will set the stop SCN in the control file equal to the corresponding start SCN in the data file header for each data file. When the database is opened the next time, Oracle makes two checks. The first check is to see if the checkpoint counter in the data file header matches its corresponding checkpoint counter in the control file. Once it is the same, it does the second check. This check compares the start SCN value in the data file header to its corresponding stop SCN in the control file. If the stop SCN equals the start SCN, then no recovery is required for that file. This check is performed for every data file and then the database is opened. As part of the open, the stop SCNs are set to infinity again.

Now, take the case in which you shut the database down hard using the **shutdown abort** command. In this case, a checkpoint is not performed and the stop SCN remains at infinity when the database goes down. During the next startup, the checkpoint counters are again matched first. If they are the same (you didn't replace the data files with a backup copy), then Oracle compares the stop and start SCNs. In this case, since the stop SCN is infinite and the start SCN has some value, Oracle determines that they are not the same, so thread recovery needs to be performed. In this case, since you are starting up the instance after a crash, crash recovery will be performed. As part of the crash recovery, Oracle reads the online log files and applies the changes to the database as part of the roll forward, and reads the rollback segment's transaction table to perform transaction recovery (roll backward). Thread recovery is discussed later in this section.

After shutting down the database, if you replace one of the data files with a backup copy, Oracle detects this as part of the checkpoint counter check and asks you to apply media recovery. From the data file header, Oracle also knows the beginning log sequence number of the archived redo log file at which recovery starts. Oracle requests that you apply media recovery starting from that log file sequence number.

### Roll Forward

Any kind of recovery (thread or media) is done in two parts. The first part is the roll forward. Roll forward involves sequentially applying the redo records to the corresponding data blocks. Oracle will apply all or none of the changes in an atomic redo record.

This is done in the following manner. First, the log file is opened for each thread that was enabled at the time the SCN was allocated. If the log file is online (as in the case of crash recovery), then it is automatically opened. If the log is an archived log file, then you are prompted to enter the name of the log file. The redo is applied from all the threads in the order it was generated, switching threads if needed. Thread switching is discussed later in the "Media Recovery" section of this chapter.

The order of application of redo records without an SCN is not precise, but it is good enough for rollback to make the database consistent. If the next log file in a thread is needed, an online copy is used if available. If not, the dirty recovery buffers are written to the disk, and the checkpoints on the data files are advanced so that the redo does not need to be reapplied— this is known as a *redo checkpoint*. Then you are prompted for the next log file. Note that redo application does occasionally need to back up and reapply redo that was skipped. This can happen when a corrupted block is repaired and redo for it was skipped.

Every data block has a version number. Every change made to the data block is recorded in the log file as a change vector. The change vector will have a version number 1 greater than that of the block. When recovery is done, for example, change 11 needs to be applied to the block that has a version number of 10. After applying the change, the block's version number will be incremented by 1, and made 11. Then change 12 needs to be applied to this block, and so on.

Figure 6-1 shows that changes 6 and 7 from the redo log file are being applied to a data block, thus rolling it forward. In this figure, you can see that in the redo log file there are two redo records that belong to block number 20 of file 10. Let's assume that at the beginning of recovery, the data block on disk has a block version of 5, and so change 6 needs to be applied from the redo log file. So, the first redo record will be applied to block 20. As part of rolling forward, after the change is applied to the block, the block's version number is now incremented to 6. Now the second redo record (corresponding to file 10, block 20) in the redo log file has change 7, which needs to be applied to the data block with version number 6. This will change the block's version number to 7, as shown in Figure 6-1.

Now, if another redo record exists for this data block that has a change number of 9, this redo record cannot be applied to the data block since the data block's version number is 7. This means that change 8 has to be applied before change 9. In other words, all changes have to be sequentially applied to the block. However, at some point in time, when change 15 needs to be applied to a block and the version of the block is, say, 19, that means the block is ahead of the redo change (i.e., the change is already in the data block). In this case, the redo is skipped and the next redo record in the redo log file is read. A data block can be in the future of the redo, for example, if database recovery is being performed but only one data file has been restored, and the other files are the current files. Then redo is applied only to that one file that really needs recovery. However, since all the redo is examined during recovery, it will try applying redo to the files that don't need recovery as well. This doesn't require Oracle to actually read the data block, but it checks the redo SCN against the checkpoint SCN of the file header. If the checkpoint SCN is ahead of the redo SCN, then Oracle realizes that the data block is in the future of the redo (which

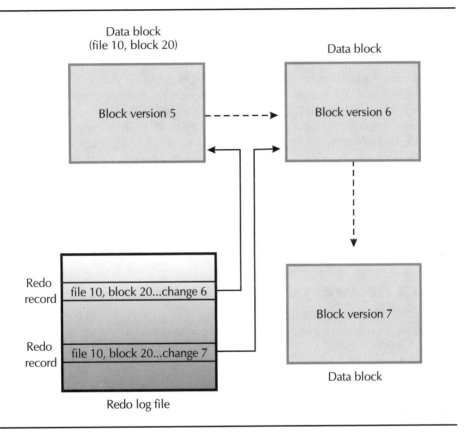

**FIGURE 6-1.** *Rolling a data block forward*

means that the block already contains the change). So, the redo record is skipped and the next record in the redo log file is examined.

## Rolling Backward

Once all the redo has been applied (rolled forward), the second part of the recovery process is the *rollback*. This process is also known as *transaction recovery*. Rollback segments are the mechanism that allows Oracle to roll back the uncommitted transactions. Because rollback segments reside in data files and are protected by the redo mechanism, all redo must be applied before any transactions can be rolled back.

Oracle finds the transaction tables by querying the base dictionary table, UNDO$. It scans the transaction tables of the rollback segments for active transactions. For each uncommitted transaction, Oracle chains through the undo and rolls back all changes. It is reasonable to see redo being generated, and thus log files being archived, if many or large transactions are being rolled back. This is because rolling back transactions causes changes to blocks inside the data files, thus generating redo.

The **init.ora** parameter ROLLBACK_SEGMENTS has no effect on this. All transactions in all the rollback segments are looked at and uncommitted transactions are rolled back. Once this is finished, all rollback segments acquired by the instance will be ONLINE, and all others OFFLINE. Rollback segments containing dead transactions that cannot be cleaned up are marked as NEEDS RECOVERY. The SYSTEM rollback segment is always ONLINE for the database to function, and should not be listed in the **init.ora** parameter ROLLBACK_SEGMENTS. At this point, transaction recovery is complete and users can log on.

The SYSTEM rollback segment is unique and special, and this has consequences for recovery. Undo generated by all transactions involving UNDO$ (the base data dictionary table, owned by the user SYS) uses the SYSTEM rollback segment. This means that SYSTEM rollback segment corruptions are very serious.

## Block Recovery

Block-level recovery is automatically performed by Oracle during normal operation of the database and is transparent to the user. When a process dies while changing a buffer, Oracle reconstructs the buffer using the online redo log files for the current thread and writes it to disk. The buffer header contains information regarding the range of redo records that needs to be applied to it.

When Oracle detects a corrupted block in the cache, it attempts to pull the block off disk and recover it using the online log files. It starts with the online log file that contains redo records that haven't been checkpointed against the data file holding the block. This is because no buffer should need recovery from any time before the last checkpoint. The redo log files are scanned in order and the redo records for the block are applied. Recovery stops at the end of the redo log file with the version number that was current during the time the block recovery started. If an error occurs in doing recovery, the block is marked as corrupted and a *corrupt block error* is signaled.

If the PMON process is performing the block recovery, Oracle does not allow it to spend large amounts of time working on the recovery of one buffer. PMON makes some progress in doing the recovery and then checks for other things to clean up (such as abnormally terminated processes or rollback transactions). To control the amount of recovery done by PMON, Oracle limits the amount of redo that is applied in one call to block recovery. The maximum number of redo blocks to apply in one call to block recovery by PMON is a port-specific constant, and users don't have control over this.

Block-level recovery is a normal operation performed automatically by Oracle during normal operation of the database and does not involve any action from the DBA.

# Thread Recovery

In this discussion, we assume that you are running the PARALLEL SERVER option and have multiple instances accessing the database. A single-instance database uses the same structures and recovery methods described below—it is just a simpler case in which only one thread exists.

If an instance crashes while it has the database open, it is necessary to do *thread recovery*. This involves applying to the database all the redo changes in the thread that have occurred since the last time the thread was checkpointed. The checkpoint SCN stored in the control file for the thread ensures that any blocks that were dirty in the buffer cache when the instance died will have the lost changes applied.

Thread recovery also does a clean close of the thread that the instance had open. If the thread was in the middle of a log switch when the instance died, thread recovery rolls back the appropriate information and calculates the *next available block*. The next available block is the block number in the redo log file from which the thread starts writing redo information. Thread recovery also calculates the highest SCN used by the dead instances.

Thread recovery is done as a part of either *instance recovery* or *crash recovery*. Instance recovery is done while the database is open and one instance detects that another instance has died. This is possible only if you are running multiple instances using the PARALLEL SERVER option. Oracle determines whether there really is a dead instance, and if so, it does thread recovery for its redo thread. It also clears the locks held by the dead instance, if any, after any required thread recovery is complete. If you restart the dead instance before instance recovery is done, then Oracle will do crash recovery. In general, the first instance to open the database after an abnormal termination (**shutdown abort** or a database crash) does crash recovery.

**NOTE**
*If you are running a single-instance database, there is only one thread. In this case, if the instance crashes, there is no concept of instance recovery as there is only one instance. When you restart the instance, thread recovery is done as part of crash recovery.*

While running the PARALLEL SERVER option, if another instance attempts to open the database while the first one is doing crash recovery, it waits until crash recovery is complete. Crash recovery determines which threads are left open and calls thread recovery to close them cleanly. The reason for this is that if crash recovery dies in the middle for some reason, a data file can be replaced with a backup that was taken just before crash recovery started. This file would then look like a current file, but it would be missing the changes for any threads that were recovered.

Remember that before attempting thread recovery, the checkpoint counter in the control file for every data file is checked with the corresponding checkpoint counter in the data file header. This ensures that none of the data files have been restored from a backup. If there is a restored file, then media recovery needs to be performed.

Each thread's redo can be applied independently because for any given block, only one cache at a time can have changes that have not been written to disk. This means that to recover a specific thread, only the redo log files for that thread are required. If multiple threads are being recovered, they will be recovered one at a time. In other words, thread recovery is single-threaded. The following example should illustrate this concept.

Let's assume that a DBA is running the PARALLEL SERVER option with two instances accessing the database, and with T1 as the thread for instance 1 and T2 as the thread for instance 2. Let's further assume that there are two transactions running simultaneously (one from each instance) and modifying the same block in the database. Figure 6-2 shows the changes recorded in the log files of T1 and T2. If the first instance crashes, thread recovery needs to be performed and can be applied independently, as mentioned earlier. You may wonder how change 5 can be applied to the block without applying change 4, which belongs to T2.

The explanation is that at the time of thread recovery, the version of the block on disk has to be at least 6. This is because when the transaction of instance 1 wants to modify the block to create change 7, the block needs to be *pinged* (pinging is the process of flushing the dirty buffer from one instance's cache to disk so that the second instance can modify it), and change 6 has to be written to disk. So, during thread recovery of T1, changes 3 and 5 will be skipped because the version of the data block on disk is ahead of the redo, and therefore these changes don't need to be applied to the data block.

For crash recovery, however, it is important to note that none of the threads are closed until all the redo from all threads is applied. If this is not done, a DBA can restore a backup copy of a data file, and Oracle wouldn't know that it needs recovery. It would be possible to have multiple instances cooperating on crash recovery. Each instance would recover one thread at a time until all threads were recovered. As shown in the above example, no thread needs to wait for another thread to apply recovery first, as in the case of thread recovery. In the next section, we will learn that media recovery is dependent on multiple threads.

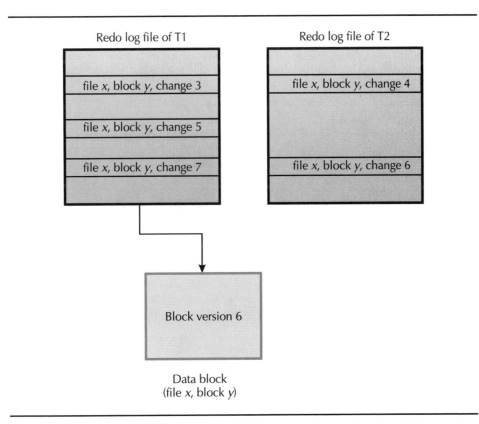

**FIGURE 6-2.** *Thread recovery*

Thread recovery doesn't attempt to apply redo that is before the checkpoint SCN of a data file. The end of a thread recovery almost always advances the data file checkpoints and always advances the checkpoint counters.

## Media Recovery

While block and thread recovery are done by the database automatically, *media recovery* is done in response to a recovery command issued by the DBA. It is used to make backup data files current or to restore changes that were lost when a data file went offline without a checkpoint. For example, if you take a tablespace offline using the IMMEDIATE option, the data files will go offline without a checkpoint being performed by Oracle. Media recovery can apply archived log files as well as online log files.

## When to Do Media Recovery

A restored data file backup always needs media recovery, even if it can be accomplished with the online log files. The same is true of a data file that went offline without a checkpoint. The database cannot be opened if any of the online data files needs media recovery. A data file cannot be brought online while the database is open if it needs media recovery. Depending on the failure and the recovery procedure you want to use, you can recover the database while a portion of the database is open; but if the database is open, the file to be recovered must be offline. We will get into details on the options that you have for doing media recovery later in this section.

## Media Recovery Operation: Database, Tablespace, and Data File Recovery

Oracle detects that media recovery is needed when the checkpoint counter in the data file header is not equal to the corresponding checkpoint counter in the control file. When you issue the **recover** command from SVRMGR, recovery starts at the lowest checkpoint SCN of the data files being recovered. This means Oracle checks for the SCN value in the file header for all data files and chooses the one that has the oldest SCN value. As we discussed earlier, associated with this checkpoint SCN is the thread that issued the checkpoint. Oracle starts applying media recovery to this file starting with this thread. The checkpoint SCN of every file is saved to eliminate applying redo from before its checkpoint. The highest stop SCN is also saved (recorded in the control file) to know whether recovery should stop before all the redo is applied.

There are primarily three options you can choose while doing media recovery. First, you can do *database recovery*. This means that you can restore all (or some) data files from the backup and recover the entire database. The second type is a *tablespace recovery*. While a portion of the database is open and running, you can perform media recovery on a specific tablespace. This means all data files that belong to the tablespace will be recovered. The third type of recovery is *data file recovery*. Here, you can recover a specific data file while the rest of the database is in use. All three of these options use the same criteria for determining if the files can be recovered.

When a process recovers a data file, first it locks the data file in EXCLUSIVE mode. If the process cannot lock the file because some other process has a lock on it (since the file is online or another process is recovering the data file), then Oracle gives you an error saying that the data file is in use. This prevents two recovery sessions from recovering the same data file, and it prevents media recovery of a file that is in use.

During media recovery, the redo of all enabled threads is applied. Oracle has an initial list of enabled threads that it has to recover. As it starts reading the redo log files, it knows if any new threads have been enabled. If so, it will apply recovery for those threads as well. The last redo record in each redo thread is an *end_of_thread* record, which tells Oracle that there is no more redo to be applied for that specific thread. Recovery for a particular thread is complete when this record is applied. Media recovery is complete when all enabled threads have been recovered through the end of each thread.

While applying redo, Oracle may have to switch between threads to roll blocks forward enough to apply the next piece of redo. Oracle may have to apply the same archive log file multiple times if it contains a lot of blocks that were modified by other threads. During media recovery, a thread's redo will be applied until it hits the end_of_thread marker or until it needs to apply a redo change that is in the future of a block. If a thread finds that it has redo in the future of a block, recovery will switch to another thread. Eventually, the block should be rolled forward enough to apply this piece of redo. The example in Figure 6-3 illustrates the concept of switching threads.

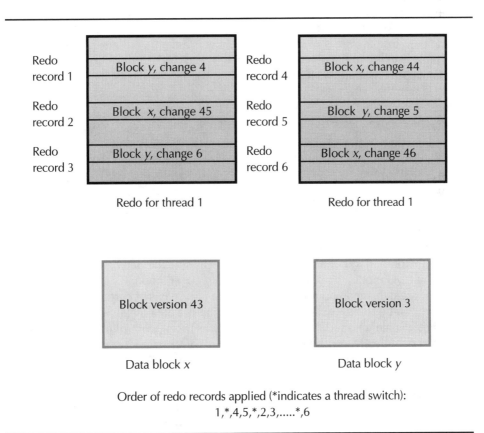

**FIGURE 6-3.** *Thread switching during recovery*

Figure 6-3 shows two database blocks and redo for two threads. Redo record 1 of thread 1 contains change 4 of data block $y$. Since data block $y$ has version number 3 on disk, this is the next change that needs to be applied. However, redo record 2 of thread 1 contains change 45, and this cannot be applied to block $x$, as the redo is in the future of the block. In other words, change 44 needs to be applied to block $x$ before change 45 can be applied, so Oracle has to switch threads and start applying recovery starting from redo record 4 of thread 2. Note that after redo record 4 is applied, Oracle continues to apply redo in this thread until it is forced to switch again or until it completes recovery for this thread. Figure 6-3 gives the order in which the redo records are applied in this example. The asterisk (*) indicates that a thread switch happened.

## Prerequisites for Using Media Recovery

If a media failure occurs while the database is operating in NOARCHIVELOG mode, complete recovery using physical backups might not be possible. In other words, if you take weekly offline backups, then you should be prepared, in a worst-case scenario, to lose a week's worth of data if there is a media failure. This is because the changes made to the database are not archived to the archive log files because the database is running in NOARCHIVELOG mode. So, running the database in this mode is suitable only if the data can be reconstructed, if necessary, during a media failure. In summary, if the DBA opts to operate the database in NOARCHIVELOG mode, the only recovery methods available are as follows:

- *Restoring from an offline backup*   This involves restoring all data files, control files, and online log files—and restarting the database.

- *Rebuilding the database using a full database export*   This method involves re-creating the schema of the database and importing all the data from a previously taken full database export.

On the other hand, if a media failure occurs while the database is operating in ARCHIVELOG mode, there are many ways to recover, depending on the types of files that are damaged and what type of media failure has occurred. Complete recovery can be done—which involves restoring the data file(s) from backup, applying *all* changes made since the backup was taken, and rolling forward the database completely—without losing any data. For the purpose of this discussion, we assume that you are operating the database in ARCHIVELOG mode.

**NOTE**
*It is very important that you run your database in ARCHIVELOG mode. Otherwise, it is almost certain that you will lose data if a media failure occurs and you lose your database files.*

As mentioned earlier, there are three kinds of recovery commands that you can use:

```
Recover database
Recover tablespace
Recover datafile
```

The recovery command to use depends on the kind of failure that occurred and whether you want to keep the database open while recovering. If you recover a data file or a tablespace when the database is open, it is called *online recovery*. If the database is closed when you perform recovery, it is called *offline recovery*. Table 6-2 summarizes which type of recovery can be performed while recovering the database, a tablespace, or a data file.

When the **recover database** command is used, the database always has to be mounted but not open. Since a tablespace is a logical entity, Oracle recognizes it only when the database is open; therefore, when using the **recover tablespace** command, the database needs to be open, but with the tablespace being recovered offline. (The SYSTEM tablespace can never be recovered using the **recover tablespace** command because it cannot be taken offline.) To recover a data file, you can use the **recover datafile** command, and the database can be open or closed, depending on the files being recovered. For example, if the SYSTEM data files are being recovered, the database has to be closed because the database cannot be open with SYSTEM data files offline. If files belonging to a USER tablespace are being recovered, the database can be open, but the files that are being recovered need to be offline.

## Database Recovery and Implementation

This section describes various media recovery options that Oracle provides to DBAs at a database-wide level. Regardless of the method used, the fundamental concept of recovery is very straightforward: *Before opening the database, all data files must be recovered to the exact same point in time and not have any changes in the future from this point.* For example, take a look at this illustration:

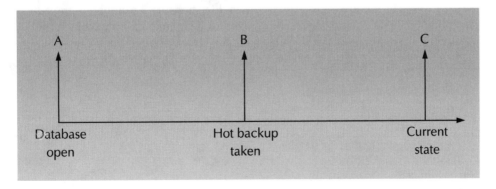

| Recovery Command | Database Online | Database Offline |
|---|---|---|
| Recover database | No | Yes |
| Recover tablespace | Yes | No |
| Recover datafile | Yes | Yes |

**TABLE 6-2.** *Online and Offline Recovery*

The database is opened at state A, a hot backup is taken at state B, and the current state of the database is state C. Let's assume that a media failure occurred and a data file belonging to the USER tablespace is lost. At this point you have two recovery options:

- You can recover all the data files from state B and recover all of them to state C by using the **recover database** command.

- The one data file that was damaged can be restored from the backup, the database mounted, the data file taken offline, and the database opened before recovering it with the **recover datafile** command.

In either case, at the end of recovery, all data files have to be at state C (or the current state, whatever it is). You should never start the database with one data file at state B and the rest of the data files at state C. This would cause database inconsistency. Oracle keeps track of the fuzziness of the files to avoid such situations. If you try to open an inconsistent database, Oracle will display an error. However, you can force Oracle to open the database, but this is not supported by Oracle Support Services.

It is possible, and might be necessary in some drastic situations, to start up the database in an inconsistent mode—such cases should be handled by an Oracle Support Services representative. In cases like this, there are a number of precautions that you need to take, and the database needs to be rebuilt after opening it. The main reason for facing such a drastic situation is usually due to the DBA not having a proper backup procedure in place. It is unlikely that DBAs who plan a good backup and recovery scheme would face a situation like this. The syntax to use database recovery is as follows:

```
RECOVER [AUTOMATIC] [FROM 'location'] [DATABASE]
    | [UNTIL CANCEL]
    | [UNTIL TIME date]
    | [UNTIL CHANGE integer]
[USING BACKUP CONTROLFILE]
```

All keywords in square brackets are optional. If the AUTOMATIC option is used, recovery is done automatically without asking the DBA for the names of the redo log files during media recovery.

Alternatively, the command **set autorecovery on/off** can be used from SVRMGR to turn on/off automatic recovery. However, when you request Oracle to do automatic recovery, the archived redo log files should be in the location specified by the **init.ora** parameter LOG_ARCHIVE_DEST, and the format of the filename should be the same as specified in the **init.ora** parameter LOG_ARCHIVE_FORMAT. If you don't want Oracle to do media recovery automatically, you should omit this option while using the **recover** command. This will force Oracle to prompt you for the next archived redo log file name, and you should specify the next log file name. Alternatively, you can use the **alter database recover** command to perform database media recovery.

**NOTE**

*Oracle recommends using the **recover** command rather than the **alter database** command with the RECOVER clause to do media recovery because it is easier to use.*

The next keyword is FROM, which is optional as well. This should be used if the file location is different from what is specified in the **init.ora** parameter LOG_ARCHIVE_DEST. If you don't use the UNTIL keyword, Oracle assumes that complete database recovery is requested. For example, the command

```
SVRMGR> RECOVER DATABASE
```

does media recovery on all the data files that are online, if required. If all instances are cleanly shut down and no backup files are restored, this command will signal an error saying no recovery is required. This command will also fail if any one of the instances has the database open, since they will have the data file locks. Database-wide recovery can be performed *only* when the database is not open and mounted.

The other options, such as UNTIL CANCEL, UNTIL TIME, and UNTIL CHANGE, will be discussed in the next section as part of incomplete recovery.

Appendix A gives complete details of the new features of release 8.1.5. A brief description of the Parallel Recovery option is discussed below.

As shown in Figure 6-4, the Oracle server uses one process to read the redo log files and dispatches the redo information to several recovery processes. The recovery processes apply the changes from the redo log files to the data files. Recovery processes are not dedicated to a specific file, but recover a range of data blocks. The **init.ora** parameter RECOVERY_PARALLELISM determines the number of recovery processes desired.

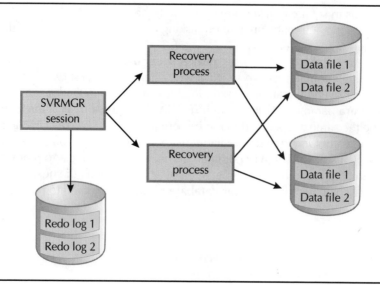

**FIGURE 6-4.** *Parallel recovery*

## Complete vs. Incomplete Recovery

Recovering the database from a media failure without losing any data is known as *complete recovery*. If you have lost some data after recovering the database, it is known as *incomplete recovery*. Complete recovery should be implemented when all the required redo log files, backup data files (for all the lost or damaged data files), and a current valid control file are available. Incomplete recovery should be used only when you cannot recover all the data completely (for example, to recover from the loss of an archived or online redo log file and the loss of control files). Incomplete recovery can also be implemented to restore the database to a previous point in time. For example, if you drop a table by accident at 10 A.M. and want to recover the table, you can restore the appropriate data files from a backup and do point-in-time, incomplete recovery to a point before 10 A.M. Chapter 10 gives a case study on point-in-time recovery. When incomplete recovery is done, the database must be opened using the **alter database open resetlogs** command. This marks the database so that the redo that was skipped can never be accidentally applied.

There are three options to choose from when doing incomplete recovery. The **recover database** command should be used with one of the following options: UNTIL CANCEL, UNTIL TIME, or UNTIL CHANGE. These options allow you to perform cancel-based, time-based, and SCN-based recovery, respectively.

If the UNTIL CANCEL option is chosen, Oracle allows you to roll forward one log file at a time. When recovery needs to be stopped, just issue the **cancel** command. Online log files are not automatically applied in this mode. If multiple threads of redo are being recovered, there may be log files in other threads that are partially applied when the recovery is canceled.

The UNTIL TIME option allows the DBA to do recovery to a specific point in time within a redo log file. The *Oracle 8i SQL Reference Release 8.1.5* manual gives the date format that needs to be specified with this command. This option works just like the UNTIL CHANGE option, except that a time is given instead of an SCN.

The UNTIL CHANGE option recovers the database to a transaction-consistent state. The SCN that is specified with this option is noted by Oracle as a reference, and any redo records that have an SCN less than the reference SCN are applied. This option terminates the redo application for any redo associated with that SCN or higher. Thus, the transaction that is committed exactly at the SCN is rolled back. If the DBA needs to recover through a transaction that committed at a specific SCN, then the DBA needs to add one to the SCN specified in this command. The following are some examples of incomplete recovery:

```
SQL> recover database until cancel;
SQL> recover database until time '2000-06-15:17:55:00';
SQL> recover database until change integer;
SQL> recover database until cancel using backup controlfile;
```

The first command above does recovery until you issue the command **cancel**. The second command does point-in-time recovery. All changes up to 5.55 P.M. on June 15th, 2000 are applied to the database. The third command does recovery up to a specific SCN, specified as an integer. The last command is the same as the first one except that a backup control file is used to do recovery. When is it appropriate to use the above commands? Let's look at the following example.

John doesn't multiplex his redo log files, and one day he lost his online redo log files due a media failure. If he opens his database now, the data will be inconsistent since data from committed transactions after the last checkpoint may or may not be in the data files on disk. As discussed earlier, the fundamental rule of recovery is that all blocks have to be at the same point in time before starting up the database. In this case, incomplete recovery needs to be done.

The recommended procedure is to restore the complete database backup from a recent online or offline backup and issue the command **recover database until cancel** from the SVRMGR prompt. Once all the archived redo log files are applied, open the database using the **alter database open resetlogs** command. This command creates the online log files for you.

**NOTE**
*From the example given here, it is clear that multiplexing online log files is very important.*

If a data file is offline during incomplete recovery, it will not be recovered. This is all right if the file is part of a tablespace that was taken offline with the NORMAL option. But if the tablespace is taken offline with the IMMEDIATE option and the data file is still offline when the RESETLOGS option is used to open the database, the tablespace containing the data file will have to be dropped and re-created. This is because the data file needs media recovery from a point before the RESETLOGS option was used. In Chapter 10, one case study shows that it is not possible to do recovery on a data file that is restored from before a point where RESETLOGS was done. In general, the view V$DATAFILE should be checked to ensure that all necessary data files are online before an incomplete recovery is done. The only data files that can be offline are files that belong to a tablespace that was taken offline with the NORMAL option or read-only data files.

Doing incomplete recovery can sometimes be tricky. The following example will make this clear. Let's assume that at time T1 a hot backup of the database was taken. At time T2, a tablespace containing file F1 was dropped. Let's assume that you need a table that resides in the tablespace that was dropped at time T2. In this case, you need to restore from the backup taken at time T1, perform point-in-time recovery, and stop before T2. Since media recovery recovers only online data files, you need to make sure that the data file you need is online; otherwise, it will not be recovered. This means that if you are using a *current* control file during recovery, you can't recover file F1, as it no longer exists.

Therefore, you must use the backup control file from time T1 (or any time before T2) to perform recovery. Another option is to create a new control file using the **create controlfile** command and then perform recovery.

**NOTE**
*Data files can be taken offline by using the **alter database datafile 'filename' offline** command; the control file can be created using the **create controlfile** command. Both these commands are described in the* Oracle8*i* SQL Reference Release 8.1.5 *manual.*

If recovery is done with a control file other than the current one, you must use the USING BACKUP CONTROLFILE option with the **recover database** command. This is the case if a control file backup was restored or if the control file was created with the RESETLOGS option. A **create controlfile** command with the NORESETLOGS option makes the new control file current. A backup control file wouldn't have valid information about the online log files and the data file stop SCNs. Therefore, Oracle can't use the online log file during recovery, and hence assumes infinite stop SCNs for the data files. In order to correct this information, when you open the database you must have the RESETLOGS option specified. An error is signaled if a NORESETLOGS option is used while opening the database.

The USING BACKUP CONTROLFILE option can be used either alone or in conjunction with an incomplete recovery option. For example, it is quite common to use a command such as **recover database until cancel using backup controlfile**. Unless an incomplete recovery option is included, all threads must be applied to the end of thread. This is validated when the log files are reset when the database is opened. Failure to specify the USING BACKUP CONTROLFILE option when it is required can frequently be detected by Oracle. The old checkpoint counter in the data file headers will never be greater than the checkpoint counter in the current control file, but this may not catch the problem if the data files are also backups. The online log file headers are also validated against their control file entries, but this too may not always catch an old control file. So, if you are using a backup copy of the control file, always use the USING BACKUP CONTROLFILE option with the **recover** command.

## RESETLOGS Option

The RESETLOGS option is needed when you open the database after one of the following is performed:

- Incomplete recovery

- Recovery using a backup control file

- Recovery with a control file that was created using the **create controlfile** command with the RESETLOGS option

When you use this option to open the database, Oracle throws away the redo that was not applied during the recovery and ensures that it can never be applied again. It also reinitializes the control file information about online log files and redo threads.

While doing complete recovery of the database, if all threads of redo have been completely applied to all online data files, then we can be sure that the database is consistent. However, when incomplete recovery is done, there is the possibility that a file was not restored from a sufficiently old backup. This is definitely the case if the file has a different checkpoint than the other files. For this reason, before you open the database with the RESETLOGS option, you have to make sure that all data files are recovered to the same point in time to ensure consistency of the database.

A *resetlogs SCN* and *counter* are kept in the control file to identify uniquely each execution of a database opened with the RESETLOGS option. The values are written into the header of every data file and redo log file as well. A redo log file cannot be applied during a recovery if its log sequence number doesn't match what is expected by Oracle. A data file can't be recovered from a backup that was taken before the database was opened with the RESETLOGS option. This ensures that changes discarded by resetting the log files do not get back into the database. So, it is very important to note that a database backup (online or offline) should be performed immediately after opening the database with the RESETLOGS option. However, read-only tablespaces and any tablespaces that were taken offline with the NORMAL option can be brought online, even after opening the database with the RESETLOGS option.

**NOTE**
*Oracle strongly recommends taking an offline or online backup of the entire database after the database is opened with the RESETLOGS option.*

Here is a brief description of what happens when you open the database using the RESETLOGS option. First, the redo is thrown away by zeroing all the online log files. This means that redo in online log files may be lost forever if it is not backed up—it would only be needed if it were decided to do the recovery all over again. One log is picked to be the current log file for every enabled thread. That log header is written as log sequence number 1. Note that the set of log files and their thread associations are picked up from the control file. If it is a backup control file, this may be different from what was current the last time the database was open.

Next, the file headers of all the online data files are updated to the new database checkpoint. The new *resetlogs* data is written into the header. The offline data files are marked as *needing media recovery* in the control file. This recovery can never be done, as no redo can be applied after the database is open with the RESETLOGS option. This means that the tablespace that contains the offline data file needs to be dropped. The only exception is if the file was taken offline using the NORMAL option. In this case, the checkpoint SCN written to the file headers is recorded in the data dictionary. Thus, no recovery is required to bring a tablespace and its files online if the files are not fuzzy and are checkpointed at exactly the SCN saved in the dictionary. The following example shows the log sequence numbers of the online log files before and after the RESETLOGS option is used to open the database:

```
SQL> archive log list
Database log mode              ARCHIVELOG
Automatic archival             ENABLED
Archive destination            c:\oracle\oradata\test\archive
Oldest online log sequence     61
Next log sequence to archive   63
Current log sequence           63
```

```
SQL> recover database until cancel;
Media recovery complete.
SQL> alter database open resetlogs;
Statement processed.
SQL> archive log list;
Database log mode              ARCHIVELOG
Automatic archival             ENABLED
Archive destination             c:\oracle\oradata\test\archive
Oldest online log sequence     0
Next log sequence to archive   1
Current log sequence           1
```

When you open the database with the RESETLOGS option, after transaction recovery, the data files listed in the data dictionary are compared with the data files listed in the control file. This is also done on the first open after executing a **create controlfile** command. Oracle does this check because there is a possibility that incomplete recovery ended at a time when the files in the database were different from those in the control file used for the recovery. Using a backup control file or creating a new control file can have the same problem.

Checking the dictionary doesn't do any harm, so it could be done on every database open; but it could be time consuming. As part of the check, the entry in **file$** is compared with the entry in the control file for every file number. Since **file$** reflects the space allocation information in the database, it is correct, and the control file might be wrong. If the file doesn't exist in **file$**, but the control file record says it does, the file is dropped from the control file. If a file exists in **file$** but not in the control file, a fake entry is created in the control file. The fake file is named MISSING*xxxx* where *xxxx* is the file number in decimal form. This file is marked as offline and needs media recovery. If this data file is unavailable, the tablespace containing the file must be dropped. If the data file is available, the entry for MISSING*xxxx* can be renamed to point to the real file. If the data file is part of a tablespace that has been taken offline with the NORMAL option, it may be brought online without recovery. Another option is to repeat the entire operation that led up to the dictionary check with the correct control file. For incomplete recovery, this would involve restoring all backups and repeating the recovery.

To summarize, opening up the database with the RESETLOGS option has many implications on the database and impacts the database backups. So you should use this option only after doing incomplete recovery or after recovering using a backup control file. The most important point to remember is that after opening the database with the RESETLOGS option, you should immediately take an online or offline backup of the entire database.

### Checklist for Complete and Incomplete Database Recovery

In this section we summarize the requirements and discuss the advantages of using database recovery. Implementation plans are described for doing complete recovery and incomplete recovery.

#### Description

- Database recovery recovers all the data files in the database that are online.

- Complete or incomplete recovery is possible.

- You can recover from an online or offline backup.

#### Requirements

- You have to do offline recovery only (i.e., database cannot be open during recovery).

- All data files to be recovered should be online.

#### Required Files

- Archived and/or online redo log files

- Current or backup control file

- Backup of data files (for the lost or damaged data files)

#### Advantages

- It recovers the database in one step.

- You can do incomplete recovery.

- You can recover data files that belong to the SYSTEM tablespace.

#### Disadvantages

- The database is inaccessible during recovery.

- It can take a long time, depending on the amount of redo to be applied and frequency of backups.

## Complete Recovery Implementation

The following steps show how to do complete recovery:

1. Restore all (or the damaged) data files at the OS level. For example, in UNIX, you can issue the following command:

   ```
   mcs% cp /home/orahome/backup/*.dbf /home/orahome/data/815
   ```

2. Start the instance in RESTRICT mode and mount the database:

   ```
   SQL> startup restrict mount [dbname];
   ```

3. This step is optional and should be used only if the original location of a lost or damaged database file has become invalid (i.e., a disk crash). The path stored in the control file must be renamed to the new restored file location. Use the following command to rename data or log files:

   ```
   SQL> alter database rename file 'old_filename' to 'new_filename';
   ```

4. Make sure that all the data files you want to recover are online. Select from the V$DATAFILE view to get the file status:

   ```
   SQL> select file#, status, name from V$DATAFILE;
   SQL> alter database datafile 'filename' online;
   ```

5. Recover the database:

   ```
   SQL> RECOVER DATABASE [dbname];
   ```

   Oracle now prompts for the names of the archived redo log files that it needs to apply, beginning with the earliest. When recovery is complete, you will see the message "Media recovery complete."

6. Now you can open the database:

   ```
   SQL> alter database [dbname] open;
   ```

**NOTE**
*A database can be opened only if all the online data files have been recovered to the same point in time.*

## Incomplete Recovery Implementation

Let's assume that a DBA running Oracle Financial Applications accidentally ran a batch job twice, thereby logically corrupting the data. This requires restoring from the backup and rolling forward to a point in time before the batch job was run the second time. The steps involved in doing this are as follows:

1. First, shut down Oracle Financial Applications and then the database, and back up all the database files in case you make an error in doing incomplete recovery of the database. This involves stopping the concurrent managers and shutting down the database clean before taking a backup:

   ```
   SQL> shutdown [dbname]
   ```

2. Restore all the data files from backup. You can use the current control file. For example, in UNIX:

   ```
   mcs% cp /home/orahome/backup/*.dbf /home/orahome/data/815
   ```

3. Start the instance in the RESTRICT mode and mount the database:

   ```
   SQL> startup restrict mount [dbname];
   ```

4. This step is optional and should be used only if the original location of a lost or damaged database file has become invalid (i.e., a disk crash). The path stored in the control file must be renamed to the new restored file location. Use the following command to rename data or log files:

   ```
   SQL> alter database rename file 'old_filename' to 'new_filename';
   ```

5. Make sure that all the data files you want to recover are online. Select from the V$DATAFILE view to get the file status:

   ```
   SQL> select file#, status, name from V$DATAFILE;
   SQL> alter database datafile 'filename' online;
   ```

6. Recover the database using the UNTIL CANCEL or UNTIL TIME option. For example, to recover up to 1:55 P.M. on the 15th of June, 2000, use the following command:

   ```
   SQL> recover database until time '2000-06-15:13:55:00';
   ```

   Oracle prompts you for redo log files, and you should get the message "Log applied" after each redo log file is applied. Recovery ends at the specified time and returns the message "Media recovery complete."

7. Open the database using the RESETLOGS option:

   ```
   SQL> ALTER DATABASE OPEN RESETLOGS;
   ```

8. Take an offline or online backup. This is a very important step.

## Tablespace Recovery

The syntax for using tablespace recovery is as follows:

```
RECOVER [AUTOMATIC] [FROM location]
 | TABLESPACE tablespace_name [, tablespace_name...]
```

It is very important to note that you can use tablespace recovery only while doing complete recovery—incomplete recovery cannot be done in Oracle7. In Oracle8 and 8*i*, you can do Tablespace Point-in-Time Recovery (TSPITR) for incomplete recovery of tablespaces.

The **recover tablespace** command does media recovery on all the data files in the tablespace(s) listed. We have learned that a tablespace is a logical entity that corresponds to one or more physical data files on the disk. Oracle knows which tablespace contains what data only when the database is open. Therefore, you can do tablespace recovery only when the database is open.

Before doing tablespace recovery, you have to take the tablespace offline. Tablespaces that cannot be taken offline (such as SYSTEM) cannot be recovered using the **recover tablespace** command. If none of the data files of a tablespace need recovery, an error is signaled.

## Checklist for Tablespace Recovery

A summary of tablespace recovery and an implementation plan are given here.

### Description

- Tablespace recovery allows online recovery of all restored data files in the listed tablespace(s).

- You can recover from an online or offline backup.

- You can do complete recovery only. (You should use TSPITR for incomplete recovery of tablespaces.)

### Requirements

- The database must be open.

- The tablespace to be recovered should be offline.

### Required Files

- Archived and online redo log files

- Current control file

- Backup of the data files (for lost or damaged files)

### Advantages

- Recovers all lost or damaged data files in the listed tablespace(s) in one step.

- It is faster than doing database recovery, since redo doesn't need to be applied to all data files.

- Other tablespaces in the database are accessible to users during recovery.

- Multiple SQL*PLUS sessions can be used to recover tablespaces in parallel.

### Disadvantages

- You cannot perform online recovery for tablespaces that cannot be taken offline, such as SYSTEM. To recover the SYSTEM tablespace, you have to use the **recover database** command.

- Incomplete recovery cannot be performed.

### Tablespace Recovery Implementation

1. Take the tablespace(s) that needs recovery offline:

   ```
   SQL> alter tablespace ts_name offline;
   ```

2. Restore all (or any) data files that belong to the tablespace(s) that needs recovery.

3. If the original location of a lost or damaged data file has become invalid (i.e., a disk crash), the path stored in the control file must be renamed to the new, restored file location:

   ```
   SQL> alter database rename file 'old_filename' to 'new_filename';
   ```

4. Recover the tablespace(s):

   ```
   SQL> RECOVER TABLESPACE ts_name [,ts_name ...]
   ```

   Oracle now prompts for the names of the archived redo log files that it needs to apply, beginning with the earliest log file needed. When all changes are applied to the database, Oracle displays a message saying "Media recovery complete."

5. Bring the tablespace online:

   ```
   SQL> alter tablespace ts_name online;
   ```

# Data File Recovery

The syntax for using data file recovery is as follows:

```
RECOVER [AUTOMATIC] [FROM location]
| DATAFILE 'filename' ['filename',...]
```

It is very important to note that you can use data file recovery only while doing complete recovery—incomplete recovery cannot be done.

The **recover datafile** command does recovery on all the data files listed. Online or offline recovery is possible as long as media recovery locks can be acquired on data files. If the database is open by any instance, then the data file recovery can recover only offline data files—online recovery cannot be performed while recovering the SYSTEM data files.

## Checklist for Data File Recovery

A summary of data file recovery and an implementation plan are given here.

### Description

■ Data file recovery allows recovery of a data file(s). You can use separate terminal sessions to perform parallel recovery of database files.

■ It allows recovery from offline or online backups.

■ Online or offline recovery (i.e., with database open or mounted) can be implemented, depending on the data files.

### Requirement

■ The data file must be taken offline for online recovery.

### Required Files

■ Archived and online redo logs

■ Current control file

■ Backup of data files (for the lost files)

### Advantages

■ Offline or online recovery can be performed.

■ Multiple SQL*PLUS sessions can be implemented to recover data files in parallel.

### Disadvantages

■ For online recovery, the data file must be taken offline. Therefore, SYSTEM data files cannot be recovered with the **recover datafile** command.

■ Cannot perform incomplete recovery.

## Online Recovery Implementation

1. Mount the database:

   ```
   SQL> startup mount [dbname]
   ```

2. Take all the damaged or lost data files offline:

   ```
   SQL> alter database datafile 'filename' offline;
   ```

3. Open the database:

   ```
   SQL> alter database open;
   ```

4. Restore the data files that need to be recovered (i.e., the files that were taken offline in step 2). If the original location of a lost or damaged database file has become invalid (i.e., a disk crash), the path stored in the control file must be renamed to the new, restored file location:

   ```
   SQL> alter database rename file 'old_filename' to 'new_filename';
   ```

5. Recover the data file(s):

   ```
   SQL> RECOVER DATAFILE 'datafile' [, 'datafile'...]
   ```

   Oracle now prompts for the names of the archived redo log files that it needs to apply, beginning with the earliest log file needed. When all changes are applied to the database, Oracle displays a message saying "Media recovery complete."

6. Bring the data file(s) online:

   ```
   SQL> alter database datafile 'filename' online;
   ```

## Offline Recovery Implementation

1. Restore any data files that need recovery. If the original location of a lost or damaged database file has become invalid (i.e., a disk crash), the path stored in the control file must be renamed to the new, restored file location:

   ```
   SQL> alter database rename file 'old_filename' to 'new_filename'
   ```

2. Mount the database:

   ```
   SQL> startup restrict mount [dbname]
   ```

3. Since the database is closed, the data files can be offline or online. You can use the following commands to take data files online or offline, respectively:

   ```
   SQL> alter database datafile 'filename' online
   SQL> alter database datafile 'filename' offline
   ```

**4.** Recover the data file(s):

```
SQL> RECOVER DATAFILE 'datafile' [, 'datafile'...]
```

Oracle now prompts for the names of the archived redo log files that it needs to apply, beginning with the earliest log file needed. When all changes are applied to the database, Oracle displays a message saying "Media recovery complete."

**5.** If the data file(s) was offline during recovery (i.e., in step 4), you need to bring it online before startup. You can skip this step if the data file(s) is online:

```
SQL> alter database datafile 'filename' online;
```

**6.** Open the database:

```
SQL> alter database [dbname] open;
```

Table 6-3 compares the three media recovery options.

| Recover Database | Recover Tablespace | Recover Data File |
|---|---|---|
| Recovers all data files of the database in one step. | Can recover one tablespace, multiple tablespaces, or all tablespaces in a single step. | Can recover a single database file, multiple database files, or all database files in one step. |
| Used with the database closed and with files to be recovered online. | Used with the database open, but with the tablespace being recovered offline. | Used with the database closed or open; if open, data files to recover should be offline. |
| Must be used if the damaged tablespace is the SYSTEM. | Cannot be used to recover a tablespace that cannot be taken offline, such as SYSTEM. | Cannot be used when the database is open to recover files in the SYSTEM tablespace. |
| Two sessions cannot recover the database simultaneously. | Can be used with multiple SQL*PLUS sessions to recover multiple tablespaces in parallel. | Can be used with multiple SQL*PLUS sessions to recover multiple data files in parallel. |
| Incomplete recovery can be done. | Complete recovery only. | Complete recovery only. |

**TABLE 6-3.** *Comparison of the Three Media Recovery Options*

## Creating Control File and Data Files

While doing media recovery, it is always suggested to use the current control file, if you have one. If the current control file is lost as part of the media failure, you can use a backup copy of the control file or create a new control file. The syntax to create a new control file is given here:

```
CREATE CONTROLFILE [REUSE] [SET]
DATABASE [dbname]
LOGFILE filespec [, filespec, ...]
RESETLOGS / NORESETLOGS
DATAFILE filespec [, filespec, ...]
[MAXLOGIFLES integer]
[MAXLOGMEMBERS integer]
[MAXLOGHISTORY integer]
[MAXDATAFILES integer]
[MAXINSTANCES integer]
[ARCHIVELOG | NOARCHIVELOG]
```

For a complete description of the keywords, refer to *Oracle8i SQL Reference*.

The **create controlfile** command can be used to create a new control file when all the existing control files are lost or corrupted. This command is very commonly used to alter some of the parameters, such as MAXDATAFILES and MAXLOGFILES. Note that these parameters are set when the database is originally created, and the only way to alter them is to re-create the database or the control file. Obviously, re-creating the entire database is impractical, so you should use the **create controlfile** command to modify these parameters.

The **create controlfile** command can be issued only after the database is started with the **startup nomount** option. After executing this command, a new control file is created and the database is automatically mounted. The new control file can then be used for recovery, if needed. The first database open will verify that the data dictionary is consistent with the information in the new control file. After the database is open, it is strongly recommended that you shut the database down cleanly and take a complete backup. This is particularly important if the RESETLOGS option was used while creating the control file. The following example illustrates how to create a new control file:

1. Take a backup of all available redo log files, data files, and control files before attempting this operation.

2. Start up the instance, but don't mount the database:

   ```
   SQL>  STARTUP NOMOUNT pfile=c:\oracle\ora81\admin\test\pfile\init.ora
   ```

3. Issue the **create controlfile** command.

**4.** Recovery may be implemented, if needed; otherwise, go to next step.

**5.** Open the database:

```
SQL> ALTER DATABASE OPEN [NO]RESETLOGS;
```

In step 3, you should specify all the data files and log files that are part of the database. It may be difficult for you to remember them unless you have written them down somewhere. For this purpose, the following command should be used:

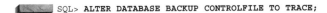

```
SQL> ALTER DATABASE BACKUP CONTROLFILE TO TRACE;
```

This command creates a SQL script that can be used to create a new control file. This command should be used as part of your backup procedure. Here is a sample trace file that is created by executing the above SQL command:

```
SQL> alter database backup controlfile to trace;
Statement processed.
```

On a Windows NT installation, the above command produced a trace file (in the directory pointed to by the USER_DUMP_DEST parameter in the **init.ora**) with the following content:

```
Dump file C:\Oracle\admin\ora8i\udump\ORA00297.TRC
Tue Jun 20 15:37:53 2000
ORACLE V8.1.5.0.0 - Production vsnsta=0
vsnsql=d vsnxtr=3
Windows NT V4.0, OS V5.101, CPU type 586
Oracle8i Enterprise Edition Release 8.1.5.0.0 - Production
With the Partitioning and Java options
PL/SQL Release 8.1.5.0.0 - Production
Windows NT V4.0, OS V5.101, CPU type 586
Instance name: test

Redo thread mounted by this instance: 1

Oracle process number: 25

Windows thread id: 297, image: ORACLE.EXE


*** SESSION ID:(22.33144) 2000.06.20.15.37.53.016
*** 2000.06.20.15.37.53.016
# The following commands will create a new control file and use it
# to open the database.
# Data used by the recovery manager will be lost. Additional logs may
# be required for media recovery of offline data files. Use this
# only if the current version of all online logs are available.
STARTUP NOMOUNT
CREATE CONTROLFILE REUSE DATABASE "ORA8I" NORESETLOGS NOARCHIVELOG
    MAXLOGFILES 32
    MAXLOGMEMBERS 2
    MAXDATAFILES 32
    MAXINSTANCES 16
```

```
     MAXLOGHISTORY 1630
LOGFILE
  GROUP 1 'C:\ORACLE\ORADATA\TEST\REDO04.LOG'   SIZE 1M,
  GROUP 2 'C:\ORACLE\ORADATA\TEST\REDO03.LOG'   SIZE 1M,
  GROUP 3 'C:\ORACLE\ORADATA\TEST\REDO02.LOG'   SIZE 1M,
  GROUP 4 'C:\ORACLE\ORADATA\TEST\REDO01.LOG'   SIZE 1M
DATAFILE
  'C:\ORACLE\ORADATA\TEST\SYSTEM01.DBF',
  'C:\ORACLE\ORADATA\TEST\USERS01.DBF',
  'C:\ORACLE\ORADATA\TEST\RBS01.DBF',
  'C:\ORACLE\ORADATA\TEST\TEMP01.DBF',
  'C:\ORACLE\ORADATA\TEST\OEMREP01.DBF',
  'C:\ORACLE\ORADATA\TEST\INDX01.DBF',
  'RMAN_TS_DATA',
  'ABCD',
  'USER_DATA',
  'RCVAT',
  'USER_DATA1'
CHARACTER SET WE8ISO8859P1
;
# Configure snapshot controlfile filename
EXECUTE
SYS.DBMS_BACKUP_RESTORE.CFILESETSNAPSHOTNAME('C:\ORACLE\TEST\DATABASE\SNCFORA8I.ORA');
# Recovery is required if any of the datafiles are restored backups,
# or if the last shutdown was not normal or immediate.
RECOVER DATABASE
# Database can now be opened normally.
ALTER DATABASE OPEN;
# Files in normal offline tablespaces are now named.
ALTER DATABASE RENAME FILE 'MISSING00008'
  TO 'USER_TEMP';
# Files in read-only tablespaces are now named.
ALTER DATABASE RENAME FILE 'MISSING00013'
  TO 'C:\LOB\DATA1';
# Online the files in read-only tablespaces.
ALTER TABLESPACE "DATA_TS" ONLINE;
# No tempfile entries found to add.
#
```

When you add a new data file to a tablespace or create a new tablespace, you should take a backup of the new data file(s) and the control file immediately. If you forget to take a copy of the data file(s) and you lose the current data file due to a media failure, you can create the data file(s) using the following command:

SQL> **ALTER DATABASE CREATE DATAFILE *'filename'*;**

This is a very useful command introduced in Oracle7. It can be used to create a new empty data file that will replace the existing one. At this point, media recovery should be performed to roll forward the data file. This means that all the changes made to the data file since its creation should be saved by retaining the necessary archived redo log files. Oracle records the SCN value in the control file when a new data file is created; so when you apply recovery, Oracle tells you where to start recovery. In order to use this command to create SYSTEM data files, the database should be created with the ARCHIVELOG option; otherwise, this command can be used only for data files that are created after the database is put in ARCHIVELOG mode. Chapter 10 provides a case study on how to use this command.

# Recovery Strategy

For smooth operation of the database and prompt recovery from failures, you need to plan a robust backup and recovery strategy. The first step in doing this is to determine the business goals. Operation requirements cannot be met if they are unknown or undefined. The second step is to do an operations review on the current backup and recovery strategy against the reliability and availability requirements stated in the business goals.

A DBA should be able to do an operations audit on the recovery strategy to identify remedial action where the present backup and recovery implementation does not meet operations requirements, or in the case of a new system, to provide a robust backup and recovery strategy. If this is done, the risk of losing data can be minimized and the DBA can have peace of mind.

The first step is to establish the requirements. You should be able to answer the following questions before planning a backup and recovery strategy:

■ How much data can I afford to lose?

■ How long can the database be offline to perform backups?

■ Should recovery be needed, how quickly do I need to recover the data?

■ What resources are available for me to do backup and recovery?

■ Do I need the capability to reverse changes made to the database?

These are all important factors. For example, if you can afford to lose a week's worth of data if a failure occurs (i.e., you can easily populate the last week's worth of data), then you can take weekly backups. Similarly, how long the database can be down while taking backups will determine whether a hot or cold backup should be taken.

The following are some issues to consider while designing a backup and recovery strategy:

■ Redo log files need to be sized according to operational requirements. The size of the online redo log files should be determined by estimating the amount of redo the transactions would be generating per hour. A point of failure in version 6 was the loss of online redo log files. So, multiplexing of online redo log files is very important (i.e., maintaining multiple log members for each log group).

■ At least three copies of the control file should be maintained on different disks. Disks should be mounted under different controllers.

■ Database design considerations, such as planning to keep archived redo log files and online log files on different disks, are important.

■ In many cases, the procedure of rolling forward a database or database file from a backup can be simplified and made faster by keeping, on disk, a recent backup of all the data files and all the associated archived redo log files. For many systems, much of the time necessary for recovery is spent restoring the data and archived redo log files from tape.

■ Operate in ARCHIVELOG mode to utilize greater flexibility in recovery options.

■ A higher level of security can be achieved by maintaining a second backup of offline archived redo log files. This copy should ideally be to tape, requiring a dedicated tape drive and some operator monitoring. Disk mirroring might not be a safe option in some cases.

■ The use of the UNIX **compress** utility should be verified with the hardware vendor.

■ The physical copying of disks to tape should detect disk errors. An additional check on database health may be achieved via the export mechanism. This has the advantage of reading and optionally analyzing all data tables. It is recommended that the production instances be automatically exported to disk prior to the nightly backup. An export should be completed with the database operating in RESTRICT mode, while no data is being modified. Two forms of export are recommended, *schema* and *full*. Both should use a parameter file including tables, synonyms, sequences, indexes, grants, and constraints.

■ In the event of object loss, it is often advantageous to have a complete set of object-creation scripts available outside the database. This is particularly useful for re-creating indexes, views, and constraints. Similarly, scripts should be maintained for grants.

■ You should have battle-tested rebuild strategies. It is highly recommended to prepare and test recovery scripts for each instance. Tests should address at least the following scenarios:

　■ Loss of a SYSTEM tablespace

　■ Loss of a non-SYSTEM tablespace

- Loss of a non-SYSTEM tablespace with active rollback segments

- Loss of redo logs (online and archived)

- Loss of static or dynamic user tables

- Loss of control file

# Logical Recovery Using import

Oracle provides the **import** utility for DBAs who rely on logical backups to restore the data. The **import** utility reads data from export files (DDL and DML SQL statements), executes them to create the tables, and populates the data into the Oracle database. **import** automatically does any character set translation (ASCII or EBCDIC) necessary.

The **import** utility can be used to restore or reorganize a database. One of the main advantages of using the **import** utility is that you can be sure that no physical data block corruptions will be imported because no data block corruptions will be propagated to the backup file when exported. This is because the **export** utility does a full table scan on all the tables that are backed up (exported). Another advantage is that data can be exported from a database on one machine and imported into another. This is useful for DBAs running a heterogeneous environment.

To view the contents of the export file without importing it, the SHOW=Y **import** option can be used. **import** can be performed from the command line or by using a parameter file (PARFILE = *parameter_file*).

To import data using the **import** utility, the DBA must have access to the CONNECT and RESOURCE roles of an Oracle database and to the export file. Only a DBA can import an export file that was exported by a DBA. Rollback segments should be sized appropriately to perform the import or it will roll back to the last commit, only partially importing the data. By default, **import** commits after loading each table unless the COMMIT=Y parameter is used to commit after each array insert. This will guarantee that data imported remains in the database (doesn't get rolled back, since **commit** is issued after an **insert**), but will have an overhead on performance.

The RECORDLENGTH parameter is required when a DBA imports into another operating system that by default uses a different value. The BUFFER size must be set high enough to import a table row containing long fields. If rows contain LONG data, only one row at a time is fetched. The *Oracle8i Utilities* guide gives complete details on the **import** utility.

## Before You Import

There are few steps, shown next, that you have to perform before you start using the **import** utility.

1. Make sure that you run the SQL script **catexp.sql** that creates the necessary internal views for **export/import** utility. It also assigns all necessary privileges such as SELECT ANY TABLE, BACKUP ANY TABLE, EXECUTE ANY PROCEDURE, and EXECUTE ANY TYPE to the IMP_FULL_DATABASE role for the **import** utility to work. This role will then be assigned to the DBA role for proper execution of export on the database. You can verify the creation of the role IMP_FULL_DATABASE and privileges assigned to it using Oracle Security Manager. If you have run the script **catalog.sql** while creating your database, you need not run the script **catexp.sql**, as **catalog.sql** automatically runs **catexp.sql**.

**NOTE**
*The actual names of the script files depend on your operating system. The script filenames and the method for running them are described in your Oracle operating system-specific documentation.*

2. As a DBA, if and when you want to assign a user to perform a full database import, he or she has to be granted the IMP_ FULL_DATABASE role. By default, this role is assigned to the DBA role.

3. If you plan to use Oracle Enterprise Manager V2.0 GUI for automating and scheduling imports on a database, you need to ensure that Oracle Intelligent Agent is running on that database and is registered with the Management Server for the **import** utility to work.

4. Space availability must be checked in the respective database/tablespace. This is very important in case of importing BFILE and tables containing LONG columns.

5. The BUFFER size must be set high enough to import a table row containing LONG fields.

6. When importing schema objects from one database to another, it is imperative that the same schema is available on the importing database.

## Executing the import Utility

The **import** utility can be invoked by using one of the following three methods at the system command prompt or from Oracle Enterprise Manager GUI:

1. By invoking **import** with import parameters that you want use. For example:

```
C:\> imp prod/password fromuser=john touser=pat file=prod.dmp tables=( Dept,Cstmr,
Cstm_det) log=user.log
```

2. By specifying the **import** utility with the parameter (PARFILE) file, as given below:

```
C:\>imp username/password PARFILE=filename
```

The PARFILE is a file containing the import parameters through which you want to control the behavior of import operation. A typical PARFILE file will look as follows:

```
FILE=prod.dmp
SHOW=n
IGNORE=n
GRANTS=y
FROMUSER=Johnn
TOUSER=pat
TABLES=(Dept,Cstmr, Cstm_det)
Log=users.log
```

3. By using Interactive mode.

Invoking the **import** utility only with username/password enables an interactive session and subsequently **import** will prompt you for the information it needs. For example:

```
C:\> imp username/password
```

This mode is supported for backward compatibility only.

   If you have installed Oracle Enterprise Manager, **import** can also be invoked from Oracle Schema Manager and Oracle Storage Manager.

## Import Parameters

Table 6-4 gives the names of the parameters that you can use with the **import** utility, their default values, and brief descriptions. For more information refer to the *Oracle8i Utilities Release 8.1.5* manual.

## Import Modes

There are four modes in which you can import database objects. The FULL import mode is the first one; it can be enabled by using the FULL=YES option in the **import** command. The second mode is the USER import mode. Using the FROMUSER and TOUSER parameters, the **import** utility enables you to import objects that are owned by other users from an export file. The third mode is the TABLE mode, in which you can use the TABLES parameter to import selected tables into the database. The fourth mode is the TABLESPACE mode, which allows you to move a set of tablespaces from one Oracle database to another. We discuss these modes now.

| Parameter | Default | Description |
|---|---|---|
| USERID | Undefined | The username/password of the user performing the import. |
| BUFFER | OS dependent | The size in bytes of the buffer used to transport data rows. |
| FILE | **expdat.dmp** | The name of the export file to import. |
| SHOW | No | A flag to indicate whether to list only the contents of the export file, and not import the table data, not create any object, and not modify the database. |
| IGNORE | Yes | A flag to indicate whether to ignore errors if the object already exists during import. |
| GRANTS | Yes | A flag to indicate whether to import grants. |
| INDEXES | Yes | A flag to indicate whether to import indexes. |
| ROWS | Yes | A flag to indicate whether to import the rows of table data. |
| FULL | No | A flag to indicate whether to import the entire file. |
| FROMUSER | Undefined | A list of user names whose objects are exported. |
| TOUSER | Undefined | A list of user names to whom data is imported. |
| TABLES | Undefined | A list of table names to import. |
| RECORDLENGTH | System dependent | The length in bytes of the file record. |
| INCTYPE | Undefined | The type of incremental import. Valid values are SYSTEM and RESTORE. |
| COMMIT | No | A flag to indicate whether to commit after each array insert. By default, **import** commits after loading each table. |
| PARFILE | Undefined | The name of an **import** parameter file that contains one or more parameter specifications. |

**TABLE 6-4.** *Description of **import** Parameters*

## Full Database Import

This mode of import is useful if you are recovering database objects from a full database export file dump. In this mode of import, all the objects found in the export file will be imported into the database. The export file may be a COMPLETE, CUMULATIVE, or INCREMENTAL database export file. The full database import mode can also be further divided into COMPLETE, CUMULATIVE, and INCREMENTAL imports. CUMULATIVE and INCREMENTAL imports take less time than COMPLETE imports and allow you to get an import of just the changed data and definitions. While doing imports, it is very important to note the order in which COMPLETE, INCREMENTAL, and CUMULATIVE exports are done. This is because a COMPLETE export must be done before performing a FULL database import. If you have taken COMPLETE export followed by INCREMENTAL or CUMULATIVE exports, while doing recovery you must perform **import** as follows.

Run an **import** from the most recent INCREMENTAL or CUMULATIVE export file by specifying INCTYPE=SYSTEM, followed by most recent COMPLETE export file by specifying INCTYPE=RESTORE, and end with an import from the most recent INCREMENTAL or CUMULATIVE exports file with the INCTYPE=RESTORE option. In this case, you are performing an import from the most recent INCREMENTAL or CUMULATIVE export file twice, once at the beginning of the recovery with INCTYPE=SYSTEM option and at the end of the recovery with INCTYPE=RESTORE option. This ensures the importing of the most recent objects of the system by specifying INCTYPE=SYSTEM and FULL=Y. It is important to note that an import from an INCREMENTAL export file drops the existing database objects before new objects are imported. In the case of a normal import, objects are not dropped, and an error is usually generated if the object already exists. All three modes should be used in a robust backup scheme.

**COMPLETE Import**    A COMPLETE import should be done as part of a full database import. To perform this type of import, you should set the parameter INCTYPE=COMPLETE in the **import** command. After each COMPLETE import, both the preceding CUMULATIVE and INCREMENTAL export files are no longer required. For example:

```
C:\imp system/manager inctype=restore full=Y file=file_spec
```

In the above example, the parameter INCTYPE=RESTORE causes the **import** utility to import all user database objects and data contained in the export file, excluding system objects. You can also use a parameter file that allows you to specify import parameters in a text file, which can easily be modified or reused. By doing this, you need not type all the parameters at the command prompt every time you want to invoke **import** with different parameter settings.

Oracle also allows you to perform an import on the remote database using the Net8 service name. The export file can be placed locally or remotely. If it is placed on a remote machine, it must be accessible to the **import** utility. In the above example, the **import** operation is performed on the database residing on a local machine. You can modify the same command to perform an import on a remote database by supplying the Net8 service name in the **import** command syntax as follows:

```
C:\imp system/manager@test.demo parfile=c:\utility\fullexp.txt
```

In this case, Oracle uses the Net8 service name "test.demo" to log on to the remote database as user SYSTEM and performs an import on the remote database.

The CUMULATIVE database import imports only tables that have been modified or created since the most recent CUMULATIVE or COMPLETE export file. An incremental import can be done in two ways: using SYSTEM or the RESTORE type. If you specify INCTYPE=SYSTEM, **import** imports only the object types and their definitions from an export file. It will not import user data or objects from an export file. If you specify the INCTYPE=RESTORE, **import** extracts all user database objects and data contained in the export file. It will not import object types and their definitions.

### Example: Re-creating the Database from an Incremental Export

Once the data is exported, you can use the following steps to import data from an incremental export:

1. Using the *most recent* export file (whether COMPLETE, CUMULATIVE, or INCREMENTAL), restore the database definitions using the following command:

   ```
   $ imp DBA/passwd inctype=system full=Y file=exp_file
   ```

2. Bring the necessary rollback segments ONLINE.

3. Import the most recent COMPLETE export file using the following command:

   ```
   $ imp DBA/passwd inctype=restore full=Y file=file_spec
   ```

   If no CUMULATIVE exports were taken, skip to step 5.

4. Import, in chronological order, all the CUMULATIVE export files since the most recent COMPLETE export:

   ```
   $ imp DBA/passwd inctype=restore full=Y file=file_spec
   ```

5. Import, in chronological order, all the INCREMENTAL export files since the most recent CUMULATIVE (or COMPLETE) export, using the following command:

   ```
   $ imp DBA/passwd inctype=restore full=Y file=file_spec
   ```

### Restrictions

■ INCREMENTAL, CUMULATIVE, and COMPLETE exports can be performed only in FULL database mode (FULL=Y).

■ Only users who have the role EXP_FULL_DATABASE can run INCREMENTAL, CUMULATIVE, and COMPLETE exports.

■ You cannot specify INCREMENTAL exports as read-consistent.

**NOTE**
*INCREMENTAL, CUMULATIVE, and COMPLETE exports are obsolete features that will be phased out in a subsequent release. You should begin now to migrate to Oracle's Recovery Manager for database backups.*

## USERMode Import

This mode of import can be used to import one or more database users' schemas. It allows the user who invokes **import** to import objects from an export file into his or her own schema and another user's schema as well, if the IMP_FULL_DATABASE role is enabled for him or her. If you don't have IMP_FULL_DATABASE role enabled, you can only import your own objects from an export file. USER mode is also appropriate if you want to move objects from one user to another.

For example, the user PROD has been assigned the IMP_FULL_DATABASE role for importing objects into his own schema and into other user's schema as well. Figures 6-5 through 6-10 show how to do import using the Data Management GUI utility from Oracle Enterprise ManagerV2. The following procedure shows how to import into your own schema as well as importing into other users' schemas.

1. After you invoke the **import** utility, you will see the Import File window, as shown in Figure 6-5. Specify the import filename and its location in the File Name field. This wizard also supports multiple import dump files. To import from multiple dump files, you should specify all the filenames in the same sequence as they were created during the export process. You can change the file sequence by selecting the file and clicking the Up and Down arrow buttons on the right side of this window. Then click the Next button.

2. In the Import Type window, select the type of import you want to perform from the available import modes, as shown in Figure 6-6. The Import wizard enables the appropriate import mode option based on the type of export mode you have chosen for creating the export dump file during export. Click the Next button.

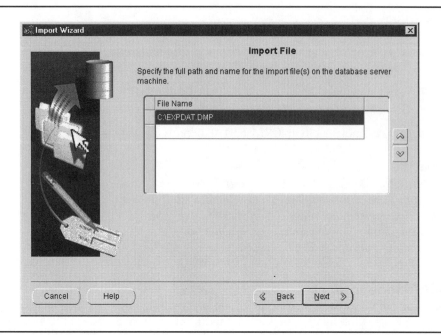

**FIGURE 6-5.** *Specifying the export file names and their location*

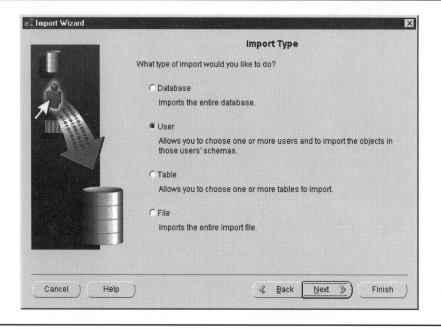

**FIGURE 6-6.** *Selecting the type of import*

3. In the User Selection window, select the users you want to import from the Available Users list. The selected user names will be displayed in the right column of the window, as shown in Figure 6-7. The wizard builds the Available Users list based on the export file content. Click the Next button.

4. The User Mapping window allows you to import objects from one user's schema into another user's schema. If you want to do so, click the Yes radio button as shown in Figure 6-8. This figure shows that we are importing the tables that belong to SCOTT into the user PROD. For further selection of objects, click the Next button. Otherwise, click Finish to complete import specifications.

5. When you click the Next button, you will see the Associated Objects window. Here you can decide exactly what you want to import. Figure 6-9 shows selected the data, grants, indexes, and the constraints of all the tables to be imported. To specify whether to import the statistics that are found in the import file or recalculate statistics and to tune the import process, click the Advanced button. Otherwise, click the Finish button to complete the process. If you click the Next button, you will see the Summary window.

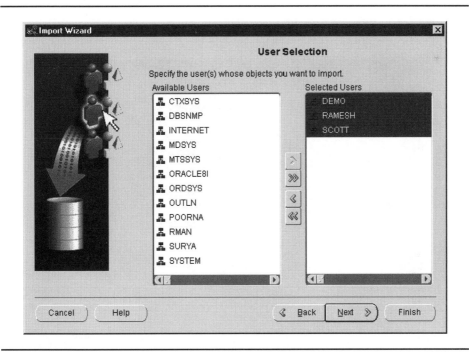

**FIGURE 6-7.** *Selecting users from available users*

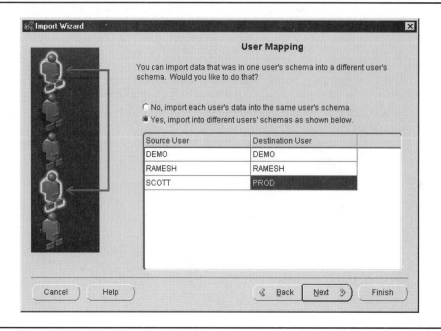

**FIGURE 6-8.** *Importing schema options*

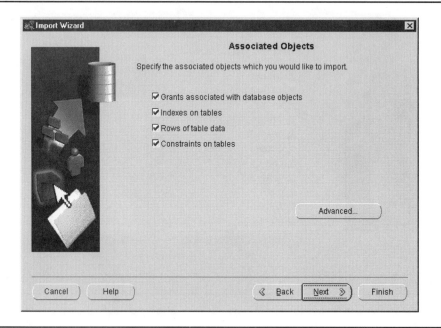

**FIGURE 6-9.** *Import object specification*

**6.** Figure 6-10 shows the summary of the import operation that we have specified. Click OK to complete the process and submit the import job to OEM for execution.

You can make use of the new feature of Oracle8*i* for importing from multiple export dump files. Oracle8*i* **export/import** utility has the ability to export and import precalculated optimizer statistics instead of recomputing the statistics at import time. This ability to export precalculated optimizer statistics helps the **import** operation to be much faster, as there is no need to estimate statistics at the time of import.

## TABLE Mode Import

TABLE mode import allows you to restore table data from an export file generated by FULL, USER and TABLE modes. This mode of import is appropriate when you want to restore only a given table's data into a user schema. In this mode, users can import tables owned by them. By default, if you invoke the **import** utility, you can import only the tables in your schema. You cannot import table definitions that are

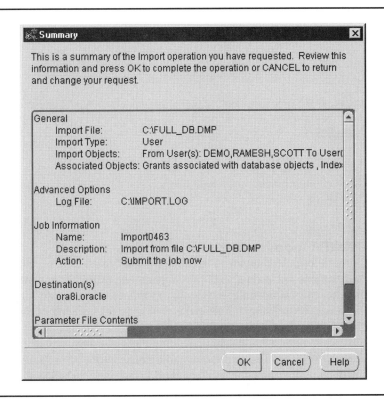

**FIGURE 6-10.** *Viewing the summary of export job*

referenced to other objects on which you don't have privileges. If you have the IMP_FULL_DATABASE role assigned to you, then you can import tables from any user's schema into the database by specifying TABLES=*schema.table_name*. If you don't specify a schema, **import** defaults to the schema from which the object was exported. For example, a TABLE-mode import can be invoked as follows:

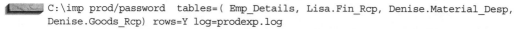

```
C:\imp prod/password  tables=( Emp_Details, Lisa.Fin_Rcp, Denise.Material_Desp,
Denise.Goods_Rcp) rows=Y log=prodexp.log
```

In this example, assume that the IMP_FULL_DATABASE role is assigned to the user PROD. PROD is importing a table called EMP_DETAILS owned by her, a table called FIN_RCP from Lisa's schema and two more tables called MATERIAL_DESP and GOODS_RCP that belong to Denise's schema. Note that the schema name for the table EMP_DETAILS is not mentioned. **import** then defaults to the schema in which it was exported.

Assume that the user PROD doesn't have the IMP_FULL_DATABASE role assigned to her and she tries to import the tables. You will see the following error:

```
C:\imp prod/password  tables=( Emp_Details, Lisa.Fin_Rcp,
Denise.Material_Desp, Denise.Goods_Rcp) rows=Y log=prodexp.log

Import: Release 8.1.5.0.0 - Production on Tue Jun 6 15:07:34 2000

(c) Copyright 1999 Oracle Corporation.  All rights reserved.


Connected to: Oracle8i Enterprise Edition Release 8.1.5.0.0 - Production
With the Partitioning and Java options
PL/SQL Release 8.1.5.0.0 - Production

Export file created by EXPORT:V08.01.05 via conventional path
IMP-00013: only a DBA can import a file exported by another DBA
IMP-00000: Import terminated unsuccessfully

C:\>
```

## TABLESPACE Mode Import

TABLESPACE mode import allows you to move a subset of an Oracle database and "plug" it in to another Oracle database. Moving data via transportable tablespaces can be much faster than performing either an import/export or unload/load of the same data, because transporting a tablespace only requires copying of data files and integrating the tablespace structural information. You can also use transportable tablespaces to move index data, thereby avoiding the index rebuilds you would have to perform when importing or loading table data. Before transporting tablespaces between databases, tablespaces must be set to READ-ONLY mode. This prevents any transactions that may alter data in the tablespace.

The following example shows how to transport a tablespace from one database to another database using a TABLESPACE import. Let us assume that you want to transport TS1, TS2, and TS3 tablespaces from the database ORA8I.ORACLE to database TEST.DEMO. To perform transporting of tablespaces, you have to create an export file as per the guidelines given in Chapter 4 for exporting tablespaces. In order to transport the tablespaces, you should do the following:

1. Copy the data files **ts1_data.dbf**, **ts2_data.dbf**, and **ts3_data.dbf** (that belong to the respective tablespaces) to the destination database TEST.DEMO.

2. Run the **import** utility as SYSDBA to complete the tablespace transport. For example:

```
C:\>IMP TRANSPORT_TABLESPACE=Y DATAFILES='C:\DATAFILES\ TS1_DATA.DBF',
'C:\DATAFILES\ TS2_DATA.DBF', 'C:\DATAFILES\ TS3_DATA.DBF' TABLESPACES= TS
1,TS2, TS3 TTS_OWNERS=PROD,VENKAT FROMUSER=PROD,VENKAT TOUSER=SCOTT, JOHN
FILE=C:\BACKUP\TS_TRANS.DMP LOG=TS_LOG.LOG
Import: Release 8.1.5.0.0 - Production on Sun May 14 12:13:05 2000
(c) Copyright 1999 Oracle Corporation.  All rights reserved.
Username: SYS AS SYSDBA
Password:
Connected to: Oracle8i Enterprise Edition Release 8.1.5.0.0 - Production
With the Partitioning and Java options
PL/SQL Release 8.1.5.0.0 - Production
Export file created by EXPORT:V08.01.05 via conventional path
About to import transportable tablespace(s) metadata...
import done in WE8ISO8859P1 character set and WE8ISO8859P1 NCHAR character set
Import terminated successfully without warnings.
```

When you enter the above **import** command, it will ask you to enter a user name. To perform the import, you should log in as "SYS AS SYSDBA" in order to update the data dictionary regarding the newly plugged tablespaces. The **import** utility reads all the tablespace definitions from the export file and updates the dictionary. TABLESPACES, TTS_OWNERS, FROMUSER, and TOUSER are optional parameters. If you do not specify FROMUSER and TOUSER, all database objects will be created under the same user as in the source database. In this case, you must ensure that those users exist in the destination database. If not, **import** will return an error. You can use the FROMUSER and TOUSER parameters to change the owners of objects. For example, if you want to import the objects in the tablespace set owned by the user PROD to user SCOTT, you must specify FROMUSER=PROD TOUSER=SCOTT in the **import** command. For more information refer to the *Oracle8i Utilities Release 8.1.5* manual.

# Partition-Level Import

A partition-level import allows you to move table data selectively from one database to another across tables and partitions. A partition-level import lets you to import one or more specified partitions or subpartitions within a table from an export dump file created in TABLE mode export. For example, if you have an export file of a partitioned table that was created in TABLE mode export and now you want to restore the table partition from the export file, you can use the partition-level import. You should ensure that the database has the required tablespaces available before you import the partitions. Enter the following **import** command to perform a partition-level import:

```
C:\>IMP PROD/PROD FILE=C:\BACKUP\PARTAB.DMP IGNORE=YES FULL=YES
LOG=C:\BACKUP\LOG\PRATABLOG.TXT

Import: Release 8.1.5.0.0 - Production on Tue Jun 6 11:14:56 2000

(c) Copyright 1999 Oracle Corporation.  All rights reserved.


Connected to: Oracle8i Enterprise Edition Release 8.1.5.0.0 - Production
With the Partitioning and Java options
PL/SQL Release 8.1.5.0.0 - Production

Export file created by EXPORT:V08.01.05 via conventional path

Warning: the objects were exported by prod1, not by you

import done in WE8ISO8859P1 character set and WE8ISO8859P1 NCHAR character set
. importing prod1's objects into prod
. . importing partition       "REGISTRATIONS_RANGE":"P1"     27344 rows imported
. . importing partition       "REGISTRATIONS_RANGE":"P2"     27984 rows imported
. . importing partition       "REGISTRATIONS_RANGE":"P3"       924 rows imported
Import terminated successfully without warnings.

C:\>
```

In the above example, all rows in the partition (p1, p2, and p3) of the table are imported.

## Importing BFILE

When you use the **import** utility to restore tables that contain BFILE columns, it imports only the data definition (such as BFILE locator), directory alias, filename, and so on that are available in the export file. This is because the **export** utility only records the names and directory aliases referenced by the BFILE columns. BFILE contents will not be recorded in the export file. As a DBA, you have to copy all the directories from the source to destination database manually before you can use the table. If you move the database to a location in which the old directories cannot be used to access the included files, you must create the directories at the O/S level and copy the BFILE files to the new location. For example, let us assume that the table IMAGE has a column of type BFILE that contains a reference to the binary file that is placed in a directory called **c:\Image1** and you have taken an export of the table. If you want to import the table to another database, you should do the following:

1. Copy the directory **Image1** that contains the image files to the destination system where you want to import the table. If you need to relocate the directory to a new location, you have to re-create the directory alias for the new location of the directory.

2. Invoke the **import** utility to import the table as follows:

```
C:\>imp lob_user/lob_user file=c:\backup\lob_user.dmp full=y ignore=y
log=c:\backup\log\lob_log.txt

Import: Release 8.1.5.0.0 - Production on Tue Jun 6 17:32:18 2000

(c) Copyright 1999 Oracle Corporation.  All rights reserved.


Connected to: Oracle8i Enterprise Edition Release 8.1.5.0.0 - Production
With the Partitioning and Java options
PL/SQL Release 8.1.5.0.0 - Production

Export file created by EXPORT:V08.01.05 via conventional path
import done in WE8ISO8859P1 character set and WE8ISO8859P1 NCHAR character
set
. importing LOB_USER's objects into LOB_USER
. . importing table                  "LOB_TABLE"            9 rows imported
Import terminated successfully without warnings.

C:\>
```

For more information refer to the *Oracle8i Utilities Release 8.1.5* manual.

# Disaster Recovery

This section gives you details on design considerations, planning, and maintenance of standby databases. Refer to the "Hot Standby Database" section in Chapter 3 for a definition of standby databases.

## Concepts and Terminology

This section describes the concepts and terminology behind the standby database feature. First, we will briefly review the recovery mechanism in Oracle8i. Emphasis is placed on areas affecting the standby mechanism. Next, we will briefly review the standby database feature and how changes are propagated from the primary to the standby database.

## Archiving and Recovery

Let us consider a production database. When the database is running, Oracle guarantees transaction durability by logging changes to data in the form of *redo*. When the Oracle recovery mechanism is invoked, redo is applied to data to restore database consistency. Redo is written to the online redo log files by *LGWR*, a background process. The online redo log is composed of two or more online redo log files. LGWR writes to one online log at a time, the *current* or *active* log. When the active log is filled, LGWR performs a *log switch* and begins writing to the next available online log. When all online logs are filled, the next available online log will be reused, and so on, in a cyclic fashion.

Let us assume that the database is now running in ARCHIVELOG mode and automatic archiving is enabled. Let us now consider the following events, diagrammed in Figure 6-11:

- At time TBackup, an *offline backup* of the database completes successfully.

- At time TFirstArchive, an archive log file is successfully created after the backup.

- At time TLastArchive, archiving successfully creates an archive log file before a failure.

- At time TFailure, a failure occurs making the database unusable, such that *media recovery* is necessary.

**NOTE**
*At the point of failure, it is possible that at least one inactive online log was being copied to an archive log file. Such archive log files are not available for recovery. If available, the online redo log can be used to recover to the last committed transaction before the failure.*

Let us now consider media recovery. After the media failure is repaired and the system is brought back online, the database is restored from the offline database backup. The backed up archive log files from time TFirstArchive to TLastArchive are also restored. Recovery commands are issued such that the archive log files are used to *apply* redo to the database. The database is now consistent up to time TLastArchive; that is, the point in time at the end of the last committed transaction in the last archive log file used in the recovery. However, the database is not completely recovered up to the time of failure, TFailure. If a valid copy of the online

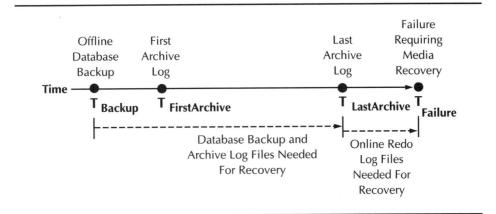

**FIGURE 6-11.**  *Backup and recovery timelines*

redo logs is available as of $T_{Failure}$, then—and only then—can those redo logs be used to recover the database up to the point in time of the failure. If the online redo logs are not available, then committed transactions that occurred after the last recovered archive log are lost—that is, transactions committed during the period $T_{LastArchive}$ to $T_{Failure}$.

## The Standby Database Feature—Overview

In this section, the standby database feature is briefly reviewed before describing how changes in the primary database are propagated to the standby. Administrative tasks are briefly outlined in this section; detailed descriptions are provided later in this section.

A *primary database* is a database that contains production data that must be protected against any kind of loss. A *standby database* is a copy of the primary database and can be brought online quickly to become the production database. When the standby database is *activated*, it becomes the production database, and the older version of the production database is no longer valid. Once the standby is activated, production users can then connect to the new production database. Figure 6-12 shows a standby database.

**Database Configuration and Implementation**    It is recommended that the hardware at the standby site be configured in exactly the same manner as the hardware at the primary site. (However, different configurations are possible, as

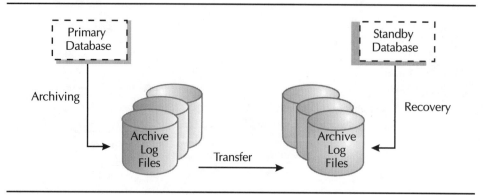

**FIGURE 6-12.** *Standby database*

discussed later in the "Database Design" section.) The only notable difference between the file structures of the two databases should be that the standby database has a special control file. Archiving must be enabled before deploying the standby feature. From that point on, archiving must remain enabled so that the standby database can be made reasonably concurrent with the primary by applying archive log files. Before setting up your standby database, you must choose which recovery mode you want keep your standby database in. Oracle provides you with two options: *manual* and *managed* recovery mode.

**NOTE**
*Although manual archiving can be used, it is always better to use automatic archiving.*

Deployment of the standby database can be briefly outlined as follows:

**I.** Primary site

    **A.** Back up initialization file(s), database files, and password file if you use remote login.

    **B.** Create standby database control file.

    **C.** If you want to enable the archive processes to archive to the standby location, configure the LOG_ARCHIVE_DEST_*n* parameters in the **init.ora** file to point to the standby database's archive destination. This will involve configuring a Net8 service name for the SERVICE attribute of the LOG_ARCHIVE_DEST_*n* parameter.

**II.** Transfer files to the standby site

**III.** Standby site

    **A.** Restore all data files that are copied from the primary site, including the standby control file.

    **B.** Create standby database instance.

    **C.** Mount the standby database using the standby control file.

    **D.** Leave the standby database either in Managed Recovery or Manual Recovery mode.

Before deploying the standby database, make sure that Net8 service configured at the primary site to connect to the standby site is working. The archive location at the standby site must be accessible from the primary site for the archive process to archive the online log files. If you make use of the LOG_ARCHIVE_DEST_$n$ parameter in the **init.ora** feature for transferring archived redo log files, Oracle uses the Remote File Server (RFS) process, using Net8 service for transferring the archived redo log files. If you choose to keep your standby database in manual recovery mode, the standby database needs to be maintained to ensure that changes (archive log files) at the primary are *propagated* to the standby database. Maintenance should be automatic so that propagation occurs quickly to ensure that the standby database is reasonably *concurrent* with the primary. How closely the standby database concurs with the primary depends on how quickly changes are propagated to the standby database.

Maintenance can be briefly outlined as follows:

    **I.** Primary site

        **A.** Continue archiving to archive log destination. This will include the archive destination at the standby site.

    **II.** Standby site

        **A.** Apply archive log files to standby database.

The redo in the archive log files from the primary is applied to the standby database. Thus, the standby database is in a constant state of recovery. This is the primary mechanism for propagating changes to the standby database.

**NOTE**
*The archive stream must not be interrupted at the primary site. If this occurs, then the standby database must be rebuilt.*

When a failure occurs, it is possible that one or more archive log files are not completed and are not available for recovery. In a standby database environment, if one or more complete archive log files are not transferred to the standby, then these archive log files are also not available for recovery. In other words, the standby database is only concurrent with the primary database to the last transaction in the last archived log file transferred and applied to the standby database. Transactions in the online log files are lost. This is a design issue that must be kept in mind when considering the transfer mechanism and the tuning of the archive log files.

**Redo Generation**    You must ensure that transactions occurring at the primary are propagated to the standby database through the archive log files. It is important to note that Oracle's redo logging and transaction consistency mechanisms work independently. The purpose of redo is to record changes to the database, which can be replayed during recovery.

A few database operations deliberately do not generate redo. For example, it is unnecessary to generate redo for sort segments because the segments are transient in nature, and changes to the segments are not needed during recovery. Furthermore, performance of some transactions can be improved by interfering with redo logging mechanism using the UNRECOVERABLE option. For details on the UNRECOVERABLE option, refer to the *Oracle8i SQL Reference Release 8.1.5* manual. Obviously, it is not possible to replay changes at the standby database that are *not* stored in the redo. In almost all cases, performing recovery at the standby database will bring the database to a state that is concurrent with the primary. For a few specific cases, as noted below, changes at the primary are recovered in a slightly different manner at the standby database. Furthermore, in some cases, it may be desirable not to propagate changes to the standby database.

**Invalidating the Standby Database**    If the archive stream is interrupted, then the standby database must be rebuilt. Any command issued at the primary that forces media recovery will interrupt the archive stream. Furthermore, media recovery is always necessary when the online redo logs are *cleared*. For more information on clearing logs, refer to the *Oracle8i Administrator's Guide Release 8.1.5* manual. Thus, *avoid using commands that interrupt the archive stream.*

**Full Propagation**    Full propagation occurs when a transaction at the primary is completely propagated to the standby database. At the primary site, almost all transactions generate the necessary redo to completely propagate a transaction. However, there are some transactions that are not completely propagated or only partially propagated through the archive log files. These transactions *can* be propagated with some extra administration. Conversely, you may choose *not* to propagate some transactions.

**Normal Propagation**    Normal propagation occurs when a complete transaction is propagated to the standby database through the archive log files. Assuming no errors occur at the standby database, normal propagation results in full propagation. This is the general case, and almost all transactions are propagated in this way.

For example, data file size changes are normally propagated. If the standby database's hardware is configured the same as the primary's hardware, then any successful data file size changes at the primary should normally result in full propagation. The standby database's hardware that is not configured the same as the primary's is more susceptible to failure. In particular, a propagated **resize** command attempting to increase the size of a data file might fail for lack of disk space. Furthermore, normal propagation that needs to increase the size of an autoextend data file might fail for lack of disk space. When a space availability problem is encountered, normal propagation can continue after freeing disk space. Normally, such problems can be avoided by ensuring that the standby database has available disk space.

We will look at how the **alter tablespace** command is propagated here:

- **Tablespace status**    Changing the status of a tablespace is normally propagated to the standby database.

- **Offline or read-only tablespaces**    The redo propagated to the standby database allows the recovery process to update the data dictionary and control file. Because no further redo is generated at the primary, no redo is subsequently propagated to the standby database. Thus, no action is needed at the standby site. If the standby database is activated, then the status in the control file is updated to OFFLINE or READ-ONLY. Note that after an OFFLINE or READ-ONLY status change, the data files can be brought online or made READ-WRITE, but only if the data files are recovered.

**Avoiding Propagation**    Sometimes, it may be desirable *not* to propagate transactions from the primary database to the standby database. For example, the redo generated for a heavily updated tablespace that is not mission-critical may slow down propagation to an unacceptable level. In this case, you can OFFLINE DROP the desired tablespace at the standby database. However, if the affected tablespace is needed when the standby database is activated, then the tablespace must be brought online at activation time and may need recovery.

**NOTE**
*Obviously, an OFFLINE DROP at the standby
database does not stop redo being generated at the
primary. The redo is still stored in the archive log
files that are transferred to the standby database, but
it is ignored by the standby recovery process.
Furthermore, even though the redo is not applied,
the standby recovery process must still read past the
redo records. Thus, the front end of the propagation
method will still affect the time to propagate, which
may heavily influence propagation times for VLDBs.
Conversely, the back end of the propagation
method, which would write to data files, does not
occur. This could be a considerable time saving
during propagation.*

**Partial Propagation**     Partial propagation occurs when application of redo does
not completely propagate the transaction at the standby database. Let us see how
partial propagation occurs when new data files are created:

The redo propagated to the standby database allows the recovery process to
update the standby control file. If the file does not exist at the standby site, the
recovery process will fail. Such a failure can be prevented by copying the data file
to the standby database before the redo is applied. However, this may not be
practical when very large data files are added at the primary. In this case, it may be
more efficient to issue the same data file creation command at the standby database
as was issued at the primary. Once the data file is created, recovery can continue.
When recovery successfully propagates the transaction, the data dictionary and file
headers are updated.

**Nonpropagation**     Some actions at the primary interfere with redo generation and
are not propagated through the archive log files to the standby database. Let us look
at a few cases where this situation can arise:

- **Renaming database files**   Renaming a data file or online log file at the
  primary does not generate redo, but only changes the file pointers in the
  primary control file. Thus, it is left to the discretion of the database
  administrator to move files to different locations without affecting the
  configuration of the standby database. (This is useful if files need to be
  migrated to larger disks.) To fully propagate *filename changes*, rename the
  files at the standby database using operating system commands and refresh
  the standby control file.

- **Online redo log configuration**   Adding or dropping online redo log files at the primary is reflected in the primary control file, but no redo is generated that will propagate the change to the standby control file. Thus, it is left to the discretion of the database administrator how the online redo log is configured at both sites. To fully propagate a changed online redo log configuration to the standby database, either refresh the standby control file or issue the same commands as issued at the primary. However, refreshing the standby control file is recommended because this guarantees that the configuration is the same for the primary and standby control files.

**NOTE**
*Reconfiguring the online redo log could invalidate the standby database.*

- **Temporary tablespaces and sort segments**   Changes to sort segments do not generate redo because such changes are not needed during recovery. Thus, at the standby database, you do not need to offline drop temporary tablespaces used *only* for sort operations.

- **Unrecoverable commands**   The UNRECOVERABLE option can be used to improve performance for some database operations, such as table creation. For such operations, a small amount of redo is generated that marks affected objects as unrecoverable. Any redo generated *after* the UNRECOVERABLE command cannot be used. Although redo is still stored in the archive log files transferred to the standby database, the redo is not applied to affected objects because they are deemed inconsistent. Thus, changes to objects at the primary after an UNRECOVERABLE command are not propagated through the archive log files to the standby database. For more information refer to the *Oracle8i Backup and Recovery Guide Release 8.1.5* manual.

# Choice, Design, and Planning

This section gives some insight into answering the following questions: Does the standby feature fulfill my business need? What design and planning issues must be resolved? What will the feature cost? Answering these questions may be apparent only after you read this section in its entirety.

## Standby Database—The Correct Choice?

What business need are you trying to fulfill? The answer should be that you are implementing a disaster recovery mechanism. Answering the following questions will help you decide whether the standby feature is a suitable choice for you.

Do you want to access data in the standby database while it is in standby mode? Unfortunately, this is not possible with the current implementation of the feature. (Once activated, the standby database cannot be reused as a standby unless it is rebuilt.) This might be changed in the future releases of Oracle. If your transaction rates are within certain limits, then replication may suit your business needs. Alternatively, you might consider incremental exports and imports to another database.

How much data can you lose? If you cannot afford to lose *any* transactions in your production database, then the standby feature may not be acceptable. However, fault-tolerant systems that guarantee no data loss tend to be extremely expensive. If well implemented, switching over to a standby database may take only a few minutes. If the transactions lost during the switch-over period are an acceptable loss, then the standby feature may be a very suitable choice. Also, if you can transfer the online redo log or archive the outstanding redo, you will not lose any committed transactions.

The number of transactions lost during switch-over to a standby database depends on the number of transactions that were not propagated to the standby database—that is, committed transactions in the online redo log and in archive log files that are not transferred to the standby database. Generally, in a well-tuned standby environment, transaction loss can be minimized.

What quantity of data must be protected? If you want to protect only a small percentage of the data in your production database, then there may be a simpler and cheaper alternative.

Let us consider a data warehouse in which one tablespace is critical. The tablespace contains calculated summary information that cannot be lost. This summary information is garnered from very large tables in other tablespaces, which are not critical because they can be easily rebuilt. The large tables are heavily updated and generate very large quantities of redo. In this case, the time to propagate the mission-critical tablespace to a standby database is adversely affected by the noncritical tablespaces. However, if the large tablespaces do not need to be propagated, then use of the UNRECOVERABLE option during loading will have a considerable impact on reducing propagation time.

MTTR—what is the desired recovery time? For a standby environment, mean time to recover (*MTTR*) is calculated as follows:

MTTR = Detection + Apply Remaining Redo + Standby Activation + Switch Users

Generally, the major influence on MTTR is the time needed to apply outstanding archive log files to the standby database. This depends on the number and size of the archive log files, which can be tuned. Activating the standby database and switching users over to the standby database should be accomplishable within minutes. Switch-over times to a standby of a few minutes are often possible.

Conversely, a large MTTR might be suitable. If the standby database is kept a couple of hours behind the primary, then it is possible to recover to a point in time before a logical corruption. For example, a logical corruption would occur if a table was loaded with obsolete data.

What will it cost? The largest direct cost will be the purchase of any new hardware. It is recommended that the standby site hardware duplicate the primary site as much as possible. Other possible direct costs are hiring an administrator, upgrading software or operating systems, and so on. One potential indirect cost might be performance on the primary database. (However, tuning the archiving mechanism on the primary database for the standby feature might actually increase performance on the primary database). Reducing risk of downtime by implementing several standby databases is sensible, but is obviously more expensive.

## Design and Planning Issues
In this subsection, design and planning issues are briefly discussed.

**Software Upgrades**    You must have Oracle7 release 7.3 or higher installed to use the standby database feature. If an upgrade is required, then it is necessary to consider the effect on your production database. You may need to upgrade your application software or your operating system. After such upgrades, system retuning is often required.

**Hardware and Oracle Version**    The primary and standby sites *must* use the same version of Oracle, for a specific operating system and platform. Preferably, the primary and standby databases should reside on systems at separate locations some distance apart and not share resources such as the same power source, hard disks, and so on. It is recommended that hardware configurations be exactly the same at the primary and standby sites. If the hardware is configured the same, then this ensures that on activation of the standby database, the same resources are available and that performance will be the same. Likewise, disk configurations and disk space usage should be the same at both sites to ensure that adding data files or increasing data file sizes at the primary also succeed at the standby database. Administration of both sites is also simplified. Although not recommended, it is possible to have different hardware configurations, in which case you must ensure that the standby database has sufficient disk space and that the standby database's initialization file is adequately tuned to reflect the available system resources.

**Lost Transactions and MTTR**    How many transactions can be lost during the MTTR? Begin by determining the maximum number of transactions that occur in a period of time and the minimum time for an archive log file to fill. (These numbers must be determined during the busiest periods of the business day and when ARCH does not fall behind LGWR.) You can then calculate an approximate maximum number of transactions that can be propagated in an archive. If only one archive is not successfully transferred at the time of a failure, then the potential number of transactions lost will not exceed twice the calculated maximum in an archive. (This assumes that the number of lost transactions in the online redo log will not exceed the maximum calculated for an archive.) Now, time how long it takes to transfer and apply an archive (filled during the busy period) to the standby database. Using the formula on the previous page, you can determine the MTTR. At this point, you have MTTR and transaction loss metrics for the configuration of the online redo log at the primary. If the metrics are too high, then you must review your archiving strategy and tune the primary or standby databases, or possibly both.

**Tuning**    Once Oracle release 7.3 or higher is available on your system, then deployment and maintenance of the standby feature can be made relatively straightforward. Tuning for the standby feature may be simple or complex. On the primary, the database is tuned to ensure that archiving does not interfere with normal operations. On the standby database, you might tune the initialization file to optimize the application of archive log files to reduce the MTTR. (When the standby database is activated, you would use another initialization file tuned to the standby hardware configuration.)

A tuning goal for the primary site is to avoid ARCH falling behind LGWR, which is normally achievable. In a standby environment, there is usually a secondary goal; that is to get the archive log files transferred and applied to the standby database as quickly as possible. These tuning goals may conflict. For example, small archive log files are ideal for speedy propagation, but this requires small online redo logs. If there are too few online redo logs, then ARCH will fall behind LGWR. Furthermore, creating small archive files is unrealistic in some processing environments (in particular, high-volume OLTP environments).

Tuning may be relatively straightforward—for example, ensuring that the online redo log and archive log files are on their own disks separate from other database files. As another example, you might consider not propagating some tablespaces to improve performance. (It is a good practice to store similar database objects in their own tablespaces and put the corresponding data files on their own disks to optimize I/O performance.)

**Transfer Mechanism**    A fast interconnect between the primary and standby database will reduce the MTTR. Other network traffic must not interfere with the transfer of archive log files. Archive log files should be transferred and applied to the standby database as soon as possible. However, you must ensure that only completely finished archive log files are transferred.

**Switching Users to the Standby Database**    You must choose a mechanism for users to switch over from the primary to the standby database. The most effective method requires that software detect a failure and choose a different network route to the standby database. The software could reside in the user application, which may need recoding.

**Standby Database Automation**    The deployment and maintenance of the standby feature should be automated as much as possible. When a failure occurs, the standby database becomes the new primary. At this point, you can switch back to the original primary or use it as a standby database. If you decide to maintain the original primary site as the standby database, the transfer and application of archive log files should be automatic. Furthermore, any partially propagated or nonpropagated changes that must be fully propagated on a regular basis should be automated. Finally, error detection should be automated.

**Error Detection**    If you opt for transferring archived log files manually from the primary to the secondary, you must implement mechanisms to detect failures automatically. First, a mechanism must initiate switch-over to the standby database when the primary site fails. Second, a mechanism must detect problems at the primary site affecting the standby feature (in particular, the archiving mechanism). Third, a mechanism must detect failures in the transfer mechanism, and fourth, a mechanism must detect failures in full propagation at the standby database.

Most of the above detection mechanisms can be accomplished by writing scripts that run at regular intervals at both the primary and standby database sites. For example, a script run at the standby database could ping the primary to detect a network failure and thus a potential break in the transfer mechanism. If the ping does not succeed but the network is not malfunctioning, this indicates that there may be a failure at the primary. At that point, a process could use a dial-out modem to page the database administrator.

A site must not be entirely responsible for detecting its own failures. Rather, *both* sites must perform bidirectional error detection. For example, the same script run at both sites can search (for example, using **grep** command in UNIX) for recovery errors in the standby database alert log file. If errors are detected, then the error log will be available at both sites, even if one of the sites becomes unavailable.

**Backups and Standby Rebuilds**    Although the standby feature is a robust disaster recovery mechanism, backups are still necessary. The standby site or sites are also susceptible to failure! Thus, you must prepare for the eventuality of performing media recovery at the primary using backups of the database files, including the archive logs. However, there is an additional benefit. The backups can be used to rebuild the standby database during strategically convenient periods.

**Training and Preventing Problems**  Application developers must be made aware of issues that will affect the standby database. For example, developers must be cautioned against usage of the UNRECOVERABLE option to modify tables that are needed after the standby database is activated.

# Preparation

This section reviews preparations before deploying the standby feature. We assume that we are using a UNIX operating system.

## Upgrading, Testing, and Automation

It is good practice to test upgrades before upgrading in a production environment. The introduction of a new system to host the standby database provides a useful opportunity to perform thorough testing before implementing the standby feature. You can experiment with a new operating system and version of Oracle8 (or Oracle8*i*) to ensure that your production system will run properly on the new system. This is also the time to determine and test any changes in client software needed to switch over to the standby database.

Scripts for automating deployment, propagation, problem prevention, and error detection must also be written and tested. You may find the following tips useful:

- **Problem prevention**  At the primary, modify the global **.login** script to halt execution of batch scripts that contain SQL commands that will interfere with the standby mechanism. The **.login** script will **grep** for commands that are listed later in this chapter, in Table 6-7. At the standby database, queue a **cron** job that regularly checks that the amount of disk space available for data files matches the space available at the primary. (This is particularly useful when the configurations for the primary and standby databases are different.) The same **cron** job can also check for unexpected changes in the data file directory at the primary.

- **Error detection**  **cron** jobs to detect errors must run at both sites (see the earlier "Error Detection" section). Scripts to detect errors at the primary or standby database can **grep** for errors in the alert logs and trace files. A **grep** for errors in the range ORA-00250 to ORA-00298 will detect archiving errors, ORA-00300 to 00369 will detect some redo log errors, and so on. Refer to the *Oracle8i Error Messages Release 8.1.5* manual for other appropriate ranges. If possible, check the online message file, which will be more up-to-date and include platform-specific messages.

## Database Design

Make any necessary changes to the database layout during the testing period. The goal is to avoid making unnecessary physical structural changes after the standby feature is implemented. Thus, now is the time to perform any reorganization or defragmentation tasks. In particular, now is the time to make any control file changes—for example, if you anticipate that MAXDATAFILES may need to be increased in the near future.

It is good practice to place similar objects in the same tablespace. This facilitates administration and performance improvements. For example, sorts using a temporary tablespace placed on its own set of disks on one disk controller will not cause I/O contention with full table scans in another tablespace.

If you choose *not* to propagate some objects, then place these objects in a separate tablespace that will be offline dropped at the standby database. Candidates for nonpropagation are tablespaces that are not needed after activation, tablespaces that can be rebuilt easily and quickly with minimal effect on the MTTR when the standby database is activated, and tablespaces not immediately needed at activation that can be rebuilt some time thereafter.

## Timing Metrics, Tuning Archiving, and Deployment Time

When testing the standby feature, keep timing metrics for major tasks. These metrics are needed to determine the MTTR and potential transaction loss (see "Lost Transactions and MTTR" in the previous section). If these numbers are unacceptable, you can tune archiving at the standby site before introducing major archiving changes at the primary. See "Tuning" in the previous section.

When deploying the standby feature, a window of opportunity is needed to perform backups at the primary. Here again, timing metrics are useful. The larger the production database, the more critical are the metrics, especially if online backups are used.

**NOTE**
*For large databases, caution must be taken when performing online backups because extra redo is generated for the backup. This will affect the archiving rate and may cause ARCH to fall behind LGWR. It may be necessary to do an online backup on a few or only one tablespace at a time.*

The backup and restore phases of deployment consume most of the time. Deployment time can be roughly calculated as follows:

```
deployment = backup + archive current logs + file transfer + restore + archive application
```

It might be possible to dramatically reduce deployment time by parallelizing the backup, transfer, and restore. For example, each data file might be copied, transferred, and restored by a single process.

**Example Metrics**    Timings for your environment will be dependent on hardware limitations and database size. However, it is useful at this point to have some numbers as a frame of reference. The following metrics are typical for Sequent machines using an FDDI network: approximately three hours for a complete standby database rebuild of a 20GB database; **ftp** transfer rate at approximately 3.5MB per second; approximately 300KB per second when archiving up to current log; and finally, for a 10-drive tape array, a backup rate of 20GB per hour. These metrics are provided by Oracle Support Services. Please note that these metrics will change based on the platform and hardware you use.

### Initialization Parameters

The standby and primary sites must have their own unique initialization files. If the two sites are configured the same, then the only difference is that CONTROL_FILES will point to the standby control file. See Table 6-5 for details.

### Standby Site Specifics

Ensure that the production database will run at the standby site. This is especially important if different configurations are used for the standby and primary databases. Also check that environment variables are correctly set—in particular, ORACLE_HOME, ORACLE_SID, and any other variable specified in your installation guide.

Ensure that the initialization parameters are set correctly for the standby site (see Table 6-5). If the two sites have different hardware configurations, then you must ensure that parameters are tuned for the standby configuration. If standby directory paths are different than at the primary, then the standby paths must be reflected in the standby control file and initialization file.

Ensure that the database directory paths for the standby database are valid and have sufficient disk space.

### Primary Site Specifics

Ensure that initialization parameters are set correctly for the primary site, as discussed earlier in this section. In particular, COMPATIBLE must be set to the right version of the database. Check that directory paths and file names are correctly set in the parameters. Ensure that automatic archiving is working correctly. Instigate measures to prevent untimely alterations to the production database during

| Initialization Parameter | Primary Site Value | Standby Site Value |
|---|---|---|
| COMPATIBLE | Must be 7.3 or higher. If you want to open standby database in read-only mode, it must be 8.1 or higher. | Identical to primary database value. |
| COMPATIBLE_NO_RECOVERY | Obsolete in 8*i*. This value must be COMPATIBLE for versions lower than 8.1.3. | Identical to primary database value. |
| LOG_ARCHIVE_DEST_*n* | As you set normally, plus at least one of these parameters should point to an archive destination in the standby site if you want to enable transferring of archived log files to standby site automatically. | Must be the same as the primary if the same configurations are used at both sites. However, this parameter may differ. |
| CONTROL_FILE | Primary control file path and name. | Standby control file path and name. |
| DB_FILES | As you set in **init.ora** parameter file. | Must be same value as that of primary. |
| DB_NAME | As set while creating the database. | Must be the same as primary. |
| %%%_DUMP_DEST ORACLE_TRACE _%%%_PATH | As needed. | Must be the same as the primary if the same configurations are used at both sites. However, these parameters may differ. |

**TABLE 6-5.** *Initialization Parameters for Primary and Standby Databases*

| Initialization Parameter | Primary Site Value | Standby Site Value |
|---|---|---|
| DB_FILE_STANDBY_NAME_CONVERT LOG_FILE_STANDBY_NAME_CONVERT | Not needed—however, if these values are set at the standby database, then it is a good policy to have these parameters identical to the standby values. | Only use these parameters if the directory paths to data files or online redo logs are different at both sites. Values are used to convert primary path names to standby path names. |
| STANDBY_ARCHIVE_DEST | Not needed. | Set the parameters STANDBY_ARCHIVE_DEST and LOG_ARCHIVE_DEST to the same value. |

**TABLE 6-5.** *Initialization Parameters for Primary and Standby Databases* (continued)

deployment, such as revoking privileges from users that can add data files. Also, start up **cron** jobs to detect if untoward changes occur to the database during deployment. (These scripts should have been written during the testing period, as described earlier in the "Upgrading, Testing, and Automation" section.) Finally, ensure that the control file is consistent.

# Deployment

This section describes how to deploy the standby database feature. Table 6-6 shows the steps involved in deploying the standby feature. The examples show real commands, but may not be complete. References to **cron** jobs assume that scripts to be queued are already available. Notes and scripting information are provided in the sections following the table.

## Deployment Notes and Scripting
This section provides useful information for the steps listed in the previous section.

**Backups**    UNIX commands **cpio**, **ufsdump**, **dd**, **tar**, and so on can be used for copying file system data files. For raw partition data files, use the **dd** command. See Chapter 3 for various backup commands in different operating systems.

| Steps Performed At/During: | Example Commands and Comments |
|---|---|
| **Primary Site**<br>Check automatic archiving. | **Archive Log List** |
| | Check ARCH is running and initialization parameter LOG_ARCHIVE_START=TRUE.<br>**select status from v$logfile**<br>  **where status is not null;** |
| | No rows should be returned. INVALID or STALE status indicates problems that need to be resolved before continuing. (Status DELETED indicates a log file is no longer used.) |
| Start change detection. | Queue **cron** job that looks for changes to the physical structure of the database. |
| Check tablespaces. | **select tablespace_name, status from dba_tablespaces;**<br>Ensure that desired tablespaces are online or READ-ONLY. |
| Backup database.<br>(Note 1, Note 2) | For offline backup, within Oracle:<br>**sqlplus <<eof**<br>**connect internal**<br>**shutdown immediate**<br>**exit**<br>**eof**<br>At O/S prompt:<br>**cp $ORACLE_HOME/dbs/*.dbf $BACKUP** |
| Archive to current online log. | **alter system archive log current;** |
| Create standby control file. | **alter database create standby controlfile as 'ctlstby.ora';** |
| **Transfer of Files to Standby Site**<br>(Note 2) | Files from *offline* backup, standby control file, and archive log files:<br>**for each FILE (`ls -1 $BACKUP`)**<br>  **dd if=$FILE \| resh $STDBYSITE of=\\$BACKUP/$FILE**<br>**end**<br>**dd if=ctlstby.ora \| resh $STDBYSITE of=\\$BACKUP**<br>**foreach FILE (`ls -1 $LOG_ARCHIVE_DEST`)**<br>  **dd if=$FILE \| resh $STDBYSITE**<br>  **of=\\$LOG_ARCHIVE_DEST/$FILE**<br>**end** |
| **Standby Site**<br>Check environment. | echo $ORACLE_HOME $ORACLE_SID<br>du $ORACLE_HOME/dbs<br>Check Oracle environment and disk space availability. |
| | **resh $PRIMARYSITE cat \\$ORACLE_HOME/dbs/init.ora \\**<br>**\| comm -3 $ORACLE_HOME/dbs/initstby.ora**<br>If both sites are configured the same, then the above comparison of initialization files should only show that the CONTROLFILE parameters are different. |

**TABLE 6-6.** *Deploying the Standby Database Feature*

| Steps Performed At/During: | Example Commands and Comments |
|---|---|
| Restore backups. (Note 2) | cp $BACKUP/*.dbf $ORACLE_HOME/dbs<br>Archive log files are already in correct directory from transfer. |
| Start standby database. | **sqlplus**<br>**connect internal**<br>**startup nomount pfile=$ORACLE_HOME/ dbs/initstby.ora** |
| Take unwanted tablespaces offline. | **alter tablespace** *unwanted* **offline drop;** |
| Start recovery. | If you want to place the standby database in manual recovery mode:<br>**recover standby database;**<br>If you want to place the standby database in managed recovery mode (in this mode, whenever the archived log files arrive at standby database, they will be applied automatically):<br>**recover managed standby database;** |
| Start failure detection. | Queue **cron** job to ping primary. (This step could be in autopropagation scripts.) |
| Start automatic propagation. | Queue **cron** job to find and transfer archive log files from primary to standby database. |
| **Both Sites** | |
| Start error detection. | Queue **cron** jobs to detect errors at either site. |

Note 1: Archive log files must also be backed up to ensure that a complete database backup is available for recovery.

Note 2: The "backup," "transfer," and "restore" steps shown in the above table could be one action—that is, copying the files directly to the standby database. However, backups are required at the primary.

**TABLE 6-6.** *Deploying the Standby Database Feature* (continued)

**Offline Backups**    Before performing an offline backup, make sure that the database is shut down cleanly by examining the alert file. A **shutdown abort** or shutdown due to a crash is not acceptable. In this case, you must restart and shut down the database until you get a clean shutdown. However, a **shutdown immediate** is acceptable.

When performing offline backups for standby database deployment, ensure that you back up all data files, control files, and initialization files. You can use the backup to rebuild the standby database or recover the primary if the standby becomes unavailable.

**Online Backups**     Online backups generate extra redo. For large databases, performing online backups for all tablespaces may not be acceptable because of the increased burden on ARCH. In this case, online backups should only be performed for a few tablespaces or only one tablespace at a time. The following script creates and executes another script that performs online backups of one tablespace at a time. The $BACKUP variable must be defined globally, probably in **.login** or **.cshrc**. Note that to conserve disk space, **compress** is used to create the backup file, which must be reversed when the files are restored at the standby database.

```
Sqlp*lus <<EOD
connect system/manager
set echo off
set termout off
set feedback off
set heading off
spool backup.sh
SELECT
'SQL*PLUS <<EOS'||CHR(10)||
'connect internal'||chr(10)||
'ALTER TABLESPACE '||TABLESPACE_NAME||' BEGIN BACKUP;'||CHR(10)||
'EXIT'||CHR(10)||
'EOS'||CHR(10)||
'compress <'||FILE_NAME||' \$BACKUP'||CHR(10)||
'SQL*PLUS <<EOS'||CHR(10)||
'connect internal'||CHR(10)||
'ALTER TABLESPACE '||TABLESPACE_NAME||' END BACKUP;'
||CHR(10)||'EXIT'||CHR(10)||
'EOS'||CHR(10)
FROM DBA_DATA_FILES WHERE STATUS = 'AVAILABLE';
spool off
EOD
chmod u+x backup.sh
backup.sh
```

**Archive up to Current Online Log**     The **alter system archive log current** command is used to ensure that all redo is archived. This forces a log switch (on all threads in a Parallel Server environment). The archive log files contain all redo at an SCN existing after the data files were backed up. This guarantees that the standby recovery process can successfully apply the archive log files against the backed up data files.

**Transfer Files to Standby Database**     Ensure that all files are transferred to the standby database. This includes backup data files, backup archive log files, and standby control files. The initialization file for the primary should not be copied because the standby database has its own initialization file. When raw partitions are used, ensure that the raw files end up in the correct location. Preferably, the locations are named the same, which simplifies administration.

When transferring to the standby database, ensure that the files are valid. While transferring offline data files or archive log files to the standby database, ensure that the files are not still being accessed by the database. The following script can be used as an outline for scripts performing such checks. Note that the following script performs the backup, transfer, and restore of the primary's archive log files:

```
foreach FILE ($LOG_ARCHIVE_DEST/arch1_*.dbf)
    echo "Backing up archive: $FILE"
    if (! -F $FILE) then
        echo "Error: `$FILE` is not a regular file."
        exit
    end
    cp $FILE $BACKUP
    if ($status == 1) then
        echo "Error: backup failed on archive `$FILE`"
        exit
    end
    cmp -s $FILE $BACKUP/$FILE
    if ($status == 1) then
        echo "Error: Oracle still using archive `$FILE`"
        rm $BACKUP/$FILE
        exit
    end
    dd if=$FILE | resh $STDBYSITE of=\$BACKUP/$FILE
    if ($status == 1) then
        echo "Error: failed to transfer archive `$FILE`"
        exit
    end
    resh $STDBYSITE cp \$BACKUP/$FILE \$ORACLE_HOME/dbs
    if ($status == 1) then
        echo "Error: restore failed at standby site for archive `$FILE`"
        exit
    end
end
```

## Maintenance

This section describes how to maintain the standby feature after deployment. Maintenance of the standby database ensures that changes made to the primary are fully propagated to the standby database. Whenever possible, these tasks should be automated with scripts that run at regular intervals. Most changes to the primary are propagated using normal propagation, which is fairly easy to automate. See the "Transferring and Applying Archive Log Files" section that follows. However, special attention is needed if partially propagated and nonpropagated changes must be fully propagated. Table 6-7 indicates whether a command is normally propagated or requires extra administrative efforts to be fully propagated.

| Command Issued at Primary Site | Effect at Standby Site |
|---|---|
| **sqlldr direct=false (RECOVERABLE)** | Propagated. |
| **sqlldr direct=false (UNRECOVERABLE)** | Not propagated. If the affected objects are needed after activation, then, at the standby database, either: 1. Rebuild the standby OR 2. Back up the affected data files at the primary and restore at the standby database. If the affected objects are not needed, then ensure that the tables exist in a tablespace that can be offline dropped at the standby database. |
| **allocate** | Not applicable—session-based command. |
| **alter cluster** | Propagated. |
| **alter database** | |
| **activate standby database** | Not applicable—rejected at primary. |
| **add logfile** | Not propagated. |
| **add logfile member** | If the online redo log configuration should be the same as at the primary, then refresh the standby control file. |
| **archivelog** | No effect. |
| **backup controlfile** | No effect. |
| **backup controlfile to trace** | No effect—unless the SQL commands in the trace file are used to re-create the primary database, which then invalidates standby if online redo logs are cleared. |
| **convert** | Invalidates standby—must rebuild. |
| **clear logfile** | Invalidates standby—must rebuild. |
| **create datafile** | Partial propagation. Recovery process at standby database will fail during application of archive if data files do not already exist. Data files should be created in advance at the standby database to prevent automatic recovery from failing However, if the recovery process fails, then the problem can be fixed by creating the data file(s) and restarting recovery. |
| **create standby controlfile** | No effect—new standby control file should be used to refresh control file at standby site. |

**TABLE 6-7.**   *Command Propagation from Primary to Secondary Database*

| Command Issued at Primary Site | Effect at Standby Site |
|---|---|
| **datafile autoextend** | Propagated—future propagation will fail if disk space is not available. |
| **datafile end backup** | Propagated—no action needed. |
| **datafile offline** | Propagated—no action needed because no further redo is generated at the primary for an offline data file. |
| **datafile online** | Propagated—only possible if complete media recovery of affected tablespace at primary was successful *before* archive log files are transferred to the standby database. |
| **datafile resize** | Propagated—command will fail if disk space available for increase in data file size is insufficient. |
| **disable thread** | Not propagated (PARALLEL SERVER option only). |
| **enable thread** | Not propagated (PARALLEL SERVER option only). |
| **drop logfile group** | Not propagated. |
| **drop logfile member** | If the online redo log configuration should be the same as at the primary, then refresh the standby control file. |
| **mount** | No effect. |
| **mount standby database** | Not applicable—rejected at primary. |
| **noarchivelog** | Invalidates standby—must rebuild because the archive stream is interrupted. |
| **open resetlogs** | Invalidates standby—must rebuild. |
| **open noresetlogs** | No effect. |
| **recover**<br>  **automatic**<br>  **datafile**<br>  **logfile**<br>  **tablespace**<br>  **until cancel**<br>  **until time**<br>  **until change**<br>  **using backup**<br>    **controlfile** | Invalidates standby if incomplete or media recovery is performed, which requires the standby database to be rebuilt. However, if you can perform complete recovery without resetting the logs, then the standby database is *not* invalidated. |

**TABLE 6-7.** *Command Propagation from Primary to Secondary Database* (continued)

| Command Issued at Primary Site | Effect at Standby Site |
|---|---|
| rename file | Not propagated—the standby control file is not updated. If the redo log configuration at the standby database is different than at the primary, then no action is needed. Else, rename as for data files.Data files at standby database must be renamed at the operating system level and then at the database level; that is, repeat the commands issued at the primary. |
| rename global_name | Not propagated—refresh control file. |
| reset compatibility | Invalidates standby—must rebuild. |
| set | Propagated. |
| alter function<br>alter index | Propagated. |
| alter index<br>rebuild recoverable | Propagated. |
| alter index<br>rebuild unrecoverable | Not propagated. See **sqlldr unrecoverable**. |
| alter package<br>procedure<br>profile<br>resource cost<br>role<br>rollback segment<br>sequence | Propagated. |
| alter session | Not applicable—session-based command. |
| alter snapshot<br>snapshot log | Propagated. |

**TABLE 6-7.** *Command Propagation from Primary to Secondary Database* (continued)

| Command Issued at Primary Site | Effect at Standby Site |
|---|---|
| alter system<br>    **archive log sequence**<br>    **archive log change**<br>    **archive log current**<br>    **archive log logfile**<br>    **archive log next**<br>    **archive log all**<br>    **archive log start** | No effect. |
|     **archive log stop** | Invalidates standby—if archive stream is interrupted. In which case, you must rebuild standby database.<br>However, if this is a temporary halt in archiving, then it has *no effect*. |
|     **switch log** | No effect. |
| **alter table** | Propagated. |
| **alter tablespace**<br>    **add datafile** | Partial propagation—treated the same as **alter database create datafile**. |
|         **begin backup** | May increase number of archive log files because extra redo is generated during the online backup. Ensure that the online backup completes at primary. |
|         **end backup** | Backed up primary tablespace can be used to refresh tablespace at standby database. |
|         **coalesce** | Propagated. |
|         **default storage** | Propagated. |
|         **rename datafile** | Not propagated—treated the same as **alter database rename file**. |
|         **offline** | Propagated—no action needed. See **alter database datafile offline**. |
|         **online** | Propagated—treated the same as **alter database datafile online**. |
|         **permanent** | Propagated. |
|         **read only** | Indirect propagation—treated the same as **alter tablespace offline normal**. |

**TABLE 6-7.** *Command Propagation from Primary to Secondary Database* (continued)

| Command Issued at Primary Site | Effect at Standby Site |
|---|---|
| read write | Propagated—no action needed. See **alter database datafile online normal**. |
| temporary | Propagated. |
| alter trigger<br>    user<br>    view | Propagated. |
| analyze | Propagated. |
| audit | |
| commit | |
| create cluster | |
| create controlfile | Invalidates standby—if the archive stream is interrupted, in which case, rebuild standby database. However, if you are performing complete recovery without resetting the online redo logs, then the standby database is not invalidated. For example, if all primary control files are lost but all other files are available, then the control file can be created with NORESETLOGS.<br>Furthermore, if you create a control file to increase maximum values, such as MAXDATAFILES, and do not reset the redo logs, then you should refresh the standby control file if the change must be propagated. |
| create database | Not propagated because primary database destroyed, which invalidates standby. If command was not intended at primary, then switch over to standby database. |
| create database<br>    link<br>    function | Propagated. |
| create index | Propagated. |

**TABLE 6-7.** *Command Propagation from Primary to Secondary Database* (continued)

| Command Issued at Primary Site | Effect at Standby Site |
|---|---|
| create index rebuild recoverable | Propagated. |
| create index rebuild unrecoverable | Not propagated. See **sqlldr unrecoverable**. |
| create package package body procedure profile role rollback segment schema sequence snapshot snapshot log synonym | Propagated. |
| create table  recoverable | Propagated. |
| create table  unrecoverable | Not propagated. See **sqlldr unrecoverable**. |
| create tablespace | Partial propagation—treated the same as **alter tablespace add datafile**. |
| create trigger user view | Propagated. |
| delete drop index drop package procedure profile role rollback segment sequence snapshot snapshot log synonym | Propagated. |

**TABLE 6-7.** *Command Propagation from Primary to Secondary Database* (continued)

| Command Issued at Primary Site | Effect at Standby Site |
|---|---|
| drop table | |
|     tablespace | |
| drop trigger | Propagated. |
|    user | |
|    view | |
| explain plan | |
| grant | |
| insert | |
| lock table | |
| noaudit | |
| rename | |
| revoke | |
| rollback | |
| savepoint | |
| select | |
| set role | |
| set transaction | |
| truncate | |
| update | |

**TABLE 6-7.** *Command Propagation from Primary to Secondary Database* (continued)

## Maintenance Notes and Scripting

This section provides some useful information for maintaining standby databases.

**Upgrades**    If it is your intention to upgrade either the operating system or the Oracle software, you must ensure that the upgrades occur at both the primary and standby databases. The safest route is to shut down both databases, upgrade, and rebuild the standby database.

**Logical Transaction Grouping**    During normal operations, there may be groups of transactions that are critical, such that it is advantageous if these transactions are propagated more quickly than usual to the standby database. To do so, after the transactions are committed, issue the **alter system archive log current** command. This forces a log switch (on all threads in a Parallel Server environment), such that all redo up to an SCN higher than the last commit in the transaction group is written out to completed archive log files. The completed archive log files can then be transferred and applied at the standby database.

**Transferring and Applying Archive Log Files**   In this section, code and script outlines are provided that can be used to transfer and apply the archive log files to the standby database automatically. The idea is to have a stored procedure running every few minutes at the primary, which writes out a file identifying the latest archive completed. On the standby database, a job runs that reads the identifier, and if the identifier is greater than the last archive applied at the standby database, the job transfers the newest archive log files and applies them at the standby database. The examples do not contain error checking and are not intended to be complete, but merely to provide you with a basis to write your own code.

In the code and scripts, it is assumed that the same configuration is used at the primary and standby sites, thus:

- Directory paths used are the same at both sites:

  LOG_ARCHIVE_FORMAT = arch%S.log

- The operating system default for %S produces four characters—for example, arch0234.log.

- The following initialization parameters are the same at both sites:

  - LOG_ARCHIVE_FORMAT

  - LOG_ARCHIVE_DEST

  - UTIL_FILE_DIR

- The following environment variable is the same at primary and standby sites:

  LOG_ARCHIVE_DEST

At the primary, the following procedure is queued to run every three minutes. This procedure writes out a file with information identifying the latest archive created. The identifying information is the latest archive sequence number. Archive sequence numbers are used in the %S part of the archive filename.

```
CREATE OR REPLACE PROCEDURE Note_Latest_Archive AS
  LatestSeqNum INT;
  fno INT;
BEGIN
  SELECT MAX(SEQUENCE#) INTO LatestSeqNum FROM V$LOG
    WHERE ARCHIVED = 'YES';
  fno :=
  UTL_FILE.FOPEN('$LOG_ARCH_DEST', 'latest.arc', 'W');
  UTL_FILE.PUTLINE(fno, LatestSeqNum);
  UTL_FILE.FCLOSE(fno);
END;
```

**NOTE**
*Archive sequence numbers do not necessarily represent the order in which archive log files are completed or applied. However, the method used in these samples works because all archive log files are eventually transferred.*

The following anonymous block can be issued in SQL*PLUS at the primary to put the above procedure in the database queue. The job then executes every three minutes.

```
VARIABLE jobno INT;
BEGIN
  DBMS_JOB.SUBMIT(:jobno,'note_latest_archive',SYSDATE,'SYSDATE + 1/480');
END;
```

At the standby site, the following script runs continuously. The script checks whether the latest archive log files at the primary site are newer than the last archive log file applied at the standby database. If so, the newest archive log files are transferred from the primary to the standby database and applied. Thereafter, the script waits three minutes and repeats the cycle.

```
while (1)
  set LastApplied = `ls -1 $LOG_ARCHIVE_DEST | tail -1`
  @ LastApplied  = `basename $LastApplied:r | cut -c7-10`
  @ NextToApply  = `expr $LastApplied + 1 `
  @ NewestArchive = `resh $PRIMARYSITE cat $LOG_ARCHIVE_DEST/latest.arc`
  if ( $NextToApply < $NewestArchive ) then
    foreach Archive (`echo $NextToApply $NewestArchive | \
         awk '{for(i=$1;i<=$2;i++) {printf("arch%04.log\n",i)} }' ` )
      resh $PRIMARYSITE dd if=$LOG_ARCHIVE_DEST/$Archive | \
           resh dd of=$LOG_ARCHIVE/$Archive
      svrmgrl <<EOF
      connect internal
      recover standby database until cancel
      auto
      cancel
      EOF
    end
  end
  sleep 180
end
```

**NOTE**
*The previous script takes only normal propagation into account. You will need to modify the previous script to fully propagate other changes. For example, you could add code to check for new data files added at the primary and if found, then copy the data files to the standby database before the recovery process starts. This prevents the recovery process from failing when a new data file is not found. However, this is impractical if very large data files are added at the primary. Thus, you should add small data files and resize the data files thereafter.*

**Initialization Parameters**    If parameter values are changed in the initialization file at the primary, then ensure that corresponding changes are made to the standby initialization file.

**Refreshing the Control File**    Refreshing the standby control file is performed as described in Table 6-8.

| Steps to be Performed at | Commands and Comments |
|---|---|
| **Primary Site:** | |
| Create new standby control file. | **alter database create standby controlfile;** |
| Archive up to current log. | **alter database archive log current;** |
| Transfer files to standby site. | Transfer the new standby control file and archive files to the standby database. |
| **Standby Site:** | |
| Shutdown recovery, if necessary. | Kill automatic maintenance script, or CANCEL if performing manual recovery. Ensure standby database is shut down normally. |
| Start and mount standby database. | **sqlplus connect internal startup mount pfile=$ORACLE_HOME/dbs/ initstby.ora** |

**TABLE 6-8.**    *Refreshing Control File*

| **Steps to be Performed at** | **Commands and Comments** |
|---|---|
| **Standby Site:** | **alter tablespace *unwanted* offline drop;** |
| Offline drop unwanted tablespaces. | Only needed if unwanted tablespaces at primary were added since last refresh. |
| Recover remaining archive log files. | **recover standby database;** |
| Restart maintenance. | Restart automatic maintenance scripts. |

**TABLE 6-8.**   *Refreshing Control File* (continued)

# Activation

This section describes how to switch over to the standby database after a failure of the production database and how to switch back once the failure is fixed. Table 6-9 shows the steps involved in activating the standby feature. The examples show real commands, but may not be complete.

| **Steps to be Performed at/during** | **Commands and Comments** |
|---|---|
| **Transfer of Files to Standby Site** | If possible, transfer any remaining archive log files to be applied from the primary. If possible, transfer the online redo log from the primary, *but only if* the online redo log configurations are the same at both sites. This will allow the standby database to be recovered up to the last transaction committed at the primary. If you have configured the primary database to transfer the archived log files to the standby database using the LOG_ARCHIVE_DEST_*n* parameter, you need not transfer archived log files manually. If automatic transfer fails, you have to manually copy them to the standby database. |

**TABLE 6-9.**   *Steps Involved in Activating a Standby Database*

| Steps to be Performed at/during Standby Site | Commands and Comments |
|---|---|
| Start and mount standby database. | **sqlplus**<br>**connect internal**<br>**startup mount**<br>**pfile=$ORACLE_HOME/dbs/**<br>**initstby.ora** |
| Recover remaining archive log files. | **recover standby database;** |
| Activate standby database. | **alter database activate standby database;** |
| Offline unwanted tablespaces. | **alter tablespace *unwanted* offline;**<br>Possibly because tablespace was offlined at primary. |
| Change tablespaces to READ-ONLY. | **alter tablespace *wanted* read only;**<br>Possibly because tablespace was read-only at primary. |
| Online tablespaces. | **alter tablespace *wanted* online;**<br>Possibly because tablespace was offline at standby database to improve performance. |
| Switch over users. | Contact users directly or initiate network switching software. |
| Instigate new standby. | Your new primary database must be safeguarded. Instigate backups and when possible, build a new standby database. |
| Open the standby database in READ-ONLY mode. | **alter database mount read only;**<br>For opening the standby database in READ-ONLY mode for query purposes. |

**TABLE 6-9.** *Steps Involved in Activating a Standby Database* (continued)

## After Activation and Switching Back to Original Production Site

After switching over to a standby database, it becomes the primary, in which case, you will need another standby site. The mechanisms you use to deploy and maintain a standby database must be flexible. Preferably, scripts will not need modification because environment variables are used to identify the primary and standby sites. Thus, after activation, you can create a new standby database simply by changing the variables to point to the new site names and running the scripts. This is particularly useful if you want to use the original site as the standby database. Furthermore, you will need to make the original site the standby site (and then activate it) if you wish that original site to house the production database once again.

## Activation Notes

Activating the standby database clears the online redo logs before opening the database unless the logs are already cleared. You can reduce your MTTR by creating in advance and clearing the online redo logs just before activation using the **alter database clear logfile** command. When the online redo logs are reset in this manner, a special flag is set. Oracle recognizes the flag at activation and does not clear the logs, thus saving time.

**Switching the Standby Database to READ-ONLY Mode**    Opening the standby database in READ-ONLY mode allows users to query the data stored in the database for reporting information. The following procedure shows how to do this:

1. Connect to the standby instance as SYSDBA and issue the CANCEL command to halt its recovery process if it is already in recovery mode. If the database is in managed recovery mode, skip to step 2.

   ```
   SQL> RECOVER CANCEL
   ```

   Skip to step 3.

2. If it is in managed recovery mode, to cancel the recovery operation, issue the following command:

   ```
   SQL> RECOVER MANAGED STANDBY DATABASE CANCEL
   ```

3. Shut down the standby database.

4. Start the standby instance in NOMOUNT mode using SQL*PLUS as follows. (In this example, the standby **init.ora** file is placed in the directory **c:\oracle\admin\test\pfile\**)

   ```
   SQL> STARTUP NOMOUNT PFILE=C:\ORACLE\ADMIN\TEST\PFILE\STANDBYINIT.ORA;
   ```

5. Once the database is started, issue the following command to mount the database in READ-ONLY mode.

   ```
   SQL> ALTER DATABASE MOUNT READ ONLY;
   ```

   This places the standby database in READ ONLY mode. This ensures that no changes will be allowed in the standby database.

**NOTE**
*When the standby database is in READ ONLY mode, transferred archived redo log files at the standby site will not be applied.  You have to resync the standby database again with the primary site by bring it to manual or managed recovery mode.*

# Failure Analysis

In today's ever-changing technological world, businesses are finding it harder to maintain high availability of crucial business information systems. This problem is further complicated by the diversity in heterogeneous networks and the increasing trend toward client/server architecture. Maintaining high availability is no small task in a client/server environment, yet many companies are moving toward a high-availability (24 hours a day, 7 days a week), mission-critical type of operation for three main reasons.

The first reason is *globalization of businesses.* These days, with international markets opening up, many companies are opening up branches in various countries; yet due to business reasons, they are keeping operations centralized. This essentially means that a database or an application running on a machine needs to be available at all times.

The second reason is competitive pressure. For example, if a bank extends its business hours to Saturdays and Sundays, other banks have to meet their competitor's challenge. This means keeping the databases up and running on Saturdays and Sundays as well.

The third and final reason why more companies are moving toward high-availability systems is cost of downtime. A survey done by SVP Strategic Research Division shows that businesses, on an average, incur $1,300 of mean revenue loss per outage minute. This survey was done on 450 companies in the manufacturing, securities, health insurance, transportation, banking, retail, and telecommunications industries. This implies that a shop that operates 24 hours a day, 7 days a week, and maintains a 99-percent availability, faces 1-percent downtime (accounts for more than 5,000 minutes of downtime), which is equivalent to six million dollars of revenue loss per year.

## System Outage Survey

A system outage survey and a down system and recovery survey conducted by Oracle Support Services found very interesting information on why systems go down, how often, and how customers recover them. Consider the following outage categories:

- Physical outages

- Design outages

- Operational outages

- Environmental outages

- Scheduled outages

The first four outage types in this list are *unscheduled* outages, according to IEEE. *Physical outages* are usually caused by hardware failures. Media failure or a CPU failure is a typical example of a physical outage. *Design outages* are caused by software failures, more commonly known as software *bugs*. Any software bug, whether in the operating system, database software, or application software, contributes to a design outage. *Operational outages,* on the other hand, are caused by human intervention. Failures attributed to poor DBA skills, user errors, inappropriate system setup, or inadequate backup procedures are examples of operational outages. Outages such as earthquakes, power surges, and failures due to abnormal temperature conditions are typical examples of *environmental outages*. The last category is the *scheduled outage,* which is necessary for the maintenance of the system—for example, configuring/reconfiguring hardware and software.

Oracle Support Services has done a survey on 30 Oracle customers running mission-critical applications. Not all customers surveyed have high-availability requirements. The operational logs at each site were reviewed with the help of the DBAs and system managers for the years 1994 through 1995. The total outage minutes were calculated at each site. Each outage was analyzed, and the cause for the outage was categorized according to the outage classes mentioned above. Under each outage class, the total amount of downtime was calculated and averaged out over 30 customers.

Figure 6-13 gives the outage categories as a percentage of the total outage time. The figure shows that the outages caused by design failures cause the most downtime (36 percent). This includes software bugs caused by the operating system, Oracle, third-party software that runs on top of Oracle, and in-house developed applications.

Figure 6-14 gives a detailed analysis of design-related outages. While documentation is the main cause and accounts for almost 50 percent of the downtime caused by design outages, the downtime for code bugs is significant (40 percent) as well.

Figure 6-13 shows that 34 percent of the outage time is caused by operational outages, an outage that you can control. As you can see, this is quite significant. Figure 6-15 gives further details on the operational outage category. While 80 percent of the operations-related downtime was due to lack of DBA skills, the

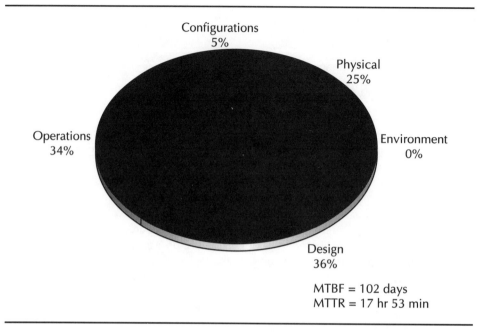

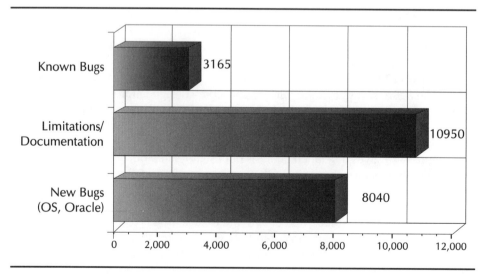

**FIGURE 6-13.** *Outage analysis survey conducted at 30 Oracle customer sites*

**FIGURE 6-14.** *Design-related outages*

survey showed that improper recovery handling, improper network setup, improper system setup, and DBA/user errors were some of the main reasons for operational outages.

Finally, Figure 6-13 shows that physical outages cause 25 percent of the total downtime. Since the survey was done on a small sample of 30 customers, the environmental outages are zero percent, which leaves the scheduled downtime to be 5 percent.

To summarize, the survey showed that of the total system downtime, 95 percent was due to unscheduled outages, and the other 5 percent of the time the systems were down due to maintenance. In addition, the average mean time between failures (MTBF) is calculated for the sample surveyed. This gives the mean time elapsed between two consecutive failures, which is calculated to be 102 days. The average mean time to recover (MTTR) when a failure occurs is estimated to be 17 hours and 53 minutes.

## Down System and Recovery Survey

Most Oracle customers might be familiar with Oracle Support Services' processes and procedures. When a customer calls into the support organization, a *technical assistance request* (or a TAR) is created to track the call. Oracle Support Services has

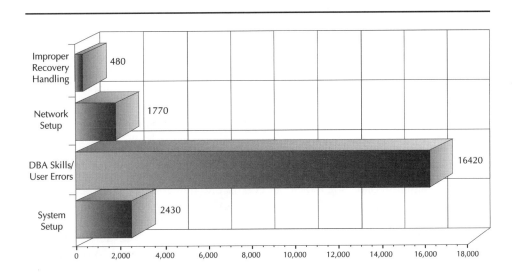

**Downtime in Minutes**

**FIGURE 6-15.** *Operations-related outages*

done a study on the priority 1 TARs that were logged by the analysts. A *priority 1 TAR* is logged when an Oracle database is not operational and critically impacts the customer's business. The total TARs surveyed were 208. Of the total TARs, 18 percent of them (38 TARs) show that DBAs had to do media recovery to bring the production database back to normal operation.

An important observation in this survey is that of the 38 TARs that ended up in doing recovery, 17 of them did *complete recovery* and the other 21 had to do *incomplete recovery*, which usually implies data loss. In these 38 cases, the root cause for doing media recovery was due to OS/hardware problems, loss of data files due to user errors, block corruptions, instance crashes, inadequate DBA skills, and Oracle bugs. Figure 6-16 gives a breakdown of these 38 TARs. Note that this survey was done on a very small sample of TARs and may have a significant margin of error.

# Recommendations for Disaster Recovery

In today's world, businesses are beginning to demand more from their information systems, while at the same time pushing the outer limits of technology. This poses a daunting challenge on the service organizations. A reactive service paradigm no longer provides adequate solutions. A proactive approach is required to meet the demands of running mission-critical operations in today's heterogeneous client/ server networks.

### Customer Requirements

The following are some general requirements you need to consider while designing disaster recovery procedures for your site. When they are properly designed, you should be able to increase or decrease the MTTR.

- Sites must have a premium level of support from their hardware and software vendors.

- Uninterrupted power supply units must be used for mission-critical systems.

- A system-monitoring tool should be used to detect problems proactively. Monitoring tools should be able to do event monitoring and problem reporting. For example, the tool should be able to beep/e-mail/fax the DBA in the event of any fatal problems. In addition, it should be able to monitor space usage and other crucial data structures in the database proactively. Various third-party tools exist that can be customized to monitor your database and applications.

| Problem | Count | Complete Recovery | Incomplete Recovery |
|---|---|---|---|
| OS/Hardware problems | 14 | 9 | 5 |
| Loss of files | 15 | 3 | 12 |
| Block Corruptions | 4 | 2 | 2 |
| Crashed Instance | 2 | 2 | |
| DBA Skills | 2 | 1 | 1 |
| Bugs | 1 | | 1 |
| | 38 | 17 | 21 |

**Recovery detail**

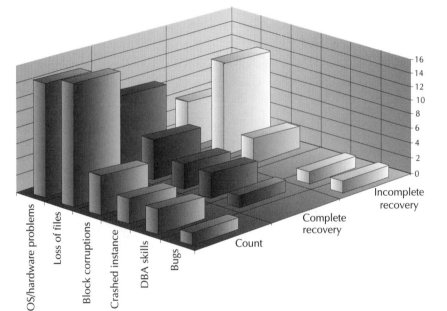

**FIGURE 6-16.** *Recovery detail graph*

■ Sites should have access to the world via the Internet. In addition, have dedicated phone lines and high-bandwidth modems connected to your machine for you to access from home or on the road. When problems occur, the hardware and software vendors can use the modem to dial into your site to monitor, diagnose, and fix problems.

■ Sites should have a qualified system administrator, and proper system administration procedures should be practiced. The system administrator must successfully complete required education programs with the hardware vendor. The DBAs should do the same with the database vendors.

■ Proper hardware protection should be available at each production site. Required hardware protection may include hard disk mirroring, keeping spare parts on site, and implementing a backup and recovery plan. RAID (redundant arrays of inexpensive disks) technology is becoming very popular for building fault tolerance and improving data availability. RAID technology is built on the fact that disk arrays generally improve performance, but how much it improves depends on the RAID level used and how the manufacturer has implemented it. The following is a brief description of the RAID levels:

   ■ **RAID 0**   A disk array that doesn't have redundancy but implements striping is referred to as RAID 0. This level doesn't offer any fault tolerance and improves speed.

   ■ **RAID 1**   Mirroring of disks is referred to as RAID 1. Mirroring is a concept where two disk drives store identical information. The system writes to both the disk drives for every write operation. When one disk fails, the other keeps working, thereby providing fault tolerance.

   ■ **RAID 2**   This level provides check disks with data bit-striped across the data and check disks. With this technology, you can detect and correct single-bit errors and detect double-bit errors. The check disks take about 30 percent of the total disk array space. RAID 2 is relatively complex to implement.

   ■ **RAID 3**   This level is commonly implemented in workstations. A parity disk is used for a group of drives and the data written to the disk array is bit-striped across the data disks. This level of RAID reduces overhead for check disks (about 80 percent of the space in the array can be used for data storage).

   ■ **RAID 4**   This level is used for transaction-processing applications, due to better optimized disk array architecture. At this RAID level, block or sector striping is done on the data disks, which allows multiple unrelated sectors to be read simultaneously. However, write operations might become a bottleneck.

   ■ **RAID 5**   The primary advantage of RAID 5 is the distributed check-data approach, which allows multiple read and write operations to take place simultaneously.

■  If using Oracle, sites must be able to operate the machine in production with all the Oracle diagnostic events turned on (if and when required), with adequate performance from the machine. If the machine performance is not adequate, the machine will have to be correctly sized.

■  All Oracle sites must be Optimal Flexible Architecture (OFA) compliant.

■  Machines running in production must be housed in a proper hazard-free environment. It is recommended that an environmental audit be requested from the hardware vendor.

■  DBAs, system managers, and application developers should analyze the in-house applications and develop clear expectations on the response time and availability goals for each application.

■  Oracle database administrators need to be certified by Oracle. The administrator is expected to have a certain knowledge level of the Oracle database. The Oracle Education Services gives a certification test and does a skills assessment when requested. They also recommend the classes a DBA should take.

■  Sites *must* maintain a test bed that should be a replica of their production environment. If running a very large database (VLDB), a percentage of the data should be maintained on test database. This is absolutely required to perform on-site testing and migration planning for future software releases. This machine should also be used for testing backup and recovery procedures at regular intervals.

■  Last, but not least, the system managers and DBAs have to maintain an operations log at each production site. Any kind of physical, design, operational, environmental, or scheduled outage should be recorded promptly. If an automated procedure doesn't exist, at least manual logging should be practiced.

# CHAPTER

# 7

## Oracle
## Recovery Manager

racle has introduced a new utility called the Recovery Manager (RMAN) in Oracle8 and the same was enhanced in Oracle8i with added features that can be used for all backup and recovery tasks. The Recovery Manager is available with a GUI as well as a command-line interface (CLI). Though Recovery Manager can work without a recovery catalog (by using the target database's control file) while managing multiple databases, we suggest that you use Recovery Manager with its recovery catalog feature to get maximum benefit from the utility. You can minimize the risks due to DBA errors considerably by using Recovery Manager as the Oracle server manages the recovery catalog. The Recovery Manager has various features that you can take advantage of, including INCREMENTAL backups. Fairly comprehensive reporting features are also available with Recovery Manager for better backup management. In this chapter, we discuss how to create and use the recovery catalog. We also show how to perform backups and recovery using Recovery Manager.

# Recovery Manager (RMAN) Concepts

Recovery Manager is an Oracle utility that facilitates the DBAs' performing backup and recovery tasks on databases and provides them with centralized control over backup and recovery operations on enterprise databases. RMAN keeps an index of backup and recovery operations that are performed on registered databases. It keeps the records of backups either in the control files of the respective target databases or in the recovery catalog if one is created. The actual physical backup copies will be stored in the specified storage system that can either be tape or disk. RMAN writes all backup data in files called "backup pieces" in an Oracle-proprietary format that can be read only by the RMAN utility. No other utility can use the RMAN backup sets for recovery purposes. If you want to backup to tape, you need to have one of the standard media managers such as Legato Storage Manager installed, configured, and integrated with Oracle. Execution of every RMAN **backup** command produces a backup set that is a logical grouping of one or more physical files called *backup pieces*. Figure 7-1 shows the basic functional components of RMAN.

For RMAN to work, the following prerequisites must be met:

■ You have to set either *password file authentication* for managing remote target databases or *O/S native authentication* that allows you to manage local databases only. We suggest setting password file authentication, since this allows you to maintain centralized backup and recovery operation on databases spread across the network. If you are using RMAN to manage a local database with O/S authentication, you have to set the following parameters:

 **1.** REMOTE_LOGIN_PASSWORDFILE to none in **init.ora** file (i.e., leave the parameter value blank).

 **2.** SQLNET.*authentication services* parameter appropriately as per the O/S requirement. For example, in Windows NT this value should be NTS in the **sqlnet.ora** for the O/S authentication to work.

- SYSDBA system privilege is necessary for a user to run RMAN and perform backup and recovery operations on a database.

- All backup devices must be accessible to RMAN in order to store the physical backup copy. If you want to use tape device storage, you must have media management software installed and integrated with the Oracle server.

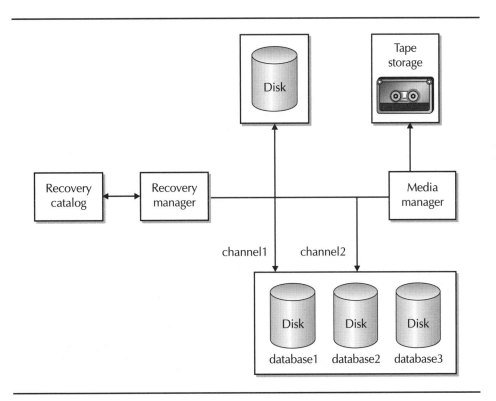

**FIGURE 7-1.** *Functional block diagram of Recovery Manager*

Recovery Manager keeps a record of all databases that are registered with RMAN. Whenever RMAN is invoked to backup or recover a database, it verifies the target database with the stored database ID available in the RMAN catalog or in the target database's control file. If that matches, RMAN establishes a minimum of two server sessions or *channels* with the target database. A channel is nothing but a remote procedure call to the target database using the PL/SQL interface to perform backup and recovery operations. RMAN compiles the commands that you have issued using its own PL/SQL engine and executes it on the target database. During execution of a command, RMAN displays the progress of the command execution. In summary, if you give an RMAN command to back up your database, first RMAN connects to the target database to verify that the database is registered with it. If not, it reports an error saying that the database is not registered and asks you to register the database. For the registered databases, RMAN establishes server sessions and compiles the commands that were issued at RMAN prompt for backup. A typical **backup** command on RMAN will be as follows (Figure 7-2 shows the output):

```
Run
{ allocate channel disk1 type disk;
backup database;
};
```

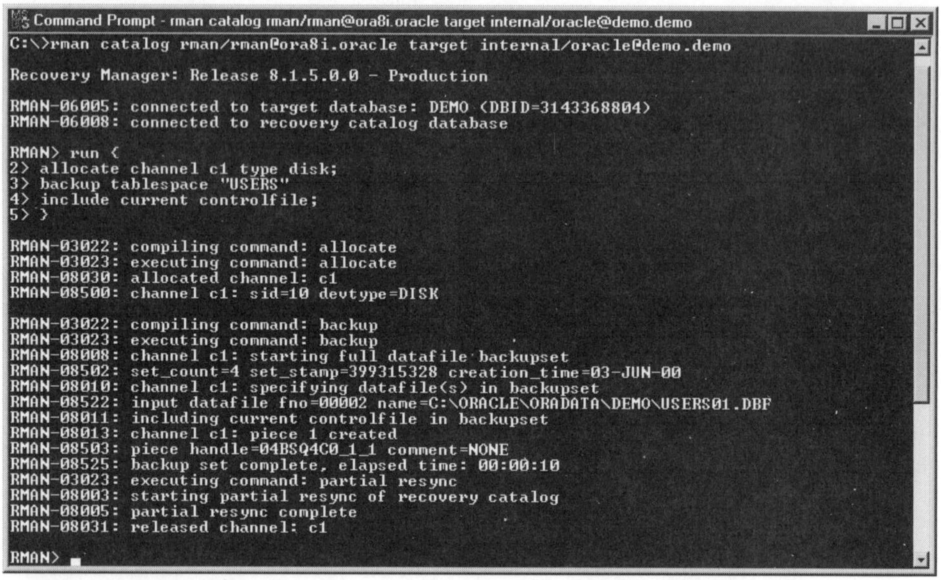

**FIGURE 7-2.** *RMAN's allocate and backup command execution at the command prompt*

When you use RMAN with Oracle Enterprise Manager (OEM) GUI, it compiles the RMAN commands and submits the job to the Oracle Intelligent Agent to execute on the target database. You can invoke Recovery Manager from Oracle Enterprise Manager from the Tools | Database Applications | Oracle Storage Manager menu.

## Advantages of Using Recovery Manager

Use of Recovery Manager for backup and recovery has the following advantages over performing backup and recovery at operating system level:

- Recovery Manager keeps track of all backup and recovery operations that were performed on databases without user intervention, thereby avoiding human errors while doing backup and recovery operations.

- RMAN can be used effectively for managing centralized backup and recovery procedures across enterprise databases.

- It supports INCREMENTAL backups.

- It has the ability to identify corrupt blocks.

- RMAN allows you to automate scheduled backups.

- It has the ability to cross-check and ensure that backed up files are intact. For example, you can verify if the required backups are available using **report need backup** command.

- It identifies the data files that require a backup based on user-specified limits.

- RMAN can generate logs of all backup and recovery operations performed.

- You can store preconfigured and compiled backup scripts that can be run anytime without recompiling the RMAN commands time and again.

- RMAN scripts are operating system independent and can be ported onto all operating systems without modification.

# The Recovery Catalog

If you wish to manage production databases that are spread across enterprise networks, it is highly advisable to run Recovery Manager with recovery catalog for backup and recovery operations. If you configure RMAN with recovery catalog, you can use all options that are available with RMAN. For example, you can:

- Check whether a particular backup set is available using RMAN's **change crosscheck** command.

- Use options such as **available**, **unavailable uncatalog**, **create script**, **delete script**, **replace script**, **print script**, etc.

The recovery catalog contains information regarding the following:

- Data file and archived redo log backup sets and backup pieces

- Data file copies

- Archived redo logs and their copies

- Tablespaces and data files on the target database

- Stored scripts, which are user-created sequences of RMAN and SQL commands

## Creating the Recovery Catalog

Before creating the recovery catalog, you should ask yourself the following question: *Do you need a separate database for holding the recovery catalog schema?*

In short, if you are using a single database, using a catalog doesn't make sense. If you have to manage multiple databases, using a catalog makes sense. Also, having the catalog in a separate database is recommended. If you have multiple databases and wish to keep the catalog in one of the existing databases, there are some ramifications to doing this. Make sure the database you use for storing the catalog is physically small (less than 1GB, as a rule of thumb). If you have multiple databases, but all of them are very large, it's a good idea to create a separate database to hold the recovery catalog. The reason for this will be clear after you read the following discussion.

Let's take an example where you have five databases: db1, db2, db3, db4, and db5. Let's assume that you have created a recovery catalog and have placed it in database, db2. The information of all the backup sets is recorded in the catalog. If any one of the databases—db1, db3, db4, or db5—crashes, and if you need to do media recovery, you can use RMAN with the recovery catalog stored in db2 and recover the crashed database(s). In case all or some of the databases crash, including db2, you cannot recover any of them using RMAN, because you lost your recovery catalog with db2. The recovery catalog needs to be available in order to recover a down database.

**NOTE**
*If you can't use RMAN to recover your database(s), you can always use SQL\*PLUS and manually do recovery of db2 using physical backups. Once db2 is recovered, you can use RMAN and the recovery catalog to recover the other databases. However, this means you must have an O/S backup of database db2.*

From the above example, it is clear that in order to safeguard your catalog database, you have to plan a backup strategy for the db2 database, as that contains the recovery catalog and that is the heart of your backup and recovery plan. One option to resolve the above situation is to create one more recovery catalog—one in db2 and another in db4. In this case, you can use RMAN to backup db1, db3, db4, and db5, and the information regarding backup sets is stored in the catalog that is stored in db2. Now, you can use RMAN to back up db2 and store the information in the catalog that's stored in db4. In summary, you are performing *cross backups* between the databases db2 and db4. While this is a better way of planning your backups, it will still create a problem if both the databases (db2 and db4) crash at the same time and if you need to perform media recovery. While the probability is very small for two databases crashing at the same time, it could happen due to an environmental outage—for example, power failure due to an earthquake. So the ideal way to plan a backup in the above example is to create catalogs in db2 and db4 and take an operating system backup (online or offline backup) of either db2 or db4.

If all the databases (db1 through db5) are very large, you will end up taking a backup of a very large database, which is not desirable. For this reason, we recommend that you create a separate database—db6—to hold the catalog, and take a physical backup of database db6. This should be fairly simple and fast as the database db6 contains only the recovery catalog and should be very small.

Following is a summary of the above discussion:

1. If you have just one database and you are using RMAN, don't use a recovery catalog. However, you must safeguard the current control file by multiplexing it to multiple locations.

2. If you have multiple databases and want to use RMAN, use the following steps:

   ■ If you want to store the recovery catalog in one of the existing databases, select the database that is smallest in size to keep the recovery catalog.

   ■ If all your databases are large, create a new database to hold the recovery catalog.

■ Include cross backups of the recovery catalog database.

■ Take an operating system backup of the recovery catalog (offline or online).

■ Run all databases in ARCHIVELOG mode and maintain multiple backup copies of archived redo log sets.

**NOTE**
*Ensure that the recovery catalog database and target databases do not reside on the same disks; if they do and you lose one database, you will lose the others.*

Let us now go through the process of creating a recovery catalog. Before trying to create a recovery catalog, you must perform the following tasks:

■ A separate tablespace must be created for the catalog schema.

■ A separate user has to be created to own the catalog schema with CONNECT and RESOURCE roles. In addition, the RECOVERY_CATALOG_OWNER role must be granted to the user. The RECOVERY_CATALOG_OWNER role provides the user with privileges to maintain and query the recovery catalog.

■ The user who owns the recovery catalog schema should be given UNLIMITED QUOTA privilege on the tablespace that was created exclusively for the recovery catalog schema.

Once the above steps are performed, you are ready to create a recovery catalog. Let us assume that you have created a tablespace named RCVCAT and a user called RMAN with CONNECT and RESOURCE privileges on the *TEST.DEMO* database (recovery catalog database). The user has also been given UNLIMITED QUOTA privilege on the tablespace RCVCAT and been granted the RECOVERY_CATALOG_ OWNER role. Creation of the recovery catalog involves the following:

```
C:\>rman catalog rman/rman@test.demo log=create_rmanlog.log

Recovery Manager: Release 8.1.5.0.0 - Production


RMAN-06008: connected to recovery catalog database
RMAN-06428: recovery catalog is not installed

RMAN>
```

After connecting to the recovery catalog database, issue the **create catalog** command to create the catalog, specifying the RCVCAT tablespace as follows:

```
RMAN> create catalog tablespace 'RCVCAT';

RMAN-06431: recovery catalog created

RMAN>
```

Note that you should enclose the tablespace name within single quotes and the name should not contain any white space. You should also note that the tablespace name is case sensitive. If you type the tablespace name in lowercase, then you will get the following error message:

```
RMAN-06004: ORACLE error from recovery catalog database: ORA-00959:
tablespace '
rcvcat' does not exist.
```

Figure 7-3 shows the creation of the RMAN schema in which various objects like tables indexes, packages, and so forth are created. In Oracle8*i*, you need not run the **catrman.sql** script in order to create the recovery catalog as you would in Oracle8. Oracle8*i* comes with new Recovery Catalog maintenance commands such as **create catalog** to create the recovery catalog. The other new commands—**upgrade catalog** and **drop catalog**—are also available in Oracle8*i*. These maintenance commands help you manage the recovery catalog effectively.

## Registering a Database

To use Recovery Manager to perform backup and recovery operations on databases, you must first register these with Recovery Manager. You cannot perform backup or recovery on a nonregistered database using RMAN. For example, let us consider that you have created a recovery catalog on the database TEST.DEMO and want to register the database ORA8I.ORACLE with RMAN. You have to perform the following steps.

1. Connect to the target database using RMAN:

```
C:\>rman catalog rman/rman@test.demo target internal/oracle@ora8i.oracle

Recovery Manager: Release 8.1.5.0.0 - Production
RMAN-06005: connected to target database: TEST (DBID=1693819414)
RMAN-06008: connected to recovery catalog database
RMAN>
```

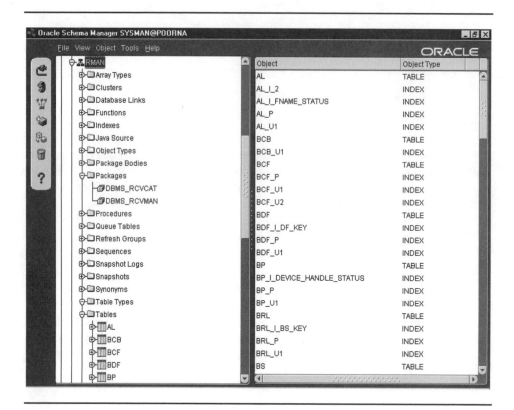

**FIGURE 7-3.** *Recovery catalog schema objects from Oracle Schema Manager*

2. Issue the **register** command at the RMAN prompt, as shown here:

```
RMAN> register database;

RMAN-03022: compiling command: register
RMAN-03023: executing command: register
RMAN-08006: database registered in recovery catalog
RMAN-03023: executing command: full resync
RMAN-08002: starting full resync of recovery catalog
RMAN-08004: full resync complete

RMAN>
```

When you connect to a nonregistered database, RMAN *does* connect to the
catalog database and the target database without giving any error message.
However, when you issue a backup or recovery command, it will tell you that that

database is not found in the recovery catalog. Let us assume that the database ORA8I.ORACLE is not registered with the recovery catalog. When you issue a **backup** command, you will get the following error message:

```
RMAN> run
2> {
3> allocate channel ch1 type disk;
4>      backup database;
5> };

RMAN-03022: compiling command: allocate
RMAN-03023: executing command: allocate
RMAN-08030: allocated channel: ch1
RMAN-08500: channel ch1: sid=10 devtype=DISK

RMAN-03022: compiling command: backup
RMAN-03026: error recovery releasing channel resources
RMAN-08031: released channel: ch1
RMAN-00571: ===========================================================
RMAN-00569: ======= ERROR MESSAGE STACK FOLLOWS ======
RMAN-00571: ===========================================================
RMAN-03002: failure during compilation of command
RMAN-03013: command type: backup
RMAN-03014: implicit resync of recovery catalog failed
RMAN-06038: recovery catalog package detected an error
RMAN-20001: target database not found in recovery catalog

RMAN-00571: ===========================================================
RMAN-00569: ======= ERROR MESSAGE STACK FOLLOWS ========
RMAN-00571: ===========================================================
RMAN-00558: error encountered while parsing input commands
RMAN-01005: syntax error: found ";": expecting one of: "allocate,
alter, beginline, catalog, change, connect, create, crosscheck, debug,
delete, drop, exit, endinline, host, {, library, list, mount, open,
print, register, release, replace, report, reset, resync, rman,
rpctest, run, set, sql, "
RMAN-01007: at line 0 column 2 file: standard input
RMAN>
```

During the database registration process, RMAN identifies the database identifier number (unique to every database that is generated by Oracle at the time of database creation) to distinguish one database from another and records its details in the recovery catalog. The recovery catalog is updated automatically when a **backup**, **copy**, **restore**, or **switch** is performed using the Recovery Manager. However, information regarding redo logs and archive log files is not automatically written to the recovery catalog. We recommend that you frequently synchronize the catalog to update it with information on log switches and archive log files. The frequency depends on the rate at which archive log files are created. On most sites, a "resync" once a week should be sufficient. Use the **resync catalog** command to accomplish this, as shown here:

```
RMAN> resync catalog;
RMAN-03022: compiling command: resync
RMAN-03023: executing command: resync
RMAN-08002: starting full resync of recovery catalog
RMAN-08004: full resync complete
```

**NOTE**
*If you are using RMAN with different target databases that have the same database name and identifier, be extremely careful to specify the correct recovery catalog schema when invoking Recovery Manager.*

You can also register databases with recovery catalog from Oracle Enterprise Manager (OEM) version 2. You can invoke RMAN from Oracle Enterprise Manager's Tools | Database Applications | Oracle Storage Manager menu. The following steps illustrate how you can perform database registration from Oracle Enterprise Manager GUI.

1. Run the Oracle Storage Manager from Oracle Enterprise Manager.

2. Invoke the Catalog Maintenance Wizard from Tools | Backup Management of Oracle Storage Manager window. The Introduction screen appears as shown in Figure 7-4. Note that you can choose not to see this page by disabling the radio button at the bottom of the screen.

3. Click the Next button to start the database registration process. You will see the Operation Choice screen. Choose the "register database"option. Figure 7-5 gives you a sample output.

4. At the Configuration screen, click Next button to view the summary of the registered job. See Figure 7-6 for the Configuration screen output.

5. At the Summary screen, click Cancel if you need to go back and change the backup configuration. If the configuration information looks fine, click OK. Figure 7-7 shows the output of the Summary screen.

6. Click OK to submit the job to OEM. You can verify the job status from the main OEM. Note that if your database is already registered with the catalog, you will get an error message as shown in Figure 7-8.

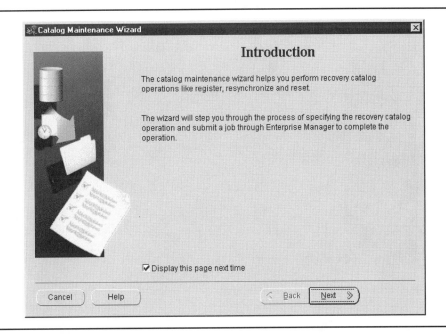

**FIGURE 7-4.**   *Startup screen of RMAN Catalog Maintenance Wizard*

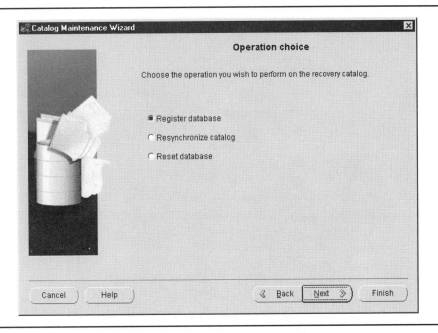

**FIGURE 7-5.**   *Operation Choice Menu of the Catalog Maintenance Wizard*

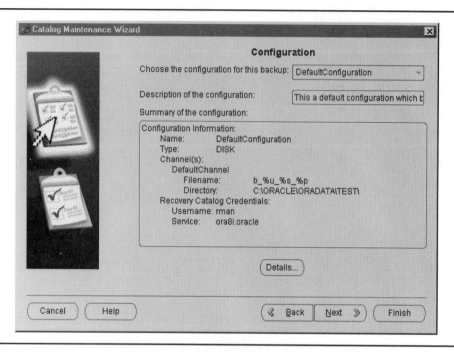

**FIGURE 7-6.** *Configuration screen of the Catalog Maintenance Wizard*

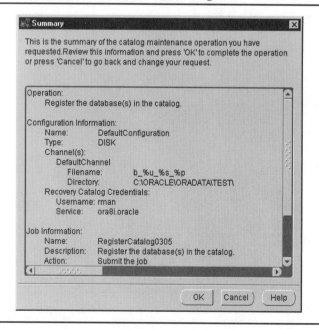

**FIGURE 7-7.** *The Summary Menu of the Catalog Maintenance Wizard*

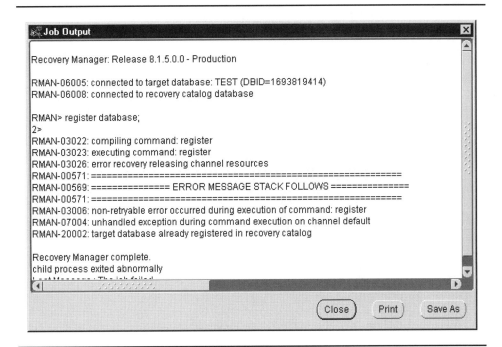

**FIGURE 7-8.**   *Job Output through OEM*

Executing Recovery Manager from Oracle Enterprise Manager needs the following components to be configured. Otherwise, all GUI-based RMAN operations will fail.

- Oracle Intelligent Agent has to be configured and running on all the databases on which you want to run RMAN jobs for backup and recovery operations.

- *Administrators preferred credentials* must be set to SYSDBA in the "Administrators preferred credentials" property sheet of OEM. You can view this from System | Preferences folder of OEM.

- Oracle Net8 has to be configured for the OEM home to connect to the databases to which you want to submit the RMAN jobs.

## Deregistering Databases from the Recovery Catalog

In certain circumstances, you need to move a database's registration from one recovery catalog to another as part of your modified backup and recovery strategy. You can do so by deregistering a database from one recovery catalog and registering it with the other recovery catalog. RMAN has the provision to deregister a database using the DBMS_RCVCAT package. You have to be very careful while deregistering a database from recovery catalog. Once you deregister, you can no longer use the backup sets that were taken with the recovery catalog for recovering the database. For deregistering a database, you need to obtain the database details such as database ID number (DB_ID) and database key (DB_KEY) as well as the list of all backup sets of the database that is stored in the recovery catalog. The database identifier number can be obtained from RMAN when you connect to the target. For example,

```
C:\>rman catalog rman/rman@test.demo

Recovery Manager: Release 8.1.5.0.0 - Production

RMAN-06008: connected to recovery catalog database

RMAN> connect target internal/oracle@test.oracle

RMAN-06005: connected to target database: TEST (DBID=1693819414)

RMAN>
```

In the preceding example, the database ID number is 1693819414. Using this number, you should get the database *key number* from the recovery catalog by querying the DB table that belongs to the recovery catalog schema.

```
SQL> select db_key, rpad(to_char(db_id),12)"DB_ID_NUMBER" from db where
db_id=1693819414;
DB_KEY DB_ID_NUMBER
------- ------------
    825 1693819414
1 row selected.
SQL>
```

In the preceding example, the **db_key** and **db_id_number** values are 825 and 1693819414, respectively. You should use these values and run the DBMS_RCVCAT package that was created during the recovery catalog creation to unregister the database as shown here:

```
SQL> execute dbms_rcvcat.unregisterdatabase(825, 1693819414);
PL/SQL procedure successfully completed.
SQL>
```

**NOTE**
*The DBMS_RCVCAT.UNREGISTERDATABASE
package works on Oracle8 and higher version
databases. For more information, refer to the*
Oracle8i Backup and Recovery Guide
Release 8.1.5 *manual.*

## Changing the Recovery Catalog

Occasionally, it is necessary to update the recovery catalog to remove references to
a backup piece, data file copy, or archive log from the recovery catalog. You can
use the **change** command in the Recovery Manager to make appropriate changes to
the catalog. You can also delete an entry in the catalog. In the following example,
we will delete a data file copy:

```
RMAN>list copy of tablespace "USERS";
RMAN-03022: compiling command: list

List of Datafile Copies
Key     File S Completion time Ckp SCN  Ckp time        Name
------- ---- - --------------- ---------- --------------- ------
1672    2    A 01-JUN-00       686690   12-MAY-00       D:\TEMP\USR1ORCL
1680    2    A 01-JUN-00       686690   12-MAY-00       D:\TEMP\RBSORCL.BAK
1681    2    A 01-JUN-00       686690   12-MAY-00       D:\TEMP\USERS01.BAK

RMAN>
RMAN>change datafilecopy 1681 delete;
RMAN-03022: compiling command: change
RMAN-08070: deleted datafile copy
RMAN-08513: datafile copy filename=D:\TEMP\USERS01.BAK recid=14 stamp=399149258
RMAN>D:\temp>DIR
 Volume in drive D has no label.
 Volume Serial Number is A045-0AEA

 Directory of D:\temp

06/01/00  09:55p       <DIR>          .
06/01/00  09:55p       <DIR>          ..
06/01/00  07:37p           2,729,984 CNTLORA.BAK
06/01/00  12:39a           2,729,984 CNTRLORA
06/01/00  12:39a           2,099,200 RBS1ORCL
06/01/00  10:02a           3,147,776 RBSORCL.BAK
06/01/00  12:38a         146,802,688 SYS1ORCL
06/01/00  12:38a           3,147,776 USR1ORCL
              8 File(s)    160,657,408 bytes
                           509,263,872 bytes free
```

In the preceding example, we determined the primary key of the backup copy D:\TEMP\USERS01.BAK and deleted it using the **change datafilecopy..delete** command of Recovery Manager.

# Taking Backups Using Recovery Manager

The Recovery Manager supports all kinds of backups except logical backups (performed using the **export** utility). If you are using a recovery catalog, backups are automatically registered in it, and the Oracle server keeps track of the backups. If you need to restore a data file or a control file, the information in the recovery catalog will be used to identify an appropriate backup that can be used to perform the required recovery operation. You can perform whole backups, tablespace backups, data file backups, control file backups, and archive log backups. You should also remember that **init.ora** files, password files, operating system files, online redo logs, and transported tablespaces (before they have been specified read-write) cannot be backed up by RMAN utility. The Recovery Manager supports three types of backup: *backup sets, data file copies* (also called *image copies*), and *operating system backups.*

Backup sets are created using the **backup** command of Recovery Manager. Backup sets can contain archive log files or data files and can be FULL or INCREMENTAL. RMAN never combines both data files and archive log files in a single backup set. Even if you choose to backup both data files and log files in a single backup operation, RMAN generates two separate backup sets each for data files and archived log files. A FULL backup contains all the blocks of a set of data files that have been used by the database. We would like to point out that a FULL backup is not a backup of the whole database. A whole database backup includes all blocks regardless of whether they are used or unused.

An INCREMENTAL backup only contains blocks that have been modified since the last backup at the same or lower level. Oracle allows you to take backups and assign a level (an integer value) to the backup. An INCREMENTAL backup will only include blocks that have changed since the previous backup at the same or lower level. A CUMULATIVE as well as nonCUMULATIVE option is also provided in INCREMENTAL backups. There is a restriction that a backup set cannot mix archive log files and data files. The **restore** command in Recovery Manager is used to restore files from a backup set.

A data file copy is created using the **copy** command of Recovery Manager. A copy of a data file is created using an Oracle server process and not the operating system. An **alter tablespace..begin backup** is not required prior to creating a data file copy. Data file copies can be directly used to replace the original file without any restoration. You have to use the **set newname** and **switch** commands in RMAN to make a data file copy the current version of the data file. This is very similar to the **alter database rename datafile** command. Media recovery, if necessary, can be performed on the data file copies.

You can also choose to use operating system utilities to create backups. Such copies can be registered in the catalog using the **catalog** command of Recovery Manager. You must use the **alter tablespace..begin backup** before you take a copy of a data file at the operating system level.

We have seen that the Recovery Manager supports backup sets, data file copies, and operating system copies. We will now take a look at how different kinds of backup can be taken using Recovery Manager. First, we will examine the creation of backup sets, and after that we will look at a few examples of data file copies and operating system copies. More examples are provided in the case studies in Chapter 10.

**NOTE**
*Even though in some of our examples we may have used the same disk to create backups, we recommend that you create all your backups on a disk other than the one that contains data files. This ensures that the backup is not lost if the disk(s) containing the database files crashes.*

# Whole Database Backups

Whole database backups containing all control files and database files can be taken with the database open or closed. The backup includes all blocks regardless of whether they have been used or not. Backup of online redo logs is not required, nor is it recommended. Restoration of online redo logs can corrupt the database, as discussed earlier.

### Creating a Backup Set for a Whole Database Backup

A backup set for a whole database backup contains all the data files and control files belonging to a database. It is necessary for a database to be in ARCHIVELOG mode to take a whole backup while the database is open. In NOARCHIVELOG mode, the database needs to be closed. The Recovery Manager will not permit you to take a whole backup if the database is open and in NOARCHIVELOG mode. Similarly, if you invoke Recovery Manager from Oracle Enterprise Manager GUI mode (for taking a whole database backup of a database that is in NOARCHIVELOG mode), RMAN shuts down the database, mounts it, takes a whole database backup, and brings it up once the backup is over. When the database is in NOARCHIVELOG mode, RMAN allows you to take only a FULL database backup and cannot perform tablespace and datafile file backups. Here is an example that attempts to create a backup set while the database is open and in NOARCHIVELOG mode.

```
RMAN> run{
2>       allocate channel disk1 type disk format
'c:\backup\%d_backup%U';
3>              backup database;
4>       sql 'ALTER SYSTEM ARCHIVE LOG CURRENT';
5>       sql 'ALTER SYSTEM ARCHIVE LOG ALL';
6> }
RMAN-03022: compiling command: allocate
RMAN-03023: executing command: allocate
RMAN-08030: allocated channel: disk1
RMAN-08500: channel disk1: sid=17 devtype=DISK
RMAN-03022: compiling command: backup
RMAN-03025: performing implicit partial resync of recovery catalog
RMAN-03023: executing command: partial resync
RMAN-08003: starting partial resync of recovery catalog
RMAN-08005: partial resync complete
RMAN-03023: executing command: backup
RMAN-08008: channel disk1: starting full datafile backupset
RMAN-08502: set_count=16 set_stamp=399055781 creation_time=31-MAY-00
RMAN-08010: channel disk1: specifying datafile(s) in backupset
RMAN-08522: input datafile fno=00001
name=C:\ORACLE\ORADATA\TEST\SYSTEM01.DBF
RMAN-08011: including current controlfile in backupset
RMAN-08522: input datafile fno=00003
name=C:\ORACLE\ORADATA\TEST\RBS01.DBF
RMAN-08522: input datafile fno=00009 name=USER_DATA3
RMAN-08522: input datafile fno=00005 name=RCVCATLOG
RMAN-08522: input datafile fno=00007 name=USER_DATA1
RMAN-08522: input datafile fno=00008 name=USER_DATA2
```

When you need to back up a database to tape devices, you have to specify the device type in the RMAN **allocate channel** command option. For example, the above RMAN **backup** command can be modified for backup on tape device as below:

```
RMAN> run{
2>       allocate channel dev1 type 'sbt_tape';
3>              backup database;
4>       sql 'ALTER SYSTEM ARCHIVE LOG CURRENT';
5>       sql 'ALTER SYSTEM ARCHIVE LOG ALL';
6> }
```

In the **allocate channel** command, the type determines what type of media Oracle process should use for read and write. The type **'disk'** indicates that the backup media is random-access disks, and Oracle attempts to read backups from or write backups to disk. If you specify type **'sbt_tape'**, then Oracle attempts to read backups from or write backups to access a media manager. For using a tape device for backup, at least one media manager must be configured and integrated with oracle to access the tape drive and the channel type must be **'sbt_tape'**.

When backing up huge databases, allocating a single channel to a single-disk media drastically increases disk I/Os and results in I/O contention. In order to avoid this kind of I/O bottleneck, you have to think of allocating multiple channels for spreading a backup set across multiple physical disk drives. You should always allocate one type of disk channel per disk drive and specify the format string so that the filenames are on different disks and thereby balancing the I/Os across disk drives. For example, you can modify the whole database backup script as shown here to spread a backup set across multiple channels:

```
run{
     allocate channel d1 type disk format 'C:\backup\%d_backups%U';
     allocate channel d2 type disk format 'D:\ %d_backups%U';
     allocate channel d3 type disk format ''E:\ %d_backups%U';
     backup database;
sql 'ALTER SYSTEM ARCHIVE LOG CURRENT';
sql 'ALTER SYSTEM ARCHIVE LOG ALL';
}
```

Two kinds of FULL database backups are possible: *consistent backup* and *inconsistent backup.* When all data files are in READ/WRITE mode and control files are consistent to a point in time (same SCN), a consistent backup can be taken. Redo logs need not be applied while restoring from a FULL consistent backup. A consistent FULL backup is the only method of backup available when a database is in NOARCHIVELOG mode. You should never perform backup on databases that are in NOARCHIVELOG mode and are not shut down using NORMAL or IMMEDIATE options.

When a database is running in ARCHIVELOG mode, you can take a full backup that is inconsistent. Redo logs need to be applied to the data files in order to restore the database to a consistent state. You need to perform the following steps in order to run the Recovery Manager from OEM with the database open and in ARCHIVELOG mode. You can run RMAN from OEM Tools | Database Applications | Oracle Storage Manager menu.

1. Run the RMAN Backup Wizard from Tools | Backup Management of Oracle Storage Manager and click Next to define the database backup process. Backup wizard gives you the options to choose a predefined backup strategy or to define your own backup strategy. Select the type of backup strategy you want to define for your backup plan as shown in Figure 7-9 and click Next to continue with the operation.

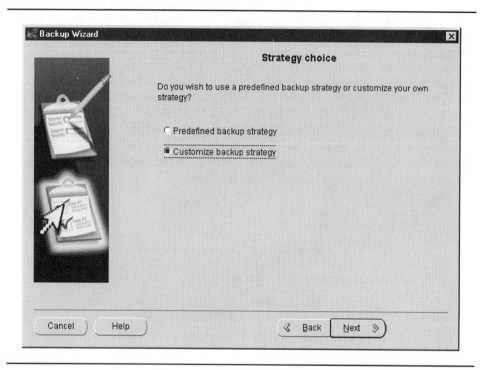

**FIGURE 7-9.** *RMAN backup plan customization wizard from OEM*

2. Select the type of backup operation you want to perform in the Backup Selection screen, as shown in Figure 7-10, and click Next.

3. In the Archive Logs screen, you need to decide whether you want to include the archive logfiles as part of your backup strategy. This is a very important step. Choose the appropriate option here. Unless there is a special reason, it is always recommended to archive *all* the log files as shown in Figure 7-11. You can also choose to delete the archived log files after they have been backed up. We strongly recommend that you don't delete the archive logs after backup until you verify that the backed up log files are functioning properly (i.e. can be used for recovery purposes during test recovery). After selecting the proper options, click Next.

4. In the Backup Options screen, choose between full database backup and incremental backup. You can also choose between the type of incremental backup and the level that you want as shown in Figure 7-12. Click on Next.

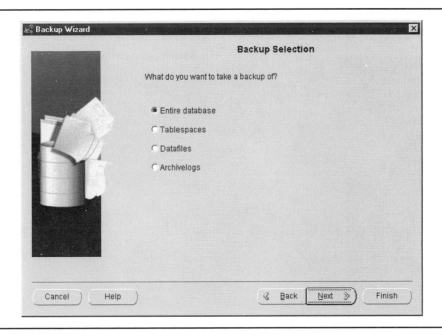

**FIGURE 7-10.**   *Backup selection screen for various RMAN backup options*

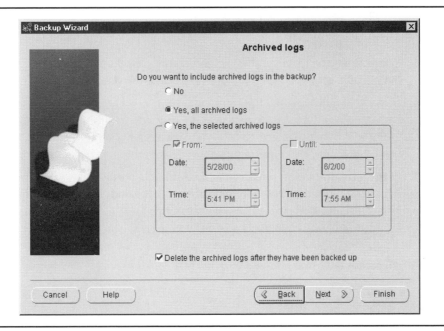

**FIGURE 7-11.**   *Choosing the time-based arvhivelogs*

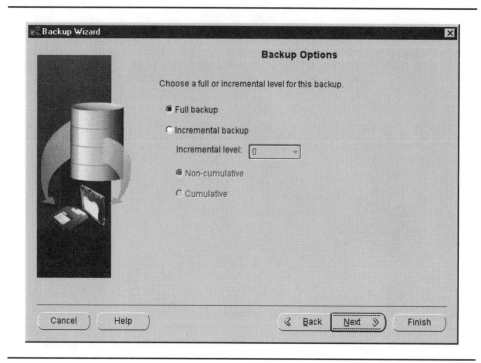

**FIGURE 7-12.** *Choosing the type of backup*

5. You will see the Configuration screen with the backup information you have requested as shown in Figure 7-13. Click Next.

6. In the Schedule screen, choose the appropriate scheduling option for your backup job to run. This Wizard also enables you to submit the job to multiple destinations. Figure 7-14 shows a sample output of the wizard. Click Next.

7. In the Job Information screen, specify a suitable name and description for the backup job to be submitted to OEM console and also specify when to submit the job as shown in Figure 7-15. Click Finish.

8. You can view the backup job information from Job Pane of OEM main screen. Click on the job that you have submitted to OEM to view its execution details as shown in Figure 7-16.

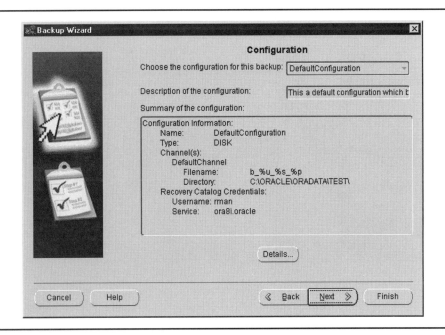

**FIGURE 7-13.** *Summary of backup configuration*

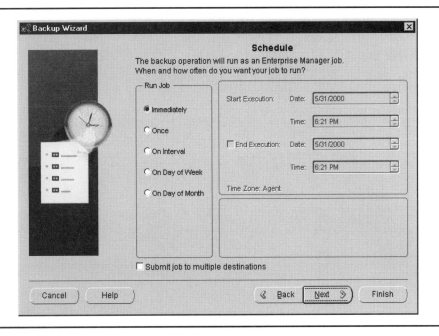

**FIGURE 7-14.** *Scheduling the backup job*

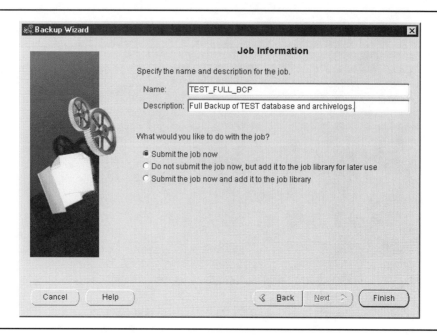

**FIGURE 7-15.** *Submitting the backup job to OEM for execution*

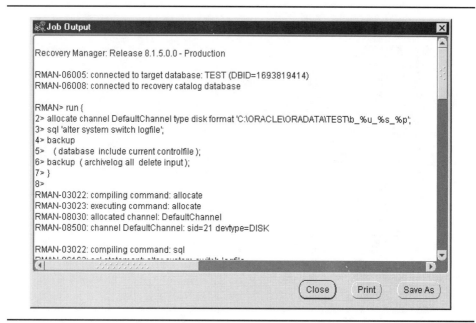

**FIGURE 7-16.** *Completion of backup job that was submitted to OEM*

Whenever you perform RMAN functions from the OEM GUI, Oracle compiles RMAN commands and submits the RMAN activities in the form of jobs to OEM, which in turn submits the jobs to Oracle Intelligent Agents that are running on the remote databases for execution. On receipt of each job, Agents on the respective databases execute the jobs and return the job's status to OEM. You can find all jobs that are submitted to OEM from the OEM jobs folder. For more information refer to the *Oracle Enterprise Manager Documentation Release 2.0* manual.

## Creating Data File Copies for a Whole Database Backup

To create data file copies for a whole database backup, copy all database files and control files individually. Before executing the **copy** command, identify the data files available in the database by generating a report on the target database schema using the **report schema** command:

```
RMAN> report schema;
RMAN-03022: compiling command: report
RMAN-03025: performing implicit partial resync of recovery catalog
RMAN-03023: executing command: partial resync
RMAN-08003: starting partial resync of recovery catalog
RMAN-08005: partial resync complete
Report of database schema
File K-bytes    Tablespace           RB segs Name
---- ---------- -------------------- ------- -------------------
1       143360 SYSTEM               YES     C:\ORACLE\ORADATA\TEST\SYSTEM01.DBF
2         3072 USERS                NO      C:\ORACLE\ORADATA\TEST\USERS01.DBF
3        25600 RBS                  YES     C:\ORACLE\ORADATA\TEST\RBS01.DBF
4         2048 TEMP                 NO      C:\ORACLE\ORADATA\TEST\TEMP01.DBF
RMAN>
```

You should note down all the data filenames in order to create an RMAN script that will copy all the data files and the current control file as well.

The following is an example of a RMAN **copy** script that performs the data file copy of a database that consists of four data files:

```
RMAN> run{
2> allocate channel c1 type disk;
3> copy datafile 1to 'd:\temp\sys1orcl.bak';
4> copy datafile 2 to 'd:\temp\usr1orcl.bak';
5> copy datafile 3 to 'd:\temp\rbs1orcl.bak';
6> copy datafile 3 to 'd:\temp\rbs1orcl.bak';
7>copy current controlfile to 'd:\temp\cntrlora.bak';
8> }

RMAN> run{
2>  allocate channel c1 type disk;
3> copy datafile 1 to 'd:\temp\sys1orcl';
4> copy datafile 2 to 'd:\temp\usr1orcl';
5> copy datafile 3 to 'd:\temp\rbs1orcl';
6> copy datafile 4 to 'd:\temp\rbs1orcl';
7> copy current controlfile to 'd:\temp\cntrlora';
8> }
```

```
RMAN-03022: compiling command: allocate
RMAN-03023: executing command: allocate
RMAN-08030: allocated channel: c1
RMAN-08500: channel c1: sid=17 devtype=DISK
RMAN-03022: compiling command: copy
RMAN-03025: performing implicit partial resync of recovery catalog
RMAN-03023: executing command: partial resync
RMAN-08003: starting partial resync of recovery catalog
RMAN-08005: partial resync complete

RMAN-03023: executing command: copy
RMAN-08000: channel c1: copied datafile 1
RMAN-08501: output filename=D:\TEMP\SYS1ORCL recid=4 stamp=399083910
RMAN-03023: executing command: partial resync
RMAN-08003: starting partial resync of recovery catalog
RMAN-08005: partial resync complete

RMAN-03022: compiling command: copy
RMAN-03023: executing command: copy
RMAN-08000: channel c1: copied datafile 2
RMAN-08501: output filename=D:\TEMP\USR1ORCL recid=5 stamp=399083915
RMAN-03023: executing command: partial resync
RMAN-08003: starting partial resync of recovery catalog
RMAN-08005: partial resync complete

RMAN-03022: compiling command: copy
RMAN-03023: executing command: copy
RMAN-08000: channel c1: copied datafile 3
RMAN-08501: output filename=D:\TEMP\RBS1ORCL recid=6 stamp=399083936
RMAN-03023: executing command: partial resync
RMAN-08003: starting partial resync of recovery catalog
RMAN-08005: partial resync complete

RMAN-03022: compiling command: copy
RMAN-03023: executing command: copy
RMAN-08000: channel c1: copied datafile 4
RMAN-08501: output filename=D:\TEMP\RBS1ORCL recid=7 stamp=399083944
RMAN-03023: executing command: partial resync
RMAN-08003: starting partial resync of recovery catalog
RMAN-08005: partial resync complete

RMAN-03022: compiling command: copy
RMAN-03023: executing command: copy
RMAN-08027: channel c1: copied current controlfile
RMAN-08505: output filename=D:\TEMP\CNTRLORA
RMAN-03023: executing command: partial resync
RMAN-08003: starting partial resync of recovery catalog
RMAN-08005: partial resync complete
RMAN-08031: released channel: c1

RMAN>
```

## Advantage of Making Image Copies

The output of the RMAN **copy** command is similar to copying files at operating system level. The difference is that the file was generated by the RMAN process. The

RMAN **copy** command also checks for physical and logical data block corruptions which OS copy commands do not. The output of the RMAN **copy** command is called an *image copy* and is not in RMAN-specific format (unlike RMAN backup sets, which need to be processed by RMAN's **recover** command only). So, the image copies can be used without any further processing for recovery purposes. Physical corruptions will be identified by default by RMAN. In order to identify the logical corruption, you have to specifically include the CHECK LOGIC option in the **copy** command. If RMAN finds any logical corruption, it logs the particular block details in the **alert.log** and the server session trace file. Like the **backup** command, RMAN continues the copy operation even if it encounters block corruptions until the total number of physical and logical corruptions is less than its **maxcorrupt** setting. **Maxcorrupt** value can be set using the **set** command preceding the **backup\copy** command as shown here:

```
run
{
set maxcorrupt for datafile 2 to 3;
allocate channel dev2 type disk;
copy check logical datafile 'c:\oracle\oradata\test\users01.dbf' to 'd:\temp\rbsorcl.bak'
tag = 'Bi_weekly_df_copy';
}
```

While processing the above command, if RMAN encounters corrupt blocks, it populates the V$BACKUP_CORRUPTION and V$COPY_CORRUPTION views with corrupt block details. If the total number of encountered corrupt blocks exceeds the **maxcorrupt** setting, then the command terminates without populating the views.

## Creating an Operating System Backup for a Whole Database Backup

The procedure involves three steps. Step 1 is to mark individual tablespaces using the **alter tablespace..begin backup** command. The second step is to use operating system utilities to copy all the data files belonging to the tablespace. The third step is to tell the database that you are done copying the data files by issuing the **alter tablespace..end backup command**. Once these copies are created, you need to register these copies in the recovery catalog. The following is an example of an operating system backup. We will only demonstrate one tablespace, called TEST. You need to perform this routine for all tablespaces that contain user data.

```
SQL> alter tablespace test begin backup;
Statement processed.
SQL> host
Microsoft(R) Windows NT(TM)
(C) Copyright 1985-1996 Microsoft Corp.
C:\ORACLE\ORADATA\TEST>copy tst1orcl.dbf d:\backup\tst1orcl.dbf
```

```
1 file(s) copied.
 C:\ORACLE\ORADATA\TEST>exit
 SQL> alter tablespace test end backup;
Statement processed.
```

After copying all the data files that belong to the tablespace, you can use the RMAN **catalog** command to register with the RMAN catalog. For example, the copied data file **tst1orcl.dbf** that is located in the directory **d:\backup** can be registered with the recovery catalog as shown here:

```
RMAN> catalog datafilecopy 'c:\backup\tst1orcl.dbf';
RMAN-03022: compiling command: catalog
RMAN-03023: executing command: catalog
RMAN-08050: cataloged datafile copy
RMAN-08513: datafile copy filename=C:\BACKUP\TST1ORCL.DBF recid=9 stamp=399121362
RMAN-03023: executing command: partial resync
RMAN-08003: starting partial resync of recovery catalog
RMAN-08005: partial resync complete
RMAN>
```

Before executing the RMAN **catalog** command, you should ensure that RMAN is connected to the desired target database. If you try to register a data file copy that doesn't belong to a database, you will get the following RMAN error:

```
RMAN-10035: exception raised in RPC: ORA-19563: datafile copy header
validation failed for file D:\RAMESH\ TST1ORCL.DBF
RMAN-10031: ORA-19563 occurred during call to DBMS_BACKUP_RESTORE.INSPECTDATAFILECOPY
```

Note that the catalog cannot support file copies that were created in Oracle7 or lower versions. Recataloging backup pieces or backup sets is also not possible with the RMAN **catalog** command. If you want remove the data file copy entries from the recovery catalog, you can do so by using the RMAN **change uncatalog** command. This command removes the record of a specified backup or copy from the recovery catalog. This command does not delete physical data files, but only removes their entries from the catalog. The **change delete** command removes entries from the recovery catalog and deletes the physical files.

You can use the RMAN **list** command to verify the data file copy registration. For example, issue the **list copy of tablespace 'users'** command at the RMAN prompt while you are connected to the target database, as given below:

```
RMAN> LIST COPY OF TABLESPACE 'USERS';
RMAN-03022: compiling command: list
List of Datafile Copies
Key    File S Completion time Ckp SCN  Ckp time   Name
-----  ---- - --------------- -------- ---------- ------
2035   2    A 01-JUN-00       683120   31-MAY-00  C:\BACKUP\ TST1ORCL.DBF
RMAN>
```

# Tablespace Backups

A tablespace backup is a backup of all data files that belong to the tablespace. You need to back up tablespaces that are read-only only once after they have been made read-only. It is not necessary to use the **alter tablespace..begin backup** command to create backup sets using Recovery Manager. This is because Recovery Manager creates a *snapshot* of the data file headers before starting a hot backup on a tablespace, thereby noting the SCN at the beginning of the backup.

## Creating a Backup Set for a Tablespace

You can normally create a backup set for a tablespace only when the database is running in ARCHIVELOG mode. The only exceptions to this rule are READ-ONLY or OFFLINE-NORMAL tablespaces. The following example illustrates a backup of a tablespace called USERS:

```
RMAN> RUN
2> {allocate channel c1 type disk;
3> backup tablespace "USERS"
4> filesperset 3
5> format 'aatst_%t%s.%p';
6> }

RMAN-03022: compiling command: allocate
RMAN-03023: executing command: allocate
RMAN-08030: allocated channel: c1
RMAN-08500: channel c1: sid=11 devtype=DISK
RMAN-03022: compiling command: backup
RMAN-03023: executing command: backup
RMAN-08008: channel c1: starting full datafile backupset
RMAN-08502: set_count=26 set_stamp=399146772 creation_time=01-JUN-00
RMAN-08010: channel c1: specifying datafile(s) in backupset
RMAN-08522: input datafile fno=00002 name=C:\ORACLE\ORADATA\TEST\USERS01.DBF
RMAN-08013: channel c1: piece 1 created
RMAN-08503: piece handle=AATST_39914677226.1 comment=NONE
RMAN-08525: backup set complete, elapsed time: 00:00:04
RMAN-03023: executing command: partial resync
RMAN-08003: starting partial resync of recovery catalog
RMAN-08005: partial resync complete
RMAN-08031: released channel: c1
RMAN>
```

We will look at the directory listing resulting from the above backup:

```
C:\ORACLE\ORA81\DATABASE>dir aatst*
Volume in drive C is MS-DOS_6
 Volume Serial Number is 2338-6CE4
 Directory of C:\ORACLE\ORA81\DATABASE
06/01/00 06:06P            12,800 AATST_31557122110.1
             1 File(s)      12,800 bytes
                        52,330,496 bytes free
```

Alternatively, you can use the **list** command in Recovery Manager to get information on the backup of tablespace USERS. The RMAN **list** command gives you a detailed listing of specified backup sets or image copies recorded in the recovery catalog or target control file. We will discuss more about this command later in this chapter. The following example gives information about the tablespace USERS using the **list** and **report** commands:

```
RMAN> list copy of tablespace "USERS";
RMAN-03022: compiling command: list
List of Datafile Copies
Key     File S Completion time  Ckp SCN    Ckp time      Name
------  ---- - --------------- ---------- ------------  ------
1987    2    A 01-JUN-00         686690    12-MAY-00    D:\TEMP\USR1ORCL
2028    2    A 01-JUN-00         686690    12-MAY-00    D:\TEMP\RBSORCL.BAK
RMAN>

RMAN> list backupset of datafile "c:\oracle\oradata\test\users01.dbf";
RMAN-03022: compiling command: list
List of Backup Sets
Key     Recid      Stamp       LV Set Stamp  Set Count  Completion Time
------  ---------- ----------  -- ---------- ---------- -----------------
2072    18         399146774   0  399146772  26          01-JUN-00
    List of Backup Pieces
    Key     Pc# Cp# Status      Completion Time        Piece Name
    ------- --- --- ----------  ---------------------- -------------------
    2074    1   1   AVAILABLE   01-JUN-00              AATST_39914677226.1
    List of Datafiles Included
    File Name                                       LV Type Ckp SCN    Ckp Time
    ---- ------------------------------------------ -- ---- ---------- ---------
    2    C:\ORACLE\ORADATA\TEST\USERS01.DBF          0  Full 686690    12-MAY-00
RMAN>
RMAN> report unrecoverable tablespace "USERS";
RMAN-03022: compiling command: report
Report of files that need backup due to unrecoverable operations
File Type of Backup Required Name
---- ---------------------- -----------------------------------
RMAN>
```

## Creating a Data File Copy of a Tablespace
A data file copy is a simple copy of all data files belonging to a tablespace. The advantage of this method is that you can use the data file copies directly without a **restore** command. This can reduce downtime considerably. Here is an example:

```
RMAN> run
2> {allocate channel c1 type disk;
3> copy datafile 'c:\oracle\oradata\test\users01.dbf' to
'd:\temp\users01.bak';
```

```
4> }
RMAN-03022: compiling command: allocate
RMAN-03023: executing command: allocate
RMAN-08030: allocated channel: c1
RMAN-08500: channel c1: sid=13 devtype=DISK
RMAN-03022: compiling command: copy
RMAN-03023: executing command: copy
RMAN-08000: channel c1: copied datafile 2
RMAN-08501: output filename=D:\TEMP\USERS01.BAK recid=14 stamp=399149258
RMAN-03023: executing command: partial resync
RMAN-08003: starting partial resync of recovery catalog
RMAN-08005: partial resync complete
RMAN-08031: released channel: c1
RMAN>
```

### Operating System Backup of a Tablespace

It is also possible to use operating system utilities to create a backup of a tablespace. The **alter tablespace..begin backup** and **alter tablespace..end backup** commands are necessary to do this. Please refer to the example in the previous subsection titled "Creating an Operating System Backup for a Whole Database Backup" under the "Whole Database Backups" section earlier in this chapter for details.

## Data File Backups

Specific data files can be backed up, if necessary, using Recovery Manager. However, this is not a very common use of Recovery Manager, as DBAs prefer to back up tablespaces rather than data files. However, in a situation where a tablespace has only one data file, it is possible to use data file backups. Also, your database needs to be in ARCHIVELOG mode unless the tablespace in question is READ-ONLY or OFFLINE-NORMAL as mentioned earlier. We will illustrate data file backups with the following example of a backup set:

```
RMAN> run
2> {allocate channel c1 type disk;
3> backup datafile 'c:\oracle\oradata\test\users01.dbf'
4> format 'aatst_%t%s.%p';
5> }
RMAN-03022: compiling command: allocate
RMAN-03023: executing command: allocate
RMAN-08030: allocated channel: c1
RMAN-08500: channel c1: sid=13 devtype=DISK

RMAN-03022: compiling command: backup
RMAN-03023: executing command: backup
RMAN-08008: channel c1: starting full datafile backupset
RMAN-08502: set_count=27 set_stamp=399149451 creation_time=01-JUN-00
```

```
RMAN-08010: channel c1: specifying datafile(s) in backupset
RMAN-08522: input datafile fno=00002 name=C:\ORACLE\ORADATA\TEST\USERS01.DBF
RMAN-08013: channel c1: piece 1 created
RMAN-08503: piece handle=AATST_39914945127.1 comment=NONE
RMAN-08525: backup set complete, elapsed time: 00:00:03
RMAN-03023: executing command: partial resync
RMAN-08003: starting partial resync of recovery catalog
RMAN-08005: partial resync complete
RMAN-08031: released channel: c1
RMAN>
```

You can also create data file copies and operating system backups for data files. The procedure is very similar to that of a tablespace. Refer to the previous section for syntax.

# Control File Backups

Control file backups are very vital to any backup strategy. You must take a backup of a control file every time you modify the schema of the database. In this section we discuss how to take a backup set of a control file as well as a file copy of the control file.

## Backup Set of a Control File

You can create a backup set of the control file separately through Recovery Manager, as shown here:

```
RMAN> run
2> {allocate channel c1 type disk;
3> backup current controlfile
4> tag = weekly_sat_backup;
5> }
RMAN-03022: compiling command: allocate
RMAN-03023: executing command: allocate
RMAN-08030: allocated channel: c1
RMAN-08500: channel c1: sid=13 devtype=DISK
RMAN-03022: compiling command: backup
RMAN-03023: executing command: backup
RMAN-08008: channel c1: starting full datafile backupset
RMAN-08502: set_count=28 set_stamp=399149748 creation_time=01-JUN-00
RMAN-08010: channel c1: specifying datafile(s) in backupset
RMAN-08011: including current controlfile in backupset
RMAN-08013: channel c1: piece 1 created
RMAN-08503: piece handle=0SBSL2LK_1_1 comment=NONE
RMAN-08525: backup set complete, elapsed time: 00:00:05
RMAN-03023: executing command: partial resync
RMAN-08003: starting partial resync of recovery catalog
RMAN-08005: partial resync complete
RMAN-08031: released channel: c1
RMAN>
```

When you perform a FULL backup, the control file automatically is included in the backup. You can also include a control file in the backup of a tablespace or data file, as shown here:

```
run {
allocate channel c1 type disk;
backup tablespace "USERS"
include current controlfile;
}
```

You can perform the same backup operation from Oracle Enterprise Manager as well. Figures 7-17 through 7-19 show how to include current control file in a tablespace backup set.

You can get the status of the tablespace backup job that we submitted from the history folder of OEM job pane of the OEM window.

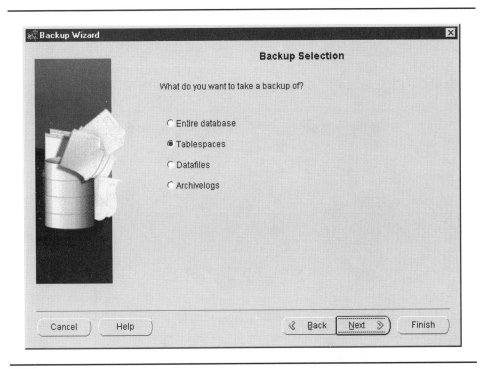

**FIGURE 7-17.** *Tablespace backup option selected for tablespace backup*

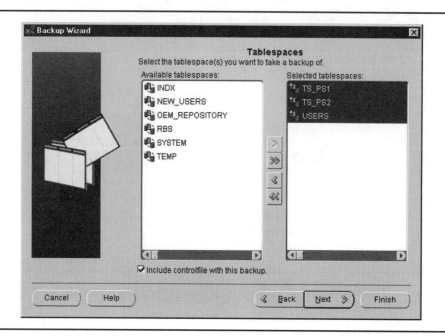

**FIGURE 7-18.** *Selected tablespaces with INCLUDE CONTROLFILE option*

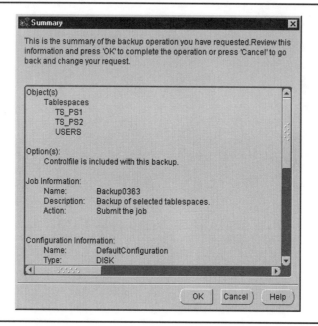

**FIGURE 7-19.** *Summary of tablespace backup with current controlfile operation*

### File Copy of a Control File

A data file copy is an image of the control file that can replace an existing control file with no changes. Here is an example that shows how to make a file copy of the control file using RMAN:

```
RMAN> run
2> {allocate channel c1 type disk;
3> copy current controlfile to 'd:\temp\cntlora.bak';
4> }
RMAN-03022: compiling command: allocate
RMAN-03023: executing command: allocate
RMAN-08030: allocated channel: c1
RMAN-08500: channel c1: sid=13 devtype=DISK
RMAN-03022: compiling command: copy
RMAN-03023: executing command: copy
RMAN-08027: channel c1: copied current controlfile
RMAN-08505: output filename=D:\TEMP\CNTLORA.BAK
RMAN-03023: executing command: partial resync
RMAN-08003: starting partial resync of recovery catalog
RMAN-08005: partial resync complete
RMAN-08031: released channel: c1
RMAN>
```

**NOTE**
*We recommend that you use the multiplexing feature of Oracle to create at least three copies of the control file on separate disks (mounted under different disk controllers, if possible) using the CONTROL_FILES parameter in the **init.ora** file.*

# Archive Log Backups

You can create a backup set of archive log files based on log sequence numbers using Recovery Manager. If you choose to back up all the archive log files you should use the ALL option. You can also create backups of archive log files based on timestamps. You must ensure that the NLS_DATE_FORMAT and NLS_LANG parameters are set properly in your client environment. The following example creates a backup of archive log files with a starting log sequence number of 3 and an ending log sequence number of 10. You can get the log sequence numbers by querying the V$ARCHIVED_LOG view:

```
RMAN> run
2> {allocate channel c1 type disk;
3> backup archivelog low logseq 3 high logseq 10 thread 1;
4> }
```

```
RMAN-03022: compiling command: allocate
RMAN-03023: executing command: allocate
RMAN-08030: allocated channel: c1
RMAN-08500: channel c1: sid=13 devtype=DISK
RMAN-03022: compiling command: backup
RMAN-03023: executing command: backup
RMAN-08009: channel c1: starting archivelog backupset
RMAN-08502: set_count=31 set_stamp=399153232 creation_time=01-JUN-00
RMAN-08014: channel c1: specifying archivelog(s) in backup set
RMAN-08504: input archivelog thread=1 sequence=6 recid=1 stamp=395415008
RMAN-08504: input archivelog thread=1 sequence=7 recid=2 stamp=395489000
RMAN-08504: input archivelog thread=1 sequence=8 recid=3 stamp=395573807
RMAN-08504: input archivelog thread=1 sequence=9 recid=4 stamp=395589355
RMAN-08504: input archivelog thread=1 sequence=10 recid=5 stamp=395654884
RMAN-08013: channel c1: piece 1 created
RMAN-08503: piece handle=0VBSL62G_1_1 comment=NONE
RMAN-08525: backup set complete, elapsed time: 00:00:02
RMAN-03023: executing command: partial resync
RMAN-08003: starting partial resync of recovery catalog
RMAN-08005: partial resync complete
RMAN-08031: released channel: c1
RMAN>
```

Figures 7-20 through 7-22 show how to use Recovery Manager from OEM for backing up archived log files. The GUI is very user friendly and some DBAs, especially novice DBAs, prefer to use it.

Optionally, you can use the **copy** command in Recovery Manager to create copies of archive log files. You must specify the full path name of the archive log files, as shown here:

```
RMAN> run{
2> allocate channel c1 type disk;
3> copy archivelog
'c:\oracle\oradata\test\archive\ORCLT0001S0000000391.ARC' to
4> 'c:\temp\arch391.bak';
5> }
```

**NOTE**
*We recommend that you keep backups of your archive log files on disk using the duplexing feature provided by Oracle8*i*. In order to do this, you can set the parameter LOG_ARCHIVE_DUPLEX_DEST in the **init.ora** file. Please refer to the Oracle8*i* Reference Release 8.1.5 manual for more information.*

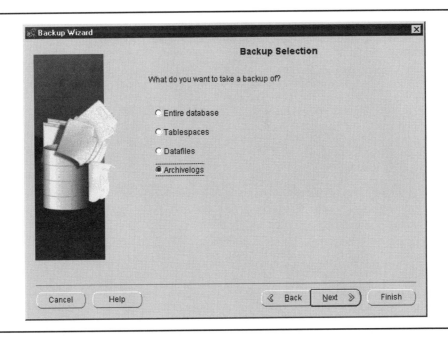

**FIGURE 7-20.** *Backup Selection menu*

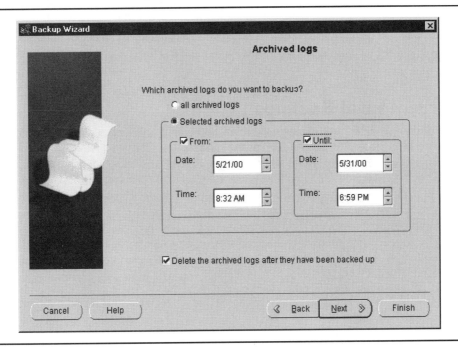

**FIGURE 7-21.** *Selecting time-based archive log backups*

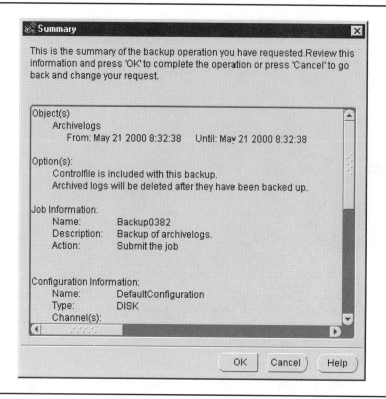

**FIGURE 7-22.**  *Summary information of selected archive logs for backup*

## Incremental Backups

An INCREMENTAL backup saves space and time as it only copies blocks that have changed since the previous backup at the same or lower level. Two kinds of INCREMENTAL backups are available: 1) CUMULATIVE INCREMENTAL backup and 2) nonCUMULATIVE INCREMENTAL backup. Cumulative backups include all blocks that were changed since the last backup at a lower level. A CUMULATIVE backup reduces the work during restoration as only one backup contains all the changed blocks. However, they consume more space. A nonCUMULATIVE backup only includes blocks that were changed since the previous backup at the same or lower level. We will illustrate these techniques with an example by backing up tablespace USERS. Incremental backups allow you to design very comprehensive backup methodologies.

Let us assume that our backup methodology creates a backup at level 0 every Sunday. We will perform a nonCUMULATIVE INCREMENTAL backup at level 2 on Mondays, Tuesdays, Thursdays, Fridays, and Saturdays. On Wednesdays, we will take a nonCUMULATIVE INCREMENTAL backup at level 1. Table 7-1 shows the backup plan.

**NOTE**
*A level 0 backup includes all blocks ever used by the database. It is not a whole database backup. Level 0 backup marks the blocks appropriately so that future INCREMENTAL backups at different levels are possible.*

| Day | Backup Type | Level of Backup | What gets backed up? |
|---|---|---|---|
| Sunday | NonCUMULATIVE INCREMENTAL | 0 | All blocks ever used by the database |
| Monday | NonCUMULATIVE INCREMENTAL | 2 | Blocks changed between Sunday and Monday |
| Tuesday | NonCUMULATIVE INCREMENTAL | 2 | Blocks changed between Monday and Tuesday |
| Wednesday | NonCUMULATIVE INCREMENTAL | 1 | All blocks changed between Sunday and Wednesday |
| Thursday | NonCUMULATIVE INCREMENTAL | 2 | Blocks changed between Wednesday and Thursday |
| Friday | NonCUMULATIVE INCREMENTAL | 2 | Blocks changed between Thursday and Friday |
| Saturday | NonCUMULATIVE INCREMENTAL | 2 | Blocks changed between Friday and Saturday |
| Sunday | NonCUMULATIVE INCREMENTAL | 0 | All blocks ever used by the database |

**TABLE 7-1.** *A Typical Backup Plan Using Non-Cumulative Incremental Backups*

On Sundays, we will run the following script:

```
RMAN> run {
2> allocate channel c1 type disk;
3> backup incremental level 0
4> format 'D:\sunday%t.%s'
5> filesperset 5
6> tablespace "USERS";
7> }
RMAN-03022: compiling command: allocate
RMAN-03023: executing command: allocate
RMAN-08030: allocated channel: c1
RMAN-08500: channel c1: sid=11 devtype=DISK
RMAN-03022: compiling command: backup
RMAN-03023: executing command: backup
RMAN-08008: channel c1: starting incremental level 0 datafile backupset
RMAN-08502: set_count=32 set_stamp=399157139 creation_time=01-JUN-00
RMAN-08010: channel c1: specifying datafile(s) in backupset
RMAN-08522: input datafile fno=00002 name=C:\ORACLE\ORADATA\TEST\USERS01.DBF
RMAN-08013: channel c1: piece 1 created
RMAN-08503: piece handle=D:\SUNDAY399157139.32 comment=NONE
RMAN-08525: backup set complete, elapsed time: 00:00:04
RMAN-03023: executing command: partial resync
RMAN-08003: starting partial resync of recovery catalog
RMAN-08005: partial resync complete
RMAN-08031: released channel: c1
RMAN>
```

This backs up all used blocks in the tablespace USERS. The FILESPERSET
parameter of **backup** command specifies the maximum number of input files to
place in one backup set to ensure that all allocated channels are equally used
for the purpose of backup. When RMAN encounters the FILESPERSET parameter,
it compares the FILESPERSET value to an internally calculated value (total number
of files requiring backups divided by the total number of allocated channels)
and takes the lowest of the two, thereby ensuring that all channels are used. On
Monday and Tuesday, we will run the following script, which will do a level 2
INCREMENTAL backup:

```
RMAN>run
  {
allocate channel c1 type disk;
backup incremental level 2
format 'level2%t.%s'
filesperset 5
tablespace "USERS";
}
RMAN-03022: compiling command: allocate
RMAN-03023: executing command: allocate
RMAN-08030: allocated channel: c1
RMAN-08500: channel c1: sid=11 devtype=DISK

RMAN-03022: compiling command: backup
```

```
RMAN-03023: executing command: backup
RMAN-08008: channel c1: starting incremental level 2 datafile backupset
RMAN-08502: set_count=35 set_stamp=399160301 creation_time=01-JUN-00
RMAN-08010: channel c1: specifying datafile(s) in backupset
RMAN-08522: input datafile fno=00002 name=C:\ORACLE\ORADATA\TEST\USERS01.DBF
RMAN-08056: skipping datafile 00002 because it has not changed
RMAN-08057: channel c1: backup cancelled because all files were skipped
RMAN-03023: executing command: partial resync
RMAN-08003: starting partial resync of recovery catalog
RMAN-08005: partial resync complete
RMAN-08031: released channel: c1
```

The above script, when run on Monday, will create an INCREMENTAL backup, which includes blocks that are changed between Sunday and Monday. Similarly, the backup of Tuesday will have changes between Monday and Tuesday. Now that we have created an INCREMENTAL backup for Monday and Tuesday, we will run a level 1 INCREMENTAL backup on Wednesday (see Table 7-1). This backup now includes all changed blocks from the last backup at an equal or lower level. This happens to be the backup taken on Sunday, which was at level 0. So, this backup on Wednesday consolidates all the changes made to the database from Sunday to Wednesday. The script for Wednesday's INCREMENTAL backup at level 1 is shown here:

```
RMAN>run {
allocate channel c1 type disk;
backup incremental level 1
format 'level1%t.%s'
filesperset 5
tablespace "USERS";
}
RMAN-03022: compiling command: allocate
RMAN-03023: executing command: allocate
RMAN-08030: allocated channel: c1
RMAN-08500: channel c1: sid=11 devtype=DISK

RMAN-03022: compiling command: backup
RMAN-03023: executing command: backup
RMAN-08008: channel c1: starting incremental level 1 datafile backupset
RMAN-08502: set_count=33 set_stamp=399159755 creation_time=01-JUN-00
RMAN-08010: channel c1: specifying datafile(s) in backupset
RMAN-08522: input datafile fno=00002 name=C:\ORACLE\ORADATA\TEST\USERS01.DBF
RMAN-08056: skipping datafile 00002 because it has not changed
RMAN-08057: channel c1: backup cancelled because all files were skipped
RMAN-03023: executing command: partial resync
RMAN-08003: starting partial resync of recovery catalog
RMAN-08005: partial resync complete
RMAN-08031: released channel: c1
```

On Thursday, Friday, and Saturday, we will run a level 2 INCREMENTAL backup that takes a backup of all blocks changed on a daily basis again. The following example shows this.

```
RMAN>run
  {
allocate channel c1 type disk;
backup incremental level 2
format 'level2%t.%s'
filesperset 5
tablespace "USERS";
}
RMAN-03022: compiling command: allocate
RMAN-03023: executing command: allocate
RMAN-08030: allocated channel: c1
RMAN-08500: channel c1: sid=11 devtype=DISK

RMAN-03022: compiling command: backup
RMAN-03023: executing command: backup
RMAN-08008: channel c1: starting incremental level 2 datafile backupset
RMAN-08502: set_count=35 set_stamp=399160301 creation_time=01-JUN-00
RMAN-08010: channel c1: specifying datafile(s) in backupset
RMAN-08522: input datafile fno=00002 name=C:\ORACLE\ORADATA\TEST\USERS01.DBF
RMAN-08056: skipping datafile 00002 because it has not changed
RMAN-08057: channel c1: backup cancelled because all files were skipped
RMAN-03023: executing command: partial resync
RMAN-08003: starting partial resync of recovery catalog
RMAN-08005: partial resync complete
RMAN-08031: released channel: c1
RMAN>
```

Finally, the cycle can be repeated with a level 0 backup on Sunday again.

## Cumulative Backups

Figures 7-23 through 7-26 show how to perform CUMULATIVE backups
using OEM.

**NOTE**
*For complete details on FULL and INCREMENTAL
backups, please refer to Chapter 8 of the* Oracle8i
Backup and Recovery Guide Release 8.1.5 *manual.
Examples of CUMULATIVE and nonCUMULATIVE
INCREMENTAL backups are also provided
in Chapter 8.*

## Proxy Copying

The PROXY option of RMAN's **backup** command allows third-party media
management software to control the database backup and recovery operations. This
relieves the burden on RMAN activities. The media management software gets all the
information such as a list of data files, their location, status, and so on from RMAN.
For each file that is specified in the **backup** PROXY command, RMAN queries the
media manager to determine whether it can copy the file. If the media manager
cannot copy the file, then RMAN uses conventional backup sets to back up the file.

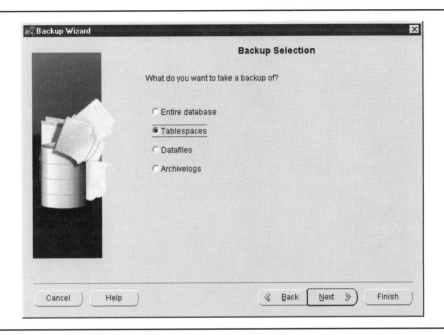

**FIGURE 7-23.** *Backup selection from the Backup Wizard*

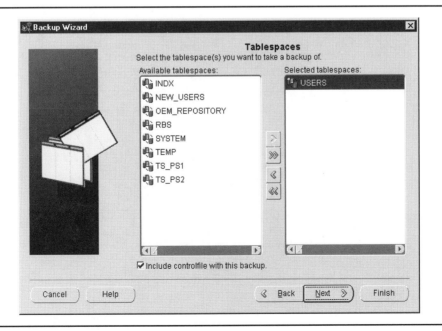

**FIGURE 7-24.** *Choosing the tablespaces to back up*

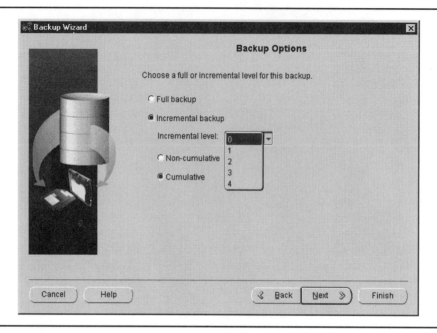

**FIGURE 7-25.** *Selection of CUMULATIVE backup level 0*

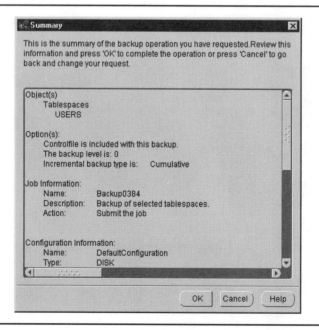

**FIGURE 7-26.** *Summary of tablespace CUMULATIVE backup*

# Reporting Features in Recovery Manager

The Oracle8*i* Recovery Manager has detailed reporting features. You can use the **list** or **report** command to produce reports on backup sets and image copies that are registered with the recovery catalog or the control file of the target database. In this section we will describe how you can best use the **list** and **report** commands for backup and recovery purposes.

## The list Command

The RMAN **list** command is one of the report commands every DBA uses to generate information about backup sets and image copies that are available with Recovery Manager. The **list** command queries the recovery catalog for the specified database and generates a list of all backup sets or image copies recorded in the RMAN's metadata that is specific to the database. If you are not using a recovery catalog, the **list** command queries the control file of the specified database. The **list** command can be used with the following options: DATABASE, TABLESPACE, DATAFILE, ARCHIVED REDO LOG, CONTROL FILE, DATAFILE COPY FILENAME, DEVICE NAME, RECOVERABILITY, TAG or BY TIME.

Let's looks at a few examples of using the **list** command:

```
RMAN>list backup of database;
RMAN-03022: compiling command: list
RMAN-03024: performing implicit full resync of recovery catalog
RMAN-03023: executing command: full resync
RMAN-08002: starting full resync of recovery catalog
RMAN-08004: full resync complete

List of Backup Sets
Key      Recid      Stamp      LV Set Stamp  Set Count  Completion Time
-------  ---------- ---------- -- ---------- ---------- ---------------
4029     1          386787093  0  386786930  1          13-JAN-00

    List of Backup Pieces
    Key     Pc# Cp# Status      Completion Time        Piece Name
    ------- --- --- ----------- ---------------------- ----------
    4032    1   1   AVAILABLE   13-JAN-00
C:\ORACLE\ORADATA\ORA8I\B_01BGRPJI_1_1

    List of Datafiles Included
    File Name                                    LV Type Ckp SCN   Ckp Time
    ---- ---------------------------------------- -- ---- ---------- ---------
    1    C:\ORACLE\ORADATA\ORA8I\SYSTEM01.DBF     0  Full 250631     13-JAN-00
    2    C:\ORACLE\ORADATA\ORA8I\USERS01.DBF      0  Full 250631     13-JAN-00
    3    C:\ORACLE\ORADATA\ORA8I\RBS01.DBF        0  Full 250631     13-JAN-00
    4    C:\ORACLE\ORADATA\ORA8I\TEMP01.DBF       0  Full 250631     13-JAN-00
    5    C:\ORACLE\ORADATA\ORA8I\OEMREP01.DBF     0  Full 250631     13-JAN-00
```

```
       6     C:\ORACLE\ORADATA\ORA8I\INDX01.DBF     0  Full 250631      13-JAN-00

List of Backup Sets
Key       Recid       Stamp       LV Set Stamp  Set Count  Completion Time
-------   ---------   ---------    -- ---------  ---------  ---------------
4030      2           388515460    0  388515278  2          02-FEB-00

      List of Backup Pieces
      Key       Pc# Cp# Status      Completion Time         Piece Name
      -------   --- --- ---------   --------------------    ------------------------
      4033      1   1   AVAILABLE   02-FEB-00               C:\BACKUP\B_02BIGHEE_2_1

      List of Datafiles Included
      File Name                                      LV Type Ckp SCN    Ckp Time
      ---- -----------------------------------       -- ---- ---------- ---------
      1    C:\ORACLE\ORADATA\ORA8I\SYSTEM01.DBF      0  Full 1106508    02-FEB-00
      2    C:\ORACLE\ORADATA\ORA8I\USERS01.DBF       0  Full 1106508    02-FEB-00
      3    C:\ORACLE\ORADATA\ORA8I\RBS01.DBF         0  Full 1106508    02-FEB-00
      4    C:\ORACLE\ORADATA\ORA8I\TEMP01.DBF        0  Full 1106508    02-FEB-00
      5    C:\ORACLE\ORADATA\ORA8I\OEMREP01.DBF      0  Full 1106508    02-FEB-00
      6    C:\ORACLE\ORADATA\ORA8I\INDX01.DBF        0  Full 1106508    02-FEB-00
      8    USER_TEMP                                 0  Full 1106508    02-FEB-00
      9    RMAN_TS_DATA                              0  Full 1106508    02-FEB-00

RMAN>
```

Similarly, the following command lists the data file copies of all files. You should look at the status column "S" in the output of **list** command. The status column output will be A for the valid and available backup sets. For unavailable backup sets, the column output will be U, and for expired backup sets the output will be E.

```
RMAN>list copy of database;
RMAN-03022: compiling command: list

List of Datafile Copies
Key       File S Completion time Ckp SCN    Ckp time         Name
-------   ---- - --------------- ---------  ---------------  --------------------
1671      1    A 01-JUN-00       1237419    01-JUN-00        D:\TEMP\SYS1ORCL
1680      2    A 01-JUN-00       686690     12-MAY-00        D:\TEMP\RBSORCL.BAK
1674      4    A 01-JUN-00       1237424    01-JUN-00        D:\TEMP\RBS1ORCL

RMAN>
```

The following example gives the backup sets of all the data files that belong to the tablespace USERS:

```
RMAN> list backup of tablespace "USERS";

RMAN-03022: compiling command: list

List of Backup Sets
Key       Recid       Stamp       LV Set Stamp  Set Count  Completion Time
-------   ---------   ---------   -- ---------  ---------  ---------------
4029      1           386787093   0  386786930  1          13-JAN-00
```

```
    List of Backup Pieces
    Key     Pc# Cp# Status      Completion Time        Piece Name
    ------- --- --- ----------- ---------------------- ----------
    4032    1   1   AVAILABLE   13-JAN-00
C:\ORACLE\ORADATA\ORA8I\B_01BGRPJI_
1_1

    List of Datafiles Included
    File Name                                     LV Type Ckp SCN   Ckp Time
    ---- -------------------------------------    -- ---- ---------- ---------
    2     C:\ORACLE\ORADATA\ORA8I\USERS01.DBF     0  Full 250631     13-JAN-00

List of Backup Sets
Key     Recid      Stamp       LV Set Stamp   Set Count  Completion Time
------- ---------- ----------  -- ----------  ---------- ---------------
4030    2          388515460   0  388515278   2          02-FEB-00

    List of Backup Pieces
    Key     Pc# Cp# Status      Completion Time        Piece Name
    ------- --- --- ----------- ---------------------- ----------------------
    4033    1   1   AVAILABLE   02-FEB-00              C:\BACKUP\B_02BIGHEE_2_1

    List of Datafiles Included
    File Name                                     LV Type Ckp SCN   Ckp Time
    ---- -------------------------------------    -- ---- ---------- ---------
    2     C:\ORACLE\ORADATA\ORA8I\USERS01.DBF     0  Full 1106508    02-FEB-00

RMAN>
```

Similarly, a listing of all copies of data files belonging to the tablespace ROLLBACK_DATA can be obtained by issuing the following command:

```
RMAN> list copy of tablespace "rollback_data";
RMAN-03022: compiling command: list
RMAN-06210: List of Datafile Copies
RMAN-06211: Key    File S Completion time Ckp SCN    Ckp time    Name
RMAN-06212: ----- ---- - --------------- ---------- --------- ------
RMAN-06213: 563    3    D 26-OCT-97                  564662     26-OCT-97   C:\ORANT\
                                                                            DATABASE\
                                                                            RBS1ORCL.ORA
```

# The report Command

The **report** command performs detailed analysis of information stored in the recovery catalog or in the control file and produces rich information on backup set or image copies. The output of the **report** command can also be stored in message log file. For saving reports in a file, you have to specify the MSGLOG or LOG option while connecting to Recovery Manager from the operating system command prompt. For example, if you want to list out all data files that are available in the target database, issue the **report** command as follows. RMAN lists out all the data files that are recorded in the current control file of the target database.

```
RMAN> report schema;

RMAN-03022: compiling command: report
Report of database schema
File K-bytes     Tablespace         RB segs Name
---- ----------  ------------------  ------- -------------------
1       143360  SYSTEM              YES     C:\ORACLE\ORADATA\TEST\SYSTEM01.DBF
2         3072  USERS               NO      C:\ORACLE\ORADATA\TEST\USERS01.DBF
3        25600  RBS                 YES     C:\ORACLE\ORADATA\TEST\RBS01.DBF
4         2048  TEMP                NO      C:\ORACLE\ORADATA\TEST\TEMP01.DBF
5        10240  RCVCAT              NO      RCVCATLOG
7         5120  USER_DATA           NO      USER_DATA1
8         5120  USER_DATA           NO      USER_DATA2
9        14336  USER_DATA           NO      USER_DATA3

RMAN>
```

You must use a recovery catalog when issuing a **report schema** command with
the AT TIME, AT SCN, or AT LOGSEQ options. Otherwise, a recovery catalog is not
required for the **report** command.

The following example reports all data files that cannot be recovered from
existing backups:

```
RMAN> report unrecoverable;
RMAN-03022: compiling command: report
Report of files that need backup due to unrecoverable operations
File Type of Backup Required Name
---- ----------------------- ----------------------------------------
1    full or incremental     C:\ORACLE\ORADATA\ORA8I\USER_DATA01.DBF
RMAN>
```

The output shows that the data file **user_data01.dbf** cannot be recovered. You
should note that RMAN considers a tablespace or data file unrecoverable only when
an unrecoverable operation has been performed against an object residing in the
data file since the last backup of the data file. For example, if you have lost a few
archived redo log files accidentally (that were generated after performing a
tablespace backup, and you don't have a backup of those lost archived log files
recorded in the recovery catalog), then this tablespace backup set will be
considered by RMAN as unrecoverable. To generate a list of backup sets or image
copies that are not needed for recovery, issue the following **report** command:

```
RMAN> report obsolete redundancy 2;

RMAN-03022: compiling command: report
Report of obsolete backups and copies
Type                    Key    Completion Time     Filename/Handle
--------------------    ------ ------------------  ----------------------------------
Backup Set              1482   27-MAY-00
Backup Piece            1486   27-MAY-00           C:\BCP2
Backup Set              1480   27-MAY-00
Backup Piece            1484   27-MAY-00           02BS6VFO_1_1
Backup Set              16     20-APR-00
```

```
Backup Piece          17    20-APR-00      01BP339H_1_1
Backup Set          1526    31-MAY-00
Backup Piece        1528    31-MAY-00      C:\BACKUP\TEST_BACKUPS0ABSI4L1_1_1
Backup Set          1481    27-MAY-00
Backup Piece        1485    27-MAY-00      C:\BACKUP\BACKUP1
RMAN>
```

The above output shows that a few backup sets, backup pieces, and data file copies are obsolete and can be deleted from the backup. RMAN considers a backup set or a data file copy or a backup piece as obsolete if there are more than two (specified by the REDUNDANCY option; in our example, redundancy is 2) recent backups or image copies.

The following command will give a list of data files that belong to the tablespace USERS that cannot be completely recovered (due to missing redo information) from backup sets using Recovery Manager:

 RMAN>report unrecoverable tablespace "USERS";

You can run reports to get information on previous backups. Here is the syntax to get a listing of all data files in the tablespace USERS that have not been backed up in the last three days:

 RMAN>report need backup days 3 tablespace "USERS";

The following example generates a report of all backup sets that can never be used:

```
RMAN>report obsolete orphan;
Backup Set          1415    27-MAY-00
Backup Piece        1439    27-MAY-00      C:\BACKUP\BACKUP1
Backup Set          1423    31-MAY-00
Backup Piece        1447    31-MAY-00      AA_1TEST.18

RMAN>
```

**NOTE**
*For more information, refer to Chapter 7 of the* Oracle8i Backup and Recovery Guide Release 8.1.5 *manual.*

# Scripts in Recovery Manager

The Recovery Manager has the ability to use stored scripts. It is highly recommended that you create scripts for regular tasks. Scripts can be stored on the file system or within the recovery catalog itself. We recommend that you store scripts within the recovery catalog since the server itself can maintain them. You can create a script in the recovery catalog by using the **create** command. You cannot create and store scripts if you don't use a recovery catalog. In order to run a stored script, you can use the **execute script** command. You can replace existing scripts using the **replace script** command.

Here is a sample script that can be used to create a FULL backup with all archived log files. Archive log files will be deleted after they have been backed up.

```
RMAN> create script Full_backup
2> {
3> allocate channel ch1 type disk;
4> allocate channel ch2 type disk;
5> allocate channel ch3 type disk;
6> allocate channel ch4 type disk;
7>  backup full
8>     tag weekly_inc_backup
9>     filesperset 6
10>     database;
11>     sql 'ALTER SYSTEM ARCHIVE LOG CURRENT';
12>     backup
13>         filesperset 10
14>         archivelog all
15>         delete input;
16> }

RMAN-03022: compiling command: create script
RMAN-03023: executing command: create script
RMAN-08085: created script Full_backup
```

To replace an existing script in the recovery catalog, issue the **replace script** command which will replace the specified script with the supplied script in the command. The following **replace script** command replaces the already existing "aa_full" script with the following script.

```
RMAN>
RMAN>replace script aa_full {
allocate channel c1 type disk;
backup full filesperset 3
(database format 'aa_full%p%d.%s');
}
RMAN-03022: compiling command: replace script
RMAN-03023: executing command: replace script
RMAN-08086: replaced script aa_full
RMAN>
```

In order to run a stored script, you must use the **execute script** command, as shown here:

```
RMAN>run {
execute script aa_full;
}
RMAN> run {
2> execute script aa_full;
3> }

RMAN-03021: executing script: aa_full

RMAN-03022: compiling command: allocate
RMAN-03023: executing command: allocate
RMAN-08030: allocated channel: c1
RMAN-08500: channel c1: sid=11 devtype=DISK
RMAN-08013: channel c1: piece 1 created
RMAN-08503: piece handle=AA_FULL1TEST.38 comment=NONE
RMAN-08525: backup set complete, elapsed time: 00:02:40
RMAN-03023: executing command: partial resync
RMAN-08003: starting partial resync of recovery catalog
RMAN-08005: partial resync complete
RMAN-08031: released channel: c1
RMAN>To delete a stored script from recovery catalog, issue the delete script command as follow:
RMAN> delete script 'Inc_backup';

RMAN-03022: compiling command: delete script
RMAN-06175: deleted script: Inc_backup

RMAN>
```

For more information refer to Chapter 11 of the *Oracle8i Backup and Recovery Guide Release 8.1.5.*

# Diagnostics in Recovery Manager

The Recovery Manager provides a fairly comprehensive set of error messages. Syntax errors are reported immediately, whereas runtime errors are shown during execution of the command.

We will illustrate an example of syntax errors here:

```
RMAN>execute script aa_full;

RMAN-00571: ===========================================================
RMAN-00569: =============== ERROR MESSAGE STACK FOLLOWS =============
RMAN-00571: ===========================================================
RMAN-00558: error encountered while parsing input commands
RMAN-01005: syntax error: found "execute": expecting one of:
"allocate, alter, beginline, catalog, change, connect, create,
crosscheck, debug, delete, drop, exit, endinline, host, {,library,
list, mount, open, print, register, release, replace, report, reset,
resync, rman, rpctest, run, set, sql, "RMAN-01007: at line 1 column 1
file: standard input
```

Here is an example of a runtime error that is obtained if insufficient disk space is available to create a backup set:

```
RMAN>run {
execute script aa_full;
}
RMAN-03021: executing script: aa_full
RMAN-03022: compiling command: allocate
RMAN-03023: executing command: allocate
RMAN-08030: allocated channel: c1
RMAN-08500: channel c1: sid=11 devtype=DISK
RMAN-03022: compiling command: backup
RMAN-03023: executing command: backup
name=C:\ORACLE\ORADATA\TEST\TEMP01.DBF
RMAN-03026: error recovery releasing channel resources
RMAN-08031: released channel: c1
RMAN-00571: ===========================================================
RMAN-00569: =============== ERROR MESSAGE STACK FOLLOWS =============
RMAN-00571: ===========================================================
RMAN-03015: error occurred in stored script aa_full
RMAN-03007: retryable error occurred during execution of command: backup
RMAN-07004: unhandled exception during command execution on channel c1
RMAN-10035: exception raised in RPC: ORA-19502: write error on file "aa_full1TES
T.42", blockno 145153 (blocksize=512)
ORA-27070: skgfdisp: async read/write failed
OSD-04016: Error queuing an asynchronous I/O request.
O/S-Error: (OS 112) There is not enough space on the disk.
RMAN-10031: ORA-19624 occurred during call to DBMS_BACKUP_RESTORE.BACKUPPIECECREATE
```

Here is another example of a runtime error that is obtained when an attempt is made to overwrite an existing script:

```
RMAN>create script aa_full {
allocate channel c1 type disk;
backup full filesperset 3
(database format 'aa_full%p%d.%s');
}
RMAN-03022: compiling command: create script
RMAN-03023: executing command: create script
RMAN-03026: error recovery releasing channel resources
RMAN-00571: ===========================================================
RMAN-00569: =============== ERROR MESSAGE STACK FOLLOWS ===============
RMAN-00571: ===========================================================
RMAN-03006: non-retryable error occurred during execution of command:
create script
RMAN-07004: unhandled exception during command execution on channel default
RMAN-20401: script already exists

RMAN>
```

# Recovery Manager and the Database Identifier

The Oracle Recovery Manager identifies catalog information in the recovery catalog by using the *database identifier* (dbid) and not the database name. This can create a problem if you have created databases by copying a master database. Here is a real-life example.

In a classroom setup, a single master database was used to create nine differently named databases (one for the instructor, eight for the students). The databases were renamed from the master using **create controlfile set database *newname***, which worked without a problem. However, all databases had the same dbid in V$DATABASE (we realize that this is not a common way to create multiple databases; however, we have seen DBAs using this method). When an attempt was made to register the databases in RMAN, an error was obtained as shown here:

```
RMAN>register database;

RMAN-03022: compiling command: register
RMAN-03023: executing command: register
RMAN-03026: error recovery releasing channel resources
RMAN-00571: ===========================================================
RMAN-00569: =============== ERROR MESSAGE STACK FOLLOWS ===============
RMAN-00571: ===========================================================
RMAN-03006: non-retryable error occurred during execution of command: register
RMAN-07004: unhandled exception during command execution on channel default
RMAN-20002: target database already registered in recovery catalog
RMAN>

RMAN>list incarnation of database;

RMAN-03022: compiling command: list
RMAN-03026: error recovery releasing channel resources
RMAN-00571: ===========================================================
RMAN-00569: =============== ERROR MESSAGE STACK FOLLOWS ===============
RMAN-00571: ===========================================================
RMAN-03002: failure during compilation of command
RMAN-03013: command type: list
RMAN-03014: implicit resync of recovery catalog failed
RMAN-06038: recovery catalog package detected an error
RMAN-20020: database incarnation not set

RMAN>
RMAN>reset database;
RMAN-03022: compiling command: reset
RMAN-03023: executing command: reset
RMAN-03026: error recovery releasing channel resources
RMAN-00571: ===========================================================
RMAN-00569: =============== ERROR MESSAGE STACK FOLLOWS ===============
RMAN-00571: ===========================================================
RMAN-03006: non-retryable error occurred during execution of command: reset
RMAN-07004: unhandled exception during command execution on channel default
RMAN-20009: database incarnation already registered
RMAN>RMAN>list incarnation of database;

RMAN-03022: compiling command: list
RMAN-03026: error recovery releasing channel resources
RMAN-00571: ===========================================================
RMAN-00569: =============== ERROR MESSAGE STACK FOLLOWS ===============
RMAN-00571: ===========================================================
```

```
RMAN-03002: failure during compilation of command
RMAN-03013: command type: list
RMAN-03014: implicit resync of recovery catalog failed
RMAN-06038: recovery catalog package detected an error
RMAN-20020: database incarnation not set

RMAN>
```

As you can see, the databases have distinct names but an identical ID. The only way to overcome this problem is to use different recovery catalog schemas in this case.

**NOTE**
*Copying databases is not a good practice, and may not be supported by Oracle Support Services.*

As seen in the few examples that we have provided, the error stack contains precise information on the nature of the error and can usually provide sufficient feedback on the error condition.

# Collecting Logs of a Recovery Manager Session

The Oracle Recovery Manager has a command-line option that allows you to capture the output of a session to a file. Here is an example that captures output of the current session to a file named **aarman.log**:

```
C:\ORACLE\DATABASE>rman80 target=\"internal/aa@prod\"
rcvcat=\"rman/aa@rcv\" msglog=\"c:\temp\aarman.log\"
```

# Corrupt Block Detection in Recovery Manager

Since the Recovery Manager uses an Oracle server process to read the blocks that are backed up, block corruptions are detected automatically. The verification checks that apply to a block that is read into the database buffer cache are also applied here. Information on corrupt blocks can be obtained by querying the views V$BACKUP_CORRUPTION and V$COPY_CORRUPTION. By default, the Recovery Manager will throw an error on detecting the first corrupt block, but you can use the **set maxcorrupt** command to bypass a few corrupt blocks. Here is an example of a backup that failed due to corrupt block detection:

```
RMAN> run {
2> allocate channel c1 type disk;
3> backup datafile '/vobs/oracle/dbs/t_db2.f'
4> format '/tmp/aa%t';
5> }
RMAN-03022: compiling command: allocate
RMAN-03023: executing command: allocate
```

```
RMAN-03022: compiling command: allocate
RMAN-03023: executing command: allocate
RMAN-08030: allocated channel: c1
RMAN-08500: channel c1: sid=10 devtype=DISK
RMAN-03022: compiling command: backup
RMAN-03023: executing command: backup
RMAN-08008: channel c1: starting datafile backupset
RMAN-08502: set_count=2 set_stamp=316236215
RMAN-08010: channel c1: including datafile 2 in backupset
RMAN-03026: error recovery releasing channel resources
RMAN-08031: released channel: c1
RMAN-00569: ================error message stack follows================
RMAN-03006: non-retryable error occurred during execution of command: backup
RMAN-07004: unhandled exception during command execution on channel c1
RMAN-10032: unhandled exception during execution of job step 1: ORA-06512: at
line 84
RMAN-10035: exception raised in RPC: ORA-19583: conversation terminated due
to error
ORA-19566: exceeded limit of 0 corrupt blocks for file /vobs/oracle/dbs/t_db2.f
ORA-06512: at "SYS.DBMS_BACKUP_RESTORE", line 399
RMAN-10031: ORA-19583 occurred during call to DBMS_BACKUP_RESTORE.
BACKUPPIECECREATE
```

We will query the table DEPT1, which contains this block, as well as V$BACKUP_CORRUPTION for details. Note that V$BACKUP_CORRUPTION is not populated as yet.

```
SQL> select * from dept1;
DEPTNO     DNAME          LOC
---------- -------------- -------------
ORA-01578: ORACLE data block corrupted (file # 2, block # 3)
ORA-01110: data file 2: '/vobs/oracle/dbs/t_db2.f'
SQL> select * from v$backup_corruption;
RECID  STAMP SET_STAMP  SET_COUNT  PIECE#  FILE#  BLOCK#  BLOCKS  CORRUPTION MAR
-----  ----- ---------  ---------  ------- -----  ------  ------  ---------------
0 rows selected.
```

By querying the DEPT1 table, we know that block #3 of file #2 is corrupted. In order to get more information on the block corruption, we will modify the RMAN script to set MAXCORRUPT to a value of 5 (greater than zero):

```
RMAN> run {
2> allocate channel c1 type disk;
3> set maxcorrupt for datafile '/vobs/oracle/dbs/t_db2.f' to 5;
3> backup datafile '/vobs/oracle/dbs/t_db2.f'
4> format '/tmp/aa%t';
5> }
RMAN-03022: compiling command: allocate
RMAN-03023: executing command: allocate
RMAN-08030: allocated channel: c1
RMAN-08500: channel c1: sid=10 devtype=DISK
RMAN-03022: compiling command: set
RMAN-03022: compiling command: backup
RMAN-03023: executing command: backup
RMAN-08008: channel c1: starting datafile backupset
```

```
RMAN-08502: set_count=3 set_stamp=316238227
RMAN-08010: channel c1: including datafile 2 in backupset
RMAN-08013: channel c1: piece 1 created
RMAN-08503: piece handle=/tmp/aatry316238227 comment=NONE
RMAN-03023: executing command: partial resync
RMAN-08003: starting partial resync of recovery catalog
RMAN-08005: partial resync complete
RMAN-08031: released channel: c1
```

We can now look at the V$BACKUP_CORRUPTION view for details:

```
SQL> select * from V$backup_corruption;
RECID   STAMP      SET_STAMP   SET_COUNT   PIECE#   FILE#   BLOCK#   BLOCKS   CORRUPTION   MAR
------  ------     ----------  ---------   ------   ------  -------  ------   ----------   ---
    1   316238233  316238227       3          1       2       3        1          0       YES
1 row selected.
```

You should contact Oracle Support Services to help you with the block corruption if you are not in a position to rebuild the data file that is corrupted.

# Testing and Validating Backup Sets and Copies

Recovery Manager has one more feature that helps you test your backup sets and image copies before you do your recovery operation. The RMAN **restore validate**, **validate,** and **change croscheck** commands let you use various options to test your database backup sets and copies and ensure that your backup sets and image copies are intact and can be used for recovery purposes. When you issue the **restore validate** command, RMAN executes a restore test run (recovery) without actually restoring the files.

### restore validate Whole Database

The RMAN **restore validate** command allows you to test your recent whole database backup set. Before issuing the command, consider the following:

- The database has to be mounted and closed for a whole database validation check. In case of validating individual tablespace and data files, the respective tablespace and data files must be taken offline for validating backup sets and copies.

- You should identify their "list key number" by issuing the **list** command. For example, let us test the restore of the entire database TEST:

  **1.** Mount the database and let that be in the closed state.

  **2.** Start Recovery Manager and connect to the recovery catalog and the target database TEST and issue the following command:
  ```
  RMAN> run {
  2> allocate channel ch1 type disk;
  ```

```
3> restore database validate;
4> }

RMAN-03022: compiling command: allocate
RMAN-03023: executing command: allocate
RMAN-08030: allocated channel: ch1
RMAN-08500: channel ch1: sid=12 devtype=DISK

RMAN-03022: compiling command: restore

RMAN-03022: compiling command: IRESTORE
RMAN-06178: datafile 2 not processed because file is offline
RMAN-03023: executing command: IRESTORE
RMAN-08096: channel ch1: starting validation of datafile backupset
RMAN-08502: set_count=2 set_stamp=399306144 creation_time=03-JUN-00
RMAN-08023: channel ch1: restored backup piece 1
RMAN-08511: piece handle=02BSPRD0_1_1 params=NULL
RMAN-08098: channel ch1: validation complete
RMAN-08096: channel ch1: starting validation of datafile backupset
RMAN-08502: set_count=3 set_stamp=399306145 creation_time=03-JUN-00
RMAN-08023: channel ch1: restored backup piece 1
RMAN-08511: piece handle=03BSPRD1_1_1 params=NULL
RMAN-08098: channel ch1: validation complete
RMAN-08031: released channel: ch1
RMAN>
```

The output of the command shows that the command has been executed successfully and the database has valid backup sets for recovery, if necessary.

### restore validate Individual Backup Sets and Backup Copies
To perform a **restore validate** operation, the target database can be either closed or the database can be open and the respective data file or tablespace must be taken offline. You should also get "list key number" by issuing the **list** command at the RMAN prompt. In the case of control file validation, you need not specify the "list key number". RMAN identifies the latest copy or backup set available in the catalog.

### restore validate the Control File
In the following example, we will validate the control file with the target database open:

1. Start Recovery Manager and connect to the catalog (ORA8I.ORACLE) and target database TEST by issuing the following command:

```
C:\ rman catalog rman/rman@ORA8I.ORACLE target internal/oracle@test.demo
Recovery Manager: Release 8.1.5.0.0 - Production
RMAN-06005: connected to target database: TEST (DBID=4103468597)
RMAN-06008: connected to recovery catalog database
RMAN>
```

2. Issue the **restore validate** command to validate the control file of the target database as follows:

```
RMAN> run {
2>    allocate channel dev1 type disk;
```

```
3>      restore controlfile validate;
4> }

RMAN-03022: compiling command: allocate
RMAN-03023: executing command: allocate
RMAN-08030: allocated channel: dev1
RMAN-08500: channel dev1: sid=25 devtype=DISK

RMAN-03022: compiling command: restore

RMAN-03022: compiling command: IRESTORE
RMAN-03023: executing command: IRESTORE
RMAN-08096: channel dev1: starting validation of datafile backupset
RMAN-08502: set_count=0 set_stamp=4294967295 creation_time=18-AUG-21
RMAN-08023: channel dev1: restored backup piece 1
RMAN-08511: piece handle=C:\BACKUP\CONTROL.CTL params=NULL
RMAN-08098: channel dev1: validation complete
RMAN-08031: released channel: dev1
RMAN>
```

**3.** After executing the above command, you should look for the following RMAN message in the command output:

```
"RMAN-08098: channel dev1: validation complete"
```

The output shows that the control file is intact and can be restored.

### restore validate Backup Sets and Image Copies

For testing tablespace and data file backup sets and copies, the target database can either be closed or open. If it is open, the tablespace and data files that you want to validate must be brought offline before you perform the **restore validate** check. Of course, you should note down the "list key number" of the backup sets and copies. You have to supply this number in the **restore tablespace validate** or **restore datafile validate** command. Now let us test the tablespace USERS that belongs to database TEST. First, take the tablespace USERS offline and issue the **list** command to get the list key number as follows:

```
RMAN> list backup of tablespace "USERS";

RMAN-03022: compiling command: list

List of Backup Sets
Key      Recid      Stamp        LV Set Stamp   Set Count   Completion Time
-------  ---------  ----------   -- ----------   ----------  ---------------
2781     1          399302049    0  399302047    1           03-JUN-00

    List of Backup Pieces
    Key     Pc# Cp# Status      Completion Time         Piece Name
    ------- --- --- ----------  ---------------------   ------------
    2782    1   1   AVAILABLE   03-JUN-00               01BSPNCV_1_1
```

```
    List of Datafiles Included
    File Name                                     LV Type Ckp SCN   Ckp Time
    ---- ------------------------------------- -- ---- ---------- ---------
     2    C:\ORACLE\ORADATA\DEMO\USERS01.DBF     0  Full 178411    03-JUN-00

List of Backup Sets
Key     Recid      Stamp      LV Set Stamp  Set Count  Completion Time
------- ---------- ---------- -- ---------- ---------- ---------------
2788    2          399306190  0  399306144  2          03-JUN-00

    List of Backup Pieces
    Key     Pc# Cp# Status      Completion Time        Piece Name
    ------- --- --- ----------- ---------------------- ------------
    2791    1   1   AVAILABLE   03-JUN-00              02BSPRD0_1_1

    List of Datafiles Included
    File Name                                     LV Type Ckp SCN   Ckp Time
    ---- ------------------------------------- -- ---- ---------- ---------
     2    C:\ORACLE\ORADATA\DEMO\USERS01.DBF     0  Full 178415    03-JUN-00

RMAN>
```

Among the listed backup sets that belong to the tablespace USERS, let us validate the backup set whose list key number is 2788:

```
RMAN> run {
2>          allocate channel ch1 type disk;
3>          validate backupset 2788;
4>      }

RMAN-03022: compiling command: allocate
RMAN-03023: executing command: allocate
RMAN-08030: allocated channel: ch1
RMAN-08500: channel ch1: sid=10 devtype=DISK

RMAN-03022: compiling command: validate
RMAN-03023: executing command: validate
RMAN-08096: channel ch1: starting validation of datafile backupset
RMAN-08502: set_count=2 set_stamp=399306144 creation_time=03-JUN-00
RMAN-08023: channel ch1: restored backup piece 1
RMAN-08511: piece handle=02BSPRD0_1_1 params=NULL
RMAN-08098: channel ch1: validation complete
RMAN-08031: released channel: ch1

RMAN>
```

In the command output, look for the RMAN message:

```
"RMAN-08098: channel ch1: validation complete"
```

In case the specified backup set is not available, you will get the following error message for the same command:

```
RMAN> run {
2>          allocate channel ch1 type disk;
3>          validate backupset 2788;
4>      }
```

```
RMAN-03022: compiling command: allocate
RMAN-03023: executing command: allocate
RMAN-08030: allocated channel: ch1
RMAN-08500: channel ch1: sid=10 devtype=DISK

RMAN-03022: compiling command: validate
RMAN-03026: error recovery releasing channel resources
RMAN-08031: released channel: ch1
RMAN-00571: ===========================================================
RMAN-00569: ============== ERROR MESSAGE STACK FOLLOWS ===========
RMAN-00571: ===========================================================
RMAN-03002: failure during compilation of command
RMAN-03013: command type: validate
RMAN-06038: recovery catalog package detected an error
RMAN-20215: backup set is missing
RMAN-06159: error while looking up backup set
RMAN>
```

## Back Up Set and Image Copy Validation Using the RMAN validate Command

In this section we will examine a backup set and understand whether it can be restored. RMAN scans all of the backup pieces in the specified backup sets and looks at the checksums to verify that the contents are intact and can be successfully restored if necessary. Note that the **validate backupset** command does not do any recovery operation unlike the **restore validate** command. The **validate backupset** command is useful when you suspect that one or more backup pieces in a backup set are missing or damaged. To specify which backup set to validate, use the **list** command. For example, to validate a backup set, connect to the catalog and target database and issue the following command:

```
RMAN>List Backup;
List of Backup Sets
Key      Recid       Stamp      LV Set Stamp  Set Count  Completion Time
-------  ----------  ---------- -- ----------  ---------- ---------------
2789     3           399306266  0  399306145   3          03-JUN-00

    List of Backup Pieces
    Key    Pc# Cp# Status      Completion Time         Piece Name
    -----  --- --- ----------  ---------------------   ------------
    2792   1   1   AVAILABLE   03-JUN-00               03BSPRD1_1_1

    List of Datafiles Included
    File Name                                       LV Type Ckp SCN   Ckp Time
    ---- -----------------------------------------  -- ---- ---------- ---------
    1    C:\ORACLE\ORADATA\DEMO\SYSTEM01.DBF         0  Full 178416     03-JUN-00
    6    C:\ORACLE\ORADATA\DEMO\INDX01.DBF           0  Full 178416     03-JUN-00
```

Note down the "list key number" to use with the RMAN **validate** command.
In this example, we are specifying a data file backup set whose list key number
is 2788:

```
RMAN> run{
2>      allocate channel ch1 type disk;
3>      validate backupset 2788;
4> }
RMAN-03022: compiling command: allocate
RMAN-03023: executing command: allocate
RMAN-08030: allocated channel: ch1
RMAN-08500: channel ch1: sid=10 devtype=DISK
RMAN-03022: compiling command: validate
RMAN-03023: executing command: validate
RMAN-08096: channel ch1: starting validation of datafile backupset
RMAN-08502: set_count=2 set_stamp=399306144 creation_time=03-JUN-00
RMAN-08023: channel ch1: restored backup piece 1
RMAN-08511: piece handle=02BSPRD0_1_1 params=NULL
RMAN-08098: channel ch1: validation complete
RMAN-08031: released channel: ch1
RMAN>
```

### crosscheck Backup

The **crosscheck** RMAN command is used to verify whether backups sets are
available or not by examining the disk storage, or by accessing the media manager
in the case of tape storage. In the following example, let us cross-check the backup
set of tablespace USERS:

```
RMAN> allocate channel for maintenance type disk;

RMAN-03022: compiling command: allocate
RMAN-03023: executing command: allocate
RMAN-08030: allocated channel: delete
RMAN-08500: channel delete: sid=9 devtype=DISK
RMAN> crosscheck backup of tablespace USERS;

RMAN-03022: compiling command: XCHECK
RMAN-08074: crosschecked backup piece: found to be 'AVAILABLE'
RMAN-08517: backup piece handle=01BSPNCV_1_1 recid=1 stamp=399302048
RMAN-08074: crosschecked backup piece: found to be 'AVAILABLE'
RMAN-08517: backup piece handle=02BSPRD0_1_1 recid=2 stamp=399306145
RMAN>
```

You can also specify a time period to verify the status of backup sets that are taken during the specified time period.

# Disaster Recovery Using Recovery Manager

Recovery Manager can be effectively used for database recovery. RMAN can perform either complete or incomplete recovery. Using the **set until** command, you can specify a time, SCN, or log sequence number as a limit for incomplete recovery. The RMAN **restore** command is used to restore data files, control files, or archived redo logs from backup sets or image copies, and the **recovery** command is used to apply redo log files for the purpose of media recovery. RMAN restores backups from disk or tape, but image copies only from disk.

## Database Recovery

Let us now consider that due to a disk crash you have lost your database called TEST. Due to multiplexing, you do have a copy of your current control file. We will illustrate how you can use OEM to recover the database completely in this section.

The following steps illustrate how you can perform a full database recovery using RMAN from OEM GUI.

1. Run the Recovery Manager's Recovery Wizard from Tools | Backup Management menu of Oracle Storage Manager window and click Next to define the full database recovery process.

2. Recovery Wizard gives you the option to choose the type of database recovery. It can be a full database recovery, tablespace or data file recovery. If you want recover the database fully, then the database must be in mounted and "not opened" state. If the database is in ARCHIVELOG mode and in the database open, then you can only perform tablespace or datafile recovery. Since we are doing full database recovery here, select the Entire Database option from the available options as shown in Figure 7-27.

3. Click Finish to recover the database to the most recent state (complete recovery). If you want to do time-based recovery, click Next. Figure 7-28 shows Restore Until screen. Since we are doing complete recovery, we did not click on the "Until" option in the figure. Click Next.

4. In the Rename screen, verify that all datafiles are present. You should not choose any file here (as shown in Figure 7-29) unless you want to restore the datafile to a different location. Click Next.

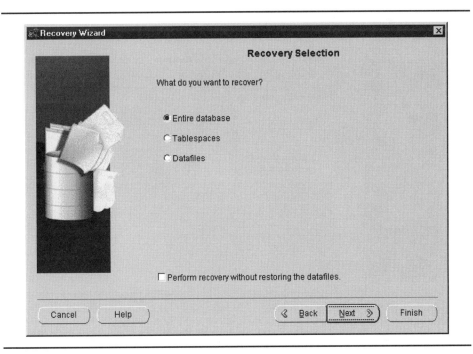

**FIGURE 7-27.** *Recovery selection in Recovery Wizard*

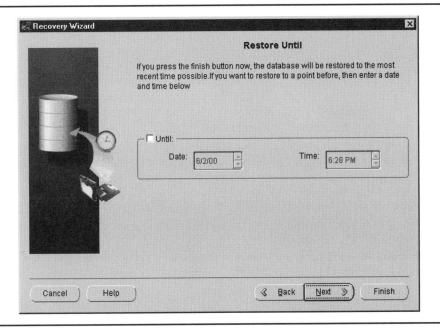

**FIGURE 7-28.** *Time-based recovery option in Recovery Wizard*

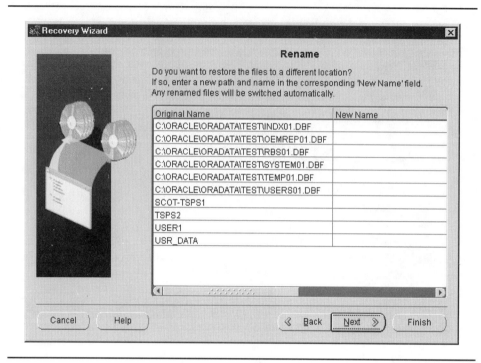

**FIGURE 7-29.** *"Rename" or "Relocate" data files option*

**5.** The Configuration screen shows configuration information as shown in Figure 7-30. Click Finish

**6.** The Summary screen shows the summary of the recovery operation that you have requested. Figure 7-31 shows the sample output. Click OK to submit the recovery job to OEM for execution.

After the recovery job is completed, you can open the database for use. Note that you can get status of recovery job from the job pane of the OEM window. In case of incomplete recovery, you should always open the database with the RESETLOGS option after performing incomplete recovery.

Here, it was just a simple loss of the database. As you would know, in the real world the problems are not so simple. What if you have lost the disk that contains the Oracle code? And what if the catalog database is at your company's HQ in Boston? How do you connect to the catalog database first before you do recovery? This complicated, yet more realistic, case study is presented in Chapter 10.

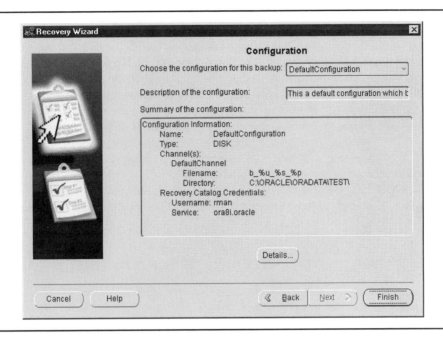

**FIGURE 7-30.**  *Configuration information in Recovery Wizard*

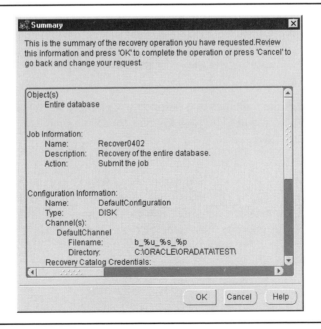

**FIGURE 7-31.**  *Summary of Recovery Operation*

# Tablespace and Data File Recovery

If two or more data files that belong to a tablespace are lost or corrupted due to a disk crash, you can use tablespace recovery option available in the Recovery Manager. Note that to perform tablespace or data file recovery, your database should be running in ARCHIVELOG mode and you should have the required archived redo log files for media recovery. The recovery procedure for tablespace recovery will differ depending on whether the database is open or closed during recovery. You must ensure that the tablespace is taken offline before attempting to recover the tablespace. The following example shows how you can perform a tablespace recovery through Recovery Manager. In this example, you have lost two data files that belong to the tablespace USERS_DATA and want to recover the tablespace when the database is open. Issue the following RMAN command:

```
run {
        allocate channel ch1 type disk;
        sql "ALTER TABLESPACE USERS_DATA  OFFLINE IMMEDIATE";
        restore tablespace USERS_DATA;
        recover tablespace USERS_DATA;
        sql "ALTER TABLESPACE USERS_DATA  ONLINE";
}
```

Executing the above script does the following:

1. RMAN allocates channel ch1 for recovery operation.

2. It takes the tablespace USERS_DATA offline.

3. RMAN then restores the data files that belong to the tablespace from the backup set.

4. It recovers the data files that belong to the tablespace USERS_DATA by applying the required archive log files for media recovery.

5. Finally, RMAN brings the tablespace USERS_DATA online.

While performing, if you cannot restore data files to the default location, use the **set newname** command before issuing the **restore** command. In this case, Oracle considers the restored data files as data file copies and performs a switch to make them the current data files. Oracle creates the filename or overwrites it if it already exists. For more information refer to the *Oracle8i Backup and Recovery Guide Release 8.1.5*.

# Control File Recovery

This section describes control file recovery options that Oracle Recovery Manager provides. Let us assume that due to a media failure you lost all copies of your control file, including even after multiplexing. In order to open the database, you must restore the control file from a recent backup. RMAN makes your life easy while restoring it from a backup if you have taken a backup of the control file using Recovery Manager. The target database must be in the NOMOUNT stage for the control file to be restored from a backup. Note that when you take a whole database backup using RMAN, it includes the current control file in the backup set. In this situation, if you want to do crash recovery and open your database, you should first restore the control file that belongs to the database from a recent backup.

Let us assume that recovery catalog is stored in the database ORA8I.ORACLE, the recovery schema is RMAN, and the database DEMO.ORACLE is the database that has lost the control file. To restore the control file of the lost database, do the following:

1. Start SQL*PLUS and, using the proper **init.ora** file, start the instance with the NOMOUNT option.

2. Start Recovery Manager and connect to recovery catalog as follows:

```
C:\>rman catalog rman/rman@ora8i.oracle

Recovery Manager: Release 8.1.5.0.0 - Production

RMAN-06008: connected to recovery catalog database

RMAN>
```

3. Connect to the target database (DEMO.ORACLE).

```
RMAN> connect target internal/oracle@demo.oracle

RMAN-06006: connected to target database:  (not mounted)

RMAN>
```

4. Once connected to the target database, issue the **restore** command to restore your control file:

```
RMAN> run {
2> allocate channel ch1 type disk;
3> restore controlfile;
}
```

```
RMAN-03022: compiling command: allocate
RMAN-03023: executing command: allocate
RMAN-08030: allocated channel: dev1
RMAN-08500: channel ch1: sid=13 devtype=DISK

RMAN-03022: compiling command: restore

RMAN-03022: compiling command: IRESTORE
RMAN-03023: executing command: IRESTORE
RMAN-08016: channel dev1: starting datafile backup set restore
RMAN-08502: set_count=0 set_stamp=0 creation_time=01-JAN-88
RMAN-08021: channel dev1: restoring controlfile
RMAN-08505: output filename=C:\ORACLE\ORADATA\DEMO\CONTROL01.CTL
RMAN-08023: channel dev1: restored backup piece 1
RMAN-08511: piece handle=D:\TEMP\DEMO_CLTL_0CBSSB0F params=NULL
RMAN-08024: channel dev1: restore complete
RMAN-08058: replicating controlfile
RMAN-08506: input filename=C:\ORACLE\ORADATA\DEMO\CONTROL01.CTL
RMAN-08505: output filename=C:\ORACLE\ORADATA\DEMO\CONTROL02.CTL
RMAN-08031: released channel: ch1
```

`RMAN>`

When you are connected in a very large network of databases, what if your database name is the same as some other database? This is quite possible, as many salespeople can create a database called DEMO in different domains to give product demonstrations to their clients. In this case, when you try to restore the control file of DEMO.ORACLE, how does Recovery Manager know which database to recover? It doesn't. So in this case, you will get an RMAN error as follows:

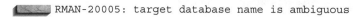 `RMAN-20005: target database name is ambiguous`

How do we resolve this kind of error? (*Hint*: We have to first figure out the database identifier [dbid] of the target database.) Refer to Chapter 10 to see a special case study on this problem.

# CHAPTER

## 8

## Replication

eplication can be considered as one of the most effective backup mechanisms for mission-critical applications. Replication ensures continuous availability of data for applications to function. It provides alternative data access options at any point of time, even when one or more data access options are not available. For example, an application might normally access a local database rather than a remote server to minimize network traffic and achieve maximum performance. In the replicated environment, the application can continue to function, even if the local server experiences a failure, while other servers with replicated data remain accessible. Figure 8-1 shows the basic structure of a replication environment. It involves a master replication site and two snapshot sites placed remotely, and each snapshot site is connected to the master database through a one-way communication channel called database link (DB_LINK). This link is used for replicating the desired set of database objects from the master database to the snapshot site. Oracle establishes a database session in the remote database on behalf of the local application's request using the database links. We will discuss basic replication and database links in this chapter.

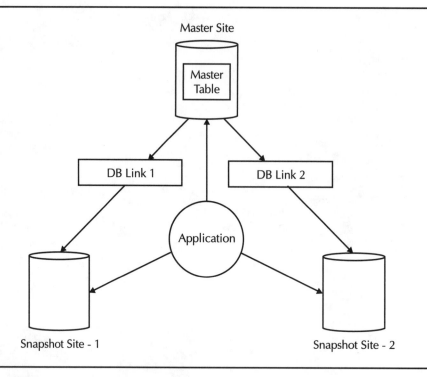

**FIGURE 8-1.** *Basic replication*

# Replication Concept

Unlike a pure distributed database system, in which a single copy of data is spread across the network, the replication technique enables you to copy and maintain database schema objects in multiple databases spread across networks to support mission-critical applications. This process gives you the option to replicate and maintain the whole database or a selected set of database objects in remote databases. While replication relies on basic distributed database technology to function, it is different from distributed databases. Replication can offer benefits to applications that are not possible within a pure distributed database environment.

While the snapshot is a transactionally consistent image of the master table, you have to update the data in the snapshot periodically. This process is called *refreshing*. You can refresh the snapshots by using a COMPLETE refresh, FAST refresh, or FORCE refresh. If you are replicating a table called Aquila from the master to the snapshot, a COMPLETE refresh completely replaces the entire table. The FAST refresh would transmit only the changes made to the master table since the last refresh. If you use the FORCE refresh, it would try to do a FAST refresh. If that fails, it would do a COMPLETE refresh. Refer to the *Oracle8i Replication Guide* for more information.

# Replication Requirements

There are a few parameters you must check before you establish a replication environment in your network:

- Ensure that GLOBAL_NAMES is set to TRUE in your **init.ora** file for advanced replication features; otherwise, it will enable basic replication features only. Each database in a replicated environment must be distinct and should have its own global database name. A global database name consists of two components: a database name of eight characters and a domain name that contains the database.

- Ensure that you have allocated enough job processes at each master site.

- Configure the Oracle Net Service Names between the master and the snapshot sites. If you are using Oracle Name Server in your Oracle network, you have to specify all the required database links (DB_LINKS) in the replication setup. The parameter GLOBAL_NAMES must be set to TRUE for each database that is participating in the replicated environment at both master and snapshot sites. Note that the value of GLOBAL_NAMES should be the same at the master and all snapshot sites.

■ Set an appropriate value for the initialization parameter JOB_QUEUE_PROCESSES in the **init.ora** file. This value specifies the number of SNP background processes per instance that are involved in the replication environment. This value ensures that Oracle can initiate the required number of job processes or SNP background processes to support various other processes such as refreshing snapshots, automatic propagation of the deferred transaction queue, purging the deferred transaction queue, and so forth. For multimaster replication, each master site will have a scheduled link to each of the other master sites. For example, if you have four master sites, each site will have scheduled links to the other three sites. You will typically need one process for each scheduled link. You may need to add an additional job process for purging the deferred transaction queue and other user-defined jobs.

■ Define one more initialization parameter JOB_QUEUE_INTERVAL in the **init.ora** file. This value determines the time interval between two consecutive job processes to execute any pending operations. The default value is set to 60 seconds and is adequate for most replicated environments. You have to adjust this to an appropriate value as per your requirement. For example, if the sites need frequent updates, then a job interval of less than 60 seconds should be set.

# Basic Replication

In the basic form of replication, Oracle enables you to replicate objects from one database—namely, the master database—to other databases (called snapshot sites), into which the replicated objects are placed. The basic replication involves a minimum of one master database, a database link between the master and snapshot sites, and a minimum of one snapshot site. The snapshot sites will hold the replicated objects as *materialized* views. The objects of the snapshot site cannot be edited—no objects can be inserted or deleted. They just provide read-only copy of the data for applications to query. A snapshot's *defining* query determines what data the snapshot should replicate from the master database. The logical data structure of table snapshots is defined by a query that references data in one or more remote master tables. Basic replication supports both ROWID snapshot and complex snapshot.

## Snapshot's Defining Query

A snapshot's defining query should be such that each row in the snapshot corresponds directly to a row or a part of a row in a single master table. Specifically, the defining query of a snapshot should not contain a distinct or aggregate function, a GROUP BY or CONNECT BY clause, a join, restricted types of subqueries, or a set operation.

## ROWID Snapshot or Primary-Key Snapshot

In this basic form of replication, the snapshot views are constructed based on the primary key of the master table. Oracle also supports ROWID snapshots based on the physical row identifiers or "ROWIDs" of rows in the master table for backward compatibility only. While creating ROWID snapshots, Oracle creates an additional index on the snapshot's base table with the name I_SNAP$_*snapshotname*. In this form of replication, Oracle replicates data based on the table ROWIDs.

## Complex Snapshots

A snapshot is considered as complex when the defining query is constructed with distinct or aggregate function, a GROUP BY or CONNECT BY clause, a join, restricted types of subqueries, or a set operation. The primary disadvantage of a complex snapshot is that Oracle cannot perform a FAST refresh of the snapshot, only a COMPLETE refresh. Consequently, use of complex snapshots can affect network performance during COMPLETE snapshot refreshes.

# Types of Replication Environments

Oracle supports three types of replication environments. They are

- Multimaster replication
- Snapshot replication
- Multimaster and snapshot hybrid configurations

## Multimaster Replication

Multimaster replication allows multiple sites, acting as equal peers, to manage replicated database objects in groups. Each site in a multimaster replication environment acts as master site.

When transactions change local data, the server automatically captures information about the modifications and queues corresponding deferred transactions to remote sites. Multimaster replication can either be asynchronous or synchronous. In an asynchronous form of replication, the updates at the master sites are stored in deferred transaction queues; from there, they will be propagated to other master sites. For this type of replication, Oracle uses its internal system of triggers, deferred transactions, deferred transaction queues, and job queues to propagate data-level changes asynchronously among master sites in an advanced replication system. In the synchronous form of replication, when a transaction updates a local table (which is being replicated), the changes will be propagated to all other sites. Each transaction that modifies the local data will ensure that the replicated data at the remote sites are also updated. In the event of any failure at any of the replicated master sites, Oracle ensures that the transaction either commits or rolls back at all master sites.

## Snapshot Replication

A snapshot replication is a process of replicating a complete or partial copy of a target master table at a single point in time. A snapshot can be updatable or read-only. In the basic replication, a snapshot gives read-only access to the replicated object that is originating from the target master table. In advance replication, all the changes that are performed at the snapshot site will be updated at the master table. That is, the changes are propagated in both directions.

## Multimaster and Snapshot Hybrid Configurations

In a multimaster and snapshot hybrid configuration, you can have any number of master sites and multiple snapshot sites for each master site. In this configuration, all replicated objects at the master sites will be updated completely, but in the case of snapshot sites, the replication can be either complete or partial.

# Setting Up a Master Replication Site

After configuring the basic database setting (as discussed earlier in this chapter) for replication, you can use either the replication management application programming interface (API) or the Oracle Replication Manager integrated with the Oracle Enterprise Manager to configure an Oracle replication environment. The API is a set of PL/SQL packages that can be executed from SQL prompt. In order to establish a master replication site, you have to perform the following steps:

1. Connect as internal at the master site and run the SQL script **CATREP.SQL**, which is available in the **%Ora_Home%\rdbms\admin** directory. Before running the script, you should ensure that the value of the initialization parameter OPEN_CURSOR is set to an appropriate value so as to create the required number of open cursors. In order to run the script successfully, you have to set the value to not less than 100 for a typical setup.

**2.** After running the script, you have to check the status of newly created objects by querying the data dictionary view ALL_OBJECTS for their validity. In case you find any invalid package in the query output, you have to compile all the listed packages manually.

**3.** A username for the replication administrator needs to be created to manage the replication site. For example, create a user named REPLICATIONADMIN. This needs to be created at each database that will participate in the replicated environment.

**4.** Grant privileges to replication administrator using the DBMS_REPCAT_ADMIN package as follows:

```
BEGIN
DBMS_REPCAT_ADMIN.GRANT_ADMIN_ANY_SCHEMA (
USERNAME => ' ReplicationAdmin ');
END;
/
```

Note that COMMENT ANY TABLE and LOCK ANY TABLE privileges need to be granted to the replication administrator if you want to create snapshot logs for any replicated table.

**5.** The replication propagator has to be registered using the package DBMS_DEFER_SYS. This package registers the user REPLICATIONADMIN as the propagator for the local database. It also grants him or her CREATE SESSION, CREATE PROCEDURE, CREATE DATABASE LINK, and EXECUTE ANY PROCEDURE privileges, so that the user can create wrappers. The propagator is responsible for propagating the deferred transaction queue to other master sites. The follow example does this for the user REPLICATIONADMIN:

```
BEGIN
   DBMS_DEFER_SYS.REGISTER_PROPAGATOR (
      USERNAME => ' ReplicationAdmin ');
END;
/
```

**6.** You should register the replication administrator REPLICATIONADMIN as the receiver for the local database. The receiver will receive the propagated deferred transactions sent by the propagator from other master sites. You can do this by using the package DBMS_REPCAT_ADMIN as follows:

```
BEGIN
   DBMS_REPCAT_ADMIN.REGISTER_USER_REPGROUP (
      USERNAME => ' ReplicationAdmin ',
      privilege_type => 'receiver',
      list_of_gnames => NULL);
END;
/
```

**7.** After setting the all parameters as described above, you are done. But, if you run the site as a master replication database, the size of the deferred transaction queue for the database will increase as the updates and new records are being added to the site and the same are being propagated to the remote sites. These successfully propagated changes are recorded in the deferred transaction queue. Hence, the log of the deferred transaction queue has to be cleaned frequently. To activate the purge activity, you have to run the DBMS_DEFER_SYS package as the replication administrator as follows:

```
BEGIN
    DBMS_DEFER_SYS.SCHEDULE_PURGE (
        next_date => SYSDATE,
        interval => 'sysdate + 1/24',
        delay_seconds => 0,
        rollback_segment => '');
END;
/
```

**8.** Though a replication administrator alone can maintain the replication environment and propagate/receive replicated changes, you may need to create additional users to manage different activities such configuring and maintaining a replication environment, propagating deferred transactions, and updating changes to the snapshots from the associated master tables. All these activities need different sets of privileges. You may need to create proxy users to manage these different activities individually on behalf of the respective site administrators. Create a proxy administrator PROXY_SNAPADMIN to perform database activities at the local master site on behalf of the snapshot administrator. The proxy refresher performs tasks at the master site on behalf of the refresher at the snapshot site. You have to be very careful with the kind of privileges granted to these proxy administrators and receivers, as they receive very powerful database privileges on behalf of their respective administrators.

**9.** Create PROXY_SNAPADMIN and grant the PROXY_SNAPADMIN privileges using the following procedure:

```
BEGIN
    DBMS_REPCAT_ADMIN.REGISTER_USER_REPGROUP (
        username => 'PROXY_SNAPADMIN',
        privilege_type => 'PROXY_SNAPADMIN',
        list_of_gnames => NULL);
END;
/
```

10. Create PROXY REFRESHER and grant CREATE SESSION and SELECT ANY TABLE privileges.

11. Create the required database links to other remote master sites as needed. Let us assume that you have created the database link AQUILASOFT.COM pointing to another master site.

12. Create a scheduled link to determine how often your deferred transaction queue is propagated to each of the other master sites. To create a scheduled link, you should connect to the database as replication administrator and execute the SCHEDULE_PUSH procedure for each database link that you created for each master site, as follows:

```
BEGIN
   DBMS_DEFER_SYS.SCHEDULE_PUSH (
       destination => AQUILASOFT.COM,
       interval => 'SYSDATE + 10 / (24 * 60)',
       next_date => SYSDATE);
END;
/
```

You should also execute the same procedures at the other master sites using the database links that are pointing to the rest of the master sites in the network. Once the master site setup is over, you can start performing replication.

## Creating a Master Group

Once the setting up of the master site is over, you can start replicating database objects such as tables, indexes, views, packages and package bodies, procedures, functions, triggers, sequences, and synonyms by creating master groups for the related objects. The following procedure illustrates how you can use Replication Manager to create a master group for placing database objects. You can access the Create Master Group Wizard from the Group | Master | Create menu bar of Oracle Replication Manager GUI.

In the General folder of the Create Master Group Wizard, enter the name and description of the master group that you want create. Optionally, you can enter a link qualifier for accessing the group. A link qualifier is a simple extension to a database link name, pointing to your master group database. Figure 8-2 shows a sample output of the wizard.

Open the Objects folder and define the database objects that you want to replicate in the group. Click the Add button at the bottom of the window to define the database objects for replication. Select the schema whose objects are to be

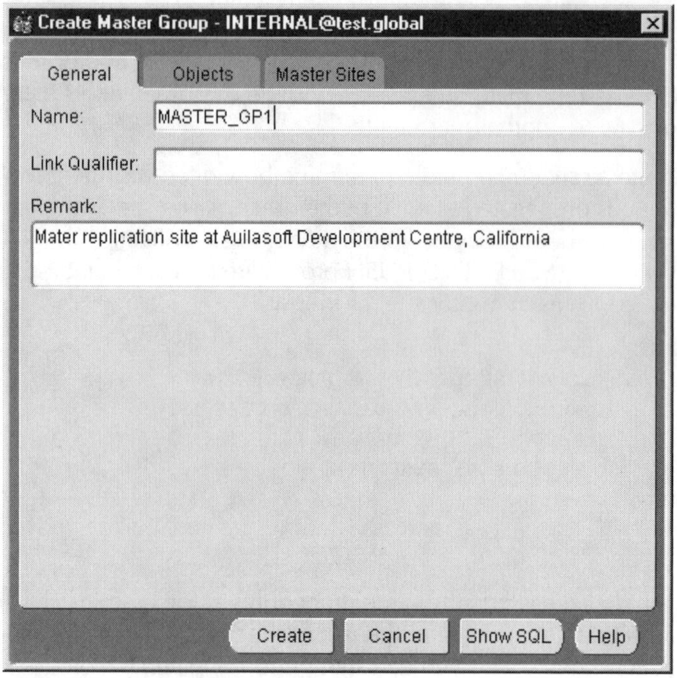

**FIGURE 8-2.** *Creating a master group*

included in the group from the drop-down list of the Schema button. Select the type
of object by enabling the respective radio button from the "Objects to display"
window. Choose the objects from the Available Object list and add them to the
Selected Objects list. Click the OK button as shown in the Figure 8-3.

If the table doesn't have primary-key constraints, the wizard will prompt you to
select an alternative key for the table. Click the Create button to create the group. In
the Master Sites window, you can define the other master sites for the group. Figure
8-4 shows a sample master group—MASTER_GROUP—and the object placed in it.

After creating the group, you have to generate replication support for the objects
that you have placed in the group. You can do this by selecting the newly created
group, opening its Operation folder, and clicking on the Generate radio button,

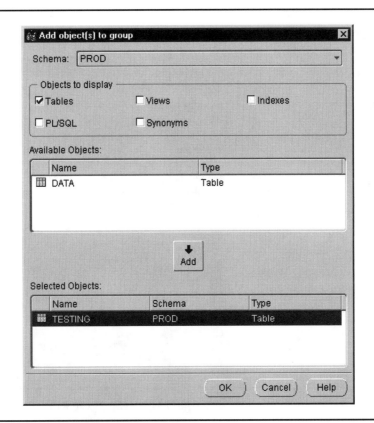

**FIGURE 8-3.**   *Adding objects to the group*

as shown in Figure 8-5. The wizard also gives you the option of editing the group's objects and adding and removing master sites for the group.

# Setting Up a Snapshot Site

Snapshot sites can be created at places where you need to provide complete or partial data of the master objects. The snapshot object must be originated from any one of the defined master sites. Read-only snapshots do not need to belong to a

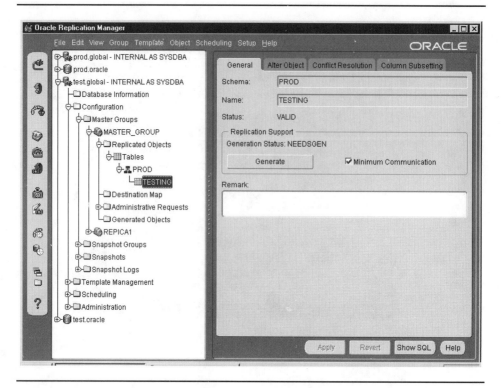

**FIGURE 8-4.** *Sample master group called MASTER_GROUP*

master group, but the updatable snapshots must be part of a snapshot group that is based on a master group at a master site.

## Snapshot Site Requirements

In addition to the points listed in the previous section, you have to create the TNSNAMES alias to connect to the required master site(s) as well as the snapshot sites that you want to create. Database links have to be created to the sites whose master groups or objects you want to replicate at the snapshot site. The snapshot environment can be set up either using the replication management API or the Oracle Replication Manager.

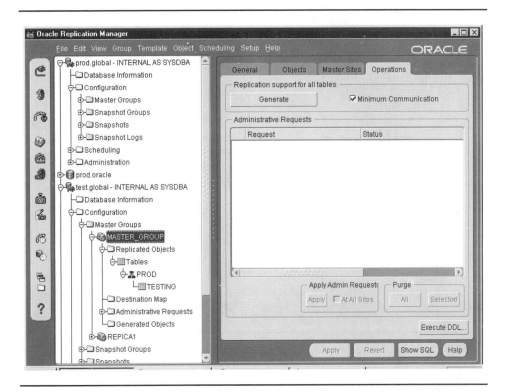

**FIGURE 8-5.**   *Generating replication support*

# Creating a Snapshot Site

The Oracle Replication Manager provides wizards to set up master and snapshot sites, in order to create master and snapshot groups and objects. You can invoke the Create Snapshot Wizard from Object | Create Snapshot menu of Replication Manager. Figure 8-6 shows the Snapshot Master Site window of the wizard. Enter the name of the TNSNAMES alias name in the Master Sites field that connects to the master site and enter the SYSTEM user account's password of the master site, as shown in Figure 8-6. Click the Next button.

In the Snapshot Sites window, click the Add button to add the snapshot site details, as shown in Figure 8-7.

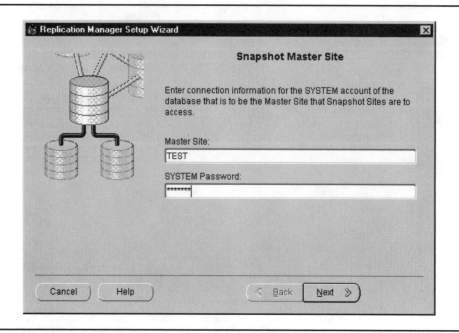

**FIGURE 8-6.** *Creating a snapshot: defining the master site*

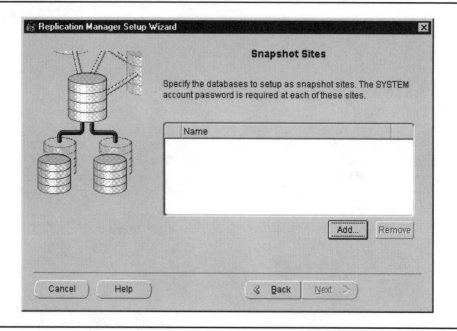

**FIGURE 8-7.** *Creating a snapshot: defining the snapshot site*

In the Add Site window, you have to specify the name of the TNSNAMES that connects to the snapshot site and the password of the SYSTEM account that belongs to the snapshot site, as shown in Figure 8-8. In this example, we want to create a snapshot site that can be accessed through the TNSNAMES alias PROD.GLOBAL After entering the details, click the Add button to see the list in the Site Adding window and make the proper choices. Click the OK button.

Click the Next button to create schemas such as snapshot site administrator and propagator to support the snapshot replication, as shown in Figure 8-9. As shown in the figure, the administrator of the snapshot site is SNAPADMIN. If you want to create a separate user account to manage the data propagation and reception at the snapshot site, you can do so by enabling the Propagator/Receiver

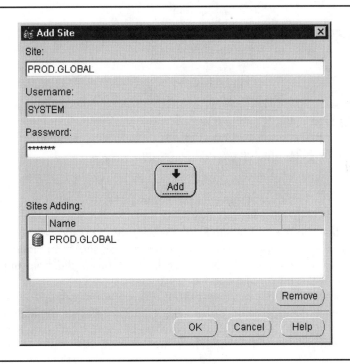

**FIGURE 8-8.** *Creating a snapshot: adding snapshot details*

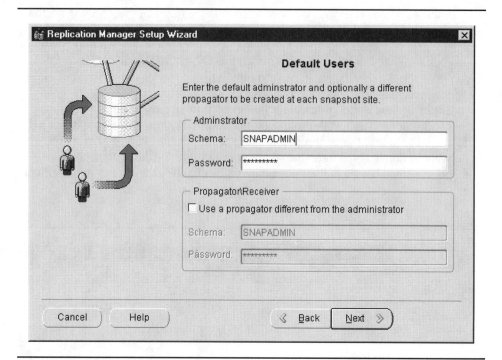

**FIGURE 8-9.** *Creating the replication administrator schema*

Radio button. If you select this, enter the name and password of the propagator account in the respective fields. Click Next.

You will see the Snapshot Site Schemas window. You should select the schemas that have replication support at the master replication site, as in Figure 8-10. In this example, we have selected the schema Test, which has replication support at the master site. Click on the Next button.

The moment you click on the Next button, you will be asked to enter the schema password to access his or her objects that are having replication support at the master site. Once you enter this, you see the Set Default Link Scheduling window. Here you can define the scheduling interval, as shown in Figure 8-11. Using the Scheduling option, different time intervals can be set to propagate changes from the snapshot site to the master site. Click the Next button.

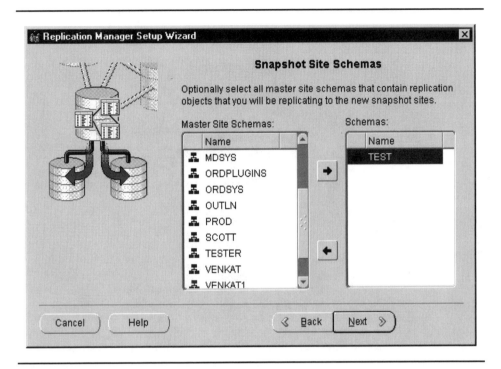

**FIGURE 8-10.** *Selecting schemas for replication*

In the Set Default Purge Job Scheduling window, you can set the time interval to purge deferred transactions. After successfully pushing a deferred transaction to its destination master site, the transaction does not have to remain in the site's deferred transaction queue. Regular purging of applied deferred transactions from a site's deferred transaction queue keeps the size of the queue manageable. You can do this in this window as shown in Figure 8-12. This wizard also allows you to define a rollback segment to be used when purging the deferred transactions from the deferred transaction queues. Click the Next button.

You can see that in Figure 8-13 PROD.GLOBAL is configured as the snapshot site. Click Next.

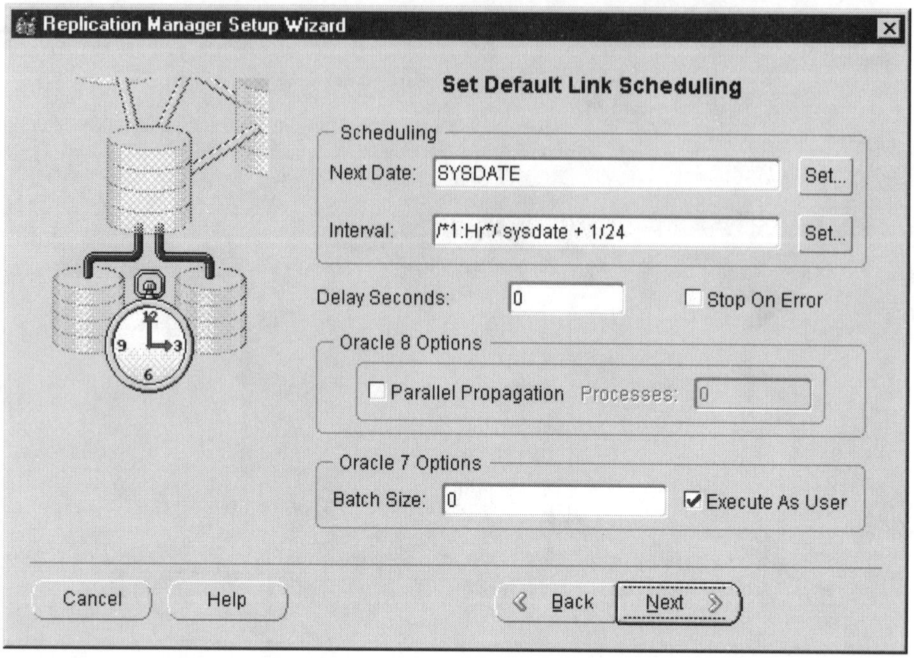

**FIGURE 8-11.** *Defining a scheduling interval*

In the next window, you will see the Record a Script button. If you want to record the setup details in PL/SQL script form, enable the Record a Script option and click the OK button to complete the snapshot site configuration, as shown in Figure 8-14.

You need to set up your master and snapshot sites per your application requirements. We have shown how Oracle Replication Manager can be used to create a master site and a read-only snapshot site. In the previous examples, we have set the initialization parameter GLOBAL_NAMES to FALSE in order to set up those sites. In advanced replication, this **init.ora** parameter needs to be set to TRUE. Oracle Replication Manager also supports replication conflict resolution. Replication conflicts can occur in an advanced replication environment that permits concurrent updates to the same data at multiple sites. For more information, refer to the *Oracle8i Replication API Reference Release 8.1.5* and *Oracle8i Replication Release 8.1.5* manuals.

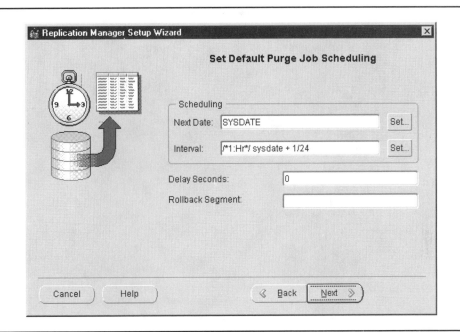

**FIGURE 8-12.** *Scheduling the interval to purge applied deferred transactions*

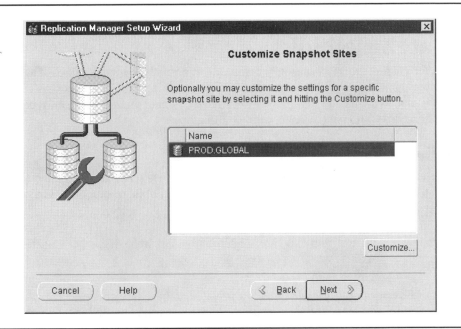

**FIGURE 8-13.** *Configuring databases for a snapshot site*

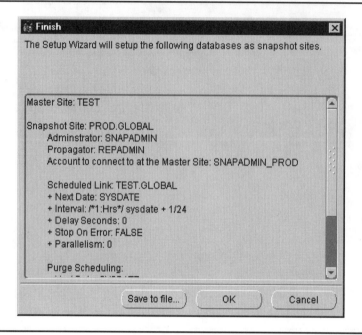

**FIGURE 8-14.** *Configuration summary*

# Database Links

A database link creates a one-way communication path from one database to another database. Typically, a database link provides an application access to data that is placed physically in a remote destination. Oracle provides various types of database links—namely, private, public, and global.

## Private Database Link

A private database link allows only the owner in whose schema it is created to access the remote database. It is more secure than a public or global database link. For example:

```
SQL> CREATE DATABASE LINK aquilasoft.com
     CONNECT TO CURRENT_USER
     USING 'finance';
```

In the above example, Oracle creates a private database link called AQUILASOFT.COM in the current user schema using the Oracle Net8 Service

Name *finance*. The database link name must be the same name as the global database name of the remote database it references as long as the initialization parameter GLOBAL_NAMES is set to TRUE. You can specify any name for the database if the parameter is set to FALSE. Before you create the database link, you should verify that the Net Service Name is working properly. The current user must be a global user with a valid account on the remote database for the link to succeed. You can also create a database link using a fixed user's login credentials who has a valid user account in the remote database. For more information, refer to the *Oracle8i SQL Reference Release 8.1.5* manual.

**NOTE**
*Keeping the **init.ora** parameter GLOBAL_NAMES to TRUE allows you to use advanced replication.*

## Public Database Link

Unlike a private database link, all users can use a public database link for accessing the remote database objects. The public database link will be created by the DBA of your database.

## Global Database Link

A global database link creates a one-way communication channel between databases in a centralized network environment (such as networks having centralized name services ) and centralized user authentication services integrated with Oracle. A global database link should be given the same name as the global database name of the remote database it references. When you set the initialization parameter GLOBAL_NAMES to TRUE, Oracle ensures that the name of the database link is the same as the global database name of the remote database. In order to create a global database link, you have to configure Oracle Name Server. To use a current user's database link, the user must be a global user authenticated by the Oracle Security Server or a non-Oracle authentication service integrated with Oracle.

# Replicable Datatypes

Replication supports the following datatypes:

| NUMBER | CHAR | RAW |
| DATE | NVARCHAR2 | ROWID |
| VARCHAR2 | NCHAR | |

Oracle doesn't support columns that use the LONG and LONG RAW datatypes, user-defined object types and external or file-based LOBs (BFILEs), binary LOBs (BLOBs), character LOBs (CLOBs), and national character LOBs (NCLOBs).

**NOTE**
*Oracle8i does not support replication of LOB datatypes in replication environments in which some sites are running Oracle7 release 7.3. For more information, refer to the Oracle8i Replication API Reference Release 8.1.5 manual.*

# CHAPTER

## 9

# Diagnostic Facilities and Debugging the RDBMS

his chapter familiarizes the DBA with the diagnostic facilities that are available in Oracle7, Oracle8, and Oracle8*i*. To diagnose any RDBMS-related problems, you should be familiar with all the debugging utilities that are provided by Oracle. In addition, certain concepts such as reading the control file dumps or reading the trace files are necessary. All the information recorded in any trace file might not be useful to the DBA or the user. Some of the information is specifically used by Oracle Support Services analysts and the Oracle development teams. We will first start off by discussing the various trace files that are generated by Oracle automatically. We will then discuss various diagnostic tools available to debug the RDBMS. Note that this chapter is dedicated to learning the diagnostic tools pertaining to the RDBMS only. Tools to debug/tune applications such as **sql_trace** and **tkprof** or database tuning scripts such as **utlbstat/utlestat** are not discussed in this chapter, as they are beyond the scope of this book.

# Oracle Trace Files

The alert log file provides crucial information about the database, and should usually be the first file to take a look at when diagnosing a database problem. If any trace files are created on the system, this information will be provided in the alert log file. The ability to use the information contained in a trace file is very dependent on your experience with the various messages printed in the file. Many messages printed to the log are not associated with any error conditions.

During startup of the database, if the alert log file doesn't exist, Oracle will create one for you. This file will be used to write information such as "DBWR started." Listing 9-1 shows the dump of an alert file (**alert.log**) after starting up the Oracle8*i* database on Microsoft Windows NT.

### Listing 9-1

```
Dump file C:\Oracle\admin\prod\bdump\prodALRT.LOG
Wed Aug 16 15:37:46 2000
ORACLE V8.1.5.0.0 - Production vsnsta=0
vsnsql=d vsnxtr=3
Windows NT V4.0, OS V5.101, CPU type 586
Starting up ORACLE RDBMS Version: 8.1.5.0.0.
System parameters with non-default values:
  processes             = 59
  shared_pool_size      = 15728640
  java_pool_size        = 20971520
  control_files         = C:\Oracle\oradata\prod\control01.ctl,
C:\Oracle\oradata\prod\control02.ctl
  db_block_buffers      = 8466
  db_block_size         = 2048
  compatible            = 8.1.0
  log_buffer            = 32768
  log_checkpoint_interval = 10000
```

```
  log_checkpoint_timeout   = 1800
  db_files                 = 1024
  db_file_multiblock_read_count= 8
  remote_login_passwordfile= EXCLUSIVE
  db_domain                = oracle
  global_names             = TRUE
  distributed_transactions = 500
  service_names            = prod.oracle
  instance_name            = prod
  mts_dispatchers          =
(ADDRESS=(PARTIAL=YES)(PROTOCOL=TCP))(DIS=1)(SES=254)(CON=254)(TIC=15)(POO=NO)(MUL=NO)(LIS=(ADDR
ESS_LIST=(ADDRESS=(PROTOCOL=IPC)(KEY=PNPKEY))(ADDRESS=(PROTOCOL=TCP)(HOST=127.0.0.1)(PORT=1521))
(ADDRESS=(PROTOCOL=IPC)(KEY=prod.oracle))))(PRE=oracle.aurora.server.SGiopServer)
  mts_servers              = 1
  open_links               = 4
  db_name                  = prod
  os_authent_prefix        =
  job_queue_processes      = 0
  job_queue_interval       = 10
  parallel_max_servers     = 5
  background_dump_dest      = C:\Oracle\admin\prod\bdump
  user_dump_dest           = C:\Oracle\admin\prod\udump
  max_dump_file_size       = 10240
  oracle_trace_collection_name=
PMON started with pid=2
DBW0 started with pid=3
LGWR started with pid=4
CKPT started with pid=5
SMON started with pid=6
RECO started with pid=7
Wed Aug 16 15:37:48 2000
starting up 1 shared server(s) ...
starting up 1 dispatcher(s) for network protocol '(ADDRESS=(PARTIAL=YES)(PROTOCOL=TCP))'...
Wed Aug 16 15:37:51 2000
create controlfile reuse set database prod
datafile 'C:\Oracle\oradata\prod\system01.dbf',
'C:\Oracle\oradata\prod\temp01.dbf',
'C:\Oracle\oradata\prod\rbs01.dbf',
'C:\Oracle\oradata\prod\indx01.dbf',
'C:\Oracle\oradata\prod\oemrep01.dbf',
'C:\Oracle\oradata\prod\users01.dbf'
logfile 'C:\Oracle\oradata\prod\redo01.log' size 1M,
'C:\Oracle\oradata\prod\redo02.log' size 1M,
'C:\Oracle\oradata\prod\redo03.log' size 1M,
'C:\Oracle\oradata\prod\redo04.log' size 1M resetlogs
Wed Aug 16 15:37:54 2000
Successful mount of redo thread 1, with mount id 4112596303.
Wed Aug 16 15:37:54 2000
Completed: create controlfile reuse set database prod
datafil
Wed Aug 16 15:37:54 2000
alter database prod open resetlogs
RESETLOGS after incomplete recovery UNTIL CHANGE 137638
Wed Aug 16 15:37:55 2000
Errors in file C:\Oracle\admin\prod\udump\ORA00181.TRC:
ORA-00313: open failed for members of log group 1 of thread 1
ORA-00312: online log 1 thread 1: 'C:\ORACLE\ORADATA\PROD\REDO04.LOG'
ORA-27041: unable to open file
OSD-04002: unable to open file
O/S-Error: (OS 2) The system cannot find the file specified.
```

```
Wed Aug 16 15:37:55 2000
Errors in file C:\Oracle\admin\prod\udump\ORA00181.TRC:
ORA-00313: open failed for members of log group 2 of thread 1
ORA-00312: online log 2 thread 1: 'C:\ORACLE\ORADATA\PROD\REDO03.LOG'
ORA-27041: unable to open file
OSD-04002: unable to open file
O/S-Error: (OS 2) The system cannot find the file specified.

Wed Aug 16 15:37:55 2000
Errors in file C:\Oracle\admin\prod\udump\ORA00181.TRC:
ORA-00313: open failed for members of log group 3 of thread 1
ORA-00312: online log 3 thread 1: 'C:\ORACLE\ORADATA\PROD\REDO02.LOG'
ORA-27041: unable to open file
OSD-04002: unable to open file
O/S-Error: (OS 2) The system cannot find the file specified.

Wed Aug 16 15:37:56 2000
Errors in file C:\Oracle\admin\prod\udump\ORA00181.TRC:
ORA-00313: open failed for members of log group 4 of thread 1
ORA-00312: online log 4 thread 1: 'C:\ORACLE\ORADATA\PROD\REDO01.LOG'
ORA-27041: unable to open file
OSD-04002: unable to open file
O/S-Error: (OS 2) The system cannot find the file specified.

Picked broadcast on commit scheme to generate SCNs
Wed Aug 16 15:37:58 2000
Thread 1 opened at log sequence 1
  Current log# 1 seq# 1 mem# 0: C:\ORACLE\ORADATA\PROD\REDO04.LOG
Successful open of redo thread 1.
Wed Aug 16 15:37:58 2000
SMON: enabling cache recovery
Wed Aug 16 15:38:00 2000
Dictionary check beginning
Dictionary check complete
Wed Aug 16 15:38:04 2000
SMON: enabling tx recovery
Wed Aug 16 15:38:05 2000
Completed: alter database prod open resetlogs
Wed Aug 16 15:38:05 2000
alter database prod character set WE8ISO8859P1
Wed Aug 16 15:38:09 2000
Thread 1 advanced to log sequence 2
  Current log# 2 seq# 2 mem# 0: C:\ORACLE\ORADATA\PROD\REDO03.LOG
Thread 1 advanced to log sequence 3
  Current log# 3 seq# 3 mem# 0: C:\ORACLE\ORADATA\PROD\REDO02.LOG
Thread 1 advanced to log sequence 4
  Current log# 4 seq# 4 mem# 0: C:\ORACLE\ORADATA\PROD\REDO01.LOG
Thread 1 advanced to log sequence 5
  Current log# 1 seq# 5 mem# 0: C:\ORACLE\ORADATA\PROD\REDO04.LOG
Wed Aug 16 15:38:22 2000
Completed: alter database prod character set WE8ISO8859P1
Wed Aug 16 15:38:22 2000
alter database prod national character set WE8ISO8859P1
Completed: alter database prod national character set WE8ISO8
Shutting down instance (normal)
License high water mark = 1
Wed Aug 16 15:38:26 2000
ALTER DATABASE CLOSE NORMAL
Wed Aug 16 15:38:27 2000
SMON: disabling tx recovery
```

```
SMON: disabling cache recovery
Wed Aug 16 15:38:29 2000
Thread 1 closed at log sequence 5
Wed Aug 16 15:38:29 2000
Completed: ALTER DATABASE CLOSE NORMAL
```

When the database is started, all the **init.ora** parameters and messages indicating that the background processes have started are recorded in the alert log file. The thread that this instance is using and the log sequence number that LGWR is currently writing to are also recorded. In general, the alert log file keeps a log of all database startups, shutdowns, tablespace creations, rollback segment creations, some **alter** statements issued, information regarding log switches, and error messages. Each entry has a timestamp associated with it, and for nonerror messages, there is usually an entry for the beginning of an action plus an entry indicating its successful completion. It is very important for you to regularly check this file for error messages. If there is an error message in the alert log file, it will often direct you to a specific trace file (or files) for more information.

In addition to the alert log file, there are two types of trace files that Oracle generates automatically. One is the *background trace file* created by background processes such as DBWR and LGWR. The background trace files might or might not be created on startup, depending on whether there is any information that the background process needs to write at that time. Initially, when the file is created, it contains some header information indicating the version numbers of the RDBMS and the operating system. These files are created in a directory specified by the **init.ora** parameter BACKGROUND_DUMP_DEST.

The second type of trace file is produced by the user connection to Oracle and is known as the *user trace file*. These files are only created when the user session encounters an error condition and information can be dumped to the trace files. In addition, if a user session requests a trace file by using the **alter session** command, they are created as a user trace as well. The user trace files are created in a directory specified by the **init.ora** parameter USER_DUMP_DEST.

Trace file names have a standard format so you can locate them easily. The names of the trace files give information that can help users locate the correct one more easily. The naming convention is operating system specific. For example, on OpenVMS, the file has the name *IMAGE_NAME_SID_PROCESS_ID*.TRC. The *IMAGE_NAME* is the name of the executable image that created the trace file. The *SID* is the system identifier of the instance. The *PROCESS_ID* is the process ID of the process that created the trace file. In the UNIX environment, the background trace file will look something like *ORA_PID_PROCESS_ID*.trc, and the user trace file has the name *PROCESS_ID*.trc. The *ORA_PID* is the Oracle process ID, and the *PROCESS_ID* is the system process ID for the process creating the trace file. Note that all messages written to the user trace files might not be critical, but it is always a good practice for the DBA to monitor the trace files at periodic intervals.

There is a lot of information contained in the trace files that the DBA can use to resolve some of the problems. Later in this chapter, we will discuss in detail some of the common errors, causes, and resolutions. But before we do that, we need to examine some of the diagnostic features and better understand how to read the information in certain trace files.

# Diagnostic Tools

Oracle provides various diagnostic tools for debugging the RDBMS. Certain events can be turned on to dump diagnostic information of various data structures to trace files. Next, some special **init.ora** parameters are available that can be used while diagnosing memory and disk corruptions. These parameters are not set during normal operation of the database, as they affect the performance of the database. A brief overview of such parameters will be given as well.

## Setting Trace Events

The Oracle RDBMS contains a facility that allows the DBA to dump information contained in various structures and to trace the occurrence of particular events. There are two ways to turn on the event trace. The first way is to set the required event in the **init.ora** file, which will turn on event trace for all the sessions. The second way is to enter the **alter session set events** command, usually from Server Manager. This will turn on event trace for just the ongoing session.

The syntax while using **init.ora** is

EVENT = "*event syntax* | ,LEVEL *n*|: *event syntax* | ,LEVEL *n*|.."

The syntax while using SQL is

ALTER SESSION SET EVENTS '*event syntax* LEVEL *n*: *event syntax* LEVEL *n*:...';

For example, to dump the complete contents of the control file, issue the following command:

```
SQL> ALTER SESSION SET EVENTS 'IMMEDIATE TRACE NAME CONTROLF LEVEL 10';
```

The *event syntax* contains multiple keywords. The first keyword of the event syntax can be an *event number* or a special keyword, **immediate**. Event numbers can be Oracle error numbers (ones prefixed by "ORA-" in the *Oracle8i Error Messages Release 8.1.5* manual) or internal *event codes* defined in the Oracle RDBMS. The event codes are implemented by logic in the kernel that takes some action depending on its value. These internal event codes can be found in the **rdbms/mesg/oraus.msg** file on UNIX, or in the **ERROR.MSG** file in the **ORA_RDBMS** directory on OpenVMS. In some operating systems, this file might be in binary format and not a text file, as in WINDOWS NT. The internal event codes are in the range 10000 to 10999. Some of the event codes that are commonly used by DBAs and Oracle Support Services will be discussed later in this chapter.

If the keyword **immediate** is specified as the first word in the event syntax, it's an indication to Oracle that it is an unconditional event, and the structure specified should be dumped to trace immediately after the command is issued. This keyword is issued in the **alter session** command (it doesn't make sense to use it in the **init.ora** file).

The second and third keywords in the event syntax are almost always **trace** and **name**, respectively. The keyword **trace** indicates that the output will be dumped to a trace file and the keyword **name** comes before the actual *event name*. There are qualifiers other than **trace** that can be used as well, but they are for internal use only by the Oracle development team. The last keyword of the event syntax is the *event name*, which is the actual structure that you want to dump.

If you are not using the **immediate** option as the first keyword in the event syntax, then you need to indicate how long the specified tracing should be enabled. Specifying the keyword **forever** will keep the event active for the life of the session or instance, depending on whether the event is set from **init.ora** or at a session level.

After the event syntax, the **level** keyword is specified for most events. An exception would be while dumping the **errorstack**, where there is no level (**errorstack** is discussed later in this section). Usually, the **level** needs to be set between 1 and 10. A value of 10 would dump all the information for that event. So, for example, setting **level** to 1 while dumping the control file would dump only the control file header, whereas setting **level** to 10 would dump the entire contents of the control file. **level** has a special meaning while using the **blockdump** keyword to dump a data block. Here, the **level** is the actual address of the data block, specified in decimal form. Oracle Support Services will advise you on what the value of **level** should be, depending on the structure you are dumping to trace.

Putting all this together, here are some examples. The following are examples that can be used while using the **init.ora** file to set events:

```
EVENT = "604 TRACE NAME ERRORSTACK FOREVER"

EVENT = "10210 TRACE NAME CONTEXT FOREVER, LEVEL 10"
```

The above two lines need to be typed in the **init.ora** file exactly as shown. The first statement dumps the error stack every time a process encounters the ORA-00604 error. The second statement is a block-checking event that checks every block's integrity when read from disk to cache. Remember that setting these events in the **init.ora** file creates a trace when the above conditions occur by any session in the database. The following are examples that can be used while using SQL to set events:

```
alter session set events 'immediate trace name blockdump level 67109037';
alter session set events 'immediate trace name controlf level 10';
alter session set events 'immediate trace name systemstate level 10';
```

The first statement dumps the data block 67109037 to a trace file. Every data block in the Oracle database is uniquely identified by a combination of block number and a file number. In the above example, 67109037 is the decimal representation of the file number and the block number. This information is operating system dependent. The second statement dumps the entire contents of the control file to trace. The third statement dumps the *systemstate* to trace, which includes all *process state* dumps (system state and process state are discussed later in this chapter). This system state dump will be useful while diagnosing *system hang* problems.

**NOTE**
*The syntax for dumping data blocks has been changed in Oracle8 and Oracle8i. See the next section.*

## Event Names

This section gives a partial list of the event names that can be set. It includes the definition of each event name, a brief description of the trace it produces, and when this event should be used.

**buffers**    Setting this trace event will dump all the buffers in the SGA buffer cache. This event is useful while diagnosing corruptions happening in memory. If a proper **level** is not set, setting this event can affect performance of the database. Setting the **level** to 1 dumps only the buffer header, whereas setting it to 10 dumps the entire contents of the buffer. Depending on the problem that is being diagnosed, Oracle Support Services will suggest the appropriate **level** to set. This event should be used only when requested by Oracle Support Services. For example,

```
alter session set events 'immediate trace name buffers level 1';
```

dumps the buffer header to trace.

**blockdump**    Use this command to dump a specific database block belonging to any segment, such as data, index, or rollback. The block's address should be specified after the **level** keyword as a decimal value. This command should be used under Oracle Support Services' supervision. This event is normally set to debug data corruptions in data or index blocks. In Oracle 7x, the syntax is

```
alter session set events 'immediate trace name blockdump level 134219181';
```

which dumps the contents of the data block that has an address of 134219181.

In Oracle8x, the syntax is

```
alter system dump datafile 11 block 9;
```

This command dumps data block 9 in data file 11.

**controlf**    This event is the one most commonly used to dump the contents of the control file. Setting the **level** to 1 will dump only the control file header. Setting the **level** to 10 will dump the entire contents of the control file. For example,

```
alter session set events 'immediate trace name controlf level 10';
```

dumps the entire control file to trace. A detailed description of control file dumps is provided in the following section.

**locks**    When set, this event dumps all locks held by the lock process. It is usually used to debug locking problems while using the PARALLEL SERVER option. For example,

```
alter session set events 'immediate trace name locks level 5';
```

dumps the information regarding the locks held by the LCK process to trace.

**redohdr**    This is also a common event, which dumps the redo log file's header to trace. Setting the **level** to 1 dumps the control file entry of the redo information only. A **level** 2 dumps the generic file header (discussed later in this chapter). Any **level** greater than 2 dumps the complete log header to trace. Sometimes while starting up the database after a media failure, Oracle reports that some data files have failed the verification checks that it performs. In such cases, using this event along with **file_hdrs** and **controlf** is useful for debugging. For example,

```
alter session set events 'immediate trace name redohdr level 10';
```

dumps the redo header information to trace.

**loghist**    This event dumps the log history entries from the control file. If **level** 1 is set, it only dumps the earliest and latest log history entries. If **level** 2 or greater is specified, it dumps the most recent 2**level** (2 to the power **level**) entries. For example,

```
alter session set events 'immediate trace name loghist level 4';
```

Here, **level** is set to 4, so 2**4 = 16 most recent log history entries would be dumped from the control file. Note that you can select from the view V$LOG_HISTORY to get the same information.

**file_hdrs**    This event dumps all data file headers to trace. The **level** setting is the same as for the event **Redohdr**. For example,

```
alter session set events 'immediate trace name file_hdrs level 10';
```

dumps the contents of all data file headers to trace.

**errorstack**    Oracle will create a stack called the *error stack* to store the information relating to a particular error that a process has encountered. Usually when an error occurs, the Oracle foreground process gets an error message. However, while running some applications (such as Oracle Forms), the foreground process might not get all the information related to the error. This event dumps the entire error stack to trace and is very useful for debugging any Oracle error. For example, if an application is failing with the ORA-00604 error,

```
alter session set events '604 trace name errorstack forever';
```

dumps the error stack and also the process stack to trace. For more information on stack traces, refer to the "Oracle Internal Errors" section later in this chapter.

**systemstate**    This event dumps the entire system state, which includes all processes' state dumps. This event is very useful for diagnosing problems when experiencing performance degradation, process hangs, or system hangs. System state and process state dumps are discussed in the "Oracle Internal Errors" section of this chapter. This event should be used under the supervision of Oracle Support Services. For example,

```
alter session set events 'immediate trace name systemstate level 10';
```

dumps the system state to trace.

**coalesce**    For DBAs, this is an extremely useful space-management event. When set, this event coalesces free space in **fet$** for the specified tablespace (**fet$** gives information regarding the free space that's available in the database, and is discussed in Chapter 2). For example, if blocks 1–5 indicate the first chunk of free space and blocks 6–10 indicate the second chunk, by setting this event, the two records can be replaced by a single record in the **fet$** table, indicating that one chunk of free space is available that contains blocks 1–10. The tablespace and number of entries to coalesce are specified after the **level** as follows:

```
alter session set events 'immediate trace name coalesce level X';
```

where $X$ is a decimal number constructed by taking the high-order two bytes as the number of extents to coalesce and the low-order two bytes as the tablespace number. So for example, let's assume that we want to coalesce up to five entries in the system tablespace. Then, the high-order two bytes in hexadecimal representation will be 0x0005. Since the system tablespace has a tablespace number of zero, the low-order two bytes are 0x0000. Combining the low-order and high-order bytes, the value in hex is 0x00050000. This represents a value of 327680 in decimal form, which is the value of $X$:

```
alter session set events 'immediate trace name coalesce level 327680';
```

**NOTE**
*This event needs to be explicitly set while using Oracle7 (7.0.x) of the RDBMS only. In Oracle8i, this feature is built into the database and has been disabled.*

Some other event names exist in addition to the ones just described, but they are not used as often. Some of them are **Latches**, **Processstate**, **Row_Cache**, **Enqueues**, and **Contextarea**.

## Event Codes

Note that some codes that are available in one version of Oracle may be changed or deleted in the following version. In addition, some of the event codes are destructive and can crash the database, so these event codes are not supported by Oracle Support Services without their guidance. It is suggested that you try some of these events on your test database, but *don't* experiment on your production database. Following is a description of some of the common event codes used by Oracle Support Services.

**Event Codes 10013 and 10015**   These event codes are used while diagnosing problems induced by a corrupted rollback segment. In such cases, the database cannot be started and gives the ORA-01578 error, indicating that a block in the database is corrupted for whatever reason. If Oracle Support Services determines the cause to be due to a rollback segment, setting the above events in the **init.ora** file creates a trace file that will be helpful in determining the bad rollback. The syntax for setting event 10015 in the **init.ora** file is

```
event = "10015 trace name context forever"
```

**Event Codes 10029 and 10030**   These event codes give information on the session logons and session logoffs, which are used by some DBAs. If you want to know the number of logons and logoffs to the database, you can use these events.

**Event Codes 10210 and 10211**   These are *block-checking* and *index-checking* events, respectively. Normally when a block is read from disk to cache, some basic integrity checks are performed. By setting these events, Oracle does additional checks, which could be very crucial while diagnosing some block corruptions. PMON always has block checking turned on. It is good practice to use the block-checking and index-checking events even during normal operation of the database, but there is an overhead involved. Running the database with these events turned on is especially advisable for customers running a VLDB shop with high availability requirements. For example,

```
event = "10210 trace name context forever, level 10"
```

turns on block checking for every data block read into the SGA.

In Oracle8*i*, for events 10210 and 10211, you need not set the events in **init.ora** file. Instead, you can set the initialization parameter DB_BLOCK_CHECKING to TRUE, which does the same job as that of the events 10210 and 10211. Since this **init.ora** parameter is dynamic, it can be set to TRUE or FALSE using the **alter system set** command.

**Event Codes 10231 and 10232**   These are probably the most important event codes. Assume that due to a physical outage, one of the blocks on disk is zeroed out—that is, all the data in that block is gone. To salvage the remaining data in that table, you need to export that table. However, a full table scan of the table would fail when the bad block is read. To work around the corruption, event 10231 needs to be set. This event skips corrupted blocks during full table scans. If event 10232 is set, these corrupted blocks are dumped to a trace file. There are certain conditions that need to be met in order for event 10231 to work:

This block should be *soft corrupted* by Oracle. This means that when Oracle detects a corrupt block, it marks the block as corrupt by setting certain bits in the block to zero. In order for Oracle to soft corrupt the block, you have to use event 10210. So, using event 10231 along with event 10210 is recommended. The **level** should be set correctly. Oracle Support Services can provide this information to you. In Oracle8*i*, you can use the DBMS_REPAIR package to soft corrupt blocks that are corrupt. This is discussed in the section "Detecting and Repairing Data Block Corruption Using the DBMS_REPAIR Package" later in this chapter.

Accessing the blocks through an index won't work. Only full table scans should be done on the table. Note that if this event is set in a session, it would work only if that session does the full table scan. If you need to export the table, then this event should be set in the **init.ora** file.

Two examples are given below. The first one is used with SQL and the second is used in the **init.ora** file.

```
alter session set events '10231 trace name context off';

event = "10231 trace name context forever, level 10"
```

The first statement turns off block checking for that session. The second statement turns on block checking database-wide for all data blocks read into the SGA by any process.

**Event Code 10061**   This event code has been added with version 7.0.15. After a database crash or a **shutdown abort** statement is issued, during next startup, SMON cleans up temporary segments. When set, this event will disable cleanup of temporary segments by SMON at startup time. Sometimes, depending on the outage that caused the failure, it might be necessary to take such an action to start the database up.

After starting up the database, Oracle Support Services analysts can troubleshoot the problem and fix it, at which point this event should be removed from the **init.ora** file and the database restarted.

# init.ora Parameters

Almost every DBA will be familiar with the documented **init.ora** parameters. Parameters such as LOG_BUFFERS, DB_BLOCK_WRITE_BATCH, and DB_FILE_ MULTIBLOCK_READ_COUNT are usually used by DBAs to tune the database (for example, tuning memory allocation or tuning I/O). Other parameters, such as SQL_ TRACE and TIMED_STATISTICS, are used while debugging or tuning application-specific problems.

The **init.ora** parameters we are about to discuss are not documented. Some DBAs know about these parameters, and may have used them as well. Any **init.ora** parameter that starts with an underscore is an undocumented, unsupported Oracle feature. The idea behind keeping these parameters undocumented should be clear—there are risks involved in using these parameters. If not used properly, the data might become inconsistent, thereby having logical corruptions in the database. Two such parameters are _OFFLINE_ROLLBACK_SEGMENTS and _CORRUPTED_ ROLLBACK_SEGMENTS.

### _OFFLINE_ROLLBACK_SEGMENTS and _CORRUPTED_ROLLBACK_SEGMENTS

These undocumented parameters help you solve problems that are related to rollback segments. For example, if you have problems opening the database due to a corrupted rollback segment, using the _CORRUPTED_ROLLBACK_SEGMENTS parameter will help you open the database. These parameters have drastic effects on the database and should be used under Oracle Support Services' supervision. Please note that _OFFLINE_ROLLBACK_SEGMENTS is made redundant from Oracle7.3 onward, due to deferred transaction recovery.

To use these parameters, set the following line in the **init.ora** file:

*parameter = (rollback segment name, rollback segment name,...)*

For example,

```
_corrupted_rollback_segments =  (rbs1, rbs2)
```

would take the rollback segments **rbs1** and **rbs2** offline while doing transaction recovery.

Due to hardware or software failures, if a block in a rollback segment gets corrupted, it will cause problems while starting up the database. Consider the following scenario: A DBA was getting the ORA-01578 error on a rollback segment block during startup. By setting events, an Oracle Support Services analyst dumped a trace file on startup, and all Oracle indicated was that Oracle error ORA-01578 was encountered while recovering transaction X. No additional information was given (such as the object name or number). By using the _OFFLINE_ROLLBACK_SEGMENTS parameter, the database was brought online. Is the database consistent at this time? Is rebuilding the database necessary? To answer these questions, you need to understand the ramifications of using these parameters.

When the _OFFLINE_ROLLBACK_SEGMENTS parameter is used, Oracle takes the rollback segment(s) offline during transaction recovery (roll backward) for those rollback segments listed in this parameter when the database is started. In other words, Oracle temporarily prevents SMON from cleaning up the uncommitted transactions in the rollback segments involved. However, when a data/index/cluster/ cluster index block, which is part of this uncommitted transaction, is needed at a later time, Oracle tries to read the block and detects a corruption. So, using this parameter gives the DBA or the Oracle Support Services analyst a chance to determine which objects still have uncommitted transactions in the rollback segment by dumping the transaction table and corresponding pieces of the rollback segment itself.

If the problem is due to an inability to roll back a transaction because an object is corrupt, it may be possible to drop the object and bring the rollback segment back online without further damage taking place, and still have any remaining uncommitted transactions roll back normally. If the status of the rollback segment changes from NEEDS RECOVERY to IN USE or AVAILABLE, then it is generally safe to say that you can continue operating the database without a rebuild. If rebuilding your database is necessary, depending on the size of the database and the kind of backup and recovery procedures used, it may sometimes be faster to go back to a good backup and recover the database instead of going through a rebuild.

When the _CORRUPTED_ROLLBACK_SEGMENTS parameter is used, it works the same way while starting up the database as described in the previous case. However, once the database is open, the blocks needing read consistency are read *as is*. In other words, the uncommitted transactions are marked as *committed*. As a result, the blocks are made *good enough*, yet might be out of sync with respect to the application data. Applications handling financial-type transactions, which need a very high degree of accuracy, can run into problems here, as the outcome of a query can give different results than expected. In addition, using this parameter can lead to worse problems down the road if, for example, a data dictionary cluster index becomes inconsistent with the clustered tables because it was only partially rolled back. Note that one of the main differences of using this parameter vs. the _OFFLINE_ROLLBACK_SEGMENTS parameter is that once the _CORRUPTED_

ROLLBACK_SEGMENTS parameter is used to corrupt the rollback segments, they can never be brought online and used again.

To summarize, using the _CORRUPTED_ROLLBACK_SEGMENTS parameter to start up the database and dropping the rollback segments involved almost immediately guarantees database inconsistency if not loss of data integrity, which may or may not be detected immediately. There is no quick and simple way to find that out ahead of time. Even a database rebuild does not guarantee user data integrity. So, you need to consider very carefully your options before using any of these parameters.

## _DB_BLOCK_COMPUTE_CHECKSUMS

_DB_BLOCK_COMPUTE_CHECKSUMS is the next **init.ora** parameter worth mentioning. This parameter is not documented before release 7.2, and is normally used to debug corruptions that happen on disk. When this parameter is set, while reading a block from disk to cache, Oracle will compute and write a checksum to the block. Next time the same block is read, Oracle computes the checksum again and compares it with the value that's in the block. If they differ, it's an indication that the block is corrupted on disk. Oracle marks the block as corrupt and signals an error. There is an overhead involved in using this parameter, and it should normally be used only when advised by Oracle Support Services

## _DB_BLOCK_CACHE_PROTECT

Another diagnostic **init.ora** parameter is _DB_BLOCK_CACHE_PROTECT. If this parameter is set to TRUE, Oracle will catch stray writes made by processes in the buffer cache. Using operating-system-dependent utilities and system calls, it forces every process to lock a block in memory before writing to it. If a process writes to a location in memory that it hasn't locked, then an access violation occurs, giving diagnostic trace information.

The _DB_BLOCK_CACHE_PROTECT parameter is not implemented on most UNIX ports, since memory management under UNIX does not make it easy to implement this parameter. On some operating systems, using this parameter might have a severe impact on performance. Refer to your operating system manual to see whether this feature is implemented on your OS.

One problem with setting any of these events or event codes in the **init.ora** file is that the database needs to be shut down and started up, which is not very practical for a lot of customers with high availability requirements. For example, if a block of a particular user's table gets corrupted, and the DBA decides to work around the corruption by setting event code 10231 and exporting the table, the DBA has to shut the database down and include this event in the **init.ora** parameter, start up the database, and, finally, export the table. In the future releases of Oracle, the **init.ora** parameter EVENT will modify the scope of the **alter session set events** command from a session level to the instance level.

# Analyzing Log Files Using LogMiner

Archived redo log files are very important, especially for database recovery. Each archived redo log file contains a set of database changes. When the database is running in ARCHIVELOG mode, every change made to the database is recorded to the online log file and is finally archived to the archive log files. The ARCH process archives the log files to a specified destination. The database change information, written in the archived log files (as redo records) is very crucial to recovery of the database. In order to read the various database changes recorded in an archived redo log file, you need to open the specified archived log file and its contents. Oracle provides a new tool called *LogMiner* for this purpose. It is of immense help to DBAs for opening the log file and reading its content. Sometimes it helps the DBAs to diagnose a problem by reading the log files. You can use this tool to open both online and archived log files. Using this tool involves the following steps:

1. Setting the environment for the tool to function

2. Creating a database dictionary file

3. Specifying a list of log files to be analyzed through ADD_LOGFILE procedure

4. Starting the LogMiner session to analyze the log file contents

5. Viewing the log file contents

6. Ending the LogMiner session

We will discuss these steps in detail.

## Setting the Environment

To establish a working environment for the tool, you must perform the following:

- Check that the **init.ora** file parameter UTL_FILE_DIR has been set to a valid directory location in your file system.

- Run the **dbmslogmnrd.sql** script in schema SYS to create the necessary package and associated procedures. You can find this script in **%Ora_Home%\ rdbms\admin** directory.

- Create a dictionary file using DBMS_LOGMNR_D.BUILD procedure. This procedure queries the dictionary tables of the database and creates a text-based file that contains dictionary table information. This file, which contains a snapshot of the database catalog, is used by the tool for analyzing log files. You should note that the dictionary file must be created in the same database that generates the log files you want to analyze.

**NOTE**
*You should have access to the archived log files*
*that you want to analyze using this tool.*

### Creating the Database Dictionary File

The database dictionary file can be created using the DBMS_LOGMNR_D.BUILD procedure as follows. In the following example, let us assume that you have the initialization parameter UTL_FILE_DIR to **c:\backup** in your **init.ora** file. Prior to running this procedure, you should have executed the **dbmslogmnrd.sql** script; otherwise, you will get the ORA-06550 error.

```
SQL> EXECUTE dbms_logmnr_d.build('dictionary.ora','c:\backup');
PL/SQL procedure successfully completed.
SQL>
```

You can verify the newly created **dictionary.ora** file in the specified directory **c:\backup**.

### Specifying a List of Log Files to be Analyzed

Before running the LogMiner tool, you should supply a list of log files that you want to analyze using the tool. You can use the ADD_LOGFILE procedure associated with the DBMS_LOGMNR package to create a list of log files for the tool.

The syntax of the procedure is as follows:

```
DBMS_LOGMNR.ADD_LOGFILE(
    LogFileName         IN VARCHAR2,
    Options             IN BINARY_INTEGER default ADDFILE );
```

When executing the procedure, you need to specify the log file name with its directory location. You also need to specify whether you want to start a new list or add the log files to an existing list, as shown above in the Options parameter. For example, to create a new list with a log file **00454AMPLE001001S00454.ARC**, which is located in the directory **c:\oracle\oradata\test\archive\**, use the following command:

```
SQL> EXECUTE DBMS_LOGMNR.ADD_LOGFILE(LogFileName
=>'c:\oracle\oradata\test\archive\00454AMPLE001001S00454.ARC',Options => dbms_logmnr.NEW);
PL/SQL procedure successfully completed.
SQL>
```

You have to execute the procedure for each log file that you want to add to the list. You can also remove a log file using the procedure DBMS_LOGMNR.REMOVEFILE.

### Starting the LogMiner Session to Analyze the Log File Contents

In order to analyze the log files that you have added, you have to start the LogMiner session. You can use the START_LOGMNR procedure option of the DBMS_LOGMNR package for this purpose. The syntax of the procedure is as follows:

```
DBMS_LOGMNR.START_LOGMNR(
    startScn          IN NUMBER default 0,
    endScn            IN NUMBER default 0,
    startTime         IN DATE default '01-jan-1988',
    endTime           IN DATE default '01-jan-2988',
    DictFileName      IN VARCHAR2 default '',
    Options           IN BINARY_INTEGER default 0 );
```

In this procedure, you have the option to specify the start and end SCN values and time parameters to filter the redo records you want to analyze. When you specify the start SCN value, LogMiner considers redo records with SCN greater than or equal to the specified start SCN value. If it is the end SCN value, then the tool considers redo records with SCN value less than or equal to the specified end SCN value; otherwise, it will fail to start the session. Timestamp specification is also the same as the start SCN and end SCN specifications. Except for the DictFileName parameter, all other parameters are optional parameters. The following is the example for using the DBMS_LOGMNR.START_LOGMNR procedure for starting the LogMiner session:

```
SQL> EXECUTE DBMS_LOGMNR.START_LOGMNR(DictFileName =>'c:\backup\dictionary.ora');
PL/SQL procedure successfully completed.
SQL>
```

After starting the LogMiner session, you can query the V$LOGMNR_CONTENTS table that contains the log file contents.

### Viewing the Log File Contents

The log file **00454AMPLE001001S00454.ARC** has been added to the list of log files that need to be analyzed, as mentioned in the earlier section, "Specifying a List of Log Files to Be Analyzed." The LogMiner tool opens the entire list of specified log files and populates the V$LOGMNR_CONTENTS table with redo record details. In the following example, the query output of the V$LOGMNR_CONTENTS table gives all the changes made by the user DEMO.

```
SQL>SELECT SCN, LOG_ID, USERNAME, SQL_REDO, SQL_UNDO FROM V$LOGMNR_CONTENTS WHERE
USERNAME='DEMO';
SCN       LOG_ID    SQL_REDO                    SQL_UNDO
------    ------    --------------------        -------------------
210148    450       set transaction
                    read write
```

```
210148    450        update DEMO.TEST       update DEMO.TEST set
                     set SNAME = 'COKE'     NAME ='PEPSI' where
                     where ROWID =          ROWID = 'AAAA+AAADAAAAAoAA4';
                     'AAAA+AAADAAAAAoAA4';
210150    450        commit;
SQL>
```

**NOTE**

*The above output has been reformatted to fit on the
printed page so that the correct information appears
in the appropriate column.*

The above query output shows that an update has been done. The value PEPSI
has been changed to COKE. You can see that a redo was generated to change the
value to COKE. An undo value is also recorded in the log file for the value PEPSI.
From this output, you can view all the changes made to the database with their
respective SCN values. You have the option to specifically query the table for all
changes made to the database by a particular user with their SCN values, including
database corruption entries. From this data, you can find the time and SCN for a
specific transaction, which can be used in change-based recovery. The V$LOGMNR_
CONTENTS table includes multiple sets of placeholder columns. Each set contains a
name column, a redo value column, and an undo value column. Each placeholder
column set can be assigned to a table and column through a LogMiner assignment
file (**logmnr.opt**). After a placeholder column is assigned, it can be used to select
changes to the assigned column and table from the redo log stream.

### Ending the LogMiner Session
After analyzing the log, you need to end the LogMiner session using the following
DBMS_LOGMNR.END_LOGMNR procedure. To end a LogMiner session, execute
the procedure as follows:

```
SQL> DBMS_LOGMNR.END_LOGMNR;
PL/SQL procedure successfully completed.
SQL>
```

# Diagnosing Database Problems Using OEM-Diagnostic Pack

Oracle Diagnostics Pack is a set of easy-to-use applications and is tightly integrated
with Oracle Enterprise Manager console. It is highly helpful in automating database
problem detection and generating reports on database resource usage. The diagnostic
pack allows DBAs to collect information on database activities, and interpret them

to pinpoint problem areas and fix them in an efficient way. In this chapter we describe how the tool can be used to trace database problems. The diagnostic pack contains the following tools:

- Oracle Advanced Events Tests

- Trace Manager

- Trace Data Viewer

- TopSessions

- Lock Manager

- Capacity Planner

- Performance Manager

**NOTE**
*Configuration issues of these applications will not be discussed in this chapter. For configuring details, please refer to* Oracle Enterprise Manager Configuration Guide Release 2.0.

**NOTE**
*The Oracle Diagnostics Pack must be separately purchased and licensed from Oracle.*

## Oracle Advanced Events Tests

The Event Management System (EMS) within Oracle Enterprise Manager assists the DBA with automatic problem detection and correction. The OEM console provides event management functionality with several event tests. Oracle EMS constantly reads the Oracle alert log file for error messages. As soon as Oracle writes an error to the alert log, the system identifies and reports this to the DBA in the form of event notification.

The Oracle Advanced Event Tests for the database and service types are grouped into the following categories:

- Fault Management Event Tests

- Space Management Event Tests

- Resource Management Event Tests

- Performance Management Event Tests

- Audit Management Event Tests

**Database Fault Management Event Tests**    Severe problems that need immediate attention and possible correction are grouped under this event test. Some examples of such problems are down database, block corruptions, and abrupt stopping of the ARCH process. For example, you can set or remove database events via Create Events from OEM toolbar. In the following example, let us assume that we have created an event in the database PROD to notify a block corruption whenever one occurs. Whenever there is a block corruption, PMON identifies and signals Oracle to write to the alert log file and subsequently the OEM Event Management System detects and notifies the designated administrator for immediate correction. The following procedure illustrates the use of this test. In this example, we set up an event for the database TEST.ORACLE.

In this example, let us see as to how we can set an event to detect any block corruption in a database using Fault Management Event Tests. You should follow the same procedure to define other events as well. From the OEM main window (shown in the Figure 9-1) select the Event | Create Events to create an event.

In this part of General tab of the Create Event window, you should define a suitable event name, a description for the event, and the type of destination (whether it is database, listener, or node). In our example, the destination must be

**FIGURE 9-1.**    *Creating an event from the OEM main menu*

a database. The set of events will differ for the type of destination. Choose the specified destination from the Available Destinations subwindow and add that to the Monitored Destinations subwindow for monitoring, as shown in Figure 9-2. Set the frequency at which the destination has to be checked for the event condition. Once these parameters are defined in this General tab of the Create Event window, click on the Tests tab for choosing the type of event.

You will see all the available tests in the Tests tab, as shown in Figure 9-3. Choose the type of event that you wish to set from the Available Tests subwindow and move that to the Selected Tests subwindow. You can also specify multiple events, if you want to. Click on the Parameters tab for setting event filters for the event test.

Figure 9-4 shows a sample output of the Parameters tab in the Create Event window. For the data block corruption event test, no parameter specification is required. Oracle Event Management System will use the default database credentials set in the preferred credential page of Edit Administrator Preferences window for destinations. You can get this Edit Administrator Preferences window from the System | Preferences toolbar of OEM. If you want to change to other login credentials, you can do so by selecting the Override Preferred Credential radio button and entering a new login name and password.

From the Permissions tab of the Create Event window, you can set permission for administrators to get notification, to view, and to edit the event. You can also enable this event notification to external SNMP (Simple Network Management protocol) services from this window. A sample window of this page property is shown in Figure 9-5.

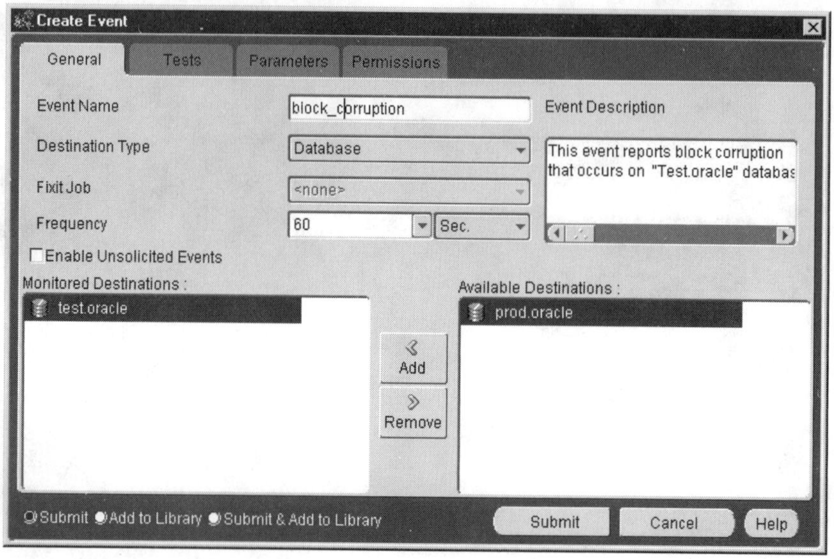

**FIGURE 9-2.** *Defining an event name and destination*

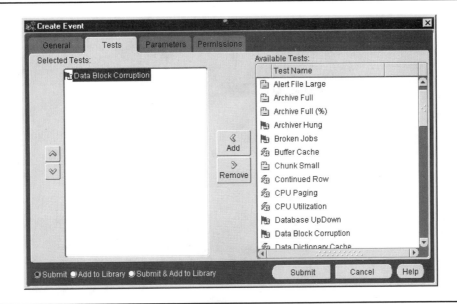

**FIGURE 9-3.**   *Choosing a Data Block Corruption test*

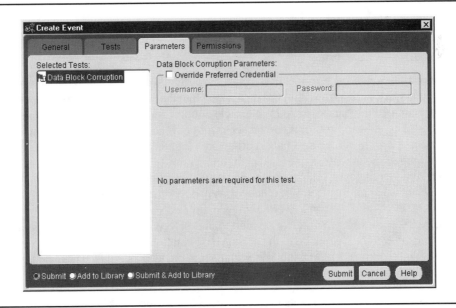

**FIGURE 9-4.**   *Parameter specification for the Data Block Corruption test*

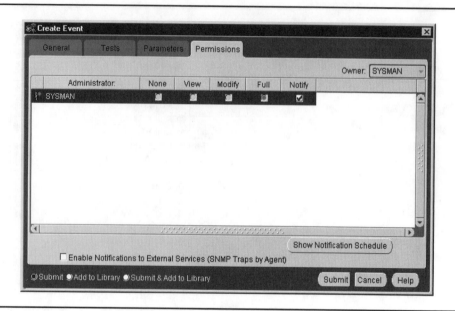

**FIGURE 9-5.**   *Setting permissions to get notification*

Click Submit. Figure 9-6 shows a sample notification of the event data Block_corruption in the OEM window.

Oracle gives you the option to set database events on other events such as Failed Jobs, Error Transactions, or Deferred Transactions to verify whether the database listener is down, the maximum user limit is reached, and so on.

**Space Management Event Tests**    This group of event tests can be set to track possible space problems within the database. Note that around 33 percent of the TARS that come into the database group in Oracle Support Services are space management related. These database events can be set to monitor the growth of the alert log file, space in the archived log destination drive that potentially affects normal database functioning, tablespace segment growth, and so on. To get an alert or warning regarding the archived log device space usage, you should specify a free space threshold value for the Archive Full event. Whenever the free space value falls below this specified threshold limit, Event Management System generates a notification. Figure 9-7 shows such a notification alert in the OEM window. This event generates an alert whenever the free space in the archived destination device falls below 25 percent of its total space (the notification tells you that the device has only 25 percent free space left). In this group, you can also set events to track the following:

■   The maximum extents limit of objects that belong to a tablespace

■   The size of the snapshot log

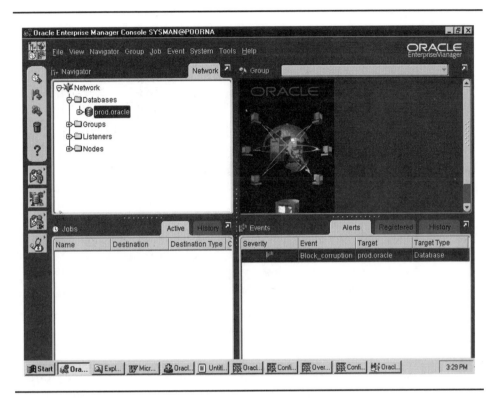

**FIGURE 9-6.** *Notification of the event Block_corruption*

**Resource Management Event Tests**    With the resource management event tests, you can monitor the number of data files limit, locks limit, processes limit, sessions limit, and users limit. You should specify the threshold value for each event while configuring these events.

**Database Performance Management Event Tests**    The Performance Management Event Tests are SYSSTAT table delta, systat table, rollback contention, redo log allocation, network I/O, library cache, in memory sort, index rebuild, free buffer, disk I/O, data dictionary cache, continued row and buffer cache. These event tests monitor the system for performance problems such as buffer cache hit ratio, data dictionary cache miss ratio, disk I/O, free buffers, in-memory sort ratio, library cache miss ratio, rollback contention, row fragmentation (using Continued Row event), and so on. Based on these event notifications, a DBA can attempt to increase performance whenever the specified performance parameters go below the threshold value. There is another set of performance event tests called Node Performance Management Event Tests available with the diagnostic pack to monitor CPU utilization and CPU paging rate.

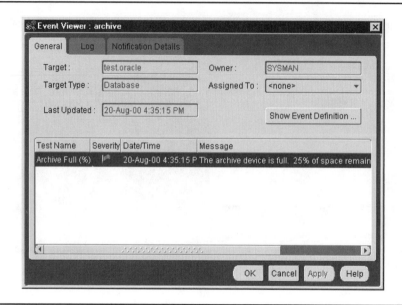

**FIGURE 9-7.** *Alert notification from the Archive Full event*

**Database Audit Management Event Test**    This category of event tests is useful for monitoring the user connection to a specified database. You can specify a single user, a list of users, or all database users in the event for notification.

> **NOTE**
> *For more information, refer to* Oracle Enterprise Manager Performance Monitoring and Planning Guide Release 2.0.

## Oracle Trace Manager

Oracle Trace Manager is a GUI application that runs on the OEM console. The Oracle Trace Manager can be used to create, schedule, and administer Oracle trace files for a specified database or for products that contain Oracle trace API calls in the form of jobs. Oracle Server release 7.3 or higher has the Oracle Trace data collection API for performance data collection. Oracle Trace Manager uses Oracle Intelligent Agent for executing the jobs. The Oracle Trace Manager is able collect a wide variety of data on SQL statements, detailed statistics on SQL events, transaction events, and other useful information for server performance tracing and correction. For collecting trace data, you need to define trace data collection sets. This can be done using Oracle Trace Collection Wizard. Oracle Diagnostic Pack gives you the Oracle Trace Data Viewer GUI application to interpret the data collected by the Trace Manager for better understanding.

**Defining Trace Data Collection Set**    The Oracle Trace Collection Wizard allows you to define the type of data collection that you want for a specified database. Each type contains a set of database events. While defining the data collection sets, you need to specify the collection name, the database on which you want gather statistics, the event sets, and the duration of data collection (start and end time). DBAs should schedule data collection only when they need to track server activities for analyzing database performance. Trace Manager generates huge amounts of data and uses up your disk space. Using Trace Manager, a DBA can collect data on point events such as user connection, occurrence of error in a process (error stack), and so on, which occur instantaneously in a database. Data on duration-based events such as the usage of CPU time, number of input/output operations (I/Os) performed, and memory usage by a query or a user can also be collected through the Oracle Trace Manager. The time-based events are grouped as duration-based events.

During a collection, Oracle Trace Manager writes event data to a collection binary file. You have to format the binary file content in a database and use the Oracle Trace Data Viewer to read the file contents. You can also store the data for future reference.

Before you run Oracle Trace, you should ensure the following:

■ The Oracle Management Server must be configured (both server and agent) and running. Oracle Intelligent Agent and data gathering services must be running on the managed nodes (on which you want to monitor).

■ All the nodes that you want to monitor using Oracle Trace must be discovered through the OEM console before running the Trace Manager.

■ The initialization parameter ORACLE_TRACE_ENABLE must be set to TRUE in the **init.ora** file for all the databases that you want to configure for Oracle Trace.

■ OEM preferred credentials must be set for nodes on which you want to collect data.

■ You must ensure that the OEM job subsystem is working on all nodes and databases that you want to configure for collection.

■ You should also ensure that the trace user account TRACESVR and the trace packages DBMS_ORACLE_TRACE_AGENT and DBMS_ORACLE_TRACE_ USER exist in the database(s). If they don't exist, you should run the **otrcsvr.sql** script manually. This will be in the **%oracle_home%\otrace\admin** directory.

■ Predefined tables (called the Oracle Trace formatter tables) should be created on any one of the databases (valid for releases of Oracle Server prior to 7.3.4 and 8.0.4). These tables are required by the Oracle Trace formatter, which converts and loads an Oracle Trace collection binary file into Oracle tables. You can create these tables in a schema that uses the Oracle Trace formatter by using the following command:

```
vobsh -c "user/password@service" -o CREATE -p "EPCFMT"
```

■ The Oracle Trace Collection Services' control files **facility.dat, collect.dat**, and **regid.dat (process.dat** is renamed to **facility.dat** in Oracle8) exist in the **%oracle_home%/otrace/admin** directory on UNIX systems and in **%oracle_home%\otrace*xx*\admin** on Windows NT on the target nodes. If the control files are missing, run the **otrccref.exe** executable file located in the **%oracle_home%\bin** subdirectory.

Figure 9-8 shows that two data collection sets—namely, poorn051 and poorn052—are configured for the database node POORNA. The General tab gives you the details such as the node, the collection duration, and the database on which the collection set is defined.

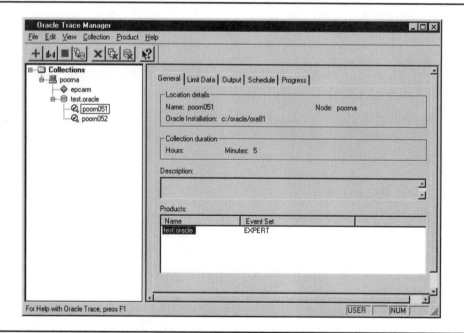

**FIGURE 9-8.** *Data collection sets for the node POORNA*

Figure 9-9 shows the output of the collection status from the Progress tab of the Trace Manager windows. This shows the type of action, the status of each action that was performed for the collection set, and the time of notification. Likewise, the Output tab gives you details of the data collection output file with the extension (**.cdf**) and its format history. You can locate this file in **%oracle_home%\otrace\ admin\cdf** directory.

## Oracle Trace Data Viewer

As mentioned earlier, the Trace Data Viewer reads and interprets the data collected by the Oracle Trace Manager. Oracle Trace Data Viewer is a tool that does the following:

- Sorts and processes large trace data collections

- Extracts and aggregates key metrics

- Presents the information in predefined data views selected by the user

The user can then perform analysis on the data. Oracle Trace Manager writes all the collected data in a flat file that cannot be read or interpreted by DBAs without the help of Oracle Trace Data Viewer. Appropriate tables have to be created in a

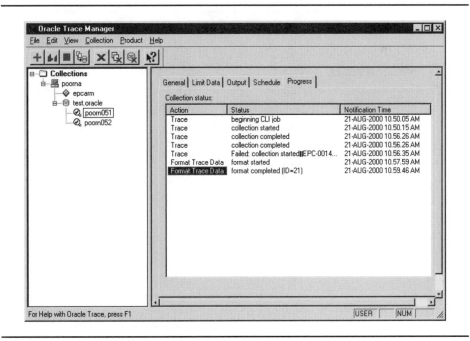

**FIGURE 9-9.** *Collection status information*

user schema for storing the data collection details. For creating these tables, you have to run **vobsh.exe** from the operating system prompt, which is available in the **%Oracle_Home\bin** directory. While executing the executable, you need to specify the designated user to hold the formatter tables. For example, If you want create all these formatter tables in a schema called OEM_DIAG, do the following:

```
C:\ vobsh.exe -c "OEM_DIAG/ OEM_DIAG @net service name" -o CREATE -p "EPCFMT"
```

A few operating systems might not accept double quotes. You should refer to the respective operating system manuals for details. For more details, refer to *Oracle Enterprise Manager Configuration Guide Release 2.0*.

Once data collection is over, you can manually run the Oracle Trace Data Viewer from Oracle Trace Manager. All the collected data will be grouped under different categories like (Disk) I/O statistics, Parse statistics, Elapsed time statistics, CPU statistics, Row statistics, and Sort statistics. Figure 9-10 shows the different categories under SQL Statistics.

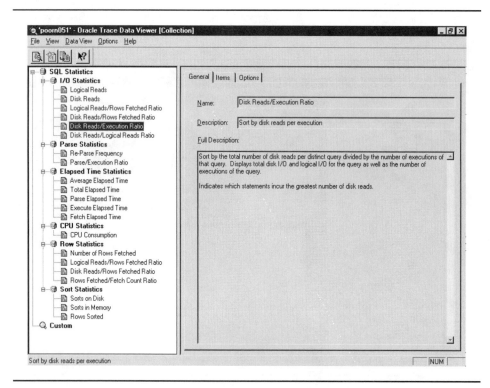

**FIGURE 9-10.** *SQL Statistics in the Oracle Trace Data Viewer*

For viewing disk reads, you should double click on the Disk Reads folder under I/O Statistics from the Oracle Trace Data Viewer window. This will give you disk read statistics for queries that were executed in the database during the data collection duration. Figure 9-11 shows a sample output of Disk Reads I/O statistics for a query.

Likewise, you can get statistics on SQL statement execution for any query that was being executed during data collection. This application also gives you an option to display only the selected statistics from the available pool of statistics. For more information refer to *Oracle Enterprise Manager Oracle Trace User's Guide Release 2.0* and *Oracle Enterprise Manager Configuration Guide Release 2.0*.

### Oracle TopSessions

Oracle TopSessions is a tool for monitoring database resources used by each database connection in real time. It is one of the powerful tools provided by Oracle to the DBAs. You can make use of this tool to get detailed statistics about database sessions and diagnose the source of any database resource problems. When a DBA

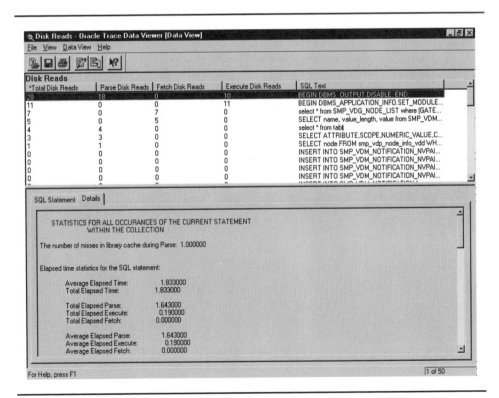

**FIGURE 9-11.** *Disk Reads I/O statistics in the Oracle Trace Data Viewer*

notices a sudden increase in resource usage such as processes, memory, locks, and so on by certain session, she or he can track those sessions using the Oracle TopSessions tool and take appropriate action. This tool also allows you to kill the problematic session. The statistics given by this tool can also be used for better system management and database resource utilization.

Before running the tool against any database (Oracle 7.0 to Oracle 8.1), you have to run the appropriate **smptsi*xx*.sql** script on the database(s) that you want monitor. The *xx* indicates the database version number. You can find these scripts in **%Oracle_OEM_Home%\sysman\admin** directory on Windows NT. Figure 9-12 shows a sample output of Oracle TopSessions running on an Oracle8*i* database called TEST.ORACLE.

The output gives you details such as:

- Each session that was established to the database TEST.ORACLE
- Username
- Oracle session ID for each session

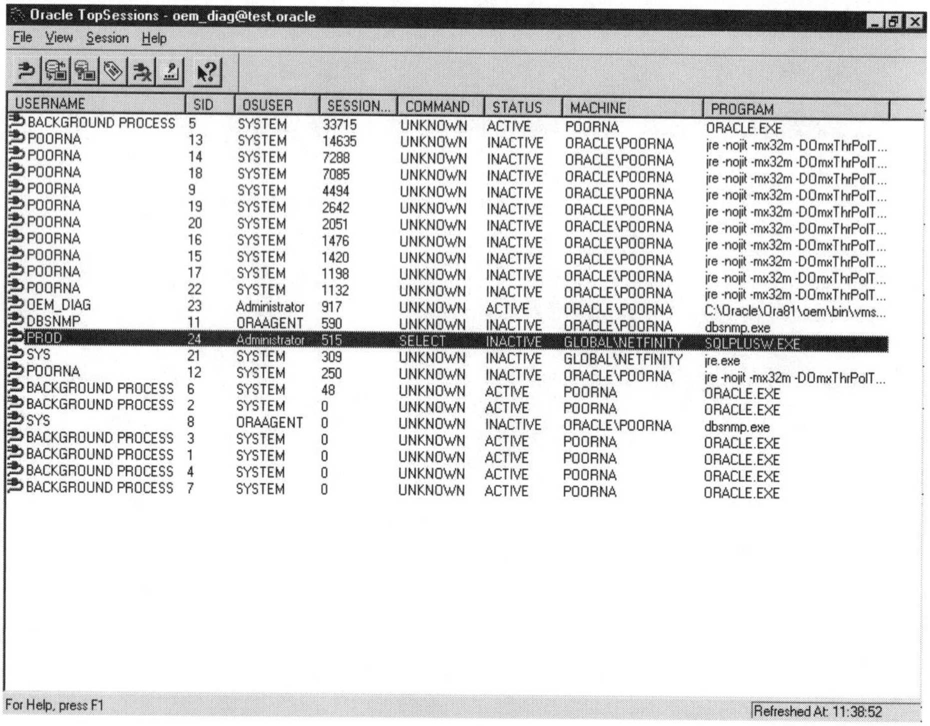


| USERNAME | SID | OSUSER | SESSION... | COMMAND | STATUS | MACHINE | PROGRAM |
|---|---|---|---|---|---|---|---|
| BACKGROUND PROCESS | 5 | SYSTEM | 33715 | UNKNOWN | ACTIVE | POORNA | ORACLE.EXE |
| POORNA | 13 | SYSTEM | 14635 | UNKNOWN | INACTIVE | ORACLE\POORNA | jre -nojit -mx32m -DOmxThrPolT... |
| POORNA | 14 | SYSTEM | 7288 | UNKNOWN | INACTIVE | ORACLE\POORNA | jre -nojit -mx32m -DOmxThrPolT... |
| POORNA | 18 | SYSTEM | 7085 | UNKNOWN | INACTIVE | ORACLE\POORNA | jre -nojit -mx32m -DOmxThrPolT... |
| POORNA | 9 | SYSTEM | 4494 | UNKNOWN | INACTIVE | ORACLE\POORNA | jre -nojit -mx32m -DOmxThrPolT... |
| POORNA | 19 | SYSTEM | 2642 | UNKNOWN | INACTIVE | ORACLE\POORNA | jre -nojit -mx32m -DOmxThrPolT... |
| POORNA | 20 | SYSTEM | 2051 | UNKNOWN | INACTIVE | ORACLE\POORNA | jre -nojit -mx32m -DOmxThrPolT... |
| POORNA | 16 | SYSTEM | 1476 | UNKNOWN | INACTIVE | ORACLE\POORNA | jre -nojit -mx32m -DOmxThrPolT... |
| POORNA | 15 | SYSTEM | 1420 | UNKNOWN | INACTIVE | ORACLE\POORNA | jre -nojit -mx32m -DOmxThrPolT... |
| POORNA | 17 | SYSTEM | 1198 | UNKNOWN | INACTIVE | ORACLE\POORNA | jre -nojit -mx32m -DOmxThrPolT... |
| POORNA | 22 | SYSTEM | 1132 | UNKNOWN | INACTIVE | ORACLE\POORNA | jre -nojit -mx32m -DOmxThrPolT... |
| OEM_DIAG | 23 | Administrator | 917 | UNKNOWN | ACTIVE | ORACLE\POORNA | C:\Oracle\Ora81\oem\bin\vms... |
| DBSNMP | 11 | ORAAGENT | 590 | UNKNOWN | INACTIVE | ORACLE\POORNA | dbsnmp.exe |
| PROD | 24 | Administrator | 515 | SELECT | INACTIVE | GLOBAL\NETFINITY | SQLPLUSW.EXE |
| SYS | 21 | SYSTEM | 309 | UNKNOWN | INACTIVE | GLOBAL\NETFINITY | jre.exe |
| POORNA | 12 | SYSTEM | 250 | UNKNOWN | INACTIVE | ORACLE\POORNA | jre -nojit -mx32m -DOmxThrPolT... |
| BACKGROUND PROCESS | 6 | SYSTEM | 48 | UNKNOWN | ACTIVE | POORNA | ORACLE.EXE |
| BACKGROUND PROCESS | 2 | SYSTEM | 0 | UNKNOWN | ACTIVE | POORNA | ORACLE.EXE |
| SYS | 8 | ORAAGENT | 0 | UNKNOWN | INACTIVE | ORACLE\POORNA | dbsnmp.exe |
| BACKGROUND PROCESS | 3 | SYSTEM | 0 | UNKNOWN | ACTIVE | POORNA | ORACLE.EXE |
| BACKGROUND PROCESS | 1 | SYSTEM | 0 | UNKNOWN | ACTIVE | POORNA | ORACLE.EXE |
| BACKGROUND PROCESS | 4 | SYSTEM | 0 | UNKNOWN | ACTIVE | POORNA | ORACLE.EXE |
| BACKGROUND PROCESS | 7 | SYSTEM | 0 | UNKNOWN | ACTIVE | POORNA | ORACLE.EXE |

**FIGURE 9-12.** *Output of Oracle TopSessions*

- OS user

- The application that was being used by the user who initiated the session

- Node name from which the session was established

To get more details for a specified session, double-click on it. Figure 9-13 gives you sample session details of a session initiated by the user PROD with session ID 515. This drill-down window of the user session gives you every detail about the session. Figure 9-13 shows information in the General tab.

The Statistics tab gives you details about SQL statistics of the user session. The Cursors tab gives you all the SQL statements executed by the session. You can also get the explain plan for the selected queries by clicking the Show Explain Plan button. The Locks tab of the TopSessions Details window provides information about locks held or requested by the session. This information is obtained from the V$LOCK and V$ROLLNAME views. For details, refer to *Using Oracle TopSessions in Oracle Enterprise Manager Performance Monitoring and Planning Guide Release 2.0*

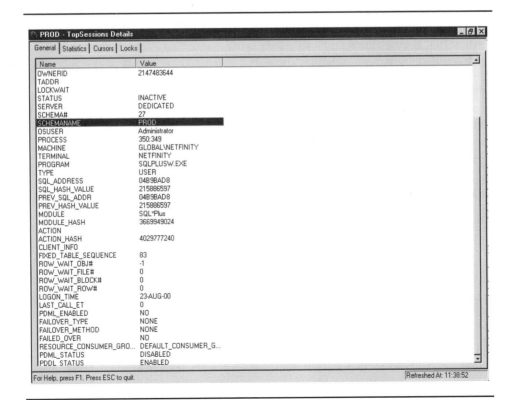

**FIGURE 9-13.** *TopSessions details for schema name PROD*

### Oracle Lock Manager

Oracle Lock Manager is an application that works closely with the Oracle Performance Manager and can be enabled from the Oracle Performance Manager window. It allows DBAs to collect statistics on all database lock details by any or all sessions in a managed database (node) in a real-time environment. You can figure out which lock holds what resources and which user session initiated the lock, in addition to other information, from this manager. It allows you to view all locks or locks created by a specific user and resolve any lock conflicts. It also allows you to terminate any locks from the application itself. It can present the collected lock details in a chart, but to enable charting facility, you need to configure your application to view the statistics in chart form. For more information, refer to *Oracle Enterprise Manager Performance Monitoring and Planning Guide Release 2.0* and *Oracle Enterprise Manager Configuration Guide Release 2.0*.

### Oracle Capacity Planner

Oracle Capacity Planner is an easy-to-use GUI application that works on Oracle Enterprise Manager. It requires the services of Oracle Intelligent Agent and data gatherer services on the managed nodes in order to collect statistics on databases. The Capacity Planner collects statistics from target databases (nodes) at regular intervals and stores the data in a binary file. At a specified interval, the application extracts data from this binary file, converts it to a readable format, and stores it in the Oracle Capacity Planner *historical database* that is configured for the Capacity Planner to store the collected data. You need to configure this application with suitable database credentials in order for the application to store the formatted data. You can configure the application to collect data at specified intervals—for example, during peak data processing hours. For more information, refer to *Oracle Enterprise Manager Performance Monitoring and Planning Guide Release 2.0*.

### Oracle Performance Manager

Oracle Performance Manager is a tool that allows system administrators and database administrators to monitor various system parameters in real time. Some important areas are as follows:

- Memory usage

- Disk I/O contention

- Resource contention

You need to focus on the key metrics of your database, so that you can easily monitor the parameters that most affect your database performance. You can launch the application from the OEM console. The Oracle Performance Manager connects to the Oracle Management Server using the same credentials used to start the OEM console. For more details, refer to *Oracle Enterprise Manager Performance Monitoring and Planning Guide Release 2.0.*

# Detecting and Repairing Data Block Corruption Using the DBMS_REPAIR Package

Selina is the DBA of a terabyte DSS database. She has a table called HISTORY that she uses every day. While working on the table one day, she got the following error:

```
ERROR at line 1:
ORA-01578: ORACLE data block corrupted (file # 22, block # 240)
ORA-01110: data file 22: 'C:\ARCHIVE_HISTORY1.DBF'
SQL>
```

How should Selina deal with this problem? The traditional way is to restore from a backup and recover the data file. This could take Selina a while, as she has 1,000 redo log files to apply. The other option is to drop the table and import it from a table export backup. Selina doesn't keep export backups. Even if she did, it would be a very slow process.

Oracle introduces the DBMS_REPAIR tool to fix block corruptions in tables, partitions, or indexes like this one. However, you need to understand the limitations of this tool before using it. Though DBMS_REPAIR is a package, it is a tool to the DBAs, so we will use the terms "tool" and "package" interchangeably for the rest of this section. By running the DBMS_REPAIR package, Oracle gives you details about corrupt blocks and tells you how to fix them. The DBMS_REPAIR package writes all the necessary details regarding the corrupt data blocks and repair directives in a special table called REPAIR_*key*, where *key* can be any name that you choose. We create the table with the name REPAIR_ADMIN. The REPAIR_ADMIN table has to be created before running the DBMS_REPAIR package against any table or index. In addition to detecting block corruptions, the tool can be used for the following purposes:

- To soft corrupt the blocks, so Oracle knows that it's a corrupted block

- To skip corrupted blocks during full table or index scans

- To manage orphan rows in an index that point to rows in corrupt data blocks

- To rebuild the freelists for the specified table or index

Before using DBMS_REPAIR, you must carefully evaluate the other available options to address data block corruptions with little or no data loss. Such options include media recovery from the most recent backup set, rebuilding the table or index from export dump file, and creating a replication site—if you have replication set up for the affected table. You should also carefully compare the pros and cons of using this tool in addressing the corruptions because running this tool has certain ramifications, which will be discussed later in this section. There are certain issues that you have to consider before using the tool to fix a corrupt block. They are as follows:

■   You cannot access rows in blocks marked corrupt by Oracle. Note that a block may be marked corrupt by Oracle, even though there are rows that you can legitimately access.

■   Referential integrity constraints may be affected when blocks are marked corrupt. In this case, you have to disable the required referential constrains and reenable them after fixing the problem.

■   Index rows might not be in sync with rows in the base table. This will result in database inconsistency. Therefore, you should evaluate how far this tool limits the problem. Running the DBMS_REPAIR tool with the DUMP_ORPHAN_KEYS procedure option can help you identify the affected rows, based on which you can fix the problem by re-creating the affected index, if necessary.

■   Freelist details stored in the data dictionary may not be useful after using this tool to fix the corruption. You need to rebuild the freelist by running the DBMS_REPAIR.REBUILD_FREELISTS procedure.

Figure 9-14 is a flow chart that shows the functionality of the DBMS_REPAIR package.

## Creating DBMS_REPAIR Administration Tables

Before using the DBMS_REPAIR package, you have to create special tables (ORPHAN_*key* and REPAIR_*key*) using the DBMS_REPAIR.ADMIN_TABLES procedure. Oracle uses these admin tables to store information about corrupted blocks in the database. The REPAIR_*key* table will contain information on corrupted blocks that belong to tables or partitioned tables. The ORPHAN_*key* table is used by Oracle to keep information on index entries that point to rows in corrupt data blocks. These details will be used by the package to rebuild corrupted data.

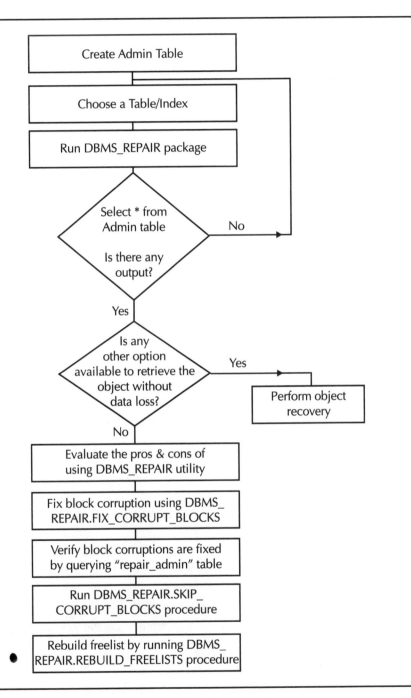

**FIGURE 9-14.** *Functionality flow chart of DBMS_REPAIR package*

The syntax for the DBMS_REPAIR.ADMIN_ TABLES procedure is as follows:

```
DBMS_REPAIR.ADMIN_TABLES (
   table_name IN    VARCHAR2,
   table_type IN    BINARY_INTEGER,
   action     IN    BINARY_INTEGER,
   tablespace IN    VARCHAR2         DEFAULT NULL);
```

Let us see how the package can be used to create DBMS_REPAIR administration tables. For creating the table, you need to perform the following steps:

1. You must log on to the database with SYSDBA privileges. Only user SYS must own the DBMS_REPAIR administration tables.

2. Create a tablespace to hold the administration tables. You can also use an existing tablespace for this purpose. However, creating a separate tablespace with a small size is advisable.

3. Run the package at the SQL*PLUS prompt with all necessary package inputs as follows:

```
DBMS_REPAIR.ADMIN_TABLES ('REPAIR_ADMIN', 1, 1,'REPAIR_TS');
```

In this example, you are directing the package to create a REPAIR_ADMIN table in the REPAIR_TS tablespace. The first variable is the name of the admin table. Note that the table name must be prefixed with "REPAIR_" or "ORPHAN_". If the second variable is 1, the package creates a REPAIR_*key* table. It should be 2 if you want to create the ORPHAN_*key* table. If the third variable is 1, the package performs a "create" operation. If it is 2, the package performs a "delete" operation, and if it is 3, it drops the table. The fourth variable is the name of the tablespace in which the table would be created. The following code shows how to create, delete, and drop the administration tables:

```
SQL> EXEC DBMS_REPAIR.ADMIN_TABLES ('REPAIR_ADMIN', 1, 1,'REPAIR_TS');
PL/SQL procedure successfully completed.
SQL>

SQL> EXEC DBMS_REPAIR.ADMIN_TABLES ('ORPHAN_ADMIN', 2, 1,'USERS');
PL/SQL procedure successfully completed.
SQL>
```

If you want to drop the ORPHAN_ADMIN table, issue the following statement:

```
SQL> EXEC DBMS_REPAIR.ADMIN_TABLES ('ORPHAN_ADMN', 2, 3, NULL);
PL/SQL procedure successfully completed.
```

If you want to clean the table (delete the rows), issue the following statement:

```
SQL> EXEC DBMS_REPAIR.ADMIN_TABLES ('ORPHAN_ADMN', 2, 2,NULL);
PL/SQL procedure successfully completed.
SQL>
```

## Scanning a Specific Table or Index Using the DBMS_REPAIR.CHECK_OBJECT Procedure

The CHECK_OBJECT procedure of the DBMS_REPAIR package should be used to check for data block corruptions that belong to the specified object (table, partition, or index). It populates the REPAIR_ADMN table with information about corruptions and repair directives if it finds any block corruptions. This procedure checks all blocks that are associated with the specified object. Optionally, you may specify a DBA (Data Block Address) range, partition name, or subpartition name when you want to check a portion of an object. To run this procedure, you must know operations such as using PL/SQL functions, variables, various datatypes, passing inputs to the procedure, and how to store the procedure output. Let us see how the procedure can be used to check an object.

First, you should decide which table you want to check for block corruptions. You should also define a variable and its type as NUMBER to store its output. The execution of the procedure will fail if you don't declare a variable prior to running the procedure to capture its output.

The syntax of the procedure is given here:

```
DBMS_REPAIR.CHECK_OBJECT (
    schema_name        IN   VARCHAR2,
    object_name        IN   VARCHAR2,
    partition_name     IN   VARCHAR2         DEFAULT NULL,
    object_type        IN   BINARY_INTEGER DEFAULT TABLE_OBJECT,
    repair_table_name  IN   VARCHAR2         DEFAULT 'REPAIR_TABLE',
    flags              IN   BINARY_INTEGER DEFAULT NULL,
    relative_fno       IN   BINARY_INTEGER DEFAULT NULL,
    block_start        IN   BINARY_INTEGER DEFAULT NULL,
    block_end          IN   BINARY_INTEGER DEFAULT NULL,
    corrupt_count      OUT BINARY_INTEGER) ;
```

The most important variables are the *object_type, repair_table_name,* and *corrupt_count.* The *object_type* can either be a table or an index. For a table (both partitioned and nonpartitioned), you should pass the variable 1 and for index type, pass 2. You must mention the admin table that you have created earlier (REPAIR_ ADMIN or ORPHAN_ADMIN). The variables such as *flags, relative_fno, block_start,* and *block_end* are optional. If you know the range of blocks within the object, you can specify that to limit the scope of the check to a particular block range. If you don't know this, you need to specify it as NULL. If you request to scan an entire table, Oracle will check every block of the table for corruptions. You have to supply the package with input variables (NULL if optional) except the variable *corrupt_count*, which is the output of the package. The *corrupt_count* output gives you the number of corruptions reported during the check. To capture its output, you must define a suitable variable with correct datatype. Once the execution is over, you can query the value of the variable to see the number of reported corruptions.

We have now created a table called DATA with 1,000 rows. Later, we will corrupt this table and run the DBMS_REPAIR package to see how the row count changes at various stages.

```
SQL> SELECT COUNT(*) FROM DATA;
COUNT(*)
----------
       992
SQL>
```

At this point, we corrupt the table DATA.

**NOTE**
*DBAs don't have any tools to corrupt tables or data files for testing. Oracle has internal tools to corrupt blocks for testing purposes. Please don't attempt to corrupt your production tables.*

In the following example, we check the table DATA (for possible corruptions) that belongs to the schema PROD. Let's assume that we have created an administration table called REPAIR_ADMIN in schema SYS. To check this table for corrupt blocks, use the following procedure:

1. Log on to the database as INTERNAL. Declare a VARIABLE with its datatype as NUMBER as follows:

   ```
   SQL> VARIABLE A NUMBER;
   SQL>
   ```

2. Execute the DBMS_REPAIR.CHECK_OBJECT procedure as follows:

   ```
   SQL> EXEC DBMS_REPAIR.CHECK_OBJECT ('PROD','DATA', NULL, 1,
   'REPAIR_ADMN', NULL, NULL, NULL, NULL,:A);
   PL/SQL procedure successfully completed.
   SQL>
   ```

3. To check whether the DBMS_REPAIR package found any block corruptions, query the value of variable A, which will give you the number of corrupt blocks that the package detected during the block check as shown here:

```
SQL> PRINT A;
        A
---------
        1
SQL>
```

This example shows that the package encountered a single block corruption.

4. Query the REPAIR_ADMN table for greater details:

```
SQL> SELECT RELATIVE_FILE_ID FILE, BLOCK_ID BLOCK,
  2, OBJECT_NAME OBJECT, CORRUPT_DESCRIPTION,
  3  REPAIR_DESCRIPTION, MARKED_CORRUPT MARKED FROM REPAIR_ADMN;

FILE BLOCK OBJECT CORRUPT_DESCRIPTION       REPAIR_DESCRIPTION   MARKED
---- ----- ------ --------------------      ------------------   ------
10   24    DATA   kdbchk: xaction header    mark block software  FALSE
                  lock count mismatch       corrupt
                  trans=1 ilk=80 nlo=79

SQL>
```

The query output shows that there is one corrupt block (BLOCK is 24), which belongs to the table DATA in schema PROD. It also tells you that the FILE number is 10. You can get the information regarding the tablespace name and data file name and its location from the data dictionary using the FILE_ID and TABLESPACE_ID for a better understanding of the block corruption and its location. Finally, the REPAIR_ DESCRIPTION column shows that the block should be marked as software corrupt. The MARKED column shows FALSE, indicating that the block is currently not software corrupt. So, the first thing we need to do is to software corrupt this block. This can be done using the FIX_CORRUPT_BLOCKS procedure option.

## Fixing Corrupt Blocks Using the DBMS_REPAIR.FIX_ CORRUPT_BLOCKS Procedure

You should use this procedure only after populating the REPAIR_ADMIN table with block corrupt information. This procedure soft corrupts the blocks mentioned in the REPAIR_ADMIN table. Before soft corrupting any block, the procedure once again checks to ensure that the block is still corrupt and then marks it as software corrupt. Then the REPAIR_ADMIN table is updated with the fix and a timestamp at which the fix was done. Let's continue with the example we started in the previous section.

Now that we have a corrupt block in the REPAIR_ADMIN table, let's fix the corruption by marking it software corrupt. The syntax for running this procedure and an example are shown here:

```
DBMS_REPAIR.FIX_CORRUPT_BLOCKS (
    schema_name       IN  VARCHAR2,
    object_name       IN  VARCHAR2,
    partition_name    IN  VARCHAR2         DEFAULT NULL,
    object_type       IN  BINARY_INTEGER DEFAULT TABLE_OBJECT,
    repair_table_name IN  VARCHAR2         DEFAULT 'REPAIR_TABLE',
    flags             IN  BINARY_INTEGER DEFAULT NULL,
    fix_count         OUT BINARY_INTEGER);

SQL> VARIABLE A NUMBER;
SQL> EXEC
DBMS_REPAIR.FIX_CORRUPT_BLOCKS('PROD','DATA',NULL,1,'REPAIR_ADMN',NULL,:A);
PL/SQL procedure successfully completed.
SQL>
```

You can query the value of the variable A to check how many corrupt blocks are fixed successfully. After the successful execution of the package, query the REPAIR_ADMIN table to check whether the block entries are marked as software corrupt. The query and its output are given here:

```
SQL> SELECT RELATIVE_FILE_ID FILE, BLOCK_ID BLOCK,
  2, OBJECT_NAME OBJECT, CORRUPT_DESCRIPTION,
  3   REPAIR_DESCRIPTION, MARKED_CORRUPT MARKED FROM REPAIR_ADMN;

FILE BLOCK OBJECT CORRUPT_DESCRIPTION       REPAIR_DESCRIPTION   MARKED
---- ----- ------ --------------------      ------------------   ------
10   24    DATA   kdbchk: xaction header    mark block software TRUE
                  lock count mismatch       corrupt
                  trans=1 ilk=80 nlo=79

SQL>
```

In this output, the MARKED column now shows a value of TRUE, indicating that the block in question has been software corrupted. Now let's try to access the table and see how many rows exist. If you recall, we had 1,000 rows when we created the table.

```
SQL> SELECT COUNT(*) FROM DATA;
SELECT COUNT(*) FROM DATA
                     *
ERROR at line 1:
ORA-01578: ORACLE data block corrupted (file # 10, block # 24)
ORA-01110: data file 10: 'C:\TEST2.DBF'
SQL>
```

While Oracle has marked the block software corrupt, you still can't do a full table scan on it. You have to run the DBMS_REPAIR.SKIP_CORRUPT_BLOCKS procedure in order to direct Oracle to skip the blocks that are marked as corrupt during full table or index scan.

You should run the DBMS_REPAIR.SKIP_CORRUPT_BLOCKS procedure immediately after running the DBMS_REPAIR.FIX_CORRUPT_BLOCKS procedure.

## Skipping Corrupt Blocks Using the DBMS_REPAIR.SKIP_ CORRUPT_BLOCKS Procedure

The following example shows how the procedure can be used to skip corrupt blocks using the DBMS_REPAIR.SKIP_CORRUPT_BLOCKS procedure. The procedure has four input variables—the *schema_name*, the *object_name*, the *object_type*, and the *flags* parameter. While the first three have been described earlier, the flags variable takes a numeric value of 1 for skip action and 2 for noskip action while doing full table scan of the corrupted table. The procedure syntax is as follows:

```
DBMS_REPAIR.SKIP_CORRUPT_BLOCKS (
      schema_name IN VARCHAR2,
      object_name IN VARCHAR2,
      object_type IN BINARY_INTEGER DEFAULT TABLE_OBJECT,
      flags       IN BINARY_INTEGER DEFAULT SKIP_FLAG);
SQL> EXEC DBMS_REPAIR.SKIP_CORRUPT_BLOCKS ('PROD','DATA',1,1);
PL/SQL procedure successfully completed.
SQL>
```

When the object specified in the above procedure is a table, skip applies to the table and its associated indexes. When the object is a cluster, it applies to all of the tables in the cluster and their respective indexes.

Coming back to our example, let's run the query on the table DATA. Here's the output:

```
SQL> SELECT COUNT(*) FROM DATA;
  COUNT(*)
----------
       840
SQL>
```

This output shows that after running the DBMS_REPAIR.SKIP_CORRUPT_BLOCKS procedure, you can have access to table data without the ORA-01578 error. Notice the ramification of running the DBMS_REPAIR tool. You have lost 160 rows of data. One main advantage of this tool is that you can retrieve the data past the corrupted block; however, we have lost 160 rows of data in the table.

**NOTE**
*Any corruption that involves the loss of data requires analysis and understanding of whether it violates your business rules. Hence, DBMS_REPAIR is not a magic wand—you must still determine whether the repair approach provided by this package is appropriate for your business. Depending on the nature of the repair, you can lose data, and logical inconsistencies can be introduced; therefore, you need to evaluate the advantages and disadvantages associated with using DBMS_REPAIR with respect to your business rules.*

## Using the DBMS_REPAIR.DUMP_ORPHAN_KEYS Procedure to View Orphaned Keys

This procedure is useful in identifying orphan keys in indexes that are pointing to corrupt rows of the table. (An orphaned key in an index is one that doesn't have a valid row in the table). On successful execution of the procedure, you should query the ORPHAN_ADMIN table and decide whether to rebuild your index or not. For each encountered orphan index key during the execution of the procedure, a row is inserted into the specified ORPHAN_ADMIN table.

The syntax of the procedure is as follows:

```
DBMS_REPAIR.DUMP_ORPHAN_KEYS (
    schema_name        IN  VARCHAR2,
    object_name        IN  VARCHAR2,
    partition_name     IN  VARCHAR2        DEFAULT NULL,
    object_type        IN  BINARY_INTEGER DEFAULT INDEX_OBJECT,
    repair_table_name  IN  VARCHAR2        DEFAULT 'REPAIR_TABLE',
    orphan_table_name  IN  VARCHAR2        DEFAULT 'ORPHAN_KEYS_TABLE',
    flags              IN  BINARY_INTEGER DEFAULT NULL,
    key_count          OUT BINARY_INTEGER);
```

For running the procedure, you have to specify the variables *schema name*, the name of the index (*object_name*) whose keys you want to check for the existence of orphans, and the *object_type* (2 for indexes). Specify the REPAIR_ADMIN and ORPHAN_ADMIN table names for the *repair_table_name* and *orphan_table_name* variables. Following is an example:

```
SQL> EXEC
DBMS_REPAIR.DUMP_ORPHAN_KEYS('PROD','SNO_IDX',NULL,2,'REPAIR_ADMIN','ORPHAN_ADMIN',NULL,:A);
PL/SQL procedure successfully completed.
SQL>
```

A sample (partial) output of the query is given here:

```
SQL> select SCHEMA_NAME, INDEX_NAME, INDEX_ID, TABLE_NAME, KEYROWID, KEY,
DUMP_TIME  from orphan_admin;
SCHEMA_NAME  INDEX_NAME  INDEX_ID TABLE_NAME  TABLE_ID
-----------  ----------  -------- ----------  --------

KEYROWID            KEY                 DUMP_TIME
-----------------   -----------------   ---------

PROD        SNO_IDX    3701     AQUILA     3700
AAAA50ACUAAAIACAgA  *BAAAAAADwgM2/g      17-AUG-00
PROD        SNO_IDX    3701     AQUILA     3700
AAAA50ACUAAAIACAkA  *BAAAAAADwgM3/g      17-AUG-00

SQL>
```

You have to drop and re-create the index SNO_IDX above to avoid any inconsistencies in your queries.

The last thing you need to do while using the DBMS_REPAIR package is to run the DBMS_REPAIR.REBUILD_FREELISTS procedure to reinitialize the freelist details in the data dictionary views. After fixing block corruptions, in order to rebuild the freelist and have access to all the free blocks, you have to run the DBMS_REPAIR.REBUILD_FREELISTS procedure on the specified table or index as follows. The syntax of the procedure is shown here:

```
DBMS_REPAIR.REBUILD_FREELISTS (
     schema_name     IN VARCHAR2,
     object_name     IN  VARCHAR2,
     partition_name  IN VARCHAR2         DEFAULT NULL,
     object_type     IN BINARY_INTEGER DEFAULT TABLE_OBJECT);
```

In this example, we are running the procedure to rebuild the freelist of the table DATA:

```
EXEC DBMS_REPAIR.REBUILD_FREELISTS('PROD','DATA',NULL,1);
SQL> EXEC DBMS_REPAIR.REBUILD_FREELISTS('PROD','DATA',NULL,1);
PL/SQL procedure successfully completed.
SQL>
```

### Limitations of the DBMS_REPAIR PACKAGE

The DBMS_REPAIR package has the following limitations:

- Tables with LOBS, nested tables, and VARRAYS are supported, but the "out of line columns" are ignored.

- Clusters are supported in the CHECK_OBJECT procedure.

- Index-organized tables and LOB indexes are not supported.

- The DUMP_ORPHAN_KEYS procedure cannot be run against bitmap indexes or function-based indexes.

- The DUMP_ORPHAN_KEYS procedure processes keys that are, at most, 3,950 bytes long.

For more information refer to *Oracle8i Supplied Packages Reference Release 8.1.5.*

# Other Diagnostic Utilities

To further collect diagnostic information, a debugger is provided in both Oracle7 and Oracle8. In releases 7.2 and earlier, there is a utility called **oradbx** (on UNIX) or **orambx** (on OpenVMS). From release 7.3 upward, the Server Manager line mode provides a utility called **oradebug**. Both **oradbx** and **oradebug** are discussed next. In addition, various V$ tables are also useful for debugging the RDBMS. A few of them are discussed here.

### ORADBX

This utility has existed for a long time and is used extensively by Oracle Support Services analysts. **oradbx** is a debugger program implemented in 6.0.29 on UNIX for debugging active Oracle processes. **oradbx** sends messages asynchronously to the active Oracle process to dump to trace information of different data structures of Oracle, such as SGA, PGA, state objects, context area, system states, stack trace, core, control file, data file, and *ipc* information. It also allows the user or DBA to turn on event trace when the process is already running. Following is the output of the help screen of **oradbx**. Note that some of these diagnostic traces can be obtained by using the **alter session set events** command as well.

```
(oradbx) help
help                    - print help information
show                    - show status
debug <pid>             - debug process
dump SGA                - dump SGA
dump PGA                - dump PGA
dump stack              - dump call stack
dump core               - dump core without crashing process
```

```
dump level 0            - dump error buffer
dump level 1            - level 0 + call stack
dump level 2            - level 1 + process state objects
dump level 3            - level 2 + context area
dump system 1           - brief system states dump
dump system 2           - full system states dump
dump ipc                - dump ipc information
dump controlfile #      - dump control file at level #
dump datafile #         - dump data file header at level #
dump procstat           - dump process statistics
event <event-trace>     - turn on event trace
unlimit trace           - unlimit the size of trace file
exit                    - exit this program
!                       - shell escape
```

The following example illustrates how to take a process state dump of a process using the **oradbx** utility:

1. Start **oradbx**.

2. Initiate a user process—for example, SQL*PLUS.

3. Determine the *pid* for the user process via a **ps** command.

4. In **oradbx**, enter **debug *pid***.

5. In **oradbx**, enter **dump level 2**.

This will create a trace file with the process state dump.

## Oradebug

Like **oradbx**, this facility in Server Manager (line mode) provides access to Oracle process memory structures, stacks, and so on. Using the **oradebug** utility, a *process state* dump can be generated. It can also be used to dump structures of the SGA. In addition, a particular event can be enabled for an already running Oracle process. The following example shows how SQL trace information for a running Oracle process can be collected in a trace file:

```
SQL> oradebug help
 HELP            [command]                  Describe one or all commands
 SETMYPID                                   Debug current process
 SETOSPID        <ospid>                    Set OS pid of process to debug
 SETORAPID       <orapid> ['force']         Set Oracle pid of process to debug
 DUMP            <dump_name> <level>        Invoke named dump
 DUMPSGA         [bytes]                    Dump fixed SGA
 DUMPLIST                                   Print a list of available dumps
 EVENT           <text>                     Set trace event in process
 SESSION_EVENT   <text>                     Set trace event in session
```

```
DUMPVAR        <p|s|uga> <name> [level]    Print/dump a fixed PGA/SGA/UGA variable
SETVAR         <p|s|uga> <name> <value>    Modify a fixed PGA/SGA/UGA variable
PEEK           <addr> <len> [level]        Print/Dump memory
POKE           <addr> <len> <value>        Modify memory
WAKEUP         <orapid>                    Wake up Oracle process
SUSPEND                                    Suspend execution
RESUME                                     Resume execution
FLUSH                                      Flush pending writes to trace file
TRACEFILE_NAME                             Get name of trace file
LKDEBUG                                    Invoke lock manager debugger
NSDBX                                      Invoke CGS name-service debugger
-G                                         OPS-command prefix
SETINST                                    set instance list
RELEASE                                    release instance list
CORE                                       Dump core without crashing process
IPC                                        Dump ipc information
UNLIMIT                                    Unlimit the size of the trace file
PROCSTAT                                   Dump process statistics
CALL           <func> [arg1] ... [argn]   Invoke function with arguments
SQL> spool off

SQL> oradebug setospid 9431
Oracle pid: 12, Unix process pid: 9431, image: oraclevk803
SQL> oradebug unlimit
Statement processed.
SQL> oradebug event 10046 trace name context forever, level 12
Statement processed.
SQL> oradebug flush
Statement processed.
```

In this example, the Server Manager process attaches to the Oracle process 9431. This means the Server Manager process has access to the private memory of the Oracle process 9431. Next, the trace file size is set to *unlimited*, and then the SQL trace event is enabled (event 10046). Note above that after attaching to the Oracle process, we can also take a process state of the Oracle process (not shown in the example). Finally, we flush the trace information collected to disk.

**NOTE**
*Avoid dumping the background processes because exiting **oradbx** or **oradebug** could kill the background process, thus killing the Oracle instance.*

## V$ Views

Oracle maintains a set of tables called *dynamic performance tables*. The data in these tables keeps changing during normal operation of the database. Though most of these tables contain data relating to the performance of the database, there are some tables that contain information regarding the control file, data files, log files, and backup information. There are a set of V_$ views created on top of these tables, and public synonyms are created on top of these views, which are prefixed with V$. Some of the V$ objects (commonly referred to as V$ views) are extremely useful when diagnosing common problems on a day-to-day basis and monitoring the normal database activity and its status. Some V$ views are very useful when diagnosing problems relating to backup and recovery. A list of some of the important V$ views is given here:

| | | |
|---|---|---|
| V$ACCESS | V$INSTANCE | V$RECOVERY_FILE |
| V$ARCHIVE | V$LOCK | V$ROLLNAME |
| V$BACKUP | V$LOG | V$ROLLSTAT |
| V$BGPROCESS | V$LOGFILE | V$SESSION |
| V$DATABASE | V$LOG_HISTORY | V$SESSION_WAIT |
| V$DATAFILE | V$PROCESS | V$THREAD |
| V$DB_OBJECT_CACHE | V$RECOVERY_LOG | V$WAITSTAT |
| V$INSTANCE_RECOVERY | V$DBFILE | V$SYSTEM_EVENT |
| V$SQLAREA | V$SGASTAT | V$SESS_IO |

## Lock Utility

Locking is an essential aspect of any dynamic system in which there are many users or many processes sharing access to a single object or resource. Depending on the applications being used, or on the circumstances of process termination, there are situations that can cause processes to hang while waiting for a particular resource. For many DBAs, determining which process is "holding up" the rest involves intense scrutiny of the MONITOR LOCK screen.

There are two types of locks that are managed by the Oracle RDBMS: internal locks and data (DML) locks.

The two categories of internal locks are *latches* and *enqueues*. Both latches and enqueues protect shared-memory data structures. Enqueues, however, protect other objects as well, such as access to control files, redo logs, and rollback segments. Latches are internal locks that are only held for short periods of time. Structures such as the LRU chain in the buffer cache are protected by this latch, so processes that make modifications to the LRU chain need to acquire this latch before doing so.

When a process wishes to acquire a latch, most of the time it tries to acquire it with a *willing to wait* request. This means that it is willing to retry in the event that it cannot acquire the latch on the first try. The overall assumption here is that since latches will be held for very short periods of time, a short waiting period followed by a retry will be successful. Enqueues are also internal locks, but they differ from latches in that there is a built-in mechanism for processes to wait in line for the resource. Enqueues can be held in shared or exclusive mode, depending on the degree of sharing allowed for the given transaction. One of the most common types of enqueue is the row cache enqueue.

Data locks, which are present to protect the consistency of the data, can be held in exclusive or shared mode at the row or table level. With row-level locking, this category of locks is the most common source of contention.

To diagnose locking problems, or systems hung on locks, Oracle provides a file called **utllockt.sql**. This script file can be quite useful for filtering out relevant information from the MONITOR LOCK screen, especially when there may be many other users whose shared locks are not really interesting to the problem at hand. The **utllockt.sql** script is normally found in the **%ora_home%/rdbms/admin** directory and clearly describes how to use this script and interpret the output. The next listing shows a sample output when script file **utllockt.sql** is run.

According to the documentation in the **utllockt.sql** script, "if a process id is printed immediately below and to the right of another process, then it is waiting for that process. The process ids printed at the left hand side of the page are the ones that everyone is waiting for." In the following table, process 10 is waiting for process 7. The lock information to the right of the process ID describes the lock that this process is waiting for. By definition, process 7 is not waiting for any locks. What this implies is that 7 is the process that is *blocking* or *holding up* the other processes from acquiring the resources that they wait for. Also shown is the fact that process 10 is waiting for a transaction (TX) lock.

| Waiting Session | Lock Type | Mode_ Requested | Mode_ Held | Lock_ ID1 | Lock_ ID2 |
|---|---|---|---|---|---|
| 7 | None | | | | |
| 10 | Transaction | Exclusive | Exclusive | 327731 | 721 |

# Debugging the RDBMS

In this section, we discuss when and why you would want to take dumps of control files, data blocks, log file headers, and data file headers using the **alter session** command. Using the **alter system** command to dump contents of redo log files is discussed as well. Then, using some sample dumps, some of the data structures useful to the DBA are discussed.

## Control File Dump

The control file can be dumped using the **alter session** statement while the database is open or mounted. Oracle Support Services uses the control file dump to diagnose various problems. Sometimes the wrong version of a data file or log file might be used by the DBA to start up the database. Oracle will normally give an error, as shown in this example:

ORA–01130: data file version num incompatible with ORACLE Version num.

Other reasons for dumping the control file would include the following:

- To check the status of the data files

- To see the status of the threads

- To see if the database was ever started using the RESETLOGS option

- To check *compatibility version*

- To see checkpointing information

- To see the status of online log file information

There is much more information that Oracle Support Services and developers use from a control file dump when debugging various RDBMS problems.

One common reason DBAs dump the control file is to see the full path names of all the data files and log files when the database is down. When the database is open or mounted, selecting from V$DATAFILE gives the same information gotten by reading the control file dump. However, more content has been added to the control files in Oracle8. Oracle7, Oracle8, and Oracle8*i* control file dumps are explained next.

# Oracle7 Control File Dump

Listing 9-2 shows a partial dump of a control file. Each line of the dump is numbered for reference in the discussion that follows. This dump is taken on an OpenVMS system running Oracle7 release 7.1.2.

**Listing 9-2**

```
 1.  Dump file ORA_DUMP:WRVMS_RDBMS5_FG_SQLDBA_009.trc
 2.  15-APR-1994 17:53:34.01:
 3.  Oracle7 Server Release 7.1.2.0.0 - Beta Release
 4.  With the procedural, distributed, parallel query and Parallel Server options
 5.  PL/SQL Release 2.1.2.0.0 - Beta
 6.  Parallel server mode inactive
 7.  Proc: 0x3d4251f0 RVELPURI2 User: [113,040] RVELPURI Term: VTA824:
 8.  Image: $1$DUA41:[V7ROOT.RDBMS]SQLDBA.EXE;8
 9.  Enqueue Quota: 200
10.  vsnsql=a vsnxtr=3
11.  cpu 4700 13000202 vms V5.5-2H4 clustered with 35 nodes
12.  scsnd: WRVMS, ndname: WRVMS, sys$node WRVMS::
13.  cpuid 13 rev 01CB00000000000013000202 archflg 38F0
14.  hwmdl: 459 hwnm: VAX 4000-700A cpus: FFFFFFFF cpush: 0 active: 1, avail: 1
```

```
15.  locktbl size 160000 max 480001 resource hash size 65535
16.  15-APR-1994 17:53:33.46:
17.  *** SESSION ID:(7.51)
18.  DUMP OF CONTROL FILES, Seq # 12181 = 2f95
19.  FILE HEADER:
20.  Software vsn=117489664=700c000, Compatibility Vsn= 117477376= 7009000
21.  Db Id=3283207049=c3b1c389, Db Name='RDBMS5'
22.  Control Seq=12181=2f95, File size=280=118
23.  File Number=0, Blksiz=512, File Type=1
24.  DATABASE ENTRY:
25.  (offset = 0x163, size = 129, max = 1, hi = 1)
26.  DF Version:creation=0x700c000 compatable=0x700b000, Date 01/08/93 11:30:17
27.  DB Name RDBMS5
28.  Database flags = 0x00000041
29.  Incmplt recovery scn: 0.00000000 Resetlogs scn: 0.00000000 count: 0x0
30.  Redo Version: creation=0x700c000 compatable=0x700c000
31.  #Data files = 8, #Online files = 5
32.  Database checkpoint: Thread=1 scn: 1f4.912955e8
33.  Threads: #Enabled=3, #Open=1, Head=1, Tail=1
34.  enabled  threads:  01110000 00000000 00000000 00000000 00000000 00000000 00000000
35.  Max log members = 2, Max data members = 1
36.  Log hist = 1134, Arch list: Head=4, Tail=1, Force scn: 1f4.01068bb6
37.  REDO THREAD ENTRIES:
38.  (offset = 0x200, size = 80, max = 16, hi = 3)
39.  THREAD #1 - status:0x7 thread links forward:0 back:0
40.  #logs:2 first:1 last:2 current:1 last used seq#:0x3c5
41.  enabled at scn: 1f4.010687d6 01/04/94 12:49:59
42.  opened at 04/14/94 23:25:04 by instance RDBMS5
43.  Checkpointed at scn: 1f4.912955e8 04/15/94 17:52:56
44.  thread:1 rba:(3c5.2.10)
45.  enabled  threads:  01110000 00000000 00000000 00000000 00000000 00000000 00000000
46.  THREAD #2 - status:0x6 thread links forward:0 back:0
47.  #logs:3 first:3 last:7 current:4 last used seq#:0x87
48.  enabled at scn: 1f4.010686fc 01/03/94 16:10:17
49.  opened at 02/14/94 17:32:22 by instance RDBMS5
50.  Checkpointed at scn: 1f4.01068b6f 02/18/94 17:18:04
51.  thread:2 rba:(87.1b.0)
52.  enabled  threads:  01110000 00000000 00000000 00000000 00000000 00000000 00000000
53.  THREAD #3.
54.  LOG FILE ENTRIES:
55.  (offset = 0x700, size = 63, max = 32, hi = 7)
56.  LOG FILE #1:
57.  (#  1) DISK$WR3:[V7ROOT.DB_RDBMS5]ORA_LOG1.RDO
58.  Thread 1 redo log links: forward=2 backward=0
59.  siz=0x3e8 seq=0x3c5 hws=0x1 bsz=512 nab=0xffffffff flg=0x8
60.  Archive links: fwrd=0 back=5 Prev scn: 1f4.912955e5
61.  Low scn: 1f4.912955e7 04/15/94 17:52:56
62.  Next scn: ffff.ffffffff 04/15/94 17:52:47
63.  LOG FILE #2:
64.  (#  2) DISK$WR3:[V7ROOT.DB_RDBMS5]ORA_LOG2.RDO
65.  Thread 1 redo log links: forward=0 backward=1
66.  siz=0x3e8 seq=0x3c4 hws=0x2 bsz=512 nab=0x2 flg=0x1
67.  Archive links: fwrd=0 back=0 Prev scn: 1f4.01068bb6
68.  Low scn: 1f4.912955e5 04/15/94 17:52:47
69.  Next scn: 1f4.912955e7 04/15/94 17:52:56
70.  LOG FILE #3.
71.  DB FILE ENTRIES:
72.  (offset = 0xee0, size = 107, max = 32, hi = 8)
```

```
73.  DATA FILE #1:
74.  (#  3) DISK$WR3:[V7ROOT.DB_RDBMS5]ORA_SYSTEM.DBS
75.  size=5120 bsize=2048 status=xf head=3 tail=3 dup=1
76.  Checkpoint cnt:888 scn: 1f4.912955e8 stop scn: ffff.ffffffff 04/14/94 23:16:33
77.  Creation Checkpointed at scn: 0.00000003 01/08/93 11:30:50
78.  thread:1 rba:(1.3.10)
79.  enabled  threads:01000000 00000000 00000000 00000000 00000000 00000000 00000000
80.  Offline scn: 0.00000000
81.  Online Checkpointed at scn: 0.00000000 01/01/88 00:00:00
82.  thread:0 rba:(0.0.0)
83.  enabled  threads:00000000 00000000 00000000 00000000 00000000 00000000 00000000
84.  DATA FILE #2:
85.  (#  4) DISK$WR3:[V7ROOT.DB_RDBMS5]ORA_SYSTEM2.DBS
86.  size=512 bsize=2048 status=xf head=4 tail=4 dup=1
87.  Checkpoint cnt:836 scn: 1f4.912955e8 stop scn: ffff.ffffffff 04/14/94 23:16:33
88.  Creation Checkpointed at scn: 80.000bc80f 01/19/93 12:52:55
89.  thread:1 rba:(27.250.192)
90.  enabled  threads:01000000 00000000 00000000 00000000 00000000 00000000 00000000
91.  Offline scn: 0.00000000
92.  Online Checkpointed at scn: 0.00000000 01/01/88 00:00:00
93.  thread:0 rba:(0.0.0)
94.  enabled  threads:00000000 00000000 00000000 00000000 00000000 00000000 00000000
95.  DATA FILE #3:
96.  (#  5) DISK$WR3:[V7ROOT.DB_RDBMS5]USERS1.DBS
97.  size=5120 bsize=2048 status=xe head=5 tail=5 dup=1
98.  Checkpoint cnt:69 scn: 1f4.912955da stop scn: ffff.ffffffff 04/14/94 23:30:37
99.  Creation Checkpointed at scn: 1f4.01068793 01/04/94 11:58:38
100. thread:2 rba:(68.25e.186)
101. enabled  threads:01100000 00000000 00000000 00000000 00000000 00000000 00000000
102. Offline scn: 1f4.912955af
103. Online Checkpointed at scn: 1f4.912955ba 04/14/94 23:32:08
104. thread:1 rba:(3c3.19c.14)
105. enabled  threads:01110000 00000000 00000000 00000000 00000000 00000000 00000000
106. DATA FILE #4:
107. (#  8) DISK$WR3:[V7ROOT.DB_RDBMS5]TEST1.DBS
108. size=1024 bsize=2048 status=x80 head=8 tail=8 dup=1
109. DATA FILE #5:
110. (#  9) DISK$WR3:[V7ROOT.DB_RDBMS5]ORA_SYSTEM3.DBS
111. size=5120 bsize=2048 status=xf head=9 tail=9 dup=1
112. DATA FILE #6:
113. (# 11) DISK$WR3:[V7ROOT.DB_RDBMS5]TEST.DBS
114. size=5 bsize=2048 status=x10 head=11 tail=11 dup=1
115. DATA FILE #7:
116. (# 14) DISK$WR3:[V7ROOT.DB_RDBMS5]TEST2.DBS
117. size=5 bsize=2048 status=x80 head=14 tail=14 dup=1
118. DATA FILE #8:
119. (# 15) DISK$WR3:[V7ROOT.DB_RDBMS5]TEST3.DBS
120. size=10 bsize=2048 status=x86 head=15 tail=15 dup=1
121. LOG FILE HISTORY ENTRIES:
122. (offset = 0x8060, size = 24, max = 1600, hi = 1134)
123. Earliest log history:
124. Record 1: Thread=1 Seq#=1 Link=1
125. Low scn: 0.00000001 01/08/93 11:30:25 Next scn: 0.00000076
126. Latest log history:
127. Record 1134: Thread=1 Seq#=964 Link=1133
128. Low scn: 1f4.912955e5 04/15/94 17:52:47 Next scn: 1f4.912955e7
129. *** END OF DUMP ***
```

Lines 1–17 of Listing 9-2 give the trace file header information. This includes information of the foreground process that created this trace file, the executable this process was running, a timestamp, the Oracle version number, and, finally, information concerning the operating system. Line 18 indicates that this is the dump of a control file. At the beginning of any file dump, Oracle records a similar set of information regarding the database files, and this is known as the *generic file header* information. Lines 19–23 give the generic file header information. Note that this generic file header information would be the same for any data file or log file in this database.

Line 20 shows the *software version* to be 0x700c000. This is the hexadecimal representation that is equivalent to 7.0.1.2.0.0 in the decimal form. This is the Oracle version under which this control file was created. Note that the current version of the software is release 7.1.2, which means that the Oracle software version has been upgraded after the original install. The *compatibility version* (7.0.9.0.0) is the lowest version of Oracle software with which the format of this control file is compatible.

The *Db Id (0xc3b1c389)* on line 21 is the database identification number, which is created by the hashed database name and creation time. This identification number is placed in all generic file headers and verified when the database is started. *Db Name* is the database name.

The control file sequence number on line 22 indicates the number of times this control file has been updated. This can be considered as the version of the control file. *File size* is the physical size of the control file in blocks. The number 280 is the decimal value and 118 is its hex representation. Note that this doesn't include the file header block. So, 281 * block size gives the size of the control file in bytes. The block size is given on the next line as 512 bytes, which is the same as the operating system block size. Oracle defines file types for control files, log files, and database files. Line 23 indicates that the control file type is 1 and the file number is zero.

After the generic file header, the control file dump is divided into five sections:

- Database entry
- Redo thread entries
- Log file entries
- Database file entries
- Log file history entries

The *database entry* portion of the control file gives information regarding the database. Lines 24–36 of Listing 9-2 contain data structures that belong to the database entry. Let's examine some of the important data structures.

Line 25 gives the *offset* in hexadecimal bytes. This is the offset at which the database entry starts in the control file, and *size* is the size of the database entry in bytes.

Line 29 is of importance to DBAs. These structures are normally updated after doing incomplete recovery. If count is a nonzero value, then Resetlogs SCN gives the SCN value at which the database was open with the RESETLOGS option. We have learned in Chapter 6 that Oracle will not allow the DBA to apply redo to this database that was created before the Resetlogs SCN. This is why the DBA must take a backup of the database after starting it up with the RESETLOGS option.

On line 31, *#Data files* gives the number of data files that belong to the database, whether offline or online. The files that are dropped from the database (using the **drop tablespace** command) are not counted. In this database, there are a total of eight data files, of which three files are offline.

Line 33 gives information regarding the total number of threads that are enabled and open. If *#open* is greater than one, this indicates that this database is running with the PARALLEL SERVER option. Note that this database is accessed by only one instance, but two more threads have been created (*#enabled=3*). The instance that started the database has one thread open. The other two threads are enabled but not open.

Line 35 shows that this database can have a maximum of two log file members per group. The parameter MAXLOGMEMBERS is specified during the creation time of the database. Note that the maximum number of data file members is one. At this time, Oracle doesn't support mirroring of data files. This is reserved for future use.

Line 36 gives the last updated entry in the circular log history table that resides in the control file. Any redo with a start SCN below the *force SCN* will be forced to archive out. The force SCN is the SCN before which all log files are archived out.

*Redo thread entries* is the second part of the control file dump, which starts at line 37. On line 38, *max* indicates the maximum number of redo threads that can be enabled and *hi* gives the number of threads currently enabled. Since three threads are enabled, the information of thread 1 follows from lines 39–45, the information of thread 2 from lines 46–52, and so on.

The status on line 39 indicates that this thread is publicly enabled and open. Note that the status of thread 1 is different from that of thread 2 (line 39 vs. line 46). This is because thread 2 is publicly enabled but not open.

Line 40 gives some important information regarding the log file groups of thread 1. The *#logs* indicates the number of log file groups that thread 1 has, and the *current* log file group that the LGWR process is writing to is log #1. This log file has a log sequence number of 0x3c5 (hex), as indicated on line 40. The SCN at which thread 1 is enabled is given, followed by the timestamp on line 41. Similarly, the next line gives the timestamp at which this thread was opened.

The third part of Listing 9-2 gives the *log file entries* information for each log file group of all the threads. As indicated on line 55 (hi = 7), there are a total of seven log file groups. The full path name of the first log file is given on line 57.

The next two lines indicate that this log file belongs to thread 1 and the size of the log file is 0x3e8 (hex). The sequence number of this log file is 0x3c5 (hex) and the log file, similar to the control file, has a block size of 512 bytes. The structure *nab* is the next available block in the log file that the LGWR process can write to. If this log file is the current log file that the LGWR process is writing to, then this value is set to infinity, as shown on line 59. When a log switch happens, a low SCN is allocated to the new log file, which is the same as the high SCN of the log file that it just filled. The high SCN of a current log is infinite. The low SCN and next SCN on lines 61 and 62 are the low and high SCN values of the log file.

The fourth part of Listing 9-2 gives the *data file entries* information for each data file, starting at line 71. Line 72 indicates, similar to the log file entries, that there are eight data files in this database. The full path name of the data file is given. When you select from the V$DATAFILE view, this is where it gets the information. The *status* indicates that this file belongs to the system tablespace.

On line 76, the checkpoint counter has a value 888. This is the number of times a checkpoint was done on this file. This counter keeps incrementing every time a checkpoint is done on this file, even when the data file is in hot backup mode. The *stop SCN* is the SCN after which no recovery is required for this file. Note that this value will be set only when the database is shut down normally. While the database is open, this value is set to infinity.

Oracle7 introduced a new **alter database create datafile** command. This command allows a DBA to create and recover a new data file when the original file is lost. So, Oracle keeps track of the SCN value from which recovery needs to be applied after creating such a file. On line 77 is the creation checkpoint SCN, meaning that this was the SCN when this file was created. When a file is taken offline (by taking the tablespace offline), the SCN at which the file is taken offline is recorded as the offline SCN in the control file. This is shown on lines 80 and 102. The offline SCN on line 80 corresponds to that of the system data file, and thus has a zero value since system data files can never be taken offline. Line 102 shows the offline SCN at which USER1.DBS is taken offline.

Similarly, when a tablespace is put in hot backup mode by using the **alter tablespace begin backup** command, a checkpoint is done on all the data files that belong to this tablespace. This is recorded as the *online checkpointed at SCN* as shown on lines 81 and 103. This information is recorded for every data file.

It is interesting to observe the status set for different data files. Note that the data files **ora_system.dbs**, **ora_system2.dbs**, and **ora_system3.dbs** belong to the SYSTEM tablespace. Every other data file belongs to its own tablespace, which has the same name as its data file. Before taking the control file dump, the following was done:

- Tablespace TEST was taken offline immediate.

- Tablespaces TEST1 and TEST2 were taken offline normal.

- Tablespace TEST3 was put in READ ONLY mode (available from release 7.1).

- Tablespace USER1 was put in HOT BACKUP mode.

Now observe the status of each data file given in Listing 9-2.

The last portion of Listing 9-2 gives the information regarding *log file history entries*. The control file dump, even when set to level 10, doesn't dump the complete log history table. There is a special event to dump the log history entries, which we discussed in the previous section. If the database is open, selecting from the V$LOG_HISTORY table gives all the entries. Line 122 indicates that a total of 1,600 log history entries can be stored in the control file, of which 1,134 records are created. Note that this is a circular table. The first and last records from this table are given when the control file is dumped. Line 124 gives the log sequence number and the thread number of the first entry. The next line gives the low and high SCNs that are recorded in this log file. Similar information is given for the latest entry of the log file history table.

# Oracle8 Control File Dump

An example of an Oracle8 control file dump is shown in Listing 9-3. Only the sections that have been added to the Oracle8 control file are explained in the following sections.

**Listing 9-3**

```
DUMP OF CONTROL FILES, Seq # 850 = 0x352
  FILE HEADER:
      Software vsn=134217728=0x8000000, Compatibility Vsn=134217728=0x8000000
      Db Id=2990569313=0xb2407761, Db Name='VK803'
      Control Seq=850=0x352, File size=260=0x104
      File Number=0, Blksiz=2048, File Type=1
      DATABASE ENTRY:
        (blkno = 0x1, size = 192, max = 1, in-use = 1, last-recid= 0)
DF Version: creation=0x8000000 compatible=0x8000000, Date  08/18/97 06:24:33
DB Name "VK803"
Database flags = 0x00006001
Controlfile Creation Timestamp  08/18/97 06:24:33
Incmplt recovery scn: 0x0000.00000000
Resetlogs scn: 0x0000.00000001 Resetlogs Timestamp  08/18/97 06:24:33
Prior resetlogs scn: 0x0000.00000000 Prior resetlogs Timestamp  01/01/88 00:00:00
Redo Version: creation=0x8000000 compatable=0x8000000
#Data files = 2, #Online files = 2
Database checkpoint: Thread=1 scn: 0x0000.000125d7
Threads: #Enabled=1, #Open=1, Head=1, Tail=1
enabled  threads:   01000000 00000000 00000000 00000000 00000000 00000000
  00000000 00000000
Max log members = 2, Max data members = 1
Arch list: Head=2, Tail=1, Force scn: 0x0000.00008966
Snapshot Controlfile filename
```

```
  (name #5) /vobs/oracle/dbs/snapcf_vk803.f
 Snapshot Controlfile checkpoint scn: 0x0000.0000d797 11/03/97 03:20:52
 Controlfile Checkpointed at scn: 0x0000.000125d7 01/01/88 00:00:00
 thread:0 rba:(0x0.0.0)
 enabled  threads:  00000000 00000000 00000000 00000000 00000000 00000000
  00000000 00000000
     CHECKPOINT PROGRESS RECORDS:
     (blkno = 0x3, size = 104, max = 1, in-use = 1, last-recid= 0)
THREAD #1 - status:0x2 flags:0x0 dirty:0
low cache rba:(0xffffffff.ffffffff.ffff) on disk rba:(0x109.a.0)
on disk scn: 0x0000.000125db 11/03/97 22:24:56
     REDO THREAD RECORDS:
     (blkno = 0x3, size = 104, max = 1, in-use = 1, last-recid= 0)
THREAD #1 - status:0x7 thread links forward:0 back:0
 #logs:2 first:1 last:2 current:1 last used seq#:0x109
 enabled at scn: 0x0000.00000001 08/18/97 06:24:33
disabled at scn: 0x0000.00000000 01/01/88 00:00:00
 opened at 11/03/97 22:24:52 by instance vk803
Checkpointed at scn: 0x0000.000125d7 11/03/97 22:24:52
 thread:1 rba:(0x109.2.10)
 enabled  threads:  01000000 00000000 00000000 00000000 00000000 00000000
  00000000 00000000
 log history: 264
     LOG FILE RECORDS:
     (blkno = 0x4, size = 72, max = 32, in-use = 2, last-recid= 2)
LOG FILE #1:
  (name #1) /vobs/oracle/dbs/t_log1.f
 Thread 1 redo log links: forward: 2 backward: 0
 siz: 0x3e8 seq: 0x00000109 hws: 0x2 bsz: 512 nab: 0xffffffff flg: 0x8 dup: 1
 Archive links: fwrd: 0 back: 2 Prev scn: 0x0000.0000d790
 Low scn: 0x0000.000125d6 11/03/97 22:24:52
 Next scn: 0xffff.ffffffff 11/03/97 03:19:56
LOG FILE #2:
...
DATA FILE #1:
  (name #3) /vobs/oracle/dbs/t_db1.f
creation size=17408 block size=2048 status=0xe head=3 tail=3 dup=1
 tablespace 0, index=1 krfil=1 prev_file=0
 unrecoverable scn: 0x0000.000082b2 08/29/97 00:38:23
 Checkpoint cnt:281 scn: 0x0000.000125d7 11/03/97 22:24:52
 Stop scn: 0xffff.ffffffff 11/03/97 15:21:22
 Creation Checkpointed at scn: 0x0000.00000003 08/18/97 06:24:40
 thread:1 rba:(0x1.3.10)
 enabled  threads:  01000000 00000000 00000000 00000000 00000000 00000000
  00000000 00000000
 Offline scn: 0x0000.00000000 prev_range: 0
 Online Checkpointed at scn: 0x0000.00000000 01/01/88 00:00:00
 thread:0 rba:(0x0.0.0)
 enabled  threads:  00000000 00000000 00000000 00000000 00000000 00000000
  00000000 00000000
 Hot Backup end marker scn: 0x0000.00000000
..
     TABLESPACE RECORDS:
     (blkno = 0x23, size = 68, max = 32, in-use = 2, last-recid= 2)
TABLESPACE #0 SYSTEM: recno=1
 First datafile link=1  Number of rollback segments=0
 Tablespace PITR mode start scn: 0x0000.00000000 01/01/88 00:00:00
 Tablespace PITR last completion scn: 0x0000.00000000 01/01/88 00:00:00
```

```
TABLESPACE #1 USERS: recno=2
...
    LOG FILE HISTORY RECORDS:
        (blkno = 0x27, size = 36, max = 224, in-use = 224, last-recid= 264)
Earliest record:
 RECID #41 Recno 41 Record timestamp  08/18/97 06:27:21 Thread=1 Seq#=41 Link-Recid=40
  Low scn: 0x0000.000018fa 08/18/97 06:27:16 Next scn: 0x0000.000019a2
Latest record:
 RECID #264 Recno 40 Record timestamp  11/03/97 22:24:52 Thread=1 Seq#=264 Link-Recid=263
  Low scn: 0x0000.0000d790 11/03/97 03:19:56 Next scn: 0x0000.000125d6
.......
RECID #41 Recno 41 Record timestamp  08/18/97 06:27:21 Thread=1 Seq#=41 Link-Recid=40
  Low scn: 0x0000.000018fa 08/18/97 06:27:16 Next scn: 0x0000.000019a2
    OFFLINE RANGE RECORDS:
        (blkno = 0x2b, size = 56, max = 36, in-use = 0, last-recid= 0)
    ARCHIVED LOG RECORDS:
        (blkno = 0x2c, size = 584, max = 100, in-use = 0, last-recid= 0)
    BACKUP SET RECORDS:
        (blkno = 0x49, size = 40, max = 50, in-use = 2, last-recid= 2)
Earliest record:
 RECID #1 Recno 1 Record timestamp  11/03/97 03:57:13
  Backup set key: stamp=316238227, count=3
  Backup contains: <full datafiles>
  Backup set is NOT part of the incremental strategy
  Blocksize=2048 Piece-Count=1 Level=0 Time:
Latest record:
 RECID #2 Recno 2 Record timestamp  11/03/97 04:03:25
  Backup set key: stamp=316238602, count=4
  Backup contains: <full datafiles>
  Backup set is NOT part of the incremental strategy
  Blocksize=2048 Piece-Count=1 Level=0 Time:
 RECID #1 Recno 1 Record timestamp  11/03/97 03:57:13
  Backup set key: stamp=316238227, count=3
  Backup contains: <full datafiles>
  Backup set is NOT part of the incremental strategy
  Blocksize=2048 Piece-Count=1 Level=0 Time:
    BACKUP PIECE RECORDS:
        (blkno = 0x4a, size = 736, max = 66, in-use = 2, last-recid= 2)
Earliest record:
 RECID #1 Recno 1 Record timestamp  11/03/97 03:57:10 piece #1
  Backup set key: stamp=316238227, count=3
  Flags: <concurrent access>
  Device: DISK
  Handle: /tmp/aatry316238227
  Media-Handle:
  Comment:
  Tag:
Latest record:
 RECID #2 Recno 2 Record timestamp  11/03/97 04:03:22 piece #1
  Backup set key: stamp=316238602, count=4
  Flags: <concurrent access>
  Device: DISK
  Handle: /tmp/aausr316238602.4
  Media-Handle:
  Comment:
  Tag:
 RECID #1 Recno 1 Record timestamp  11/03/97 03:57:10 piece #1
  Backup set key: stamp=316238227, count=3
```

```
      Flags: <concurrent access>
      Device: DISK
      Handle: /tmp/aatry316238227
      Media-Handle:
      Comment:
      Tag:
        BACKUP DATAFILE RECORDS:
          (blkno = 0x62, size = 116, max = 69, in-use = 2, last-recid= 2)
Earliest record:
 RECID #1 Recno 1 Record timestamp  11/03/97 03:57:13 File=2 Incremental backup level=0
   File is NOT part of the incremental strategy
   Backup set key: stamp=316238227, count=3
   Creation checkpointed at scn: 0x0000.000083a6 11/03/97 02:46:54
   File header checkpointed at scn: 0x0000.0000d7a6 11/03/97 03:57:10
   Resetlogs scn and time scn: 0x0000.00000001 08/18/97 06:24:33
   Incremental Change scn: 0x0000.00000000
   Absolute Fuzzy scn: 0x0000.00000000
   Newly-marked media corrupt blocks  1 Total media corrupt blocks 1
   Total logically corrupt blocks 0  Block images written to backup 22
   Blocks scanned for backup 5120  Block size 2048
   Low Offline Range Recid 0
Latest record:
 RECID #2 Recno 2 Record timestamp  11/03/97 04:03:25 File=2 Incremental backup level=0
   File is NOT part of the incremental strategy
   Backup set key: stamp=316238602, count=4
   Creation checkpointed at scn: 0x0000.000083a6 11/03/97 02:46:54
   File header checkpointed at scn: 0x0000.0000d7ac 11/03/97 04:03:22
......
 RECID #1 Recno 1 Record timestamp  11/03/97 03:57:13 File=2 Incremental backup level=0
   ......
      BACKUP LOG RECORDS:
        (blkno = 0x66, size = 76, max = 79, in-use = 0, last-recid= 0)
      DATAFILE COPY RECORDS:
        (blkno = 0x69, size = 660, max = 64, in-use = 0, last-recid= 0)
      BACKUP DATAFILE CORRUPTION RECORDS:
        (blkno = 0x7e, size = 44, max = 46, in-use = 2, last-recid= 2)
Earliest record:
 RECID #1 Recno 1 Record timestamp  11/03/97 03:57:13 File=2 Piece #1 Starting block #3
Block count=1
   Backup set key: stamp=316238227, count=3
   Flags: <newly corrupt>
   For logically corrupt block: scn of corrupting change: scn: 0x0000.00000000
Latest record:
RECID #2 Recno 2 Record timestamp  11/03/97 04:03:25 File=2 Piece #1 Starting block #3
Block count=1
   Backup set key: stamp=316238602, count=4
   Flags: <newly corrupt>
   For logically corrupt block: scn of corrupting change: scn: 0x0000.00000000
 RECID #1 Recno 1 Record timestamp  11/03/97 03:57:13 File=2 Piece #1 Starting block #3
Block count=1
   Backup set key: stamp=316238227, count=3
   Flags: <newly corrupt>
   For logically corrupt block: scn of corrupting change: scn: 0x0000.00000000
      DATAFILE COPY CORRUPTION RECORDS:
        (blkno = 0x7f, size = 40, max = 50, in-use = 0, last-recid= 0)
      DELETION RECORDS:
        (blkno = 0x80, size = 20, max = 101, in-use = 0, last-recid= 0)
*** END OF DUMP ***
```

## Checkpoint Progress Records

Checkpoint progress records are used to record the state of the buffer cache efficiently in case instance or crash recovery is required. Each record occupies one block in the control file and contains information about the buffer cache of the owning instance. This information is used along with the thread record to determine how much redo needs to be applied by thread recovery. In this record, the *low cache rba* indicates a redo value (an address within the redo log file) at which recovery can begin. All buffers with lower redo values have been written already. The *on-disk-rba* is the highest redo value that is on disk. Instance recovery will have to apply redo up to this point. Finally, *on-disk-scn* is the corresponding SCN at the *on-disk-rba*. It is needed in the case that the *on-disk-rba* points to a block that was never written. In this situation, the *on-disk-scn* will become the high SCN of the thread. Following is an example of the *checkpoint progress record* in the control file:

```
CHECKPOINT PROGRESS RECORDS:
     (blkno = 0x3, size = 104, max = 1, in-use = 1, last-recid= 0)
THREAD #1 - status:0x2 flags:0x0 dirty:0
low cache rba:(0xffffffff.ffffffff.ffff) on disk rba:(0x109.a.0)
on disk scn: 0x0000.000125db 11/03/97 22:24:56
```

## Tablespace Records

Each tablespace is listed in the *tablespace record*. A link to the first data file in the tablespace is shown. Tablespace Point-In-Time Recovery (TSPITR) start SCN and completion SCN are also recorded. The fixed view V$TABLESPACE also reports this information:

```
TABLESPACE RECORDS:
     (blkno = 0x23, size = 68, max = 32, in-use = 2, last-recid = 2)
TABLESPACE #0 SYSTEM: recno=1
 First datafile link=1  Number of rollback segments=0
 Tablespace PITR mode start scn: 0x0000.00000000 01/01/88 00:00:00
 Tablespace PITR last completion scn: 0x0000.00000000 01/01/88
 00:00:00
TABLESPACE #1 USERS: recno=2
```

## Offline Range Records

When a tablespace is taken *offline* with the NORMAL option or is made *read only* and brought back *online* or *read-write*, an offline range record is created in the control file. This record contains information such as the file number that is taken offline, along with a timestamp, the SCN at which the data file is taken offline, and the last SCN at which it is checkpointed. You can see more information on these records using the fixed view V$OFFLINE_RANGE. No offline range record is created if a data file is individually taken offline or a tablespace is taken offline with the IMMEDIATE option. The following code is part of the control file that describes this record:

```
    OFFLINE RANGE RECORDS:
        (blkno = 0x4b, size = 56, max = 36, in-use = 3, last-recid= 3)
Earliest record:
 ......
Latest record:
 RECID #3 Recno 3 Record timestamp  10/27/97 17:38:18 File=4 Link-Recid=2
 Offline scn: 0x0000.00036dbf
 Online checkpointed at scn: 0x0000.00036dc3 10/01/97 20:54:33
 thread:1 rba:(0x151.dd.bc)
```

## Archived Log Records

When an online redo log is archived successfully or cleared, an archived log record is created. Also, when an archive log is restored from a backup set or a copy, an archived log record gets created. The *thread number*, *log sequence number*, and *resetlogs change number* are written to the archived log record when a log file is updated. This information can also be viewed using the fixed view V$ARCHIVED_LOG.

## Backup Set Records

When Recovery Manager completes a backup set successfully, a backup set record is created in the control file(s). This record shows the *backup set stamp*, an ordered count of the backup set, contents of backup set (archive logs, incremental or a full data file), block size, and the number of backup pieces. More information on each backup set completion can be obtained by using the fixed view V$BACKUP_SET.

```
    BACKUP SET RECORDS:
        (blkno = 0x49, size = 40, max = 50, in-use = 2, last-recid= 2)
Earliest record:
 ......
Latest record:
 RECID #2 Recno 2 Record timestamp  11/03/97 04:03:25
   Backup set key: stamp=316238602, count=4
   Backup contains: <full datafiles>
   Backup set is NOT part of the incremental strategy
   Blocksize=2048 Piece-Count=1 Level=0 Time:
```

## Backup Piece Records

A backup piece record is created for every piece in a successfully completed backup set using Recovery Manager. Information shown in the following dump can also be viewed using the fixed view V$BACKUP_PIECE:

```
       BACKUP PIECE RECORDS:
           (blkno = 0x4a, size = 736, max = 66, in-use = 2, last-recid= 2)
    Earliest record:
    ......
    Latest record:
     RECID #2 Recno 2 Record timestamp  11/03/97 04:03:22 piece #1
       Backup set key: stamp=316238602, count=4
       Flags: <concurrent access>
       Device: DISK
       Handle: /tmp/aausr316238602.4
       Media-Handle:
       Comment:
       Tag:
```

## Backup Data File Records

A backup data file record is created in the control file for every data file in a backup set taken using Recovery Manager. The information shown in this dump includes a *file identifier, backup set stamp, count, creation checkpoint scn, file header checkpoint scn, resetlogs scn, newly marked media corrupt blocks, total media corrupt blocks,* and *total logical block corruptions.* The same information can also be viewed using the fixed view V$BACKUP_DATAFILE.

```
       BACKUP DATAFILE RECORDS:
           (blkno = 0x62, size = 116, max = 69, in-use = 2, last-recid= 2)
    Earliest record:
    ......
    Latest record:
     RECID #2 Recno 2 Record timestamp  11/03/97 04:03:25 File=2 Incremental backup level=0
       File is NOT part of the incremental strategy
       Backup set key: stamp=316238602, count=4
       Creation checkpointed at scn: 0x0000.000083a6 11/03/97 02:46:54
       File header checkpointed at scn: 0x0000.0000d7ac 11/03/97 04:03:22
       Resetlogs scn and time scn: 0x0000.00000001 08/18/97 06:24:33
       Incremental Change scn: 0x0000.00000000
       Absolute Fuzzy scn: 0x0000.00000000
       Newly-marked media corrupt blocks  1 Total media corrupt blocks 1
       Total logically corrupt blocks 0  Block images written to backup 22
       Blocks scanned for backup 5120  Block size 2048
       Low Offline Range Recid 0
```

## Backup Log Records

When a backup containing archived logs is completed successfully using Recovery Manager, a record is inserted for each log in the backup set. These records can also be viewed using the fixed view V$BACKUP_REDOLOG. The information includes *backup set stamp, count, thread number, log sequence number,* SCN at which this log is switched into, SCN at which this log is switched out of, and the size of the log file.

## Data File Copy Records

When a data file is copied using Recovery Manager successfully, a data file copy record is inserted into the control file(s). These records can also be viewed using the fixed view V$DATAFILE_COPY. The information in the following dump includes *datafile copy record stamp, name, tag, datafile absolute number, tablespace relative datafile number,* and all the information shown in backup datafile records:

```
   DATAFILE COPY RECORDS:
      (blkno = 0x23a, size = 660, max = 64, in-use = 3, last-recid= 3)
Earliest record:
.......
Latest record:
 RECID #3 Recno 3 Record timestamp  11/05/97 19:42:17
  File=4 (4) database id=1189248130 block size=2048
  Flags: <deleted>
  Filename: C:\TEMP\TST.BAK
  Creation checkpointed at scn: 0x0000.00003c4c 11/02/97 11:09:27
  File header checkpointed at scn: 0x0000.0002ae03 11/05/97 19:42:15
  Resetlogs scn and time scn: 0x0000.00000001 11/02/97 09:11:30
  Recovery Fuzzy scn and time scn: 0x0000.00000000 01/01/88 00:00:00
  Absolute Fuzzy scn: 0x0000.00000000
  Newly-marked media corrupt blocks 0  Total media corrupt blocks 0
  Total logically corrupt blocks 0  Block images written to backup 512
  Low Offline Range Recid 0
```

## Backup Datafile Corruption Records

During the creation of a backup set, Recovery Manager performs a sanity check on each block before copying it. During this check, if it encounters any corrupted blocks, they are recorded in the control file(s). This dump shows *backup set stamp, count, file#, backup piece number,* the starting block, and number of blocks that are corrupted. These records can also be viewed using the fixed view V$BACKUP_ CORRUPTION.

```
BACKUP DATAFILE CORRUPTION RECORDS:
      (blkno = 0x7e, size = 44, max = 46, in-use = 2, last-recid= 2)
Earliest record:
.......
Latest record:
 RECID #2 Recno 2 Record timestamp  11/03/97 04:03:25 File=2 Piece #1 Starting
block #3 Block count=1
  Backup set key: stamp=316238602, count=4
  Flags: <newly corrupt>
  For logically corrupt block: scn of corrupting change: scn: 0x0000.00000000
 RECID #1 Recno 1 Record timestamp  11/03/97 03:57:13 File=2 Piece #1 Starting
block #3 Block count=1
  Backup set key: stamp=316238227, count=3
  Flags: <newly corrupt>
  For logically corrupt block: scn of corrupting change: scn: 0x0000.00000000
```

## Data File Copy Corruption Records

If Recovery Manager comes across any corruption in a data file during a data file copy execution, it inserts copy corruption records into the control file(s). They can also be viewed using the fixed view V$COPY_CORRUPTION. The information displayed in this dump is the same as in backup corruption records.

## Deletion Records

These records are created to facilitate Recovery Manager's catalog *resync* operation. These records are created when an archived log, a data file copy, or a backup piece is deleted. These records can also be viewed using the fixed view V$DELETED_OBJECT.

```
DELETION RECORDS:
     (blkno = 0x251, size = 20, max = 1619, in-use = 3, last-recid= 3)
Earliest record:
......
Latest record:
 RECID #3 Recno 3 Record timestamp  11/05/97 19:42:45
   Object type=16  Object recid=3  Object timestamp=3 11/05/97 19:42:17
......
```

# Oracle8*i* Control File Dump

An Oracle8*i* control file dump is almost identical to the Oracle8 control file dump, with the exception of the proxy copy record. Listing 9-4 gives a partial dump (beginning and ending portion) of the Oracle8*i* control file. The proxy copy record is explained here.

Oracle records a record for each proxy-copied file in the control file. RMAN uses this information to resynchronize the recovery catalog. The V$PROXY_DATAFILE view gives details about the backup information of a data file and control file that are generated using the proxy copy feature of the RMAN **backup** command. Each row in this view represents a backup of one database file. Similarly, the V$PROXY_ARCHIVEDLOG view gives details about archived log files that are backed up using RMAN's **backup proxy copy** command. Proxy copy is a backup created by a media manager. Backup of the proxy copy can be generated using the RMAN's **backup** command.

### Listing 9-4

```
Dump file C:\Oracle\admin\test\udump\ORA00349.TRC
Sat Aug 12 14:19:59 2000
ORACLE V8.1.6.0.0 - Production vsnsta=0
vsnsql=e vsnxtr=3
Windows NT Version 4.0 Service Pack 5, CPU type 586
```

```
Oracle8i Enterprise Edition Release 8.1.6.0.0 - Production
With the Partitioning option
JServer Release 8.1.6.0.0 - Production
Windows NT Version 4.0 Service Pack 5, CPU type 586
Instance name: test

Redo thread mounted by this instance: 1

Oracle process number: 15

Windows thread id: 349, image: ORACLE.EXE


*** 2000-08-12 14:19:59.296
*** SESSION ID:(17.93) 2000-08-12 14:19:59.281
DUMP OF CONTROL FILES, Seq # 1551 = 0x60f
 FILE HEADER:
      Software vsn=135266304=0x8100000, Compatibility
      Vsn=134217728=0x8000000
      Db Id=1702542330=0x657abbfa, Db Name='TEST'
      Control Seq=1551=0x60f, File size=1598=0x63e
      File Number=0, Blksiz=2048, File Type=1 CONTROL
    .


**********************************************************************
PROXY COPY RECORDS
**********************************************************************
 (blkno = 0x22e, size = 852, max = 572, in-use = 0, last-recid= 0)
*** END OF DUMP ***
```

# Redo Log File Dump

In this section, we will examine the file dump of a redo log file header. To diagnose some of the data corruptions, it is often necessary for Oracle Support Services analysts to take a look at the contents of the redo log file as well. You should use the **alter system** command to dump the contents (redo information) of a redo log file. This command is given in this section.

### File Header

Listing 9-5 gives the output of a redo log file header dump. Note that the **alter system** command dumps the header information to the trace file for every online log file.

Most of the data structures in Listing 9-5 should be familiar to you by now. Lines 1–14 give the header of the trace file. Line 15 indicates that this is a log file header dump. There are three log groups in this database. When the log file or data file header is dumped, the trace file contains not only the header information of the requested file but also its corresponding entries from the control file. In Listing 9-5, lines 16–22 are taken from the *log file entries* portion of the control file for this log group. Lines 23–27 give the *generic file header* stored in the log file. The information in lines 28–35 is derived from the log file header. In other words, the data structures given between lines 16–22 and 28–35 should be identical.

## Listing 9-5

```
1.   Dump file C:\Oracle\admin\test\udump\ORA00346.TRC
2.   Tue Aug 22 14:33:28 2000
3.   ORACLE V8.1.6.0.0 - Production vsnsta=0
4.   vsnsql=e vsnxtr=3
5.   Windows NT Version 4.0 Service Pack 5, CPU type 586
6.   Oracle8i Enterprise Edition Release 8.1.6.0.0 - Production
7.   With the Partitioning option
8.   JServer Release 8.1.6.0.0 - Production
9.   Windows NT Version 4.0 Service Pack 5, CPU type 586
10.  Instance name: test
11.  Redo thread mounted by this instance: 1
12.  Oracle process number: 15
13.  Windows thread id: 346, image: ORACLE.EXE
14.  *** SESSION ID:(16.1867) 2000-08-22 14:50:53.140
15.  DUMP OF LOG FILES: 3 logs in database
16.  LOG FILE #1:
17.  (name #1) C:\ORACLE\ORADATA\TEST\REDO01.LOG
18.  Thread 1 redo log links: forward: 2 backward: 0
19.  siz: 0x800 seq: 0x000001de hws: 0x5 bsz: 512 nab: 0x2e flg: 0x1 dup: 1
20.  Archive links: fwrd: 0 back: 0 Prev scn: 0x0000.0006fb70
21.  Low scn: 0x0000.000749c1 08/21/2000 09:36:02
22.  Next scn: 0x0000.00079811 08/22/2000 08:54:14
23.  FILE HEADER:
24.  Software vsn=135266304=0x8100000, Compatibility Vsn=135266304=0x8100000
25.  Db Id=1702542330=0x657abbfa, Db Name='TEST'
26.  Control Seq=1641=0x669, File size=2048=0x800
27.  File Number=1, Blksiz=512, File Type=2 LOG
28.  descrip:"Thread 0001, Seq# 0000000478, SCN 0x0000000749c1-0x000000079811"
29.  thread: 1 nab: 0x2e seq: 0x000001de hws: 0x5 eot: 0 dis: 0
30.  reset logs count: 0x181a977a scn: 0x0000.00000001
31.  Low scn: 0x0000.000749c1 08/21/2000 09:36:02
32.  Next scn: 0x0000.00079811 08/22/2000 08:54:14
33.  Enabled scn: 0x0000.00000001 07/31/2000 12:11:42
34.  Thread closed scn: 0x0000.00079810 08/21/2000 09:36:38
35.  Log format vsn: 0x8000000 Disk cksum: 0xf4c5 Calc cksum: 0xf4c5
36.  LOG FILE #2:
37.  (name #2) C:\ORACLE\ORADATA\TEST\REDO02.LOG
38.  Thread 1 redo log links: forward: 3 backward: 1
39.  siz: 0x800 seq: 0x000001df hws: 0x3 bsz: 512 nab: 0xad flg: 0x1 dup: 1
40.  Archive links: fwrd: 0 back: 0 Prev scn: 0x0000.000749c1
41.  Low scn: 0x0000.00079811 08/22/2000 08:54:14
42.  Next scn: 0x0000.0007986e 08/22/2000 14:40:02
```

```
43.    FILE HEADER:
44.    Software vsn=135266304=0x8100000, Compatibility Vsn=135266304=0x8100000
45.    Db Id=1702542330=0x657abbfa, Db Name='TEST'
46.    Control Seq=1645=0x66d, File size=2048=0x800
47.    File Number=2, Blksiz=512, File Type=2 LOG
48.    descrip:"Thread 0001, Seq# 0000000479, SCN 0x000000079811-0x00000007986e"
49.    thread: 1 nab: 0xad seq: 0x000001df hws: 0x3 eot: 0 dis: 0
50.    reset logs count: 0x181a977a scn: 0x0000.00000001
51.    Low scn: 0x0000.00079811 08/22/2000 08:54:14
52.    Next scn: 0x0000.0007986e 08/22/2000 14:40:02
53.    Enabled scn: 0x0000.00000001 07/31/2000 12:11:42
54.    Thread closed scn: 0x0000.00079811 08/22/2000 08:54:14
55.    Log format vsn: 0x8000000 Disk cksum: 0x2fcf Calc cksum: 0x2fcf
56.    LOG FILE #3:
57.    (name #3) C:\ORACLE\ORADATA\TEST\REDO03.LOG
58.    Thread 1 redo log links: forward: 0 backward: 2
59.    siz: 0x800 seq: 0x000001e0 hws: 0x1 bsz: 512 nab: 0xffffffff flg: 0x8 dup: 1
60.    Archive links: fwrd: 0 back: 0 Prev scn: 0x0000.00079811
61.    Low scn: 0x0000.0007986e 08/22/2000 14:40:02
62.    Next scn: 0xffff.ffffffff 08/21/2000 09:36:02
63.    FILE HEADER:
64.    Software vsn=135266304=0x8100000, Compatibility Vsn=135266304=0x8100000
65.    Db Id=1702542330=0x657abbfa, Db Name='TEST'
66.    Control Seq=1645=0x66d, File size=2048=0x800
67.    File Number=3, Blksiz=512, File Type=2 LOG
68.    descrip:"Thread 0001, Seq# 0000000480, SCN 0x00000007986e-0xffffffffffff"
69.    thread: 1 nab: 0xffffffff seq: 0x000001e0 hws: 0x1 eot: 1 dis: 0
70.    reset logs count: 0x181a977a scn: 0x0000.00000001
71.    Low scn: 0x0000.0007986e 08/22/2000 14:40:02
72.    Next scn: 0xffff.ffffffff 08/21/2000 09:36:02
73.    Enabled scn: 0x0000.00000001 07/31/2000 12:11:42
74.    Thread closed scn: 0x0000.0007986e 08/22/2000 14:40:02
75.    Log format vsn: 0x8000000 Disk cksum: 0x8e52 Calc cksum: 0x8e52
```

Line 28 gives the most important information that a DBA needs. It indicates that this log group belongs to thread 1, has a log sequence number of 478, a low SCN of 0x0000000749c1, and the next SCN of 0x000000079811. Line 48 shows that the low SCN (79811) of log file #2 is the same as the high SCN of log file #1. Note that the line 68 gives information about the log file #3. The next SCN of infinity (0xffffffffffff) indicates that this is the current online log that the LGWR process is writing to. In Oracle8*i*, one extra line is printed containing the *log format version, disk checksum,* and the *calculated checksum* for each log file. For example, line 35 shows that this log file belongs to version 8 of Oracle. If the disk checksum doesn't match the calculated checksum, there is a possibility that the block got corrupted on disk.

## Dumping Redo

The **alter system** command can be used to dump the contents of a redo log file into your session's trace file. The command can be issued when the database is in a *nomount, mount,* or *open* state. The records from an online or offline log file can be dumped. A redo log file that belongs to a different database on the same operating system can be dumped to trace as well. This is very useful, as many times Oracle Support Services asks the customer to send the complete log file and dumps the contents of it in-house. The complete syntax of this command is given here:

```
ALTER SYSTEM DUMP LOGFILE 'filename' option option...;
option  =  rba min seqno . blockno |
           rba max seqno . blockno |
           dba min fileno . blockno |
           dba max fileno . blockno |
           time min value |
           time max value |
           layer value |
           opcode value
```

Note that the statement is not an **alter session** statement but an **alter system** statement. If no options are specified, this statement dumps the entire contents (redo records) of a log file (online or archive) to trace. The *filename* is the name of the log file to be dumped and should be specified in single quotes. The *rba* is the address of the redo information. If a minimum and maximum value of rba is specified, Oracle dumps only the redo records specified between the addresses to the trace file. Alternatively, if the min and max values of a *dba* (data block address) are specified, Oracle dumps all the changes (redo) for that range of data blocks to trace. Specifying a time range dumps the redo created within that time frame. *Layer* and *opcode* should be specified to dump a particular type of redo—for example, all commit records or end hot backup redo records. The values for the opcode, layer, dba, or rba will be supplied by the Oracle Support Services analyst when needed. The following example illustrates the use of this command:

```
SQL> alter system switch logfile;
Statement processed.
SQL> update backup set c2 = 'phy_backup';
2 rows processed.
SQL> commit;
Statement processed.
SQL> select * from backup;
C1          C2
----        ----
1           phy_backup
2           phy_backup
2 rows selected.
SQL> archive log list
Database log mode              NOARCHIVELOG
Automatic archival             ENABLED
Archive destination            C:\Oracle\oradata\test\\ARCHIVE
Oldest online log sequence 8
```

```
Current log sequence        9
SVRMGR> alter system dump logfile
'C:\Oracle\oradata\test\wdblog2.log';
Statement processed.
SQL> exit
```

In this example, we have opened a new log file by switching logs. An **update** statement has modified two rows and then the transaction is committed. The **archive log list** command shows that the online redo log file with sequence number 9 contains the change made to the table backup. From views V$LOG and V$LOGFILE, the name of the redo log file can be found. The **alter system** statement dumps this online log file. Listing 9-6 shows the output of the trace file created by the **alter system** command.

**Listing 9-6**

```
DUMP OF REDO FROM FILE 'C:\ORACLE\ORADATA\TEST\REDO02.LOG'
 Opcodes *.*
 DBA's: (file # 0, block # 0) thru (file # 2000000, block # 4194303)
 RBA's: 0x000000.00000000.0000 thru 0xffffffff.ffffffff.ffff
 SCN's scn: 0x0000.00000000 thru scn: 0xffff.ffffffff
 Times: creation thru eternity
 FILE HEADER:
       Software vsn=135266304=0x8100000, Compatibility Vsn=135266304=0x8100000
       Db Id=1702542330=0x657abbfa, Db Name='TEST'
       Control Seq=1645=0x66d, File size=2048=0x800
       File Number=2, Blksiz=512, File Type=2 LOG
 descrip:"Thread 0001, Seq# 0000000479, SCN 0x000000079811-0x00000007986e"
 thread: 1 nab: 0xad seq: 0x1df eot: 0 dis: 0
 reset logs count: 0x181a977a Reset scn: 0x0000.00000001
  Low scn: 0x0000.00079811 08/22/2000 08:54:14
 Next scn: 0x0000.0007986e 08/22/2000 14:40:02

REDO RECORD - Thread:1 RBA: 0x0001df.00000002.0010 LEN: 0x0038 VLD: 0x01
SCN scn:  0x0000.00079812 08/22/2000 08:54:14
CHANGE #1 MEDIA RECOVERY MARKER SCN:0x0000.00000000 SEQ:  0 OP:17.3
Crash Recovery at scn:  0x0000.00079810

REDO RECORD - Thread:1 RBA: 0x0001df.00000003.0010 LEN: 0x0254 VLD: 0x01
SCN scn:  0x0000.00079813 08/22/2000 08:54:16
CHANGE #1 TYP:0 CLS:11 AFN:1 DBA:0x00400002 SCN:0x0000.000749e0 SEQ:  1 OP:5.2
ktudh redo: slt: 0x0013 sqn: 0x000000c0 flg: 0x0412 siz: 208 fbi: 0
            uba: 0x004001b2.003b.02    pxid:  0x0000.000.00000000
CHANGE #2 TYP:0 CLS:12 AFN:1 DBA:0x004001b2 SCN:0x0000.000749df SEQ:  2 OP:5.1
ktudb redo: siz: 208 spc: 1796 flg: 0x0012 seq: 0x003b rec: 0x02
            xid:  0x0000.013.000000c0
ktubl redo: slt: 19 rci: 0 opc: 11.1 objn: 15 objd: 15 tsn: 0
Undo type:  Regular undo    Begin trans    Last buffer split:  No
Temp Object:  No
Tablespace Undo:  No
             0x00000000  prev ctl uba: 0x004001b2.003b.01
prev ctl max cmt scn:  0x0000.0006fb8f  prev tx cmt scn:  0x0000.000749c4
KDO undo record:
KTB Redo
```

```
op: 0x04  ver: 0x01
op: L  itl: scn:  0x0000.011.000000c1 uba: 0x004001b2.003b.01
                   flg: C---    lkc:  0      scn: 0x0000.000749e0
KDO Op code: URP  xtype: XA  bdba: 0x0040009e  hdba: 0x0040009d
itli: 1  ispac: 0  maxfr: 1177
tabn: 0 slot: 1(0x1) flag: 0x2c lock: 0 ckix: 0
ncol: 12 nnew: 11 size: 0
col  1: [ 4]  52 42 53 30
col  2: [ 2]  c1 02
col  3: [ 2]  c1 03
col  4: [ 2]  c1 03
col  5: [ 4]  c3 2e 4d 20
col  6: [ 1]  80
col  7: [ 3]  c2 03 13
col  8: [ 2]  c1 32
col  9: [ 1]  80
col 10: [ 2]  c1 04
col 11: [ 2]  c1 02
CHANGE #3 TYP:2 CLS: 1 AFN:1 DBA:0x0040009e SCN:0x0000.000749e0 SEQ:  1 OP:11.5
KTB Redo
op: 0x11  ver: 0x01
op: F  xid: 0x0000.013.000000c0    uba: 0x004001b2.003b.02
Block cleanout record, scn:  0x0000.00079813 ver: 0x01, entries follow...
  itli: 1  flg: 2  scn: 0x0000.000749e0
KDO Op code: URP  xtype: XA  bdba: 0x0040009e  hdba: 0x0040009d
itli: 1  ispac: 0  maxfr: 1177
tabn: 0 slot: 1(0x1) flag: 0x2c lock: 1 ckix: 0
ncol: 12 nnew: 11 size: 0
col  1: [ 4]  52 42 53 30
col  2: [ 2]  c1 02
col  3: [ 2]  c1 03
col  4: [ 2]  c1 03
col  5: [ 4]  c3 30 4d 50
col  6: [ 1]  80
col  7: [ 3]  c2 03 13
col  8: [ 2]  c1 32
col  9: [ 1]  80
col 10: [ 2]  c1 03
col 11: [ 2]  c1 02
CHANGE #4 MEDIA RECOVERY MARKER SCN:0x0000.00000000 SEQ:  0 OP:5.19
session number    = 13
serial  number    = 1
current username = SYS
login   username =
client info       =
OS username       =
Machine name      =
OS terminal       =
OS process id     =
OS program name   =
```

# Data File Dump

Data file dumps are very similar to log file dumps. Data file headers can be dumped
to a trace file using the **alter session** command. All data file header information will
be dumped to the trace file. In this section, a dump of a data file header is shown.
Then, a brief description of a data block dump follows.

## File Header

We first discuss the Oracle7 data file header, and then the new structures added in Oracle8 and 8*i*.

**Oracle7 Data File Header**     Listing 9-7 shows a partial dump of Oracle7 data file headers. The lines are numbered to reference the data structures in the discussion to follow.

Similar to the log file header dump, the dump of a data file header also dumps the control file entry for that data file. This information is derived from the *data file entry* portion of the control file. Information derived from the control file is shown between lines 10 and 19. Information between lines 25 and 31 is derived from the data file header. The *checkpointed at SCN* in the file header (line 29) should match the *SCN* in the control file (line 12). Similarly, the checkpoint counter (indicated as *chkpt cnt* on line 28) in the data file header should match the counter in the control file (indicated as *checkpoint cnt* on line 12). If an old data file is restored before starting up the database, this is how Oracle knows that media recovery for that file is required.

### Listing 9-7

```
1.  Dump file C:\ORACLE7\RDBMS70\trace\ORA07655.TRC
2.  Tue Nov 29 07:01:09 1994
3.  ORACLE V7.0.16.6.0 - Beta vsnsta=1
4.  vsnsql=7 vsnxtr=3
5.  MS-WINDOWS Version 3.10
6.  Tue Nov 29 07:01:09 1994
7.  *** SESSION ID:(6.5)
8.  DUMP OF DATA FILES: 4 files in database
9.  DATA FILE #1:
10. (#  6) C:\ORACLE7\DBS\wdbsys.ora
11. size=4096 bsize=2048 status=xf head=6 tail=6 dup=1
12. Checkpoint cnt:136 scn: 0.0000199a stop scn: ffff.ffffffff 11/27/94 09:20:25
13. Creation Checkpointed at scn: 0.00000003 07/04/94 19:54:13
14. thread:0 rba:(0.0.0)
15. enabled  threads:  00000000 00000000 00000000 00000000 00000000 00000000 00000000
16. Offline scn: 0.00000000
17. Online Checkpointed at scn: 0.00000000 01/01/88 00:00:00
18. thread:0 rba:(0.0.0)
19. enabled  threads:  00000000 00000000 00000000 00000000 00000000 00000000 00000000
20. FILE HEADER:
21. Software vsn=117507584=7010600, Compatibility Vsn= 117485568= 700b000
22. Db Id=1082323460=4082f204, Db Name='ORACLE'
23. Control Seq=386=182, File size=4096=1000
24. File Number=1, Blksiz=2048, File Type=3
25. Creation   at   scn: 0.00000003 07/04/94 19:54:13
26. Backup taken at scn: 0.00000000 01/01/88 00:00:00 thread:0
27. reset logs count:0xd06f592 scn: 0.000018aa recovered at 11/24/94 09:21:45
28. status:0x104 root dba:0x01000179 chkpt cnt: 136 ctl cnt:135
29. Checkpointed at scn: 0.0000199a 11/29/94 06:51:54
30. thread:1 rba:(6.5d.10)
31. enabled  threads:  01000000 00000000 00000000 00000000 00000000 00000000 00000000
32. DATA FILE #2:(4)Oracle8i Data File Header
```

Listing 9-8 shows a partial dump of an Oracle8*i* data file header. There are a few changes to the file headers in Oracle8*i*, and they are discussed here. The lines are numbered to reference the data structures in the discussion that follows.

### Listing 9-8

```
 1.  Dump file C:\Oracle\admin\test\udump\ORA00204.TRC
 2.  Tue Aug 22 10:49:21 2000
 3.  ORACLE V8.1.6.0.0 - Production vsnsta=0
 4.  vsnsql=e vsnxtr=3
 5.  Windows NT Version 4.0 Service Pack 5, CPU type 586
 6.  Oracle8i Enterprise Edition Release 8.1.6.0.0 - Production
 7.  With the Partitioning option
 8.  JServer Release 8.1.6.0.0 - Production
 9.  Windows NT Version 4.0 Service Pack 5, CPU type 586
10.  Instance name: test
11.  Redo thread mounted by this instance: 1
12.  Oracle process number: 14
13.  Windows thread id: 204, image: ORACLE.EXE
14.  *** 2000-08-22 10:49:21.015
15.  *** SESSION ID:(13.891) 2000-08-22 10:49:21.015
16.  DUMP OF DATA FILES: 11 files in database
17.  DATA FILE #1:
18.  (name #4) C:\ORACLE\ORADATA\TEST\SYSTEM01.DBF
19.  creation size=29696 block size=2048 status=0xe head=4 tail=4 dup=1
20.  tablespace 0, index=1 krfil=1 prev_file=0
21.  unrecoverable scn: 0x0000.00000000 01/01/1988 00:00:00
22.  Checkpoint cnt:543 scn: 0x0000.00079812 08/22/2000 08:54:14
23.  Stop scn: 0xffff.ffffffff 08/21/2000 09:36:38
24.  Creation Checkpointed at scn:  0x0000.00000004 07/31/2000 12:11:59
25.  thread:1 rba:(0x1.3.10)
26.  enabled  threads:  01000000 00000000 00000000 00000000 00000000 00000000
27.  00000000 00000000
28.  Offline scn: 0x0000.00000000 prev_range: 0
29.  Online Checkpointed at scn:  0x0000.00000000
30.  thread:0 rba:(0x0.0.0)
31.  enabled  threads:  00000000 00000000 00000000 00000000 00000000 00000000
32.  00000000 00000000
33.  Hot Backup end marker scn: 0x0000.00000000
34.  FILE HEADER:
35.  Software vsn=135266304=0x8100000, Compatibility Vsn=134217728=0x8000000
36.  Db Id=1702542330=0x657abbfa, Db Name='TEST'
37.  Control Seq=1642=0x66a, File size=53056=0xcf40
38.  File Number=1, Blksiz=2048, File Type=3 DATA
39.  Tablespace #0 - SYSTEM  rel_fn:1
40.  Creation   at   scn: 0x0000.00000004 07/31/2000 12:11:59
41.  Backup taken at scn: 0x0000.00000000 01/01/1988 00:00:00 thread:0
42.  reset logs count:0x181a977a scn: 0x0000.00000001 recovered at 08/22/2000 08:54:11
43.  status:0x4 root dba:0x00400219 chkpt cnt: 543 ctl cnt:542
44.  begin-hot-backup file size: 0
45.  Checkpointed at scn:  0x0000.00079812 08/22/2000 08:54:14
46.  thread:1 rba:(0x1df.2.10)
47.  enabled  threads:  01000000 00000000 00000000 00000000 00000000 00000000
48.  00000000 00000000
49.  Backup Checkpointed at scn:  0x0000.00000000
50.  thread:0 rba:(0x0.0.0)
51.  enabled  threads:  00000000 00000000 00000000 00000000 00000000 00000000
```

```
52.  00000000 00000000
53.  External cache id: 0x0 0x0 0x0 0x0
54.  Absolute fuzzy scn: 0x0000.00000000
55.  Recovery fuzzy scn: 0x0000.00000000 01/01/1988 00:00:00
```

Line 21 shows the unrecoverable SCN for a data file in the control file section of the dump. This SCN (in control file) is updated when an unrecoverable direct write (skipping buffer cache) is written to disk successfully. DBAs can use this SCN to determine whether or not a file needs backup, and which of the existing old backups are useless. Any backup with an SCN lower than this SCN cannot be used for recovery and is therefore useless.

Line 39 shows the tablespace number and name to which a data file belongs and the data file's relative file number within the tablespace. Line 44 shows the *begin-hot-backup file size*, which is the size of the file at the beginning of the hot backup. This is done to make sure file checks do not fail, even if the file is extended in the middle of hot backup. A nonzero number for this structure indicates that this particular data file is in hot backup mode. Line 49 shows the backup checkpoint SCN. We have learned in Chapter 6 that when a file is in hot backup mode, the checkpoint is not advanced. In order to track the checkpoint updates that were not done, the backup checkpoint is advanced instead. If the database crashes or the file goes *offline immediate,* the *backup checkpoint* can be copied to the *normal checkpoint* in the current file. Note that the checkpoint information in the file header is not frozen when you use RMAN to do online backups. Some more Oracle internal SCN information is documented on lines 54 and 55.

## Block Dump in Oracle7

While diagnosing block corruptions, it is common to examine the data, index, and rollback segment blocks. The **alter session** command can be used to take block dumps of such segments in Oracle7 and the **alter system** command in Oracle8*i*. In Oracle7, calculating the address of the data block is operating system dependent because the number of bits representing the file number and block number is different for different operating systems. Oracle Support Services analysts usually give the address in decimal form to DBAs when a block dump is required. However, in Oracle8 an Oracle8*i*, the syntax has become significantly easy as you can specify the file number and the block number in the **alter system** command. The following example illustrates using the **alter session** command to take a block dump in Oracle7.

Let's assume that a table called BACKUP has two rows. We are interested in dumping the data block of this table. The contents of the table are as follows:

```
SQL> select * from backup;
C1        C2
----      ----
1         log_backup
```

```
2        phy_backup
2 rows selected.
SQL> alter session set events 'immediate trace name blockdump level 33554650';
Statement processed.
```

The above **alter session** command will dump the data block to a trace file. Listing 9-9 gives the output of the trace. Note that this is an Oracle7 database.

### Listing 9-9

```
Dump file C:\ORACLE7\RDBMS70\trace\ORA12447.TRC
Wed Nov 30 10:08:58 1994
ORACLE V7.0.16.6.0 - Beta vsnsta=1
vsnsql=7 vsnxtr=3
MS-WINDOWS Version 3.10
Wed Nov 30 10:08:58 1994
*** SESSION ID:(6.1)
buffer dba: 20000DA inc: 65 seq: 10 ver: 1 type: 6=trans data
Block header dump: dba: 20000da
Object id on Block? Y
seg/obj: 35d  csc: 00.19d1  itc: 1  flg: O  typ: 1 - DATA
fsl: 0  fnx: 0
itl 01:  xid: 01.18.21  uba: 1000734.28.04  flg: C--- lkc: 0  scn: 0.19d1
data_block_dump
===============
tsiz: 0x7b8
hsiz: 0x16
pbl=81ac04a4
bdba: 020000da
flag=---------
ntab=1
nrow=2
frre=-1
fsbo=0x16
fseo=0x796
avsp=0x780
tosp=0x780
0xe:pti[0]  nrow=2  offs=0
0x12:pri[0] offs=0x7a7
0x14:pri[1] offs=0x796
block_row_dump:
tab 0, row 0, @0x7a7
tl=17 fb: --H-FL-- lb: 0x0 cc: 2
col 0: [2]
c1 02
col 1: [10]
6c 6f 67 5f 62 61 63 6b 75 70
tab 0, row 1, @0x796
tl=17 fb: --H-FL-- lb: 0x0 cc: 2
col 0: [2]
c1 03
col 1: [10]
70 68 79 5f 62 61 63 6b 75 70
end_of_block_dump
```

### Block dump in Oracle8*i*

In Oracle8*i*, you can use the following command to dump a data block in the database:

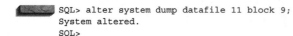

```
SQL> alter system dump datafile 11 block 9;
System altered.
SQL>
```

This will dump the ninth Oracle block in data file 11. Listing 9-10 gives a partial output of the above query:

### Listing 9-10

```
*** 2000.09.20.14.34.59.301
Start dump data blocks tsn: 7 file#: 11 minblk 9 maxblk 9
buffer tsn: 7 rdba: 0x02c00009 (11/9)
scn: 0x0000.00080b09 seq: 0x02 flg: 0x00 tail: 0x0b090602
frmt: 0x02 chkval: 0x0000 type: 0x06=trans data

Block header dump:  0x02c00009
 Object id on Block? Y
 seg/obj: 0x11ca  csc: 0x00.80b08  itc: 1  flg: -  typ: 1 - DATA
     fsl: 0  fnx: 0x0 ver: 0x01

 Itl          Xid                 Uba          Flag Lck       Scn/Fsc
 0x01   xid:  0x0002.013.00000319  uba: 0x00000000.0000.00  ----    0  fsc 0x0000.00000000

data_block_dump
===============
tsiz: 0x7b8
hsiz: 0xae
pbl: 0x08fcac44
bdba: 0x02c00009
flag=-----------
ntab=1
nrow=78
frre=-1
fsbo=0xae
fseo=0x1a1
avsp=0xf3
```

# Oracle Errors and Resolution

This section is divided into two parts. The first part focuses on common errors that a DBA encounters on a day-to-day basis in the areas of space management and general database administration. These common errors, their background and resolution, and some proactive measures are discussed. Oracle internal errors are uncommon yet severe, and may cause down production database or applications. Such internal errors are usually due to various data structure corruptions caused by hardware and software failures. Such problems are categorized and diagnostic actions to DBAs are suggested. Next, a few examples are provided to illustrate how to deal with block corruptions.

# Common Oracle Errors

A user approaches the DBA and tells him or her that he can't add rows to his table because Oracle is giving some error. This is a very common scenario, and one of the less stressful situations compared to some others that DBAs face. In this section, we discuss some of the typical problems that you face on a day-to-day basis, such as space management issues with tables and indexes. Errors due to memory fragmentation problems with shared pool area, problems with snapshots, and, finally, rollback segment management are discussed in this section. Problem resolutions or workarounds are suggested where applicable.

## ORA-1545

When we see a rollback segment with NEEDS RECOVERY status, it means precisely that—the rollback segment needs to be recovered. Here is some useful information on the issue and how to work around it.

In Chapter 6, we learned that on instance startup, Oracle performs crash recovery. This leaves the database in a state in which the roll forward is complete and there is no more redo to be applied. Then, the rollback segments are scanned to roll back all the uncommitted or active transactions that are detected by looking at the transaction table of the rollback segments. If undo can be applied to all the uncommitted transactions, the rollback will be successful and complete. If Oracle cannot, for any reason, apply the undo, then the rollback segment is not recovered completely and will be put in the NEEDS RECOVERY state. The best way to detect this is to set the diagnostic events 10013 and 10015, as discussed earlier in this chapter. When these events are set, the transaction table is dumped to the trace file for all the rollback segments both before and after recovery. For rollback segments that are completely recovered, there will be a dump for both—that is, before and after recovery of the rollback segment. But for irrecoverable rollback segments, there will be a *before image* dump with a stack trace. By scanning the transaction table before recovery, you should see active transaction entries. In the trace file, there will also be an Oracle error, ORA-01135, somewhere after the transaction table dump. This error indicates that a particular data file is offline, and looks something like the following:

```
ORA-01135 file name accessed for DML/query is off-line
```

This indicates that there is a data file that is offline and undo needs to be applied to this file. If the **init.ora** file specifies a rollback segment to be acquired for the instance, which is marked as NEEDS RECOVERY, you will get the ORA-01545 error, which says

```
ORA-01545 rollback segment #'name' was not available
```

Unfortunately, the message doesn't say why it is unavailable. By simply taking the rollback segment name off of the ROLLBACK_SEGMENTS parameter list in **init.ora**, you should be able to start up the database if that's the only segment that needs recovery. The DBA might find that there is more than one rollback segment in NEEDS RECOVERY state, but this gets you over the problem temporarily. The important question you might ask is, "Why can't undo be applied while rolling back?" The most probable reason is that the DBA either has taken a tablespace offline using the IMMEDIATE option, or has made a file offline before opening the database, while mounted. This problem can be permanently resolved in one of two ways:

- Bring the tablespace online so that the **alter tablespace.online** command will cause the undo to be applied and change the status of the rollback segment.

- Drop the tablespace so that the **alter tablespace drop** command will trash the undo, as it is no longer required. Obviously, this action can be taken only if the tablespace can be rebuilt.

Either of the above actions can be taken while the database is open. If neither can be used, then bringing the database up without the rollback segments specified in the **init.ora** and leaving the database open for a while (maybe 30 minutes) will change the rollback segment's status from NEEDS RECOVERY to AVAILABLE. This undercover job is done by SMON, which, among other things, looks at the rollback segments and copies the unapplied undo to *saveundo* (a deferred rollback segment). The DBA needs to make sure that there is sufficient free space in the system tablespace for this to happen. The save undo will stay there until the tablespace in question is available again. If the system rollback segment has a transaction that is active and can't be rolled back because of a tablespace being offline, then the DBA needs to go back to a backup. Needless to say, this should be a rare case and possible only if this database contains a single rollback segment.

## ORA-165X

The ORA-0165X error message simply says that a specific object in the database could not be extended. In Oracle 7.0, this message used to be ORA-1547. Starting with release 7.1 and higher, the specific object in question is pointed out in the error text. The following are the error numbers relating to space management. For the remainder of this section, we will refer to these errors as ORA-0165X errors.

| | |
|---|---|
| ORA-01652 | No more space is available to allocate to a temporary segment. |
| ORA-01653 | No more space is available to allocate to a table. |
| ORA-01654 | No more space is available to allocate to an index. |
| ORA-01655 | No more space is available to allocate to a cluster. |

Some new concepts in space management have been introduced in release 7.2 that will reduce the administrative overhead while doing space management. One of these is the concept of dynamically resizing data files. Without adding a data file, the DBA can manually extend a file to add more space or shrink a file to reclaim the free space in the database. Appendix A discusses the new features introduced in Oracle8 and Oracle8*i*.

The ORA-0165X error is possibly the most common Oracle error message a DBA will see. You need to understand under what circumstances it arises and the options you have to resolve the error. In Chapter 2, you learned that Oracle uses the logical *tablespace* unit; however, the physical aspect of the tablespace unit is the data file. The data file, which is created physically on disk, is where all objects within that tablespace reside. In order to add space to the tablespace, you must add a data file. When the ORA-0165X error arises, the problem is due to lack of space in a particular tablespace. The error message gives two parameters: SIZE, which tells the DBA how many Oracle blocks the system was not able to find, and TABLESPACE, which tells the user where the space is needed. Oracle will always try to allocate contiguous space. Although the tablespace may have enough free space, if it is not contiguous, the error will still occur.

In order to see the free space available for a particular tablespace (say, USERS), you must use the view SYS.DBA_FREE_SPACE. Within this view, each record represents one fragment of free space. For example,

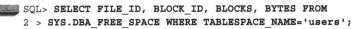

```
SQL> SELECT FILE_ID, BLOCK_ID, BLOCKS, BYTES FROM
2 > SYS.DBA_FREE_SPACE WHERE TABLESPACE_NAME='users';

FILE_ID    BLOCK_ID    BLOCKS    BYTES
--------   ----------  -------   -------
4          2           20        40960
4          1465        72        147456
4          22          25        51200
4          147         1318      2699264

4 rows selected.
```

This query tells you that there are four chunks of free space within the tablespace USERS and gives each of their sizes in Oracle blocks and bytes. The above query doesn't, however, properly display the contiguous chunks of free space. If you alter the query a bit by adding an ORDER BY clause, the output will be easy to read:

```
SQL> SELECT FILE_ID, BLOCK_ID, BLOCKS, BYTES FROM
2 > DBA_FREE_SPACE WHERE TABLESPACE_NAME='USERS'
3 > ORDER BY BLOCK_ID;
```

```
FILE_ID    BLOCK_ID    BLOCKS    BYTES
--------   ---------   -------   -------
4          2           20        40960
4          22          25        51200
4          147         1318      2699264
4          1465        72        147456
```

4 rows selected.

You can see that there are really two chunks of contiguous space instead of four. If you carefully examine the output, you see that at block #2 there are 20 blocks of free space. The next chunk of free space starts with block #22, which makes those two chunks contiguous. The same thing applies to block #147. When you add the number of blocks at that location, you see that they end at block 1464, which is adjacent to the next chunk of space.

The information in this view is very important to understand. Under Oracle7, the SMON background process wakes up every five minutes and coalesces the free space. We have seen in the "Setting Trace Events" section that the DBA can set events to coalesce space immediately. Note that this is completely automated in Oracle8*i*.

Using the same example from above, if you try and create a table of 1,325 Oracle blocks (or 2,650K), the free space is coalesced:

```
SQL> CREATE TABLE bulletin (y NUMBER) STORAGE (INITIAL 2650K)
2 > TABLESPACE users;

Table created.

SQL> SELECT FILE_ID, BLOCK_ID, BLOCKS, BYTES FROM
2 > DBA_FREE_SPACE WHERE TABLESPACE_NAME='USERS'
3 > ORDER BY BLOCK_ID;

FILE_ID    BLOCK_ID    BLOCKS    BYTES
-------    ---------   ------    -----
4          2           45        92160
4          1472        65        133120

2 rows selected.
```

In addition, it is important to understand how the space algorithm works internal to Oracle. The RDBMS initially tries to find an exact-sized extent. If this doesn't exist, it will then break up an extent of a larger size. Finally, if it still is not able to find space, it will coalesce. Note that dropping the object has no effect on coalescing. Consider the following example:

```
SQL> DROP TABLE bulletin;

Table dropped.
```

```
SQL> SELECT FILE_ID, BLOCK_ID, BLOCKS, BYTES FROM
2 > DBA_FREE_SPACE WHERE TABLESPACE_NAME='USERS'
3 > ORDER BY BLOCK_ID;

FILE_ID  BLOCK_ID  BLOCKS  BYTES
-------  --------  ------  -----
4        2         45      92160
4        147       1325    2713600
4        1472      65      133120

3 rows selected.
```

A simpler approach is simply to see what is the biggest chunk of free space you have, and see if it is smaller than the size the error is giving. This is the only approach needed for Oracle7.

Perform the following query:

```
select max(blocks) from sys.dba_free_space where tablespace_name='name';
```

This will return one record that shows the biggest chunk of space free in the tablespace in question. This number will be lower than the one returned by the error. If you wish to compare the contiguous space with total space, perform the following query:

```
select sum(blocks) from sys.dba_free_space where tablespace_name='name';
```

This also returns one record. This value can be compared to the above to see how much of the total space is contiguous. Note that if there is no space in a tablespace, no records will be retrieved from the SYS.DBA_FREE_SPACE view.

Sometimes a user might try to do an **insert** into one tablespace and get an error on another tablespace. To understand this, let's examine the objects that can grow in the database.

**Data Dictionary**    The ORA-0165X error will occur if the data dictionary objects need to extend but there is not enough space in the system tablespace for them to do so. This situation presents the ORA-00604 error before the ORA-0165X error. For example, if creating a table forces the dictionary table **tab$** to extend, and if the SYSTEM tablespace doesn't have enough space, the create table will receive the ORA-00604 error followed by the ORA-0165X error.

**Tables and Indexes**    The ORA-0165X error will occur if additional space is needed to satisfy an **insert** or **update** of an object. If this error arises on the creation of an index or table, the specified storage or tablespace default storage parameters need to be investigated.

**Rollback Segments** If the error occurs with a rollback segment, the ORA-01650 error will always precede the ORA-0165X error. The ORA-01650 error indicates that it couldn't extend the rollback segment and the reason is the ORA-0165X error (not enough space). The ORA-01650 error message is given here:

```
01650, 00000, "unable to extend rollback segment %s by %s in tablespace %s"
// *Cause:  Failed to allocate an extent for rollback segment in tablespace.
// *Action: Use ALTER TABLESPACE ADD DATAFILE statement to add one or more
//          files to the tablespace indicated.
```

**Temporary Tables** Temporary tables are created by the Oracle kernel to do a sort on behalf of the user. A user can tell that he or she is running out of space for a temporary table, based on the operation he or she is performing (such as creating an index or doing a query with an ORDER BY clause or a lengthy *join* statement). In this case, the temporary tablespace of the user needs to be found using the following query:

```
select temporary_tablespace from sys.dba_users where username = 'username';
```

If the space being used seems excessive, you may want to investigate the default storage for the temporary tablespace, as it is possible that the defaults are too large. To see the default storage, perform the following query:

```
select initial_extent, next_extent, min_extents, pct_increase from
sys.dba_tablespaces where tablespace_name='name';
```

The default storage of the temporary (or any) tablespace can be altered using the following SQL command:

```
alter tablespace name default storage (initial xxx next yyy);
```

Rather than add space to the temporary tablespace, you may opt to alter the user so that he or she uses a tablespace you know has more free space. If you wish to change the temporary tablespace for the user, issue the following command:

```
alter user username temporary tablespace new_tablespace_name;
```

Space can be added to a tablespace using the **alter tablespace** command. This statement will create a database file on disk and add the file to the tablespace. The **alter tablespace** statement can be performed on any tablespace (including system) without shutting down the database or taking the tablespace offline. Immediately following the completion of the statement, the space is available for the DBA. Once a data file is added, it cannot be deleted, short of dropping the tablespace.

While adding a data file to a tablespace, a DBA might accidentally add a bigger file than is needed. In such cases, some DBAs tend to shut the database down, mount it, and use the **alter database** command to take the file offline and then open the database. Then, they drop the data file they just added. This is a very dangerous operation. It will work as long as Oracle doesn't allocate any space from this data file. Note that even if the file is taken offline, Oracle will still try to allocate space to it, as the free space is seen by Oracle in the **fet$** table. So, the only solution to such problems is to export the data in that tablespace, drop the tablespace, re-create the tablespace with the right file sizes, and, finally, import the data back. A data file can be added to the tablespace using the following command:

```
alter tablespace tablespace_name add datafile 'filename' size size_of_file;
```

To get an idea of the naming conventions or locations for existing files, perform the following query:

```
select file_name from sys.dba_data_files where tablespace_name='name';
```

Often, users receive the ORA-0165X error while running an import. Some of the common reasons are discussed here.

**Compress Option**     Exporting with COMPRESS=Y modifies the INITIAL EXTENT storage parameter to be equal to the space that the table has allocated at the time of export. If a user tries to import specific tables into an existing database, the import often fails because it cannot find contiguous space. Consider the scenario in which a table is spread across four extents of 10MB each. When this table is exported with COMPRESS=Y, the INITIAL EXTENT for this table is now 40MB. The user drops the table, then tries to import. The RDBMS cannot find 40MB of contiguous space, which raises an ORA-0165X error. Although the table existed in the tablespace, import can no longer re-create it.

To work around this problem without adding space to the tablespace, the DBA can do one of the following:

- Export the table and specify COMPRESS=N. This preserves the table's original storage parameters.

- Pre-create the table with specific storage parameters before importing.

- Truncate the table before importing the data rather than dropping it.

**Creating Indexes**     If the import fails when creating the indexes, you need to modify your temporary tablespace. The solution is to create enough space for the RDBMS to do the sorting for the index. One workaround is to pre-create the table and index before importing. This should only be used if it is not possible to add the space, even for a short period of time. This method also has a grave effect on the import's performance because every time a row is inserted, the index tree needs to be traversed to insert the key. If you are using SQL*LOADER to load data, a better workaround is to pre-create the index with the NOSORT option. Then, you need to presort the data at the OS level before loading it into the table.

**Rollback Segments**     By default, the **import** utility commits at the end of each table; therefore, it is very likely your rollback segments will run out of space. To work around this problem without adding space to the rollback segment tablespace, you can specify the COMMIT=Y option on import. This overrides the default and commits at the end of each *buffer* (also an **import** parameter), rather than at the end of the table. This will impact performance because every commit forces the LGWR process to write the commit record to the log file on disk, hence doing more I/O.

## ORA-01555

There are various reasons why users can get the ORA-01555 error. The most common reason is that the rollback segments are too small, but there are other reasons as well. The following discussion gives a complete summary of all the situations that would cause the ORA-1555 error and how to resolve them. In order to understand the discussion, you need to be familiar with some of the internal mechanisms of Oracle, so a brief explanation about read consistency and block cleanouts is given.

Oracle always enforces statement-level read consistency. This guarantees that the data returned by a single query is consistent with respect to the time when the query began. Therefore, a query never sees the data changes made by transactions that commit during the course of execution of the query.

We have learned in Chapter 6 that an SCN can be defined as the state of the database at any given point in time. To produce read consistency, Oracle marks the current SCN as the query enters the execution phase. The query can only see the snapshot of the records as of that SCN. Oracle uses rollback segments to reconstruct the read-consistent snapshot of the data. Whenever a transaction makes any changes, a snapshot of the record before the changes were made is copied to a rollback segment and the data block header is marked appropriately with the address of the rollback segment block where the changes are recorded. The data block also maintains the SCN of the last committed change to the block. As data blocks are read on behalf of the query, only blocks with a lower SCN than the query SCN will be read. If a block has uncommitted changes of other transactions, or changed data with a more recent SCN, then the data is reconstructed using the saved snapshot from the rollback segments. In some rare situations, if the RDBMS is not able to reconstruct the snapshot for a long-running query, the query results in the ORA-01555 error.

A rollback segment maintains the snapshot of the changed data as long as the transaction is still active (commit or rollback has not been issued). Once a transaction is committed, the RDBMS marks it with the current SCN and the space used by the snapshot becomes available for reuse. Therefore, the ORA-01555 error will result if the query is looking for a snapshot that is so old that the rollback segment doesn't contain it due to wraparound or overwrite.

There are four main reasons why the ORA-01555 error occurs.

**Few and Small Rollback Segments**    If a database has many concurrent transactions changing data and committing very often, then the chances of reusing the space used by a committed transaction is higher. A long-running query then might not be able to reconstruct the snapshot due to wraparound and overwrite in rollback segments. Larger rollback segments in this case will reduce the chance of reusing the committed transaction slots.

**Corrupted Rollback Segments**    Corrupted rollback segments can cause this error as well. If the rollback segment is corrupted and cannot be read, then a statement needing to reconstruct a before-image snapshot will result in this error.

**Fetch Across Commits**    A fetch across commit is a situation in which a query opens a cursor, loops through fetching, changes data, and then commits the records on the same table. For example, suppose a cursor was opened at an SCN value of 10. The execution SCN of the query is then marked as SCN=10. Every fetch by that cursor now needs to get the read-consistent data from SCN=10. Let's assume that the user program fetches *x* number of records, changes them, and then commits them with an SCN value of 20. If a later fetch happens to retrieve a record that is in one of the previously committed blocks, then the fetch will see that the SCN value is 20. Since the fetch has to get the snapshot from SCN=10, read consistency needs to be performed on the data using the rollback segment. If it cannot roll back to SCN 10, the ORA-01555 error occurs. Committing less often in this case will result in larger rollback segments and *reduce* the probability of getting the error.

**Fetch Across Commits with Delayed Block Cleanout**    When a data or index block is modified in the database and the transaction is committed, Oracle does a fast commit by marking the transaction as committed in the rollback segment header, but does not clean the locks in the data blocks that were modified. The next transaction that does a select on the modified blocks will do the actual cleanout of the block. This is known as a *delayed block cleanout*.

Now let's take the same example as with fetch across commits, but instead of assuming one table, let's assume that there are two tables that the transaction uses— in other words, the cursor is opened, and then, in a loop, fetches from one table, changes records in another, and commits. Even though the records are getting committed in another table, it can still cause the ORA-01555 error because cleanout has not been done on the table from which the records are being fetched. This is possible because some other transaction has modified this table before we did the **select**. For this case, a full table scan before opening and fetching through the cursor will help.

An effective solution for both the fetch across commit cases would be to add an ORDER BY clause to the driving cursor **select** statement. The sorted *rowsource* would be kept in a temporary segment, which is a good enough snapshot for the life of the cursor, hence ORA-01555 will not occur.

Note that fetch across commits, as explained in the last two cases, is not supported by ANSI SQL standards. According to the standard, a cursor is invalidated when a commit is performed, and should be closed and reopened before fetching again. Though not ANSI SQL standard, Oracle, unlike some other database vendors, allows users to do fetch across commits, but users should be aware that this might result in the ORA-01555 error.

## ORA-01594

The most probable cause of the ORA-01594 error is small extent sizes. Shrinking of extents is started when a request is made for an undo block and the kernel detects that the current extent of the rollback segment is reaching the end of its free space. If several extents are to be freed, this can generate substantial undo, which may eventually wrap into the extent that is being freed up. This will cause the ORA-01594 error to occur. Having a smaller number of larger extents is a good way of dealing with this problem.

## ORA-04031

Fragmentation of shared-pool memory area is a common problem that application programmers and DBAs often face, and the ORA-04031 error is commonly a result of such fragmentation. Here, we will discuss some of the workarounds that are available today and future enhancements that are under consideration.

Imagine the SHARED_POOL being similar to a tablespace. While you may get the ORA-165X error when you cannot get sufficient contiguous free space in the tablespace, you will get the ORA-04031 error when you cannot get contiguous free space in the SHARED_POOL (SGA). Application programmers usually get this error while attempting to load a big package or while executing a very large procedure and there is not sufficient contiguous free memory available in the shared pool. This may be due to fragmentation of the shared-pool memory or insufficient memory in the shared pool.

If it is due to fragmentation, one needs to flush the shared pool and/or break up the package or procedure into smaller blocks. If the shared pool is badly fragmented, even using small packages or procedures can result in this error. Flushing the shared pool might not help all the time because it will not flush the PINNED buffers that are being changed at that time.

If it is due to insufficient memory, SHARED_POOL_SIZE should be increased from the default value, which is 3.5MB. Increasing the SHARED_POOL parameter might not be a viable solution in some shops that have high availability requirements because you allocate the size of the shared pool during startup time, and increasing the SHARED_POOL parameter means shutting down and restarting the database. Unfortunately, this size is fixed and cannot be extended on the fly.

Current workarounds include the following:

- Utilize the **dbms_shared_pool** package, available with Oracle versions 7.0.13 and higher. This package allows users to display the sizes of objects in the shared pool and mark them for pinning (discussed in Chapter 2) in the SGA in order to reduce memory fragmentation. The DBA must grant to user SYS the EXECUTE privilege on the package in order to keep the package in the shared pool. Procedures are run under the schema of the owner; therefore, if user SYS does not have EXECUTE privileges on the package, SYS will get an error stating that the object doesn't exist.

- Increase the SHARED_POOL_SIZE, as the current default tends to be a low estimate when utilizing the PROCEDURAL option.

There are plans in the future to change the functionality to reduce the occurrence of this problem. At the current time, Oracle needs one contiguous chunk of memory to process a given package or procedure. In future releases of Oracle, the PL/SQL code will be modified such that it will request a certain amount of memory and will accept several smaller contiguous chunks for the same package or procedure, thereby reducing the probability of this error.

At times, ORA-04031 can be very annoying to application programmers and DBAs. However, with the help of the DBMS_SHARED_POOL package, and careful planning and administration, the DBA can eliminate this error for good.

## ORA-07445

You might have seen this error reported in your alert log if you are using ORACLE 7.2 or a newer release. This error means an operating system exception has occurred, and the exception is shown as an argument to this error. A trace file name is also listed in the alert log. The trace provides a *stack trace* and the *process state* for the process that generated the error. The trace also shows the SQL that caused the error. Additionally, a *core dump* file is created in the *core dump destination*. The name of the core directory contains the process PID in it so you can identify it easily.

This error normally is caused by an Oracle code bug. Such errors should be reported to Oracle Support Services immediately.

**Core Dump**    When a process performs an illegal operation, the operating system dumps the memory and the stack frames of the offending process into an operating system file, famously known as a *core*.

Sometimes the process can corrupt memory badly, causing Oracle trace functions to fail in generating the trace file. In such circumstances, debugging the problem can become quite complicated, but not impossible if the core file and the executable causing the *core* are preserved.

A debugger provided by the operating system can be used to pull the *stack trace* from the *core* file. On some operating systems like Digital UNIX, *stack trace* can provide the line number at which the *exception signal* is received. The most common signals received are *Signal 11* (segmentation violation) and *Signal 10* (address is not aligned to the word boundary). Other possible *signals* can be seen in **/usr/include/sys/signal.**

## ORA-12004

You need to understand the concepts of *snapshots* and *procedures* before you read this section. Please refer to the *Oracle8i Application Developer's Guide* for details on snapshots and procedures. This section gives some debugging information on snapshots. Most of the snapshot problems can be approached this way.

An ORA-12004 error occurs when you try to do a *fast refresh,* and the attempt fails because Oracle could not use the snapshot log. For example, assume that the procedure **dbms_snapshot.set_up** is executed (remotely) at the master site. One query in the procedure is

```
Select log, oldest, youngest+1/86400
from mlog$ where master = :2 and mowner = :1 for update;
```

This procedure retrieves the log name and updates the timestamps in the snapshot log. If the **update** fails, if you are not able to get the log name, or if any other error occurs, then this procedure does not return a log name, and the ORA-12004 error is signaled.

Consider the scenario in which the procedure **dbms_snapshot.get_log_age** is executed (again, remotely at the master site). This procedure returns a date defined by

```
Select oldest into oldest from sys.mlog$ where mowner = mow and master = mas;
```

This date (call it *log_date*) is then compared to the date of this snapshot's most recent refresh (call it *snap_date*). The *snap_date* is given by the SNAPTIME column in the **snap$** base data dictionary table. If *snap_date* is earlier than *log_date*, then the ORA-12004 error is signaled.

To summarize, there are two possible causes for the ORA-12004 error. Either you were unable to retrieve the name of the log file (from **dbms_snapshot.set_up**) or the log is out of date, possibly because the snapshot log has been purged. (Snapshot logs can be purged manually using **dbms_snapshot.purge_log**; Oracle also purges the log automatically after refreshes, but the automatic purge shouldn't age out any other snapshots.)

To debug this problem, you can run **dbms_snapshot.set_up** by hand. The name of the log table is an *out* variable. So, consider the following procedure:

```
create table foo (a varchar(30));

declare
owner varchar(30);
master varchar(30);
log varchar(30);
snapshot date;
snaptime date;
begin
    snapshot := SYSDATE;
    snaptime := SYSDATE;
    owner := 'SCOTT';
    master := 'EMP';
    dbms_snapshot.set_updblink(owner, master, log, snapshot, snaptime);
    insert into foo(a) values (log);
end;
```

After executing this, the log name for the master table should be in *foo*. This can be verified as follows:

```
SQL> select * from foo;
A
-------------------
MLOG$_EMP
1 row selected.
```

As a side effect, this procedure will cause the master site (and **mlog$** and snapshot logs) to believe that a snapshot has occurred, and will result in future refreshes, possibly returning the ORA-12004 error for out-of-date reasons. So, be prepared to do full refreshes on your snapshots after running this test.

If **dbms_snapshot.set_up** appears to be running correctly, then you can attempt to figure out why your log tables are outdated using the above queries. Please refer to Chapter 8 of this book for more information on setting up master sites and snapshot sites.

## Oracle Internal Errors

Internal to Oracle Support Services, all high-priority problems reported by customers are divided into seven categories. Most of the time, these problems are kernel related. However, some major functionality not working in an application could potentially stop a production or development workshop, resulting in a high-priority problem as well. These kinds of problems need to be diagnosed as soon as possible, and some initial diagnostics can be taken by DBAs. This section gives information on Oracle internal errors, such as the ORA-00600 error. Next, an overview of the various categories of priority 1/priority 2 problems and the standard diagnostics a DBA can collect before calling Oracle Support Services are discussed. Last, some examples illustrate how to deal with memory or block corruptions.

## ORA-00600

As discussed earlier in this chapter, the main purpose of trace files is to record information when error conditions occur. All errors that are signaled by Oracle have a code associated with them. While some common errors are displayed onscreen to the users, some fatal or internal errors are recorded in the alert file in addition to creating a trace file. For example, the ORA-01578 error means that a block has been corrupted. All of the *ORA-* errors are documented in the *Oracle8i Error Messages Release 8.1.5* manual. There is a special Oracle error code that has meaning only to Oracle Support Services and Oracle Development. The ORA-00600 error is signaled when a sanity check fails within the Oracle code. To illustrate what is meant by a sanity check, examine the following pseudocode:

```
/* Pseudo-code to get file# F, block# B from the database */

get(F,B)
Begin
If (F > MAX_NUMBER_OF_FILES)
signal ("ORA 00600 [2858] [F]");
exit ( )
endif;
......
end
```

In this code segment, the *if* statement tests for the validity of the file number requested. If the file number requested is out of range for possible file numbers, the program will signal the error and exit. Note that this is not the complete meaning of the actual ORA-00600 [2858] error, but an illustration of a sanity check.

The first argument in the ORA-00600 error is used as a tag for the location in the code where the error is signaled. Each first argument is unique to one section of the code. The second through fifth arguments are used to give additional information, such as the file number in the previous example.

The ORA-00600 error message informs Oracle Support Services where the error occurred in the code, but doesn't indicate what the RDBMS was doing when it entered the routine containing the error. The *stack trace dumps* help to determine what was happening at the time the error occurred. The *stack trace* is a dump of the execution stack of a process. It contains the names of all active routines and the values of the arguments passed to those routines. Stack traces are read from the bottom up, with the top routine usually being the routine that prints out the stack trace. The arguments on the stack trace of an Oracle process are usually not very helpful, since they are mostly address pointers and not the values of actual data structures. But the routine names help Oracle Support Services determine what type of activity led up to this error. For example, it can be determined that a corrupted block was found during the act of building a consistent read block if the routine that builds consistent read blocks is on the stack.

The dump of a stack trace is done by making a call to the operating system that Oracle is currently running on. This causes the appearances of stack traces to look different from one platform to another. On UNIX platforms, the dump of the stack trace will include the routine names, whereas on OpenVMS the stack trace is dumped with the routine names encrypted as addresses in the code. To make the stack trace readable, the DBA should format the trace file using the **trcfmt** command on the machine on which the trace file is created. This will convert the addresses to routine names and will be in a human-readable format.

The ORA-00600 error is often followed by state dumps in the trace files. There are two types of state dumps, *system state* and *process state*. A system state will give information about objects currently held by the Oracle RDBMS. A process state dump will show objects held by a particular process. These dumps are usually large in size and difficult to decipher. But one of the key pieces of the information contained in these dumps is the blocks held by each process. When a process hits an error condition, it is often due to some information it has extracted from a block it is holding. If we know the blocks held by the errant process, it is easier to track down the source of the problem. By using the data block addresses in the system or process state dump, we can see what objects are encountering the signaled errors. If more information is required, Oracle Support Services will request that the DBA dump more information concerning a block, a process state, or a system state, depending on the error (the syntax for dumping the system state and the process state are discussed earlier in this chapter).

## Categories of Priority 1/Priority 2 Problems and Diagnostic Actions

Following are the various categories of problems that could impact the availability of the database or question the data integrity of the database. This is followed by a description and the diagnostic actions that a DBA needs to take before calling Oracle Support Services. Note that it might be necessary to take some of the actions with the help of an Oracle Support Services analyst.

- Data corruptions
- Logical corruptions
- System hangs
- Performance problems

- System crashes
- Critical functionality not available
- Memory corruptions

**Data Corruptions**     *Data corruptions* include all block format corruptions, invalid index entries, and corruptions of metadata (such as the data dictionary). An example is a user getting the ORA-00600 [3339] error on a system data file when selecting from a table. There could be various reasons why data corruptions occur. For example, it could be the hardware vendor's operating system problem with clustered disks. Standard or typical diagnostic actions for these kinds of problems include the following:

- Collecting trace files (and formatting them where applicable) if the corruption is reported as an internal error.

- Dumping the redo logs corresponding to the time of corruption. If you are not sure how many log files to dump, saving all the redo log files and contacting Oracle Support Services is suggested.

- Asking the system manager for complete hardware diagnostics to be carried out if there is a reason to suspect vendor OS problem.

- Where appropriate, determining if the problem is generic or port specific.

**NOTE**
*Some of these actions might be appropriate for Oracle Support Services analysts as well.*

**Logical Corruptions**     *Logical corruptions* refer to the case where the data (either as stored or as returned by a query) is incorrect, although it isn't necessary that an error be returned externally. Typical examples of a logical corruption would be phantom rows in a table after updating a column to null, or a query returning different results when using different types of optimizers. Logical corruptions are very dangerous, as they are difficult to detect. Standard diagnostic actions to DBAs include the following:

- Trying to create a reproducible test case
- Collecting trace files (and formatting them where applicable) if the corruption is reported as an internal error (such as ORA-00600 [13004])
- When appropriate, determining if the problem is generic or port specific

**Hangs**    A hang can be described as a situation in which *no work is getting done.* A typical symptom is when an Oracle user realizes that a session is not responding to his or her request. In such situations, a DBA needs to identify any of the following if they are occurring:

- Machine is hanging.

- Machine is accepting connections, but Oracle is not.

- Machine and Oracle are accepting connections, but the complaining user's session is frozen.

In the first case, operating system specialists should be involved to diagnose the problem, whereas in the second scenario it is safe to conclude that the entire Oracle *instance* is hanging. In such a state, it is more than likely that Oracle is waiting for some resource that is not available.

**Instance Hangs**    When the entire instance hangs, we need to collect diagnostics to identify the cause of the hang, and maybe take necessary action to alleviate the problem. The **alert.log** should be checked for messages that indicate situations like when the *ARCH* process is stuck or the *DBWR* is stuck because a write to the disk did not return. If the message in the **alert.log** reveals the problem, necessary corrective action can be taken immediately. If a helpful message is not available in the **alert log**, then the next step would be to try and connect as INTERNAL using SQL*PLUS. Check if any of the fixed views such as V$LICENSE provide helpful information. When you query V$LICENSE, and if a row is returned, then we would know how many sessions are connected to this instance at this time. The following query can be used to identify the wait type and the number of sessions waiting on each type:

```
select event, count(*) from  V$SESSION_WAIT group by event;
```

The output of the above query suggests the distribution of a session across wait events. If the event *latch free* has an unusual number of sessions waiting on it, then we need to get the distribution of sessions by *latch numbers*. The following query can be used:

```
select p2, count(*) from V$SESSION_WAIT where event = 'latch free'
group by p2;
```

If the bulk of the sessions are waiting on a single latch number, then the session holding the latch needs to be identified using the V$LATCHHOLDER view. Before that, we should get the latch name and address by querying the V$LATCH view. The latch number information from the above query can be used in this situation.

Using the V$SESSION_WAIT view, you can determine if a session is waiting for an event. We can repeat these above steps until the offending session is identified.

**Session Hangs**     Once the session is identified, a *process state dump* of that process should be taken using **oradebug**. The trace file would be in the directory pointed to by the USER DUMP DESTINATION in the **init.ora**. The trace file might reveal the reason for the hang. Also, the process should be tracked using an operating system tool to capture the system calls made by the process. Some of the popular tools on UNIX are **truss**, *trace*, and **glance**. For example, **truss** on a process might reveal that there is no system call being made at all. This indicates that the process may be in a tight loop within Oracle code. It is also possible that a system call did not return from the operating system.

The information collected can be provided to Oracle Support Services for an in-depth analysis of the problem. Temporarily, the problem can be alleviated by terminating the offending session.

**Performance Problems**     Performance problems can be classified into two categories. General cases of deterioration in response times or batch completion times represent the first. The second is performance degradation on increase in concurrent activity. These kinds of problems are generally time-consuming and require patience. Poor response times can sometimes be due to waits for library cache pins. Standard diagnostic actions include the following:

- Documenting performance degradation in terms of specific indicators such as response time, batch completion time, number of concurrent logins supported, efficiency of shared-pool management, and so on.

- Providing a reproducible test case, if possible, or documenting in detail the environment and factors leading to poor performance. For example, in the case where reproducibility depends on concurrency in a production environment, it is appropriate to document circumstances surrounding degradation, such as number of logins, average memory usage, typical functionality invoked, I/O activity, and dynamic statistics on Oracle activity.

- Setting up a modem for Oracle Support Services personnel to dial in and monitor if the problem is reproducible only at your site with reasonable frequency.

- When appropriate, determining if the problem is generic or port specific.

**System Crashes**     *System crashes* include cases in which the database crashes, usually due to one of the background processes dying. These kinds of problems are not common; but if the database crashes, DBAs should make the following diagnostics:

■ Check the alert file to see if any ORA-00600 errors have occurred, and if so, get the trace files and format them, if necessary.

■ Find out what the users were doing at the time of the crash or what applications were running at that time. If a specific application is isolated, try reproducing the problem by running the application on a test machine.

■ When appropriate, determine if the problem is generic or port specific.

**Critical Functionality Not Available**  *Critical functionality not available* refers to all situations in which functionality or vital features that rely on a production application become unavailable, typically due to a bug in the database software or any third-party software that runs on top of Oracle. Some examples that fall into this category include cases in which Oracle utilities core dump or the applications error out. In some cases, a function not available might affect the availability of the database indirectly. For example, consider a case in which a database is being recovered from a full database export, and import from multiple tapes doesn't work correctly, thereby preventing a database rebuild of a production database. Again, the standard diagnostics in this case include the following:

■ Collecting trace files and dumping relevant redo log files, depending on the error (under Oracle Support Services guidance), and documenting the circumstances leading up to the error.

■ Providing a reproducible test case if possible.

■ Providing detailed information, such as utilities used, storage structures accessed, DDL/DML performed, and procedures or packages executed during the time the error occurred, is necessary if providing a reproducible test case is not possible.

■ When appropriate, determining if the problem is generic or port specific.

**Memory Corruptions**  *Memory corruptions* include internal errors signaling memory leaks, corruptions of memory data structures, and cache corruptions. Diagnostic actions include the following:

■ Collecting a trace file if the error produces one

■ Providing a reproducible test case if possible, or documenting circumstances that caused the error, such as the following:

■ Details of OCI, or the Oracle tool/utility or the precompiler used in the application

- Operating system tools or third-party tools used in conjunction with the application

- Triggers fired by the application

- Packages or procedures executed

## Resolving Block Corruptions

Data corruption can occur for numerous reasons, and in most cases it goes undetected at the time the corruption occurs. It is only later, when that piece of information is needed, that the corruption is detected. The Oracle RDBMS keeps its information, including data, in block format. The Oracle data block can be (and in many cases is) composed of several operating system blocks. For instance, if the Oracle block size is 2,048 bytes and the operating system block size is 512 bytes, then the Oracle block is composed of four operating system blocks. The **init.ora** parameter DB_BLOCK_SIZE will indicate the current Oracle block size.

Each block of an Oracle data file is formatted with a fixed header that contains information about the particular block. This information provides a means to ensure the integrity for each block and, in turn, the entire Oracle database. One component of the fixed header of a data block is the *data block address*. This structure is a 32-bit integer that stores the file number of an Oracle database and the Oracle block number offset relative to the beginning of the file. Whenever there is a problem with the data block address while reading a block from disk to cache, Oracle will signal an internal error along with two internal arguments. The error message will look something like the following:

```
ORA-00600 [3339] [arg1] [arg2] [] [] [] []
ORA-01578: Data block corrupted in file # x block # y
```

The first argument (*arg1*) is the data block address that Oracle found in the data block just read from disk. The second argument (*arg2*) is the data block address that Oracle expects to find in that data block. If they are different, then the ORA-00600 error is displayed, as shown above. This error is typically caused by some form of operating system or hardware malfunction.

Oracle uses standard C system function calls to read/write blocks from all the files it maintains. This includes system calls such as **lseek( )**, **read( )**, **readv( )**, **write( )**, and **writev( )**. Once the block is read, it is mapped to shared memory (the SGA) by the operating system. Oracle then does sanity checks on the block to ensure the integrity of the fixed header. The data block address check is the first check Oracle makes on the fixed header.

In some cases, *arg1* is displayed as 0, while *arg2* is a 32-bit number. This means that the data block address component for the block just read is 0. Usually, this is because a portion of the Oracle block has been zeroed out. Typically, the first operating system block piece of an Oracle block is zeroed out when there is a soft error on disk and the operating system attempted to repair its block. In addition, disk-repairing utilities will also cause this zeroing-out effect. One known Oracle software bug specific to UNIX platforms is caused by running multiple database writers (**init.ora** parameter DB_WRITERS > 1) and was addressed in versions 6.0.33.2 and higher. Note that the ORA-01578 error message does not necessarily accompany the ORA-00600 error.

In other cases, both arguments of the ORA-00600 error display large numbers. This implies that the data block address in the physical block on disk is incorrect. There are various reasons why this can happen.

One reason why this can happen is if the block is corrupted in memory and is written to disk. This situation is quite rare. In most cases, it is caused by memory faults that go undetected. If the DBA suspects that there may be memory problems with the system, he or she should enable further sanity block checking by placing the event codes 10210 and 10211 in the **init.ora** file. The syntax is given in the "Setting Trace Events" section of this chapter. However, when these events are set, and if the DBWR process detects a corrupted block in cache prior to writing it to disk, it will signal the ORA-00600 [3398] error and will *crash* the instance. The block in question is thus never written to disk, thereby preventing the database from corruptions. Various arguments including the data block address are passed to the ORA-00600 [3398] error. The DBA should simply restart the instance and contact Oracle Support Services with the trace files.

A second reason is that blocks are sometimes written into the wrong places in the data file. This is called *write blocks out of sequence*. In this case, both data block addresses given in the arguments are valid. This typically happens when the operating system's I/O mechanism fails to write the block in the proper locations that Oracle requests via the **lseek( )** system call. Some hardware/operating system vendors support *large files* or *large file systems*. These can contain physical files as large as 4.2GB. This is larger than what can be represented by a 32-bit, unsigned number. Oracle doesn't support files larger than 2GB. Hence, the operating system must translate the *offset* transparent to the application (that is, Oracle). On such configurations, even smaller Oracle data files suffer corruptions caused by blocks being written out of sequence because the **lseek( )** system call did not translate the correct location.

A third cause is I/O error. In this case, both of the data block addresses are valid but the data block address in argument 1 of the error (*arg1*) is from the previous block read into the SGA prior to this read request. The calls that Oracle makes to **lseek( )** and **read( )** are checked for return error codes. In addition, Oracle checks to see whether the number of bytes read by the **read( )** system call is a multiple of BLOCK SIZE bytes. If these checks appear to be successful, Oracle assumes that the direct read succeeded. Upon sanity checking, the data block address is incorrect and the database operation request fails due to the fact that I/O read really never took place. In this case, the data block address that Oracle reads is really the address of another block in the database.

The fourth reason you may get the ORA-00600 error with valid data block addresses for both its arguments is because of reading a wrong block from the same disk drive. Typically, this is caused by a very busy disk. In some cases, the block read is off by one block, and can range into several hundreds of blocks. Note that the data block addresses of both the arguments are valid. Since this occurs when the disk is very busy and under high load conditions, ensuring that the disk drive has the current EPROM release helps. No doubt, there could be other reasons why block corruptions happen. The preceding four reasons are from my personal experience.

Note that in the third and fourth cases above, the database will not be corrupted, and the operation can be tried again with success. However, if a data block does get corrupted, a DBA should know how to retrieve data from that table. Retrieving data from a corrupt table can be done in different ways. The following example illustrates how data can be retrieved from a corrupt table using index scans:

```
Select distinct(key) from corrupt_table
where key > (lowest value for the key)
and substr(rowid,1,8) = corrupt_block_id
order by 1;
```

This method can be used only if the corrupt table has an index. The first step involves selecting all the distinct key values that are in the corrupted block. Note that since we cannot do a full table scan, the key values will be selected from the index leaf block. The following query will give the key values that belong to the corrupt block.

Note that *key* is the name of the column on which the index is created and *corrupt_table* is the name of the corrupted table. *Corrupt_block_id* is the actual hexadecimal value that identifies the corrupt block. When the corrupt block is first detected by the Oracle process or a user process, the ORA-01578 error message is displayed. As part of the error message, the block number of the corrupted block is given. This is the value that *corrupt_block_id* should be equated to. The above query will be fully satisfied by an index scan, since both *rowid* and *key* are in the index. Note that in the WHERE clause, the predicate *key > (lowest value for the key)* is a dummy clause that forces Oracle to do an index scan.

The second step involves selecting all the data from the table before the *lowest key value* in the corrupted block and after the *highest key value* in the corrupted block, and putting that into a new table. This can be done by the following query:

```
create new_table as select * from corrupt_table
where key > (lowest value for the key)
and key NOT IN (key list)
```

The *key list* is the list of key values that we derived from the previous **select** statement.

For nonunique indexes, this method may cause some data loss if the duplicates are located in blocks that are not corrupted, but this can be managed to some extent by using descending index scans. For example, if key value 100 has four occurrences and one of them has a ROWID pointing to the bad block, and if the other three keys in the index leaf block are *after* this bad key, then these three keys can be retrieved using the following query:

```
Select /*+ use descending scan on index */ *
from corrupt_table where key = 'duplicate key' and
rownum < 4;
```

Finding the number of occurrences of a key should not be a problem, because we can still use index scans to count the occurrences of the key. The first query in this example will give the distinct keys that are in the block. Do a **count** on each one of them. If more than one key is pointing to the bad block, this can be solved by doing the above query iteratively, changing the ROWNUM until the query succeeds. Now in the above example, if the occurrences are mixed, then both ascending and descending scans may have to be used in a *trial-and-error* fashion. For keys that reside between the bad blocks in the index page, there seems to be no other way short of dumping some blocks. In this case, it is suggested that the DBA contact Oracle Support Services.

# CHAPTER
## 10

## Case Studies of Backup and Recovery

t just couldn't get any better. The Cleveland Indians were making a comeback in the bottom half of the ninth. Matt Williams was at the plate; one hit could put the Indians in the World Series.

Beep...beep....beep...beep.....

Shaken by the annoying sound of the beeper, we came back to reality and picked up the phone to call Henry.

"Henry, what's up?"

"Hi Rama! We have a customer on the line. The disk controller failed and they lost their data files. They have a backup from last week. They don't want to lose any data and they can't be down for more than three hours. They want to know what is the best and fastest way to recover. Can you assist?"

If you don't want to be in a situation like this, you should read this chapter carefully.

# Case Studies

In this chapter, we discuss some of the case studies of backup and recovery that are based on different kinds of failures that have occurred in real life at customer sites and recovery procedures that Oracle Support Services has recommended. Each case study has several sections and is presented in the following format:

- **Scenario**  The Scenario section presents the kinds of backups taken at the site, their frequency, and other background information, including the version of the database.

- **Problem**  This section describes the kind of failure that occurred or the situation the DBA is facing while operating the database.

- **Solution**  This section gives all possible alternatives to recover the database for the specified failure.

- **Test using Oracle Server Manager**  In this section, the recommended solution is tested on the Oracle database using SQL commands in Server Manager. For this purpose, we will provide one or more tests that simulate a particular kind of failure and the recovery procedure that is applied. We have conducted most of our tests on UNIX and Windows NT, but the procedures used are very generic and can be applied on most operating systems.

- **Test using Oracle Recovery Manager** In some cases, we provide a test based on Oracle Recovery Manager. In one case we will use the GUI, and in some others we will use the command-line interface—that is, RMAN.

- **Observation** Here, we summarize the situation and the important points to learn from the test that we performed earlier.

We will start with some simple cases and study more difficult cases as we go along.

# Case 1: NOARCHIVELOG Mode and Recovery

The purpose of this case study is to show the ramifications of operating the database in NOARCHIVELOG mode. There are some risks involved in operating in this mode, and this case study should make them clear.

## Scenario

John uses an Oracle database to maintain the inventory of his grocery store. Once every week he runs a batch job to insert, update, and delete data in his database. He uses a stand-alone Windows NT machine running Oracle8. John starts the database up in the morning at 8 A.M., shuts it down at 5 P.M., and operates the database all day in NOARCHIVELOG mode. He takes an offline (cold) backup of the database once a week, on every Sunday, by copying all the data files, online log files, and control files to tape.

## Problem

On a Wednesday morning, John realized that he had lost a data file that contained all the user data. He tried to start up the database using the **startup open** command and got the following error:

```
ORA-01157: cannot identify data file 4 - file not found
ORA-01110: data file 4: 'd:\orant\database\usr1orcl.ora'
```

He realized that he had accidentally deleted one of the data files while trying to free up some space on the disk.

## Solution

One solution in this case is to restore the complete database from the recent offline backup taken on Sunday and start up the database.

**NOTE**
*If you use this solution, you will lose the data
entered Monday and Tuesday.*

Follow these steps:

1. Take a backup of all the current data files, online log files, and control files. This is a precautionary step, in case your backup data files are bad.

2. Delete all the control files, data files, and online log files.

3. Restore all the control files, data files, and online log files from Sunday's offline backup.

4. Start up the database using the **startup open** command.

### Test Using Oracle Recovery Manager

We will use the GUI of Recovery Manager in this example. Take a cold backup of the database using Windows NT Backup Manager. Figure 10-1 shows the dialog box for the cold backup. Remember that your database is in NOARCHIVELOG mode and therefore must be shut down with the NORMAL option for this to be a valid backup.

Verify that the backup was completed by checking the directory listing of the backup directory. Figure 10-2 shows the listing of the backup for our test case.

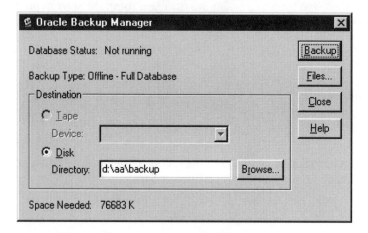

**FIGURE 10-1.** *Cold backup with Windows NT Backup Manager*

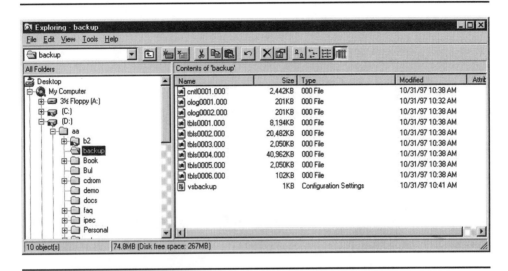

**FIGURE 10-2.** *Directory listing of cold backup*

Let's create a test table in the **user_data** tablespace and insert some records into this table. After this, we will delete the file **usr1orcl.ora** using the Windows Explorer to simulate a lost data file belonging to the **user_data** tablespace.

```
SVRMGR> create table case1 (c1 number) tablespace user_data;
Statement processed.
SVRMGR> insert into case1 values (1);
1 row processed.
SVRMGR> commit;
Statement processed.
SVRMGR> select tablespace_name, file_name, status from dba_data_files where
    2> tablespace_name = 'USER_DATA';
TABLESPACE_NAME                 FILE_NAME                    STATUS
-----------------------------   --------------------         ---------
USER_DATA                       D:\ORANT\DATABASE\USR1ORCL.ORA   AVAILABLE
1 row selected.
SVRMGR> shutdown abort
ORACLE instance shut down.
SVRMGR> host del d:\orant\database\usr1orcl.ora
```

We can now attempt to restore the **usr1orcl.ora** data file using Recovery Manager. Figure 10-3 shows the dialog box for Recovery Manager on Windows NT. Select <latest backup> and click on the OK button.

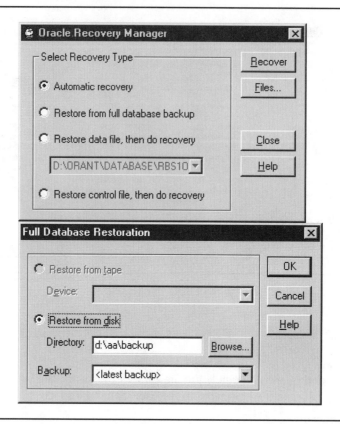

**FIGURE 10-3.** *Dialog box for database restoration in Recovery Manager*

Figure 10-4 shows that the recovery of the tablespace **user_data** was successful. Note that RMAN has simply restored the most recent cold backup since the database is in NOARCHIVELOG mode. It is very clear that the table **case1** is lost, as it did not exist when the cold backup was taken.

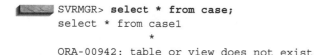
```
SVRMGR> select * from case;
select * from case1
              *
ORA-00942: table or view does not exist
```

### Observation
When the database is operating in NOARCHIVELOG mode, the changes made to the database are not archived to the archive log files. So in this case, after John restores the database, it is current as of Sunday. All the changes he made to the database from Monday through Wednesday are lost, and he needs to reenter the

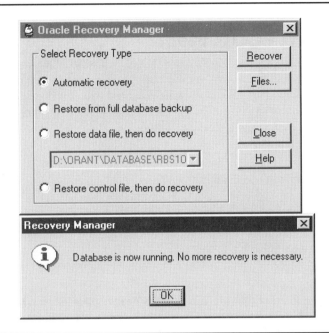

**FIGURE 10-4.**   *Successful restoration of database*

data. If the data file that is lost doesn't contain any data (such as a data file belonging to the TEMPORARY tablespace), you can start the database by taking the data file offline and rebuilding the tablespace. This is discussed in the next case study. In addition to the offline backup taken once a week, if John takes a full database export every week and an incremental export every night, a second solution can be considered here, as follows:

1. Back up all data files, control files, and redo log files as a precautionary measure.

2. Delete all database files, re-create the database, and import the data using the *complete* and *incremental export* backups. The database will now be current as of Tuesday night.

**NOTE**
*John backs up the online log files as part of his cold backup. Oracle does not recommend backing up online log files during cold or hot backups. You can always start up the database using the RESETLOGS option, which will create new online logs for you.*

## Case 2: Dropping Data Files in NOARCHIVELOG Mode

Even when you are operating the database in NOARCHIVELOG mode, depending on the type of data file that is lost, it might be possible to survive a media failure without any data loss. This case study tells you how you can do this. However, operating the database in NOARCHIVELOG mode is not recommended if you don't want to lose your data when a media failure occurs.

### Scenario

Consider the same scenario used in Case 1.

### Problem

The disk crashed and one of the data files was lost. In this case, the data file belonged to the TEMPORARY tablespace.

### Solution

In Chapter 2, we learned that the TEMPORARY tablespace is used by Oracle to do the intermediate work while executing certain commands that require sorting of data. For example, creating an index of certain SQL commands that include ORDER BY or GROUP BY clauses requires Oracle to store the sorted data in the data file that belongs to the TEMPORARY tablespace. No user tables or indexes should be stored in this data file, so it is OK to drop this data file and start up the database. To drop the data file, you need to use the **alter database datafile '*filename*' offline drop** command. Note that after opening the database, the tablespace is online, but the data file is offline. Any other data files that belong to this tablespace are online and can be used. However, Oracle recommends re-creating the tablespace. There is a specific reason for this, and it will be discussed later in Case 9.

### Test Using Server Manager

Let's perform a test by setting the database in the ARCHIVELOG mode, switching log files, and shutting down the database using the ABORT option. To simulate the loss of the data file, we will delete **tmp1orcl.ora** at the OS level and then try to take the data file offline while the database is mounted.

```
C:\ORANT\DATABASE>svrmgr30
Oracle Server Manager Release 3.0.3.0.0 - Production
(c) Copyright 1997, Oracle Corporation.  All Rights Reserved.
Oracle8 Release 8.0.3.0.0 - Production
With the Partitioning and Objects options
PL/SQL Release 8.0.3.0.0 - Production
```

```
SVRMGR> connect internal
Password:
Connected.
SVRMGR> startup mount
ORACLE instance started.
Total System Global Area        12071016 bytes
Fixed Size                         46136 bytes
Variable Size                   11090992 bytes
Database Buffers                  409600 bytes
Redo Buffers                      524288 bytes
Database mounted.
SVRMGR> archive log list
Database log mode               Archive Mode
Automatic archival              Enabled
Archive destination             C:\ORANT\database\archive
Oldest online log sequence      46
Next log sequence to archive    47
Current log sequence            47
SVRMGR> alter database noarchivelog;
Statement processed.
SVRMGR> alter database open;
Statement processed.
SVRMGR> alter system switch logfile;
Statement processed.
SVRMGR> alter system switch logfile;
Statement processed.
SVRMGR> shutdown abort
ORACLE instance shut down.
SVRMGR> host
Microsoft(R) Windows NT(TM)
(C) Copyright 1985-1996 Microsoft Corp.
C:\ORANT\DATABASE>del tmp1orcl.ora
C:\ORANT\DATABASE>exit
SVRMGR> startup mount
ORACLE instance started.
Total System Global Area        12071016 bytes
Fixed Size                         46136 bytes
Variable Size                   11090992 bytes
Database Buffers                  409600 bytes
Redo Buffers                      524288 bytes

Database mounted.
SVRMGR> alter database open;
alter database open
*
ORA-01157: cannot identify data file 4 - file not found
ORA-01110: data file 4: 'C:\ORANT\DATABASE\TMP1ORCL.ORA'
SVRMGR> alter database datafile 'c:\orant\database\tmp1orcl.ora' offline;
alter database datafile 'c:\orant\database\tmp1orcl.ora' offline
*
ORA-01145: offline immediate disallowed unless media recovery enabled
SVRMGR> alter database archivelog;
alter database archivelog
*
ORA-00265: instance recovery required, cannot set ARCHIVELOG mode
SVRMGR> alter database datafile 'c:\orant\database\tmp1orcl.ora' offline drop;
Statement processed.
SVRMGR> alter database open;
```

```
Statement processed.
SVRMGR> drop tablespace temporary_data including contents;
Statement processed.
SVRMGR> create tablespace temporary_data datafile 'c:\orant\database\tmp1orcl.ora' size 1m;
Statement processed.
```

### Observation

Note that first we tried to take the data file offline using the following command:

```
SVRMGR> alter database datafile 'c:\orant\database\tmp1orcl.ora' offline;
```

This failed because in Oracle7 and above, this command can be used only if the database is operating in ARCHIVELOG mode. Since the error indicates this, we tried to put the database in ARCHIVELOG mode. This failed because the database needs to be shut down cleanly before we can change the mode of the database. Since we shut the database with the ABORT option, until crash recovery is performed, Oracle will not allow us to put the database in ARCHIVELOG mode. However, we can't start up the database unless we have recovered the lost data file; so the only option is to take the data file offline by issuing the **alter database datafile.offline drop** command. This command bypasses the check to see whether the database is in ARCHIVELOG mode. Once we took the data file offline, the database opened fine. Note that we have to re-create the tablespace as shown in the test by dropping and re-creating the TEMPORARY_DATA tablespace. You might ask the question, "Why can't we just add another data file and keep using the database?" Why do we need to re-create the tablespace? These questions will be answered in Case 9.

Note that this procedure can be used, even if a data file that belongs to the USER tablespace or INDEX tablespace is lost. However, since the tablespace needs to be re-created, you need to make sure that you have the data to re-create the tablespace. If it is a USER tablespace, you need to re-create all the tables and insert data manually. Alternatively, you can restore the backup database onto a test machine, export the data of the USER tablespace, and import it into the production database. If it is the INDEX tablespace, you can just re-create the indexes.

# Case 3: Loss of a System Data File

There are only a limited number of recovery options that you have if some of the crucial data files such as the SYSTEM data files are lost. A solid backup procedure is the only way out of such disasters. This case study shows how to recover your database when the data file belonging to the SYSTEM tablespace is lost.

### Scenario

Moe is the DBA of a real-time call-tracking system. He uses Oracle7 release 7.3 of the database on a VAX/OpenVMS system and takes an online backup of the database every night. (Note that online backups can be performed only if the database is running in ARCHIVELOG mode.) The total database size is 5GB, and the real-time call-tracking system is a heavy OLTP (online transaction processing) system, with the maximum activity primarily between 9 A.M. and 9 P.M. every day. At 9 P.M., a batch job runs a command procedure that puts the tablespaces in *hot backup* mode, takes the backup of all the data files to tape at the operating system level, and then issues the **alter tablespace end backup** command in SVRMGR.

## Problem

One afternoon a disk crashed, losing the SYSTEM data file residing on the disk. As this happened at peak processing time, Moe had to keep the downtime to a minimum and open the database as soon as possible. He wanted to start the database first and then restore the data file that was lost, so he took the system data file offline. When he tried to open the database, he got the following error:

```
ORA-01147: SYSTEM tablespace file 1 is offline

ORA-01110: data file 1: 'DISK$WR3:[RDBMSPT.ORACLE.DATA]SYSTEM.DBS'
```

## Solution

A data file can be taken offline and the database started up, with the exception of the data files belonging to the SYSTEM tablespace. In this case, the data file that was lost belongs to the SYSTEM tablespace. The only solution here is to restore the SYSTEM data file from the previous night's online backup and then perform database recovery. Note that if the disk crash has damaged several data files, then all the damaged data files need to be restored from the online backup. The database needs to be mounted and the **recover database** command issued before the database can be opened.

### Test Using Oracle Recovery Manager

We will conduct a test that recovers the database from a full backup to simulate the loss of a data file belonging to the SYSTEM tablespace on Windows NT. We will demonstrate two recovery methods: using a backup set and using a data file copy.

We will first create a full backup set as shown here:

```
RMAN> run {
2> allocate channel c1 type disk;
3> backup database filesperset 3
4> format 'aa_full%t.%s';
5> }
RMAN-08031: released channel: c1
RMAN-03022: compiling command: allocate
RMAN-03023: executing command: allocate
```

```
RMAN-08030: allocated channel: c1
RMAN-08500: channel c1: sid=14 devtype=DISK
RMAN-03022: compiling command: backup
RMAN-03023: executing command: backup
RMAN-08008: channel c1: starting datafile backupset
RMAN-08502: set_count=2 set_stamp=318296969
RMAN-08010: channel c1: including datafile 1 in backupset
RMAN-08010: channel c1: including datafile 2 in backupset
RMAN-08010: channel c1: including datafile 3 in backupset
RMAN-08013: channel c1: piece 1 created
RMAN-08503: piece handle=AA_FULL318296969.2 comment=NONE
RMAN-08008: channel c1: starting datafile backupset
RMAN-08502: set_count=3 set_stamp=318297039
RMAN-08011: channel c1: including current controlfile in backupset
RMAN-08013: channel c1: piece 1 created
RMAN-08503: piece handle=AA_FULL318297039.3 comment=NONE
RMAN-03023: executing command: partial resync
RMAN-08003: starting partial resync of recovery catalog
RMAN-08005: partial resync complete
RMAN-08031: released channel: c1
```

We will now simulate a loss of the data file named **sys1orcl.ora** by deleting the file on the production database. If you now try to start the database, you should get an error similar to the one shown below:

```
SVRMGR> startup
ORACLE instance started.
Total System Global Area      12071016 bytes
Fixed Size                       46136 bytes
Variable Size                 11090992 bytes
Database Buffers                409600 bytes
Redo Buffers                    524288 bytes
Database mounted.
ORA-01157: cannot identify data file 1 - file not found
ORA-01110: data file 1: 'C:\ORANT\DATABASE\SYS1ORCL.ORA'
```

We will now use RMAN to recover the database using the backup set that we have created. Note that the production database (*prod*) is in a mounted stage but is not open, whereas the database that contains the recovery catalog (*rcv*) is open and available. We can open the *prod* database after restoring the SYSTEM tablespace.

```
D:\ORANT\DATABASE> rman80 target=\"internal/oracle@prod\"
rcvcat=\"rman/rman@rcv\"
Recovery Manager: Release 8.0.3.0.0 - Production
RMAN-06005: connected to target database: ORACLE
RMAN-06008: connected to recovery catalog database
```

```
RMAN> run {
2> allocate channel c1 type disk;
3> restore tablespace "system";
4> recover tablespace "system";
5> sql 'alter database open';
6> }
RMAN-03022: compiling command: allocate
RMAN-03023: executing command: allocate
RMAN-08030: allocated channel: c1
RMAN-08500: channel c1: sid=12 devtype=DISK
RMAN-03022: compiling command: restore
RMAN-03023: executing command: restore
RMAN-08016: channel c1: starting datafile backupset restore
RMAN-08502: set_count=2 set_stamp=318296969
RMAN-08019: channel c1: restoring datafile 1
RMAN-08509: destination for restore of datafile 1:
C:\ORANT\DATABASE\SYS1ORCL.ORA
RMAN-08023: channel c1: restored backup piece 1
RMAN-08511: piece handle=AA_FULL318296969.2 params=NULL
RMAN-08024: channel c1: restore complete
RMAN-03023: executing command: partial resync
RMAN-03022: compiling command: recover
RMAN-03022: compiling command: recover(1)
RMAN-03022: compiling command: recover(2)
RMAN-03022: compiling command: recover(3)
RMAN-03023: executing command: recover(3)
RMAN-08054: starting media recovery
RMAN-08055: media recovery complete
RMAN-03022: compiling command: recover(4)
RMAN-03023: executing command: partial resync
RMAN-08003: starting partial resync of recovery catalog
RMAN-08005: partial resync complete
RMAN-03022: compiling command: sql
RMAN-06162: sql statement: alter database open
RMAN-03023: executing command: sql
RMAN-06162: sql statement: alter database open
RMAN-03023: executing command: sql
RMAN-08031: released channel: c1
```

This recovery method works well. This method can be somewhat slow, especially if the backup set is stored on tape and not on disk. However, recovery can be much faster if you restore from a data file copy. Remember that a *data file copy* is a copy of the data file that is available on disk. Also, it is important that you make a data file copy on a different disk (preferably mounted under a different controller) than the one that contains the data file to protect yourself from a disk or controller failure. Let's first create a data file copy of the **sys1orcl.ora** data file.

```
RMAN> run {
2> allocate channel c1 type disk;
3> copy datafile 'c:\orant\database\sys1orcl.ora' to 'd:\temp\sys1orcl.bak';
4> }
RMAN-03022: compiling command: allocate
RMAN-03023: executing command: allocate
RMAN-08030: allocated channel: c1
RMAN-08500: channel c1: sid=12 devtype=DISK
RMAN-03022: compiling command: copy
RMAN-03023: executing command: copy
RMAN-08000: channel c1: copied datafile 1
RMAN-08501: output filename=D:\TEMP\SYS1ORCL.BAK recid=2 stamp=318298021
RMAN-03023: executing command: partial resync
RMAN-08003: starting partial resync of recovery catalog
RMAN-08005: partial resync complete
RMAN-08031: released channel: c1
```

We will now use the backup copy **sys1orcl.bak** to recover the lost data file that belongs to the SYSTEM tablespace:

```
RMAN> run {
2> allocate channel c1 type disk;
3> restore (datafile 1) from datafilecopy;
4> recover tablespace "system";
5> sql 'alter database open';
6> }
RMAN-03022: compiling command: allocate
RMAN-03023: executing command: allocate
RMAN-08030: allocated channel: c1
RMAN-08500: channel c1: sid=12 devtype=DISK
RMAN-03022: compiling command: restore
RMAN-03023: executing command: restore
RMAN-08019: channel c1: restoring datafile 1
RMAN-08507: input datafilecopy recid=2 stamp=318298021 filename=D:\TEMP\SYS1ORCL.BAK
RMAN-08509: destination for restore of datafile 1: C:\ORANT\DATABASE\SYS1ORCL.ORA
RMAN-08007: channel c1: copied datafilecopy of datafile 1
RMAN-08501: output filename=C:\ORANT\DATABASE\SYS1ORCL.ORA recid=3 stamp=318298232
RMAN-03023: executing command: partial resync
RMAN-08003: starting partial resync of recovery catalog
RMAN-08005: partial resync complete
RMAN-03022: compiling command: recover
RMAN-03022: compiling command: recover(1)
RMAN-03022: compiling command: recover(2)
RMAN-03022: compiling command: recover(3)
RMAN-03023: executing command: recover(3)
RMAN-08054: starting media recovery
RMAN-08055: media recovery complete
RMAN-03022: compiling command: recover(4)
RMAN-03023: executing command: partial resync
RMAN-08003: starting partial resync of recovery catalog
RMAN-08005: partial resync complete
RMAN-03022: compiling command: sql
RMAN-06162: sql statement: alter database open
RMAN-03023: executing command: sql
RMAN-08031: released channel: c1
```

## Observation

In this case, it took Moe approximately 45 minutes to bring the database to normal operation without Recovery Manager. This included the time to restore the SYSTEM data file from tape to disk and roll forward the data file. The restore took approximately 43 minutes and the roll forward took only 2 minutes. One way to reduce the MTTR (mean time to recover) is by maintaining a backup copy of all the database files on disk, thereby reducing the time to restore the data file from backup. Another option is to use the operating system's disk mirroring option. Comparatively, recovery with Recovery Manager took only 10 minutes, using a backup set from disk that contained the **sys1orcl.ora** file, since the backup set was on disk. Recovery using the datafile copy was even faster, as Oracle was able to use a copy of the data file **sys1orcl.bak** without any changes.

One very important point to note in this scenario is the backup scheme Moe uses. The batch job puts all the tablespaces in hot backup mode and then takes an OS backup of all the data files. This is not the recommended procedure. Oracle Support Services suggests doing hot backup of one tablespace at a time.

# Case 4: Loss of a Non-SYSTEM Data File Without Rollback Segments

As a DBA, you have a lot of options when you lose a non-SYSTEM data file that doesn't contain rollback segments. This case study gives you three recovery methods that you can use and discusses the advantages and disadvantages of each method.

## Scenario

Lisa is the DBA for an Oracle8 database on Windows NT 4.0 that holds an inventory control system. She takes a weekly offline backup on Sundays at midnight and also performs an online daily backup. She runs the database in ARCHIVELOG mode. The database is about 2.5GB and consists of a USER_DATA tablespace that is 2GB, a temporary tablespace called TEMPORARY_DATA, a tablespace for indexes called INDEX_DATA, and a tablespace for rollback segments called ROLLBACK_DATA. The USER_DATA tablespace is made up of four data files, each 500MB in size. All the non-SYSTEM rollback segments reside in the tablespace ROLLBACK_DATA.

## Problem

One of the data files that belong to the USER_DATA tablespace is lost in a disk crash. This tablespace does not have any rollback segments. Lisa wants to recover the data file as soon as possible.

**NOTE**
*Recovery of a data file that contains rollback
segments is discussed in Case 5.*

## Solution

When a non-SYSTEM data file is lost, there are three manual methods by which
the data file can be recovered. First, as discussed in Case 3, the **recover database**
command can be used. This requires the database to be mounted but not open,
which means offline recovery needs to be performed. The second method is to
use the **recover datafile** command. Here, the data file needs to be offline but the
database can be open or mounted. The third method is to use the **recover tablespace**
command, which requires the tablespace to be offline and the database to be open.
We will test all the above three methods in the next section.

   If you are using Recovery Manager, you can recover from a backup set as well
as from a data file copy.

## Test Using Server Manager

The Windows NT machine contains an Oracle8 database. In the first part of the
test, let's create a table and insert data into the table. Then, let's simulate the loss
of a non-SYSTEM data file by deleting the data file at the operating system level
and shutting down the database. After this, we will demonstrate all three methods
of recovery.

```
C:\ORANT\DATABASE>svrmgr30
Oracle Server Manager Release 3.0.3.0.0 - Production
(c) Copyright 1997, Oracle Corporation.  All Rights Reserved.
Oracle8 Release 8.0.3.0.0 - Production
With the Partitioning and Objects options
PL/SQL Release 8.0.3.0.0 - Production
SVRMGR> connect internal
Password:
Connected.

SVRMGR> create table case4(c1 number) tablespace user_data;
Statement processed.
SVRMGR> insert into case4 values(1);
1 row processed.
SVRMGR> insert into case4 values(2);
1 row processed.
SVRMGR> commit;
Statement processed.
SVRMGR> alter system switch logfile;
Statement processed.
SVRMGR> shutdown abort
ORACLE instance shut down.
SVRMGR> host
Microsoft(R) Windows NT(TM)
(C) Copyright 1985-1996 Microsoft Corp.
C:\ORANT\DATABASE>del usr1orcl.ora
C:\ORANT\DATABASE>copy backup\usr1orcl.ora
        1 file(s) copied.
C:\ORANT\DATABASE>exit
```

```
SVRMGR> startup
ORACLE instance started.
Total System Global Area      12071016 bytes
Fixed Size                       46136 bytes
Variable Size                 11090992 bytes
Database Buffers                409600 bytes
Redo Buffers                    524288 bytes
Database mounted.
ORA-01113: file 2 needs media recovery
ORA-01110: data file 2: 'C:\ORANT\DATABASE\USR1ORCL.ORA'
```

## Method 1: Database Recovery    Now, let's test the first method in recovering this database by using the **recover database** command:

```
SVRMGR> startup mount
ORACLE instance started.
Total System Global Area      12071016 bytes
Fixed Size                       46136 bytes
Variable Size                 11090992 bytes
Database Buffers                409600 bytes
Redo Buffers                    524288 bytes
Database mounted.
SVRMGR> recover database;
ORA-00279: change 319914 generated at 10/15/97 23:21:08 needed for thread 1
ORA-00289: suggestion : C:\ORANT\DATABASE\ARCHIVE\ORCLT0001S0000000055.ARC
ORA-00280: change 319914 for thread 1 is in sequence #55

 Specify log: {<RET>=suggested | filename | AUTO | CANCEL}
<enter>
Log applied.
ORA-00279: change 319948 generated at 10/15/97 23:51:42 needed for thread 1
ORA-00289: suggestion : C:\ORANT\DATABASE\ARCHIVE\ORCLT0001S0000000056.ARC
ORA-00280: change 319948 for thread 1 is in sequence #56
ORA-00278: log file 'C:\ORANT\DATABASE\ARCHIVE\ORCLT0001S0000000055.ARC' no longer needed for this recovery
 Specify log: {<RET>=suggested | filename | AUTO | CANCEL}
auto
Log applied.
ORA-00279: change 339951 generated at 10/15/97 23:55:17 needed for thread 1
ORA-00289: suggestion : C:\ORANT\DATABASE\ARCHIVE\ORCLT0001S0000000057.ARC
ORA-00280: change 339951 for thread 1 is in sequence #57
ORA-00278: log file 'C:\ORANT\DATABASE\ARCHIVE\ORCLT0001S0000000056.ARC' no longer needed for this recovery
 Log applied.
Media recovery complete.
SVRMGR> alter database open;
Statement processed.
SVRMGR> select * from case4;
C1
----------
         1
         2
2 rows selected.
```

## Method 2: Data File Recovery    This method involves taking the data file offline and opening the database before issuing the **recover datafile** command:

```
SVRMGR> startup mount;
ORACLE instance started.
Total System Global Area      12071016 bytes
Fixed Size                       46136 bytes
Variable Size                 11090992 bytes
Database Buffers                409600 bytes
Redo Buffers                    524288 bytes
```

```
Database mounted.
SVRMGR> alter database open;
ORA-01113: file 2 needs media recovery
ORA-01110: data file 2: 'C:\ORANT\DATABASE\USR1ORCL.ORA'
SVRMGR> alter database archivelog;
Statement processed.
SVRMGR> alter database datafile 'c:\orant\database\usr1orcl.ora' offline;
Statement processed.
SVRMGR> alter database open;
Statement processed.
SVRMGR> recover datafile 'c:\orant\database\usr1orcl.ora';
ORA-00279: change 319914 generated at 10/15/97 23:21:08 needed for thread 1
ORA-00289: suggestion : C:\ORANT\DATABASE\ARCHIVE\ORCLT0001S0000000055.ARC
ORA-00280: change 319914 for thread 1 is in sequence #55
 Specify log: {<RET>=suggested | filename | AUTO | CANCEL}
auto
Media recovery complete.
SVRMGR> alter database datafile 'c:\orant\database\usr1orcl.ora' online;
Statement processed.
SVRMGR> select * from case4;
C1
----------
        1
        2
2 rows selected.
```

### Method 3: Tablespace Recovery

You could also perform a tablespace recovery. This method requires that the tablespace in question is offline and the database is open:

```
SVRMGR> startup mount
ORACLE instance started.
Total System Global Area      12071016 bytes
Fixed Size                       46136 bytes
Variable Size                 11090992 bytes
Database Buffers                409600 bytes
Redo Buffers                    524288 bytes
Database mounted.
SVRMGR> alter database archivelog;
Statement processed.
SVRMGR> alter database open;
alter database open
*
ORA-01113: file 2 needs media recovery
ORA-01110: data file 2: 'C:\ORANT\DATABASE\USR1ORCL.ORA'
SVRMGR> alter database datafile 'c:\orant\database\usr1orcl.ora' offline;
Statement processed.
SVRMGR> alter database open;
Statement processed.
SVRMGR> alter tablespace user_data offline;
Statement processed.
SVRMGR> recover tablespace user_data;
ORA-00279: change 319914 generated at 10/15/97 23:21:08 needed for thread 1
ORA-00289: suggestion : C:\ORANT\DATABASE\ARCHIVE\ORCLT0001S0000000055.ARC
ORA-00280: change 319914 for thread 1 is in sequence #55
 Specify log: {<RET>=suggested | filename | AUTO | CANCEL}
auto
Log applied.
Media recovery complete.
SVRMGR> select * from case4;
C1
----------
ORA-00376: file 2 cannot be read at this time
ORA-01110: data file 2: 'C:\ORANT\DATABASE\USR1ORCL.ORA'
SVRMGR> alter tablespace user_data online;
```

```
Statement processed.
SVRMGR> select * from case4;
C1
----------
         1
         2
2 rows selected.
```

## Test Using Oracle Recovery Manager

We will now illustrate the recovery of the data file **c:\orant\database\usr1orcl.ora** using Oracle Recovery Manager. First, we will attempt to recover the tablespace USER_DATA directly. This results in an error similar to the one shown here. The data file must be restored before attempting recovery of the tablespace.

```
RMAN> run {
2> recover tablespace "user_data";
3> }
RMAN-03022: compiling command: recover
RMAN-03025: performing implicit partial resync of recovery catalog
RMAN-03023: executing command: partial resync
RMAN-08003: starting partial resync of recovery catalog
RMAN-08005: partial resync complete
RMAN-03022: compiling command: recover(1)
RMAN-03022: compiling command: recover(2)
RMAN-03026: error recovery releasing channel resources
RMAN-00569: ================error message stack follows================
RMAN-03002: failure during compilation of command
RMAN-03013: command type: recover
RMAN-03002: failure during compilation of command
RMAN-03013: command type: recover(2)
RMAN-06094: datafile 2 must be restored
```

We will now restore data file 2 from a backup set before attempting recovery of the tablespace USER_DATA:

```
RMAN> run {
> allocate channel c1 type disk;
> restore (datafile 2);
> recover tablespace "user_data";
> sql 'alter tablespace user_data online';
> }
MAN-03022: compiling command: allocate
MAN-03023: executing command: allocate
MAN-08030: allocated channel: c1
MAN-08500: channel c1: sid=17 devtype=DISK
MAN-03022: compiling command: restore
MAN-03023: executing command: restore
MAN-08016: channel c1: starting datafile backupset restore
MAN-08502: set_count=6 set_stamp=315562781
MAN-08019: channel c1: restoring datafile 2
MAN-08509: destination for restore of datafile 5: C:\ORANT\DATABASE\USR1ORCL.ORA
MAN-08023: channel c1: restored backup piece 1
MAN-08511: piece handle=AA_FULL1ORACLE.6 params=NULL
MAN-08024: channel c1: restore complete
MAN-03023: executing command: partial resync
RMAN-08003: starting partial resync of recovery catalog
RMAN-08005: partial resync complete
RMAN-03022: compiling command: recover
RMAN-03022: compiling command: recover(1)
RMAN-03022: compiling command: recover(2)
RMAN-03022: compiling command: recover(3)
```

```
RMAN-03023: executing command: recover(3)
RMAN-08054: starting media recovery
RMAN-08515: archivelog filename=C:\ORANT\DATABASE\ARCHIVE\ORCLT0001S0000000381.A
RC thread=1 sequence=381
RMAN-08515: archivelog filename=C:\ORANT\DATABASE\ARCHIVE\ORCLT0001S0000000382.A
RC thread=1 sequence=382
RMAN-08515: archivelog filename=C:\ORANT\DATABASE\ARCHIVE\ORCLT0001S0000000383.A
RC thread=1 sequence=383
RMAN-08515: archivelog filename=C:\ORANT\DATABASE\ARCHIVE\ORCLT0001S0000000384.A
RC thread=1 sequence=384
RMAN-08515: archivelog filename=C:\ORANT\DATABASE\ARCHIVE\ORCLT0001S0000000385.A
RC thread=1 sequence=385
RMAN-08055: media recovery complete
RMAN-03022: compiling command: recover(4)
RMAN-03023: executing command: partial resync
RMAN-08003: starting partial resync of recovery catalog
RMAN-08005: partial resync complete
RMAN-03022: compiling command: sql
RMAN-06162: sql statement: alter tablespace user_data online
RMAN-03023: executing command: sql
RMAN-08031: released channel: c1
```

You could also use a data file copy to recover the tablespace. This would be an even faster method to perform such a recovery. Here is the same example again using a copy of **usr1orcl.ora** for recovery. First, we will make a file copy of the data file:

```
RMAN> run {
2> allocate channel c1 type disk;
3> copy datafile 'c:\orant\database\usr1orcl.ora' to 'd:\temp\usr1orcl.bak';
4> }
RMAN-03022: compiling command: allocate
RMAN-03023: executing command: allocate
RMAN-08030: allocated channel: c1
RMAN-08500: channel c1: sid=13 devtype=DISK
RMAN-03022: compiling command: copy
RMAN-03025: performing implicit partial resync of recovery catalog
RMAN-03023: executing command: partial resync
RMAN-08003: starting partial resync of recovery catalog
RMAN-08005: partial resync complete
RMAN-03023: executing command: copy
RMAN-08000: channel c1: copied datafile 2
RMAN-08501: output filename=D:\TEMP\USR1ORCL.BAK recid=8 stamp=316023468
RMAN-03023: executing command: partial resync
RMAN-08003: starting partial resync of recovery catalog
RMAN-08005: partial resync complete
RMAN-08031: released channel: c1
```

The recovery process is shown here:

```
RMAN> run {
2> allocate channel c1 type disk;
3> restore (datafile 2) from datafilecopy;
4> recover tablespace "user_data";
5> sql 'alter database open';
6> }
RMAN-03022: compiling command: allocate
RMAN-03023: executing command: allocate
RMAN-08030: allocated channel: c1
RMAN-08500: channel c1: sid=13 devtype=DISK
RMAN-03022: compiling command: restore
RMAN-03025: performing implicit partial resync of recovery catalog
RMAN-03023: executing command: partial resync
```

```
RMAN-08003: starting partial resync of recovery catalog
RMAN-08005: partial resync complete
RMAN-03023: executing command: restore
RMAN-08019: channel c1: restoring datafile 2
RMAN-08507: input datafilecopy recid=8 stamp=316023468 filename=D:\TEMP\USR1ORCL.BAK
RMAN-08509: destination for restore of datafile 2: C:\ORANT\DATABASE\USR1ORCL.ORA
RMAN-08007: channel c1: copied datafilecopy of datafile 2
RMAN-08501: output filename=C:\ORANT\DATABASE\USR1ORCL.ORA recid=11 stamp=316024158
RMAN-03023: executing command: partial resync
RMAN-08003: starting partial resync of recovery catalog
RMAN-08005: partial resync complete
RMAN-03022: compiling command: recover
RMAN-03022: compiling command: recover(1)
RMAN-03022: compiling command: recover(2)
RMAN-03022: compiling command: recover(3)
RMAN-03023: executing command: recover(3)
RMAN-08054: starting media recovery
RMAN-08515: archivelog filename=C:\ORANT\DATABASE\ARCHIVE\ORCLT0001S0000000585.ARC thread=1 sequence=585
RMAN-08515: archivelog filename=C:\ORANT\DATABASE\ARCHIVE\ORCLT0001S0000000586.ARC thread=1 sequence=586
RMAN-08055: media recovery complete
RMAN-03022: compiling command: recover(4)
RMAN-03023: executing command: partial resync
RMAN-08003: starting partial resync of recovery catalog
RMAN-08005: partial resync complete
RMAN-03022: compiling command: sql
RMAN-06162: sql statement: alter database open
RMAN-03023: executing command: sql
RMAN-08031: released channel: c1
```

## Observation

There are a few important points to note in these tests. In method 1 (of recovery without RMAN), note that when Oracle requested archive log **C:\ORANT\ DATABASE\ARCHIVE\ORCLT0001S0000000055.ARC**, we pressed the ENTER key, and this applied only the suggested log file. When Oracle asked for the second log, we entered **auto**, which turned *autorecovery* on. This means Oracle will automatically apply the log files if it can find them in the archive destination. If you are doing complete recovery and have to apply a lot of log files, it's easy for you to use autorecovery. Also, in method 1 we have done database recovery, which requires the database to be mounted but not open (offline recovery).

Methods 2 and 3 show how to do online recovery. Note that the database is open before doing recovery. However, the data file to be recovered was offline during recovery. While doing tablespace recovery, all files belonging to the tablespace should be offline. In method 3, after recovery, the **select** statement failed because the data file was still offline. Once the tablespace was brought online, the **select** statement succeeded.

So, which method should you use? To determine that, you need to ask yourself, "How many log files do I need to apply, and can I afford to keep the database down for that long?" If you can, then use method 1, in which the database is not open during recovery. However, if you have to open the database so that users can use other parts of the database, then you have to do online recovery by choosing method 2 or method 3.

How do you determine when to use data file recovery, as opposed to tablespace recovery? If you have a number of data files that belong to a tablespace and one of them is lost, you might want to do data file recovery (method 2) because you can keep the other data files of the tablespace available to the users. Note that if an application tries to read data from the offline data file, it will fail.

If most of the data files that belong to a tablespace are lost, using data file and tablespace recovery methods has its own advantages. For example, if a tablespace has 20 data files and all of them are lost, by using data file recovery you can parallelize recovery, but you need to issue the **recovery** command 20 times. Even if you recover multiple data files in one command, you still have to type the full path name of each data file. On the other hand, if you decide to do tablespace recovery, you have to issue the **recovery** command just once. Note that Oracle releases 7.1 and later provide parallel recovery.

An alternative method to recover a lost non-SYSTEM data file is to use the **alter database create datafile** command. This method will be discussed in Case 12.

# Case 5: Loss of a Non-SYSTEM Data File with Rollback Segments

If a non-SYSTEM data file that is lost contains rollback segments, recovery needs to be performed with care. You should understand the ramifications of recovering from such disasters, especially if you decide to do online recovery. This case study gives you some helpful hints while trying to recover non-SYSTEM data files that contain rollback segments. The overall procedure is very similar to Case 4.

### Scenario
This is the same as in Case 4. Note that all non-SYSTEM rollback segments are in the tablespace ROLLBACK_DATA.

### Problem
On Monday morning, due to a media failure, all the data files that belong to the rollback segments tablespace ROLLBACK_DATA were lost. It is the beginning of the week, and a lot of applications need to be run against the database, so Lisa (the DBA) decides to do online recovery. Once she took the data files offline and opened the database, she tried to select from a user table and got the Oracle error:

```
ORA-00376: file 2 cannot be read at this time
```

File 2 happens to be one of the data files that belong to the rollback segment tablespace.

### Solution
If the data file that is lost belongs to a rollback segment tablespace, recovery could be tricky. Since Lisa decided to do online recovery, she did the right thing by taking

all the data files offline that were lost during the media failure. This means that all the rollback segments that belong to the data file need to be recovered. However, while recovery is being performed, no rows that are involved in an active transaction that points to the rollback segments can be accessed. Until you recover the data files that contain the rollback segments, you need to create some temporary rollback segments to process the new applications. The following test will make the process of recovering the data files that contain rollback segments clear.

### Test Using Server Manager
In this test, to simulate the loss of data files, we will shut the database down with the ABORT option and delete the data file belonging to the ROLLBACK_DATA tablespace at the OS level:

```
C:\ORANT\DATABASE>svrmgr30
Oracle Server Manager Release 3.0.3.0.0 - Production
(c) Copyright 1997, Oracle Corporation.  All Rights Reserved.
Oracle8 Release 8.0.3.0.0 - Production
With the Partitioning and Objects options
PL/SQL Release 8.0.3.0.0 - Production
SVRMGR> connect internal
Password:
Connected.
SVRMGR> create table case5 (c1 number) tablespace user_data;
Statement processed.
SVRMGR> select * from case5;
C1
----------
0 rows selected.
SVRMGR> set transaction use rollback segment rb1;
Statement processed.
SVRMGR> insert into case5 values(5);
1 row processed.
SVRMGR> shutdown abort
ORACLE instance shut down.
SVRMGR> exit
C:\ORANT\DATABASE>del rbs1orcl.ora
C:\ORANT\DATABASE>copy backup\rbs1orcl.ora
        1 file(s) copied.
```

Before we start recovery, a very important step needs to be performed here. The **init.ora** file needs to be modified, and the ROLLBACK_SEGMENTS parameter needs to be commented out. If this is not done, Oracle will not be able to find the existing rollback segments and you won't be able to open the database.

```
C:\ORANT\DATABASE>svrmgr30
Oracle Server Manager Release 3.0.3.0.0 - Production
(c) Copyright 1997, Oracle Corporation.  All Rights Reserved.
Oracle8 Release 8.0.3.0.0 - Production
With the Partitioning and Objects options
PL/SQL Release 8.0.3.0.0 - Production
SVRMGR> connect internal
Password:
Connected.
SVRMGR> startup mount;
ORACLE instance started.
Total System Global Area      12071016 bytes
Fixed Size                       46136 bytes
Variable Size                 11090992 bytes
Database Buffers                409600 bytes
Redo Buffers                    524288 bytes
Database mounted.
SVRMGR> alter database datafile 'C:\orant\database\rbs1orcl.ora' offline;
Statement processed.
SVRMGR> alter database open;
Statement processed.
SVRMGR> create rollback segment temp1 tablespace system;
Statement processed.
SVRMGR> create rollback segment temp2 tablespace system;
Statement processed.
SVRMGR> alter rollback segment temp1 online;
Statement processed.
SVRMGR> alter rollback segment temp2 online;
Statement processed.
SVRMGR> select * from case5;
C1
----------
ORA-00376: file 3 cannot be read at this time
ORA-01110: data file 3: 'C:\ORANT\DATABASE\RBS1ORCL.ORA'
SVRMGR> select segment_name, status from dba_rollback_segs;
SEGMENT_NAME                    STATUS
------------------------------  ----------------
SYSTEM                          ONLINE
RB_TEMP                         OFFLINE
RB1                             NEEDS RECOVERY
RB2                             NEEDS RECOVERY
RB3                             NEEDS RECOVERY
RB4                             NEEDS RECOVERY
RB5                             NEEDS RECOVERY
RB6                             NEEDS RECOVERY
RB7                             NEEDS RECOVERY
RB8                             OFFLINE
RB9                             OFFLINE
RB10                            OFFLINE
RB11                            OFFLINE
RB12                            OFFLINE
RB13                            OFFLINE
RB14                            OFFLINE
RB15                            OFFLINE
RB16                            OFFLINE
TEMP1                           ONLINE
```

```
TEMP2                         ONLINE
20 rows selected.
SVRMGR> recover tablespace rollback_data;
ORA-00279: change 319914 generated at 10/15/97 23:21:08 needed for thread 1
ORA-00289: suggestion : C:\ORANT\DATABASE\ARCHIVE\ORCLT0001S0000000055.ARC
ORA-00280: change 319914 for thread 1 is in sequence #55
 Specify log: {<RET>=suggested | filename | AUTO | CANCEL}
auto
Log applied.
ORA-00279: change 339951 generated at 10/15/97 23:55:17 needed for thread 1
ORA-00289: suggestion : C:\ORANT\DATABASE\ARCHIVE\ORCLT0001S0000000057.ARC
ORA-00280: change 339951 for thread 1 is in sequence #57
ORA-00278: log file 'C:\ORANT\DATABASE\ARCHIVE\ORCLT0001S0000000056.ARC' no
longer needed for this recovery
 Log applied.
ORA-00279: change 359990 generated at 10/16/97 15:42:48 needed for thread 1
ORA-00289: suggestion : C:\ORANT\DATABASE\ARCHIVE\ORCLT0001S0000000058.ARC
ORA-00280: change 359990 for thread 1 is in sequence #58
ORA-00278: log file 'C:\ORANT\DATABASE\ARCHIVE\ORCLT0001S0000000057.ARC' no
longer needed for this recovery
 Log applied.
ORA-00279: change 380035 generated at 10/16/97 16:04:22 needed for thread 1
ORA-00289: suggestion : C:\ORANT\DATABASE\ARCHIVE\ORCLT0001S0000000059.ARC
ORA-00280: change 380035 for thread 1 is in sequence #59
ORA-00278: log file 'C:\ORANT\DATABASE\ARCHIVE\ORCLT0001S0000000058.ARC' no longer needed for this recovery
 Log applied.
Media recovery complete.
SVRMGR> select * from case5;
C1
----------
ORA-00376: file 3 cannot be read at this time
ORA-01110: data file 3: 'C:\ORANT\DATABASE\RBS1ORCL.ORA'
SVRMGR> alter tablespace rollback_data online;
Statement processed.
SVRMGR> select * from case5;
C1
----------
0 rows selected.
SVRMGR> select segment_name,status from dba_rollback_segs;

SEGMENT_NAME                   STATUS
------------------------------ ----------------
SYSTEM                         ONLINE
RB_TEMP                        OFFLINE
RB1                            NEEDS RECOVERY
RB2                            NEEDS RECOVERY
RB3                            NEEDS RECOVERY
RB4                            NEEDS RECOVERY
RB5                            NEEDS RECOVERY
RB6                            NEEDS RECOVERY
RB7                            NEEDS RECOVERY
RB8                            OFFLINE
RB9                            OFFLINE
RB10                           OFFLINE
RB11                           OFFLINE
RB12                           OFFLINE
RB13                           OFFLINE
```

```
RB14                              OFFLINE
RB15                              OFFLINE
RB16                              OFFLINE
TEMP1                             ONLINE
TEMP2                             ONLINE
20 rows selected.
SVRMGR> alter rollback segment rb1 online;
Statement processed.
SVRMGR> alter rollback segment rb2 online;
Statement processed.
SVRMGR> alter rollback segment rb3 online;
Statement processed.
SVRMGR> alter rollback segment rb4 online;
Statement processed.
SVRMGR> alter rollback segment rb5 online;
Statement processed.
SVRMGR> alter rollback segment rb6 online;
Statement processed.
SVRMGR> alter rollback segment rb7 online;
Statement processed.
SVRMGR> alter rollback segment temp1 offline;
Statement processed.
SVRMGR> alter rollback segment temp2 offline;
Statement processed.
SVRMGR> drop rollback segment temp1;
Statement processed.
SVRMGR> drop rollback segment temp2;
Statement processed.
```

Be sure to restore the ROLLBACK_SEGMENTS parameter in the **init.ora** file.

## Test Using Oracle Recovery Manager
The same recovery from a backup set is performed using Recovery Manager, as shown here:

```
RMAN> run {
2> allocate channel c1 type disk;
3> restore (datafile 3);
4> recover tablespace "rollback_data";
5> sql 'alter tablespace rollback_data online';
6> }
RMAN-03022: compiling command: allocate
RMAN-03023: executing command: allocate
RMAN-08030: allocated channel: c1
RMAN-08500: channel c1: sid=17 devtype=DISK
RMAN-03022: compiling command: restore
RMAN-03022: compiling command: allocate
RMAN-03023: executing command: allocate
RMAN-08030: allocated channel: c1
RMAN-08500: channel c1: sid=17 devtype=DISK
RMAN-03022: compiling command: restore
RMAN-03023: executing command: restore
RMAN-08016: channel c1: starting datafile backupset restore
RMAN-08502: set_count=5 set_stamp=315562680
RMAN-08019: channel c1: restoring datafile 3
```

```
RMAN-08509: destination for restore of datafile 3: C:\ORANT\DATABASE\RBS1ORCL.ORA
MAN-08023: channel c1: restored backup piece 1
MAN-08511: piece handle=AA_FULL1ORACLE.6 params=NULL
RMAN-08024: channel c1: restore complete
RMAN-03023: executing command: partial resync
RMAN-08003: starting partial resync of recovery catalog
RMAN-08005: partial resync complete
RMAN-03022: compiling command: recover
RMAN-03022: compiling command: recover(1)
RMAN-03022: compiling command: recover(2)
RMAN-03022: compiling command: recover(3)
RMAN-03023: executing command: recover(3)
RMAN-08054: starting media recovery
RMAN-08515: archivelog filename=C:\ORANT\DATABASE\ARCHIVE\ORCLT0001S0000000381.A
RC thread=1 sequence=381
RMAN-08515: archivelog filename=C:\ORANT\DATABASE\ARCHIVE\ORCLT0001S0000000382.A
RC thread=1 sequence=382
RMAN-08515: archivelog filename=C:\ORANT\DATABASE\ARCHIVE\ORCLT0001S0000000383.A
RC thread=1 sequence=383
RMAN-08515: archivelog filename=C:\ORANT\DATABASE\ARCHIVE\ORCLT0001S0000000384.A
RC thread=1 sequence=384
RMAN-08515: archivelog filename=C:\ORANT\DATABASE\ARCHIVE\ORCLT0001S0000000385.A
RC thread=1 sequence=385
RMAN-08515: archivelog filename=C:\ORANT\DATABASE\ARCHIVE\ORCLT0001S0000000386.A
RC thread=1 sequence=386
RMAN-08515: archivelog filename=C:\ORANT\DATABASE\ARCHIVE\ORCLT0001S0000000387.A
RC thread=1 sequence=387
RMAN-08515: archivelog filename=C:\ORANT\DATABASE\ARCHIVE\ORCLT0001S0000000388.A
RC thread=1 sequence=388
RMAN-08055: media recovery complete
RMAN-03022: compiling command: recover(4)
RMAN-03023: executing command: partial resync
RMAN-08003: starting partial resync of recovery catalog
RMAN-08005: partial resync complete
RMAN-03022: compiling command: sql
RMAN-06162: sql statement: alter tablespace rollback_data online
RMAN-03023: executing command: sql
RMAN-08031: released channel: c1
```

Remember to bring the rollback segments online using the **alter rollback segment.online** command.

## Observation

In this test, we first created a table and inserted a row into it. Before we committed the transaction, we shut down the database with the ABORT option. This means that the rollback segment's transaction table will now show that the transaction is active. Also, note that before we inserted the data, we made sure that the transaction uses rollback segment **rb1**, which resides in the data file that belongs to the rollback segment tablespace. The **set transaction use rollback...** command is used for this purpose.

Now, after the database is open, the **select \* from case5** command tries to read the data block. Oracle cannot read the block because recovery has finished the roll forward but not the roll back of uncommitted transactions. This means that Oracle cannot determine whether the row we have inserted is committed or rolled back. This is because we have taken the data files that contain the rollback segments offline. Note that the rollback segments show that they are in NEEDS RECOVERY state. Once we have finished tablespace recovery, the rollback segments are still in NEEDS RECOVERY. However, since recovery has rolled back the uncommitted transactions, we can select from the table **case5**. At this point, we need to bring all the rollback segments online using the **alter rollback segment** command. Also note that we have created two temporary rollback segments, **temp1** and **temp2**, during the recovery process. These rollback segments can be used by applications while the ROLLBACK_DATA tablespace is being recovered.

An alternative way to do recovery in this scenario is to do data file recovery. Case 4 discusses the advantages and disadvantages of using data file recovery and tablespace recovery.

# Case 6: Loss of an Unarchived Online Log File

Any online log file that hasn't been archived yet by the ARCH process is called an *unarchived online log file*. Losing these files can cause data loss if you don't multiplex the online logs. This case study gives you information on how to recover from such failures.

## Scenario

Sarah works in a software company as a DBA administering a small development database on a UNIX machine. She created a 500MB database with Oracle7 release 7.3. She decided to mirror the control files but not the online log files, so she created the database with three log groups with one member each. Her backup strategy includes taking online backups twice a week and a full database export once a week.

## Problem

A power surge caused the database to crash and also caused a media failure, losing all the online log files. All the data files and the current control files are intact.

## Solution

Although the data files are OK after the crash, these files cannot be used because crash recovery cannot be performed (since all online log files are lost). Forcing the database open in a situation like this can cause database inconsistency. If any of the unarchived log files are lost, crash recovery cannot be performed and, instead, media recovery needs to be performed. In this case, all the data files need to be restored from an online (or offline) full backup and rolled forward until the last available archived log file is applied. Since this is *incomplete recovery*, tablespace or data file recovery is not possible. The only option is to use the **recover database** command.

## Test Using Server Manager

This test simulates the loss of online log files by shutting down the database with the ABORT option and deleting all the online log files. The backup data files are restored, and the current control file is used to do incomplete recovery.

```
SVRMGR> shutdown abort
ORACLE instance shut down.
SVRMGR> exit
Server Manager complete.
cosmos% rm /home/orahome/data/733/*.log
cosmos% cp /home/orahome/backup/*.dbf /home/orahome/data/733
cosmos% svrmgrl
Oracle Server Manager Release 2.3.3.0.0 - Production
Copyright (c) Oracle Corporation 1994, 1995. All rights reserved.
Oracle7 Server Release 7.3.3.0.0 - Production Release
With the distributed, replication, parallel query and Spatial Data options
PL/SQL Release 2.3.3.0.0 - ProductionSVRMGR> connect internal
Connected.
SVRMGR> startup mount
ORACLE instance started.
Database mounted.
SVRMGR> recover database until cancel;

ORA-00279: Change 6232 generated at 02/03/95 08:45:58 needed for thread 1
ORA-00289: Suggestion : /home/orahome/product/733/dbs/arch1_50.dbf
ORA-00280: Change 6232 for thread 1 is in sequence #50
Specify log: {<RET>=suggested | filename | AUTO | FROM logsource | CANCEL}
enter
Applying suggested logfile...
Log applied.
ORA-00279: Change 6269 generated at 02/03/95 19:46:32 needed for thread 1
ORA-00289: Suggestion : /home/orahome/product/733/dbs/arch1_51.dbf
ORA-00280: Change 6269 for thread 1 is in sequence #51
ORA-00278: Logfile '/home/orahome/product/733/dbs/arch1_50.dbf' no longer needed for this recovery

Specify log: {<RET>=suggested | filename | AUTO | FROM logsource | CANCEL}
enter
Applying suggested logfile...
Log applied.
```

..........(Log files 52 through 55 are applied)

```
ORA-00279: Change 6310 generated at 02/03/95 22:55:43 needed for thread 1
ORA-00289: Suggestion : /home/orahome/product/733/dbs/arch1_56.dbf
ORA-00280: Change 6310 for thread 1 is in sequence #56
ORA-00278: Logfile '/home/orahome/product/733/dbs/arch1_55.dbf' no longer needed for this recovery
Specify log: {<RET>=suggested | filename | AUTO | FROM logsource | CANCEL}
cancel
Media recovery cancelled.
```

```
SVRMGR> alter database open resetlogs;
Statement processed.
SVRMGR> shutdown
Database closed.
Database dismounted.
ORACLE instance shut down.
SVRMGR> exit
 cosmos% ls
control01.ctl  rbs01.dbf   redo03.log    test1.dbf
control02.ctl  redo01.log  system01.dbf  tools01.dbf
control03.ctl  redo02.log  temp.dbf      users01.dbf
```

## Observation

Note that all the data files need to be restored from the backup before applying recovery. The **recover database until cancel** command lets you apply the log files one at a time, and you can cancel when the last archive log file is applied. Alternatively, the **recover database until change** or **recover database until time** command can be used if you want to roll forward to a specific SCN (system change number) or time. After recovery, the **ls** command on the UNIX operating system shows the database files in the directory. Note that Oracle created the online log files **redo01.log**, **redo02.log**, and **redo03.log** automatically when the database was opened with the RESETLOGS option.

The best way to protect the database from losing the online log files is to mirror them. We have learned in Chapter 2 that each log group can have multiple members, and each member should be placed on a different disk drive mounted under a separate disk controller. Multiplexing the log files is strongly recommended by Oracle Corporation.

# Case 7: Database Crash During Hot Backups

If the database crashed while taking online backups, recovery was unnecessarily complicated with Oracle RDBMS releases prior to release 7.3. This case study is presented to illustrate the new functionality introduced in 7.3 with which a data file can be put in end backup mode when the database is not open. The mean time to recover (MTTR) will improve drastically, as there is no recovery that needs to be done. This feature is available in version 7.3 and later.

## Scenario

Kevin is one of the DBAs of a Fortune 500 financial company and maintains one of the company's most crucial databases. A UNIX machine is used to store a 500GB database using Oracle7 release 7.3. The database operates 24 hours a day, 7 days a week, with 200 to 250 concurrent users on the system at any given time. There are 250 tablespaces, and the backup procedure involves keeping the tablespaces in hot backup mode and taking an online backup. Each log file is 10MB. Between issuing the **begin backup** and **end backup** commands, Oracle generates about 50 archive log files.

## Problem

On Friday afternoon, while taking hot backups, the machine crashed, bringing the database down. As this is a mission-critical workshop, Kevin needed to bring the database up as quickly as possible. Once the machine was booted, he tried to start the database and Oracle asked for media recovery starting from log file sequence number 2300. The current online log file had sequence number 2335, which meant that about 35 log files needed to be applied before the database could be opened. Realizing that this would require a significant amount of database downtime, Kevin nervously reached for the phone to call Oracle Support Services.

## Solution

Oracle introduced a wonderful new functionality in release 7.2 that gives the DBAs the ability to end the backups of data files that are in hot backup mode by using the **alter database datafile '*file_name' end backup*** command.

However, in the case of release 7.1, you still need to apply recovery when the database crashes while taking online backups. You might wonder what happens if the data file is replaced with a backup data file before issuing the above command. The next section will perform this test.

## Test Using Server Manager

This test puts the tablespace TEST in begin backup mode. After taking the backup of the data file at the OS level, data is inserted into the table that resides in the tablespace TEST. Then the database is shut down with the ABORT option to simulate the database crash.

```
cosmos% svrmgrl
Oracle Server Manager Release 2.3.3.0.0 - Production
Copyright (c) Oracle Corporation 1994, 1995. All rights reserved.
Oracle7 Server Release 7.3.3.0.0 - Production Release
With the distributed, replication, parallel query and Spatial Data options
PL/SQL Release 2.3.3.0.0 - Production

SVRMGR> connect internal
Connected.
SVRMGR> startup
ORACLE instance started.
Database mounted.
Database opened.

Total System Global Area       4481448 bytes
    Fixed Size                   47152 bytes
    Variable Size              4016504 bytes
    Database Buffers            409600 bytes
    Redo Buffers                  8192 bytes
```

```
SVRMGR> archive log list
Database log mode               ARCHIVELOG
Automatic archival              ENABLED
Archive destination             /home/orahome/product/7.3.3/dbs/arch
Oldest online log sequence      53
Next log sequence to archive    55
Current log sequence            55

SVRMGR> alter tablespace test begin backup;
Statement processed.
SVRMGR> host

cosmos% cp /home/orahome/data/733/test1.dbf /home/orahome/backup/hot
cosmos% exit
SVRMGR> create table case7 (c1 number) tablespace test;
Statement processed.
SVRMGR> insert into case7 values(7);
Statement processed.
SVRMGR> commit;
Statement processed.
SVRMGR> alter system switch logfile;
Statement processed.
SVRMGR> shutdown abort
ORACLE instance shut down.
```

Now we will perform two tests. The first test involves attempting to open the database with the current data file, **test01.dbf**. The second test involves replacing the current data file, **test01.dbf**, with the backup version of this file and trying to fool Oracle into thinking that it's the current file.

### Test 1: Using the Current Data File

```
SVRMGR> startup mount
ORACLE instance started.
Database mounted.
SVRMGR> alter database open;
ORA-01113: file 5 needs media recovery
ORA-01110: data file 5: '/home/orahome/data/733/test1.dbf'
SVRMGR> alter database datafile '/home/orahome/data/733/test1.dbf' end backup;
Statement processed.
SVRMGR> alter database open;
Statement processed.
SVRMGR> select * from case7;
C1
----------
         7
1 row selected.
```

### Test 2: Using the Backup Data File

```
cosmos% rm /home/orahome/data/733/test1.dbf
cosmos% cp /home/orahome/backup/hot/test1.dbf /home/orahome/data/733
SVRMGR> startup mount
ORACLE instance started.

Database mounted.
SVRMGR> alter database open;
ORA-01113: file 5 needs media recovery
ORA-01110: data file 5: '/home/orahome/data/733/test1.dbf'
SVRMGR> alter database datafile '/home/orahome/data/733/test1.dbf' end backup;
ORA-01235: END BACKUP failed for 1 file(s) and succeeded for 0
ORA-01122: database file 5 failed verification check
ORA-01110: data file 5: '/home/orahome/data/733/test1.dbf'
ORA-01208: data file is an old version - not accessing current version

SVRMGR> recover database
Media recovery complete.
SVRMGR> alter database open;
Statement processed.
SVRMGR> select * from case7;
C1
----------
         7
1 row selected.
SVRMGR> exit
```

## Observation

Note that when a tablespace is in hot backup mode, only some data structures in the data file header (or headers, if multiple data files exist for that tablespace) are updated, while the others are frozen. However, the contents of the file are current. For example, if an update is done on a table in this data file, the update is not blocked. But when a checkpoint is done, the *checkpointed at SCN* value is not written to the file header. This means that if a crash occurs during a hot backup, Oracle really needs to update only the file header and not the contents of the data file while opening the database. Issuing the **alter database datafile filename end backup** command does exactly that.

   In the second test that we performed, we tried to replace the data file with a backup copy. Oracle can distinguish between a current data file in hot backup mode and a restored copy of the data file by comparing the checkpoint counters in the file header and the control file. So, to summarize, you should not replace the data file, since the file contents are perfectly fine and all you need to do is just mount the database and end the backup before opening the database.

Note that the error that we received while trying to open the database for the first time after the crash is not very helpful—it just indicates that media recovery is required for a specific file(s) but doesn't tell us why. If you want to know if any data files are in hot backup mode, use the V$BACKUP view in the data dictionary. This view will give you the status of all the files. If the status says ACTIVE, then the file is in hot backup mode. For example:

```
SVRMGR> select file#, status from v$backup;
FILE#        STATUS
-----        ------
1            ACTIVE
2            NOT ACTIVE
3            NOT ACTIVE
4            NOT ACTIVE
4 rows selected.
```

# Case 8: Recovery with a Backup Control File

When using a backup control file, recovery can be tricky. You should always try to do recovery with the current control file if possible; the second best option is to create a new control file. Using the backup control file should be the last option to use, as the database needs to be started up with the RESETLOGS option. This case study gives a clear explanation of why this is necessary and the precautions you should take after starting up the database.

### Scenario

Jane uses Oracle7 release 7.3 for Windows NT on her PC for her home business. She maintains a small 20MB database and takes regular cold backups. Her backup procedure involves shutting down the database and copying the data files, log files, and control file to floppy disks. She maintains only one copy of the control file and doesn't mirror the control file because she thinks mirroring the control file doesn't make sense, since she has only one hard disk.

### Problem

Jane accidentally deleted her control file. Since she didn't have a copy of the control file, she copied the backup control file and tried to start up the database. While opening the database, Oracle complained that an old control file was being used.

### Solution

In this case, Jane has two options. Since all her data files and online log files are safe, she can create a new control file using the **create controlfile** command, perform recovery if required, and start up the database. Alternatively, she can use the backup control file. If you use a backup control file, you need to perform media recovery. Also, Oracle will force you to use the *using backup controlfile* option. Once recovery is done, you must start up the database with the RESETLOGS option, and you have to take a complete backup of your database. For this reason, it's a better idea to use the first solution in this case.

## Test Using Server Manager

In this section we will test the second option that was just described in the Solution section, since quite a few users try this option. We will first show how to use this in the interactive mode using Server Manager. Then we use RMAN to repeat the same recovery process.

```
c:\orant\bin> svrmgr23
Oracle Server Manager Release 2.3.3.0.0 - Production
Copyright (c) Oracle Corporation 1994, 1995. All rights reserved.
Oracle7 Server Release 7.3.0.0.0 - Production Release
With the distributed, replication, parallel query and Spatial Data options
PL/SQL Release 2.3.3.0.0 - Production

SVRMGR> connect internal
Connected.
SVRMGR> startup open
ORACLE instance started.
Database mounted.
Database opened.
Total System Global Area       4480888 bytes
    Fixed Size                   47152 bytes
    Variable Size              4015944 bytes
    Database Buffers            409600 bytes
    Redo Buffers                  8192 bytes

SVRMGR> select name, status, enabled from v$datafile;
NAME                                 STATUS       ENABLED
-----                                ------       ----------
C:\ORANT\DATABASE\SYS1ORCL.ORA       SYSTEM       READ WRITE
C:\ORANT\DATABASE\USR1ORCL.ORA       ONLINE       READ WRITE
C:\ORANT\DATABASE\RBS1ORCL.ORA       ONLINE       READ WRITE
C:\ORANT\DATABASE\TMP1ORCL.ORA       ONLINE       READ WRITE
C:\ORANT\DATABASE\TST1ORCL.ORA       ONLINE       READ ONLY
5 rows selected.

SVRMGR> create table case8 (c1 number) tablespace user_data;
Statement processed.

SVRMGR> insert into case8 values (8);
1 row processed.
SVRMGR> commit;
Statement processed.
SVRMGR> alter system switch logfile;
Statement processed.
SVRMGR> alter system switch logfile;
Statement processed.
SVRMGR> alter system switch logfile;
```

```
Statement processed.
SVRMGR> shutdown abort
ORACLE instance shut down.
SVRMGR> exit
c:\orant\database> copy c*.ora backup
c:\orant\database> svrmgr23
Oracle Server Manager Release 2.3.3.0.0 - Production
Copyright (c) Oracle Corporation 1994, 1995. All rights reserved.
Oracle7 Server Release 7.3.3.0.0 - Production Release
With the distributed, replication, parallel query and Spatial Data options
PL/SQL Release 2.3.3.0.0 - Production
SVRMGR> startup mount
ORACLE instance started.
Database mounted.
SVRMGR> alter database open;
ORA-01122: database file 1 failed verification check
ORA-01110: data file 1: 'c:\orant\database\sys1orcl.ora'
ORA-01207: file is more recent than control file - old control file

SVRMGR> recover database
ORA-00283: Recovery session canceled due to errors
ORA-01122: database file 1 failed verification check
ORA-01110: data file 1: ' c:\orant\database\sys1orcl.ora '
ORA-01207: file is more recent than control file - old control file

SVRMGR> recover database using backup controlfile;
ORA-00283: Recovery session canceled due to errors
ORA-01233: file 5 is read only - cannot recover using backup controlfile
ORA-01110: data file 5: 'c:\orant\database\tst1orcl.ora'

SVRMGR> alter database datafile 'c:\orant\database\tst1orcl.ora' offline;
Statement processed.

SVRMGR> recover database using backup controlfile;
ORA-00279: change 319914 generated at 10/15/97 23:21:08 needed for thread 1
ORA-00289: suggestion : C:\ORANT\DATABASE\ARCHIVE\ORCLT0001S0000000055.ARC
ORA-00280: change 319914 for thread 1 is in sequence #55

 Specify log: {<RET>=suggested | filename | AUTO | CANCEL}
<auto>
Log applied.
Media recovery complete.
SVRMGR> alter database open;
ORA-01589: must use RESETLOGS or NORESETLOGS option for database open
SVRMGR> alter database open noresetlogs;
ORA-01588: must use RESETLOGS option for database open
SVRMGR> alter database open resetlogs;
Statement processed.

SVRMGR> archive log list
Database log mode              ARCHIVELOG
Automatic archival             ENABLED
Archive destination            C:\ORANT\database\archive
Oldest online log sequence     1
Next log sequence to archive   1
Current log sequence           1

SVRMGR> select name, status, enabled from v$datafile;
```

```
NAME                                   STATUS       ENABLED
-----                                  ------       -----------
C:\ORANT\DATABASE\SYS1ORCL.ORA         SYSTEM       READ WRITE
C:\ORANT\DATABASE\USR1ORCL.ORA         ONLINE       READ WRITE
C:\ORANT\DATABASE\RBS1ORCL.ORA         ONLINE       READ WRITE
C:\ORANT\DATABASE\TMP1ORCL.ORA         ONLINE       READ WRITE
C:\ORANT\DATABASE\TST1ORCL.ORA         OFFLINE      READ ONLY
5 rows selected.
SVRMGR> alter tablespace test online;
Statement processed.
SVRMGR> select * from case8;
c1
-
8
1 rows selected.
```

## Test Using Oracle Recovery Manager

The Oracle Recovery Manager allows you to include the control file in a backup set. We will restore the control file using RMAN in the next test. First, we will create a backup set that includes a control file as shown here:

```
RMAN> run {
2> allocate channel c1 type disk;
3> backup tablespace "test" include current controlfile
4> format 'aatst%s';
5> }
RMAN-03022: compiling command: allocate
RMAN-03023: executing command: allocate
RMAN-08030: allocated channel: c1
RMAN-08500: channel c1: sid=16 devtype=DISK
RMAN-03022: compiling command: backup
RMAN-03023: executing command: backup
RMAN-08008: channel c1: starting datafile backupset
RMAN-08502: set_count=13 set_stamp=316025242
RMAN-08010: channel c1: including datafile 5 in backupset
RMAN-08011: channel c1: including current controlfile in backupset
RMAN-08013: channel c1: piece 1 created
RMAN-08503: piece handle=AATST13 comment=NONE
RMAN-03023: executing command: partial resync
RMAN-08003: starting partial resync of recovery catalog
RMAN-08005: partial resync complete
RMAN-08031: released channel: c1
```

After creating the backup set, we will delete the control file **ctl1orcl.ora** and attempt to start up the database. The following error results:

```
SVRMGR> startup
ORACLE instance started.
Total System Global Area      12071016 bytes
Fixed Size                       46136 bytes
Variable Size                 11090992 bytes
Database Buffers                409600 bytes
Redo Buffers                    524288 bytes
ORA-00205: error in identifying controlfile, check alert log for more info
```

We will now restore the control file using RMAN. Note that the target database is not mounted yet.

```
D:> ORANT\DATABASE> rman80 target=\"internal/oracle@prod\" rcvcat=\"rman/rman@rcv\"
Recovery Manager: Release 8.0.3.0.0 - Production
RMAN-06006: connected to target database: oracle (not mounted)
RMAN-06008: connected to recovery catalog database
RMAN> run {
2> allocate channel c1 type disk;
3> restore controlfile to 'c:\orant\database\ctl1orcl.ora';
4> }
RMAN-03022: compiling command: allocate
RMAN-03023: executing command: allocate
RMAN-08030: allocated channel: c1
RMAN-08500: channel c1: sid=13 devtype=DISK
RMAN-03022: compiling command: restore
RMAN-03023: executing command: restore
RMAN-08016: channel c1: starting datafile backupset restore
RMAN-08502: set_count=1 set_stamp=11384480
RMAN-08021: channel c1: restoring controlfile
RMAN-08505: output filename=C:\ORANT\DATABASE\CTL1ORCL.ORA
RMAN-08023: channel c1: restored backup piece 1
RMAN-08511: piece handle=AATST13 params=NULL
RMAN-08024: channel c1: restore complete
RMAN-08031: released channel: c1
```

At this point, you will need to issue a **recover database using backup controlfile** command and open the database with the RESETLOGS option as shown in the most recent "Test Using Server Manager" section. Remember to schedule a full backup of the database immediately, since you are using the RESETLOGS option. Also, remember to create a new incarnation record in the recovery catalog by using the **reset database** command. We present an example here:

```
RMAN> register database;
RMAN-03022: compiling command: register
RMAN-03023: executing command: register
RMAN-08006: database registered in recovery catalog
RMAN-03023: executing command: full resync
RMAN-08029: snapshot controlfile name set to default value: %ORACLE_HOME%\
DATABASE\SNCF%ORACLE_SID%.ORA
RMAN-08002: starting full resync of recovery catalog
RMAN-08004: full resync complete
RMAN> list incarnation of database;
RMAN-03022: compiling command: list
RMAN-06240: List of Database Incarnations
RMAN-06241: DB Key   Inc Key DB Name  DB ID        CUR Reset SCN  Reset Time
RMAN-06242: -------  ------- -------- ------------ --- ---------- -------
RMAN-06243: 1        2       ORACLE   1189192555   YES 1          01-NOV-97
```

After crashing the above database intentionally and performing an incomplete recovery, we opened the database using **alter database open resetlogs.** At this point, the recovery catalog needs to be reset as shown next. Note the new output of the **list incarnation** command.

```
RMAN> reset database;
RMAN-03022: compiling command: reset
RMAN-03023: executing command: reset
RMAN-08006: database registered in recovery catalog
RMAN-03023: executing command: full resync
RMAN-08002: starting full resync of recovery catalog
RMAN-08004: full resync complete
RMAN> list incarnation of database;
RMAN-03022: compiling command: list
RMAN-06240: List of Database Incarnations
RMAN-06241: DB Key  Inc Key DB Name  DB ID          CUR Reset SCN  Reset Time
RMAN-06242: ------- ------- -------- -------------- --- ---------- -------
RMAN-06243: 1       2       ORACLE   1189192555     NO  1          01-NOV-97
RMAN-06243: 1       982     ORACLE   1189192555     YES 102646     01-NOV-97
```

Note that the *Inc Key* (incarnation key) 982 will be used for future recovery, as indicated by the *CUR* column. Also note that the *CUR* column shows *NO* for the *Inc Key* of 2, which was created before the **alter database open resetlogs**.

## Observation

When you use a backup control file, you must use the USING BACKUP CONTROLFILE option with the **recover database** command. Oracle will not allow you to do recovery without this option. Also, after finishing media recovery, you must start up the database with the RESETLOGS option. The error message that you receive while trying to open the database is not very clear, since it says that you have to open the database with either the RESETLOGS or the NORESETLOGS option. However, if you try to open the database with the NORESETLOGS option, Oracle tells you that you should open the database with the RESETLOGS option. The reason you have to start the database with the RESETLOGS option if you use a backup control file is that Oracle needs to update certain data structures in the backup control file before opening the database, and this is done during RESETLOGS. After the database is open, you should *immediately* take a full online or offline backup of the database because you cannot restore any of the data files from before RESETLOGS and try to roll forward through a RESETLOGS, as described in Case 11. There is a way for you to roll forward through RESETLOGS if you are using a version of Oracle equal to or higher than release 7.3.3. This must be done with the assistance of Oracle Support Services. We have discussed this feature in Case 11.

Another important point to note is that if the backup control file indicates that the status of a data file is read-only, you should take the file offline before recovery and the tablespace online after startup. This is because read-only data files will not have any changes to be applied, hence no recovery is required.

Last but not least, even when you have only one disk, it is advisable to mirror control files, as it might help you with some failures, such as accidentally deleting a control file.

## Case 9: Space Management in Release 7.1

This case study discusses an issue that stems more from space management than backup and recovery. However, it is presented here due to the fact that many DBAs make the mistake of deleting data files without rebuilding the tablespace. The ramifications of this could be severe. The discussion here applies to Oracle7 release 7.1. Case 10 discusses an alternative solution to this problem for release 7.2 and higher.

### Scenario

Matt, the DBA of a financial firm, administers a 100GB database on an IBM mainframe running Oracle7 release 7.1. Matt operates the database in ARCHIVELOG mode. Every night, the system manager takes an operating system backup of the system. As part of this backup, all Oracle database files are copied from DASD to tape. The Oracle database is shut down before the backups are taken. In addition, Matt takes a full database export once every three months and incremental exports once a month.

### Problem

One day, while doing space management, Matt added a small data file to a tablespace, then decided that he really needed more space. He didn't want to add another data file, but instead decided to replace the smaller data file with a new, bigger data file. Since a data file cannot be dropped, he merely took the new data file offline and added a larger data file to the same tablespace. He deleted the data file at the OS level, assuming that Oracle would never need the file since he hadn't added any data to it, and also because it was offline. Shortly after he started running an application, he got the following error during an **insert** operation:

```
ORA-00376: file 6 cannot be read at this time
```

He found out that the data file Oracle is referring to (file 6) is the same data file that he had taken offline and deleted earlier.

### Solution

When you take a data file offline and open the database, you have to apply one of the following three methods:

1. Restore the data file that was taken offline from a backup and do data file recovery.

2. If no backups exist, create the data file using the **alter database create datafile** command and then recover it.

3. Rebuild the tablespace.

To apply method 1, you need to have a backup of the data file from an online or offline backup, and you need to have all the archived and online log files to recover the file. To use method 2, you need to have all the redo log files that are generated from the time the data file was originally created. In addition, the current control file or a backup control file that recognizes the offline data file should be used. Even if one of the archived log files is missing, methods 1 and 2 cannot be performed and the only option is to use method 3, which involves dropping the tablespace to which the offline data file belongs and re-creating it.

With Oracle7 releases 7.2 and higher, there is no need to take the data file offline if you want to modify the size of the data file. There is a new RESIZE option that can be used to modify the size of the data file in the **alter database..datafile** command. Case 10 discusses this option.

## Test Using Recovery Manager

Note that this test is performed on an Oracle7 database running release 7.1.4. Case 10 provides a better solution for resizing data files. The tablespace in question is called ROTEST, and it contains two data files. With the database open, one of two files is taken offline. Then, data is inserted into the ROTEST tablespace until Oracle tries to allocate space from the data file that is taken offline.

```
SQLDBA> connect internal
Statement processed
SQLDBA> alter database datafile '/mcsc2/orahome/data/PROD/rotest.dbf' offline;
Statement processed.
SQLDBA> select tablespace_name, status from dba_tablespaces;
TABLESPACE_NAME      STATUS
---------------      ------
SYSTEM               ONLINE
RBS                  ONLINE
TEMP                 ONLINE
TOOLS                ONLINE
USERS                ONLINE
ROTEST               ONLINE

SQLDBA> select name, status from v$datafile;
NAME                                             STATUS
----                                             ------
/mcsc2/orahome/data/PROD/system01.dbf            SYSTEM
/mcsc2/orahome/data/PROD/rbs01.dbf               ONLINE
/mcsc2/orahome/data/PROD/temp01.dbf              ONLINE
/mcsc2/orahome/data/PROD/tools01.dbf             ONLINE
/mcsc2/orahome/data/PROD/users01.dbf             ONLINE
/mcsc2/orahome/data/PROD/rotest.dbf              RECOVER
/mcsc2/orahome/data/PROD/rotest2.dbf             ONLINE

SQLDBA> insert into rotab3 select * from scott.dept;
ORA-00376: file 6 cannot be read at this time
ORA-01110: data file 6: '/mcsc2/orahome/data/PROD/rotest.dbf'
SQL> select * from fet$ where ts#= 5;
TS#      FILE#      BLOCK#      LENGTH
---      ----       ------      ------
5        6          17          1008
```

```
SQLDBA> alter tablespace rotest add datafile
'/mcsc2/orahome/data/PROD/rotest3.dbf' size 50k;
Statement processed.
SQLDBA> select * from fet$ where ts#=5;
TS#       FILE#       BLOCK#       LENGTH
---       -----       ------       ------
5         6           17           1008
5         8           2            24

SQLDBA> insert into rotab3 select * from scott.dept
ORA-00376: file 6 cannot be read at this time
ORA-01110: data file 6: '/mcsc2/orahome/data/PROD/rotest.dbf'
SQLDBA> create table rotab4 (c1 number) tablespace rotest;
ORA-00376: file 6 cannot be read at this time

ORA-01110: data file 6: '/mcsc2/orahome/data/PROD/rotest.dbf'

SQLDBA> alter database datafile '/mcsc2/orahome/data/PROD/rotest.dbf' online;
ORA-01113: file 6 needs media recovery
ORA-01110: data file 6: '/mcsc2/orahome/data/PROD/rotest.dbf'
SQLDBA> recover tablespace rotest;
ORA-00283: Recovery session canceled due to errors
ORA-01124: cannot recover data file 7 - file is in use or recovery
ORA-01110: data file 7: '/mcsc2/orahome/data/PROD/rotest2.dbf'
SQLDBA> recover datafile '/mcsc2/orahome/data/PROD/rotest.dbf';
ORA-00279: Change 11852 generated at 09/14/94 12:22:45 needed for thread 1
ORA-00289: Suggestion : /mcsc2/orahome/admin/PROD/arch/arch.log1_13.dbf
ORA-00280: Change 11852 for thread 1 is in sequence #13
Specify log: {<RET>=suggested | filename | AUTO | FROM logsource | CANCEL}

Applying suggested logfile...
Log applied.
Media recovery complete.
SQLDBA> alter database datafile '/mcsc2/orahome/data/PROD/rotest.dbf' online;
Statement processed.
SQLDBA> insert into rotab3 select * from scott.dept where rownum <2;
1 row processed.
```

## Observation

When a data file is taken offline, the file cannot be written to or read by Oracle. The control file indicates that the file is offline. However, when doing space management, Oracle will look at the base data dictionary table FET$ (free extents table) to figure out how much free space is available in the database. Even when the data file is taken offline, its free space can be seen from this table since this file is still part of the database. Even though a new datafile was added to ROTEST, the space in it could not be used because the space search algorithm scans FET$ sequentially from top to bottom. File 6 will be selected, even though it is offline because the code module responsible for scanning FET$ has no knowledge of the file's status. An error is only generated when another code module is called to allocate blocks from the extent in file 6, so the newly added space in file 8 is effectively unusable.

The only way to remove files from a tablespace reliably is to re-create the tablespace with fewer component files and use export/import to rebuild the data. Offlining the unwanted files (or OFFLINE DROP when running in NOARCHIVELOG mode) will allow access to data in the remaining files, but when space allocation is required, the scenario outlined above could easily occur—making it necessary to re-create the tablespace.

# Case 10: Resizing Data Files in Release 7.2 and Later

Release 7.2 introduced the concept of *resizing* data files to help DBAs reduce administrative time. This case study shows you how to use this feature on Oracle8.

### Scenario
Consider a similar scenario to that in Case 9 on Windows NT.

### Problem
Consider the same problem as in Case 9.

### Solution
Data file sizes can grow dynamically in Oracle7 release 7.2 and later. The RESIZE option can be used to change the size of a data file manually, or the AUTO EXTEND option can be used to allow the files to grow dynamically when more space is required. An upper boundary can be set for the file size.

### Test Using Server Manager
In this section we show how to use the RESIZE option to resize the existing data files.

```
C:\ORANT\DATABASE>svrmgr30
Oracle Server Manager Release 3.0.3.0.0 - Production
(c) Copyright 1997, Oracle Corporation.  All Rights Reserved.
Oracle8 Release 8.0.3.0.0 - Production
With the Partitioning and Objects options
PL/SQL Release 8.0.3.0.0 - Production
SVRMGR> connect internal
Password:
Connected.
SVRMGR> startup mount
ORACLE instance started.
Total System Global Area      12071016 bytes
Fixed Size                       46136 bytes
Variable Size                 11090992 bytes
Database Buffers                409600 bytes
Redo Buffers                    524288 bytes
```

```
Database mounted.
SVRMGR> archive log list
Database log mode               Archive Mode
Automatic archival              Enabled
Archive destination             C:\ORANT\database\archive
Oldest online log sequence      72
Next log sequence to archive    73
Current log sequence            73
SVRMGR> alter database open;
Statement processed.
SVRMGR> select file#, blocks, ts# from file$;
FILE#     BLOCKS     TS#
--------- ---------- ----------
       1      15360          0
       2       1536          1
       3       5120          2
       4        512          3
4 rows selected.
SVRMGR> alter tablespace user_data add datafile 'c:\orant\database\usr2orcl.ora'
size 10k;
Statement processed.
SVRMGR> select file#, blocks, ts# from file$;
FILE#     BLOCKS     TS#
--------- ---------- ----------
       1      15360          0
       2       1536          1
       3       5120          2
       4        512          3
       5          5          1
5 rows selected.
SVRMGR> host
Microsoft(R) Windows NT(TM)
(C) Copyright 1985-1996 Microsoft Corp.
C:\ORANT\DATABASE>dir usr*
 Volume in drive C is MS-DOS_6
 Volume Serial Number is 2338-6CE4
 Directory of C:\ORANT\DATABASE
10/19/97  07:29a             3,147,776 USR1ORCL.ORA
10/19/97  05:08p                12,288 USR2ORCL.ORA
              2 File(s)      3,160,064 bytes
                           42,827,776 bytes free
C:\ORANT\DATABASE>exit
SVRMGR> alter database datafile 'c:\orant\database\usr2orcl.ora' resize 1m;
Statement processed.
SVRMGR> select file#, blocks, ts# from file$;
```

```
FILE#      BLOCKS     TS#
---------- ---------- ----------
        1      15360          0
        2       1536          1
        3       5120          2
        4        512          3
        5        512          1
5 rows selected.
SVRMGR> host
Microsoft(R) Windows NT(TM)
(C) Copyright 1985-1996 Microsoft Corp.
C:\ORANT\DATABASE>dir usr*
 Volume in drive C is MS-DOS_6
 Volume Serial Number is 2338-6CE4
 Directory of C:\ORANT\DATABASE
10/19/97  07:29a           3,147,776 USR1ORCL.ORA
10/19/97  05:15p           1,050,624 USR2ORCL.ORA
               2 File(s)    4,198,400 bytes
                           41,156,608 bytes free
```

## Observation

Note that the data file's size is increased from 10KB to 1MB. The size of the data file is updated in the base data dictionary table FILE$. The actual physical size is also changed at the OS level, as shown by the **dir** command. When the data file size is changed, a redo record is written to the log file. In the future, if this data file is lost due to a media failure, the backup of the data file should be restored and recovery applied as usual. Note that recovery will change the size of the data file as well. When the RESIZE option is used and the file size is changed, it is not necessary for you to take a backup of the data file, as this change is propagated through redo.

# Case 11: Recovery Through RESETLOGS

Using the RESETLOGS option to open a database should be the last option for DBAs; but if it is inevitable, you should understand the ramifications of doing so. This case study illustrates the steps that you need to take before and after using this option to open the database. In continuation of this case study, we have Case 11(a), which gives a workaround when your database crashes before taking a backup after the database was opened with the RESETLOGS option.

## Scenario

Bob works as a DBA in a telecommunications company. He maintains an Oracle7 database in the human resources department. The database is installed on a UNIX server. Bob takes regular cold backups of the database. His backup procedure involves shutting down the database, making a disk-to-disk copy of the database files, and starting up the database. Then he copies all the database files from the backup disk to tape.

## Problem

Figure 10-5 shows the time line and various events that occurred in a sequential order. The log sequence numbers at various times are pointed out as well.

At point A, Bob has taken a cold backup of the database and opened the database for normal operation. At point B, a media failure occurred and he lost all the online log files. Since Bob doesn't multiplex the online log files, he had to do incomplete recovery. So, Bob restored the database as of point A and recovered the database using the **recover database until cancel** command. He applied recovery until the last archive log file and started up the database with the RESETLOGS option at point B. As shown in Figure 10-5, the *current log sequence number* was reset to 1 again at point B.

After a few days (at point C), another media failure occurred and Bob lost data file 5. All the online log files and the control files were intact, so Bob restored the backup data file for file 5 from point A and tried to do recovery. Oracle complained that data file 5 is from a point before B. Bob tried to restore the backup control file and recover the database. This time, Oracle complained that file 1 is from a point after B. Not knowing what was going on, Bob decided to restore all the data files

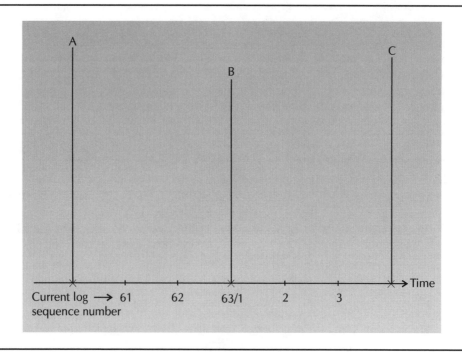

**FIGURE 10-5.** *Database events at various points in time*

and the control file from the cold backup (from point A) and tried to do recovery again. Recovery went fine until point B, but he couldn't go past point B, since Oracle didn't recognize the log files after point B. If Bob couldn't recover up to point C, he would lose all the data that he had inserted from point B to point C.

## Solution

It's absolutely necessary to take a backup of the database after the database is started with the RESETLOGS option. In this scenario, Bob should have taken a cold backup at point B. Since he hasn't done so, Bob now has only the following two options:

■ At point C, take the data file 5 offline, open the database, and export all the data from the tablespace (all objects in file 5 will be inaccessible), drop and re-create the tablespace, and import all the data taken from the export. Then shut the database down and take a cold backup. This way, Bob will lose all the data that was ever entered in file 5.

■ Restore all data files and the control file from the offline backup (point A) and roll forward up to point B. Then start up the database with the RESETLOGS option. This way, Bob will have all the data as of point B, but the data inserted between points B and C will be lost. After startup, shut down the database and take a full database backup.

We will use the second option to simulate the above scenario.

### Test Using Server Manager

Since this test is a bit complicated, we will comment after every important step of the test.

 cosmos% **svrmgrl**
```
Oracle Server Manager Release 2.3.3.0.0 - Production
Copyright (c) Oracle Corporation 1994, 1995. All rights reserved.
Oracle7 Server Release 7.3.3.0.0 - Production Release
With the distributed, replication, parallel query and Spatial Data options
PL/SQL Release 2.3.3.0.0 - Production

SVRMGR> connect internal
Connected.
SVRMGR> startup
ORACLE instance started.
Database mounted.
Database opened.
Total System Global Area        4480888 bytes
```

```
Fixed Size                      47152 bytes
Variable Size                  015944 bytes
Database Buffers               409600 bytes
Redo Buffers                     8192 bytes
SVRMGR> create table case11 (c1 number) tablespace users;
Statement processed.
```

The above **create** statement is created in the current online log file, which has sequence number 61. Next, switch the log file and make the current log sequence number 62. An insert will be done so the redo for the insert will be in log sequence number 62. Another switch will change the current log sequence number to 63. Note that at this point, we have the archive log files for log sequence numbers 61 and 62.

```
SVRMGR> alter system switch logfile;
Statement processed.
SVRMGR> insert into case11 values (11);
1 row processed.
SVRMGR> commit;
Statement processed.
SVRMGR> alter system switch logfile;
Statement processed.
SVRMGR> shutdown
Database closed.
Database dismounted.
ORACLE instance shut down.
SVRMGR> startup mount
ORACLE instance started.
Database mounted.

SVRMGR> archive log list
Database log mode              ARCHIVELOG
Automatic archival             ENABLED
Archive destination            /home/orahome/product/7.3.3/
                               dbs/arch
Oldest online log sequence     61
Next log sequence to archive   63
Current log sequence           63

SVRMGR> recover database until cancel;
Media recovery complete.
SVRMGR> alter database open resetlogs;
Statement processed.
SVRMGR> archive log list;
Database log mode              ARCHIVELOG
Automatic archival             ENABLED
Archive destination            /home/orahome/product/7.3.3/
                               dbs/arch
Oldest online log sequence     0
Next log sequence to archive   1
Current log sequence           1
```

```
SVRMGR> insert into case11 values(11);
1 row processed.
SVRMGR> commit;
Statement processed.
SVRMGR> alter system switch logfile;
Statement processed.
```

Note that the second row is inserted into table **case11**, and the redo for this insert is in log sequence number 1.

```
SVRMGR> shutdown
Database closed.
Database dismounted.
ORACLE instance shut down.
SVRMGR> host
cosmos% rm /home/orahome/data/733/users01.dbf
cosmos% cp /home/orahome/backup/users01.dbf /home/orahome/data/733
cosmos% exit
cosmos%
SVRMGR> startup mount
ORACLE instance started.
Database mounted.
SVRMGR> recover database
ORA-00283: Recovery session canceled due to errors
ORA-01190: control file or data file 4 is from before the last RESETLOGS
ORA-01110: data file 4: '/home/orahome/data/733/users01.dbf'
```

The above recovery statement failed because the control file and all data files are from a point after the RESETLOGS was done, except for the **users01.dbf** file, which was restored from the backup. So, Oracle is complaining that file 4 is from before point B of Figure 10-5.

```
SVRMGR> shutdown
ORA-01109: database not open
Database dismounted.
ORACLE instance shut down.
SVRMGR> host
cosmos% cp /home/orahome/backup/control01.ctl /home/orahome/data/733
cosmos% exit
cosmos%
SVRMGR> startup mount
ORACLE instance started.
Database mounted.
SVRMGR> recover database using backup controlfile;
ORA-00283: Recovery session canceled due to errors
ORA-01190: control file or data file 1 is from before the last RESETLOGS
ORA-01110: data file 1: '/home/orahome/data/733/system01.dbf'
```

The above recovery statement failed because we have restored a backup of the control file and data file **users01.dbf**, but all other data files are from after point B of

Figure 10-5. Oracle is complaining that file 1 is after point B. If, for example, you replace file 1 with the backup data file, then it will complain about file 2 not being from the backup, and so on. This means that all the data files and control files need to be from the backup. So, now let's restore all the data files from backup and see what happens:

```
SVRMGR> shutdown
ORA-01109: database not open
Database dismounted.
ORACLE instance shut down.
SVRMGR> host
cosmos% cp /home/orahome/backup/*.* /home/orahome/data/733
cosmos% exit
cosmos%

SVRMGR> startup mount
ORACLE instance started.
Database mounted.
SVRMGR> archive log list
Database log mode              ARCHIVELOG
Automatic archival             ENABLED
Archive destination            /home/orahome/product/7.3.3/dbs/arch
Oldest online log sequence     59
Next log sequence to archive   61
Current log sequence           61

SVRMGR> recover database using backup controlfile;
ORA-00283: Recovery session canceled due to errors
ORA-01233: file 5 is read only - cannot recover using backup controlfile
ORA-01110: data file 5: '/home/orahome/data/733/test1.dbf'
```

The recovery failed for a different reason this time. The backup control file shows the status of file 5 as read-only. Recall from Case 8 that while doing media recovery, we cannot have any read-only data files online. So, let's take this data file offline:

```
SVRMGR> alter database datafile '/home/orahome/data/733/test1.dbf' offline;
Statement processed.

SVRMGR> recover database using backup controlfile;
ORA-00279: Change 6406 generated at 02/04/95 17:36:35 needed for thread 1
ORA-00289: Suggestion : /home/orahome/product/7.3.3/dbs/arch1_61.dbf
ORA-00280: Change 6406 for thread 1 is in sequence #61
Specify log: {<RET>=suggested | filename | AUTO | FROM logsource | CANCEL}

Applying suggested logfile...
Log applied.
ORA-00279: Change 6422 generated at 02/07/95 10:34:53 needed for thread 1

ORA-00289: Suggestion : /home/orahome/product/7.3.3/dbs/arch1_62.dbf
ORA-00280: Change 6422 for thread 1 is in sequence #62
```

```
ORA-00278: Logfile '/home/orahome/product/7.3.3/dbs/arch1_61.dbf' no longer needed for this recovery
Specify log: {<RET>=suggested | filename | AUTO | FROM logsource | CANCEL}

Applying suggested logfile...
Log applied.
ORA-00279: Change 6425 generated at 02/07/95 10:35:26 needed for thread 1

ORA-00289: Suggestion : /home/orahome/product/7.3.3/dbs/arch1_63.dbf
ORA-00280: Change 6425 for thread 1 is in sequence #63
ORA-00278: Logfile '/home/orahome/product/7.3.3/dbs/arch1_62.dbf' no longer needed for this recovery
Specify log: {<RET>=suggested | filename | AUTO | FROM logsource | CANCEL}
/home/orahome/product/7.3.3/dbs/arch1_1.dbf
Applying logfile...
ORA-00310: archived log contains sequence 1; sequence 63 required
ORA-00334: archived log: '/home/orahome/product/7.3.3/dbs/arch1_1.dbf'
Specify log: {<RET>=suggested | filename | AUTO | FROM logsource | CANCEL}
cancel
Media recovery canceled.
```

Note that in the above recovery procedure, we have applied log sequence numbers 61 and 62. At this point, RESETLOGS was done so the next log sequence number that is available to us is log sequence number 1. When we applied this log, Oracle didn't recognize it, since it was looking for log sequence number 63. This proves that we cannot cross this point (at which RESETLOGS was done), so we try to stop recovery here and open the database:

```
SVRMGR> alter database open resetlogs;
ORA-01113: file 1 needs media recovery
ORA-01110: data file 1: '/home/orahome/data/733/system01.dbf'
```

Note that we cannot open the database because we are doing complete recovery. We started doing recovery by issuing the **recover database** command, so Oracle will open the database only if all the redo for the thread is applied. Since we don't have all the redo for the thread, we should do incomplete recovery by issuing the command **recover database.until cancel**. So, let's try doing recovery again with the right recovery options:

```
SVRMGR> recover database using backup controlfile until cancel;
ORA-00279: Change 6425 generated at 02/07/95 10:35:26 needed for thread 1
ORA-00289: Suggestion : /home/orahome/product/7.3.3/dbs/arch1_63.dbf
ORA-00280: Change 6425 for thread 1 is in sequence #63
Specify log: {<RET>=suggested | filename | AUTO | FROM logsource | CANCEL}
cancel
Media recovery cancelled.
SVRMGR> alter database open resetlogs;
Statement processed.
```

Note that when we tried to do recovery again, Oracle didn't request the changes starting all the way from log sequence number 61, but asked for the latest log sequence number, which is 63. This shows that when you stop and start media recovery again, Oracle continues from where you left off.

```
SVRMGR> select * from case11;
C1

--
11
1 row selected.
```

Since we recovered only until point B and didn't cross this point, the second row that we inserted into this table was lost. So, the **select** statement shows only one row in the table, which is expected.

### Observation

There are some very important points to note from this test:

- If RESETLOGS is done at a point in time, you cannot restore the backup of the database from before the RESETLOGS and recover through the RESETLOGS point. This means that any time the database is opened with the RESETLOGS option, you should take another backup immediately.

- If you want to do incomplete recovery, you should use the UNTIL CANCEL option in the **recover database** command.

- If you are using a backup control file, all the read-only data files should be offline. In addition, the USING BACKUP CONTROLFILE option should be used with the **recover database** command.

# Case 11(a): Recovery Through RESETLOGS (continued)

In Case 11 we mentioned that after starting the database with RESETLOGS option, you must take an immediate hot or cold backup of the entire database. Let's assume that you are taking a hot backup after a RESETLOGS and there is an outage and the backup was not successful. What do you do then? This case study gives you a workaround to recover *through* RESETLOGS in such cases.

**CAUTION**
*This is not an alternative for not backing up your database after a RESETLOGS! This method should be used only in emergencies!*

### Solution

This is a new feature found in Oracle7 versions 7.3.3 or higher. It makes it possible to pass a RESETLOGS if you have a copy of a control file after the RESETLOGS point. This is especially useful when there is an outage prior to successfully backing up your database after a RESETLOGS. Oracle Support Services recommends that a backup be taken after a RESETLOGS; however, this feature provides a workaround for customers who cannot take the time to do a cold backup immediately after doing recovery with RESETLOGS. If the hot backup (or future backups) did not complete successfully, this feature provides a legitimate workaround.

This feature should only be used under the following conditions:

- Oracle versions 7.3.3 and higher.

- Previous recovery with RESETLOGS has been successful.

- No consistent backup after the RESETLOGS is present.

- A consistent backup (cold or hot) prior to RESETLOGS is present.

- Control file after the RESETLOGS is present.

- All archive log files and online redo logs are present for recovery.

### Workaround 1 (Recommended by Oracle)

The recommended way to recover from such a failure is to take a cold (consistent) backup just before opening the database with the RESETLOGS option. Refer to Figure 10-5. Here, a backup was taken at point A, and the database was opened with the RESETLOGS option at point B. Before opening the database at point B, the following steps should be done:

1. Shut down the database using the IMMEDIATE (or NORMAL) option.

2. Back up all data files and the control file.

3. Start up mount.

4. Open the database using the **alter database open resetlogs** command.

Now, while taking a backup of the database after RESETLOGS, if a failure occurs (point C in Figure 10-5), you can restore the backup from point B (taken just before the RESETLOGS) and use the control file after point B and do recovery as usual.

### Workaround 2

If you do not have any backups after point A, then recovery is a bit complicated, as you need to find out the exact SCN (at point B) at which RESETLOGS was done. Again from Figure 10-5, if you have a backup from point A (and no other backups after that point), and the database was started with the RESETLOGS option at point B, and another failure occurred at point C, then the following method should be used to recover the database through RESETLOGS.

If the current control file (any control file after point B) is available, it is possible to use the backup taken before the RESETLOGS (at point A) and do the following:

1. Find the SCN immediately before the database was opened with RESETLOGS. This SCN is reported in the alert log just before the database is opened. Look for *RESETLOGS after incomplete recovery UNTIL CHANGE xxxxx* or *RESETLOGS after complete recovery through change xxxxx.* You should also query this information from any control file that is valid after the RESETLOGS point by using the following query:

   ```
   select RESETLOGS_CHANGE# - 1   from v$database;
   ```

   The SCN in the alert log and the SCN from your query should return the same number. You will be recovering the database to this SCN.

2. Shut down the database.

3. Copy the current control file to a safe location. (You *must* have a copy of the control file that was taken after the RESETLOGS was performed—it does not have to be the current control file.)

4. Restore the whole database and the control file from the backups before the RESETLOGS (point A of Figure 10-5).

5. Recover the database using the command **recover database using backup controlfile until change x** (where *x* is the SCN found in step 1).

6. Shut down the database.

7. Copy the control file from after RESETLOGS to all locations in the CONTROL_FILES parameter in the **init.ora**.

8. Start up mount the database.

9. Use the appropriate **recover database** command and recover normally. Oracle should now ask for archive log sequence number 1.

## Hints

- Always take a backup of your control file *after* RESETLOGS.
- Always back up all archive logs *before* attempting this operation.

## Dangers

It is possible (but not likely) that you may have conflicting archive log sequence numbers (the same log sequence number from before the RESETLOGS point and after the RESETLOGS). You must be very careful not to overwrite one with the other, especially if they are not backed up.

### Best Practices

- Always back up the database after RESETLOGS. This workaround is *not* an alternative for not backing up your database.

- Safeguard previous backups of the database before the RESETLOGS at least until a consistent backup is created after the RESETLOGS.

- Create control file backups immediately after RESETLOGS.

- Back up all archive logs and online redo logs that were used in recovery before opening the database with RESETLOGS.

- Record CHANGE# after point-in-time recovery.

- Back up the **alert.log** after doing a RESETLOGS.

# Case 12: Creating Data Files

It is comforting to have the option of creating a data file when you lose one, but there are ramifications of doing so. This case study gives you an idea when, why, and how to use this option.

### Scenario

Tom is the DBA of a pharmaceutical company. He administers a 20GB database on a Sun SPARC Solaris machine running Oracle7 release 7.3. His backup procedure includes taking a hot backup of the database once a week. Every Sunday night he submits a batch job that puts the tablespaces in hot backup mode, one at a time. The data files are then copied to multiple tapes.

### Problem

On a Monday afternoon, while running an application, Tom got an Oracle error saying that there is no more space in a specified tablespace. He then added a data file to that tablespace. Since the application does a lot of DML operations and modifies a lot of tables, he decided to wait until the application finished so that he could take a backup of the data file he just added. On Friday morning, a media failure occurred, and Tom lost the new data file he had added on Monday. He then realized that he forgot to take a backup of the data file on Monday. He could take the file offline and start up the database, but he would lose a lot of data that the application had inserted into that data file. Tom could restore from the backup and roll forward, but this wouldn't work because the backup doesn't have the new data file he added on Monday.

## Solution

This is a perfect scenario for re-creating the data file. To re-create the data file, Tom needs the current control file or a backup control file that recognizes the new data file that was added on Monday. Next, all the archive log files and online log files need to be available. All Tom needs to do is mount the database and issue the **alter database create datafile** command to re-create the data file. Once the file is created, he needs to apply the redo (roll forward) from the time the file was created to the present time. The following test illustrates this scenario.

## Test Using Server Manager

In this section we show how to use the **create datafile** command to create a data file that has not been backed up. Note that this command is for emergency use only.

```
cosmos% svrmgrl
Oracle Server Manager Release 2.3.3.0.0 - Production
Copyright (c) Oracle Corporation 1994, 1995. All rights reserved.
Oracle7 Server Release 7.3.3.0.0 - Production Release
With the distributed, replication, parallel query and Spatial Data options
PL/SQL Release 2.3.3.0.0 - Production

SVRMGR> connect internal
Connected.
SVRMGR> startup open
ORACLE instance started.
Database mounted.
Database opened.
Total System Global Area        4480888 bytes
    Fixed Size              47152 bytes
    Variable Size         4015944 bytes
    Database Buffers        09600 bytes
    Redo Buffers             8192 bytes

SVRMGR> alter tablespace users add datafile '/home/orahome/data/733/users02.dbf' size 40k;
Statement processed.
SVRMGR> alter system switch logfile;
Statement processed.
SVRMGR> alter system switch logfile;
Statement processed.
SVRMGR> alter system switch logfile;
Statement processed.
SVRMGR> shutdown abort
 ORACLE instance shut down.

SVRMGR> host
cosmos% rm /home/orahome/data/733/users02.dbf
cosmos% exit

SVRMGR> startup
```

```
ORACLE instance started.
Total System Global Area        12071016 bytes
Fixed Size                         46136 bytes
Variable Size                   11090992 bytes
Database Buffers                  409600 bytes
Redo Buffers                      524288 bytes
Database mounted.
ORA-01157: cannot identify data file 5 - file not found
ORA-01110: data file 5: '/home/orahome/data/733/users02.dbf'
SVRMGR> alter database create datafile '/home/orahome/data/733/users02.dbf';
Statement processed.
SVRMGR> recover datafile '/home/orahome/data/733/users02.dbf'
ORA-00279: Change 6420 generated at 02/07/95 11:00:51 needed for thread 1
ORA-00289: Suggestion : /home/orahome/product/7.3.3/dbs/arch1_62.dbf
ORA-00280: Change 6420 for thread 1 is in sequence #62
Specify log: {<RET>=suggested | filename | AUTO | FROM logsource | CANCEL}
<enter>
Applying suggested logfile...
Log applied.
Media recovery complete.
SVRMGR> alter database open;
Statement processed.
SVRMGR> host
cosmos% ls -l /home/orahome/data/733/users02.dbf
-rw-r-----   1 oracle7  dba         43008 Feb  7 13:09
/home/orahome/data/733/users02.dbf
```

## Observation

The **alter database create datafile** command expects the use of a control file that has the file entry for the data file to be re-created. It is therefore important to have one of the following:

- The current control file.

- The backup control file that has the file entry for the data file to be re-created—this means you should take a backup of the control file immediately after a schema change.

Also, note in this test that the **alter database create datafile** command actually creates the data file for you at the OS level, and the **recover datafile** command reads the changes from the redo log file and applies them to the data blocks.

# Case 13: System Clock Change and Point-in-Time Recovery

This case study is probably the toughest one to understand. Point-in-time recovery is a type of incomplete recovery. To complicate matters, if this kind of recovery is done after the system clock is changed, you can run into problems. If you take a full

online or offline backup of your database after you change the system clock, you
will never face the situation discussed in this case study.

### Scenario

Richard is the DBA of an Oracle7 database at a blood bank. He administers a 10GB
database on a UNIX machine. The database contains 10 tablespaces, and the
backup procedure involves taking an online backup once every week on Sunday.
Richard doesn't take any logical backups of the database.

### Problem

Wednesday morning at 1:58 A.M., one of the users accidentally dropped a very
important table. He didn't have an export backup of the table. The user called
Richard and requested that his table be restored from the backup. Since the user
was inserting a lot of data into the table before he dropped it, he wanted the table to
be recovered as close as possible to 1:58 A.M. Richard decided to do time-based
recovery from the most recent online backup, with the intention of halting recovery
at 1:55 A.M. To further complicate the issue, the system clock was moved back an
hour at 2 A.M. (from 2 A.M. to 1 A.M.) on Wednesday morning (see Figure 10-6).
Richard was unable to get close to the drop time, so he had to stop recovery an
hour before the table was dropped. The user lost more than an hour's worth of data.

### Solution

At point A, the online backup of the database was taken. At point B, the system
clock was changed from 2 A.M. to 1 A.M. At point C, the user accidentally dropped
his table. The transaction numbers, the SCN allocated to the transaction, and the
timestamps when the transactions were committed are shown between points A and
B, as well as B and C. For example, transaction T1 committed at time 1 A.M. and an
SCN = 10 was allocated to it. Transaction T9, with SCN = 18, committed at 1:58
A.M. (at point C), which dropped the user's table. Since the table was dropped at
point C (in Figure 10-6), Richard wanted to roll forward up to T8 and stop.

The only solution here is to restore the online backups from point A and roll
forward up to transaction T4. The reason for this is that when point-in-time recovery
is performed, Oracle uses SCNs to do recovery. However, to determine which SCN
to roll forward to, it looks at the timestamps in the redo records. In this scenario, if
recovery is to stop before 1:58 A.M. (point C in Figure 10-6, where the table is
dropped), you would issue the following command:

```
recover database until time 'yyyy-mm-dd:01:58:00';
```

This command rolls forward the database and stops before 1:58 A.M. Since the
redo log files are scanned sequentially, looking at the time line in Figure 10-6,
Oracle will read the redo generated by T4; and since its timestamp is greater than

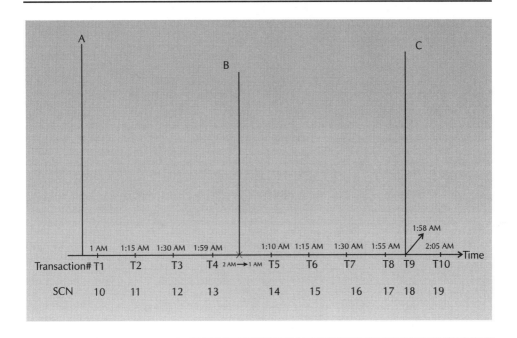

**FIGURE 10-6.**  *Database events at various points in time*

1:58 A.M., it stops after applying the changes made by T3. For example, if you change the time in the recovery statement to 2:00 A.M., looking again at Figure 10-6, you can see that all transactions have a timestamp less than 2 A.M. except T10. That means Oracle will apply all changes to the database made by transactions up to T9. But that doesn't help, since transaction T9 has dropped the table.

Note that in this case if you do complete recovery, all transactions will be applied. However, if you decide to do point-in-time recovery, you might not be able to roll forward to a point that lies between points B and C of Figure 10-6. This depends on the activity in the database. For example, in Figure 10-6, if we didn't have any transactions between points A and B, then it's quite possible to roll forward to a point that lies between points B and C. So, it is important to note that you should take a backup of the database after changing the system clock if you ever intend to use the backup and do point-in-time recovery.

## Test Using Server Manager

We will perform two tests here, both using Server Manager. The first test demonstrates how to do a simple point-in-time recovery. The second test involves changing the system clock in addition to doing point-in-time recovery. After every important step, some explanation is given.

**Test 1: Simple Point-In-Time Recovery**    Table TIMER has two columns. The first column (column A) gives the record number, and the second column (column B) gives the timestamp at which the record was inserted.

```
cosmos% svrmgrl
Oracle Server Manager Release 2.3.3.0.0 - Production
Copyright (c) Oracle Corporation 1994, 1995. All rights reserved.
Oracle7 Server Release 7.3.3.0.0 - Production Release
With the distributed, replication, parallel query and Spatial Data options
PL/SQL Release 2.3.3.0.0 - Production

SVRMGR> connect internal
Connected
SVRMGR> select a, to_char(b, 'hh24:mi:ss') time from timer;
A        TIME
--       ----
1        17:48:59
2        17:50:36
3        17:51:07
4        17:52:00
5        17:53:05
6        17:54:45
7        17:56:37
7 rows selected.
```

Now the database is shut down with the NORMAL option and we restored the backup data files that were taken at 17:45. The current control file and redo log files are used for recovery.

```
SVRMGR> connect internal
Connected.
SVRMGR> startup mount
ORACLE instance started.
Database mounted.
SVRMGR> recover database until time '1994-09-15:17:55:00';
Media recovery complete.
SVRMGR> alter database open resetlogs;
Statement processed.
SVRMGR> select a, to_char(b, 'hh24:mi:ss') time from timer;
A        TIME
--       ----
1        17:48:59
2        17:50:36
3        17:51:07
4        17:52:00
5        17:53:05
6        17:54:45
6 rows selected.
```

**Test 2: System Clock Change and Point-In-Time Recovery**    Table TIMER has three columns. The first column gives the record number, the second column gives the timestamp at which an operation happened, and the third column gives the name of the operation that was done at that time.

```
SQL> select a, to_char(b, 'HH24:MI:SS') time, c from timer;
A    TIME           C
--   --------       ----------
1    15:49:02       Switched Logs
2    15:51:51       Insert
3    15:55:38       Insert
4    15:57:29       Switched Logs
5    16:00:31       Insert
6    16:02:03       Insert
7    16:04:44       Switched Logs
8    15:04:34       Time Switch
9    15:07:27       Insert
10   15:09:35       Switched Logs
11   16:05:38       Time Change
12   15:05:25       Time Change
13   15:08:14       Switched Logs
13 rows selected.
SVRMGR> connect internal
Connected.
SVRMGR> startup mount
ORACLE instance started.
Database mounted.
SVRMGR> archive log list;
Database log mode              ARCHIVELOG
Automatic archival             ENABLED
Archive destination            /mcsc2/orahome/admin/PROD/arch/arch.log
Oldest online log sequence     7
Next log sequence to archive   9
Current log sequence           9

SVRMGR> recover database until time '1994-09-16:16:05:00';
ORA-00279: Change 13388 generated at 09/16/94 14:26:25 needed for thread 1
ORA-00289: Suggestion : /mcsc2/orahome/admin/PROD/arch/arch.log1_3.dbf
ORA-00280: Change 13388 for thread 1 is in sequence #3
Specify log: {<RET>=suggested | filename | AUTO | FROM logsource | CANCEL}

Applying suggested logfile...
Log applied.
ORA-00279: Change 13427 generated at 09/16/94 15:46:33 needed for thread 1
ORA-00289: Suggestion : /mcsc2/orahome/admin/PROD/arch/arch.log1_4.dbf
ORA-00280: Change 13427 for thread 1 is in sequence #4
ORA-00278: Logfile '/mcsc2/orahome/admin/PROD/arch/arch.log1_3.dbf' no longer needed for this recovery
Specify log: {<RET>=suggested | filename | AUTO | FROM logsource | CANCEL}

Applying suggested logfile...
Log applied.
ORA-00279: Change 13446 generated at 09/16/94 15:48:55 needed for thread 1
ORA-00289: Suggestion : /mcsc2/orahome/admin/PROD/arch/arch.log1_5.dbf
ORA-00280: Change 13446 for thread 1 is in sequence #5
ORA-00278: Logfile '/mcsc2/orahome/admin/PROD/arch/arch.log1_4.dbf' no longer needed for this recovery
Specify log: {<RET>=suggested | filename | AUTO | FROM logsource | CANCEL}
```

```
Applying suggested logfile...
Log applied.
ORA-00279: Change 13451 generated at 09/16/94 15:57:13 needed for thread 1
ORA-00289: Suggestion : /mcsc2/orahome/admin/PROD/arch/arch.log1_6.dbf
ORA-00280: Change 13451 for thread 1 is in sequence #6
ORA-00278: Logfile '/mcsc2/orahome/admin/PROD/arch/arch.log1_5.dbf' no longer needed for this recovery
Specify log: {<RET>=suggested | filename | AUTO | FROM logsource | CANCEL}
Applying suggested logfile...
Log applied.
Media recovery complete.

SVRMGR> alter database open;
ORA-01589: must use RESETLOGS or NORESETLOGS option for database open
SVRMGR> alter database open resetlogs;
Statement processed.

SQL> select a, to_char(b, 'HH24:MI:SS') time, c from timer;
A      TIME                   C
-      --------               ----------
1      15:49:02               Switched Logs
2      15:51:51               Insert
3      15:55:38               Insert
4      15:57:29               Switched Logs
5      16:00:31               Insert
6      16:02:03               Insert
7      16:04:44               Switched Logs
8      15:04:34               Time Switch
9      15:07:27               Insert
10     15:09:35               Switched Logs
10 rows selected.
```

## Observation

Test 1 is straightforward. Point-in-time recovery was done up to 17:55. Since record 7 was inserted after this time, recovery is done only up to record 6. The **select** statement shows that there are six records in the table after recovery.

In test 2, we have moved the system clock back twice—once from 16:04 to 15:04, and again after an hour from 16:05 to 15:05. Point-in-time recovery was done until 16:05:00. Note that record 7 shows that a log switch happened at 16:04:44, which is less than 16:05:00. After that, the timestamp goes back to 15:04. The first record that has a timestamp greater than or equal to 16:05:00 is record 11. So, recovery has rolled forward through the first system clock change but stopped at record 10. Therefore, the **select** statement shows that ten records exist in the table. In this example, if we had done point-in-time recovery until 16:04:00, we would have recovered only the first six records.

**NOTE**
*With Oracle8 and above,, we can do point-in-time recovery for individual tablespaces. Case 18 discusses this.*

# Case 14: Offline Tablespaces and Media Recovery

As a DBA, you need to be careful when you do media recovery. Sometimes you might finish doing recovery, but when you start the database up, you might realize, to your surprise, that roll forward did not happen to some of the data files. This case study gives you a scenario in which this could happen and what to do to prevent it.

## Scenario

Nancy administers a large database of 150GB at a factory. She uses Oracle7 release 7.3 on a UNIX server and takes weekly offline backups of the database. She triple mirrors her disk drives, and once a week she shuts the database down, unlinks one of the mirrors, and starts up the database. At this point, the database is double mirrored. She then uses tape drives to copy the database files onto the tape. She also keeps a copy of the database on a separate set of disk drives. Once the copying is done, she connects the third mirror to the double mirror. Nancy runs the database in ARCHIVELOG mode. Every day, about 100 archived log files are generated. An automated process copies the archived log files to tape at regular intervals (Oracle8 introduced a new feature that allows duplexing of archive log files), and one week's worth of archived log files are kept online on disk. The control files and online log files are multiplexed.

## Problem

On Sunday, an offline backup of the database was taken. Nancy observed that the current log sequence number was 100. Thursday morning, one of the tablespaces (TS1) was taken offline and the current log sequence number at that time was 450. On Thursday afternoon, due to a disk controller problem, some of the data files were lost. The current log sequence number at the time of the failure was 500.

Nancy decided to delete all the data files, restore data files from the offline backup from Sunday, and roll forward. She restored all the data files from the cold backup and used the current control file to do database recovery. Nancy issued the **recover database** command and applied around 400 archived log files. Since all the archived log files were in the archive destination, Nancy issued the **auto** command and Oracle automatically applied all 400 archived log files. The recovery took about 13 hours, and Nancy could finally bring the database to normal operation.

Once the database was open, she decided to bring tablespace TS1 online. Oracle asked for recovery for all the data files that belong to tablespace TS1. Nancy expected Oracle to ask for recovery starting at log sequence number 450, since that's when the tablespace was taken offline. However, when she issued the **recover tablespace** command, she realized that Oracle asked for recovery starting from log sequence number 100, all the way from when the backup was taken. Worrying that this would take another 13 hours, Nancy picked up the phone to call Oracle Support Services.

## Solution

Note that when a control file indicates that a data file is offline, that data file will not be recovered during database recovery. Since Nancy used the current control file, which shows that all the data files that belong to tablespace TS1 are offline, recovery did not recover any of the data files that belong to that tablespace. Since all the files were restored from backup, tablespace recovery for TS1 asked for recovery starting from the offline backup.

In this scenario, Nancy has to apply all the archived log files again to make the data files that belong to tablespace TS1 current. However, recovery will be shorter than 13 hours this time, since all the changes are already applied to the data blocks except for the changes that belong to tablespace TS1. Also, since tablespace TS1 was taken offline at log sequence number 450, there will not be any redo that needs to be applied between log sequence numbers 450 and 500. The exact time to recover depends on the number of changes that need to be applied to TS1. In this case, it took Nancy two hours to roll forward the second time.

A better recovery solution in a situation like this is to do the following:

1. Restore all data files from the cold backup (or selected data files, depending on which data files are lost).

2. Mount the database and select from the V$DATAFILE view to see if any of the data files are offline.

3. If any data files are offline, bring them online.

4. Recover the database using the **recover database** command and open the database.

5. Bring the tablespace online.

## Test Using Server Manager

The following test simulates this scenario. We first start up the database, take a tablespace offline, and shut the database down using the ABORT option. We then delete all the data files and restore the data files from a cold backup.

```
cosmos% svrmgrl
Oracle Server Manager Release 2.3.3.0.0 - Production
Copyright (c) Oracle Corporation 1994, 1995. All rights reserved.
Oracle7 Server Release 7.3.3.0.0 - Production Release
With the distributed, replication, parallel query and Spatial Data options
PL/SQL Release 2.3.3.0.0 - Production
```

```
SVRMGR> connect internal
Connected.
SVRMGR> startup open
ORACLE instance started.
Database mounted.
Database opened.
Total System Global Area        4480888 bytes
    Fixed Size                    47152 bytes
    Variable Size                 15944 bytes
    Database Buffers             409600 bytes
    Redo Buffers                   8192 bytes

SVRMGR> archive log list
Database log mode               ARCHIVELOG
Automatic archival              ENABLED
Archive destination             /home/orahome/product/7.3.3/dbs/arch
Oldest online log sequence      60
Next log sequence to archive    62
Current log sequence            62

SVRMGR> alter system switch logfile;
Statement processed.
SVRMGR> alter system switch logfile;
Statement processed.
SVRMGR> alter tablespace USERS offline;
Statement processed.
SVRMGR> alter system switch logfile;
Statement processed.
SVRMGR> archive log list
Database log mode               ARCHIVELOG
Automatic archival              ENABLED
Archive destination             /home/orahome/product/7.3.3/
                                dbs/arch
Oldest online log sequence      63
Next log sequence to archive    65
Current log sequence            65
SVRMGR> shutdown abort
ORACLE instance shut down.

SVRMGR> host
cosmos% rm /home/orahome/data/733/*.dbf
cosmos% cp /home/orahome/backup/*.dbf /home/orahome/data/733
cosmos% exit
```

Next, we present two recovery methods. The first method is the recovery procedure used by Nancy in this example. The second recovery method is a better way of doing recovery and is recommended by Oracle, since the log file(s) needs to be applied only once.

## Recovery Method 1

 SVRMGR> **startup mount**
ORACLE instance started.
Database mounted.

SVRMGR> **recover database**
ORA-00279: Change 6420 generated at 02/07/95 11:00:51 needed for thread 1
ORA-00289: Suggestion : /home/orahome/product/7.3.3/dbs/arch1_62.dbf
ORA-00280: Change 6420 for thread 1 is in sequence #62
Specify log: {<RET>=suggested | filename | AUTO | FROM logsource | CANCEL}

Applying suggested logfile...
Log applied.
Media recovery complete.

SVRMGR> **alter database open;**
Statement processed.
SVRMGR> **alter tablespace users online;**
ORA-01113: file 4 needs media recovery
ORA-01110: data file 4: '/home/orahome/data/733/users01.dbf'
SVRMGR> **recover tablespace users;**
ORA-00279: Change 6420 generated at 02/07/95 11:00:51 needed for thread 1
ORA-00289: Suggestion : /home/orahome/product/7.3.3/dbs/arch1_62.dbf
ORA-00280: Change 6420 for thread 1 is in sequence #62
Specify log: {<RET>=suggested | filename | AUTO | FROM logsource | CANCEL}

Applying suggested logfile...
Log applied.
Media recovery complete.
SVRMGR> **alter tablespace users online;**
Statement processed.

## Recovery Method 2

 SVRMGR> **startup mount**
ORACLE instance started.
Database mounted.
SVRMGR> **select * from v$datafile;**

SVRMGR> **select name,  status,  enabled from v$datafile;**

| NAME | STATUS | ENABLED |
|------|--------|---------|
| /home/orahome/data/733/system01.dbf | SYSTEM | READ WRITE |
| /home/orahome/data/733/rbs01.dbf | ONLINE | READ WRITE |
| /home/orahome/data/733/tools01.dbf | ONLINE | READ WRITE |
| /home/orahome/data/733/users01.dbf | OFFLINE | DISABLED |
| /home/orahome/data/733/test1.dbf | ONLINE | READ WRITE |
| /home/orahome/data/733/temp.dbf | ONLINE | READ WRITE |

6 rows selected.

SVRMGR> **alter database datafile '/home/orahome/data/733/users01.dbf' online;**
Statement processed.
SVRMGR> **recover database**
ORA-00279: Change 6420 generated at 02/07/95 11:00:51 needed for thread 1

```
ORA-00289: Suggestion : /home/orahome/product/7.3.3/dbs/arch1_62.dbf
ORA-00280: Change 6420 for thread 1 is in sequence #62
Specify log: {<RET>=suggested | filename | AUTO | FROM logsource | CANCEL}

Applying suggested logfile...
Log applied.
Media recovery complete.

SVRMGR> select name, status, enabled from v$datafile;
NAME                                   STATUS     ENABLED
--------------------------------       ------     -------
/home/orahome/data/733/system01.dbf    SYSTEM     READ WRITE
/home/orahome/data/733/rbs01.dbf       ONLINE     READ WRITE
/home/orahome/data/733/tools01.dbf     ONLINE     READ WRITE
/home/orahome/data/733/users01.dbf     ONLINE     DISABLED
/home/orahome/data/733/test1.dbf       ONLINE     READ WRITE
/home/orahome/data/733/temp.dbf        ONLINE     READ WRITE
6 rows selected.

SVRMGR> alter database open;
Statement processed.
SVRMGR> select tablespace_name, status from dba_tablespaces;
TABLESPACE_NAME        STATUS
---------------        ------
SYSTEM                 ONLINE
RBS                    ONLINE
TOOLS                  ONLINE
USERS                  OFFLINE
TEST                   ONLINE
TEMP                   ONLINE
6 rows selected.

SVRMGR> create table case14 (c1 number) tablespace users;
ORA-01542: tablespace 'USERS' is offline, cannot allocate space in it
SVRMGR> alter tablespace users online;
Statement processed.
SVRMGR> create table case14 (c1 number) tablespace users;
Statement processed.
SVRMGR> exit
SQL*DBA complete.
```

## Observation

Note that in method 2 in the above test, once the database is opened, the tablespace USERS is offline but its underlying data file is online. This is because we have placed the data file online while the database is mounted. However, Oracle has no knowledge of the status of the tablespace when the database is not open. This is because *tablespace* is a logical entity, as we discussed in Chapter 2.

In this scenario, a slight variation to method 2 would be to use the backup control file. Then, the data file doesn't need to be brought online because the backup control file indicates that all data files are online. However, the disadvantage of doing recovery with a backup control file is that once recovery is done, you must open the database with the RESETLOGS option, which means a cold backup needs to be taken immediately.

# Case 15: Read-Only Tablespaces and Recovery

If you are using read-only tablespaces, there are some special considerations when doing media recovery. This case study is dedicated to doing testing on media recovery when using read-only tablespaces. We will present three scenarios and perform a total of six tests. We will test these scenarios using the current control file and repeat them using the backup control file.

## Scenario

Figure 10-7 gives the three scenarios in which read-only tablespaces are used. In all three scenarios, point A denotes the time when a cold backup (or a hot backup) of the database is taken. Also, at point A, Figure 10-7 shows whether the tablespace in question is in read-only or read-write mode at the time the cold backups are taken. Point B is where the tablespace is changed from read-only mode to read-write mode or vice versa, depending on the scenario. Point C indicates a media failure in which all the data files are lost. In all cases, we restore the data files from point A and perform media recovery. We test the three scenarios, first with the current control file and then with a backup control file. Note that if we are using the current control file, this is the control file at point C in Figure 10-7. If using a backup control file, the asterisk (*) in Figure 10-7 indicates the point at which the backup of the control file is taken.

## Tests Using Server Manager

Following are the six tests that we will perform:

1. Tablespace is in read-only mode at backup and also before the failure occurred, and media recovery is done with the current control file.

2. Tablespace is in read-write mode at backup, but is changed to read-only mode before the failure occurred; and media recovery is done with the current control file.

3. Tablespace is in read-only mode at backup, but is changed to read-write mode before the failure occurred, and media recovery is done with the current control file.

4. Tablespace is in read-only mode at backup and also before the failure occurred, and media recovery is done with the backup control file.

5. Tablespace is in read-write mode at backup, but is changed to read-only mode before the failure occurred, and media recovery is done with the backup control file.

6. Tablespace is in read-only mode at backup, but is changed to read-write mode before the failure occurred, and media recovery is done with the backup control file.

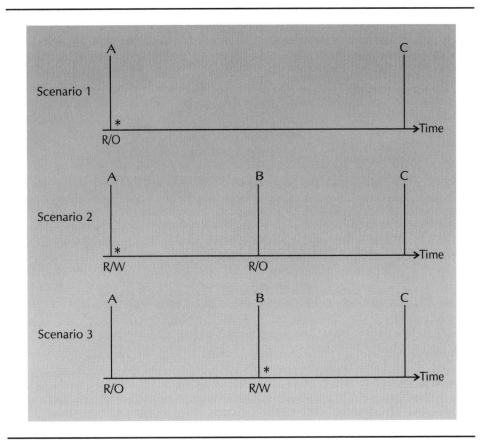

**FIGURE 10-7.** *Three different scenarios for read-only and read-write tablespaces*

Note that tests 1–3 are identical to tests 4–6, except the first three use the current control file, and the second three tests use the backup control file.

### Test 1

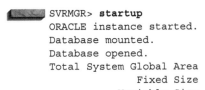

```
SVRMGR> startup
ORACLE instance started.
Database mounted.
Database opened.
Total System Global Area    4480888 bytes
           Fixed Size         47152 bytes
        Variable Size       4015944 bytes
     Database Buffers        409600 bytes
         Redo Buffers          8192 bytes
```

```
SVRMGR> select name, enabled from v$datafile;
NAME                                  ENABLED
-------------------------------       -------
/home/orahome/data/733/system01.dbf   READ WRITE
/home/orahome/data/733/rbs01.dbf      READ WRITE
/home/orahome/data/733/tools01.dbf    READ WRITE
/home/orahome/data/733/users01.dbf    READ ONLY
/home/orahome/data/733/test1.dbf      READ WRITE
/home/orahome/data/733/temp.dbf       READ WRITE
6 rows selected.

SVRMGR> alter system switch logfile;
Statement processed.
SVRMGR> alter system switch logfile;
Statement processed.
SVRMGR> alter system switch logfile;
Statement processed.

SVRMGR> shutdown abort
ORACLE instance shut down.
SVRMGR> host
cosmos% rm /home/orahome/data/733/*.dbf
cosmos% cp /home/orahome/backup/*.dbf /home/orahome/data/733
cosmos% exit
SVRMGR> startup mount
ORACLE instance started.
Database mounted.
SVRMGR> recover database
ORA-00279: Change 6420 generated at 02/07/95 11:00:51 needed for thread 1
ORA-00289: Suggestion : /home/orahome/product/7.3.3/dbs/arch1_62.dbf
ORA-00280: Change 6420 for thread 1 is in sequence #62
Specify log: {<RET>=suggested | filename | AUTO | FROM logsource | CANCEL}

Applying suggested logfile...
Log applied.
Media recovery complete.
SVRMGR> alter database open;
Statement processed.
SVRMGR> select name, enabled from v$datafile;
NAME                                  ENABLED
-------------------------------       -------
/home/orahome/data/733/system01.dbf   READ WRITE
/home/orahome/data/733/rbs01.dbf      READ WRITE
/home/orahome/data/733/tools01.dbf    READ WRITE
/home/orahome/data/733/users01.dbf    READ ONLY
/home/orahome/data/733/test1.dbf      READ WRITE
/home/orahome/data/733/temp.dbf       READ WRITE
6 rows selected.
```

## Test 2

```
SVRMGR> startup
ORACLE instance started.
Database mounted.
Database opened.
Total System Global Area        4480888 bytes
              Fixed Size          47152 bytes
           Variable Size        4015944 bytes
        Database Buffers         409600 bytes
             Redo Buffers           8192 bytes

SVRMGR> select name, enabled from v$datafile;
NAME                                  ENABLED
--------------------------------      -------
/home/orahome/data/733/system01.dbf   READ WRITE
/home/orahome/data/733/rbs01.dbf      READ WRITE
/home/orahome/data/733/tools01.dbf    READ WRITE
/home/orahome/data/733/users01.dbf    READ WRITE
/home/orahome/data/733/test1.dbf      READ WRITE
/home/orahome/data/733/temp.dbf       READ WRITE
6 rows selected.

SVRMGR> alter system switch logfile;
Statement processed.
SVRMGR> alter system switch logfile;
Statement processed.
SVRMGR> alter tablespace USERS read only;
Statement processed.
SVRMGR> alter system switch logfile;
Statement processed.

SVRMGR> shutdown abort
ORACLE instance shut down.
SVRMGR> host
cosmos% rm /home/orahome/data/733/*.dbf
cosmos% cp /home/orahome/backup/*.dbf /home/orahome/data/733
cosmos% exit
SVRMGR> startup mount
ORACLE instance started.
Database mounted.
SVRMGR> recover database
ORA-00279: Change 6507 generated at 02/12/95 18:33:31 needed for thread 1
ORA-00289: Suggestion : /home/orahome/product/7.3.3/dbs/arch1_70.dbf
ORA-00280: Change 6507 for thread 1 is in sequence #70
Specify log: {<RET>=suggested | filename | AUTO | FROM logsource | CANCEL}

Applying suggested logfile...
Log applied.
Media recovery complete.
```

```
SVRMGR> alter database open;
Statement processed.
SVRMGR> select name, enabled from v$datafile;
NAME                              ENABLED
--------------------------------  -------
/home/orahome/data/733/system01.dbf  READ WRITE
/home/orahome/data/733/rbs01.dbf     READ WRITE
/home/orahome/data/733/tools01.dbf   READ WRITE
/home/orahome/data/733/users01.dbf   READ ONLY
/home/orahome/data/733/test1.dbf     READ WRITE
/home/orahome/data/733/temp.dbf      READ WRITE
6 rows selected.
```

## Test 3

```
SVRMGR> startup
ORACLE instance started.
Database mounted.
Database opened.
Total System Global Area      4480888 bytes
              Fixed Size        47152 bytes
           Variable Size      4015944 bytes
        Database Buffers       409600 bytes
            Redo Buffers         8192 bytes

SVRMGR> select name, enabled from v$datafile;
NAME                              ENABLED
--------------------------------  -------
/home/orahome/data/733/system01.dbf  READ WRITE
/home/orahome/data/733/rbs01.dbf     READ WRITE
/home/orahome/data/733/tools01.dbf   READ WRITE
/home/orahome/data/733/users01.dbf   READ ONLY
/home/orahome/data/733/test1.dbf     READ WRITE
/home/orahome/data/733/temp.dbf      READ WRITE
6 rows selected.

SVRMGR> alter system switch logfile;
Statement processed.
SVRMGR> alter system switch logfile;
Statement processed.
SVRMGR> alter tablespace USERS read write;
Statement processed.
SVRMGR> alter system switch logfile;
Statement processed.

SVRMGR> shutdown abort
ORACLE instance shut down.
SVRMGR> host
cosmos% rm /home/orahome/data/733/*.dbf
cosmos% cp /home/orahome/backup/*.dbf /home/orahome/data/733
```

```
cosmos% exit
SVRMGR> startup mount
ORACLE instance started.
Database mounted.
SVRMGR> recover database
ORA-00279: Change 6551 generated at 02/12/95 18:39:37 needed for thread 1
ORA-00289: Suggestion : /home/orahome/product/7.3.3/dbs/arch1_72.dbf
ORA-00280: Change 6551 for thread 1 is in sequence #72
Specify log: {<RET>=suggested | filename | AUTO | FROM logsource | CANCEL}

Applying suggested logfile...
Log applied.
Media recovery complete.
SVRMGR> alter database open;
Statement processed.
SVRMGR> select name, enabled from v$datafile;
NAME                                  ENABLED
------------------------------        -------
/home/orahome/data/733/system01.dbf   READ WRITE
/home/orahome/data/733/rbs01.dbf      READ WRITE
/home/orahome/data/733/tools01.dbf    READ WRITE
/home/orahome/data/733/users01.dbf    READ WRITE
/home/orahome/data/733/test1.dbf      READ WRITE
/home/orahome/data/733/temp.dbf       READ WRITE
6 rows selected.
```

## Test 4

```
SVRMGR> select name, enabled from v$datafile;
NAME                                  ENABLED
------------------------------        -------
/home/orahome/data/733/system01.dbf   READ WRITE
/home/orahome/data/733/rbs01.dbf      READ WRITE
/home/orahome/data/733/tools01.dbf    READ WRITE
/home/orahome/data/733/users01.dbf    READ ONLY
/home/orahome/data/733/test1.dbf      READ WRITE
/home/orahome/data/733/temp.dbf       READ WRITE
6 rows selected.

SVRMGR> alter system switch logfile;
Statement processed.
SVRMGR> alter system switch logfile;
Statement processed.
SVRMGR> shutdown abort
ORACLE instance shut down.
SVRMGR> host
cosmos% rm /home/orahome/data/733/*.dbf
cosmos% rm /home/orahome/data/733/*.ctl
cosmos% cp /home/orahome/backup/*.dbf /home/orahome/data/733
cosmos% cp /home/orahome/backup/*.ctl /home/orahome/data/733
```

```
cosmos% exit
SVRMGR> startup mount
ORACLE instance started.
Database mounted.

SVRMGR> recover database using backup controlfile;
ORA-00283: Recovery session canceled due to errors
ORA-01233: file 4 is read only - cannot recover using backup controlfile
ORA-01110: data file 4: '/home/orahome/data/733/users01.dbf'

SVRMGR> alter database datafile '/home/orahome/data/733/users01.dbf' offline;
Statement processed.
SVRMGR> recover database using backup controlfile;
ORA-00279: Change 6522 generated at 02/12/95 18:34:54 needed for thread 1
ORA-00289: Suggestion : /home/orahome/product/7.3.3/dbs/arch1_70.dbf
ORA-00280: Change 6522 for thread 1 is in sequence #70
Specify log: {<RET>=suggested | filename | AUTO | FROM logsource | CANCEL}

Applying suggested logfile...
Log applied.
ORA-00279: Change 6539 generated at 02/13/95 16:19:08 needed for thread 1
ORA-00289: Suggestion : /home/orahome/product/7.3.3/dbs/arch1_71.dbf
ORA-00280: Change 6539 for thread 1 is in sequence #71
ORA-00278: Logfile '/home/orahome/product/7.3.3/dbs/arch1_70.dbf' no longer needed for this recovery
Specify log: {<RET>=suggested | filename | AUTO | FROM logsource | CANCEL}

Applying suggested logfile...
Log applied.
ORA-00279: Change 6542 generated at 02/13/95 16:19:38 needed for thread 1
ORA-00289: Suggestion : /home/orahome/product/7.3.3/dbs/arch1_72.dbf
ORA-00280: Change 6542 for thread 1 is in sequence #72
ORA-00278: Logfile '/home/orahome/product/7.3.3/dbs/arch1_71.dbf' no longer needed for this recovery
Specify log: {<RET>=suggested | filename | AUTO | FROM logsource | CANCEL}
/home/orahome/data/733/redo03.log
Applying logfile...
Log applied.
Media recovery complete.

SVRMGR> alter database open resetlogs;
Statement processed.
SVRMGR> alter tablespace users online;
Statement processed.
SVRMGR> select name, enabled from v$datafile;
NAME                              ENABLED
--------------------------------  -------
/home/orahome/data/733/system01.dbf    READ WRITE
/home/orahome/data/733/rbs01.dbf       READ WRITE
/home/orahome/data/733/tools01.dbf     READ WRITE
/home/orahome/data/733/users01.dbf     READ ONLY
/home/orahome/data/733/test1.dbf       READ WRITE
/home/orahome/data/733/temp.dbf        READ WRITE
6 rows selected.
```

## Test 5

```
SVRMGR> archive log list
Database log mode               ARCHIVELOG
Automatic archival              ENABLED
Archive destination             /home/orahome/product/7.3.3/
                                dbs/arch
Oldest online log sequence      69
Next log sequence to archive    71
Current log sequence            71

SVRMGR> select name, enabled from v$datafile;
NAME                                  ENABLED
--------------------------------      -------
/home/orahome/data/733/system01.dbf   READ WRITE
/home/orahome/data/733/rbs01.dbf      READ WRITE
/home/orahome/data/733/tools01.dbf    READ WRITE
/home/orahome/data/733/users01.dbf    READ WRITE
/home/orahome/data/733/test1.dbf      READ WRITE
/home/orahome/data/733/temp.dbf       READ WRITE
6 rows selected.

SVRMGR> create table test_5 (c1 number) tablespace users;
Statement processed.
SVRMGR> insert into test_5 values(5);
1 row processed.
SVRMGR> commit;
Statement processed.

SVRMGR> alter system switch logfile;
Statement processed.
SVRMGR> alter tablespace USERS read only;
Statement processed.
SVRMGR> archive log list
Database log mode               ARCHIVELOG
Automatic archival              ENABLED
Archive destination             /home/orahome/product/7.3.3/
                                dbs/arch
Oldest online log sequence      70
Next log sequence to archive    72
Current log sequence            72

SVRMGR> alter system switch logfile;
Statement processed.
SVRMGR> shutdown abort
ORACLE instance shut down.
SVRMGR> host
cosmos% rm /home/orahome/data/733/*.dbf
cosmos% rm /home/orahome/data/733/*.ctl
cosmos% cp /home/orahome/backup/*.dbf /home/orahome/data/733
cosmos% cp /home/orahome/backup/*.ctl /home/orahome/data/733
cosmos% exit

SVRMGR> startup mount
ORACLE instance started.
Database mounted.
```

```
SVRMGR> recover database using backup controlfile;
ORA-00279: Change 6539 generated at 02/13/95 17:02:34 needed for thread 1
ORA-00289: Suggestion : /home/orahome/product/7.3.3/dbs/arch1_71.dbf
ORA-00280: Change 6539 for thread 1 is in sequence #71
Specify log: {<RET>=suggested | filename | AUTO | FROM logsource | CANCEL}

Applying suggested logfile...
Log applied.
ORA-00279: Change 6562 generated at 02/13/95 17:05:37 needed for thread 1
ORA-00289: Suggestion : /home/orahome/product/7.3.3/dbs/arch1_72.dbf
ORA-00280: Change 6562 for thread 1 is in sequence #72
ORA-00278: Logfile '/home/orahome/product/7.3.3/dbs/arch1_71.dbf' no longer needed for this recovery
Specify log: {<RET>=suggested | filename | AUTO | FROM logsource | CANCEL}

Applying suggested logfile...
Log applied.
ORA-00279: Change 6566 generated at 02/13/95 17:07:27 needed for thread 1
ORA-00289: Suggestion : /home/orahome/product/7.3.3/dbs/arch1_73.dbf
ORA-00280: Change 6566 for thread 1 is in sequence #73
ORA-00278: Logfile '/home/orahome/product/7.3.3/dbs/arch1_72.dbf' no longer needed for this recovery
Specify log: {<RET>=suggested | filename | AUTO | FROM logsource | CANCEL}
/home/orahome/data/733/redo01.log
Applying logfile...

Log applied.
Media recovery complete.

SVRMGR> select name, enabled from v$datafile;
NAME                                ENABLED
-------------------------------     -------
/home/orahome/data/733/system01.dbf   READ WRITE
/home/orahome/data/733/rbs01.dbf      READ WRITE
/home/orahome/data/733/tools01.dbf    READ WRITE
/home/orahome/data/733/users01.dbf    READ WRITE
/home/orahome/data/733/test1.dbf      READ WRITE
/home/orahome/data/733/temp.dbf       READ WRITE
6 rows selected.

SVRMGR> alter database open resetlogs;
Statement processed.
SVRMGR> select * from test_5;
C1

_
5
1 row selected.
SVRMGR> select name, enabled from v$datafile;
NAME                                ENABLED
-------------------------------     -------
/home/orahome/data/733/system01.dbf   READ WRITE
/home/orahome/data/733/rbs01.dbf      READ WRITE
/home/orahome/data/733/tools01.dbf    READ WRITE
/home/orahome/data/733/users01.dbf    READ ONLY
/home/orahome/data/733/test1.dbf      READ WRITE
/home/orahome/data/733/temp.dbf       READ WRITE
6 rows selected.
```

## Test 6

```
SVRMGR> archive log list
Database log mode               ARCHIVELOG
Automatic archival              ENABLED
Archive destination             /home/orahome/product/7.3.3/
                                dbs/arch
Oldest online log sequence      68
Next log sequence to archive    70
Current log sequence            70

SVRMGR> select name, enabled from v$datafile;
NAME                                  ENABLED
-------------------------------       -------
/home/orahome/data/733/system01.dbf   READ WRITE
/home/orahome/data/733/rbs01.dbf      READ WRITE
/home/orahome/data/733/tools01.dbf    READ WRITE
/home/orahome/data/733/users01.dbf    READ ONLY
/home/orahome/data/733/test1.dbf      READ WRITE
/home/orahome/data/733/temp.dbf       READ WRITE
6 rows selected.
SVRMGR> alter system switch logfile;
Statement processed.
SVRMGR> alter tablespace users read write;
Statement processed.
SVRMGR> alter database backup controlfile to '/home/orahome/backup/rw_control.ctl';
Statement processed.

SVRMGR> create table test_6 (c1 number);
Statement processed.
SVRMGR> insert into test_6 values (6);
1 row processed.
SVRMGR> commit;
Statement processed.
SVRMGR> alter system switch logfile;
Statement processed.
SVRMGR> archive log list
Database log mode               ARCHIVELOG
Automatic archival              ENABLED
Archive destination             /home/orahome/product/7.3.3/
                                dbs/arch
Oldest online log sequence      70
Next log sequence to archive    72
Current log sequence            72

SVRMGR> shutdown abort
ORACLE instance shut down.
SVRMGR> host
cosmos% rm /home/orahome/data/733/*.dbf
cosmos% rm /home/orahome/data/733/*.ctl
cosmos% cp /home/orahome/backup/*.dbf /home/orahome/data/733
cosmos% cp /home/orahome/backup/rw_control.ctl /home/orahome/data/733/control01.ctl
cosmos% exit

SVRMGR> startup mount
ORACLE instance started.
Database mounted.
```

```
SVRMGR> recover database using backup controlfile;
ORA-00279: Change 6507 generated at 02/12/95 18:33:31 needed for thread 1
ORA-00289: Suggestion : /home/orahome/product/7.3.3/dbs/arch1_70.dbf
ORA-00280: Change 6507 for thread 1 is in sequence #70
Specify log: {<RET>=suggested | filename | AUTO | FROM logsource | CANCEL}

Applying suggested logfile...
Log applied.
ORA-00279: Change 6532 generated at 02/13/95 16:48:01 needed for thread 1
ORA-00289: Suggestion : /home/orahome/product/7.3.3/dbs/arch1_71.dbf
ORA-00280: Change 6532 for thread 1 is in sequence #71
ORA-00278: Logfile '/home/orahome/product/7.3.3/dbs/arch1_70.dbf' no longer needed for this recovery
Specify log: {<RET>=suggested | filename | AUTO | FROM logsource | CANCEL}

Applying suggested logfile...
Log applied.
ORA-00279: Change 6545 generated at 02/13/95 16:50:06 needed for thread 1
ORA-00289: Suggestion : /home/orahome/product/7.3.3/dbs/arch1_72.dbf
ORA-00280: Change 6545 for thread 1 is in sequence #72
ORA-00278: Logfile '/home/orahome/product/7.3.3/dbs/arch1_71.dbf' no longer needed for this recovery
Specify log: {<RET>=suggested | filename | AUTO | FROM logsource | CANCEL}
/home/orahome/data/733/redo03.log
Applying logfile...
Log applied.
Media recovery complete.

SVRMGR> select name, enabled from v$datafile;
NAME                                   ENABLED
------------------------------         -------
/home/orahome/data/733/system01.dbf    READ WRITE
/home/orahome/data/733/rbs01.dbf       READ WRITE
/home/orahome/data/733/tools01.dbf     READ WRITE
/home/orahome/data/733/users01.dbf     READ WRITE
/home/orahome/data/733/test1.dbf       READ WRITE
/home/orahome/data/733/temp.dbf        READ WRITE
6 rows selected.

SVRMGR> alter database open resetlogs;
Statement processed.
SVRMGR> select * from test_6;
C1

-
6
1 row selected.
```

## Observation

Test 1 shows that when doing media recovery with one of the data files in read-only mode, Oracle does recovery as it normally would. In this case, all the data files are taken from point A (see scenario 1 of Figure 10-7) and the current control file is used. However, in test 4 we performed the same test but used the backup control file from point A as well. When you use a backup control file, you have to start up the database with the RESETLOGS option. Any read-only files should be offline; otherwise, the RESETLOGS option has to write to read-only files. For this reason, when you use the backup control file, Oracle asks you to take the read-only data files offline. Note that the read-only tablespace can be brought online again once we open the database with the RESETLOGS option. It is very important to note that Oracle will not allow you to read any files from before a RESETLOGS was done, with the exception of read-only tablespaces and any tablespaces that are taken offline with the NORMAL option.

For test 2, we did media recovery by restoring the data files from point A and using the current control files. After the recovery is done and the database opened, tablespace USERS is in read-only mode. Test 5 is identical to test 2, except a backup of the control file from point A is used. If you use a backup control file from point B in this case, recovery won't work because you have to take USER's data files offline. This is because the control file from point B will identify USER's data files as read-only. So, we need to have a backup copy of the control file that recognizes the files as being in read-write mode from point A.

In test 3, as opposed to test 2, some of the restored data files from point A have a read-only status. If the current control file is used, you don't need to worry about the recovery because it doesn't matter if there are any data files with read-only status. However, as shown in test 6, when a backup control file is used, it cannot be from point A but has to be from point B (or anywhere between points B and C). The reason for this is that if you use the backup control file from point A, the control file identifies USER's data files as being in read-only mode, so you have to take them offline. If the data files are taken offline, the changes made to the data files between points B and C are not applied as part of recovery.

To summarize the above tests, you need to note the following points:

- If you are using the current control file, crash recovery or media recovery with a read-only data file is no different from a read-write file. There is nothing special you need to do. Oracle will recognize the files and do the appropriate recovery automatically.

- If the data file is in read-only mode and doesn't change to read-write during media recovery, the file should be offline during recovery if you are using a backup control file. You should bring the tablespace online after recovery.

- If you are doing media recovery and any data files switch between read-only and read-write modes during recovery, you should use the current control file if available. If you don't have a current control file, then use a backup control file that recognizes the files in read-write mode. If you don't have a backup control file, then create a new control file using the **create controlfile** command.

- From the above three points, it should be clear that you *should* take a backup of the control file every time you switch a tablespace from read-only mode to read-write mode, and vice versa.

# Case 16: Problem Solving with Standby Databases

The purpose of this case study is to show solutions to commonly encountered problems when using the standby database feature with Oracle7 release 7.3. In this case study, we discuss four common problem areas. Under each problem area, we will discuss some of the common *symptoms* and the suggested *solutions*.

## Different Operating System Configurations on Standby and Primary Databases

If different configurations are used for the primary and standby databases, then problems can occur at the standby database. Using different operating systems usually does not work because of different storage formats.

**Symptoms**    Typical symptoms are that you cannot start or mount the standby database, and initialization parameters are reported as invalid.

**Solution**    Problems caused by different configurations will usually show up when the standby database is started. Errors reporting that *initialization parameters are not recognized* usually indicate that the parameters are not supported by Oracle on that platform. Whenever problems are encountered when starting or mounting the standby database, check that the versions of the operating system and Oracle software match those at the primary. If errors are reported when the standby database is mounted, then check that all control files are present and current.

## Activating

When the primary database fails, you need to activate the standby database.

**Symptom**    A typical symptom is that you cannot open the standby database.

```
alter database open;
*
ORA-01666: controlfile is for a standby database
```

**Solution**    This is an easy mistake to make through force of habit. To activate the standby database, use the **alter database activate standby database** command.

## Control Files

Because the standby database has a different control file than the primary, it's easy to run into some common problems with control files.

**Symptom**   A typical symptom is that the control file is rejected at startup.

```
alter database mount standby database;
*
ORA-01665: controlfile is not a standby controlfile
```

**Solution**   The most common problem when starting a standby database is attempting to use the wrong control file. For example, the primary control file was copied to the standby site instead of the standby control file. Use a control file created with the **alter database create standby controlfile** command.

**Symptom**   A typical symptom is that the control file is not found at startup.

```
alter database mount standby database;
*
ORA-00205: error in identifying control file
'/ds1/oracle/7.3.1/dbs/ctl1stby.ctl'
ORA-07360: sfifi: stat error, unable to obtain information about file.
SEQUENT DYNIX/ptx Error: 2: No such file or directory
```

**Solution**   Ensure that a standby control file is available. If necessary, you can copy and rename the control files to match those specified in the standby initialization file.

## Application of Archive Log Files
During maintenance of the standby database, if the primary database continues to run but an archive is lost before application at the standby database, then the standby database cannot be made concurrent with the primary; that is, the standby database must be rebuilt.

**Symptom**   Suppose the recovery process rejects an archive log file as invalid.

```
ORA-00279: Change 7799 generated at 09/13/95 16:46:06 needed for thread 1
ORA-00289: Suggestion : /ds1/oracle/7.3.1/dbs/arch/arch1_42.dbf
ORA-00280: Change 7799 for thread 1 is in sequence #42
ORA-00308: cannot open archived log /ds1/arch/arch1_42.dbf
ORA-07366: sfifi: invalid file, file does not have valid header block
```

**Solution**   This error occurs because the physical structure of the file is not recognized. Check that the file was transferred correctly. This error can occur if **ftp** was used to transfer the file but the *binary* option was not used. Another possibility is that the file format is incompatible with the standby operating system. Check that the same operating system and version are operating at the primary.

**Symptom**    The recovery process cannot find an archive log file.

```
ORA-00279: Change 7176 generated at 09/13/95 16:46:06 needed for thread 1
ORA-00289: Suggestion : /ds1/oracle/7.3.1./dbs/arch/arch1_41.dbf
ORA-00280: Change 7176 for thread 1 is in sequence #41
Specify log: {<RET>=suggested \ filename | AUTO | CANCEL}

ORA-00308: cannot open archived log /ds1/arch/arch_41.dbf
ORA-07360: sfifi: stat error, unable to obtain information about file
SEQUENT DYNIX/ptx Error: 2: No such file or directory
```

**Solution**    Usually, the needed archive log file was not transferred to the standby database.

If you use an automatic mechanism to transfer and apply archives, then check that the automatic transfer script is running and that the network and primary database are working properly. If so, ensure the needed archive log file is transferred to continue with automatic propagation and archive application.

If you are manually applying archives, ensure that the archive log file is transferred and type **auto** to continue.

If you cannot obtain the needed archive log file because the primary has failed, you must consider activating the standby database to make it the primary database.

**Symptom**    When manually applying archive log files, the recovery process rejects an archive log file.

```
ORA-00279: Change 8087 generated at 09/13/95 16:46:06 needed for thread 1
ORA-00289: Suggestion : /ds1/oracle/7.3.1./dbs/arch/arch1_57.dbf
ORA-00280: Change 8087 for thread 1 is in sequence #57
Specify log: {<RET>=suggested \ filename | AUTO | CANCEL}
/ds1/logs/log2st73.dbf
ORA-00310: archived log contains sequence 56; sequence 57 required
ORA-00334: archived log: '/ds1/logs/log2st73.dbf'
```

**Solution**    Find the needed archive log file and type **auto** to continue. Ensure that the needed archive log file was transferred correctly. If a **copy** command was used to transfer the archive across a network, check that the filename is correct for the needed archive log file.

**Symptom**    The recovery process rejects the archive log file as corrupted.

```
ORA-00279: Change 7799 generated at 09/13/95 16:46:06 needed for thread 1
ORA-00289: Suggestion : /ds1/oracle/7.3.1/dbs/arch/arch1_42.dbf
ORA-00280: Change 7799 for thread 1 is in sequence #42
Specify log: {<RET>=suggested | filename | AUTO | CANCEL}
```

```
ORA-00283: Recovery session canceled due to errors
ORA-00333: redo log read error block 2 count 256
```

**Solution**   Assuming that the correct file was transferred, it is possible that the file became corrupt because of the transfer mechanism. Check that the file transfer mechanism is not inappropriately converting the file to the wrong format. Ensure that the transfer is not occurring when the archive log files are being created. Reobtain the completed archive log file from the primary database and restart recovery at the standby database.

**Symptom**   The data file is not found.

```
ORA-00279: change 22130 generated at 09/13/95 06:46:01 needed for thread 1
ORA-00289: Suggestion : /ds1/oracle/7.3.1/arch/arch1_71.dbf
ORA-00280: Change 22130 for thread 1 is in sequence #71
Specify log: {<RET>=suggested | filename | AUTO | FROM logsource| CANCEL
...
ORA-00283: Recovery session canceled due to errors
ORA-01670: new datafile 8 needed for standby database recovery
```

**Solution**   This problem occurs when a data file was added to the primary and not previously created at the standby database. The problem can be fixed at the standby database by creating the data file and restarting recovery. Note that the recovery process only detects the problem after it has updated the standby control file, which now has all relevant information needed for the missing data file. Thus, the V$DATAFILE can be used to obtain the missing data file name, as follows:

```
SELECT NAME FROM V$DATAFILE WHERE FILE# = filenumber;
```

This command can be issued while the standby database is mounted. You don't need to activate the database. Use the *filenumber* shown in the ORA-1670, which in this example is 8. Thereafter, you create the data file using the **alter database create datafile** command, but *without* the SIZE option. The size information is available in the standby control file.

# Case 17: Loss of a Data Partition in Oracle8

The goal of this case study is to demonstrate how partitions in Oracle8 can help minimize outage due to a media loss. Recall that partitions belonging to a table can be placed in separate tablespaces, and these tablespaces can reside on different disks. In the event that one of the disks fails, the remaining partitions will continue to be available. This ensures partial failure of applications based on the table in question. Please refer to Chapter 8 of *Oracle8 Server Concepts Manual*.

## Scenario

Lisa manages the sales database for a small shoe company. The database and the applications are on Windows NT. The majority of the sales data resides in a table called SALES that is organized into four partitions, one for each quarter. The partitions are placed in separate tablespaces that are on four disks. One afternoon she notices that the data file belonging to the tablespace Q2 is offline. Upon further investigation, she determines that the disk drive containing this data file has crashed.

## Solution

Since the table is partitioned and only one of the partitions residing in tablespace Q2 is not available, the solution here is to restore the tablespace Q2 and recover it. The existing applications can continue to function normally. There is no need to bring down the database.

## Test Using Recovery Manager

Let's create a table with two partitions and place them in separate tablespaces. We will then delete the data file belonging to one of the tablespaces and ensure that one of the partitions is not available anymore. We will restore the lost data file and recover the tablespace online.

First, let's create a table with two partitions using Server Manager:

```
SVRMGR> create table case17 (c1 number)
     2> partition by range(c1)
     3> (partition p1 values less than (10) tablespace user_data,
     4> partition p2 values less than (20) tablespace test);
Statement processed.
SVRMGR> select partition_name, high_value, tablespace_name
     2> from user_tab_partitions where table_name='CASE17';
PARTITION_NAME                        HIGH_VALUE          TABLESPACE_NAME
------------------------------        --------------      ---------------
P1                                    1                   USER_DATA
P2                                    20                  TEST
2 rows selected.
SVRMGR> shutdown abort
ORACLE instance shut down.
SVRMGR> host del c:\orant\database\tst1orcl.ora
SVRMGR> startup mount
ORACLE instance started.
Total System Global Area        12071008 bytes
Fixed Size                         46136 bytes
Variable Size                   11090984 bytes
Database Buffers                  409600 bytes
Redo Buffers                      524288 bytes
Database mounted.
```

```
SVRMGR> alter database datafile 'c:\orant\database\tst1orcl.ora' offline;
Statement processed.
SVRMGR> alter database open;
Statement processed.
SVRMGR> select * from case17;
C1
----------
ORA-00376: file 4 cannot be read at this time
ORA-01110: data file 4: 'C:\ORANT\DATABASE\TST1ORCL.ORA'
SVRMGR> select * from case17 partition (p1);
C1
----------
0 rows selected.
SVRMGR> insert into case17 partition(p1) values (1);
1 row processed.
SVRMGR> commit;
Statement processed.
SVRMGR> insert into case17 partition(p2) values (15);
ORA-00376: file 4 cannot be read at this time
ORA-01110: data file 4: 'C:\ORANT\DATABASE\TST1ORCL.ORA'
```

Note that we are allowed all DML operations against partition P1, but we cannot perform a full table scan nor can we perform any DML against P2. We will now recover the tablespace TEST using RMAN.

```
C:\ORANT\DATABASE>rman80 target=\"internal/oracle@prod\" rcvcat=\"rman/aa@rcv\"
Recovery Manager: Release 8.0.3.0.0 - Production
RMAN-06005: connected to target database: ORACLE
RMAN-06008: connected to recovery catalog database
RMAN> run{
2> allocate channel c1 type disk;
3> restore datafile 'c:\orant\database\tst1orcl.ora';
4> recover tablespace "test";
5> sql 'alter tablespace test online';
6> }
RMAN-03022: compiling command: allocate
RMAN-03023: executing command: allocate
RMAN-08030: allocated channel: c1
RMAN-08500: channel c1: sid=17 devtype=DISK
RMAN-03022: compiling command: restore
RMAN-03025: performing implicit partial resync of recovery catalog
RMAN-03023: executing command: partial resync
RMAN-08003: starting partial resync of recovery catalog
RMAN-08005: partial resync complete
RMAN-03023: executing command: restore
RMAN-08016: channel c1: starting datafile backupset restore
RMAN-08502: set_count=5 set_stamp=316242849
RMAN-08019: channel c1: restoring datafile 4
RMAN-08509: destination for restore of datafile 4: C:\ORANT\DATABASE\TST1ORCL.ORA
RMAN-08023: channel c1: restored backup piece 1
```

```
RMAN-08511: piece handle=AATST316242849.5 params=NULL
RMAN-08024: channel c1: restore complete
RMAN-03023: executing command: partial resync
RMAN-08003: starting partial resync of recovery catalog
RMAN-08005: partial resync complete
RMAN-03022: compiling command: recover
RMAN-03022: compiling command: recover(1)
RMAN-03022: compiling command: recover(2)
RMAN-03022: compiling command: recover(3)
RMAN-03023: executing command: recover(3)
RMAN-08054: starting media recovery
RMAN-08515: archivelog filename=C:\ORANT\DATABASE\ARCHIVE\ORCLT0001S0000000611.ARC
thread=1 sequence=611
RMAN-08055: media recovery complete
RMAN-03022: compiling command: recover(4)
RMAN-03023: executing command: partial resync
RMAN-08003: starting partial resync of recovery catalog
RMAN-08005: partial resync complete
RMAN-03022: compiling command: sql
RMAN-06162: sql statement: alter tablespace test online
RMAN-03023: executing command: sql
RMAN-08031: released channel: c1
```

We can now verify that partition P2 is available for use again.

```
SVRMGR> insert into case17 partition (p2) values (15);
1 row processed.
SVRMGR> select * from case17 partition (p2);
C1
----------
        15
1 row selected.
```

### Observation

The partitioning feature of Oracle8 can considerably improve availability because partitions can be placed in separate tablespaces. The recovery procedure is unchanged. The data file recovery procedure was identical to Case 4. An additional advantage is that DBAs can set different storage parameters for the partitions.

## Case 18: Recovery of a Table/Partition via Tablespace Point-in-Time Recovery (TSPITR)

Tablespace point-in-time recovery (TSPITR) is a new feature in Oracle8 that enables recovery of one or more non-SYSTEM tablespaces to a point in time that is different than that of the rest of the database. This feature is useful in cases when you erroneously drop a table and recover it or you want to undo an application that has modified part of the database. This feature is especially useful for DBAs who have very large databases (VLDBs), as it would drastically reduce MTTR because the time to restore a single tablespace is lot shorter than that of the entire database. A detailed description on how to use TSPITR is available in a file called **readme.pit** (text file) on your installation. On UNIX installations, you can find it in the **$ORACLE_HOME/rdbms/doc** directory. On Windows NT, the file is in the **orant\rdbms80** folder.

## Scenario

Louis is one of the DBAs of a transportation company and maintains one of the most crucial databases of the company. A UNIX machine is used to store a 600GB database using Oracle8. The database operates 24 hours a day, 7 days a week, with 200 to 250 concurrent users on the system at any given time. There are 250 tablespaces, and the backup procedure involves keeping the tablespaces in hot backup mode and taking an online backup. Each redo log file is 10MB.

## Problem

One night one of the users accidentally dropped one of his tables. He immediately beeped Louis and said that he needed the table within 24 hours. The table resides in a tablespace called AUTO that is used only by this user. The user acknowledged that he didn't need to use the tablespace immediately and no data had been added to the tablespace after dropping the table.

## Solution

This is a perfect situation to use tablespace point-in-time recovery to recover the dropped table. TSPITR enables us to roll back tablespace AUTO to the point before the table was dropped, whereas the other tablespaces in the database remain at the current time.

## Test 1

In the first test (test 1), we will simulate the problem of dropping a table and will use TSPITR to recover the lost table. Then, we will repeat the test to recover a dropped partition. Please refer to Chapter 8 in the *Oracle8 Server Concepts* manual for concepts on table and index partitions.

On the primary database:

```
SVRMGR>
SVRMGR> select to_char(sysdate,'YY-MON-DD:HH24:MI:SS') from dual;

TO_CHAR(SYSDATE,'Y
--------------------------------
97-JUL-05:15:50:49

SVRMGR>
```

```
SVRMGR> select table_name,tablespace_name from sys.user_tables;

TABLE_NAME                      TABLESPACE_NAME
------------------------------  -------------------
DEPT                            WEEK1
EMP                             WEEK1

SVRMGR> connect internal;
Connected.
SVRMGR> archive log list;
Database log mode               Archive Mode
Automatic archival              Enabled
Archive destination             /u03/app/oracle/product/8.0.3/
                                dbs/arch
Oldest online log sequence      2
Next log sequence to archive    4
Current log sequence            4
SVRMGR>
SVRMGR>
SVRMGR> select to_char(sysdate,'YY-MON-DD:HH24:MI:SS') from dual;
TO_CHAR(SYSDATE,'Y
------------------------------
97-JUL-05:15:53:21
1 row selected.
SVRMGR> alter database backup controlfile to '/home/usupport/gsinghal/clone/backup01.ctl';
Statement processed.
SVRMGR> connect gs/gs
Connected.
SVRMGR> select * from dept;
DEPTNO     DNAME                                 LOC
---------- ------------------------------------  -------------
       10  ACCOUNTING                            NEW YORK
       20  RESEARCH                              DALLAS
       30  SALES                                 CHICAGO
       40  OPERATIONS                            BOSTON
4 rows selected.

SVRMGR> select * from emp;

EMPNO ENAME  JOB         MGR  HIREDATE   SAL   COMM  DEPTNO
----- ------ ----------- ---- ---------- ----- ----- ------
7369  SMITH  CLERK       7902 17-DEC-80  800          20
7499  ALLEN  SALESMAN    7698 20-FEB-81  1600  300    30
7521  WARD   SALESMAN    7698 22-FEB-81  1250  500    30
7566  JONES  MANAGER     7839 02-APR-81  2975         20
7654  MARTIN SALESMAN    7698 28-SEP-81  1250  1400   30
7698  BLAKE  MANAGER     7839 01-MAY-81  2850         30
7782  CLARK  MANAGER     7839 09-JUN-81  2450         10
7788  SCOTT  ANALYST     7566 09-DEC-82  3000         20
7839  KING   PRESIDENT        17-NOV-81  5000         10
7844  TURNER SALESMAN    7698 08-SEP-81  1500  0      30
7876  ADAMS  CLERK       7788 12-JAN-83  100          20
7900  JAMES  CLERK       7698 03-DEC-81  950          30
7902  FORD   ANALYST     7566 03-DEC-81  3000         20
7934  MILLER CLERK       7782 23-JAN-82  1300         10
14 rows selected.
SVRMGR> connect internal;
Connected.
```

```
SVRMGR> shutdown;
Database closed.
Database dismounted.
ORACLE instance shut down.
SVRMGR> exit
```

Now, a cold backup of the database is taken at this point. Later, when we do TSPITR, we will use this backup as the starting point to roll forward the tablespace WEEK1.

```
SVRMGR> connect internal;
Connected.
SVRMGR> startup;
ORACLE instance started.
Total System Global Area        5131060 bytes
Fixed Size                        44924 bytes
Variable Size                   4152248 bytes
Database Buffers                 409600 bytes
Redo Buffers                     524288 bytes
Database mounted.
Database opened.
SVRMGR> connect gs/gs;
Connected.
SVRMGR>
SVRMGR> alter table dept modify (dname varchar2(30));
Statement processed.
SVRMGR> insert into dept values (50,'ADVANCED ANALYSIS','CA');
1 row processed.
SVRMGR> insert into dept values (60,'PIC','CA');
1 row processed.
SVRMGR> insert into dept values (70,'ESCALATIONS CENTER','CA');
1 row processed.
SVRMGR> insert into dept values (50,'SERVER TECHNOLOGY','CA');
1 row processed.
SVRMGR> commit;
Statement processed.
SVRMGR> select * from dept;
DEPTNO     DNAME                          LOC
---------- ------------------------------ -----------
        10 ACCOUNTING                     NEW YORK
        20 RESEARCH                       DALLAS
        30 SALES                          CHICAGO
        40 OPERATIONS                     BOSTON
        50 ADVANCED ANALYSIS              CA
        60 PIC                            CA
        70 ESCALATIONS CENTER             CA
        50 SERVER TECHNOLOGY              CA
8 rows selected.
SVRMGR>
SVRMGR>
SVRMGR> select to_char(sysdate,'YY-MON-DD:HH24:MI:SS') from dual;
TO_CHAR(SYSDATE,'Y
------------------------------
97-JUL-05:16:07:28
1 row selected.
SVRMGR> drop table emp;
```

```
Statement processed.
SVRMGR>
SVRMGR>
SVRMGR> create table salgrade tablespace week1 as select * from scott.salgrade;
Statement processed.
SVRMGR>
```

Note that the table SALGRADE is created after the EMP table is dropped. When we finish the recovery, we stop just before the EMP table was dropped. So the table SALGRADE will not be recovered. You should always check which objects will be lost before doing TSPITR. Refer to the **$ORACLE_HOME/rdbms/doc/readme.pit** file on your installation for details. Now let's see how we can determine that the SALGRADE table will not be recovered.

```
SVRMGR> select owner, name, tablespace_name,
2> to_char(creation_time, 'YYYY-MM-DD:HH24:MI:SS')
3> from sys.ts_pitr_objects_to_be_dropped
4> where tablespace_name in ('WEEK1')
5> and
6> creation_time > to_date('97-JULY-05:16:07:28','YY-MON-DD:HH24:MI:SS')
7> order by tablespace_name, creation_time;
OWNER           NAME              TABLESPACE_NAME          TO_CHAR(CREATION_TI
-----------     ---------------   ----------------------   -------------------
GS              SALGRADE          WEEK1                    1997-07-05:16:09:21
1 row selected.
SVRMGR>
SVRMGR> alter tablespace week1 offline immediate;
Statement processed.
```

The above command is very important. It will take the tablespace that you are about to recover offline, thereby preventing objects from being added.

```
SVRMGR> select * from v$log;
GROUP#    THREAD#    SEQUENCE#    BYTES    MEMBERS    ARC    STATUS      FIRST_CHAN    FIRST_TIM
------    -------    ---------    -----    -------    ---    ------      ----------    ---------
1         1          4            512000   1          NO     CURRENT     125997        05-JUL-97
2         1          2            512000   1          YES    INACTIVE    125870        05-JUL-97
3         1          3            512000   1          YES    INACTIVE    125987        05-JUL-97
3 rows selected.
SVRMGR> alter system archive log current;
Statement processed.
```

The above command will archive the current active online log file in case TSPITR needs the current log for recovery.

```
SVRMGR> select * from v$log;
GROUP#    THREAD#    SEQUENCE#    BYTES    MEMBERS    ARC    STATUS      FIRST_CHAN    FIRST_TIM
-------   -------    ---------    -----    -------    ---    ------      ----------    ----------
1         1          4            512000   1          YES    INACTIVE    125997        05-JUL-97
2         1          5            512000   1          NO     CURRENT     126170        05-JUL-97
3         1          3            512000   1          YES    INACTIVE    125987        05-JUL-97
```

```
3 rows selected.
SVRMGR> select * from v$logfile;
GROUP#      STATUS  MEMBER
---------- ------- -------------------------------
1                  /u03/oradata/V803/redoV80301.log
2                  /u03/oradata/V803/redoV80302.log
3                  /u03/oradata/V803/redoV80303.log
3 rows selected.
```

Now we continue the test on the clone database. You need to add new
parameters to the following **initCLONE.ora** file, such as DB_FILE_NAME_CONVERT
and LOG_FILE_NAME_CONVERT, depending on where you are restoring the data
files. For details, refer to the "Prepare the Parameter Files for the Clone" section in
the **readme.pit** document available on your installation.

```
%setenv ORACLE_SID CLONE
%cp initV803.ora initCLONE.ora

%cp configV803.ora configCLONE.ora

SVRMGR> connect internal;
Connected.
SVRMGR> startup nomount pfile=/home/usupport/gsinghal/clone/initCLONE.ora
ORACLE instance started.
Total System Global Area          5131060 bytes
Fixed Size                          44924 bytes
Variable Size                     4152248 bytes
Database Buffers                    409600 bytes
Redo Buffers                        524288 bytes

SVRMGR> alter database mount CLONE database;
alter database mount CLONE database
*
ORA-01696: controlfile is not a clone controlfile
SVRMGR> shutdown abort;
ORACLE instance shut down.
```

This test is to prove that you cannot use the control file of the production
database. Now we will use the backup control file **backup01.ctl** and try to mount
the clone database again. Note that the **initCLONE.ora** file needs to be modified to
point to the backup control file.

```
SVRMGR> connect internal;
Connected.
SVRMGR> startup nomount pfile=/home/usupport/gsinghal/clone/initCLONE.ora
ORACLE instance started.
Total System Global Area          5131060 bytes
Fixed Size                          44924 bytes
Variable Size                     4152248 bytes
Database Buffers                    409600 bytes
Redo Buffers                        524288 bytes

SVRMGR> alter database mount CLONE database;
Statement processed.
```

```
SVRMGR> select name,status from v$datafile;
NAME                                                STATUS
-------------------------------------------         -------
/home/usupport/gsinghal/clone/system01.dbf          SYSOFF
/home/usupport/gsinghal/clone/rbs01.dbf             OFFLINE
/home/usupport/gsinghal/clone/temp01.dbf            OFFLINE
/home/usupport/gsinghal/clone/tools01.dbf           OFFLINE
/home/usupport/gsinghal/clone/users01.dbf           OFFLINE
/home/usupport/gsinghal/clone/obj.dbf               OFFLINE
/u03/app/oracle/product/8.0.3/sqlplus/doc/obj/week1.dbf OFFLINE
7 rows selected.
SVRMGR> alter database rename file
'/u03/app/oracle/product/8.0.3/sqlplus/doc/obj/week1.dbf' to
'/home/usupport/gsinghal/clone/week1.dbf';
Statement processed.

SVRMGR> alter database datafile '/home/usupport/gsinghal/clone/system01.dbf' online;
Statement processed.
SVRMGR> alter database datafile '/home/usupport/gsinghal/clone/rbs01.dbf' online;
Statement processed.
SVRMGR> alter database datafile '/home/usupport/gsinghal/clone/temp01.dbf' online;
Statement processed.
SVRMGR> alter database datafile '/home/usupport/gsinghal/clone/week1.dbf' online;
Statement processed.
SVRMGR> select name,status from v$datafile;
NAME                                                       STATUS
-------------------------------------------------------    -------
/home/usupport/gsinghal/clone/system01.dbf                 SYSTEM
/home/usupport/gsinghal/clone/rbs01.dbf                    ONLINE
/home/usupport/gsinghal/clone/temp01.dbf                   ONLINE
/home/usupport/gsinghal/clone/tools01.dbf                  OFFLINE
/home/usupport/gsinghal/clone/users01.dbf                  OFFLINE
/home/usupport/gsinghal/clone/obj.dbf                      OFFLINE
/home/usupport/gsinghal/clone/week1.dbf                    ONLINE
7 rows selected.

SVRMGR> recover database using backup controlfile until time '1997-07-05:16:07:28';
ORA-00279: change 126084 generated at 07/05/97 13:44:33 needed for thread 1
ORA-00289: suggestion : /u03/app/oracle/product/8.0.3/dbs/arch1_4.dbf
ORA-00280: change 126084 for thread 1 is in sequence #4
Specify log: {<RET>=suggested | filename | AUTO | CANCEL}
Log applied.
Media recovery complete.
SVRMGR> alter database open resetlogs;
Statement processed.
SVRMGR> connect gs/gs
Connected.
SVRMGR> select * from emp;
EMPNO ENAME   JOB        MGR  HIREDATE   SAL   COMM  DEPTNO
----- ------  ---------  ---- ---------- ----- ----- ------
7369  SMITH   CLERK      7902 17-DEC-80  800         20
7499  ALLEN   SALESMAN   7698 20-FEB-81  1600  300   30
7521  WARD    SALESMAN   7698 22-FEB-81  1250  500   30
7566  JONES   MANAGER    7839 02-APR-81  2975        20
7654  MARTIN  SALESMAN   7698 28-SEP-81  1250  1400  30
7698  BLAKE   MANAGER    7839 01-MAY-81  2850        30
7782  CLARK   MANAGER    7839 09-JUN-81  2450        10
7788  SCOTT   ANALYST    7566 09-DEC-82  3000        20
```

```
7839  KING    PRESIDENT         17-NOV-81  5000          10
7844  TURNER  SALESMAN    7698  08-SEP-81  1500   0       30
7876  ADAMS   CLERK       7788  12-JAN-83  100            20
7900  JAMES   CLERK       7698  03-DEC-81  950            30
7902  FORD    ANALYST     7566  03-DEC-81  3000           20
7934  MILLER  CLERK       7782  23-JAN-82  1300           10
14 rows selected.

SVRMGR> select * from dept;
DEPTNO     DNAME                           LOC
---------- ------------------------------- -----------
        10  ACCOUNTING                      NEW YORK
        20  RESEARCH                        DALLAS
        30  SALES                           CHICAGO
        40  OPERATIONS                      BOSTON
        50  ADVANCED ANALYSIS               CA
        60  PIC                             CA
        70  ESCALATIONS CENTER              CA
        50  SERVER TECHNOLOGY               CA
8 rows selected.

SVRMGR> select TABLESPACE_NAME,STATUS  from dba_tablespaces;
TABLESPACE_NAME                STATUS
------------------------------ ---------
SYSTEM                         ONLINE
RBS                            ONLINE
TEMP                           ONLINE
TOOLS                          ONLINE
USERS                          ONLINE
OBJ                            ONLINE
WEEK1                          ONLINE
7 rows selected.
SVRMGR> select SEGMENT_NAME,STATUS from dba_rollback_segs;
SEGMENT_NAME                   STATUS
------------------------------ ----------------
SYSTEM                         ONLINE
R01                            OFFLINE
R02                            OFFLINE
R03                            OFFLINE
R04                            OFFLINE
5 rows selected.
SVRMGR> alter rollback segment R01 online;
alter rollback segment R01 online
*
ORA-01698: a clone database may only have SYSTEM rollback segment online

%exp sys/change_on_install point_in_time_recover=y recovery_tablespaces=week1

Export: Release 8.0.3.0.0 - Production on Sat Jul 5 17:15:37 1997

(c) Copyright 1997 Oracle Corporation.  All rights reserved.
Connected to: Oracle8 Enterprise Edition Release 8.0.3.0.0 - Production
With the Partitioning and Objects options
PL/SQL Release 8.0.3.0.0 - Production
Export done in US7ASCII character set and US7ASCII NCHAR character set
Note: table data (rows) will not be exported

About to export Tablespace Point-in-time Recovery objects...
```

```
For tablespace WEEK1 ...
. exporting cluster definitions
. exporting table definitions
. . exporting table              DEPT
. . exporting table              EMP
. exporting referential integrity constraints
. exporting triggers
. end point-in-time recovery
Export terminated successfully without warnings.
```

The dump of the **expdat.dmp** file will show the following:

```
EXPORT:V08.00.03
DSYS
RTPITR
1024
0
530
4000
EXECUTE sys.dbms_pitr.beginImport('8.0.0.0.0',3404103021,105867,305725322,126177);
EXECUTE sys.dbms_pitr.beginTablespace(7,126081);
EXECUTE sys.dbms_pitr.doFileVerify(7,7,126177,126156,305743714,5242880);
EXECUTE sys.dbms_pitr.endTablespace(126177,126156,305743714);
EXECUTE sys.dbms_pitr.commitPitr;
CONNECT GS
TABLE "DEPT"
CREATE TABLE "DEPT" ("DEPTNO" NUMBER(2, 0), "DNAME" VARCHAR2(30), "LOC" VARCHAR2(13))
PCTFREE 10 PCTUSED 40 INITRANS 1 MAXTRANS 255 LOGGING STORAGE(SEG_FILE 7 SEG_BLOCK 7
OBJNO_REUSE 3057 INITIAL 10240 NEXT 10240 MINEXTENTS 1 MAXEXTENTS 121 PCTINCREASE 50
FREELISTS 1 FREELIST GROUPS 1 BUFFER_POOL DEFAULT) TABLESPACE "WEEK1"
TABLE "EMP"
CREATE TABLE "EMP" ("EMPNO" NUMBER(4, 0) NOT NULL ENABLE, "ENAME" VARCHAR2(10), "JOB"
VARCHAR2(9), "MGR" NUMBER(4, 0), "HIREDATE" DATE, "SAL" NUMBER(7, 2), "COMM" NUMBER(7,
2), "DEPTNO" NUMBER(2, 0))  PCTFREE 10 PCTUSED 40 INITRANS 1 MAXTRANS 255 LOGGING
STORAGE(SEG_FILE 7 SEG_BLOCK 2 OBJNO_REUSE 3056 INITIAL 10240 NEXT 10240 MINEXTENTS 1
MAXEXTENTS 121 PCTINCREASE 50 FREELISTS 1 FREELIST GROUPS 1 BUFFER_POOL DEFAULT)
TABLESPACE "WEEK1"
ENDTABLE
EXECUTE sys.dbms_pitr.endImport;
EXIT
```

We have finally extracted the data we need from the tablespace. Now we need to import this data that modifies the data dictionary. Note that **export** and **import** don't actually transfer any user data. Now the following test is performed on the primary database again:

```
SVRMGR> select TABLESPACE_NAME,STATUS from dba_tablespaces;
TABLESPACE_NAME                 STATUS
------------------------------- ------
SYSTEM                          ONLINE
RBS                             ONLINE
TEMP                            ONLINE

TOOLS                           ONLINE
```

```
USERS                    ONLINE
OBJ                      ONLINE
WEEK1                    OFFLINE
7 rows selected.
SVRMGR>

SVRMGR> select name,status from v$datafile;
NAME                                                        STATUS
----------------------------------------------------------- ------
/u03/oradata/V803/system01.dbf                              SYSTEM
/u03/oradata/V803/rbs01.dbf                                 ONLINE
/u03/oradata/V803/temp01.dbf                                ONLINE
/u03/oradata/V803/tools01.dbf                               ONLINE
/u03/oradata/V803/users01.dbf                               ONLINE
/u03/oradata/V803/obj.dbf                                   ONLINE
/u03/app/oracle/product/8.0.3/sqlplus/doc/obj/week1.dbf     RECOVER
7 rows selected.

SVRMGR> connect gs/gs
Connected.
SVRMGR> select * from emp;
select * from emp
              *
ORA-00942: table or view does not exist

%imp sys/change_on_install point_in_time_recover=y log=imp.log

Connected to: Oracle8 Enterprise Edition Release 8.0.3.0.0 - Production
With the Partitioning and Objects options
PL/SQL Release 8.0.3.0.0 - Production

Export file created by EXPORT:V08.00.03 via conventional path
About to import Tablespace Point-in-time Recovery objects...
IMP-00017: following statement failed with ORACLE error 29300:
 "BEGIN   sys.dbms_pitr.beginTablespace(7,126081); END;"
IMP-00003: ORACLE error 29300 encountered
ORA-29300: ORACLE error, tablespace point-in-time recovery
ORA-29314: tablespace 'WEEK1' is not OFFLINE FOR RECOVER nor READ ONLY
IMP-00017: following statement failed with ORACLE error 1403:
 "BEGIN   sys.dbms_pitr.commitPitr; END;"
IMP-00003: ORACLE error 1403 encountered
ORA-01403: no data found
ORA-06512: at "SYS.DBMS_PITR", line 1115
ORA-06512: at line 1

. importing GS's objects into GS
IMP-00017: following statement failed with ORACLE error 1187:
 "CREATE TABLE "DEPT" ("DEPTNO" NUMBER(2, 0), "DNAME" VARCHAR2(30), "LOC" VAR"
 "CHAR2(13))  PCTFREE 10 PCTUSED 40 INITRANS 1 MAXTRANS 255 LOGGING STORAGE(S"
 "EG_FILE 7 SEG_BLOCK 7 OBJNO_REUSE 3057 INITIAL 10240 NEXT 10240 MINEXTENTS "
 "1 MAXEXTENTS 121 PCTINCREASE 50 FREELISTS 1 FREELIST GROUPS 1 BUFFER_POOL D"
 "EFAULT) TABLESPACE "WEEK1""
IMP-00003: ORACLE error 1187 encountered
ORA-01187: cannot read from file 7 because it failed verification tests
ORA-01110: data file 7: '/u03/app/oracle/product/8.0.3/sqlplus/doc/obj/week1.dbf'
IMP-00017: following statement failed with ORACLE error 1187:
 "CREATE TABLE "EMP" ("EMPNO" NUMBER(4, 0) NOT NULL ENABLE, "ENAME" VARCHAR2("
 "10), "JOB" VARCHAR2(9), "MGR" NUMBER(4, 0), "HIREDATE" DATE, "SAL" NUMBER(7"
```

```
", 2), "COMM" NUMBER(7, 2), "DEPTNO" NUMBER(2, 0))  PCTFREE 10 PCTUSED 40 IN"
"ITRANS 1 MAXTRANS 255 LOGGING STORAGE(SEG_FILE 7 SEG_BLOCK 2 OBJNO_REUSE 30"
"56 INITIAL 10240 NEXT 10240 MINEXTENTS 1 MAXEXTENTS 121 PCTINCREASE 50 FREE"
"LISTS 1 FREELIST GROUPS 1 BUFFER_POOL DEFAULT) TABLESPACE "WEEK1""
IMP-00003: ORACLE error 1187 encountered
ORA-01187: cannot read from file 7 because it failed verification tests
ORA-01110: data file 7: '/u03/app/oracle/product/8.0.3/sqlplus/doc/obj/week1.dbf'
IMP-00017: following statement failed with ORACLE error 29301:
"BEGIN   sys.dbms_pitr.endImport; END;"
IMP-00003: ORACLE error 29301 encountered
ORA-29301: wrong DBMS_PITR package function/procedure order
ORA-06512: at "SYS.DBMS_PITR", line 1131
ORA-06512: at line 1
Import terminated successfully with warnings.

svrmgr> alter tablespace week1 offline for recover;

%imp sys/change_on_install point_in_time_recover=y log=imp.log

Connected to: Oracle8 Enterprise Edition Release 8.0.3.0.0 - Production
With the Partitioning and Objects options
PL/SQL Release 8.0.3.0.0 - Production

Export file created by EXPORT:V08.00.03 via conventional path
About to import Tablespace Point-in-time Recovery objects...
. importing GS's objects into GS
. . importing table                       "DEPT"
. . importing table                       "EMP"
Import terminated successfully without warnings.
SVRMGR> select tablespace_name,status from dba_tablespaces;


TABLESPACE_NAME                 STATUS
------------------------------  ------
SYSTEM                          ONLINE
RBS                             ONLINE
TEMP                            ONLINE
TOOLS                           ONLINE
USERS                           ONLINE
OBJ                             ONLINE
WEEK1                           OFFLINE
7 rows selected.
SVRMGR> select name,status from v$datafile;
NAME                                                          STATUS
------------------------------------------------------------  ------
/u03/oradata/V803/system01.dbf                                SYSTEM
/u03/oradata/V803/rbs01.dbf                                   ONLINE
/u03/oradata/V803/temp01.dbf                                  ONLINE
/u03/oradata/V803/tools01.dbf                                 ONLINE
/u03/oradata/V803/users01.dbf                                 ONLINE
/u03/oradata/V803/obj.dbf                                     ONLINE
/u03/app/oracle/product/8.0.3/sqlplus/doc/obj/week1.dbf       RECOVER
7 rows selected.
SVRMGR> connect gs/gs
Connected.
SVRMGR> select * from emp;
EMPNO ENAME   JOB        MGR  HIREDATE    SAL   COMM  DEPTNO
----- ------  ---------- ---- ----------  ----- ----- ------
ORA-00376: file 7 cannot be read at this time
```

```
ORA-01110: data file 7: '/u03/app/oracle/product/8.0.3/sqlplus/doc/obj/week1.dbf'
SVRMGR> alter tablespace week1 online;
Statement processed.

SVRMGR> select * from emp;
EMPNO ENAME  JOB         MGR  HIREDATE   SAL   COMM  DEPTNO
----- ------ ----------  ---- ---------- ----- ----- ------
7369  SMITH  CLERK       7902 17-DEC-80  800         20
7499  ALLEN  SALESMAN    7698 20-FEB-81  1600  300   30
7521  WARD   SALESMAN    7698 22-FEB-81  1250  500   30
7566  JONES  MANAGER     7839 02-APR-81  2975        20
7654  MARTIN SALESMAN    7698 28-SEP-81  1250  1400  30
7698  BLAKE  MANAGER     7839 01-MAY-81  2850        30
7782  CLARK  MANAGER     7839 09-JUN-81  2450        10
7788  SCOTT  ANALYST     7566 09-DEC-82  3000        20
7839  KING   PRESIDENT        17-NOV-81  5000        10
7844  TURNER SALESMAN    7698 08-SEP-81  1500  0     30
7876  ADAMS  CLERK       7788 12-JAN-83  100         20
7900  JAMES  CLERK       7698 03-DEC-81  950         30
7902  FORD   ANALYST     7566 03-DEC-81  3000        20
7934  MILLER CLERK       7782 23-JAN-82  1300        10
14 rows selected.

SVRMGR> select * from dept;
DEPTNO     DNAME                          LOC
---------- ------------------------------ ---------
        10 ACCOUNTING                     NEW YORK
        20 RESEARCH                       DALLAS
        30 SALES                          CHICAGO
        40 OPERATIONS                     BOSTON
        50 ADVANCED ANALYSIS              CA
        60 PIC                            CA
        70 ESCALATIONS CENTER             CA
        50 SERVER TECHNOLOGY              CA
8 rows selected.
```

## Test 2

In this test, we will try to recover a partition that was dropped. Again, we start the test with the primary database.

```
SVRMGR> connect internal;
Connected.
SVRMGR>
SVRMGR> select to_char(sysdate,'YY-MON-DD:HH24:MI:SS') from dual;
TO_CHAR(SYSDATE,'Y
------------------
97-JUL-06:15:04:19
1 row selected.
SVRMGR> alter database backup controlfile to
'/home/usupport/gsinghal/clone/backup01.ctl';
Statement processed.
SVRMGR> shutdown;
Database closed.
Database dismounted.
ORACLE instance shut down.
```

Now we take a cold backup of the entire database.

```
SVRMGR> connect internal;
Connected.
SVRMGR> startup
ORACLE instance started.
Total System Global Area            5131060 bytes
Fixed Size                            44924 bytes
Variable Size                       4152248 bytes
Database Buffers                     409600 bytes
Redo Buffers                         524288 bytes
Database mounted.
Database opened.
SVRMGR> select tablespace_name,status from dba_tablespaces;
TABLESPACE_NAME                 STATUS
------------------------------  ---------
SYSTEM                          ONLINE
RBS                             ONLINE
TEMP                            ONLINE
TOOLS                           ONLINE
USERS                           ONLINE
OBJ                             ONLINE
WEEK1                           ONLINE
WEEK2                           ONLINE
WEEK3                           ONLINE
WEEK52                          ONLINE
10 rows selected.
SVRMGR> select name,status from v$datafile;
NAME                                                     STATUS
-------------------------------------------------------  -------
/u03/oradata/V803/system01.dbf                           SYSTEM
/u03/oradata/V803/rbs01.dbf                              ONLINE
/u03/oradata/V803/temp01.dbf                             ONLINE
/u03/oradata/V803/tools01.dbf                            ONLINE
/u03/oradata/V803/users01.dbf                            ONLINE
/u03/oradata/V803/obj.dbf                                ONLINE
/u03/app/oracle/product/8.0.3/sqlplus/doc/obj/week1.dbf  ONLINE
/u03/app/oracle/product/8.0.3/sqlplus/doc/obj/week2.dbf  ONLINE
/u03/app/oracle/product/8.0.3/sqlplus/doc/obj/week3.dbf  ONLINE
/u03/app/oracle/product/8.0.3/sqlplus/doc/obj/week52.dbf ONLINE
10 rows selected.

SVRMGR> connect gs/gs
Connected.
SVRMGR> select * from sales partition(p1);
ACCT_NO    PERSON                          SALES_AMOU  WEEK_NO
---------- ------------------------------- ----------  ----------
1000       JACK                            10000       3
1 row selected.
SVRMGR> insert into sales values (5000,'DAWN',9999999,2);

1 row processed.
SVRMGR> commit;
Statement processed.
SVRMGR> select * from sales partition(p1);
ACCT_NO    PERSON                          SALES_AMOU  WEEK_NO
---------- ------------------------------- ----------  ----------
1000       JACK                            10000       3
```

```
5000      DAWN                       9999999     2
2 rows selected.
SVRMGR>
SVRMGR>
SVRMGR> select to_char(sysdate,'YY-MON-DD:HH24:MI:SS') from dual;
TO_CHAR(SYSDATE,'Y
------------------
97-JUL-06:15:14:48
1 row selected.
SVRMGR> alter table sales drop partition p1;
Statement processed.
SVRMGR>
SVRMGR>
SVRMGR> select TABLE_NAME,PARTITION_NAME,HIGH_VALUE, TABLESPACE_NAME from
sys.user_tab_partitions;

TABLE_NAME         PARTITION_NAME        HIGH_VALUE        TABLESPACE_NAME
-----------------  --------------------  ----------------  ---------------
SALES              P2                    8                 WEEK2
SALES              P3                    12                WEEK3
SALES              P4                    MAXVALUE          WEEK52
3 rows selected.
SVRMGR> alter tablespace week1 offline;
Statement processed.
SVRMGR> insert into sales values (6000,'GAUTAM',9999999,1);
ORA-01502: index 'GS.SYS_C00965' or partition of such index is in unusable state
SVRMGR>
SVRMGR>
SVRMGR> select INDEX_NAME,PARTITION_NAME,HIGH_VALUE,STATUS,
2> TABLESPACE_NAME from sys.user_ind_partitions;

INDEX_NAME   PARTITION_NAME    HIGH_VALUE      STATUS     TABLESPACE_NAME
-----------  ----------------  --------------  ---------  ----------------
0 rows selected.
SVRMGR> select index_name,index_type,table_name,status from sys.user_indexes;

INDEX_NAME         INDEX_TYPE    TABLE_NAME                     STATUS
-----------------  ------------  -----------------------------  --------
SYS_C00965         NORMAL        SALES                          UNUSABLE
1 row selected.

SVRMGR> alter system archive log current;
Statement processed.
SVRMGR> select tablespace_name,status from sys.dba_tablespaces;
TABLESPACE_NAME                STATUS
-----------------------------  ---------
SYSTEM                         ONLINE
RBS                            ONLINE
TEMP                           ONLINE
TOOLS                          ONLINE
USERS                          ONLINE
OBJ                            ONLINE
WEEK1                          OFFLINE
WEEK2                          ONLINE
WEEK3                          ONLINE
WEEK52                         ONLINE
10 rows selected.
```

Now we continue the test on the clone database. We use the proper **init.ora** file and the backup control file and start the instance.

```
SVRMGR> startup nomount pfile=/home/usupport/gsinghal/clone/initCLONE.ora
ORACLE instance started.
Total System Global Area             5131060 bytes
Fixed Size                             44924 bytes
Variable Size                        4152248 bytes
Database Buffers                      409600 bytes
Redo Buffers                          524288 bytes
SVRMGR> alter database mount CLONE database;
Statement processed.
SVRMGR> select name,status from v$datafile;
NAME                                                      STATUS
------------------------------------------                -------
/home/usupport/gsinghal/clone/system01.dbf                SYSOFF
/home/usupport/gsinghal/clone/rbs01.dbf                   OFFLINE
/home/usupport/gsinghal/clone/temp01.dbf                  OFFLINE
/home/usupport/gsinghal/clone/tools01.dbf                 OFFLINE
/home/usupport/gsinghal/clone/users01.dbf                 OFFLINE
/home/usupport/gsinghal/clone/obj.dbf                     OFFLINE
/u03/app/oracle/product/8.0.3/sqlplus/doc/obj/week1.dbf   OFFLINE
/u03/app/oracle/product/8.0.3/sqlplus/doc/obj/week2.dbf   OFFLINE
/u03/app/oracle/product/8.0.3/sqlplus/doc/obj/week3.dbf   OFFLINE
/u03/app/oracle/product/8.0.3/sqlplus/doc/obj/week52.dbf  OFFLINE
10 rows selected.
SVRMGR> alter database rename file
'/u03/app/oracle/product/8.0.3/sqlplus/doc/obj/week1.dbf' to
'/home/usupport/gsinghal/clone/week1.dbf';
Statement processed.
SVRMGR> alter database rename file
'/u03/app/oracle/product/8.0.3/sqlplus/doc/obj/week2.dbf' to
'/home/usupport/gsinghal/clone/week2.dbf';
Statement processed.
SVRMGR> alter database rename file
'/u03/app/oracle/product/8.0.3/sqlplus/doc/obj/week3.dbf' to
'/home/usupport/gsinghal/clone/week3.dbf';
Statement processed.
SVRMGR> alter database rename file
'/u03/app/oracle/product/8.0.3/sqlplus/doc/obj/week52.dbf' to
'/home/usupport/gsinghal/clone/week52.dbf';
Statement processed.
SVRMGR> alter database datafile '/home/usupport/gsinghal/clone/system01.dbf' online;
Statement processed.
SVRMGR> alter database datafile '/home/usupport/gsinghal/clone/rbs01.dbf' online;
Statement processed.
SVRMGR> alter database datafile '/home/usupport/gsinghal/clone/temp01.dbf' online;
Statement processed.

SVRMGR> alter database datafile '/home/usupport/gsinghal/clone/week1.dbf' online;
Statement processed.
SVRMGR> select name,status from v$datafile;
NAME                                                      STATUS
------------------------------------------------------    ----------
/home/usupport/gsinghal/clone/system01.dbf                SYSTEM
/home/usupport/gsinghal/clone/rbs01.dbf                   ONLINE
```

```
/home/usupport/gsinghal/clone/temp01.dbf                    ONLINE
/home/usupport/gsinghal/clone/tools01.dbf                   OFFLINE
/home/usupport/gsinghal/clone/users01.dbf                   OFFLINE
/home/usupport/gsinghal/clone/obj.dbf                       OFFLINE
/home/usupport/gsinghal/clone/week1.dbf                     ONLINE
/home/usupport/gsinghal/clone/week2.dbf                     OFFLINE
/home/usupport/gsinghal/clone/week3.dbf                     OFFLINE
/home/usupport/gsinghal/clone/week52.dbf                    OFFLINE
10 rows selected.
SVRMGR>
SVRMGR> recover database using backup controlfile until time '1997-07-06:15:14:48';
ORA-00279: change 126282 generated at 07/05/97 16:11:44 needed for thread 1
ORA-00289: suggestion : /u03/app/oracle/product/8.0.3/dbs/arch1_5.dbf
ORA-00280: change 126282 for thread 1 is in sequence #5
Specify log: {<RET>=suggested | filename | AUTO | CANCEL}
Log applied.
Media recovery complete.
SVRMGR> alter database open resetlogs;
Statement processed.

SVRMGR> create table swap_p1 (acct_no number(5),person varchar2(30),
sales_amount number(8), week_no number(2)) tablespace week1;
create table swap_p1 (acct_no number(5),person varchar2(30), sales_amount number(8),
*
ERROR at line 1:
ORA-01552: cannot use system rollback segment for non-system tablespace 'WEEK1'

SVRMGR> create table swap_p1 (acct_no number(5) unique,person varchar2(30),
sales_amount number(8),  week_no number(2)) tablespace system;

Table created.

SVRMGR> select index_name,table_name,tablespace_name,status from sys.user_indexes;

INDEX_NAME              TABLE_NAME         TABLESPACE_NAME    STATUS
--------------------    ---------------    ----------------   ------
SYS_C00965              SALES              TOOLS              VALID
SYS_C00966              SWAP_P1            SYSTEM             VALID

SVRMGR> alter table sales exchange partition p1  with table swap_p1;
alter table sales exchange partition p1
*
ERROR at line 1:
ORA-14097: column type or size mismatch in ALTER TABLE EXCHANGE PARTITION

SVRMGR> desc sales;
 Name                           Null?            Type
 --------------------           ----------       ------------
 ACCT_NO                                         NUMBER(5)
 PERSON                         NOT NULL         VARCHAR2(30)
 SALES_AMOUNT                   NOT NULL         NUMBER(8)
 WEEK_NO                        NOT NULL         NUMBER(2)

SVRMGR> desc swap_p1;
 Name                                 Null?       Type
 -----------------------------        ------      ------
 ACCT_NO                                          NUMBER(5)
 PERSON                                           VARCHAR2(30)
```

```
SALES_AMOUNT                                        NUMBER(8)
WEEK_NO                                             NUMBER(2)

SVRMGR> drop table swap_p1;

Table dropped.

SVRMGR> create table swap_p1 (acct_no number(5) unique,person varchar2(30) not
null, sales_amount NUMBER(8) NOT NULL,week_no NUMBER(2) NOT NULL) tablespace system;

Table created.

SVRMGR> alter table sales exchange partition p1 with table swap_p1;

Table altered.

%exp sys/change_on_install point_in_time_recover=y recovery_tablespaces=week1

Connected to: Oracle8 Enterprise Edition Release 8.0.3.0.0 - Production
With the Partitioning and Objects options
PL/SQL Release 8.0.3.0.0 - Production
Export done in US7ASCII character set and US7ASCII NCHAR character set
Note: table data (rows) will not be exported

About to export Tablespace Point-in-time Recovery objects...
EXP-00008: ORACLE error 29308 encountered
ORA-29308: view TS_PITR_CHECK failure
ORA-06512: at "SYS.DBMS_PITR", line 745
ORA-06512: at line 1
EXP-00000: Export terminated unsuccessfully

SVRMGR> select TABLE_NAME,PARTITION_NAME,HIGH_VALUE, TABLESPACE_NAME from
sys.user_tab_partitions;
```

| TABLE_NAME | PARTITION_NAME | HIGH_VALUE | TABLESPACE_NAME |
| --- | --- | --- | --- |
| SALES | P1 | 4 | SYSTEM |
| SALES | P2 | 8 | WEEK2 |
| SALES | P3 | 12 | WEEK3 |
| SALES | P4 | MAXVALUE | WEEK52 |

Now we should check to see if any dependent objects exist before exporting. Refer to **$ORACLE_HOME/rdbms/doc/readme.pit** for details on formatting the columns and a sample script for checking dependencies.

```
SVRMGR> select owner1, name1, obj1type, ts1_name, name2, obj2type, owner2,
2>  ts2_name, reason from sys.ts_pitr_check
3>  where (ts1_name in ('WEEK1')
4>  and ts2_name not in ('WEEK1'))
5>  or
6>  (ts1_name not in ('WEEK1')
7>  and ts2_name in ('WEEK1'));
```

| owner1 | name1 | obj1type | ts1_name | name2 | obj2type | owner2 | ts2_name | reason |
|--------|-------|----------|----------|-------|----------|--------|----------|--------|
| ------ | ------ | -------- | -------- | ---------- | -------- | ------- | -------- | ---------- |
| GS | SWAP_P1 | TABLE | WEEK1 | SYS_C00984 | INDEX | GS | SYSTEM | Tables and associated indexes not fully contained in the recovery set |

```
SVRMGR> alter table swap_p1 drop constraints SYS_c00984;

Table altered

%exp sys/change_on_install point_in_time_recover=y recovery_tablespaces=week1

EXPORT:V08.00.03
DSYS
RTPITR
1024
0
530
4000

EXECUTE sys.dbms_pitr.beginImport('8.0.0.0.0',3404103021,105867,305725322,126490);
EXECUTE sys.dbms_pitr.beginTablespace(7,126081);
EXECUTE sys.dbms_pitr.doFileVerify(7,7,126490,126333,305826450,5242880);
EXECUTE sys.dbms_pitr.endTablespace(126490,126333,305826450);
EXECUTE sys.dbms_pitr.commitPitr;
CONNECT GS
TABLE "DEPT"
CREATE TABLE "DEPT" ("DEPTNO" NUMBER(2, 0), "DNAME" VARCHAR2(30), "LOC" VARCHAR2(13))
PCTFREE 10 PCTUSED 40 INITRANS 1 MAXTRANS 255 LOGGING STORAGE(SEG_FILE 7 SEG_BLOCK 7
OBJNO_REUSE 3057 INITIAL 10240 NEXT 10240 MINEXTENTS 1 MAXEXTENTS 121 PCTINCREASE 50
FREELISTS 1 FREELIST GROUPS 1 BUFFER_POOL DEFAULT) TABLESPACE "WEEK1"
TABLE "EMP"
CREATE TABLE "EMP" ("EMPNO" NUMBER(4, 0) NOT NULL ENABLE, "ENAME" VARCHAR2(10), "JOB"
VARCHAR2(9), "MGR" NUMBER(4, 0), "HIREDATE" DATE, "SAL" NUMBER(7, 2), "COMM" NUMBER(7,
2), "DEPTNO" NUMBER(2, 0)) PCTFREE 10 PCTUSED 40 INITRANS 1 MAXTRANS 255 LOGGING
STORAGE(SEG_FILE 7 SEG_BLOCK 2 OBJNO_REUSE 3056 INITIAL 10240 NEXT 10240 MINEXTENTS 1
MAXEXTENTS 121 PCTINCREASE 50 FREELISTS 1 FREELIST GROUPS 1 BUFFER_POOL DEFAULT)
TABLESPACE "WEEK1"
TABLE "SWAP_P1"
CREATE TABLE "SWAP_P1" ("ACCT_NO" NUMBER(5, 0), "PERSON" VARCHAR2(30) NOT NULL ENABLE,
"SALES_AMOUNT" NUMBER(8, 0) NOT NULL ENABLE, "WEEK_NO" NUMBER(2, 0) NOT NULL ENABLE)
PCTFREE 10 PCTUSED 40 INITRANS 1 MAXTRANS 255 LOGGING STORAGE(SEG_FILE 7 SEG_BLOCK 12
OBJNO_REUSE 3074 INITIAL 1048576 NEXT 1048576 MINEXTENTS 1 MAXEXTENTS 121 PCTINCREASE
0 FREELISTS 1 FREELIST GROUPS 1 BUFFER_POOL DEFAULT) TABLESPACE "WEEK1"
ENDTABLE
EXECUTE sys.dbms_pitr.endImport;
EXIT
```

Now we perform the import on the production database.

```
%imp sys/change_on_install point_in_time_recover=y log=imp.log

Connected to: Oracle8 Enterprise Edition Release 8.0.3.0.0 - Production
With the Partitioning and Objects options
PL/SQL Release 8.0.3.0.0 - Production

Export file created by EXPORT:V08.00.03 via conventional path
About to import Tablespace Point-in-time Recovery objects...
. importing GS's objects into GS
. . importing table                      "DEPT"

. . importing table                       "EMP"
. . importing table                    "SWAP_P1"
Import terminated successfully without warnings.
```

Now let's select the partitions of the table.

```
SVRMGR>
SVRMGR> select TABLE_NAME,PARTITION_NAME,HIGH_VALUE,
    TABLESPACE_NAME from sys.user_tab_partitions;

Table        Partition  High Value            Tablespace
----------   ---------- --------------------  ----------
SALES        P2         8                     WEEK2
SALES        P3         12                    WEEK3
SALES        P4         MAXVALUE              WEEK52

SVRMGR> select * from swap_p1;
select * from swap_p1
              *
ERROR at line 1:
ORA-00376: file 7 cannot be read at this time
ORA-01110: data file 7:
'/u03/app/oracle/product/8.0.3/sqlplus/doc/obj/week1.dbf'

SVRMGR> alter tablespace week1 online;

Tablespace altered.

SVRMGR>  select * from swap_p1;

ACCT_NO    PERSON                 SALES_AMOUNT    WEEK_NO
---------- ---------------------- --------------- ---------------
1000       JACK                   10000           3
5000       DAWN                   9999999         2

SVRMGR>
SVRMGR> alter table sales split partition P2 at (4) into ( partition P1 tablespace
week1,partition P2);

Table altered.
SVRMGR>
SVRMGR> select TABLE_NAME,PARTITION_NAME,HIGH_VALUE,
TABLESPACE_NAME from sys.user_tab_partitions;

Table        Partition  High Value            Tablespace
----------   ---------- --------------------  ----------
SALES        P2         8                     WEEK2
SALES        P3         12                    WEEK3
```

```
SALES     P4         MAXVALUE           WEEK52
SALES     P1         4                  WEEK1

SVRMGR> select * from sales partition (p1);

no rows selected

SVRMGR> alter table sales exchange partition p1 with table swap_p1;

Table altered.

SVRMGR> select * from sales partition(p1);
ACCT_NO    PERSON                       SALES_AMOU    WEEK_NO
---------- ---------------------------- ----------    ----------
1000       JACK                         10000         3
5000       DAWN                         9999999       2

SVRMGR> drop table swap_p1;

Table dropped.
```

## Observation

In this case, we have demonstrated how a table or partition that has been erroneously dropped or truncated can be recovered through TSPITR. We have seen how backups of the data files belonging to the SYSTEM tablespace and a backup control file are used in TSPITR. This case study also highlights the need to have a separate tablespace for rollback segments. It is much easier to recover rollback segments if you can identify the tablespaces and data files to which rollback segments belong. Proper creation of the *clone* database is critical to the success of TSPITR. We strongly recommend that you read the **readme.pit** file before attempting TSPITR. Pay special attention to the sections "Terminology and Restrictions of TSPITR" in **readme.pit**. This method does not work under certain situations that are documented in the file.

# Case 19: Export and Import with QUERY clause

The purpose of this case study is to show the new feature of exporting a subset of a table from one database to another using the **export/import** utility in Oracle8*i*. This case study should make you clear as to how the new feature can be applied in a production environment.

## Scenario

Peter is the DBA for an Oracle8*i* database version 8.1.6 running on Windows NT 4.0. The database holds corporate data, which has many departments such as manufacturing, customer care, HR, R&D, sales, finance, and so on. Due to recent restructuring, the Telecom division has moved to the Detroit office. As part of this move, the data that holds project information of the Telecom division has to be copied (for decentralization and backup purposes) to a new database based in Detroit. All the data related to the Telecom division is stored in the DEPT_DTL and DEPT_PRS tables, along with other departments' data. These two tables have a common column called DIV_ID. Peter wants to copy only the records that belong to the Telecom department and populate the new database in Detroit.

### Problem
Peter planned for an export from the main database and an import into the new database at Detroit. However, the company business rule dictates that he cannot export data of other organizations—only that of the Telecom division.

### Solution
Identify the common column(s) (or primary key) of both tables (DEPT_DTL and DEPT_PRS). Ensure that you can select all the records, using the common column of these tables in the WHERE clause. Peter should use Oracle Enterprise Manager or the **export** utility with the WHERE clause option in the **export** command to export only the records that belong to the Telecom division.

### Test Using export/import with Query Parameter
The following test shows you how to export data using a WHERE clause. For this test, we have created two tables called DIVISION_DETAILS and DIVISION_MASTER.

```
SQL> DESC  DIVISION_DETAILS;
 Name                            Null?    Type
 ---------------------------     -----    ------------
 DIVISION_ID                              NUMBER(5)
 PRODUCT                                  VARCHAR2(15)
 COLOR                                    VARCHAR2(10)
 WEIGHT                                   NUMBER(5,3)
 MFG_DATE                                 DATE
 QUALITY_TEST                             VARCHAR2(10)

SQL> DESC  DIVISION_MASTER;
 Name                            Null?    Type
 ---------------------------     -------  ---------------
 DIVISION_ID                     NOT NULL NUMBER(5)
 DIVISION_NAME                            VARCHAR2(15)
 LOCATION                                 VARCHAR2(15)
 INCHARGE_NAME                            VARCHAR2(20)

SQL>
```

Check total records in each table:

```
SQL> select count(*) from DIVISION_DETAILS;
  COUNT(*)
----------
    500000
SQL>
SQL> select * from DIVISION_MASTER;
DIVISION_ID DIVISION_NAME  LOCATION         INCHARGE_NAME
----------- -------------- ---------------- ---------------
       1001 TELECOM        Detroit          Matthews
       2001 EARTHMOVERS    Texas            Robert
       3001 POWERSYSTEMS   Ohio             Williams
       4001 COMPUTERS      New York         Garry
       5001 CARS           New Jersey       Alex
SQL>

 SQL> select count(*) from DIVISION_DETAILS
  2  where DIVISION_ID=1001;
  COUNT(*)
----------
     50000
```

The output shows that DIVISION_DETAILS holds 50,000 records that belong to the Telecom division. You need to export these records only. Create a parameter file called **tel.dat**. The contents of this file should be as follows:

```
FILE=c:\divisions\telecom.dmp
Log=c:\divisions\tel_30-08-00.log
TABLES=(division_details,division_master)
Grants=y
Indexes=y
Rows=y
Constraints=y
COMPRESS=Y
Query='where division_id=1001'
```

Now run the export as shown here:

```
c:\exp prod/prod@test.oracle parfile=c:\tel.dat
Connected to: Oracle8i Enterprise Edition Release 8.1.6.0.0 - Production
With the Partitioning option
JServer Release 8.1.6.0.0 - Production
Export done in WE8ISO8859P1 character set and WE8ISO8859P1 NCHAR character set
About to export specified tables via Conventional Path ...
. . exporting table          DIVISION_DETAILS       50000 rows exported
. . exporting table          DIVISION_MASTER            1 rows exported
Export terminated successfully without warnings.
```

At the Detroit site, create a parameter file called **imp.dat** that you can use to import the data. The sample contents of the **imp.dat** are as follows:

```
FILE=C:\divisions\telecom.DMP
LOG=C:\divisions\IMPORT.LOG
FROMUSER=(PROD)
TABLES=(DIVISION_DETAILS, DIVISION_MASTER)
GRANTS=y
INDEXES=y
ROWS=y
CONSTRAINTS=y
```

Invoke **import** utility to import the data as shown here:

```
c:\imp.exe prod/prod@prod parfile=c:\imp.dat
Connected to: Oracle8i Enterprise Edition Release 8.1.6.0.0 - Production
With the Partitioning option
JServer Release 8.1.6.0.0 - Production
Export file created by EXPORT:V08.01.06 via conventional path
import done in WE8ISO8859P1 character set and WE8ISO8859P1 NCHAR character set
. importing PROD's objects into PROD
. . importing table        "DIVISION_DETAILS"        50000 rows imported
. . importing table        "DIVISION_MASTER"         1 rows imported
About to enable constraints...
Import terminated successfully without warnings.

SQL> select * from tab;
TNAME                           TABTYPE  CLUSTERID
------------------------------- -------- ----------
DIVISION_DETAILS                TABLE
DIVISION_MASTER                 TABLE

SQL> select * from DIVISION_MASTER;

DIVISION_ID DIVISION_NAME  LOCATION        INCHARGE_NAME
----------- -------------- --------------- -------------
       1001 TELECOM        Detroit         Matthews

SQL>
SQL> select * from DIVISION_DETAILS where DIVISION_ID not in(1001);
no rows selected
SQL>
```

This query will list any record from the table whose DIVISION_ID is other than 1001. The output of the query shows that there is no other record other than Telecom.

## Observation

In this type of situation, to support DBAs like Peter, Oracle provides the **export/import** utility with the QUERY option. This option of the **export** utility enables DBAs to export only a select set of records from one or multiple tables provided the query must be applicable to all specified tables involved in the **export** procedure. The query will be executed against each table individually. In this example, the query part of the **export** utility (WHERE DIVISION_ID = 1001) can be applicable to both tables individually, and so is valid. Oracle selects all the rows and exports them to a dump file. The **import** utility imports associated grants, constraints, and so on into the tables.

# Case 20: Transporting Tablespace(s) Between Databases

The purpose of this case study is to illustrate a new feature called transportable tablespaces in Oracle8*i* to transfer tablespaces between databases.

## Scenario

Debra is the DBA who looks after the Oracle8*i* (Enterprise Edition 8.1.6) database that runs on Sun Solaris. The database contains details about all products, product specific problems, and problem solutions. The master database has several huge tables that belong to the schema SERVICE that are created in the tablespace TECH_SUPPORT. Since support activities are being expanded to the Asia Pacific and Europe regions, Debra needs to set up databases in Singapore and London for the local support organizations, and replicate the technical support data. The data centers, globally, should be in a homogeneous environment using the same version of the database.

## Problem

Debra wanted to use **export** and **import** utilities to transfer the data in tablespace TECH_SUPPORT. After analysis, she found that it would take her several days to export and import the data, as it is several gigabytes in size.

## Solution

Instead of performing export and import for data transferring, you can *transport* the tablespaces between databases, a new feature of Oracle8*i*. Moving data via transportable tablespaces can be much faster than using either **import/export** or **unload/load** utilities. Transporting a tablespace only requires the copying of data files and integrating the metadata into the new database. For transporting a tablespace, you need to perform the following steps:

1. Perform tablespace mode export at the master database and copy the export dump file to the destination database(s).

2. Copy the physical data files that belong to the tablespace TECH_SUPPORT to the destination database(s).

3. Import the tablespace at the destination database using the export dump file that was copied from the master database.

### Test Using export/import

A few validity checks have to be performed before transporting the tablespaces TECH_SUPPORT.

You need to run the PL/SQL package DBMS_TTS, to determine whether the tablespace TECH_SUPPORT is self-contained or not. See the next "Observation" section for details.

```
SQL> exec dbms_tts.transport_set_check('TECH_SUPPORT', TRUE);
```

Query the TRANSPORT_SET_VIOLATIONS view to see whether the tablespace is self-contained or not. If the set of tablespaces is self-contained, this query result will be empty. If the set of tablespaces is not self-contained, this view lists all the violations.

```
SQL>select * from TRANSPORT_SET_VIOLATIONS;
No rows returned
SQL>
```

Determine the status of the tablespace TECH_SUPPORT as follows:

```
SQL> SELECT TABLESPACE_NAME, STATUS from DBA_TABLESPACES
     WHERE TABLESPACE_NAME=' TECH_SUPPORT''
  TABLESPACE_NAME STATUS
  ---------------- -------
TECH_SUPPORT      READ
SQL>
```

List the data files in the tablespace as shown here:

```
SQL> SELECT A.FILE#, A.NAME LOCATION, C.NAME TABLESPACE FROM V$DATAFILE A,V$TABLESPACE
C WHERE A.tS#=C.TS# AND C.NAME='TECH_SUPPORT'
  FILE# LOCATION                             TABLESPACE
  ------ ------------------------------------ -----------
      3 D:\SERVICE\SERVICE_DF.DBF            TECH_SUPPORT
SQL>
```

List the tables and indexes that are created in the tablespace:

```
SQL> SELECT TABLE_NAME FROM DBA_TABLES WHERE
TABLESPACE_NAME='TECH_SUPPORT'
SQL>
TABLE_NAME
------------------------------
PROD_ISSUES
CUSTOMER_DTL
SQL> SELECT INDEX_NAME FROM ALL_INDEXES WHERE TABLESPACE_NAME='TECH_SUPPORT';
INDEX_NAME
------------------------------
PROD_PK
```

Now perform tablespace mode export for the tablespace TECH_SUPPORT as follows:

```
C:\ EXP TRANSPORT_TABLESPACE=y TABLESPACES= TECH_SUPPORT
            TRIGGERS=y CONSTRAINTS=y GRANTS=y FILE=C:\SERVICE\S_SUPPORT.DMP
LOG=C:\EX_TS.LOG
C:\ >EXP TRANSPORT_TABLESPACE=Y TABLESPACES=DATA_TS  FILE=DATATS.DMP  LOG=DATATS.LOG
Export: Release 8.1.6.0.0 - Production on Thu Aug 31 16:23:02 2000
(c) Copyright 1999 Oracle Corporation.  All rights reserved.

Username: SYS AS SYSDBA
Password:
Connected to: Oracle8i Enterprise Edition Release 8.1.6.0.0 - Production
With the Partitioning and Java options
PL/SQL Release 8.1.6.0.0 - Production
Export done in WE8ISO8859P1 character set and WE8ISO8859P1 NCHAR character set
Note: table data (rows) will not be exported
About to export transportable tablespace metadata...
For tablespace TECH_SUPPORT...
. exporting cluster definitions
. exporting table definitions
. . exporting table                    PROD_ISSUES
. . exporting table                    CUSTOMER_DTL
. . exporting index                    PROD_PK
. exporting referential integrity constraints
. exporting triggers
. end transportable tablespace metadata export

Export terminated successfully without warnings.
```

Copy the export file **s_support.dmp** from the directory **c:\service** to the destination database.

Perform the following steps at the destination database:

1. Copy the data files and the export dump files to a desired location the file system.

2. Check whether the user schema SERVICE exists in the destination database in order to import the tablespace in that schema.

```
SQL> select * from all_users where username='SERVICE';
USERNAME  USER_ID CREATED
--------- ------- --------
SERVICE2  6       30-AUG-00
SQL>
```

3. Invoke the **import** utility to complete the tablespace import.

```
C:\ IMP TRANSPORT_TABLESPACE=y DATAFILES='d:\service\service_df.ora'
            TABLESPACES=TECH_SUPPORT_FILE=D:\SERVICE\SERVICE.DMP
LOG=d:\SERVICE\TR_TS.LOG
Import: Release 8.1.6.0.0 - Production on Thu Aug 31 16:31:06 2000
(c) Copyright 1999 Oracle Corporation.  All rights reserved.
```

```
Username: SYS AS SYSDBA
Password:
Connected to: Oracle8i Enterprise Edition Release 8.1.6.0.0 - Production
With the Partitioning and Java options
PL/SQL Release 8.1.6.0.0 - Production
Export file created by EXPORT:V08.01.06 via conventional path
About to import transportable tablespace(s) metadata...
import done in WE8ISO8859P1 character set and WE8ISO8859P1 NCHAR character set
Import terminated successfully without warnings.

SQL> SELECT TABLE_NAME FROM DBA_TABLES WHERE TABLESPACE_NAME='TECH_SUPPORT';
SQL>

TABLE_NAME
------------
PROD_ISSUES
CUSTOMER_DTL
```

## Observation

You have seen that we can transfer a single tablespace or a set of tablespaces between databases within a very short span of time as compared to exporting and importing the same data. When performing tablespace export, the **export** utility will not export any data from the tablespace. It exports only the tablespace's metadata stored in the data dictionary. Similarly, while importing at the destination database, **import** updates only the data dictionary tables and doesn't import any table data. So, irrespective of the size of the tablespace(s), the **export/import** process will take very little time. The limitations of using this feature are as follows:

- It is not possible to transfer tablespaces between databases in a heterogeneous environment.

- You can't transfer tablespaces between two databases that have different database block sizes or different character sets.

- The tablespace should be self-contained, meaning that no objects within the tablespace or the tablespace set should point to other tablespaces that are external to the specified tablespace or tablespace set. For example, let us assume that a table called PROBLEM is created in the tablespace TECH_SUPPORT and the table has an index called INX, which is created in another tablespace called IDX_TS. Since a table in TECH_SUPPORT references an index in another tablespace, TECH_SUPPORT alone is not self-contained. In this case, when you transport the tablespaces, you should consider both the tablespaces TECH_SUPPORT and IDX as a set. If you consider both the tablespaces as a set, then you can consider the tablespace set as self-contained.

■ The tablespace or tablespace set must be in read-only mode before performing the transportation. In this case, the tablespace TECH_SUPPORT must be in read-only mode before performing

# Case 21: Recovering a Database with a Shared Database Name

Recovering a database using RMAN is a simple task. In some special circumstances, it might be more complicated to recover a database. This case study is a little complicated by the fact that you have three databases in three domains, but all of them with the same database name. If one of the databases crashes, how does RMAN know which database to recover? The purpose of this case study is to show how you can recover from a database crash using RMAN, when many databases use a single database name in a network.

## Scenario

Global Marketing Inc. is a marketing company that markets many software products for its customers. Andrew is the DBA who looks after the application servers and databases that are specifically set up for demonstration purposes. There are three databases named DEMO.ORACLE, DEMO.WORLD, and DEMO.GLOBAL (three domains which have the same database name) for giving demonstration to local, national, and international customers. Andrew has another small database called ORA8I.ORACLE in which he has created the recovery catalog of RMAN. He uses this database to back up all the other databases in the company. The recovery catalog holds the backup details of all the databases DEMO.ORACLE, DEMO.WORLD, and DEMO.GLOBAL. Andrew takes weekly full backups of all databases, including their respective control files. Marketing executives can go to any of these three databases and give demos to customers.

## Problem

One day, one of the marketing executives, Jim, was giving a demo to his customers on the database DEMO.ORACLE. There was a power surge and the database crashed. Two disks that were mounted under a controller had a fault due to disk controller failure. All the control files that belong to the database DEMO.ORACLE were on these two disks. The problem was reported to Andrew immediately. After the hardware failure was fixed, Andrew started the DEMO.ORACLE database with the NOMOUNT option and tried to recover the database using RMAN, and got an error:

```
RMAN-20005: target database name is ambiguous
```

The remaining databases, DEMO.WORLD and DEMO.GLOBAL, are up and running.

## Solution

In a network, you can have multiple domains. Each domain can have multiple databases. The database name has to be unique in a given domain. In this example, we have three domains. All of them have a database called DEMO. RMAN registers the database name and database ID (DB_ID) in the recovery catalog. If multiple databases have the same name, RMAN will not know which database to recover and gives the RMAN-20005 error. In this case, you have to specify the DB_ID.

## Test Using Oracle Recovery Manager

In this test, DEMO.ORACLE is shut down. We have DEMO.WORLD and DEMO.GLOBAL up and running. First, we need to connect to RMAN's recovery catalog (which is in the database ORA8I.ORACLE) and try to figure out the database ID numbers (DB_ID) of the databases that are up and running, as shown below:

```
C:\>rman catalog rman/rman@ora8i.oracle

Recovery Manager: Release 8.1.6.0.0 - Production

RMAN-06008: connected to recovery catalog database

RMAN> connect target internal/oracle@demo.global

RMAN-06005: connected to target database: DEMO (DBID=1693819414)

RMAN>

RMAN> connect target internal/oracle@demo.world

RMAN-06005: connected to target database: DEMO (DBID=4111044599)

RMAN>
```

Note the DB_ID numbers of the two databases that are up and running. Now let's look at the recovery catalog to see what database ID numbers are registered with RMAN:

```
SQL>Connect RMAN/RMAN@ora8i.oracle
SQL> SELECT  A.dB_KEY, TO_CHAR (A.DB_ID)"DB_ID", B.DB_NAME FROM DB A, DBINC B
WHERE A.DB_KEY=B.DB_KEY;

DB_KEY          DB_ID                    DB_NAME
-----------    --------------------     --------------------
3185            4103468597               ORA8I
2765            1693819414               DEMO
2245            4111044599               DEMO
1495            4103715043               DEMO
3 rows selected.
SQL>
```

From this query, you can deduce that the DB_ID of DEMO.ORACLE is 4103715043. Now set the target database to DB_ID 4103715043 from the RMAN command prompt, as shown here:

```
RMAN> set dbid=4103715043

RMAN-03022: compiling command: CSET

RMAN>
```

At this point of time, the DEMO.ORACLE database is down. Start the database instance with the NOMOUNT option. You don't have the current control file to mount the database.

```
RMAN> connect target internal/oracle@demo.oracle

RMAN-06006: connected to target database:  (not mounted)

RMAN>
RMAN> run {
2> allocate channel ch1 type disk;
3> restore controlfile;
4> alter database mount;
5> restore database;
}

RMAN-03022: compiling command: allocate
RMAN-03023: executing command: allocate
RMAN-08030: allocated channel: dev1
RMAN-08500: channel ch1: sid=13 devtype=DISK

RMAN-03022: compiling command: restore

RMAN-03022: compiling command: IRESTORE
RMAN-03023: executing command: IRESTORE
RMAN-08016: channel dev1: starting datafile backup set restore
RMAN-08502: set_count=0 set_stamp=0 creation_time=01-JAN-88
RMAN-08021: channel dev1: restoring controlfile
RMAN-08505: output filename=C:\ORACLE\ORADATA\DEMO\CONTROL01.CTL
RMAN-08023: channel dev1: restored backup piece 1
RMAN-08511: piece handle=D:\TEMP\DEMO_CLTL_0CBSSB0F params=NULL
RMAN-08024: channel dev1: restore complete
RMAN-08058: replicating controlfile
RMAN-08506: input filename=C:\ORACLE\ORADATA\DEMO\CONTROL01.CTL
RMAN-08505: output filename=C:\ORACLE\ORADATA\DEMO\CONTROL02.CTL
RMAN-03022: compiling command: IRESTORE
RMAN-03023: executing command: IRESTORE
RMAN-08016: channel ch1: starting datafile backupset restore
RMAN-08502: set_count=2 set_stamp=399248780 creation_time=02-JUN-00
RMAN-08089: channel ch1: specifying datafile(s) to restore from backup set
RMAN-08523: restoring datafile 00001 to C:\ORACLE\ORADATA\ORA8I\SYSTEM01.DBF
RMAN-08523: restoring datafile 00002 to C:\ORACLE\ORADATA\ORA8I\USERS01.DBF
RMAN-08523: restoring datafile 00003 to C:\ORACLE\ORADATA\ORA8I\RBS01.DBF
RMAN-08523: restoring datafile 00004 to C:\ORACLE\ORADATA\ORA8I\TEMP01.DBF
RMAN-08523: restoring datafile 00005 to C:\ORACLE\ORADATA\ORA8I\OEMREP01.DBF
RMAN-08523: restoring datafile 00006 to C:\ORACLE\ORADATA\ORA8I\INDX01.DBF
```

```
RMAN-08031: released channel: ch1
RMAN>
```

Now connect to the database DEMO.ORACLE and open the database with the RESETLOGS option:

```
SQL> ALTER DATABASE OPEN RESETLOGS;
Database altered
SQL>SELECT  COUNT(*) FROM TAB;

COUNT(*)
--------------
  1969

SQL>
```

## Observation

This type of critical situation rarely arises in a production environment. This test shows that RMAN identifies a database by its name and not the DB_ID. An important point to note here is that when you mirror your control files, make sure you keep them on different disks mounted under different controllers. Also note that since we have recovered the database from a backup control file, you have to open the database with the RESETLOGS option. After starting the database in this mode, you need to take an immediate backup of your database.

# Case 22: Setting Up a Standby Database

In this case study, we will discuss setting up a standby database in managed recovery mode with automatic archive log file transfer enabled.

### Scenario

Felix at CT bank is a DBA who handles a 500GB database (Oracle8i version 8.1.6) in New York. Since the main database experienced many shutdowns (scheduled and unscheduled) in the last one month, they decided to have a standby database to cut down the mean time to recover (MTTR). Also, availability is a major issue because all the banking applications need to make use of the replicated databases at remote sites.

### Problem

It is the responsibility of Felix to ensure better database availability and minimum downtime. The database creates redo log files at regular intervals throughout the day and night. Felix works from 9 A.M. to 6 P.M. Though there is another DBA at night, he is not as experienced as Felix. So, Felix needs an automated standby recovery process.

## Solution

Establish a standby database and mount it in managed recovery mode.

## Test

In this case study, the primary node is SALES1. We will refer to this node as the primary site. The standby is created on a node called NETFINITY. We will refer to this node as the secondary site or the standby site. Both the databases have the same directory structure, and are using Oracle 8.1.5 on Windows NT. We will give a step-by-step procedure at each site to set up the standby database.

### Starting with the Primary site

1. Create an **init.ora** file for the standby database by copying the production **init.ora** file to the standby database. Let us assume that you have mapped a logical drive **d:\** to the Oracle directory on the standby system. Copy the **init.ora** file to **d:\admin\test\pfile**. Now the logical drive **d:\** is the Oracle directory in the standby database. This file location must be the same as that of the primary database.

   ```
   C:\>copy c:\oracle\admin\test\pfile\init.ora d:\admin\test\pfile
   1 file(s) copied.
   C:\>
   ```

2. Take cold backup of all data files that constitute the primary database and copy to the standby database. To obtain the list of data files available in the database, do the following:

   ```
   SQL> SELECT NAME FROM V$DATAFILE;

   NAME
   ------------------------------------------------
   C:\ORACLE\ORADATA\TEST\SYSTEM01.DBF
   C:\ORACLE\ORADATA\TEST\RBS01.DBF
   C:\ORACLE\ORADATA\TEST\USERS01.DBF
   C:\ORACLE\ORADATA\TEST\TEMP01.DBF
   C:\ORACLE\ORADATA\TEST\INDX01.DBF
   C:\ORACLE\ORADATA\TEST\OEMREP01.DBF
   C:\ORACLE\ORADATA\TEST\DR01.DBF
   C:\ORACLE\ORADATA\TEST\USER_DATA.DBF
   8 rows selected.

   SQL>
   ```

**3.** Shut down the database in normal mode by issuing the **shutdown normal** command at the SQL prompt. You can also use the **shutdown** command with IMMEDIATE option.

```
SQL> SHUTDOWN NORMAL
Database closed.
Database dismounted.
ORACLE instance shut down.
SQL>
```

**4.** Take a backup of all the data files listed in step 2 at the operating system level by copying them to the standby location. For our example, we copy these files to the location **d:\oradata\test** directory using the operating system **copy** utility. The directory should be the same as that of the primary database. (Copy the password file as well, if the database has password file configuration.)

```
C:\>copy c:\ oracle\oradata\test\*.dbf d:\ oradata\test
c:\oracle\oradata\test\system01.dbf
c:\oracle\oradata\test\rbs01.dbf
c:\oracle\oradata\test\users01.dbf
c:\oracle\oradata\test\temp01.dbf
c:\oracle\oradata\test\indx01.dbf
c:\oracle\oradata\test\oemrep01.dbf
c:\oracle\oradata\test\dr01.dbf
c:\oracle\oradata\test\user_data.dbf

        8 file(s) copied.
```

**NOTE**
*As an optional step, keep a copy of all these files on a tape as backup.*

**5.** Start the database and open it from SQL prompt as follows:

```
SQL> STARTUP OPEN PFILE=C:\ORACLE\ADMIN\PROD\PFILE\INIT.ORA
ORACLE instance started.

Total System Global Area   296431564 bytes

Fixed Size                     65484 bytes
Variable Size               37486592 bytes
Database Buffers           258805760 bytes
Redo Buffers                   73728 bytes
Database mounted.
Database opened.
SQL>
```

**6.** Note the last archived log file name by querying the V$ARCHIVED_LOG view. All the archived redo log files generated from this point of time till we enable the standby are needed at the standby site.

```
SQL> SELECT NAME, SEQUENCE#, ARCHIVED FROM V$ARCHIVED_LOG;
NAME                                           SEQUENCE# ARC
---------------------------------------------- --------- ---
C:\ORACLE\ORADATA\TEST\ARCHIVE\00552.ARC        552       YES
C:\ORACLE\ORADATA\TEST\ARCHIVE\00553.ARC        553       YES
C:\ORACLE\ORADATA\TEST\ARCHIVE\00554.ARC        554       YES
C:\ORACLE\ORADATA\TEST\ARCHIVE\00555.ARC        555       YES
C:\ORACLE\ORADATA\TEST\ARCHIVE\00556.ARC        556       YES
C:\ORACLE\ORADATA\TEST\ARCHIVE\00557.ARC        557       YES
C:\ORACLE\ORADATA\TEST\ARCHIVE\00558.ARC        558       YES
7 rows selected.

SQL>
```

Note that the last archived log sequence number is 558. Starting from sequence number 559, until we enable the standby database, any redo log files generated have to be copied to the standby site mentioned in the STANDBY_LOG_ARCHIVE_DEST parameter of the standby **init.ora** file.

**7.** Now create a standby control file for the standby database:

```
SQL>ALTER DATABASE CREATE STANDBY CONTROLFILE AS "D:\ORADATA\TEST\TESTSTANDBY.CTL'
SYSTEM ALTERED
SQL>
```

## Preparing the Standby Site

**1.** Edit the **init.ora** file of the standby and update the parameters CONTROL_FILES and STANDBY_ARCHIVE_DEST as shown in Table 10-1. All other parameter values must be the same as that of the primary site.

| Parameter Value at Primary site | Parameter Value at Secondary Site |
| --- | --- |
| control_files = ("C:\Oracle\oradata\test\control01.ctl", "C:\Oracle\oradata\test\control02.ctl") | control_files = ("C:\Oracle\oradata\test\teststandby.ctl") |
| log_archive_dest_1='LOCATION=c:\ORACLE\oradata\test\archive' | log_archive_dest = c:\ORACLE\oradata\test\archive |
| LOG_ARCHIVE_DEST_2='SERVICE=TEST. GLOBAL MANDATORY REOPEN=10' | No entries |
| No entries | standby_archive_dest = c:\ORACLE\oradata\test\archive |
| LOG_ARCHIVE_DEST_STATE_1 = ENABLE | No entries |
| LOG_ARCHIVE_DEST_STATE_2= ENABLE | No entries |

**TABLE 10-1.** *New **ini.ora** Parameters at the Primary and Standby Sites*

Don't change the **init.ora** file of the primary site at this time—only the standby site. We will update the **init.ora** file of the primary site later.

2. Create a new instance at the standby using the **oradim** utility as follows:

```
C:\>oradim -new -sid test -intpwd oracle -startmode auto -pfile
c:\oracle\admin\test\pfile\init.ora
C:\>
```

At this point, the new TEST instance service is created. You can view this from Service Applet window of the control panel in Windows NT system.

3. Start the instance using **oradim** utility as follows:

```
C:\> oradim -startup -sid  test -starttype srvc -pfile
c:\oracle\admin\test\pfile\init.ora
C:\> set oracle_sid=test
```

Now the new instance has started using the standby **init.ora** file that we copied and edited earlier. Also, the Oracle sid is set to TEST.

4. Start SQL*PLUS and connect to the database with SYSDBA privileges and shut down the database with the IMMEDIATE option. Then start it up in the NOMOUNT option.

```
SQL> SHUTDOWN IMMEDIATE
Database closed.
Database dismounted.
ORACLE instance shut down.
SQL>startup nomount pfile=c:\oracle\admin\test\pfile\init.ora
```

5. Configure the Oracle Net Service for the TEST instance (registering with the listener) using Oracle Net8 Assistant. Figure 10-8 shows that the listener service LISTENER is configured on port 1521 on the system NETFINITY (standby database site).

**NOTE**
*You can select the Net8 Assistant from Tools | Database Applications | Net8 Assistant from the OEM main menu starting from Oracle 8.1.6. In Oracle 8.1.5 you have to start it from the OS Start menu in NT.*

Figure 10-9 shows that the TEST database is configured for the listener to service the database

### Preparing the Primary Database

1. In order to transfer the archived log files automatically from the primary site to the standby site via Net Service Name, you should create a new Net Service Name to connect to the standby instance TEST. Figure10-10 shows the Net Service Name TEST.ORACLE has been configured for the standby database.

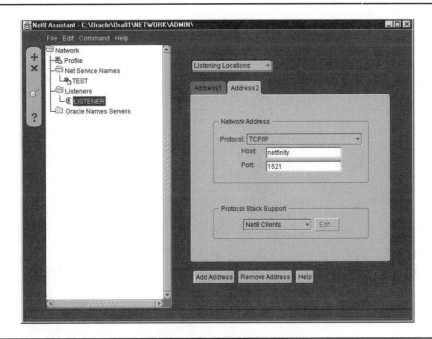

**FIGURE 10-8.** *Listener configuration*

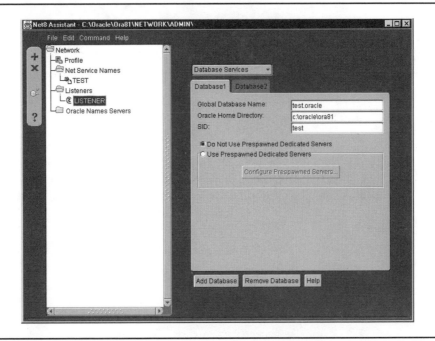

**FIGURE 10-9.** *TEST database configuration for the listener*

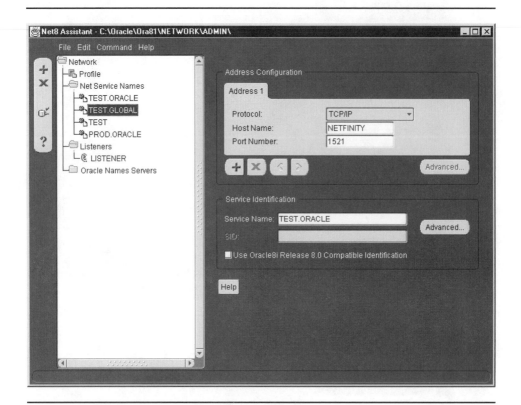

**FIGURE 10-10.** *Net Service Name configuration*

2. Verify that you can establish connection to the standby database using the newly created Net Service Name. You can test a Net Service Name by using on the Command menu of the Net8 Assistant window (see Figure 10-10), selecting the appropriate service name, and clicking on the Test Net Service Name button. The test result is shown in Figure10-11 for the Net Service Name TEST.ORACLE.

**NOTE**
*You should log on as SYSDBA because the TEST database is in NOMOUNT state.*

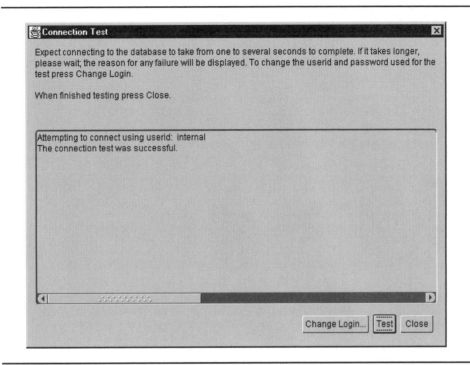

**FIGURE 10-11.** *Testing Net Service Name connection*

**At the Standby Database**    In order to put the standby database in managed recovery mode, follow the steps given below. Note that the database is in NOMOUNT state.

 **1.** Mount the database:

```
SQL> ALTER DATABASE MOUNT STANDBY DATABASE;
Database altered.
```

 **2.** Put the standby database in managed recovery mode:

```
SQL> RECOVER MANAGED STANDBY DATABASE
```

When you issue the above command, the database will be put in managed recovery mode. From this point of time, the standby database waits for the archived log files to arrive from the primary database.

**At the Primary Database**     Perform the following steps:

**I.** In order to enable automatic transferring of archived log files from this site to the standby site, edit the **init.ora** file at the primary site and add the following lines:

```
LOG_ARCHIVE_DEST_2='SERVICE=TEST.GLOBAL MANDATORY REOPEN=10'
LOG_ARCHIVE_DEST_STATE_2=ENABLE
service_names = test.global
```

The **init.ora** file for the primary database is shown in the following code:

```
service_names = test.global
db_files = 1024
control_files = ("C:\Oracle\oradata\test\control01.ctl",
"C:\Oracle\oradata\test\control02.ctl")
db_file_multiblock_read_count = 8
db_block_buffers = 5378
shared_pool_size = 15728640
log_checkpoint_interval = 10000
log_checkpoint_timeout = 1800
processes = 200
parallel_max_servers = 5
log_buffer = 32768
#audit_trail = true  # if you want auditing
#timed_statistics = true  # if you want timed statistics
max_dump_file_size = 10240  # limit trace file size to 5M each
log_archive_start = true

log_archive_dest_1='LOCATION=c:\ORACLE\oradata\test\archive'

LOG_ARCHIVE_DEST_STATE_1 = ENABLE

LOG_ARCHIVE_DEST_2='SERVICE=TEST.GLOBAL mandatory reopen=10'

LOG_ARCHIVE_DEST_STATE_2 = ENABLE
```

**2.** Archive the current online log file:

```
SQL> ALTER SYSTEM ARCHIVE LOG CURRENT;

SYSTEM ALTERED
SQL>

SQL> SELECT NAME, SEQUENCE#, ARCHIVED FROM V$ARCHIVED_LOG WHERE
SEQUENCE#>557;

NAME                                       SEQUENCE# ARC
------------------------------------------ --------- --------------------
C:\ORACLE\ORADATA\TEST\ARCHIVE\00558.ARC   558       YES
C:\ORACLE\ORADATA\TEST\ARCHIVE\00559.ARC   559       YES
C:\ORACLE\ORADATA\TEST\ARCHIVE\00560.ARC   560       YES

3 rows selected.
SQL>
```

The query output shows that two new archived files (559 and 560) were created from the time we took the cold back.

3. Copy these archived log files to the archived destination mentioned in the STANDBY_ARCHIVE_DEST parameter of **init.ora** file of standby database.

4. Enable the archiving process to archive online log files to the standby site automatically:

```
SQL>SHTUDOWN IMMEDIATE
SQL> STARTUP OPEN PFILE=C:\ORACLE\ADMIN\PROD\PFILE\INIT.ORA
ORACLE instance started.

Total System Global Area   296431564 bytes
Fixed Size                     65484 bytes
Variable Size               37486592 bytes
Database Buffers           258805760 bytes
Redo Buffers                   73728 bytes
Database mounted.
Database opened.
SQL>
```

At this point, the primary database starts archiving online log files to both local and the remote standby database locations. The standby database lags behind the primary database by the online log files.

**Activating the Standby Database**     In the event of failure at the primary database, you can activate the standby database and make the standby database your production database. Perform the following steps to activate the standby database. You should note that the standby database is kept in managed recovery mode. You have to log on to the database as SYSDBA from the SQL*PLUS command prompt and issue the following commands:

```
SQL> ALTER DATABASE ACTIVATE STANDBY DATABASE;
Database altered.
SQL>
```

Activating a standby database creates the necessary online redo log files on the standby database.

## Observation
In Oracle8*i*, the standby database features are improved considerably. Oracle8*i* allows you to establish automatic archiving at the standby database by keeping the database in managed recovery mode. In the event of failure of the primary database, the standby database can guarantee you all the data that has been applied from the

archived log files of the primary site. Once the standby database is activated, it will become the production (primary) database. Activating a standby database resets the online logs of the standby database. The activated standby database cannot be put back to standby mode again. You need to re-create the standby database all over again.

# Summary

The preceding case studies should give you an idea of the kinds of failures that happen in the real world and how you should recover with minimal (or better yet, no) data loss. Here are some points you should remember while designing backup procedures or recovering a database from a failure:

- Always mirror control files.

- Always multiplex online redo log files and keep a copy on different disk drives mounted under different controllers.

- Try to take online or offline backups (or both) at frequent intervals, depending on your business needs. Automate all backup procedures. Keep a copy of all database files on tape as well as an online copy, if possible.

- Try to take logical backups of your database whenever you can. If it's a very big database, try taking exports of the important tables at least, if possible.

- Copy the archive log files to tape very frequently in addition to keeping a copy on disk. Mirror the disk that has the archived log files at the OS level. If you are using Oracle8 or higher, duplex the archive log files using the LOG_ARCHIVE_DUPLEX_DEST parameter in the **init.ora**.

- At least once every three months (or whenever appropriate), use a test machine to restore from a backup. Simulate various failures and try restoring the database.

- If the schema of the database changes (adding or dropping data files), always take a backup of the new data file(s) that you add and also a backup of the control file *immediately*. Also, update your automated backup procedures to include the new data file(s) that you added to the database.

- When a failure occurs, always check to see if you can do complete recovery. If not, then perform incomplete recovery. Always remember that you will lose data when you do incomplete recovery.

- Always check to see if you can do online recovery. If not, then perform offline recovery.

- Make sure that all the appropriate data files are online before attempting recovery. The view V$DATAFILE will help you get this information.

- Always try to use the current control file while trying to do recovery, if possible. If the current control file is not available, try creating a new control file. Use the backup control file as the last option because you have to start up the database with the RESETLOGS option.

- If you start the database with the RESETLOGS option, *immediately* plan for an offline or an online backup.

- If you change the system time, plan for a full online or offline backup immediately.

- If you are using Oracle8 or higher, we recommend that you use Oracle Recovery Manager with a recovery catalog if you are administering more than two databases, or if you are using VLDBs. This reduces the risks of user errors during recovery as well as allowing you to take advantage of features like incremental backup, which is much faster.

- Before calling Oracle Support Services, make sure you gather all the diagnostics, as described in Chapter 9.

- Most importantly, be prepared for disasters. Don't think you will never see a failure. Every DBA will experience a database failure. It's just a matter of time. Good Luck.

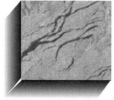

# APPENDIX
# A

## New Features
## of Oracle8i

his appendix lists all the references in this book to new features of Oracle8*i*. While all of the features are briefly discussed, some the features that relate to backup and recovery and troubleshooting the RDBMS are already discussed in detail in this book.

# Backup and Recovery

Following are the new features in Oracle8*i* Recovery Manager (RMAN):

- RMAN Uses the Target Database's Control File. RMAN now uses the control file of the target database for backup and recovery operations. The recovery catalog is no longer mandatory but optional. When using a recovery catalog, RMAN can perform a wider variety of automated backup and recovery functions.

- Control File Character Set Enables the Recovery Manager to interpret correctly tablespace names for recovery when the character set is other than the default. If the control file is lost, recovery is still possible. The DBA may specify the character set as an argument in the **create controlfile** command.

- Duplexed Backup Sets and Unique Naming Recovery Manager can now create up to four concurrent copies of each backup piece. Also, a backup piece will no longer be overwritten if an attempt is made to create a backup piece with the same name as an existing one. RMAN now issues an error.

- Tablespace Point-in-Time Recovery TSPITR can now be performed without a recovery catalog with certain restrictions.

- New Views Two new views—V$BACKUP_SYNC_IO and V$BACKUP_ASYNC_IO—are available to monitor the progress and performance of Recovery Manager backups.

- Proxy Copy The **backup** command's PROXY option allows media management vendor software to take over the entire data movement involved in a backup or restore.

- Media Pool Selection Some media management software allows backup media to be arranged into storage pools based on media type, retention period, or other criteria. RMAN has the feature to support version 2.0 of the Oracle Media Management API, commonly referred to as system backup to tape API, or SBT.

- Vendor Identification and Improved Error Messages When a channel is allocated, RMAN will display in its log a text message identifying the media management product that will be used to take backups with that channel.

When the media manager encounters an error, it will return a text error message explaining the error, which will be displayed in the RMAN log.

- New **send** Command   The new **send** command allows commands to be sent directly from an RMAN session to the media management software. Typically, this command is used to control runtime options of the media manager that cannot otherwise be controlled using RMAN.

- New **change...crosscheck** Command   The **crosscheck backup** and **delete expired backup** commands allow synchronization of the recovery catalog with the media manager's catalog. The new **change...crosscheck** command can perform crosschecks on both backup sets and image copies.

- The **list** and **report** Commands   The **list backup** command can't print the list of backups belonging to a backup set in a separate section of the report from the list of data files or archived logs included in the backup set. A new command, **report need backup redundancy**, has been implemented.

- New Recovery Catalog Maintenance Commands   Now you can use the **create catalog** command to create the recovery catalog. It replaces running the **catrman.sql** and associated scripts in the **admin** directory, which had to be run manually to create the recovery catalog schema in Oracle8.

- The **upgrade catalog** Command   RMAN recovery catalog can now be upgraded using the **upgrade catalog** command. This command upgrades the recovery catalog from any prior version.

- The **drop catalog** Command   Removes the recovery catalog schema.

- Startup and Shutdown Operations   It is no longer necessary to exit RMAN to shut down, start up, mount, or open the database. You can use the **startup** and **shutdown** commands with RMAN now. The following two forms of the **alter database** command are also supported:

```
alter database...mount
alter database...open
```

- The **duplicate** Command   Allows creation of a replicated database using the backups of another database.

- Node Affinity Detection   When backing up on multiple nodes in a parallel server environment, it is possible that some disks have affinity to certain nodes in the cluster such that access to those disks is faster from those nodes than from other nodes in the cluster. RMAN recognizes node affinity, if it exists, and will attempt to schedule data file backups on channels allocated at nodes that have affinity to those files.

# New SQL Statements

The following are the new SQL commands/clauses introduced in Oracle8*i*:

- **create dimension** Defines a parent-child relationship between pairs of column sets, where all the columns of a column set must come from the same table. To change the hierarchical relationships or dimension attributes, you can use the **alter dimension** command.

- **create outline** A stored outline is a set of attributes used by the optimizer to generate an execution plan. You can then instruct the optimizer to use a set of outlines to influence the generation of execution plans whenever a particular SQL statement is issued, regardless of changes in factors that can affect optimization. Use the **create outline** SQL command to create an outline for SQL statements.

- **call** Enables you to execute a stand-alone procedure or function, or a procedure or function defined within a type or package from within SQL.

- **context** Used to create a namespace for a set of application-defined attributes that validates and secures an application and to associate the namespace with the externally created package that sets the context.

- **create indextype** Indextype is an object that specifies the routines that manage a domain (application-specific) index. Indextypes reside in the same namespace as tables, views, and other schema objects. It binds the indextype name to an implementation type, which in turn specifies and refers to user-defined index functions and procedures that implement the indextype. The **create indextype** and **drop indextype** commands can create and delete indextypes.

- The ROLLUP Clause ROLLUP is a simple extension to the **select** statement's GROUP BY clause. It creates subtotals at any level of aggregation needed, from the most detailed up to a grand total.

- CUBE An extension similar to ROLLUP, enabling a single statement to calculate all possible combinations of subtotals. CUBE can generate the information needed in crosstab reports with a single query.

- GROUPING Using a single column as its argument, GROUPING returns 1 when it encounters a NULL value created by a ROLLUP or CUBE operation. That is, if the NULL indicates the row is a subtotal, GROUPING returns a 1. Any other type of value, including a stored NULL, will return a 0.

■ The **analyze** Command    Now, the improved functionality of **analyze** command can make a call to a user-specified statistics collection function whenever a domain index is analyzed. User-defined statistics collection functions can also be defined for individual columns of a table and for user-defined datatypes.

■ The **sample** Function    The FROM clause in a query has been modified with a **sample** clause to allow the user to specify that the results are to be based on a random (row or block) sample of a whole table.

■ Function-Based Indexes    Indexes can now be created on functions and expressions that involve one or more columns in the table being indexed.

■ Drop Column    A new drop column capability allows the DBA to easily remove unused columns in the database. New syntax for the **alter table** statement allows a column to be marked as unusable without freeing up space in the table, or to be dropped from the table with the data deleted.

■ Descending Indexes    The DESC keyword in the **create index** statement is no longer ignored. It specifies that the index should be created in descending order of keys. DESC cannot be specified for a bitmapped index.

# Constraints

■ New Constraint Functionality    In Oracle8*i*, allows you to modify the attributes of an existing constraint through the MODIFY CONSTRAINT clause of the **alter table** command.

■ DISABLE VALIDATE Constraint State    Saves space because it requires no index on a unique or primary key, yet it guarantees the validity of all existing data in the table.

■ Index-Organized Tables    Provides full-table functionality for index-organized tables. It also provides the ability to do key compression.

■ Logical ROWIDs    Oracle8*i* introduces primary key-based logical identifiers called logical ROWIDs. ROWIDs provide the fastest possible access to a row in a table

# Extensibility Framework

Oracle8i supports user-defined operators and extensible indexing. It provides an interface that enables developers to define domain-specific operators and indexing schemes and integrate them into the Oracle database server.

The extensible optimizer functionality has been extended to allow authors with user-defined functions and domain indexes to create statistics collection, selectivity, and cost functions that will be used by the optimizer in choosing a query plan.

Oracle8i supports the creation, freeing, accessing, and updating of temporary LOBs.

# Java

Java is becoming the standard language of the Internet. In Oracle8i, Oracle delivers an enterprise-class Java platform to develop and deploy Internet applications. Additionally, Oracle is making a significant strategic commitment to Java and is integrating it with its products.

# Automated Standby Databases

The standby databases have the following new features:

- Automatic Archival    With the new automated standby database feature, the archived redo logs can be automatically transferred and applied at the standby database. This eliminates the need for manual procedures to copy and transmit the redo logs and the need for the operator at the backup site to manually specify which logs to apply.

- Read-Only Databases    This option can be used to make a standby database a read-only database available for queries and reporting, even while archive logs are being copied from the primary database site.

- Database SUSPEND/RESUME    Provides a mechanism by which all I/O in the database can be stopped, enabling copies of the database to be made without I/O interference. The **alter system suspend** statement stops new lock and I/O activity from being initiated. The creation of backups or archived logs is not affected. The database remains suspended until an **alter system resume** statement is issued.

# WebDB

WebDB is an HTML-based development tool for building HTML Web pages with content based on data stored in the Oracle database.

■ Oracle Internet File System (iFS)   Combines the power of Oracle8*i* with the ease of use of a file system. Completely integrated with Oracle8*i*, the Internet File System is a Java application that runs within the Oracle8*i* Java Virtual Machine. It enables the database to become an Internet development and deployment platform.

## Oracle8*i* interMedia

Oracle8*i* interMedia adds support that enables the database server to manage multimedia content, both for Internet and traditional applications that require access to image, audio, video, text, and location information. Oracle8*i* interMedia allows multimedia data to be managed in an integral part of the enterprise data. Applications can access interMedia through both object and relational interfaces. Database applications written in Java, C++, or traditional 3GLs can interface to interMedia through class libraries, PL/SQL, and the Oracle Call Interface (OCI).

## Oracle8*i* Spatial

Spatial data is like any other data with a location component. The location component could be the *geocoded* addresses of customers or suppliers, the course of a river and the outline of its floodplain, the locations of thousands of utility poles, or X and Y coordinates on a blueprint. Spatial data is not limited to the land surface, but includes the subsurface, aquatic, marine, and lower atmospheric regions.

## Oracle8*i* Visual Information Retrieval

Oracle8*i* Visual Information Retrieval provides content-based retrieval for images stored in Oracle8*i*. Oracle8*i* Visual Information Retrieval includes foundational datatype support for images in Oracle8*i*, which complements and is completely compatible with Oracle8*i* interMedia.

Oracle8*i* Time Series provides the following kinds of functions:

■ Calendar functions provide a convenient mechanism for defining time-related operations and ensuring the validity of time-related data.

■ Time series functions provide analysis of time series data and include support for complex aggregation (such as moving average), mathematical operations (such as cumulative sum and cell-by-cell arithmetic operations), and data verification.

# Data Warehousing and Very Large Data Bases (VLDB)

Oracle8*i*'s database Resource Manager feature provides new resource management functions to control and limit the total amount of processing resources available to a given user or set of users. DBAs use the functions to implement database resource management. These are as follows:

- Resource consumer groups
- Resource plans
- Resource allocation methods
- Resource plan directives

# Summary Management Using Materialized Views

With the Oracle8*i* summary management feature, the Oracle database server automatically rewrites queries to use the summary data, rather than retrieving data from detail tables by doing expensive joins and aggregate operations. This query rewrite facility is totally transparent to the application, which is not aware of the existence of the materialized view.

# Transportable Tablespaces

This feature allows a DBA to move a subset of an Oracle database from one database to another using the **export/import** utility. However, the data is actually not exported; only the metadata is exported. It is therefore possible to clone a tablespace in one database and plug it into another, thereby copying the tablespace between databases. This feature is extremely useful while using very large databases.

# Locally Managed Tablespaces

Oracle introduces a new mechanism for managing space within a tablespace called "locally managed tablespaces." The extent map information is tracked in the tablespace itself, using bitmaps.

# Online Index Creation, Rebuild, and Defragmentation

Oracle8*i* supports the online creation or rebuilding of an index that works for partitioned or nonpartitioned B*-tree indexes, including index-organized tables. New SQL syntax specifies the online index creation or rebuild. Specifically, the ONLINE keyword may be specified in the **create index** or **alter index** statement.

The new COALESCE keyword may be specified to defragment the index. In either case, performance will be improved and space recovered.

# Nonpartitioned Table Reorganization

A new MOVE clause can be used in an **alter table** statement to reorganize a nonpartitioned table easily by allowing the user to move data into a new segment while preserving all views, privileges, and so on defined on the table. The operation is performed offline.

# Online Read-Only Tablespaces

Now a tablespace in Oracle8*i* can be placed in read-only mode when there are no outstanding transactions in that tablespace.

# New Architecture

A new "diskless" ping architecture, called cache fusion, has been introduced that provides copies of blocks directly from the holding instance's memory cache to the requesting instance's memory cache. This functionality greatly improves interinstance communication. Cache fusion is particularly useful for databases in which updates and queries on the same data tend to occur simultaneously and where, for whatever reason, the data and users have not been isolated to specific nodes so that all activity can take place on a single instance. With cache fusion, there is less need to concentrate on data or user partitioning by instance.

Oracle8*i* has deeper integration of the distributed lock manager (DLM) into the database engine, thereby increasing the efficiency of parallel cache management.

## DBMS_REPAIR Package

Oracle8*i* provides enhanced block corruption repair capability through the new DBMS_REPAIR package. It provides the DBA with a three-stage approach to addressing corruptions:

1. Detect and report corruptions.

2. Make the object usable.

3. Repair corruptions and rebuild lost data.

## Redo Log Analysis Using LogMiner

LogMiner allows online and archived redo log files to be read, analyzed, and interpreted from SQL prompt by a user. It can be used to track specific sets of changes based on a transaction, user, table, time, and so forth. It is possible to determine who modified a database object and what the state of an object was before and after the modification. Please refer to Chapter 9 of this book for more details.

## Partitioning Enhancements

New range partitioning enhancement syntax is available for merging and updating partitions.

- Merging Partitions   A new statement, **alter table...merge partitions**, can be used to merge the contents of two adjacent partitions of a table using the range method.

- Updatable Partition Keys   A new clause, ENABLE ROW MOVEMENT, of the **alter table** or **create table** statement allows rows to be moved between partitions.

The new partitioning methods introduced in Oracle8*i* are hash and composite. Hash partitioning provides a very simple way to break data into evenly sized containers to be spread across multiple I/O devices, or even multiple machines in a shared-nothing cluster.

Composite (range/hash) partitioning provides the manageability and availability benefits of range partitioning with the data distribution advantages of hash partitioning.

- **Enhanced Partition Elimination**  Partition elimination is skipping of unnecessary index and data partitions (or subpartitions) in a query. Enhanced partitioning features of Oracle8*i* provide the database with greater knowledge of data placement, thereby performing more advanced partition elimination.

- **Partition-Wise Join**  In Oracle8, when two tables are joined in parallel, each table is split into some number of separate pieces, scanned, and then redistributed on the join column. In Oracle8*i*, the redistribution step can be skipped if the data is already partitioned on the join key. This reduces memory and temporary storage requirements and increases overall performance.

- **Partitioned Table LOB Support**  Full support for partitioned tables with LOB columns is now provided. The LOB value can be stored inline in the row or out of line in a separate segment. All LOB types are supported: BLOB, CLOB, NCLOB, and BFILE.

- **Partitioning of Index-Organized Tables**  Very large databases, historical databases, and OLTP databases with special availability requirements can benefit from the partitioning of index-organized tables (IOTs). Oracle8*i* supports partitioning of IOTs and the secondary indexes defined on IOTs. The bulk loading of partitioned IOTs with secondary indexes via SQL*Loader direct path is the most efficient way of loading data.

# Index

## M

Knowledge is power. To which we say,

# crank up the power.

## Are you ready for a power surge?

Accelerate your career—become an **Oracle Certified Professional** (OCP). With Oracle's cutting-edge *Instructor-Led Training*, *Technology-Based Training*, and this *guide*, you can prepare for certification faster than ever. Set your own trajectory by logging your personal training plan with us. Go to **http://education.oracle.com/tpb**, where we'll help you pick a training path, select your courses, and track your progress. We'll even send you an email when your courses are offered in your area. If you don't have access to the Web, call us at 1-800-441-3541 (Outside the U.S. call +1-310-335-2403).

**Power learning has never been easier.**

ORACLE®
University

# Get Your FREE Subscription to *Oracle Magazine*

*Oracle Magazine* is essential gear for today's information technology professionals. Stay informed and increase your productivity with every issue of *Oracle Magazine*. Inside each **FREE,** bimonthly issue you'll get:

- Up-to-date information on Oracle Database Server, Oracle Applications, Internet Computing, and tools
- Third-party news and announcements
- Technical articles on Oracle products and operating environments
- Development and administration tips
- Real-world customer stories

# Three easy ways to subscribe:

**1. Web**   **Visit our Web site at www.oracle.com/oramag/.
You'll find a subscription form there, plus much more!**

**2. Fax**   Complete the questionnaire on the back of this card and fax the questionnaire side only to **+1.847.647.9735.**

**3. Mail**   Complete the questionnaire on the back of this card and mail it to P.O. Box 1263, Skokie, IL 60076-8263.

If there are other Oracle users at your location who would like to receive their own subscription to *Oracle Magazine*, please photocopy this form and pass it along.

# YES! Please send me a FREE subscription to *Oracle Magazine*.  ☐ NO

'ES! Please send me a FREE subscription to *Oracle Magazine*, you must fill out the entire card, sign it, and date it (incomplete cards cannot be processed or acknowledged). You can also fax your application to +1.847.647.9735. Or subscribe at our Web site at www.oracle.com/oramag/

| SIGNATURE (REQUIRED) | X | DATE | |
|---|---|---|---|

| NAME | TITLE |
|---|---|
| COMPANY | TELEPHONE |
| ADDRESS | FAX NUMBER |
| CITY | STATE | POSTAL CODE/ZIP CODE |
| COUNTRY | E-MAIL ADDRESS |

☐ From time to time, Oracle Publishing allows our partners exclusive access to our e-mail addresses for special promotions and announcements. To be included in this program, please check this box.

## You must answer all eight questions below.

**1 What is the primary business activity of your firm at this location?** *(check only one)*
- ☐ 03 Communications
- ☐ 04 Consulting, Training
- ☐ 06 Data Processing
- ☐ 07 Education
- ☐ 08 Engineering
- ☐ 09 Financial Services
- ☐ 10 Government—Federal, Local, State, Other
- ☐ 11 Government—Military
- ☐ 12 Health Care
- ☐ 13 Manufacturing—Aerospace, Defense
- ☐ 14 Manufacturing—Computer Hardware
- ☐ 15 Manufacturing—Noncomputer Products
- ☐ 17 Research & Development
- ☐ 19 Retailing, Wholesaling, Distribution
- ☐ 20 Software Development
- ☐ 21 Systems Integration, VAR, VAD, OEM
- ☐ 22 Transportation
- ☐ 23 Utilities (Electric, Gas, Sanitation)
- ☐ 98 Other Business and Services

**2 Which of the following best describes your job function?** *(check only one)*
**CORPORATE MANAGEMENT/STAFF**
- ☐ 01 Executive Management (President, Chair, CEO, CFO, Owner, Partner, Principal)
- ☐ 02 Finance/Administrative Management (VP/Director/ Manager/Controller, Purchasing, Administration)
- ☐ 03 Sales/Marketing Management (VP/Director/Manager)
- ☐ 04 Computer Systems/Operations Management (CIO/VP/Director/ Manager MIS, Operations)

**IS/IT STAFF**
- ☐ 07 Systems Development/ Programming Management
- ☐ 08 Systems Development/ Programming Staff
- ☐ 09 Consulting
- ☐ 10 DBA/Systems Administrator
- ☐ 11 Education/Training
- ☐ 14 Technical Support Director/ Manager
- ☐ 16 Other Technical Management/Staff
- ☐ 98 Other _____

**3 What is your current primary operating platform?** *(check all that apply)*
- ☐ 01 DEC UNIX
- ☐ 02 DEC VAX VMS
- ☐ 03 Java
- ☐ 04 HP UNIX
- ☐ 05 IBM AIX
- ☐ 06 IBM UNIX
- ☐ 07 Macintosh
- ☐ 09 MS-DOS
- ☐ 10 MVS
- ☐ 11 NetWare
- ☐ 12 Network Computing
- ☐ 13 OpenVMS
- ☐ 14 SCO UNIX
- ☐ 24 Sequent DYNIX/ptx
- ☐ 15 Sun Solaris/SunOS
- ☐ 16 SVR4
- ☐ 18 UnixWare
- ☐ 20 Windows
- ☐ 21 Windows NT
- ☐ 23 Other UNIX _____
- ☐ 98 Other _____
- 99 ☐ **None of the above**

**4 Do you evaluate, specify, recommend, or authorize the purchase of any of the following?** *(check all that apply)*
- ☐ 01 Hardware
- ☐ 02 Software
- ☐ 03 Application Development Tools
- ☐ 04 Database Products
- ☐ 05 Internet or Intranet Products
- 99 ☐ **None of the above**

**5 In your job, do you use or plan to purchase any of the following products or services?** *(check all that apply)*
**SOFTWARE**
- ☐ 01 Business Graphics
- ☐ 02 CAD/CAE/CAM
- ☐ 03 CASE
- ☐ 05 Communications
- ☐ 06 Database Management
- ☐ 07 File Management
- ☐ 08 Finance
- ☐ 09 Java
- ☐ 10 Materials Resource Planning
- ☐ 11 Multimedia Authoring
- ☐ 12 Networking
- ☐ 13 Office Automation
- ☐ 14 Order Entry/Inventory Control
- ☐ 15 Programming
- ☐ 16 Project Management
- ☐ 17 Scientific and Engineering
- ☐ 18 Spreadsheets
- ☐ 19 Systems Management
- ☐ 20 Workflow

**HARDWARE**
- ☐ 21 Macintosh
- ☐ 22 Mainframe
- ☐ 23 Massively Parallel Processing
- ☐ 24 Minicomputer
- ☐ 25 PC
- ☐ 26 Network Computer
- ☐ 28 Symmetric Multiprocessing
- ☐ 29 Workstation

**PERIPHERALS**
- ☐ 30 Bridges/Routers/Hubs/Gateways
- ☐ 31 CD-ROM Drives
- ☐ 32 Disk Drives/Subsystems
- ☐ 33 Modems
- ☐ 34 Tape Drives/Subsystems
- ☐ 35 Video Boards/Multimedia

**SERVICES**
- ☐ 37 Consulting
- ☐ 38 Education/Training
- ☐ 39 Maintenance
- ☐ 40 Online Database Services
- ☐ 41 Support
- ☐ 36 Technology-Based Training
- ☐ 98 Other _____
- 99 ☐ **None of the above**

**6 What Oracle products are in use at your site?** *(check all that apply)*
**SERVER/SOFTWARE**
- ☐ 01 Oracle8
- ☐ 30 Oracle8*i*
- ☐ 31 Oracle8*i* Lite
- ☐ 02 Oracle7
- ☐ 03 Oracle Application Server
- ☐ 04 Oracle Data Mart Suites
- ☐ 05 Oracle Internet Commerce Server
- ☐ 32 Oracle *inter*Media
- ☐ 33 Oracle JServer
- ☐ 07 Oracle Lite
- ☐ 08 Oracle Payment Server
- ☐ 11 Oracle Video Server

**TOOLS**
- ☐ 13 Oracle Designer
- ☐ 14 Oracle Developer
- ☐ 54 Oracle Discoverer
- ☐ 53 Oracle Express
- ☐ 51 Oracle JDeveloper
- ☐ 52 Oracle Reports
- ☐ 50 Oracle WebDB
- ☐ 55 Oracle Workflow

**ORACLE APPLICATIONS**
- ☐ 17 Oracle Automotive
- ☐ 35 Oracle Business Intelligence System
- ☐ 19 Oracle Consumer Packaged Goods
- ☐ 39 Oracle E-Commerce
- ☐ 18 Oracle Energy
- ☐ 20 Oracle Financials
- ☐ 28 Oracle Front Office
- ☐ 21 Oracle Human Resources
- ☐ 37 Oracle Internet Procurement
- ☐ 22 Oracle Manufacturing
- ☐ 40 Oracle Process Manufacturing
- ☐ 23 Oracle Projects
- ☐ 34 Oracle Retail
- ☐ 29 Oracle Self-Service Web Applications
- ☐ 38 Oracle Strategic Enterprise Management
- ☐ 25 Oracle Supply Chain Management
- ☐ 36 Oracle Tutor
- ☐ 41 Oracle Travel Management

**ORACLE SERVICES**
- ☐ 61 Oracle Consulting
- ☐ 62 Oracle Education
- ☐ 60 Oracle Support
- ☐ 98 Other _____
- 99 ☐ **None of the above**

**7 What other database products are in use at your site?** *(check all that apply)*
- ☐ 01 Access
- ☐ 02 Baan
- ☐ 03 dbase
- ☐ 04 Gupta
- ☐ 05 IBM DB2
- ☐ 06 Informix
- ☐ 07 Ingres
- ☐ 08 Microsoft Access
- ☐ 09 Microsoft SQL Server
- ☐ 10 PeopleSoft
- ☐ 11 Progress
- ☐ 12 SAP
- ☐ 13 Sybase
- ☐ 14 VSAM
- ☐ 98 Other _____
- 99 ☐ **None of the above**

**8 During the next 12 months, how much do you anticipate your organization will spend on computer hardware, software, peripherals, and services for your location?** *(check only one)*
- ☐ 01 Less than $10,000
- ☐ 02 $10,000 to $49,999
- ☐ 03 $50,000 to $99,999
- ☐ 04 $100,000 to $499,999
- ☐ 05 $500,000 to $999,999
- ☐ 06 $1,000,000 and over

If there are other Oracle users at your location who would like to receive a free subscription to *Oracle Magazine*, please photocopy this form and pass it along, or contact Customer Service at +1.847.647.9630

Form 5

OPRE